Explorations and Proposals toward Market Socialism and World Government

Explorations and Proposals toward Market Socialism and World Government:

A Visionary Odyssey

By

James A. Yunker

Cambridge Scholars Publishing

Explorations and Proposals toward Market Socialism and World Government:
A Visionary Odyssey

By James A. Yunker

This book first published 2022

Cambridge Scholars Publishing

Lady Stephenson Library, Newcastle upon Tyne, NE6 2PA, UK

British Library Cataloguing in Publication Data
A catalogue record for this book is available from the British Library

ISBN (10): 1-5275-8860-2
ISBN (13): 978-1-5275-8860-8

CONTENTS

List of Figures vii

Chapter 1
Epiphany in the Bronx 1

Chapter 2
Reality Sets In 27

Chapter 3
Union Card 53

Chapter 4
Publish or Perish 84

Chapter 5
The Vision in Print: Articles 108
- Pragmatic Market Socialism 109
- Global Economic Development 127
- Federal World Government 137
- Near Misses 146
  - Comprehensive Incentives Analysis 150
  - Beyond Global Governance 167

Chapter 6
The Vision in Print: Early Books 177
- The First Wave 182
  - Socialism Revised and Modernized 194
  - World Union on the Horizon 208
  - Additional First Wave Books 219

Chapter 7
The Vision in Print: Later Books 224
The Second Wave 227
The Next Step/Political Globalization 231
The Third Wave 246
The Grand Convergence 248
The Idea of World Government 259
Global Marshall Plan 284
Evolutionary World Government 287

Chapter 8
Pragmatic Market Socialism 301
Background 307
Blueprint 320
Evaluation 332

Chapter 9
Federal World Government 376
Background 385
Blueprint 398
Evaluation 428

Index 453

LIST OF FIGURES

2.1 World Population 1000-2000 47

5.1 WEEP Model Baseline Simulation Results 134

5.2 Nash Social Welfare Functions under Capitalism and Socialism 161

5.3 Nash Social Welfare as a Function of the Output Elasticity of Capital Management Effort (ν) 162

9.1 Per Capita Income (PCY) Growth, 1980-2010, United States, Japan, China, India 417

9.2 Graphical Comparison: Weighted Mean PCY Growth for Seven Income Groups, Projected 2010-2060, with and without GMP 424

1

EPIPHANY IN THE BRONX

During the academic year of 1961-62, I was a freshman student at the Rose Hill campus of Fordham University, located in the heart of the Bronx, the only one of the five boroughs comprising New York City located on the mainland of the United States. My family home at that time was in Tervuren, Belgium, a suburb of Brussels, where my father had recently taken up an executive position with International Telephone and Telegraph (ITT). Although I had never before lived so far away from home, I adapted to student life at Fordham fairly quickly. In addition to making friends among my fellow students at Mrs. Peters' rooming house near the campus, there were some obvious advantages to living in one of the world's great cities. Among other things, a short ride on the subway would convey me to the Metropolitan Museum of Art in Manhattan, filled to overflowing with the great masterworks of art history.

At the time I started at Fordham University in September 1961, my background and beliefs were quite conventional. Specifically with respect to "socialism," my opinion was thoroughly negative. One had only to look carefully and objectively at the Soviet Union and Red China, so I thought, for it to become completely obvious that socialism was decidedly inferior to the Western system of democratic capitalism, as exemplified by the United States, the nations of Western Europe, and several others around the world. While a socialistic system need not become immediately prostrated, as witnessed by the fact that the Soviet Union and Red China were at that time mounting a very serious geopolitical and military challenge against the Western world, communistic socialism was nevertheless decidedly inferior to Western capitalism both economically and politically.

My harsh judgment on communism had been clearly expressed in a 1958 essay I had written for an English class at Cranwell Prep in Lenox, Massachusetts. The tone of this diatribe was set in the first paragraph, which referenced the then-recent Hungarian revolt against Soviet occupation:

> Just over two years ago, the myth of the communist utopia was shattered in a rain of bullets as mechanized Russian forces cut down inexperienced, underarmed Hungarian Freedom Fighters on the bloody streets of Budapest. For a month the world watched astounded as the oppressed Hungarians erupted in a seething revolt that tore the lid off the communist Big Lie. Never before had there been such a dramatic demonstration of the failure of the "glorious socialism" that the commies claim will inherit the world. For all time the working class—the "proletariat" that is the supposed "beneficiary" of communism—gave emphatic refutation to communism's falsehoods.

I still have a copy of that English essay in my files of juvenilia. The teacher gave me an A and added the notation "Good." That was indeed the way I thought at the beginning of the 1961-62 academic year. But by the end of that year my judgment on "socialism" was—to say the least—far more nuanced than it had been. Indeed, I had come to the firm conclusion that the term "socialism," after all, could refer to a number of very different things—not all of them necessarily bad.

Turning to "world government," I don't have any preserved teenaged writings documenting my negative attitude toward the idea, but I remember it clearly enough. The dire threat from communistic socialism was in the newspapers almost every day. On the other hand, there was no immediate prospect for world government. Thus, as did most people, I gave it very little thought. But to the extent that I gave any consideration at all to world government, I dismissed the possibility as, at best, a misguided and thoroughly utopian delusion, and at worst, a despicable communist plot to destroy freedom and democracy throughout the world. If a world government were established, I had no doubt that the international communist movement would exert every effort to gain complete control over it. And should this effort be successful, I had no doubt also that human existence throughout the world would be reduced to the lowest level of oppression and misery.

But by the end of my freshman year in June of 1962, I had radically revised my opinion of both socialism and world government. From my former opinion that they were both highly undesirable, I had migrated 180 degrees to the opinion that they were both indeed highly desirable—presuming, of course, that they were *properly implemented*. By what is meant "properly implemented"? With respect to socialism, for example, this meant that while undemocratic, centrally planned socialism as practiced at that time in the Soviet Union and Red China was clearly dysfunctional, a system of politically democratic, market-oriented socialism—defining "socialism" as no more nor less than public ownership of the preponderance of land and capital—did indeed hold great promise as a socio-economic reform in the West.

With respect to world government, my ideas on proper implementation were at that time far less evolved than they were with respect to socialism. But I had an instinct that if the West would transform itself into a democratic market socialist society, the path would thereby be cleared to some form of meaningful and effective world government within a relatively brief period of time. The adoption of democratic market socialism by the West would rip up the roots of the ideological confrontation between the communist and non-communist blocs of nations. More than likely, this fundamental transformation in the West would inspire the communist nations to abandon communist party dominion in favor of genuine democracy. As a result of the much-augmented mutual respect and trust among the superpowers, major progress on disarmament would become possible. Some of the savings from reduced military expenditure could then be transferred to economic development assistance programs, enabling the less developed nations to make more rapid progress toward a much higher level of prosperity. With ideological conflict reduced to a manageable level, and global economic inequality rapidly decreasing, the practical obstacles to world government would thereby be so much diminished that the establishment of such a government would become far more likely.

It could be done! It should be done!

The emotional impact of these fundamental changes in my belief system was easily the equivalent of religious conversion. It was an epiphany of the highest order. I never experienced anything like it either before or after. No doubt several factors contributed to this remarkable transformation, but one factor in particular stands out clearly in my memory. I sometimes wonder whether it would have happened without this one factor.

The immediate catalyst to the chain of thought leading to this diametrical reversal of mind and heart was a casual reading, late in the fall semester of 1961, of *The Power Elite* by the noted sociologist C. Wright Mills, published by Oxford University Press in 1956. By 1961 the book was well established as one of the most important sociological contributions of the recent past.

Exactly what it was about the Mills treatise that precipitated my own personal drastic reappraisal of reality, I cannot say for sure. While Mills was definitely leftwing in his basic ideological orientation, he was by no means a genuine radical. His purpose was not to preach the need for major social transformations, either domestic or international. It was rather merely to put people on their guard against excessive manipulation by the "power elite" of wealthy capitalists, corporation executives, high military officers and government officials—what President Dwight D. Eisenhower memorably labeled the "military-industrial complex."

In my case, however, recognition of the possibility that my prior thinking on policy issues might have been manipulated by those with an especially strong interest in maintaining the status quo thoroughly disturbed me: it thoroughly dislodged my previously orderly structure of conventional political and economic judgments. The winter and spring of 1962 was a period of intense intellectual activity, the culmination of which was a fairly comprehensive vision of democratic market socialism as a steppingstone to world government.

In order to fully understand and appreciate this vision, it is necessary to understand and appreciate the condition of the world as it was in the early 1960s. This is not so easy for people today. The collapse and dissolution of the Soviet Union took place in 1991, well over a quarter of a century ago. Prior to that historic event, the Cold War between the communist and non-communist nations had the world perched on the edge of nuclear catastrophe for several long, perilous decades. Following the development and first use of atomic bombs against the Japanese cities of Hiroshima and Nagasaki toward the end of World War II in 1945, an arms race immediately commenced between the United States and the Soviet Union. As powerful as atomic bombs were, they were soon superseded by hydrogen bombs of a qualitatively greater level of destructiveness. Meanwhile, delivery systems were radically improved. Relatively slow airplanes were replaced by ballistic missiles. A few hours of warning of a nuclear surprise attack dwindled to a few minutes. By the start of the 1960s, it was universally acknowledged that an unrestrained nuclear war would kill hundreds of millions of people. There were differences of opinion as to precisely how many hundreds of millions would be killed, and as to what the precise odds were of such a horrific event actually happening. But almost everyone was well aware that if it *did* occur, the degree of death and destruction throughout the world would be unprecedented.

The consensus everywhere in the world was that this situation seemed fully insane: that it defied common sense that humanity would have invented such terrifying weapons of mass destruction, and at the same time built up such a level of hostility and distrust within itself that there was a non-negligible possibility that a nuclear holocaust might actually occur. But there seemed to be no escape. Communist ideology insisted that the capitalist system was rotten and evil and destined inevitably to collapse. Non-communist ideology insisted that, to the contrary, it was the communist system that was rotten and evil, and that any effort to impose it on the non-communist nations would be met by any and all means necessary, up to and including all-out nuclear war.

But what about the possibility of arranging an international conference of experts to freely discuss and decide on the merits of the ideological issue: to determine which was the better system from the standpoint of overall social welfare, or perhaps to recommend some sort of compromise social system that would combine the positive elements from both the communist and non-communist systems? Surely that would have been the rational thing to do.

Perhaps that would have been the rational thing to do—but no authoritative political leader on either side ever suggested such a thing. Both sides continued to blast away at each other with propagandistic proclamations. According to its apologists, capitalism guarantees the blessings of economic prosperity and political freedom. According to the exponents of communism, what capitalism actually guarantees is the freedom of a handful of plutocratic capitalists to exploit the general population. As for capitalist democracy, that (according to these same communist exponents) is a hypocritical sham: only political candidates acceptable to the capitalist plutocracy have any chance whatever of being elected to any important government office. Not only did the capitalist plutocracy own and control the means of communication, they also controlled access to and usage of political power by means of campaign contributions and bribery.

In the face of this kind of vociferous debate employing half-truths, oversimplifications, misrepresentations, obfuscations, and outright prevarication, it seemed, and indeed probably was, futile to hope that any sort of rational argumentation, based on objective, factual evidence, would be successful in resolving the critical issues. So it was simpler just to carry on with the arms race, in hopes that somehow, someday, unforeseen and unforeseeable developments would eventually bring the Cold War to a peaceful conclusion before ultimate disaster intervened.

As we now know, humanity got lucky. The Cold War was brought to a peaceful conclusion in 1991 when the Soviet people gave up on Marxism, and decided that—even after all that—they in fact now wanted Western-style capitalism and democracy for themselves. The policy of containment of communism, formulated and inaugurated by the Truman administration shortly after the end of World War II, had finally worked as intended. The driving force behind the international communist movement, the Soviet Union, had finally seen the light of reason, and given up on its misguided effort to bring the communist economic and political system to the entire world. It had finally become clear to them that this messianic motivation was not only deeply perverse but extremely, unacceptably hazardous.

Around the world were heard deep sighs of relief that nuclear disaster had been averted.

There is no doubt that the world is a much safer place now than it was prior to 1991. But it is not as safe as it could be and should be. Although the stockpile of nuclear-tipped missiles at the ready is much smaller than it used to be, it is by no means insignificant. And although the issue of communism versus capitalism is no longer important, nations still have many disagreements, many conflicts of interest. The "communist menace" came about in 1917 as a result of the Russian revolution. But humanity had been regularly inflicting warfare on itself for millennia prior to 1917. With the disappearance of the "communist menace" in 1991, the propensity toward conflict, violence and warfare was appreciably diminished—but it was by no means abolished. The possibility of nuclear disaster, while much smaller, is still very much with us.

Back in 1961-62, however, the eventual demise of the Cold War in 1991 was far off in the unknown future. At that time, the nuclear threat was a clear and present danger—to some a very imminent danger. People coped with this awful reality as best they could, some more successfully than others. But even the most sanguine knew that if ever announcements came through the airwaves that a nuclear war had commenced, they would be filled with terror as they searched desperately for someplace to shelter. Of course, the bigger the city, the more tempting a target it would be for the other side. And New York City, the place in which I had come to reside in September 1961, was the biggest, juiciest, most tempting target in the entire world for communist nuclear missiles.

Early in my teenage years, I had developed a taste for science fiction. For a while back then, I consumed large quantities of the stuff. In fact, I was so smitten with it that during my high school years at Cranwell Prep, I even produced a few sci-fi short stories of my own, as well as a substantial "future history textbook" covering the story of human endeavor from the present into the era of interstellar expansion.

Dissociative identity disorder (DID) is the technical psychiatric term for what is commonly known as multiple personality disorder (aka split-personality disorder). In his 1886 novel *The Strange Case of Dr. Jekyll and Mr. Hyde*, Robert Louis Stevenson authored a lurid fictionalization of the condition. I would contend that the science fiction genre also manifests a split personality. On the bright side, you have the abundant stories that optimistically envision the human race expanding out into the stars, into the galaxy, into the universe. On the dark side, you have the abundant stories that pessimistically envision humanity never getting off planet Earth owing to a catastrophic nuclear holocaust and/or environmental collapse.

On the one hand, you have The Stars; on the other you have Doomsday.

There are some unsettling technical considerations that suggest that in the real world, the Doomsday prospect is more plausible than The Stars prospect. According to Albert Einstein, whose early twentieth century cogitations laid the groundwork for nuclear weapons: as any moving object approaches the speed of light (186,000 miles per second, or 6 trillion miles per year—the distance denoted by the term "light-year"), its mass approaches infinity. Thus the speed of light is the maximum upper limit of velocity: nothing can travel faster than the speed of light. But the distances between the stars are so vast that they are measured in light-years. For example, the nearest star to our sun is Alpha Centauri, which is 4.37 light-years away. For another example, the estimated diameter of our own galaxy, known as the Milky Way, is between 100,000 and 180,000 light-years across. Of course, in the "space opera" sci-fi sub-genre exemplified by the several *Star Wars* movies, spaceships are depicted as zipping about among the stars in about the same amount of time it takes to get between various destinations on the surface of planet Earth. But unless future science can somehow get around Einstein's conclusions regarding velocity, such visions must be deemed fantasies, as something which is known to be impossible.

On the other hand, we know for a fact that nuclear doomsdays are quite possible in the here and now. The existence and the readiness of the weaponry is no fantasy. Even in the post-Cold War era, considerations of national security in the United States, the Russian Federation, and several other nuclear-armed nations around the world, require that this weaponry be kept in a constant state of readiness, and that under certain conditions, its utilization could not be long delayed. But the danger was far worse back in the 1960s, when ideologues on both sides were proclaiming that if necessary, universal death and destruction would be preferable to living under the odious socioeconomic system of the other side.

No one knew in the 1960s what the consequences would be of an all-out nuclear war, any more than anyone knows today what would happen. The consensus among the experts, foremost among whom was Herman Kahn, RAND Corporation strategist and author of such bestsellers as *On Thermonuclear War* (1959) and *Thinking about the Unthinkable* (1962), was that while the death and destruction caused by a nuclear war would be unprecedented in the history of mankind, it was unlikely to lead to the short-term extinction of humanity. The general tenor of *On Thermonuclear War* was upbeat in a sense: that nuclear war was definitely survivable, and possibly even winnable. As such, it constituted an influential rebuttal to the "we'll all die" jeremiads of hardline pacifists proposing unilateral disarmament. Naturally, critics accused *On Thermonuclear War*—despite its ostensible purpose as a warning to all mankind—of making nuclear war more rather than less likely.

From the very beginning of the nuclear age, the Doomsday Tale became an important sub-genre within the overall science fiction genre. Perhaps the best-known example of this sub-genre was *On the Beach*, a best-selling novel by Nevil Shute, published in 1957 and soon afterwards produced as a film of the same name (1959). The premise is that an all-out nuclear war would not cause the immediate extinction of the human race via the heat and blast effects created by the nuclear explosions themselves, but rather these explosions would produce so much radioactive fallout that all the survivors would eventually perish of radiation sickness. (In his writings on nuclear war, Herman Kahn opined that this premise was implausible.) Personally, I found both the novel and the film to be somewhat sanitized depictions of the potential consequences of nuclear war: the focus was on the thoughts and activities of people in Australia who had been spared the initial conflagration, but who were now waiting for the death-dealing radioactive cloud to envelop their country. Among other things, there was no depiction of the agonizing consequences of radiation sickness.

Personally I found another entry in the Doomsday literature of the period to be far more frightening than *On the Beach*: *Level 7*, by Mordecai Roshwald, published in 1959. The premise of this novel was the same as that of *On the Beach*: following the initial conflagration, radioactive fallout would be so heavy and universal that every human being on the planet would succumb. The last survivors were in the lowest level (Level 7) of a multi-level underground shelter, some 4,000 feet below the surface. The sole responsibility of the Level 7 personnel is—in the event of nuclear war—to unleash their entire nuclear missile arsenal against the enemy. It is left ambiguous who is the enemy is: Level 7 personnel are designated by codes rather than names, and no hint is provided as to whether they are American or Russian. The novel takes the form of a diary kept by X-127, one of the officers in charge of launching nuclear attacks or counterattacks.

Of course, nuclear war does break out—by "technical accident." The accident leads to the unintentional launching by the other side of twelve intercontinental ballistic missiles, of which two fall on cities. Before a message is received apologizing for the accident, a retaliatory strike is on its way. Despite efforts by human decision-makers on both sides to stop the escalation, computerized automatic response systems take over. Within less than three hours, the nuclear armories on both sides have been entirely expended, and much of the world's population on the surface is already dead. The remaining surface survivors will soon succumb to radiation sickness.

But at this point there is apparently no imminent danger to the survivors sheltering in the various underground levels. Of these levels, Level 7 is the safest. Its designers have estimated that its occupants will be safe for 500 years, long enough for surface radiation to become harmless. Unfortunately, the designers were wrong. Deadly radiation begins seeping down lower and lower into the ground, and one by one the people in the higher levels die off. Eventually everyone in Level 7 succumbs to radiation sickness. According to the story, the nuclear war takes place on June 9, and on October 12, the last survivor, X-127, passes away. Instead of 500 years, Level 7 had held out a mere four months. The author, Mordecai Roshwald, did a fine job, through the accumulation of a host of realistic details, of making it all seem very plausible, very believable. A sense of claustrophobic doom builds steadily as the story unfolds.

So this was the kind of thing that contributed to my unease as I settled in to my college studies at Fordham University in New York. If the missiles ever started flying, some of them, clearly, would head straight for the Big Apple. But would that ever happen? Would any of the leaders of the superpowers ever be so rash, so misguided, so *stupid* as to permit circumstances to arise under which nuclear war would be possible, even probable? Probably not—but there were certain things going on in the world at that time that might have given considerable pause to any sensible person.

In the fall of 1961, the most obvious danger point was the city of Berlin. The post-World War II settlement had left Germany a divided country and Berlin a divided city. East Germany and East Berlin were both occupied by Soviet Russian forces, assisted by their East German allies. Following the war, Joseph Stalin had seen to it that most territory occupied by the Red Army was forcibly communized in the interest of protecting the Soviet Union itself with a buffer zone of "friendly" regimes. Among the forcibly communized Eastern European countries was East Germany. Unfortunately for the cause of peace and stability, the erstwhile capital of Germany, Berlin, was not on the border between East Germany and West Germany. Rather it was entirely within the boundaries of East Germany, the nearest West German territory being almost 100 miles distant from the city's borders.

From the start, the postwar German partition was a public relations disaster for the communist leadership. The Soviet occupation of East Germany was exceptionally harsh owing to residual bitterness left over from the epic struggle on the Eastern front between Nazi Germany and

Soviet Russia. During the postwar years, a large gap opened up between living standards in West Germany, at that time benefiting from Marshall Plan aid, and East Germany. Quite aside from the rigors of foreign occupation by the Red Army, the economic gap alone motivated hundreds of thousands of East Germans to migrate to the West. Berlin became the most important loophole: East Berliners would cross over into West Berlin, and then use road or rail connections to relocate themselves to cities and towns within West Germany. This out-migration was an acute embarrassment for the communist leadership both in Soviet Russia and East Germany.

In a November 1958 speech, Nikita Khrushchev proclaimed that this situation had to end—within six months. Berlin must become a "free city" with no foreign occupiers. The Eisenhower administration interpreted Khrushchev's speech as an ultimatum: with American and other allied forces removed from the city, the East German communist regime would have no difficulty shutting off the out-migration. Khrushchev's demand was therefore rejected as unacceptable. This uneasy status quo continued until in August 1961, the East German regime under Walter Ulbricht forced the issue by constructing the Berlin Wall to forcibly shut down the out-migration. Not long afterwards, on the night of October 27, as a consequence of a dispute between the Americans and the Russians over whether diplomatic personnel needed to present their credentials to border guards, a standoff occurred at Checkpoint Charlie on the Friedrichstrasse between Russian and American tanks and soldiers. Both sides had loaded weapons and were under instructions to return fire if fired upon. The possibility was on everyone's mind that a small-scale border shooting incident might somehow blossom out into a nuclear World War III. Fortunately, both Kennedy and Khrushchev did not want that to happen. Informal agreements were hastily reached: the Soviets and East Germans would withdraw their demands that Berlin become a "free city," and in return the Americans would abandon any temptations they might have had toward interfering with the Berlin Wall. This arrangement persisted peaceably until finally, almost three decades later, the Berlin Wall was dismantled on November 9, 1989.

However, that "everything would turn out fine in the end" was not at all evident to me, reading my *New York Times* on an NYC park bench, on the morning of October 28, 1961. How many more of these confrontations were going to take place in the future? Would they all end peacefully? This is most definitely an unsatisfactory situation. Is there nothing at all that can be done to reduce the peril? Nothing at all?

And what about "the Russians"? True, they were our deadly enemies, with whom, upon a moment's notice, we might have to fight to the death. But from an early age, I had been a "World War II buff," and I was fully aware that not too many years before, we had stood shoulder to shoulder with the Russians against the Nazi menace. And I knew enough about the Eastern front from 1941 to 1945 to know that Russian losses during those desperate years dwarfed those of all the other allies combined. It was true, of course, that the Stalin dictatorship had much in common with the Hitler dictatorship. But at least Soviet communism, unlike German Nazism, had not openly scorned the democratic principle. Stalin's 1930s purges were monstrous, but they were not as horrific as Hitler's 1940s Holocaust against Jews and other "racial undesirables."

That the Soviet Union was dangerously paranoid could hardly be doubted, but to some extent the paranoia was understandable. Following the Russian revolution, throughout the interwar period, the Soviet Union had been the sole socialist nation in the entire world. And although most anti-socialists outside the Soviet Union assumed that it would eventually collapse owing to the weakness of its Marxist underpinnings, there were some who felt that the collapse should be hastened along by outside military intervention. And when Hitler's armies eventually invaded the Soviet Union in June 1941, a large part of the public relations justification provided for this to the world by the Nazi regime was the purported need to eliminate the "Bolshevik menace."

Even granting that the current Russian leadership was dangerously misguided, what about the historical tradition of Russian culture? What about Dostoevsky and Tolstoy in literature, and Shiskin and Repin in art, and Tchaikovsky and Prokofiev in music? Could a nation so rich in culture be now so hopelessly immured in evil as to be past redemption? And what about the Russian people? Like people everywhere, most of them were probably good and kind at heart.

The cinema is often a revealing guide to the ordinary people of any given society. As part of the ongoing cultural exchange programs of the period, a Soviet film produced in 1960, with the English title *A Summer to Remember*, was shown in New York City in the winter of 1961-62. The protagonist is a little 5-year-old tyke by the name of Seryozka, only son of the recently war-widowed Maryana. Along comes Korostelyov, ex-Red Army officer, who takes over as director of the collective farm and marries Maryana. Korostelyov is a formidable figure, but soon manifests a heart of gold where little Seryozka is concerned. When it is comes time for Korostelyov to go with Maryana to a new assignment, leaving Seryozka behind temporarily in the care of his grandparents, the cute little kid is heartbroken. But in the end it is the imposing Korostelyov who crumbles. In the midst of a raging blizzard he has the truck turned around to go back to pick up Seryozka. To his ecstatic joy, little Seryozka, together with his beloved mother Maryana and stepfather Korostyelov, will be all together in their new home! Talk about heart-warming! I came out of that New York movie theater on that cold winter's night with tears in my eyes, and with the overpowering conviction that it would be a dirty rotten shame if we were forced to wage nuclear war against people like these.

It was not long after the Checkpoint Charlie standoff that I started reading the book that changed my life forever: *The Power Elite* by C. Wright Mills. At first I didn't find anything particularly surprising about it. Any sensible person has to realize that every large-scale, organized society must have a "power elite" of responsible, authoritative leaders. This is true of the United States just as it is true of every other country in the world. So what?

But as I continued turning the pages, absorbing what Mills was trying to convey, I began to experience thoughts and feelings that I had never before thought or felt. Surely capitalism was a fine thing in a general sense, but as it had developed in the United States and the other leading capitalist nations, it had created a great deal of economic inequality, especially in the distribution of capital property. Most people possessed little or nothing in the way of stocks, bonds, and other property income-producing instruments, while at the same time a small minority of the population possessed huge amounts of this kind of property. Moreover, this situation has political implications as well as economic implications. Clearly, very wealthy people have disproportionate influence in the workings of governance even in what is ostensibly a fully democratic republic—as well as having disproportionate financial resources with which to acquire the good things in life.

And was it true, as I had always previously believed, that there was absolutely nothing at all of value within the socialist critique of capitalism? Could it be that there was not one single little iota of validity in this critique that had inspired millions upon millions of people all around the world over several generations of humanity? Could they have all been totally deluded, totally misguided, totally wrong? Somehow that proposition seemed unlikely—increasingly unlikely. These kinds of borderline heretical thoughts increasingly troubled me as I made my way through the pages of *The Power Elite*.

The first salient point emphasized by Mills is that the power elite suffers from a superiority complex that seriously weakens its ability to empathize with the rank and file of society, the "common people." Although the power elite described by Mills are generally rich, they did not all necessarily come by their wealth via inheritance and family connections. Nevertheless, whatever the source of their wealth and power, they all possess a deeply ingrained elitist attitude (Mills, pp. 283-295 passim):

> All the structural coincidence of their interests as well as the intricate, psychological facts of their origins and their education, their careers and their associations make possible the psychological affinities that prevail among them, affinities that make it possible for them to say of one another: He is, of course, one of us. And all this points to the basic, psychological meaning of class consciousness. Nowhere in America is there as great a "class consciousness" as among the elite.

Granted for the sake of argument that the interests of the "power elite" do not necessarily coincide entirely with those of "society at large," is this necessarily a problem? Are there effective means by which the power elite might impose their own preferences on the overall society even within an ostensibly fully democratic political system? Mills suggests that this is indeed the case, albeit the imposition is not by force but rather by persuasion. The means of persuasion operate through the privately-owned and operated mass communications media, upon which the general population is dependent for its information and viewpoints (Mills, pp. 296-315 passim):

> So long as the media are not entirely monopolized, the individual can play one medium off against another; he can compare them, and hence resist what any one of them puts out. The more genuine competition there is among the media, the more resistance the individual might be able to command. But how much is this now the case? *Do* people compare reports on public events or policies, playing one medium's content off against another's?
>
> The answer is: generally no, very few do: (1) We know that people tend strongly to select those media which carry contents with which they already agree. There is a kind of selection of new opinions on the basis of prior opinions. No one seems to search out counter-statements as may be found in alternative media offerings. Given radio programs and magazines and newspapers often get a rather consistent public, and thus reinforce their messages in the minds of that public. (2) This idea of playing one medium off against another assumes that the media really have varying contents. It assumes genuine competition, which is not widely true. The media displays an apparent variety and competition, but on closer view they seem to compete more in terms of variations on a few standardized themes than clashing issues. The freedom to raise issues effectively seems more and more to be confined to those few interests that have ready and continual access to these media.

In his concluding Chapter 15 ("The Higher Immorality"), Mills opines that the phenomena he describes are by no means neutral, by no means benign. They are rather highly dysfunctional: they are guiding society in a direction that is not consistent with its best interests (Mills, pp. 360-361):

> America—a conservative country without any conservative ideology—appears now before the world a naked and arbitrary power, as in the name of realism, its men of decision enforce their often crackpot definitions upon world reality. The second-rate mind is in command of the ponderously spoken platitude. In the liberal rhetoric, vagueness, and in the conservative mood, irrationality, are raised to principle. Public relations and the official secret, the trivializing campaign and the terrible fact clumsily accomplished, are replacing the reasoned debate of political ideas in the privately incorporated economy, the military ascendancy, and the political vacuum of modern America.

Two years following the publication of *The Power Elite* in 1956, Mills published another book, much shorter but even more vehement, entitled *The Causes of World War Three* (Ballantine Books, 1958). In this book Mills expressed his acute concern over the hazardous trend of international relations, which seemed to have humanity on a collision course with nuclear holocaust. Whereas most intellectuals of the period tended to assign responsibility for this unsatisfactory situation to the unimaginative and irrational tendencies within every human being, Mills was more specific. To him it was primarily the *leadership* that was at fault. Not just the leadership of the West, as dissected in *The Power Elite*, but the leadership of the East. Although Mills was willing to give communism some credit for commendable ideals, he had no sympathy for it as actually practiced in the Soviet Union, Red China, and elsewhere. Like most Western critics of the Western non-communist system at that time, he was of the firm opinion that no matter how bad the Western non-communist system might be, the Eastern communist system was even worse. There, the perverse policies laid down by the leadership were enforced on the people not by indirect trickery and persuasion, but rather by direct intimidation and coercion.

But whatever the means by which the Western and Eastern power elites controlled their respective societies, they are very much alike in one critical respect: lack of imagination. As the holders of wealth and power, they are too conservative, too suspicious of change, too attached to the status quo—even though that status quo is headed for disaster. By separate means, they have created for themselves "mass societies" of blissfully uncomprehending citizens marching like cattle toward the slaughterhouse.

The 1950s and 60s were the early days of the Cold War, and while almost everyone agreed that the nuclear arms race was not a healthy development, and that it could justly be described as mad, stupid, insane, idiotic, and so on and so forth, very little in the way of practical recommendations for ameliorating the problem were being put forward. Certainly Mills, for one, had no specific, operational ideas. For the non-communist world, there was one and only one course to be followed, containment: "We must hold out until the communists see the error of their ways and stop pushing for global communization." The situation was analogous in the communist world: "We must hold out until the people of the non-communist nations see the error of their ways and stop defending capitalism." As to the possibility that nuclear holocaust might intervene before either of these objectives could be reached—well, that risk was just the price we had to pay to protect and preserve our hallowed way of life, whatever it might be.

It was not as if at any point during the winter and spring of 1962, I sat down calmly and said to myself: "Apparently no one is thinking seriously about what sort of ideological compromise might be possible between communism and non-communism—therefore I shall undertake this." It was more that a vision emerged, step by step—but not gradually. The process was actually quite rapid, more like a "flash of intuition" than a piecemeal evolutionary development. While the overall outline was fairly clear from the beginning, the fine details of the vision took time to develop—many long years, in fact.

The starting point was that—contrary to my firm belief up to that time—"socialism" was not in fact a thoroughly malign, completely perverse concept. Always before I had identified "socialism" with "communism," and "communism" with both political tyranny (communist party dominion) and economic inefficiency (central planning). But then it came to me: "socialism" per se, as could be confirmed by reference to almost any dictionary, referred primarily to public ownership of the non-human factors of production, land and capital. True, socialism had become identified with communist party dominion and central planning owing to its historical association with communism as implemented first in Soviet Russia, and more recently in Red China. But this identification was very likely an accident of history—not something necessarily implied by the basic public ownership principle. Socialism in its pure sense need not imply central planning, and need not imply the absence of Western-style political democracy. The implications of this seminal insight were far-reaching.

During my freshman year at Fordham University, I took the standard two semester sequence in principles of economics: macroeconomics in the first (fall) semester, microeconomics in the second (spring) semester. The textbook for the course was Paul Samuelson, *Economics: An Introductory Analysis*, fourth edition (McGraw-Hill, 1958). Buried away within this encyclopedic tome, in an appendix to Chapter 30 ("Profits and Incentives") entitled "Review of Commodity and Factor Pricing: General Equilibrium and the Parable of Ideal Welfare Pricing," were several passages that caught my attention. The basic premise advanced by Samuelson in this material was that, hypothetically, a socialist economy could utilize much the same market mechanisms as utilized by the capitalist economy. Public ownership of capital did not necessarily imply that the economy must be centrally planned by a government agency—as was the case in the Soviet Union and Red China. Samuelson advanced the idea, derived from the much earlier work of Oskar Lange, that the non-human factors of production could be managed much as they were in the capitalist economy. Economic rationality demanded that these factors be paid a return—but that return did not necessarily have to be paid to private owners. Instead, the return paid to the non-human factors of production could be collected by the government and paid out to the general population as a "social dividend." This could lead to a far more egalitarian distribution of capital property income, one that might seem much fairer to most people.

As was the case with all economics students during the 1960s and for several decades thereafter, I had immense respect for Paul Samuelson. Not only were the many editions of his principles textbook, the first edition of which was published in 1948, widely utilized from the 1950s through the 1990s, he was a prolific contributor to the professional journal literature: his collected scientific papers run to seven thick volumes. His Ph.D. dissertation (*Foundations of Economic Analysis*), a survey of mathematical applications in economic theory, had been published by Harvard University Press in 1947. In 1970 he was awarded a Nobel Prize in Economics.

Nevertheless, despite his Olympian prestige, I had my doubts about the validity of Samuelson's bottom-line judgment that the problems of capitalism, especially that of "improper" distribution of income, could (as he said) "be ameliorated by appropriate policies, within the framework of the capitalistic system." Perhaps this particular problem could be "ameliorated"—but could it be "abrogated"?

In principle, it would be simple enough to deal with the problem: If the distribution of capital property income is considered excessively unequal, then simply apply a high rate of income taxation to capital income in the form of dividends, interest, and capital gains. But this simplistic notion takes no account of the political power and influence of wealthy capitalists whose personal incomes are dominated by exactly these types of income. These people would not be happy to see their personal incomes gutted by high rates of taxation on capital income, and they possess the power and influence to see to it that this does not happen. High rates of capital income taxation might well be in the interests of the general population, most of whom receive little or no capital property income, because higher taxation of capital income could enable lower taxation of wage and salary income, such labor income components as dominate the incomes of the vast majority of households. But the levers of influence—especially the mass media—controlled by the capitalist minority might be sufficient to blind the non-capitalist majority to their own interests in the matter. In other words, perhaps a more realistic and effective way to get at the problem of maldistribution of capital wealth and income would be public ownership of capital property, i.e. socialism.

Nowhere in the fourth edition of Samuelson's principles textbook was there any mention of Oskar Lange. But very early on in my study of economics at Fordham University, I became aware of Lange's reputation as the "father of market socialism." Back in the 1930s, Lange had authored a lengthy essay entitled "On the Economic Theory of Socialism," first published as a two-part article in the *Review of Economic Studies* (1936-37), and shortly afterwards as the major component of a book of the same title published by the University of Minnesota Press (1938). Lange's work was the focus of Chapter 12, "Socialist Economics," authored by Abram Bergson and included in the extremely influential *A Survey of Contemporary Economics* sponsored by the American Economic Association.

Although Lange did not coin the term "market socialism," it was soon applied by others to his proposed system. Lange was also responsible for popularizing the term "social dividend." The basic idea of what I later designated "Langian market socialism" envisioned an economy that would function very similarly to its "capitalist twin," with the principal exception that the interest and other property income components paid by the publicly-owned business enterprises for the use of capital would go to a public collection agency, which would then pay most of it out to the general public as a "social dividend." As each citizen would be a part owner of the commonly owned capital stock, each citizen would thereby be entitled to a social dividend based on the earnings of that capital stock. For the large majority of the population in a modern, industrialized economy, what they would receive as social dividend under market socialism would greatly exceed what they are currently receiving under contemporary capitalism as personal capital income.

Even as the basic concept of and motivation for market socialism crystallized in my mind during the spring of 1962, I realized that many details would have to be worked out before the idea could be convincingly presented, especially to skeptical minds—and most minds in the Western world were indeed highly skeptical of socialism. What exactly would be the mechanisms of governance for the publicly-owned business enterprises? What would ensure their efficient operation? How exactly would capital property income be collected by a public ownership agency and disbursed to the general public? Should the distribution be on a simple lump-sum basis (the same social dividend to every household or individual), or would another distribution method be superior?

And what about capitalist apologetics? The idea of socialism had been around for at least 150 years, and during all that time the defenders of the capitalist system had been busy coming up with justifications of the status quo. To the many apologists of capitalism, socialism would bring about all kinds of disabilities and disasters: the loss of entrepreneurship and the cessation of technical progress, such a degree of economic leveling as would completely destroy incentives to effort and result in an economy of stagnant mediocrity, the crushing of individuality under an immense burden of bureaucracy, the imposition of communistic totalitarianism, the suppression of the human soul, the ruination of humanity—and so on and so forth. It would be necessary to refute this formidable body of myth and misconception. And the first step toward that would be the formulation of a plausible institutional plan for market socialism.

At that point, my thinking on market socialism was in an embryonic state, and my study, research, and writing on the subject would go on not just for years afterwards, but for decades. Eventually I would publish no less than five books focused principally on market socialism, as well as approximately 25 journal articles on the subject. In chronological order, the books were as follows: *Socialism in the Free Market* (Nellen, 1978); *Socialism Revised and Modernized: The Case for Pragmatic Market Socialism* (Praeger, 1992); *Capitalism versus Pragmatic Market Socialism: A General Equilibrium Evaluation* (Kluwer, 1993); *Economic Justice: The Market Socialist Vision* (Rowman and Littlefield, 1997); and *On the Political Economy of Market Socialism: Essays and Analyses* (Ashgate, 2001). The last title on this list was a selection of 14 of my previously published journal articles on the subject.

When the Soviet Union abandoned Marxist communism and dissolved itself in 1991, thus bringing the Cold War to an abrupt and very welcome end, it was immediately apparent to me that there was no longer any role whatsoever for market socialism as a potential bridge over the ideological gap between communism and non-communism. Although there was still a significant internal case to be made for market socialism as a potential reform of the contemporary capitalist socioeconomic system, the case was no longer critical for the external purpose of reducing the threat of nuclear holocaust. Throughout the 1990s and thereafter, my principal research and writing interest turned to the world government possibility, and its economic corollary, a global economic development effort. Market socialism would be neither necessary nor sufficient for either of these.

In chronological order, my books on these subjects were as follows: *World Union on the Horizon: The Case for Supernational Federation* (University Press of America, 1993); *Common Progress: The Case for a World Economic Equalization Program* (Praeger, 2000); *Rethinking World Government: A New Approach* (University Press of America, 2005); *Political Globalization: A New Vision of Federal World Government* (University Press of America, 2007); *The Grand Convergence: Economic and Political Aspects of Human Progress* (Palgrave Macmillan, 2010); *The Idea of World Government: From Ancient Times to the Twenty-First Century* (Routledge, 2011); *Global Marshall Plan: Theory and Evidence* (Lexington, 2014); *Beyond Global Governance: Prospects for Global Government* (University Press of America, 2014); and *Evolutionary World Government: A Pragmatic Approach to Global Federation* (Hamilton, 2018). Of these books, two (*Rethinking World Government* and *Beyond Global Governance*) were collections of my professional journal articles on world government.

Of course, back in the spring of 1962, all this was far off in the remote and unknowable future. All I knew then was that there was a great deal of work to be done in order to flesh out the vision, give it structure and substance, make it as clear and compelling to other people as it was to me. This would not be easy or quick. I was going to have to concentrate my personal resources in a manner never before attempted. That skepticism was likely to be the dominant reaction among most people to their initial exposure to the thrust of what I soon came to term "the Project," soon became apparent to me as I endeavored to explain the concept to some of my fellow Fordham students. But I remained confident that if I could just find the means of properly clarifying the vision, dubious skepticism would eventually be replaced by enthusiastic acceptance.

I never gave any serious consideration to the possibility that the skeptics were fundamentally right and I was fundamentally wrong—in the sense that neither market socialism nor world government would, if implemented, be beneficial in terms of human welfare. I might have been willing to concede that the real-world force of "ignorance" (which I soon revised to "erroneous misconception") might prove so strong that it would prevent these advances from taking place anytime within the foreseeable future, even though they *would* be beneficial if they *did* take place. But I never entertained serious doubts, either then or at any subsequent time, that these two particular institutional innovations, market socialism and world government—*presuming they were properly designed and implemented*—would significantly improve the condition and prospects of human civilization everywhere in the world.

I set myself the task of constructing the elements of a case so comprehensive and compelling as to be virtually irresistible, at least on grounds of reason and rationality. I needed to greatly increase my knowledge of relevant aspects of economics, sociology, psychology, politics, history—even philosophy. (At Fordham University at that time, all undergraduates were required to complete a minor in philosophy. I didn't mind, because literally everything was grist for my mill—no aspect of human thought and activity was entirely irrelevant.) I read voraciously. For example, in a hand-written record book entitled "Journal of Personal Progress" (a kind of diary), covering the interval from October 1, 1962, through December 15, 1962, the first entry records a "partial" list of books read over the preceding nine months. Some of the 43 books on the list:

Arthur P. Mendel, ed. *Essential Works of Marxism.*
Edmund Wilson. *To the Finland Station.*
Sidney Hook. *Marx and the Marxists.*
Isaiah Berlin. *Karl Marx.*
Robert Freedman. *Marx on Economics.*
Milovan Djilas. *The New Class.*
Wesley Clair Mitchell. *Business Cycles and Their Causes.*
Isaac Deutscher. *The Great Contest.*
Seymour Melman. *The Peace Race.*
Barry Goldwater. *Conscience of a Conservative.*
Louis M. Hacker. *American Capitalism.*
John McConnell. *Economists Past and Present.*
Walt Whitman Rostow. *The Stages of Economic Growth.*
Gottfried Haberler, ed. *Readings in Business Cycle Theory.*
John Kenneth Galbraith. *The Affluent Society.*
Dennis Wong. *Population and Society.*
Charles Wright. *Mass Communication.*
E. K. Nottingham. *Religion and Society.*
Jesse Clarkson. *A History of Russia.*
George F. Kennan. *Russia and the West under Lenin and Stalin.*
Alan Moorehead. *The Russian Revolution.*
Matthew Josephson. *The Robber Barons.*
Richard Hofstadter. *Social Darwinism in American Thought.*

Considering that very few of these books were directly relevant to any of my courses, it is something of a wonder that I managed to do as well as I did in assigned course work. But the fact was that I was *driven* to a degree I had never experienced before, or ever experienced after. It was a dizzying experience, at the same time exhilarating and exhausting. Various factoids, observations, and insights went into the handwritten Journals of Personal Progress, and some went into typed essays, mostly single-spaced. As the writing piled up, my thinking gradually firmed up. In the substantial files of preserved documentation from my Fordham years, the single longest and most comprehensive manuscript is an 86-page, single-spaced typed tract, dated August 1963, with the grandiose title "Introduction to the New World." The "New World" elucidated in the manuscript, obviously, should not be confused with the "New World Order" proclaimed in the aftermath of the Soviet collapse and the end of the Cold War. My "New World" greatly predated the "New World Order" of three decades later. Clearly, however, the "new world" phrase has considerable appeal to visionary futurists. The contents page of that document is as follows:

INTRODUCTION TO THE NEW WORLD

I. Introduction
   1. The World Crisis
   2. The Solution

II. Capitalist Democracy

III. Socialism in Theory and Practice
   1. Introduction: Capitalism and Socialism
   2. Justice
   3. Efficiency
   4. Blueprint for an American Socialist System
   5. Democracy
   6. Summary

IV. Unified World Government
   1. The Need
   2. The Communist World
   3. The Post-Conciliation Program
   4. The Politically United World

V. Summary and Conclusion
   1. Summary of the Plan
   2. The Twentieth Century Council
   3. Prospects
   4. The Need for Courage and Humanity

When I review that manuscript today, I wince. It is too full of youthful enthusiasm, of dogmatic certitude, of burning anguish, towering rage, and borderline-psychotic optimism. It did not help that I consistently misspelled "ideological" as "idealogical." Moreover, the essay is disconcertingly vague on many important practical questions. Nevertheless, it contained in embryonic form the fundamental theses on market socialism and world government which I put forward much later in various publications of a more polished nature.

Later on I normally utilized the term "pragmatic market socialism" to describe the proposed socialist economy. A principal reason for this was to distinguish the proposal from "Langian market socialism" as expounded by Oskar Lange in the 1930s. "Introduction to the New World" did not cite Lange by name, but it did discuss—and reject—"marginal cost socialism," which was what Lange, and a few others, had proposed as the operational embodiment of "market socialism." Even at that early date, I had already dismissed marginal cost socialism as impractical, as too much influenced by textbook economic theory. It soon became clear to me that the publicly-owned business enterprises must be profit-maximizers, because profits were an observable success criterion, and were necessary for purposes of efficient allocation of scarce capital. Almost all socialists prior to Lange had condemned profits as clear evidence of economic exploitation. But Lange argued—compellingly in my judgment—that there was nothing inherently wrong with profits. The problem was (and is) that under contemporary capitalism, with its extraordinary concentration of capital wealth ownership, the lion's share of profits were (and are) claimed by a very small minority of wealthy capitalists. Under market socialism, in contrast, the profits produced by the publicly-owned business enterprises, would be returned via a social dividend, in a relatively egalitarian manner, to the entire population. It was not profits themselves that were bad—it was the maldistribution of profits under capitalism.

Of course, for the pragmatic market socialist economy to work successfully, the executives of the publicly-owned corporations must be motivated to do what they already do under capitalism: pursue profits energetically. Under capitalism, corporation executives are inspired to pursue profits by both the carrot (salaries and bonuses) and the stick (the possibility of dismissal). It would be the same under pragmatic market socialism, with the exception that instead of the profit motive being enforced on the executives by the class of private capitalists, it would be enforced upon them by a public ownership agency. Since nothing quite like pragmatic market socialism had ever existed in the real world, exactly what would be the nature of the public ownership agency, and exactly how it would operate, would have to be explicated in considerable detail.

In the 1963 "Introduction," I suggested that two federal government agencies, the "National Investment Banking System" and the "Central Economic Council," would work in tandem to maintain profit discipline within the publicly-owned business enterprise sector. Several years later, specifically during the 1972-1973 academic year, at which time I was an economics professor at Western Illinois University, I produced a large manuscript (unpublished) that modified the proposed institutional structure of pragmatic market socialism. The "National Investment Banking System" was supplemented by a "National Entrepreneurial Investment Board," but neither of these two would be directly responsible for profit enforcement. That specific task would be handled by a "Bureau of Public Ownership"—the name inspired by the "Bureau of Land Management," a real-world U.S. federal government agency concerned with efficient utilization of federally owned land. As for the "Central Economic Council" proposed in the 1963 "Introduction," by 1973 I had dispensed with that idea, on grounds that its functions could be adequately handled by existing government agencies, such as (in the United States) the Federal Reserve System, the Treasury, and the Council of Economic Advisers.

In addition to institutional modifications between 1963 and 1973, there were differences in emphasis. In 1963, for example, I had placed considerable emphasis on the argument that under socialism better control would be possible over the recurring problem of business recessions and depressions, and thus the dynamic performance of the economy would be significantly improved. By 1973, I had pretty much abandoned this particular argument, on grounds that Keynesian anticyclical policy under capitalism was likely to be virtually as effective as Keynesian anticyclical policy under socialism.

Considerable emphasis was also placed in 1963 on the argument that the extravagantly unequal capital wealth distribution was directly responsible for an equally extravagantly unequal distribution of political power, such as was making a mockery of the democratic ideals of which we citizens of the United States were so proud. Capitalists not only controlled who could, and who could not, run successfully for political office through the bestowal or withholding of campaign contributions, but they could also control what the public thought through their ownership and control of the communications media. Through these means, taxation of capital income was kept at a modest level, and any appreciable stirrings of interest in the socialist alternative were quickly squelched.

By 1973, I had backed off on emphasis on these factors as explanations for the persistence of capitalism despite the fact that the best interests of the general public lay with some form of market socialism. These means of thought control and political control had been going on for so long and so successfully that the general public's acceptance of the pro-capitalist, anti-socialist line was so thoroughly ingrained as to render needless any sort of conscious censorship or political favoritism. Virtually every serious candidate for political office, whatever his or her social origin and status, was already in favor of capitalism and against socialism. And executives in the publishing and broadcasting industries were totally unconscious of the effect their predispositions in favor of capitalism and against socialism might be having on their business decisions and practices.

Despite this obliviousness to reality among mass media executives, the situation still existed that control of the mass media implies control of the public's perceptions and preferences. And just as the capitalists were able to use the mass media to forestall any serious socialist threat—without conscious awareness that they were doing so, so too under market socialism the party in power in the national government could potentially forestall any threat from an opposition political party by the same means—in this case consciously. As early as the 1963 "Introduction," I was well aware of this potential problem of market socialism, and I proposed to counter the threat by making media corporations independent of any direct government control by the National Investment Banking System or the Central Economic Council. The managers of these corporations would be elected by their employees, and would be responsible only to the employees. In other words, the principle of what has been variously termed self-management, employee control, or cooperative market socialism, would be applied to the media corporations. They would not be subjected to the same sort of profit discipline as would the managers of non-media corporations. Whatever losses in efficiency this might entail would be more than compensated for by its guarantee of a more genuinely democratic political system. This exception to the general rule with respect to corporate control and governance has always been a basic component of the pragmatic market socialist concept.

Although in later work I greatly amplified and solidified the critique to be offered against the various propositions of capitalist apologetics, the basics of this critique were clearly enunciated at the outset. I addressed the propositions that capital property income was a return to saving, that it was a return to managerial effort, that it was a return to entrepreneurship, that it was a return to risk-taking, that its distribution was not unduly unequal (people's capitalism), that capitalism was necessary for the preservation of democracy and/or human dignity, that no matter how bad capitalism was, any socialist alternative would be far worse. As described later in this account, I took on these various arguments one by one, over the years, in numerous articles and several books.

But as I gradually found out, I was never able to muster a convincing argument against the following objection: "The objective arguments to be made against capitalism and in favor of market socialism, no matter how appealing they may seem upon serious reflection, are moot, irrelevant, and beside the point. This is because the overwhelming consensus against any and all forms of socialism, among the political leadership, the intelligentsia, and the general public, is so strong and consistent, that very few people will ever undertake serious reflection on these arguments. Therefore no form of public ownership socialism, market or otherwise, will become a significant political possibility in the capitalist nations within the foreseeable future." All I could really offer against this was: "Yes, but ... This is not right! Perhaps someday, somehow, it will become possible after all to snap people out of the trance they are in at the present time."

As mentioned above, upon the collapse of the Soviet Union and the dissipation of the "communist menace" in 1991, I gradually phased out my research and writing efforts on market socialism. Although I still think, and no doubt always will, that a properly designed market socialist system would enable a significant improvement over the market capitalist system of today, I am enough of a realist to concede that the increase in social welfare would probably not be particularly noticeable or verifiable. Now that the existence of Western capitalism is no longer a contributing factor to an international ideological confrontation that threatens to unleash a nuclear holocaust upon the world, the continuation of its existence does not represent an existential threat. The same cannot be said of the current international regime of relatively unconstrained national sovereignty. The persistence of this regime in today's world generates a continuing danger of nuclear war. The most effective way to reduce this threat would be the foundation of a properly designed federal world government. This was the argument in the 1963 "Introduction" manuscript, and the argument was later much refined, amplified, and elucidated in various book and article manuscripts, some unpublished but most published, in the years since 1962. My most recent book on world government was published in 2018: *Evolutionary World Government: A Pragmatic Approach to Global Federation*. Unlike the existence or non-existence of market socialism, the existence or non-existence of a federal world government potentially has a very significant bearing on the future destiny of global human civilization. It is indeed an existential matter.

Of all the arguments that could have been put forward back in 1963 against the possibility of federal world government, only one is no longer relevant in today's world. However, that particular argument was an extremely important argument. That extremely important argument was that federal world government was either impossible, or at least extremely improbable, owing to the vehement ideological confrontation between communism and non-communism. Even though that particular argument has been relegated to insignificance, there are several other very weighty arguments against the feasibility and desirability of world government: the remaining ideological confrontation between the democratic principle and various forms of political elitism, economic inequalities among nations, historical grievances, and various heterogeneities among nations beyond the economic gap: racial, religious, linguistic, and cultural. Even though the 1963 "Introduction" tract concentrated heavily on market socialism and lightly on world government, a start was made toward dealing with these various additional objections to world government.

Toward the end of the 1963 "Introduction" manuscript, as part of the "New World" plan, I proposed a "Twentieth Century Council" and a "New World Society." The Twentieth Century Council would be a large-scale think tank analogous to the RAND Corporation or the Council on Foreign Relations. Its numerous personnel, among whom I imagined that I myself would be either director or a highly influential colleague, would busy themselves working out the details of the New World plan, and providing a compelling body of evidence and argumentation supporting it. The task would be too large and complex to be successfully undertaken by one person—that "one person" being me. The New World Society, on the other hand, was going to be a mass organization, a political pressure group whose objective would be the implementation of the New World plan developed by the Twentieth Century Council. Neither organization ever came about.

The obvious motivation behind the "Twentieth Century Council" and the "New World Society" was that I personally wanted—desperately wanted—friends, companions, colleagues, comrades, to help me rise to the challenge. Alas, eventually reality set in. Eventually, reluctantly, I accepted that most likely I would remain on my own in this endeavor into the indefinite future—possibly forever.

2

Reality Sets In

When I mentioned in a March 1962 letter home that when I endeavored to explain the New World concept to various people, they would normally voice "reservations," that was a decided understatement. The typical reaction could be more accurately described as stunned disbelief: "Surely you jest!" From time to time I would become depressed that I couldn't seem to get through: that no matter what I said, whoever I was conversing with would take issue. If I said the sky is blue, so it seemed, they would say no, the sky is turquoise. I began to suspect that I was cursed with the opposite of charisma: namely, "anti-charisma." Instead of being inclined to agree with me, people felt an overwhelming urge to disagree.

But it was with a certain amount of relief that I soon concluded that the problem, after all, was not with the messenger but rather with the message. Here I was challenging people's deeply ingrained beliefs, telling them they were wrong, mistaken, misguided, misinformed. Most normal people don't want to hear that sort of thing. When you consider the various historical figures who marshaled followers with their golden oratory, one secret of their success was that they told people things they wanted to hear. Great religious figures such as Christ and Mohammed promised eternal life to their adherents—everyone wants some means of avoiding the finality of death. Successful political leaders follow an analogous strategy. For example, back in the 1920s and 30s, Adolf Hitler promised the German people that he would "make Germany great again"—a welcome promise to the many Germans who felt personally humiliated by Germany's defeat in World War I. The implication of this for me was that since the New World plan was in opposition to so much solidly entrenched opinion, it was not going to be at all easy to get it across.

Only the handful of Fordham students who were my fellow residents in Mrs. Peters' rooming house during my freshman year seemed to take my ideas seriously. But perhaps the reason for that was that they were in a sense a captive audience. Perhaps they soon concluded that it was easier to nod agreement than to engage in debate. While it was true that they had any number of objections to my plan, they eventually found from experience that it was also true that I had any number of responses to these objections. It may have been simply too much trouble to debate the matter, to take issue. Did I truly persuade them with my cogent and compelling argumentation, I wondered—or just exhaust them?

At the end of my freshman year, when I returned to my family home in Tervuren for the summer vacation of 1962, I encountered further evidence of the difficulty of getting people to understand and perceive the power and beauty of the grand design. A major problem at that time was that the precise role of "socialism" within the grand design was still quite vague. By the summer of 1962, my opinion of socialism, which was to be the launching pad for the whole process, could reasonably be described as "there's a lot more to it than most Americans believe." I was quite confident that *some* type of socialism would be superior to capitalism, though I wasn't yet sure just what type. The whole issue was still quite cloudy in my mind.

As anyone who has ever seriously studied the real-world and intellectual history of the socialist idea in human affairs will attest, this is a complicated, multi-faceted subject. In the real world, there is communistic socialism as practiced in the Soviet Union, Red China, and elsewhere, quite differently in each case. Also in the real world, there is social democratic socialism as practiced in various Western European nations and elsewhere. These social democratic parties, at some times and places quite successful, claim to be "Marxist" and "socialist" even though they have long since abandoned both Marx's prediction of revolution, and his prescription of public ownership of land and capital. Finally, in the theoretical realm, you have market socialist concepts not yet implemented anywhere in the real world, such as Oskar Lange's "marginal cost pricing" socialism and my own "pragmatic market socialism." (Possibly the contemporary real-world economy of the People's Republic of China, which has become such an important component of the global economy, might be deemed a variant of "market socialism." But this is uncertain. Certainly the defenders of capitalism will maintain that to the extent that China is successful, it is only because its economy is "capitalism under another name.")

Aside from the institutional embodiment of socialism, which apparently could be any of a number of things, you have the question of the purposes of socialism. Socialism is in favor of greater economic equality: that much is clear. But should this greater equality be pursued primarily by means of public ownership of the non-human factors of production, land and capital? Or should it be pursued primarily by means of progressive income taxation and social welfare programs, neither of which would require public ownership of land and capital? Socialism is also clearly in favor of reducing the costs imposed on society by business depressions. Should this objective be pursued by means of direct public ownership and control of business enterprises, as under centrally planned, communistic socialism? Or should it be pursued through Keynesian anticyclical policy within a capitalist private-ownership framework, as in the United States and Europe? Furthermore, is there any hard and fast relationship between socialism and democracy? On the one hand, do the undemocratic regimes in the communist nations mean that socialism is naturally in conflict with democracy? Or is it true that the extreme concentration of capital wealth under contemporary capitalism implies a parallel concentration of political power of such a degree as to make a mockery of the democratic ideal? And what about the numerous diverse reform ideas historically associated with various branches of the socialist movement? For example, how much need socialism imply—if anything—in the way of public regulation of business enterprise, or social welfare programs, or social policy in general? As of the summer of 1962, I was still struggling to make sense of all this, to arrive at a clear and sensible formulation of the specific variety of socialism needed for the New World.

The rented house in which my family was then living during the summer of 1962 was indeed a very pleasant residence, a residence that would be described by U.S. real estate agents as "executive bracket." That designation was appropriate, in that my Dad was indeed a business executive for International Telephone and Telegraph. Not only was the house quite pleasant, so also was the village of Tervuren, the city of Brussels, the country of Belgium, and the continent of Europe—by the 1960s almost fully recovered, economically at least, from the devastation of World War II. As a result of all this pleasantness, my summer vacation of 1962 would also have been quite pleasant—if it had not been for all the dissension at home provoked by my recently revised system of beliefs.

In particular, my Dad and I engaged in a number of bitter arguments over the question of "socialism," arguments that were none the less vehement for being exceedingly murky and confused. Basically what it came down to is that I thought socialism was "good" while he thought it was "bad." Neither of us were clear on anything else but that, and we both dragged into our debates all manner of intellectual hodgepodge, most of which was quite tangential to the real question at issue. Things were further obscured by the fact that neither of us were in fact precisely clear what the real question at issue actually *was*. All I knew for sure was my father was a blindly short-sighted and intellectually microscopic bourgeois, and all Dad knew for sure was that his son was a wild-eyed, fuzzy-headed, sentimental, utopian, wrong-headed pseudo-intellectual pinko who was a bit too big for his juvenile britches. Our arguments became quite personal and vicious at times. I would be beside myself with rage at not being able to make this parental fool understand my visionary concepts. For his part, my Dad would be beside himself with rage at this egotistical, strutting prophet his formerly puppy-dog son had become.

By the following summer of 1963, I had my ideas on socialism sorted out more clearly, and I was much calmer about the whole thing. Specifically, what I now had in mind was "pragmatic market socialism," a system that would be almost identical to the existing democratic market capitalist system in the United States and Western Europe—except with respect to the distribution of capital property return. This information was quite reassuring to my parents, and consequently the need for argument was much reduced. From that time onwards through the following years and decades, my parents remained dubious about my visions of global progress, but they acknowledged that what I was proposing was not inherently absurd, and they respected what I was trying to accomplish.

On the basis of my experiences both at home and at school during the early 1960s, I fairly soon concluded that it was impractical to try to disseminate these ideas via one-on-one oral communication. The concept was too complex, there were too many facets to it. Only by seeing the concept as a whole, by appreciating the interconnections among its various components, could a person ever achieve any sort of understanding and appreciation of the big picture. What was needed, therefore, was a written document, preferably a published book. Ideas need printed form to make them respectable, plausible, acceptable. Print is not a sufficient condition to make a controversial policy proposal attractive, but it is a necessary condition.

Very early on in my college career, even as a freshman student, I concluded that I needed to write a book. I thought that if I applied myself steadily to the project throughout my sophomore and junior years, in my senior year I would write a book and submit it for publication. Between freshman and sophomore years, during the summer of 1962, I made an initial effort at a substantial essay, to serve as the basis for the anticipated book. The following summer of 1963, between my sophomore and junior years, I produced the even more substantial essay previously described: "Introduction to the New World." This document was produced long before word processing, and the typed text was sufficiently messy as to preclude convenient OCR scanning. Thus I do not have today an electronic file of the work and cannot ascertain the exact word-count. However, on the basis of cleaning up and correcting scans of a few sample pages, I estimate the total word-count of "Introduction" at somewhere in the neighborhood of 45,000. Therefore at that point I was well on my way to a book-length manuscript.

But in my senior year at Fordham, I did *not* undertake the writing of a book. Aside from the fact that undertaking such a demanding project at that point in my undergraduate career might have had a severely adverse effect on my grade-point average, there was an even more significant impediment. In the face of such overpowering skepticism, I was beginning to have serious doubts that the New World plan set forth in "Introduction" was, even by the remotest stretch of the imagination, in the slightest bit practicable.

At the root of the issue lay a simple question: If indeed pragmatic market socialism would be objectively beneficial to the overwhelming majority of the United States population, then how is it that the overwhelming majority of the United States population is adamantly opposed to socialism? My answer was simple enough: Through their control of the communications media, and their financial influence on political processes, the small minority of wealthy capitalists had succeeded, whether or not consciously and intentionally, in poisoning the minds of the American people against socialism. What was not so clear to me in the early days was how incredibly successful this poisoning had been. But I gradually came to realize that every last little component of what I termed "capitalist apologetics," no matter how trivial and esoteric, had been thoroughly ingrained in the minds of every component and stratum of the population. As this grim reality gradually sank in, I began to believe that even if I traveled down to the Bowery and engaged some random alcoholic staggering along the sidewalk in a discussion of socialism, I would get the very same contentions I was getting from my fellow Fordham students.

Perhaps the most fundamentally effective of the various anti-socialist prejudices and preconceptions that had been implanted in people was the belief that life under socialism would inevitably be rather dull, rather blah. While people might concede that the nightmarish conditions during Joseph Stalin's dictatorship in the Soviet Union were unlikely to be replicated under an American version of socialism, still they tended to believe that the egalitarian principles of a socialist society would make it difficult if not impossible for people to get ahead—even very talented and productive people. Everyone would have the same (rather low) consumption standards no matter what his or her special achievements and accomplishments. It would be impossible to dream of great wealth and luxury, of life-long leisure, of palaces and yachts. To my mind it was pristinely clear that this complaint could apply only very feebly—if at all—to the pragmatic market socialist system I was advocating. This should have been obvious simply from the various institutional details of the proposal. But I found it extremely difficult, if not impossible, to get this point across to people.

Most of my debates/dialogues with various people regarding socialism in those early days pertained only to practical matters having to do with the daily lives of people under a potential pragmatic market socialist system. Usually they did not get into higher-level conceptual issues such as whether or not capital property income is economically and ethically legitimate as a return to entrepreneurship, or capital management effort, or saving, or risk-taking. In later years, as a professor of economics I was able to examine most of these questions using formal economic theory, including mathematical methods. My analysis was explicated in a substantial number of published articles and books. Not that this analysis was definitive in any sense. From my own study of the capitalism versus socialism matter over many years, I have concluded without a doubt that no resolution either for or against either capitalism or socialism is possible on the basis of a priori economic theory. The indications on this question from pure theory are necessarily ambiguous. What would be needed to resolve the matter is empirical evidence that we do not have.

In the final analysis, the only truly worthwhile empirical evidence would be provided by an experiment with a real-world pragmatic market socialist economy. We, as a society, could establish such a system on an experimental basis. If it performs well, then we could conclude with confidence that social welfare is higher under pragmatic market socialism than under capitalism. If it performs poorly, then we would conclude the opposite. In the latter case, we would return to capitalism—such a return would not be difficult because of the very minor institutional differences between the two systems. Even from a very early stage, I was at pains to emphasize this particular point to skeptics. It did not appear to have much effect. Experimentation on this scale is hard to imagine, and in any case there was the unyielding conviction among skeptics that any such experimentation with socialism was not only dangerous—it was bound to fail.

During my sophomore year at Fordham University (1962-63), I shared an apartment with Charlie Bowman and Jerry Brooks, all three of us former residents of Mrs. Peters' rooming house. The apartment, located on the first floor of a two-story house, a few blocks away from our previous location, was relatively capacious compared to our earlier lodgings. There were two bedrooms, a bathroom, a kitchen with a dining table, and a large living room at the front of the house equipped with a convertible sofa that served as my bed. It was reasonably clean considering its location, although it was, alas, home to a substantial contingent of cockroaches.

Throughout my first two years at Fordham, my one ally was Charlie Bowman. He had been au courant with the progress of the New World concept almost from the start, and was my one real confidante. Jerry Brooks had also known about it, but was rather too dubious, and anyway his educational future seemed problematic at best. Peter Treadway, who replaced Jerry Brooks as our apartment mate for the 1963-64 academic year, also knew about it and found it all highly amusing. Charlie Bowman, on the other hand, was the one person in the world who seemed to take me seriously, and who was intelligent and educated enough to possibly become a valuable future ally. He was possibly the only person in the world who wouldn't dissolve in laughter when I confided my secret desire to one day make the New York Stock Exchange into an anti-capitalism museum.

Charlie and I entertained various plans together, most of them highly premature. For example, I began sophomore year planning momentarily to post notices around the campus in an attempt to attract more associates to the project. Heeding Charlie's advice, however, I kept putting it off, until finally I ended up postponing it to the following academic year—and then the following academic year went through practically the same process. Although I quite liked and respected Charlie Bowman, as time went on, I became more and more doubtful about him. The fact that we shared an apartment in some ways placed a strain of the relationship. I was neat, tidy, and conscientious about cleaning duties. Charlie was none of these things. It irritated me to think that one of the main reasons for his lack of concern about the apartment was that his family home was located in nearby New Haven, Connecticut, and he could and did retreat to it whenever life became too disorganized and messy in the apartment. In contrast, my family home was 3,000 miles away across the Atlantic Ocean, and my visits there were confined to the annual summer vacation.

In some ways Charlie increasingly got on my nerves. For example, drink affected Charlie adversely by bringing out his neuroticism—it made him moody and maudlin, liable to violent verbal outbursts. One time he invited some friends of his from New Haven to our apartment for a "party." The guest of honor, Charlie's "best friend," was an offbeat, totally irresponsible chap by the name of Cornelius. Not surprisingly, the party ended in drunkenness and much smashed glassware. Cornelius himself made a profound symbolic statement of some sort by throwing a heavy object—I think a radio—at the wall, gouging out a large chuck of plaster. Experiences like these eroded a lot of my confidence in Charlie, as much as I hated to see the confidence go because I was psychologically so dependent on him.

At the start of my junior year (1963-64), Jerry Brooks was replaced in the apartment by Peter T. Treadway. Treadway was a born-and-bred Republican in attitude, filled with contempt for his inferiors, of whom there were many. He introduced me to the term "sniveling liberal," and while it may fit in some cases, Treadway used it indiscriminately to describe anyone even marginally left-of-center. He had a bad influence on Charlie Bowman, aggravating what I considered Charlie's negative personality traits. For example, under Peter's influence, Charlie adopted a highly dilatory approach to "Introduction to the New World." I had returned from my 1963 summer vacation with several photocopies of this substantial tract, one of which I handed to Charlie with the request that he read it carefully. (In one of my earlier works which he *had* read, he had come across a typo in which I had rendered "big capitalists" as "bug capitalists." Admittedly, the mental image of an insect dressed up like the Monopoly man, top hat and all, was indeed rather risible. But I did not think it was quite as hilarious as Charlie made it out to be.) In any case, for whatever reason, Charlie couldn't seem to find the time to make even a start on "Introduction." Weeks went by and the manuscript remained untouched on his dresser. He had recently acquired a promising new girlfriend (whom he shortly thereafter married), and between courting that young lady and keeping up with his studies, there simply wasn't sufficient time, allegedly, to undertake my opus—which in fairness, would have constituted a heavyweight reading project. Despite such excuses, I began reluctantly to conclude that Charlie Bowman was a lost cause.

Just how lost a cause he was became forcibly evident late in the fall semester of 1963, when the apartment arrangement was suddenly terminated. For weeks things had been going from bad to worse. Treadway and Bowman were very casual about everything, including the apartment. They were very reluctant to clean the place, and treated it with all the contempt born of having a real home not far away and within easy access. To me, of course, the apartment was an actual home, the only place within thousands of miles to lay my head. I wanted the place respected by my apartment mates, kept clean and orderly. Apparently my attitude got on their nerves just as much as their attitude got on mine. Without a word to me, they provided themselves with another apartment. There was a lease, but the landlord was only too happy to break it and let us go. He was sick and tired of all the noise, disturbances and general disorder in his downstairs apartment. I couldn't blame him.

Left to myself, I applied to Fordham's housing office and soon found acceptable lodgings in a rooming house at 2505 Marion Avenue, just a few doors down from the Peters address at 2511. But the parting with

Bowman and Treadway was bitter. I was deeply hurt that the two of them had so blithely and carelessly provided for themselves, without even so much as a word of consultation with me. It was a direct slap in the face from two people I had once considered friends. Possibly neither of them really intended or wanted to hurt my feelings. Presumably I could change my lodgings just as easily as they could. Possibly also they may have wanted to get back at me to some extent for my nagging them regarding the condition of the apartment—not to mention nagging them with my New World obsession.

Although the incident was painful at the time, even a bit traumatic, in the long run the effect was favorable for me, and in retrospect I was happy it happened. Through it I managed to shed once and for all an environment and some people who were inimical to effective work and study. The new home in which I came to rest was a third-floor room in Mrs. Vambakos' rooming house, which corresponded exactly to my room at the Peters house—top floor back. The place was very quiet and peaceful. Mrs. Vambakos was a very elderly widow lady. Her single roomer prior to my arrival was an equally elderly gentleman who worked as a night clerk in a downtown hotel, kept to himself, and whose path rarely crossed mine. For the first time at Fordham, I had a residence of total peace, quiet, and privacy. It did me a world of good.

At about the same time that I experienced a personal mini-trauma in the form of my rupture with Bowman and Treadway, the United States experienced a national maxi-trauma in the form of the assassination of President John F. Kennedy on November 22, 1963. Many people who were alive on that fateful day—including me—remember exactly where they were and what they were doing when they learned of the assassination. It was a Friday afternoon, and at the actual moment of the shooting I was in Professor Cammerosano's Intermediate Microeconomic Theory class. My first premonition that something was seriously wrong came when I noticed, as I walked back across the campus headed for the apartment, anticipating a quiet weekend of reading and study, a large group of people standing around a car listening to its radio. I wondered what might be the matter—were Soviet missiles on the way? Luckily Soviet missiles were not on the way—but John F. Kennedy had been shot in Dallas, Texas. I did not join the group around the car, but a little farther on, I overheard someone talking about the line of presidential succession. At that point I began to suspect the worst. My fears were confirmed when I reached home at about 2 PM and turned on the radio. At about 2:30 came the final news of the President's death.

In the years since that tragic event, innumerable conspiracy theories have been put forward in an attempt to evade the awful truth that the president of the United States, the commander-in-chief and leader of the free world, had been gunned down by an unbalanced loser by the name of Lee Harvey Oswald, using a mail-order rifle, whose principal motivation seems to have been to do something that would impress his attractive young Russian wife Marina. I remember a fellow student saying at the time that the absurdity of it all was the same as if "a brick had fallen on him." Never at that time nor at any subsequent time have I put the slightest credence in any of the thousand-and-one alternatives to the "lone gunman" theory, nor believed that Oswald's motivation was anything other than personal self-esteem. When surveys are done that purport to demonstrate that the majority of Americans today believe that Kennedy was the victim of a conspiracy, I suspect that what the majority of Americans actually believe is that it is *conceivable* that Kennedy was the victim of a conspiracy. Given the volume of the conspiracy literature, it is understandable that many if not most people believe that a conspiracy is *conceivable*. But "conceivable" is far short of "probable."

Personally, I had never been as smitten with Kennedy as most Americans in the early 1960s. The 1960 election had been very close, with Kennedy defeating Nixon by an extremely narrow margin. Nevertheless, in the two and a half years that he had been in office, and despite serious missteps such as the Bay of Pigs, Kennedy had won over the large majority of people with his youthful good looks, photogenic family, energetic manner, and eloquent oratory. His assassination pretty much earned him posthumous sainthood. Even though at that time his relentless infidelity was largely unknown, I had my own reservations about the man. While I thought he was doing a creditable job as president, and I was not aware of any other public figure who was likely to do a better job, I couldn't quite get past the fact that his family wealth had been instrumental to his meteoric rise. True, he was handsome, intelligent, industrious, and charismatic, but those qualities in themselves were unlikely to have propelled him into the presidency of the United States. In some ways, therefore, his ascendancy was evidence of the undue influence of wealth in American politics—which was a serious defect of the capitalist status quo.

Be that as it may, I was as shocked, horrified, and demoralized as most of my fellow American citizens by Kennedy's assassination. As the fall of 1963 advanced, a fall that I remember as especially gray and gloomy, I was seriously depressed by two things: Kennedy's assassination, and the fact that my New World project was getting nowhere. Ever since my freshman year, I had been planning a large tome that would present my ideas about global progress coherently and compellingly. As the great magnitude of the projected research/writing task became more and more evident, I sought associates to share the effort: assistants, collaborators, co-authors. In a word, I needed *help*. But my efforts to get help were unpromising to say the least. The best prospect I had ever had was Charlie Bowman, and he deserted me because, among other things, I kept harassing him about keeping our apartment clean and tidy. A bad sign indeed.

During the fall of 1963, however, I had one other prospect in mind—and this was not a mere student, but an actual Fordham faculty member in good standing: Professor John J. Klein. During my sophomore year, Professor Klein had been my instructor in the upper division course in money and banking. I had earned an A in that course, and seemed to be on good terms with him, or at least on as good terms as could be expected between a faculty member and a lowly student. Moreover, Klein possessed what were probably the best credentials of any Fordham University economics department faculty member at that time. He had received his Ph.D. from the University of Chicago, and an article based on his dissertation ("German Money and Prices, 1932-44") was one of only five papers included in *Studies in the Quantity Theory of Money* (1956), a seminal volume edited by the illustrious Chicago monetarist and conservative Milton Friedman. In 1960 he had published an article entitled "Price-Level and Money-Denomination Movements" in the prestigious *Journal of Political Economy*. He was also author of the widely adopted money and banking textbook *Money and the Economy*, which afterwards went through several editions. If I could attract the sympathetic attention of a personage so exalted as Professor John J. Klein, there was no telling what might become possible. Therefore at some point during the fall semester of 1963, I screwed up my courage and decided I would acquaint him with my New World project.

Although I did not commence a regular diary until the fall semester of 1964, prior to that I had been making occasional diary-style entries in my "Journal of Personal Progress." On the basis of one of these entries, dated Tuesday, November 19, 1963, three days prior to Kennedy's assassination, I am able to state with confidence that it was on that day that I finally caught up with the good Professor Klein, presented him with a copy of INW ("Introduction to the New World"), and requested humbly that he look at it and give me his opinion. He was noticeably dismayed by the prodigious length of the document (86 single-spaced typed pages), but promised (unenthusiastically) to try to get to it, with the proviso that "it is on the bottom of my list of priorities." Of course, that was sufficient for me. He happened to notice the title and commented "Looks like a way-out topic." I had to agree, but I tried to give him to understand that while I realized the "Introduction" was quite likely a lot of hogwash, at the same time I hoped that it *might* contain some value—otherwise I would not have troubled him since I knew how busy he was.

A few days later, in the stunned aftermath of the President's death, while scribbling anxious, disconnected comments on the tragedy in my Journal, I finally recorded in writing my accumulating doubts that the New World scheme was even remotely possible. The outpouring of sincere emotion all around the world impressed upon me a clearer recognition that I myself very much wanted to make a significant personal contribution—as John F. Kennedy had done—to the advancement of the global human prospect. But quite possibly there was no hope whatsoever of accomplishing this if I persisted with the New World project in its existing form. In particular, socialism might have to go:

> Capitalism is probably too strongly entrenched in the West to be uprooted. The same goes for Communism in the East. So – "Politics is the art of the possible." Human unity might be achieved even within the framework of present ideological disunity. There's no sense in becoming a martyr for the original version of the NW. True, a mass movement toward world rationality and unity is needed, but does it have to be exactly the one I first conceived? Capitalism may be too solidly entrenched in America. True, socialism would be better, but who knows that? Why should I beat my head against a stone wall? The abolition of capitalism is not absolutely necessary to world unity. To be sure, if I become convinced that the cause of real socialism in the West is hopeless, I will abandon it quicker than the wink of an eye. So what if the world is not perfect? So what if unjustified privilege exists? So what if the people believe lies? Let them believe lies. If Klein turns thumbs down on pragmatic socialism, I will be well on my way to a decision.

The "decision" referred to would be the definite abandonment of pragmatic market socialism as the key catalytic element within the New World scheme. From time to time thereafter, I reiterated my appeal to Professor Klein to read and ponder my New World essay. Weeks passed—then months—still he kept "trying to get to it." In the wake of the assassination of President Kennedy which horrified the nation and alarmed the world, followed by the breakup of the Briggs Avenue apartment which sent me personally back on my own to an almost deserted rooming house with no other student residents, I increasingly lost faith in the New World—or at least in my own personal ability to accomplish anything like it. Perhaps someone possessed of transcendent personal charisma could do it—but not me. Still, I simply had to know what Professor Klein thought of my magnum opus.

I know from a preserved letter home that near the end of February 1964, I finally cornered Professor Klein in his campus office, and he agreed to talk with me for a while about my New World tract. I said in the letter that it was a fairly long conversation, about two hours in length, but it may be that I exaggerated the length of the exchange in order to save face with my family. According to my letter home, Klein vigorously defended the capitalistic status quo, but he conceded that since most capital property income appears to be unearned, capitalism in that sense may contain an exploitative element. But in return he got me to concede that the exploitative element was rather small in a quantitative sense—perhaps so small that it would not justify the transition costs of a change to market socialism. Professor Klein also extracted from me the admission that I was not absolutely, definitely, 100 percent certain that market socialism would improve on market capitalism. But I assured my family that I had been gradually getting the upper hand in the debate, and that a second round had been scheduled for the following Monday.

As it turned out, the scheduled second round never took place. I suspect that what had happened prior to the above-described debate was that Professor Klein had skimmed "Introduction to the New World" just enough to know that it was preaching socialism, and he absolutely knew, as did practically everyone else in the United States, Western Europe, and throughout the non-communist world, that socialism, in any form whatever, was a bad idea. It was at this point that he had had a relatively lengthy debate with a student (me) who was far better informed about the deficiencies of contemporary capitalism and the potential merits of market socialism than he was. Debating the matter with this impudent, importunate, know-it-all student he likely found tiresome. He may have made an appointment for a follow-up debate, but when the time came he simply wasn't in the mood.

So it was that when I entered his office that Monday afternoon, he was just putting on his overcoat in preparation for leaving. He was in a hurry and didn't have time for further discussion of the matter. He handed me my manuscript and said that while he hadn't had a chance to read the whole thing closely, he had in fact arrived at a definite judgment on it, as follows: "This doesn't have a snowball's chance in hell!" Then he walked out. This constituted the effective termination of the debate on grounds that debate on this particular issue was pointless, useless, moot, irrelevant, beside the point. Socialism simply was not on the agenda—and never would be.

Although in senior year I took a corporation finance course from Professor John J. Klein, I never again mentioned to him the "Introduction to the New World." *Snowball's chance in hell!* Everyone knows the old expression: "cut like a knife." That's what it did to me: "snowball's chance in hell" did indeed "cut like a knife." Ever since that moment, I have had uncharitable feelings toward John J. Klein. He might have sat me down, leaned back in his chair and said gently something like: "Jim, this work is an impressive example of your intellect and sensitivity, and it does you credit as an idealist. Although I doubt that the world is ready for this level of visionary thought, I congratulate you and wish you the best of luck." He could have then added, in tones of sincere regret, "But I fear that in the here and now, things being the way they are, this work doesn't have a snowball's chance in hell." That would have been more considerate.

So, as of the spring of 1964, it had become inescapably apparent to me that any plan to establish socialism in the advanced Western countries was practically impossible—among other factors, the ownership and control of the communications media by capitalists interested in preserving the capitalist status quo was a virtually impregnable obstacle. Maybe some superman would be capable of implementing my plan of "creating a subsidiary communications network to convey the one bit of information that socialism is preferable to capitalism," but I doubted that such a superman existed. I knew *I* certainly wasn't him.

Naturally I was depressed by the apparent failure of the New World scheme, but not as much as one might expect. Messianic aspirations had been part of my life for so long by this time that I just couldn't bear to abandon them altogether. If not one way, then another. In fact, long before I concluded that the game was up on the New World approach, I had begun to think about an alternative plan—something that would be of great historical importance and benefit to humanity, but which would *not* require anything so difficult to achieve as the establishment of public-ownership socialism in the non-communist nations of the West.

Starting in early 1964, I started making notes toward a large, multi-volume work with the working title *Our Time*. Most components of the earlier New World were included, with the principal exception of pragmatic market socialism. Some things were added: most prominently some consideration of philosophical issues. Although the initial explorations in this new line of thought dated from early 1964, it wasn't until the summer of 1965 that I got around to writing a formal outline of it. In other words, for almost a year and a half the grand design was put on the back burner. There were two principal reasons for this. First, it was necessary that I buckle down seriously to my coursework in the interest of achieving good grades in my final semesters of undergraduate study. Early on I had decided that the best way to earn a living and at the same time continue my visionary research and writing was to pursue an academic career—and to pursue an academic career one needed a Ph.D. So in junior and senior years I had my eyes firmly fixed on graduate school.

In spite of the fact that I had excised pragmatic market socialism from the grand design to be laid out in *Our Time*, I continued researching and pondering the subject, which I found inherently fascinating, and which might possibly, depending on developments, become politically significant at some future time. During the spring semester of 1965, in fact, I wrote a lengthy essay on pragmatic market socialism and submitted it to a competition for the annual Economics Department Essay Award. During the latter part of the semester I fretted a great deal over whether or not I would get that award. In the end it was given to me, to my considerable relief. The single copy of the essay was returned to me just before graduation—but on an ill-considered impulse I gave it away to a fellow student who expressed mild interest. It was never returned. Very soon thereafter I greatly regretted that lapse in judgment. I suppose it was just a matter of idle curiosity, but long afterwards I would have liked to know what the status of my thought on pragmatic market socialism was as of the spring semester of 1965.

In any case, in what was the final entry in the Journal of Personal Progress made prior to the commencement of the diary, written sometime during the spring of 1964, I drafted a possible introduction to a future book on pragmatic market socialism. This draft might have served as the introduction to the lost essay on pragmatic market socialism. The first paragraph is as follows:

> Pragmatic market socialism is an economic system which attempts to reconcile the fundamental socialist principle of common, social, or state ownership of the means of production with the basically free enterprise, profit motive system of allocation of scarce resources used by the advanced capitalist countries. The basic idea is that where the rent, profit and interest generated by this type of allocation process go, under the capitalist system, to private property-owners of the non-human means of production (land and capital), under the pragmatic market socialist system, this property-return would go to the government, which would then distribute it equitably to the people at large in the form of a social dividend disbursement. This system is distinct from authoritarian socialism (the type presently existing in Russia and China), and marginal cost socialism (the type usually proposed by socialist theorists such as Oskar Lange).

Although in later years I added quite a lot in the way of institutional detail to the pragmatic market socialist proposal, the above capsule definition would remain basically accurate.

Just as the former grand design had a name (the "New World"), so too the post-New World grand design needed a name. In a flash of intuition that I later came to regret, I decided on "Plan Alpha." "Plan Alpha" was so designated because this was going to be the *first* plan of coordinated global action to gain better control over future developments. Why not call it Plan A? I guess the only possible explanation for that is that the Greek alphabet is "classier" than the Roman alphabet. Possibly Plan Alpha, the first plan, would eventually be followed by Plan Beta, Plan Gamma, and so on. That was a matter for our descendants. The name "Plan Alpha" was a classic example of "it seemed like a good idea at the time."

In September 1964, my father, accompanied by his family, had returned from Belgium to the United States, to take up a new position as CEO of a recently acquired subsidiary of International Telephone and Telegraph: ITT Cannon, an electronics firm with headquarters in Los Angeles, California. The new family home was a sprawling upscale ranch-style house with a swimming pool, located in Pasadena. As soon as I graduated from Fordham University in June of 1965, with considerable relief I said farewell forever to the Bronx and headed westward to the golden California shores on the blue Pacific Ocean. It was there, in August 1965, that I completed a two-part document, the first part an outline of Plan Alpha itself, and the second part an outline of *Our Time*, the four-volume tome that would announce and explain Plan Alpha to the waiting world. The two documents together were a little shy of 5,000 words.

A year later, in August 1966, I completed a much expanded document (almost 20,000 words), entitled simply "Plan Alpha." The intervening academic year of 1965-66 I had spent at the University of California at Berkeley, earning a master's degree in economics. In September 1966, my wife Penelope (Penny) and I headed east toward Evanston, Illinois, where I would undertake doctoral studies at Northwestern University. My one year of master's level study at UC Berkeley was very similar to my senior year at Fordham in that work on the grand design was minimal. This was for the same reason as before: the need to earn decent grades (significantly more difficult than it had been at Fordham, since UC Berkeley was among the premier universities in the nation).

I mentioned above that many years later when I looked back at the "Introduction to the New World," I was horrified by the almost fanatic tone of the work, no less than by the incompetent typing job. In retrospect, it is no wonder, with such a weak production, that I was unable to attract interest. Similarly, when I later looked back at "Plan Alpha," I was again horrified. This time, however, it wasn't so much the typing, since my Dad's executive secretary had retyped it neatly from my original draft. The principal problem with Plan Alpha was that it incorporated into the grand design elements that were both unnecessary and off-putting to the average person. True, pragmatic socialism was out of the picture, but whatever credibility might have been gained by that excision, was lost by the addition of these other extraneous elements. I've already mentioned the extraneous element of the poor name choice: "Plan Alpha" has a pretentious tone, as if it were part of some grandiosely preposterous science fiction epic. But there were a number of other, even more serious problems.

The two core proposals of Plan Alpha were for: (1) a global economic development program (what I later designated the "World Economic Equalization Program," and still later the "Global Marshall Plan"), and (2) a federal world government (what I later designated the "Federal Union of Democratic Nations"). Although obviously I have been unable, as yet, to bring either of these proposals into the realm of plausible real-world possibilities, the fact remains that it was (and remains) possible to advocate these things in a calm, balanced, reasonable manner—in such a manner as to make possible published book and article contributions to the professional literature. Not as yet to the popular—or "trade"—literature. But once certain ideas are established in the professional literature, it becomes possible that they might someday, somehow, leak out into the popular literature.

The central problem with Plan Alpha, aside from the name, is that it did not focus on these two core proposals. It brought in other ideas of a far more problematic nature, ideas that could not assist in the advancement of the core proposals, but that could (and did) detract from them. To illustrate some of these, I will provide below some direct quotes from the 1966 Plan Alpha tract, along with explanations (if any are really needed) of why they did more harm than good. Within the first few pages, a reader would encounter the following:

> Therefore, in general, the Goal of Plan Alpha is the <u>maximization of individual human welfare subject to the constraint that the human race as a whole survives and expands.</u> Given the general goal, the precise meaning of "welfare" must be specified, and a specific goal in terms of this definition formulated.
>
> For purposes of Plan construction, the Whole Man Hypothesis will provide the basic definition of welfare. To the extent that human individuals become more fully "Whole Men," to that extent is individual human welfare improved. According to the Hypothesis, the Whole

> Man is: (1) Materially Content; (2) Economically Productive; (3) Intellectually Aware and Creative; (4) Part of a Great and Growing Social Whole; (5) Possessor of a Philosophy of Life. It is obvious from this enumeration that the Whole Man concept is relative rather than absolute. That is, one is not either a Whole Man or not a Whole Man, but one is a Whole Man to a greater or lesser degree. For example, at the present time, there are probably very few humans who are not, to some extent at least, Whole Men. On the other hand, there are probably very few humans at the present time who are Whole Men to the degree that their natural capabilities would permit were the environment optimal.

What is wrong with this passage? To begin with, one does not have to be a hardline feminist to notice the consistent usage of "man" and "men," where "person" or "persons" might have served just as well. It was not too long after this early writing that I learned to use sex-neutral terminology whenever possible. For example, "humanity" or "humankind" is much better than "mankind." Aside from that, even if we replaced "Whole Man" with "Whole Person," there is no need to define this concept in order to make a case for any specific reform proposal. Some of the items on the list seem so obvious as to make their explication almost silly: for example, "Materially Content." Others seem debatable: "Part of a Great and Growing Social Whole" and "Possessor of a Philosophy of Life"? And why all the capitalizations? Even if we drop the capitalizations, the question remains: What is the point of trying to define such concepts as happiness and contentment? Most people have an adequate intuitive sense of the meaning of these things.

Further on there is a discussion of goals and means, as follows:

> The four means to the Plan Alpha Goal are formulated on the basis of concreteness and practicality. Just as it makes little sense setting out goals which are either without meaningful content or impossible to achieve, it would be the same constructing means which either have nothing to do with the goals or are incapable of implementation. The four Plan Alpha Means are these: (1) Construction of the Technological Civilization; (2) Population Control; (3) Establishment of the World State; (4) Institution of the Policy of Stellar Expansion. These Means are separate but closely interrelated. They are only to be conceived of, in fact, as a unified system.

Now we are getting into *really* serious problems. This is no longer a matter of sexist terminology or excessive capitalization. One can easily change sexist terms to sex-neutral terms, and one can easily change from uppercase to lowercase. Of the four "Plan Alpha Goals" enumerated in the foregoing, only one is a core proposal—that for a world state. Of course, it need not be belabored that most people back in the 1960s, even more than people today, were of the firm opinion that any sort of world government was a utopian fantasy—and an extremely dangerous one at that. Nevertheless, it so happens that a *properly designed* world government would have been successful back then, even as it would be successful today. (What I mean by "proper design" will be explicated at various appropriate points in the following.) *That* was the proposition to be emphasized, to be elaborated and argued. The other three Plan Alpha Goals are all highly controversial in and of themselves, are fully irrelevant to the world government goal, and needlessly weaken the case to be made for world government.

"Construction of the Technological Civilization" suggests that everyone should become a scientist or engineer. But what about the arts, literature, philosophy, the humanities? Are all we humans to become the equivalent of mechanical robots? Well, of course the intent of the "technological civilization" term was nothing so unappealing as that. The basic idea was that a higher rate of technological progress, to be fueled by a higher rate of investment in education, especially technical education, would enable less reliance on manual labor and more reliance on mental labor. For example, writers today mostly rely on microcomputer hardware and word processing software to create their works rather than pen and paper—even if these works be on non-technical topics in literature, art history, philosophy, and so on. My idea was hardly to eliminate the humanities, but rather to enable the humanities to be pursued with more technically advanced tools. But why then use the term "technological civilization" to represent this idea? As with the term "Plan Alpha," it seemed like a good idea at the time.

If any one thing might be singled out as most harmful to the credibility of Plan Alpha, it was probably specification of "Institution of the Policy of Stellar Expansion" as one of the four Plan Alpha Means. More than any other single factor, this made the whole Plan Alpha concept seem like nothing more than the perfervid imagining of a drug-addled science fiction writer. Of course, it is not too difficult to see why it seemed like a good idea at the time. In science fiction literature and cinema, rocket-ships had been gallivanting around the galaxy for decades. Moreover, John F. Kennedy had excited the nation and the world with his vow that the United States would send men to the moon, and bring them back safely, before the end of the decade. The vow was indeed fulfilled, but the motivation behind that exploit was the Cold War competition between the communist East and the non-communist West. It is hardly surprising that now that the Cold War is history, space exploration has gone to bottom of most people's priority list. Any knowledgeable astronomer will affirm that there is probably little of economic value to be found within our own solar system, and furthermore, that the technical problems involved in travelling to the stars are so daunting that there is little prospect that they will be surmounted within the foreseeable future.

The second of the four Means, "Population Control," is worthy of more serious consideration. There was only one graphical figure included in the 1966 Plan Alpha document: a hand-drawn illustration labeled "Estimated population of the world from 1 A.D. to 1960 A.D. and the projected population to 2000 A.D." The accompanying text is as follows:

> Population Control. The present rate of population growth cannot be maintained indefinitely. A mere glance at the accompanying graph, which represents the most generally accepted demographic estimates presently available, should be enough to establish this with most reasonable persons. The question is not whether or not the present rate of population growth will someday decline. The question is as to when and how the present rate of population growth will decline. And the related policy question is: should the size of population and the rate of population growth be left to take care of themselves, or should the human race attempt to establish some sort of rational control over them? It is the implicit position of the Plan, of course, that a policy of rational control would be desirable. The Plan position is not that social neglect of population would necessarily be disastrous, and a policy of control is absolutely necessary to any sort of progress, but only that, on the basis of present knowledge, a policy of control would be wiser than a policy of neglect.

Figure 2.1 displayed below, a recent equivalent to the 1966 Plan Alpha figure, is based on data in a Wikipedia post titled "Estimates of historical world population." Although more recent data show a slight reduction in the population growth rate since about 2000, before that population growth was clearly explosive from about 1800 onwards. On the basis of this indication, I am forced to conclude that excessive population growth does indeed represent a very serious threat to the future of humanity, almost as much a threat today as it was back in the 1960s. Whether or not humanity will cope successfully with the problem in the future is uncertain. Perhaps the biggest single difficulty is that the most effective means of population control, such as contraception and abortion, are regarded as heinously immoral by substantial subgroups, usually on religious grounds. Such indirect methods of population control as the implementation of economic disincentives to fertility are rejected by many people, even those who have no objections to contraception, on grounds that the government should not be interfering with people's natural rights with respect to procreation. Thus far the only country to have implemented truly drastic methods of population control is the People's Republic of China, and many observers would argue that this was possible only because the Chinese political system is basically undemocratic, not to say totalitarian.

Figure 2.1: World Population 1000-2000

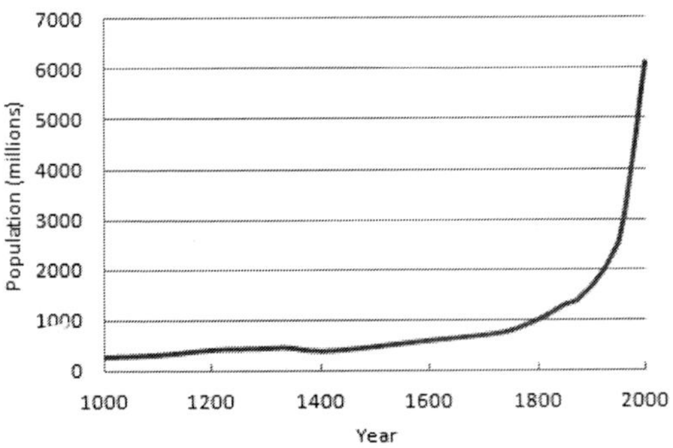

To reiterate, the two core proposals of Plan Alpha—that I still consider to be relevant and valid even today—were for: (1) a global economic development program, and (2) a federal world government. These two proposals are only weakly related to population control. My own opinion is that if both (1) and (2) were undertaken, this would increase the probability that an effective population control policy will be implemented before it is too late. But I also believe that it would be unwise to present this possibility as an important reason for undertaking global economic development and establishing a world government. This is because population control is too delicate, too sensitive, too controversial. Too many people who might otherwise be in favor of global economic development and world government, would be put off if population control were pushed too vigorously.

It is now quite clear that the mid-twentieth century "standing room only" jeremiahs were excessively alarmist. Not only has the predicted mass starvation not happened, but living standards in most nations of the world, as measured by per capita income, are increasing at a respectable rate. Arguably living standards would be rising more quickly if population growth were lower, but this is not as powerful an argument against rapid population growth as that it might cause mass starvation. In other words, population is not a critical issue for the current generation of humanity, nor probably for the next two or three generations as well. It is possible, of course, that the population problem will eventually "cure itself"—benignly—without the need for any sort of governmental intervention. Personally, I suspect that at some point the need for governmental intervention will become compellingly obvious. But that point might not be reached for another fifty years, one hundred years, possibly even longer. In the meantime, the case for global economic development and federal world government will probably be stronger if the population issue is skirted.

Getting back to the 1966 Plan Alpha document, its concluding sections presented an appeal to the reader to consider contributing to the cause by means of joining the "Twentieth Century Council," an organization exactly analogous to the "Twentieth Century Council" proposed within the New World scheme. Also included was a "Plan Alpha Society" analogous to the "New World Society." The only difference was that while the New World Twentieth Century Council would proceed directly to writing articles and books supportive of the concept, the Plan Alpha Twentieth Century Council would have, initially, a more limited mission: the writing of a proposal for financial support, to be presented to various philanthropic organizations.

Needless to say, my forecasts made in 1966 proved well wide of the mark. Not only was the Twentieth Century Council not established by the early 1970s, it was never established. It was also forecast that the Implementation Stage, which was to follow upon the Planning Stage, would commence by the early 1980s. Similarly, the Implementation Stage never happened. If the spring of 1964 might be specified as marking the death of the New World project, the spring of 1968 can be specified as marking the death of the Plan Alpha project. My two academic years of residency in the economics doctoral program at Northwestern University commenced in September 1966 and were completed in June 1968. It was at the start of those two academic years that I made a serious, sustained effort to attract friends, associates, colleagues, and comrades to help me rise to the Plan Alpha challenge. This was analogous to the effort I had made some years earlier at Fordham to find allies to help me rise to the New World challenge. As before, the effort was not merely unsuccessful—it was crushingly, humiliatingly unsuccessful.

In September 1966 I had brought with me to Northwestern University 50 photocopies of the Plan Alpha tract that had been completed in August. If needed, I could make additional copies. As it happened, additional copies were not needed. By late November 1966, I had managed to distribute approximately 20 copies of it, accompanied by various personal approaches of varying nature and length. It soon became obvious that despite the excision of pragmatic market socialism, Plan Alpha was just as unattractive as the New World had been. My prospects were mostly fellow graduate students, and while some of them offered kind words to the effect that while the Plan Alpha intentions were noble and some of the ideas might hold promise, as a whole the project was completely unfeasible. The bottom line, therefore, was that while they wished me luck, they most definitely declined to become personally involved.

A typical example was Howard Schachter, a classmate of mine in the Socialist Economic Theory course being given by Professor George Dalton. He was curious enough to read the Plan Alpha document, and afterwards wanted to talk about it. Although he granted that it had an admirably progressive tone, he initially had two major qualms: (1) the proposed world state might tend to be totalitarian; (2) the Plan as a whole was thoroughly unfeasible. He allowed as how Plan Alpha just didn't "reach" him, it wasn't "meaningful" to him. He preferred to work on shorter-run, more feasible causes, such as the civil rights crusade. He also mentioned a "meaningful" United Nations. I asked what he meant by a "meaningful" U.N. After long thought, he replied "a U.N. that would cut out this bullshit of the U.S. being in Vietnam." This was in late 1966, and while the U.S. effort in Vietnam was obviously not going well, I personally thought at that time that it would be somewhat premature to pull the plug on it. It took several more months for me personally to conclude that Vietnam was costing the United States more than it was worth. But what bothered me most about Schachter's assertion, aside from the unprofessional term "bullshit," is that Vietnam was clearly an ephemeral problem of exactly the sort that Plan Alpha was intended to ameliorate. Moreover, how could the United Nations be able to keep the United States out of Vietnam without becoming the kind of totalitarian world state he claimed to fear? Although disappointed and irritated, I resisted the temptation to escalate the argument and the meeting ended cordially. I wished him luck in his work and he in mine. But afterwards I felt depressed. I asked myself: Isn't there *anyone* in this world besides myself who is willing to look at the long run, to take the broad view?

At around the time that all this was going on, an incident occurred that was at the same time amusing and sobering. My diary records that on the afternoon of Monday, October 10, 1966, on my way home from the campus, I stopped in for a haircut at the "Golden Rule Barber Shop," a one-man establishment. That man, an older gentleman by the name of Christian H. McEntire who appeared to be about 85 years of age, turned out to be something of a screwball—in a nice way. Obviously delighted to have a captive audience, he reminisced at considerable length, rather vaguely but floridly, about his experiences as a proponent of script in Illinois during the early days of the Great Depression. From there he worked around to his current passions, which focused on the evils of smoking tobacco, one-arm driving, and tailgating. Against tailgating, he had devised a device which, when operated by a button on the dashboard, would raise a neon sign from the trunk warning the tailgater: "Not so close, please!" Against one-arm driving, he had written a poem entitled (sarcastically) "Genius at the Wheel," illustrated by a cartoon of a chimpanzee smoking a cigarette while one-handedly driving a car. The following stanza conveys the gist of the poem:

> I love to drive "chimpanzee style."
> Such nonchalance—it's so worthwhile!
> My wheel-draped wrist well does the steering—
> Why should I care 'bout nitwits jeering?

Christian pressed upon me a pamphlet, entitled "Unsafe on Any Highway," which contained not only the poem itself, but also an extended account, heartfelt but somewhat rambling, of his efforts to gain wider currency for this and other brainchildren of his. For example, he had contacted the president of the National Safety Council with a plan to print "Genius at the Wheel" periodically in all NSC publications, and to supplement this with the mass distribution of a "pinup" featuring the chimpanzee driving a car along with the text of "Genius at the Wheel," for posting on bulletin boards in schools, libraries, post offices, police stations, and sundry other public buildings, throughout the length and breadth of the nation.

Christian also provided me with a copy of a letter he had sent to President Lyndon B. Johnson (with a copy to Lady Bird Johnson) suggesting that a copy of "Unsafe on Any Highway" be sent to every holder of a driver's license in the country. He helpfully suggested that Mr. Johnson should instruct the automobile manufacturers of the country to finance this distribution in order to reduce the number of traffic accidents. Should they prove unwilling, then the federal government itself should do it (the printing could be done by the U.S. Government Printing Office to save on costs). After receiving polite but noncommittal replies from the offices of both the President and Lady Bird, Mr. McEntire assumed those doors were closed—he explained that when he sent his letter, Johnson was at his Texas ranch and probably never saw it. His latest gambit was a letter to his local Congressman asking that he say "the right words in the right places" to unblock national distribution of "Unsafe on Any Highway." That letter was sent out only in late September, so as of October he was still awaiting a reply.

However, Christian was none too sure about getting assistance from high government officials—and he thought he knew why. As it happened, Christian was a non-smoker, and he was thoroughly convinced of the pernicious effect of smoking tobacco, having been persuaded of this by scientific evidence. As a matter of fact, he used to have many discussions on the subject with none other than Jack Dempsey, who came into his barber shop regularly for a shave and a trim. As Christian pondered the matter, it gradually became clear to him who was behind all this obstructionism against his worthy campaign against one-armed driving: big tobacco manufacturers. You see, many people drive with one hand because they are smoking, and if they become convinced of the evils of one-handed driving, they wouldn't smoke while driving—and thereby the profits of the big tobacco manufacturers would plummet. You had to admit it made sense, in a way.

When I got home, my wife Penny and I had a good laugh over "Unsafe on Any Highway" and the other supporting documentation Christian had laid on me. Christian H. McEntire would reasonably be described by most sensible people as a delightful lunatic, a harmless eccentric, an entertaining crackpot. Here is a man who refuses to decline into senility—he prefers to go out as a noble old man nobly insane. I must admit I admired him—a zany to the very end!

But after the chuckles subsided, a rather sobering thought occurred to me. This man is an obvious nut to me—but am *I* an obvious nut to everyone looking at me from the outside? I wondered: Does my Plan Alpha appear to everyone else as scatterbrained and ridiculous as Mr. McEntire's grand plan to crush out the evils of tailgating and one-arm driving? Penny assured me that this was not the case—that I was objectively and without a doubt far more sane and sensible than Mr. McEntire. But still I couldn't help wondering. After all, Penny was my wife, and wives, as a rule, tend to be far more understanding and forgiving of their husbands than the rest of the world. So, after the amusement petered out, it was replaced by a disconcerting premonition that Plan Alpha would never amount to anything more than an exercise in futility.

Gradually I came to accept the reality that from here on in, I was going to have to go it alone into the indefinite future—possibly forever. It was also a reality that it would be thoroughly useless for me to approach the Ford Foundation, or any other foundation, all by myself with a request to provide substantial financial support for anything so controversial as the visionary projects I was developing. Financial support from a foundation might be possible in the future, but only if I had reputable publications in hand explaining and defending these ideas. In other words, just as I had realized way back in the winter of 1961-62 at Fordham University, it was necessary that I write and publish a book. It would have to be a big book, and I now accepted that I would have no appreciable assistance in producing this big book. That was the way it had to be. There was no alternative.

But I *should* do it, I *could* do it, and I *would* do it!

3

UNION CARD

In academia, the term "union card" refers to the Ph.D. It is *possible* to have a career as a faculty member in the American higher education system even if one does not have "Ph.D." following one's name, but it is definitely not recommended. Only at the lowest level among community colleges will lack of a doctorate not be a serious deficiency. Among the higher strata of community colleges, and on upwards through middle and upper level colleges and universities, it is absolutely necessary that one possess a Ph.D. in order to be able to walk down the corridors with one's head held high, and to be able to speak freely among one's colleagues in the conference rooms and faculty lounges. It is true that students are normally unconcerned about the academic credentials of their teachers. But that is a minor consolation to those unfortunate souls who are teaching in the higher education system without doctorates. Far more important than student opinion to the typical faculty member's sense of self-worth, is the respect of his or her faculty peers. And such respect is likely to be minimal unless one is in possession of a Ph.D. from a reputable university.

The acquisition of a Ph.D. is normally a long and rigorous undertaking. Except in extremely rare cases of geniuses and near-geniuses capable of publishing in the professional literature without benefit of a great deal of formal education, it is absolutely essential to have a Ph.D.—or be near to having one—in order to be employed as a faculty member at a reputable institution of higher education. The usual time requirement is anywhere from three years following receipt of the bachelor's degree, on up to five, seven, or even ten years. The doctoral tribulation lore is full of horror stories about students working steadily for many years and then, through some fluke of adverse fortune, failing to complete degree requirements. Sometimes this is because the dissertation advisor to whom they have attached themselves leaves the university for a better position, or most inconsiderately, just up and dies. Or sometimes it is owing to the fact that the Ph.D. candidate, after performing dazzlingly in all course and other pre-dissertation requirements, and being regarded by all as a student of great promise, finds himself or herself unable to produce the necessary "significant original contribution to knowledge." This might be because the candidate is too much of a perfectionist to be satisfied with anything less than the absolute best. But more likely it is because a recalcitrant dissertation committee refuses to deem whatever has been produced to be a "significant" original contribution to knowledge, or even to be any sort at all of an original contribution to knowledge.

Within the more technical disciplines, there is always the chance that one might be torpedoed by a technical slipup. I remember one of my fellow economics Ph.D. students at Northwestern relating with great glee a particularly chilling tale, as if he were a scoutmaster telling an especially scary ghost story to a group of little boys gathered around a campfire. Seems there once was a graduate student who was deemed exceptionally brilliant by everyone on campus. His dissertation was a masterpiece of technical virtuosity, containing hundreds and hundreds of impressive mathematical expressions. But then at the final oral defense, one member of his dissertation committee pointed out that in one of these expressions, the inequality sign was pointing in the wrong direction. With that, concluded the narrator with stunning finality, the candidate's "argument collapsed."

Of course, this tale is quite possibly apocryphal. For one thing, committee members rarely take the trouble to work through mathematical derivations: if they don't like the conclusions, it is much easier simply to object to one or more of the assumptions on which the conclusions are based. For another thing, even if the intended argument *had* collapsed, what was to prevent the alternative argument from being supported? After all, it is often the case in the field of economics that conclusions do not need to be intuitively plausible to any significant degree—it is enough that they are supported by error-free mathematical manipulations.

In my own case, it took a little over six academic years from being handed my bachelor's diploma by Fordham University in June 1965, to being handed my doctoral diploma by Northwestern University in August 1971. Of the six years, three were spent "in residence": one at the University of California at Berkeley (1965-66), and two at Northwestern University in Evanston, Illinois (1966-68). During the final three years (1968-71), I was an ABD ("all but dissertation") at Western Illinois University in Macomb, Illinois. Looking back on it, it may have been somewhat precipitous on my part to have taken a job starting in the fall of 1968. Most of my class stayed on for an additional year of residency on the Northwestern campus, and most of them finished their degree requirements one or two years ahead of me. My three academic years as an ABD at Western Illinois University were quite stressful. I had a sense that none of the Northwestern economics faculty were particularly concerned whether I finished my degree or not. If I had stopped communicating with them, they certainly would not have continued communicating with me. Indeed, if I had not kept at it with a degree of tenacity that bordered on the fanatical, I might well have never been awarded my doctorate.

Ironically, it was my strong interest in market socialism that was one of the things that got me into trouble at Northwestern. Originally, during my development of the "New World" project at Fordham in the early 1960s, market socialism was an integral part of the grand design. But by the time I graduated from Fordham in 1965, I had encountered so much staunch resistance to market socialism simply because it was a form of "socialism" and nothing else mattered, that I decided to jettison it from the grand design and explore an alternative design free from the stigma of socialism. Thus the origin of "Plan Alpha." From the fall of 1965 through the fall of 1967, I endeavored to attract sympathetic colleagues to assist me with the further development of Plan Alpha. As mentioned above, these endeavors were utterly fruitless. So I decided: What the hell, since the grand design *without* market socialism was apparently no more attractive than the grand design *with* market socialism, I might as well re-insert market socialism into the grand design.

After all, market socialism was (and remains) a good idea in and of itself, quite aside from its role within the larger grand design. And it was, after all, the starting point, the veritable linchpin, of the entire grand design as originally conceived. It was what made the grand design unique, without precedent. Obviously it was going to be difficult to "sell" a grand design of any sort to a sluggish, unperceptive, inert general public. So it might as well be a grand design that included market socialism, since in actual fact a properly designed market socialist system would be in the direct financial interest of the vast majority of the general public—even though the vast majority of the general public had, for the moment, been blinded to its true interests. So I would not be trying to "sell" something to the general public that was not actually in its own true interests. How difficult could it be, after all, when all was said and done, at the end of the day, in the final analysis, to awaken the general public to its own true interests? (*Very* difficult, as I gradually learned.)

And so, within a year or so of my matriculating at Northwestern in the fall of 1966, market socialism had been fully reinstated. As part of my Ph.D. program, it would be necessary to write a dissertation. What better topic on which to write an economics dissertation than market socialism? Although this was a perfectly straightforward and reasonable intention possessed of considerable apparent attractiveness at the time, it was probably a big mistake in terms of reducing the probability that I would leave Northwestern with doctoral degree in hand.

Basically this was because the market socialist concept had not yet attracted sufficient attention from mainstream economists to have accumulated an adequate professional literature. Despite the 1930s contribution by Oskar Lange, and despite Abram Bergson's article on "Socialist Economics" in the 1948 AEA publication *A Survey of Contemporary Economics*, the idea was still too young, too vague, too underdeveloped, too lacking in any sort of technical content. Not to mention that it was tainted simply by being a form of *socialism*, and as most people were firmly convinced, no conceivable socialist system could possibly improve on capitalism. None of the "high-powered" faculty at Northwestern in the 1960s, people such as Robert Eisner, Robert Strotz, and Dale Mortensen, exemplars of the type of faculty member who publishes impressive technical work in the leading economics journals, would have been interested in working with me on such a fuzzy, ill-defined, and inherently controversial topic as market socialism.

My dissertation adviser was Karl de Schweinitz, an older faculty member devoid of technical expertise and economic theory publications. He was reasonably well-published, but had no publications with mathematical content. And even Professor de Schweinitz was dubious about my project. As it was, as a "non-mathematical" economist his status at Northwestern was already relatively low, and he was apprehensive that associating himself with a dissertation project on market socialism would drag it down even further. Even more so, because the potential student author of the dissertation (myself) was apparently of the borderline-heretical opinion that a properly designed market socialist system might actually outperform the market capitalist status quo in the United States. Nevertheless, after a certain amount of early waffling, Professor de Schweinitz did eventually honor his clear-cut academic responsibility, and agreed to chair my thesis committee.

Under his sponsorship and tutelage, I did eventually succeed in producing, by the summer of 1971, an acceptable dissertation entitled "The Administrative Costs of Langian Socialism." But this was not the kind of work that would capture the imagination or inspire the respect of the more reputable Northwestern faculty members. Very importantly, it had zero mathematical content, zero statistical content, and zero programming content. As it happened, some 22 years after my doctoral degree was awarded by Northwestern University, I published a book entitled *Capitalism versus Pragmatic Market Socialism: A General Equilibrium Evaluation* (Kluwer

Academic Publishers, 1993) that, had it been my doctoral dissertation, would likely have deeply impressed the hotshot Northwestern economics faculty members back in the late 1960s. *General Equilibrium Evaluation* was based on computer simulations of an innovative and sophisticated economic model, and for purposes of the numerical model simulations it employed a sophisticated estimate of the size distribution of capital wealth in the United States using Federal Reserve System data published in the Survey of Consumer Finances (SCF). But back in the late sixties and early seventies when I was laboring on my dissertation, I had neither the mathematical skills, the statistical skills, nor the programming skills necessary for the work presented in *General Equilibrium Evaluation*. Moreover, the Federal Reserve System had not yet started publishing data from the Survey of Consumer Finances. The fact is that the professional skills at my disposal at the time I wrote my dissertation were rather rudimentary. Neither my performance in the economics courses I took at Northwestern, nor the quality of my dissertation, were such as to impress the more accomplished faculty. Several of my classmates at Northwestern went on to academic careers at prestigious, Ph.D.-granting universities. I was not among them. My first job was at a mid-level regional university in the rural backwoods of Illinois, and that was where I stayed.

In later years, I consoled myself that many of my contributions in economics and other areas were so inherently controversial that even if I *had* been affiliated with a top-ranked university, those contributions would not have been taken seriously. At the height of my career, I might have published in the better journals and been somewhat better-known within the profession, but that would not have translated into any measurable impact on the real world. I recall having a conversation once with a faculty colleague at Western Illinois University, Steve Rock, about my serious interest in market socialism. I told him that my fondest hope was to achieve a degree of recognition within the economics profession equivalent to that of Oskar Lange, whose 1935 essay "On the Economic Theory of Socialism" had established the basic market socialist concept as a serious idea, at least in a theoretical sense. Whereas Lange had established market socialism as a *theoretical* possibility, my hope was to upgrade the concept to the status of serious *practical* possibility. But I admitted that despite Lange being recognized widely within economics as a brilliant economist whose ideas would ordinarily be considered worthy of respect, the fact that he advocated a form of socialism made him, in the eyes of almost all mainstream economists, a "fruitcake." "Yes," said Steve Rock after a pause, "but a *well-known* fruitcake!" I thought to myself ruefully: "Steve is right—even if I *do* achieve what I am hoping to achieve, I will still be just a *well-known* fruitcake."

I mentioned above that my determination to write a dissertation on market socialism was "one of the things" that got me into trouble at Northwestern University. The other two things that did this were my missionary activities on behalf of Plan Alpha, and the deficiencies in my mathematical skills. Since I came to Northwestern with a master's degree in economics in hand from the University of California at Berkeley, I was essentially a transfer student into the economics doctoral program at Northwestern. Because I was an MA graduate of a university even higher in the prestige pecking order than Northwestern, great things were expected of me. I was awarded a two-year fellowship with no teaching or other responsibilities. But from the point of view of the Northwestern faculty, after my arrival I failed sadly to live up to expectations. Of course it got back to some of the faculty that their new student acquisition from the glittering UC Berkeley campus was going around pestering their other doctoral students, trying to get them involved with some kind of silly crackpot nonsense bearing the ludicrously pretentious designation "Plan Alpha." That was bad enough, but even worse than that was the fact that I was distinctly second-rate in terms of mathematical proficiency.

This came to light in my course work, and even more tellingly, in my lackluster performance on the written comprehensive in economic theory. This was the general qualifying exam in macroeconomic and microeconomic theory taken in the spring by all second-year doctoral students. It was also known as the "written prelim," because it was preliminary to starting work on a dissertation. This exam was devised by the instructors in the first-year macro and micro courses. Those were courses from which I had been exempted on the assumption that my training in these subjects at UC Berkeley had been at least as thorough as that delivered by the Northwestern professors. In actual fact, the mathematical content of the Berkeley first-year economic theory courses had been surprisingly limited. And my only significant prior exposure to quantitative methods in economics were two courses I had taken at Fordham in my senior year there: math econ in the fall semester, and econometrics in the spring semester. These two courses were fairly basic—hardly cutting-edge in terms of coverage and sophistication.

And so, as the theory prelim loomed up before me in the spring of 1967, I was reduced to a condition of high anxiety. I was weak in math and I knew it. To make matters worse, the exam material would be based on courses which I had not taken. At that time, mathematics had not yet completely taken over economic pedagogy—as it did soon afterwards. Thus it was possible to answer most questions reasonably satisfactorily "in words," without necessarily adding the mathematical expressions that would be helpful to fully clarify the meaning of "the words." This crucial examination was administered on Tuesday, March 8, 1967. I realized that I was in danger because of my sparse usage of mathematical expressions in my answers. If I hadn't passed it, I would have been dismissed from the Northwestern economics doctoral program at the end of the spring term. That would most likely have been the end of my hopes for an academic career—and the end of my hopes in general. I might as well get it over with: enlist in the Army and be sent to Vietnam. If I survived that, I could look forward to a prosaic career as an insurance salesman or some such thing. Thus I was a nervous wreck at the time of the examination.

As it turned out, I passed the examination, but with a grade of B rather than A. The fact that I had not passed this critical examination with an A was not lost on the Northwestern faculty. If there had been any doubt before that I was a second-rate doctoral student, the B on the prelim put that doubt to rest. Likely this goes far to explain why I had an unusual amount of difficulty in completing an acceptable dissertation. My experience with the theory prelim greatly chastened me. I vowed to stop wasting so much time on extra-curricular activities and projects completely unrelated to my coursework. I also vowed to take drastic measures to bring my mathematical skills up to speed. During the following summer session of 1967, I took three undergraduate courses, for credit, given by the Northwestern math department: differential calculus, integral calculus, and matrix algebra. In addition, during the following 1967-68 academic year, I took additional courses in mathematics, though these courses were audit only. In the early fall of 1967, I took the standard written mathematics exam for the econ Ph.D. program, and had no difficulty with it. I was finally starting to get a decent handle on mathematics. Not a moment too soon.

But I still confronted one final hurdle before attaining the coveted Ph.D.: the doctoral dissertation. This is a very high hurdle which many Ph.D. aspirants fail to clear. On the other hand, the best students often consider the dissertation a golden opportunity to get their career in academia off to a flying start. The thing to do is to determine which among the current faculty are the most active and successful in placing articles in the leading economics journals. Inevitably, the work of these luminary faculty is heavily mathematical and/or econometric. Then the work of one or more of these luminaries must be studied with great intensity. Once the requisite level of familiarity has been achieved, the student must approach the selected luminary with the humble request to be allowed to do a dissertation in the luminary's principal area of expertise, with the luminary as dissertation advisor and chair of the thesis committee. If things go well, the dissertation will be completed with no fuss or complications, the faculty luminary and the student will share a co-authored article based on the dissertation in a prestigious journal, the student will be hired by a major Ph.D.-granting university on the basis of glowing recommendation letters, and a successful career will be launched.

Needless to say, I was unable to follow this particular yellow brick road to fame and fortune—or at least to what passes for fame and fortune in the low-key world of higher education. To begin with, I did not have the math skills to get an adequate grip on the technically advanced work of the Northwestern luminaries. And even if I had, I was bound and determined to do my dissertation on market socialism. To me, market socialism was not some esoteric theoretical abstraction, the main value of which was to provide an opportunity for demonstrating one's technical proficiency. Rather it was an inherently intriguing idea with potentially immense significance for global human civilization. After all, underpinning the Cold War which was threatening to unleash nuclear Armageddon on the world, was an ideological dispute between capitalism and communism. Market socialism offered a potential bridge between these two ideologies that were locked into a potentially deadly confrontation. This was a possibility definitely worth pursuing.

Of course it would not do to admit to the Northwestern faculty that a major motivation for my interest in market socialism was the possibility that it might provide a bridge between capitalism and communism. The very notion of building such a bridge would be deemed pie-in-the-sky nonsense. If there was one thing my futile experiences with trying to recruit Plan Alpha allies and associates had taught me by this time, it was that I had better keep my mouth shut about Plan Alpha. And by extension, I had better keep my mouth shut about the possibility that market socialism might be a bridge over the ideological gulf between capitalism and communism.

But while I could not make reference to the potential role of market socialism in the context of world politics, I believed there was a sufficient amount of general interest in the topic, and a sufficient amount of published professional literature on it, to make it a viable topic for a doctoral dissertation. In this I was correct: it did turn out to be a "viable" topic—but just barely. Relative to the more successful doctoral aspirants (those who had received an A on the written theory prelim and who went on to successful careers at important Ph.D.-granting universities), I was not able to come up with a dissertation proposal that would have been deemed interesting by any of the luminaries among the 1960s Northwestern economics faculty.

The 8-page dissertation proposal I produced in the fall of 1967 had very little to recommend it from the point of view of potentially publishable research. To begin with, it was much too long and too diffuse for a thesis proposal. The lack of adequate focus was suggested by the fact that at the head of the document, three possible titles were proposed: (1) "Free Market Socialism and Economic Analysis"; (2) "A Reconsideration of Free Market Socialism"; (3) "The Theory of Free Market Socialism." This was not the kind of thing that would excite luminary faculty such as Robert Eisner, Robert Strotz, and Dale Mortensen. It was a mushy topic area, and the result of my venture into it would almost certainly be equally mushy. The best I could offer was that "hopefully" my work would "facilitate future efforts toward a scientific evaluation of free market socialism." Even at best, therefore, this was far short of actually *being* a scientific evaluation of free market socialism. On top of that, it was almost universally assumed among competent mainstream economists that if ever a truly scientific evaluation of free market socialism became possible, it would clearly and unambiguously demonstrate the inferiority of free market socialism to free market capitalism.

But assuming that I could not be dissuaded from my feckless interest in market socialism, the logical choice for dissertation advisor was Karl de Schweinitz, among whose teaching responsibilities was a course in "Socialist Economic Theory." Normally the term "economic theory" implies mathematical models and manipulations—but not necessarily, as there are some topics on which thinking is still in the pre-quantitative stage. This was the attitude of Professor de Schweinitz: he was not only unfamiliar with higher mathematics, he was decidedly skeptical about its applicability to the key issues within the field of comparative economic systems. At the same time, I was working hard to improve and deepen my skills in higher mathematics, and I had hoped that I might apply these skills to my Ph.D. dissertation. This was one basic problem in terms of my achieving a smooth working relationship with Professor de Schweinitz.

Another problem involved our varying perceptions of the available professional literature bearing on market socialism in general and the Langian market socialist proposal in particular. He was of the opinion that the relevant literature was "vast," while I was of the opinion that it was quite limited. It was on this particular question that we soon came to loggerheads. Appended to my initial dissertation proposal was a bibliography of about twenty titles, of which only two were directly and entirely focused on the Langian concept of market socialism: Oskar Lange's original 1936 essay "On the Economic Theory of Socialism," and Abram Bergson's 1948 article "Socialist Economics." De Schweinitz reacted to this list that it was ridiculously inadequate: there were "tons" of published writings that I was missing. I said I would love to have more references: so would he be kind enough to give me specific items? No, said de Schweinitz, this is *your* dissertation, and it is up to *you* to find relevant material. This went back and forth for quite a while, and eventually became rather heated. Finally the good professor, irritated beyond endurance, said to me: "I am not putting up with this, Yunker. Go find yourself another advisor!"

And so with heavy heart I made the rounds, starting with the graduate advisor, Dale Mortensen. When I suggested that possibly they should let me go ahead and write a dissertation on my own, without an advisor, and then look at it to see if it was acceptable, Professor Mortensen said that simply wasn't the way things were done. But to soften the blow, he added that he would think about advising me himself. After a suitable interval for reflection, he informed me regretfully that the subject of market socialism was too far outside his areas of interest, thus he was unable to provide useful assistance. He suggested some other possible faculty members, but they also regretfully declined my appeal that they become my dissertation advisor. Eventually I returned to de Schweinitz, hat in hand, with the humble request that he reconsider and take me on as advisee. I suspect that in the meantime someone in authority within the department had suggested to Professor de Schweinitz that this eager young fellow Yunker was deeply interested in market socialism, and since he (de Schweinitz) was the department's economic systems specialist, he and I should really be working together on my dissertation. That would explain his conciliatory manner when I went to see him. Sure, he said, let's work together to get this job done. I promised to be less arrogant, more open to input, and more assiduous in finding relevant literature. So, now with Professor Karl de Schweinitz as my advisor, it was necessary to add two additional faculty members to fill out the three-person dissertation committee. Since normally membership on a dissertation committee does not involve a great deal of work for anyone other than the dissertation advisor, it was not difficult to recruit two additional people: Walter D. Fisher and Colin Wright.

Except for a handful of superstar students, I suppose it is the nearly universal experience of Ph.D. aspirants that their thesis committee members have a much lower sense of urgency about getting the job done and the student graduated, than does the student himself. I did not keep count of the number of dissertation proposals I wrote during the 1967-68 academic year, but I suspect it was at least three or four. I would distribute these to the committee members, wait a decent interval to allow them a chance to look at it (at least two weeks, usually more), finally elicit from them a few vague and generally unhelpful comments, on the basis of which another proposal would be written, and the process started all over again. Throughout this period, all three of my committee members were agreed on only one critical point: the dissertation I was proposing was much too broad, it had to be focused much more tightly.

According to established procedures, I was not supposed to begin actual work on the dissertation until I had passed the "oral prelim," at which I would answer questions about the dissertation proposal I had previously distributed to the committee, and if my answers were satisfactory, they would approve my proposal and I could then commence work. But it was common knowledge that many students, particularly the better ones, would complete the basic substantive work on their dissertations and have results in hand even before writing up their proposals. In reality these proposals were based on the dissertation, not the other way around. My problem was that my proposals were skimpy, and the committee was not sure that I could flesh out these skimpy proposals to a dissertation worthy of sitting on the shelves of the Northwestern University library, along with all the other dissertations from decades past. Once a dissertation was accepted and put on the shelves, it would be there more or less forever. And if perchance one of those dissertations should contain errors or inadequacies, and if perchance some future researcher should discover those errors or inadequacies, how embarrassing would that be for the university!

By the late winter of 1968, my wife and I were scheduled to spend the summer vacation out in California with my family, and moreover, I had an assistant professor job waiting for me at Western Illinois University, starting in September. For a long time I had assumed that if I worked hard, I could have the dissertation chore wrapped up by the end of the 1967-68 academic year. And here the end of the year was growing nigh, and I was still entangled in this vicious circle with my committee. I could not prove to them that I was capable of writing a decent dissertation without actually writing the dissertation, and they were reluctant to let me start writing the dissertation because my dissertation proposals were insufficiently "focused." So I decided to try to break out of the circle by means of a drastic maneuver: going ahead and writing the damn thing. In March I commenced work on a manuscript with the heading "Rough Draft of a Proposed Dissertation to be entitled Economic Efficiency and Langian Socialism." The completed manuscript, dated April 25, 1968, consisted of 134 typed pages. Since I had been incapable of producing the customary 5-page proposal to persuade them that I was ready, willing, and able to produce an actual dissertation of the appropriate length (usually between 125 and 150 pages) and focus, perhaps a 134-page document would do the trick.

Not surprisingly, this gambit was unsuccessful. The committee did not agree that my 134-page document was worthy even of preliminary consideration as a Northwestern University Ph.D. dissertation. In fact, it wasn't even close. I needed to rethink the whole project—in effect, to start over from scratch. They were adamant that I was trying to rush them, to get them to sign off on work that was not nearly as refined and mature as it needed to be. They thought my topic was interesting and worth pursuing, but I seemed to be in too much of a hurry to do a really good job on it.

That I was not advanced to candidacy was a disappointment to be sure, but hardly a crushing disappointment. It was quite common for people to complete their degree requirements after they had embarked on their first jobs. What I was being required to do wasn't all that unusual or risky. One of the reasons I chose Western Illinois University for my first job was that Macomb was geographically fairly close to Evanston, so that it would not be difficult to maintain contact with my dissertation committee. I hadn't really been counting on completing all degree requirements by June of 1968, or even by the end of that summer. Although it had not been a short-run success, my "Rough Draft" gambit may have been a success in a larger, long-run sense. My 134-page document demonstrated to the committee, in a tangible way, that I was capable of producing a substantial manuscript on the assigned topic of market socialism. And while the effort may have been seriously flawed in a number of respects, given the rather mushy nature of the subject matter, not to mention its highly controversial nature, I had produced a reasonably promising first try.

In the end it did take a lot longer than I would have preferred to complete degree requirements for the Ph.D. To start with, it wasn't until late in the following fall that I was finally deemed to have passed the oral prelim and "advanced to candidacy," meaning that I was now officially authorized to commence work on my dissertation. At the prelim the attitude of my committee members was rather cold and formal. I attributed this to the fact that they did not know enough about market socialism to make a reliable judgment on my work. They could not bring themselves to reject it because that might have been an injustice to me (for that I was grateful), but at the same time they felt uncomfortable about passing me forward because my work might actually have been devoid of value. Many years would elapse before I had published a sufficient amount on market socialism in the professional literature for my work on the subject to be deemed, at a minimum, reasonably competent. But by then my connection with Northwestern University was history. The dissertation committee that sent me on my way, I suspect, did so more to get rid of a troublesome pest than anything else. Oh well, whatever their thoughts and motivations about me may have been, I was extremely grateful that they eventually signed the necessary papers for me to get my "union card" from the prestigious Northwestern University.

Counting the initial "Rough Draft," the four regular drafts (not "rough"), and the final version of the dissertation as it now sits of the shelves of the Northwestern University library, there were six versions of it, as follows:

"Economic Efficiency and Langian Socialism," rough, April 1968, 134 pp.
"The Administrative Costs of Langian Socialism," draft, Jan. 1969, 155 pp.
"The Administrative Costs of Langian Socialism," draft, Jan. 1970, 124 pp.
"The Administrative Costs of Langian Socialism," draft, Dec. 1970, 242 pp.
"The Administrative Costs of Langian Socialism," draft, May 1971, 329 pp.
"The Administrative Costs of Langian Socialism," final, Aug. 1971, 261 pp.

The title switch from the original "Economic Efficiency and Langian Socialism" to "The Administrative Costs of Langian Socialism" was the result of the dissertation committee's unanimous insistence that that my dissertation be restricted in scope and focused on a single, manageable issue. Luckily, Lange had himself provided the perfect choice for this "manageable issue" by calling attention to a possible problem with his market socialist proposal: a possible tendency toward the "bureaucratization of economic life." Predictably, this phrase has routinely been invoked by generations of critics as irrefutable proof that the Langian plan would not work. The logic is impeccable, as exemplified in the following syllogism:

Socialism inevitably produces bureaucracy.
Bureaucracies are inevitably inefficient.
Langian market socialism is a form of socialism.
Ergo: Langian socialism is inevitably bureaucratic and inefficient.

Should anyone object to this logic on grounds that one or both of the "inevitably" terms may not be completely accurate, the logic can be supported by irrefutable *empirical* evidence, as in the following:

Soviet socialism was obviously bureaucratic.
Soviet socialism was obviously inefficient.
Soviet socialism and Langian socialism are alike in being socialist.
Ergo: Langian socialism would obviously be bureaucratic and inefficient.

Should anyone object that Lange was at pains to emphasize that his proposal was fundamentally distinct from Soviet-style centrally planned socialism, and that it was for *market* socialism, this would be met with the dogmatically unequivocal proclamation that any conceivable form of socialism must inevitably and invariably be bureaucratic and inefficient, and this is so compellingly clear from such an overwhelming mass of theoretical and empirical evidence that to raise any doubts about it constitutes evidence either of abysmal ignorance or conspicuous mental deficiency. Arguments of this sort are what is generally known as "begging the question," a disreputable mode of argumentation—although quite often highly effective in practice.

What Oskar Lange actually wrote in "On the Economic Theory of Socialism" (1938, pp. 109-110) is the following:

> There is also the argument that might be raised against socialism with regard to the efficiency of public officials as compared with private entrepreneurs as managers of production. Strictly speaking, these public officials must be compared with corporation officials under capitalism, and not with private small-scale entrepreneurs. The argument thus loses much of its force. The discussion of this argument belongs to the field of sociology rather than of economic theory and must therefore be dispensed with here. By doing so, however, we do not mean to deny its great importance. It seems to us, indeed, that ***the real danger of socialism is that of a bureaucratization of economic life***, and not the impossibility of coping with the problem of allocation of resources. Unfortunately, we do not see how the same, or even greater, danger can be averted under monopolistic capitalism. Officials subject to democratic control seem preferable to private corporation executives who practically are responsible to nobody.

Lange wrote this in the 1930s, and by the 1930s it was evident to any objective observer that if "bureaucracy" was the arch-enemy of human civilization, then it was too late to do anything about it: "bureaucracy" had already triumphed. There were bureaucracies everywhere: corporations were bureaucracies, governments were bureaucracies, schools were bureaucracies, philanthropies were bureaucracies, armies and navies were bureaucracies, religious organizations were bureaucracies, social organizations were bureaucracies, virtually any form of "organization" at all was a "bureaucracy." But to most people there is no problem with this, since most people are not pathologically paranoid, and thus recognize the vital role that bureaucracy plays in human civilization. Bureaucracy is simply another name for "organization," and without organization, clearly, we would all be lost. On the other hand, all of us have at one point or another in our lives been inconvenienced—or more seriously harmed—by being forced to abide by various rules and regulations that have no obvious useful purpose. It is convenient to blame these adversities on "bureaucracy." They might just as easily be blamed on the uncaring universe, but "bureaucracy" is more satisfying. If "bureaucracy" is the problem, then resentment can be focused on human "bureaucrats," who are far more vulnerable than the uncaring universe.

Immediately following his expression of concern about the bureaucratization problem, Lange qualified it with two sentences that have been ignored by most of his critics: "Unfortunately, we do not see how the same, or even greater, danger can be averted under monopolistic capitalism. Officials subject to democratic control seem preferable to private corporation executives who practically are responsible to nobody." To my mind, this qualification demonstrates that Lange was not genuinely concerned that "bureaucratization of economic life" was any more of a problem under his market socialist system than it already was under the industrially advanced market capitalist system. He coined the phrase "bureaucratization of economic life" as a kind of catch-all category into which the various problems of any industrially advanced economy could be conveniently relegated. Having then expressed the concern that "bureaucratization of economic life" might be a serious problem under his socialist system (as under any industrially advanced system), Lange was conveniently absolved of the potential accusation that he had "ignored" these problems.

Of course, it wouldn't do to take this dismissive attitude in my dissertation toward Lange's "bureaucratization of economic life" phrase. And within the critical literature on Langian market socialism, there were certain specific issues that had been raised that could be interpreted as "bureaucratic" issues. My dissertation committee liked my suggestion that such issues could also be described as "administrative costs." As a form of socialism, Langian socialism would presumably create a bureaucracy that would not be necessary under market capitalism, and the operating costs of this new bureaucracy were the "administrative costs" that would weigh down the socialist economy. Thus the logic behind the revised title: "The Administrative Costs of Langian Socialism." Once these costs were added into the overall accounting, it would then be clear that no form of socialism, including Lange's market socialist scheme, could possibly be as efficient as capitalism. Basically this was the proposition that my dissertation committee expected my dissertation to support.

My actual intentions, however, were rather at odds with this expectation. I was convinced that neither "bureaucracy," nor any other spurious objection manufactured by capitalist apologetics, would necessarily condemn socialism to inefficiency relative to contemporary capitalism. But it had to be a *properly designed* socialism. With his proposal for "market" socialism, Lange was definitely on the right track: at a minimum an efficient socialist economy needed to dispense entirely with central planning as implemented under Soviet communism. But even years before at Fordham, I had concluded that the *specifics* of Lange's market socialist scheme were thoroughly impractical. A "properly designed" socialist economy would be a *pragmatic* market socialist system. This meant dispensing entirely with Lange's "CPB pricing system" and his "production rules" for firm managers. Once these and a few other oddities had been purged from the market socialist concept as originally devised by Lange, and the system could now be correctly described by the term "pragmatic market socialism," virtually the entire bureaucratic bugaboo would be consigned to oblivion.

Of course, I could not let this viewpoint shine through clearly within the dissertation, which by committee fiat must be confined strictly and solely to the Langian scheme. After all, this was the only form of market socialism widely known within the economics profession. Almost all mainstream economists had never given a moment's thought to anything remotely resembling my "pragmatic" market socialist concept. It was unknown, there was no literature on it—obviously, therefore, it could not be used as the basis for a dissertation. I mentioned earlier that many years later, in 1993, I published a book entitled *Capitalism versus Pragmatic Market Socialism: A General Equilibrium Evaluation*, that probably would have been acceptable as a doctoral dissertation to the Northwestern economics faculty in the late 1960s and early 1970s.

The year before *General Equilibrium Evaluation*, I had published another book, *Socialism Revised and Modernized: The Case for Pragmatic Market Socialism* (Praeger, 1992), that would likely also have been an acceptable doctoral dissertation. My original intention had been that the substantive content of the 1993 book would be included as one of the analytical appendices of the 1992 book. However, that was ruled out because of length considerations. But the 1992 book, even without this additional material, was quite a comprehensive assessment of pragmatic market socialism, and with its various analytical appendices contained an adequate sufficiency of technical content. These two books of 1992 and 1993 were based literally on two decades worth of intensive thought and research on the pragmatic market socialist concept: in a sense they were distillations from numerous published articles in the professional literature.

But none of that thought and research, and none of those publications, were available to me during the 1968-71 period during which I labored to produce an acceptable dissertation. I was forced to restrict the analysis to the Langian plan, and despite my personal reservations about that plan, I did my best to shine a favorable light on it. But my heart wasn't in it, and the resultant dissertation, despite considerable effort on my part, was inherently weak. It is fairly common for new Ph.D.s to try to get parts of their dissertations published in articles, or perhaps the whole thing as a book. A first-rate dissertation could potentially be a gold mine of publishable material. But even as I was working on my own dissertation, I was conscious that this would most likely not be the case with "The Administrative Costs of Langian Socialism."

Nevertheless, as soon as it started becoming evident to me that my dissertation committee had a rather low opinion of my potential, and that this could become a serious hindrance to my doctoral objective, it occurred to me that maybe if I could publish one or two articles based on material in my dissertation drafts, it would change their attitude toward me, and make them less dilatory in allowing me to finish. In the spring and summer of 1968, therefore, I extracted from the "Rough Draft" two manuscripts: "A Simulation-Type Experiment on Pareto Optimality" and "An Appraisal of Langian Socialism," and started submitting them to potential publishers.

The "Simulation-Type Experiment" paper was a revision of an analytical appendix to Chapter 2 in the "Rough Draft" ("Criteria of Welfare and Allocational Efficiency"). Pareto optimality (or equivalently, Pareto efficiency) is the most widely recognized and generally accepted welfare criterion in theoretical economics. Developed by Vilfredo Pareto (1848-1923), an Italian economist, mathematician, and social philosopher, it lays down the following principle: "A system may be said to be Pareto optimal if a situation has been reached wherein it is impossible to make one entity better off without making another entity worse off." The "entity" might be a private household, a business enterprise, or any other form of human organization. Technically, the principle is made operational using the differential calculus methodology of constrained optimization. The first-order conditions for the maximization of the welfare of one entity subject to the constraint of a specified level of welfare for the other entity, are referred to as the "Pareto optimality" or "Pareto efficiency" conditions. The conditions themselves, and the methodology for deriving them using differential calculus, have been instilled into generations of economic theory students.

The reason why the Pareto optimality conditions are "generally accepted" is that they are seemingly so completely unobjectionable. After all, if it were possible to make one person better off without making a second person worse off, what possible objection could be made to doing so? Of course, one problem immediately suggests itself. If it is possible to make the first person richer without making the second person poorer, in a financial sense the second person is no worse off—but he may be worse off in a psychological sense if he is envious of the first person, especially if the first person is already much richer than the second person. If envious resentment (or altruistic concern) are actual human emotions (as they apparently are), this creates "interdependencies" between people's welfare ("utility"), and these interdependencies greatly complicate the Pareto optimality conditions, relative to their formulation when these interdependencies are ignored.

But the biggest single shortcoming of Pareto optimality is that it cannot be applied to resolve *political* issues. Political issues are those involving conflicts of interest. For example, a more progressive income tax system reduces the effective income of the wealthier strata while it increases the effective income of the middle-income and lower-income strata. Moving to greater progressiveness will hurt the wealthy, while moving to lesser progressiveness will hurt the less wealthy. According to the Pareto principle, both changes are ruled out because they hurt *somebody*. When one thinks about it, one realizes that every single political issue (that is, an issue eliciting political controversy) that ever has occurred or ever will occur within human societies, involves a conflict of interest, and hence cannot be resolved on the basis of the Pareto principle.

To be sure, Pareto optimality is "generally accepted," because it is unassailable in a pure theory sense, and because its handsome equations are impressively scientific-looking. Unfortunately, the concept is vacuous in terms of the multitude of political issues confronting society, from whether the tax on gasoline should be increased by fifty cents a gallon, to whether pragmatic market socialism should replace contemporary market capitalism. To have any chance of shedding useful illumination on any of the host of real-world political issues, one must necessarily apply some form or other of "social welfare optimization." To some economists, social welfare optimization is disreputable because it involves "unscientific" interpersonal comparisons of utility. These economists tend to be political conservatives, because the one and only policy course approvable on Pareto grounds is to remain with the status quo indefinitely—because any tiny deviation from the status quo will hurt *somebody*. The impracticality of such a conclusion will be entirely evident to anyone with even the faintest suspicion that it is possible, in some matters, to improve on the status quo. This would apply not only to progressives of various stripes, but also to strict conservatives who think that things were much better 50 years ago, or 100 years ago, or maybe even earlier.

Of course, it can readily be appreciated that rigid insistence upon the validity and relevance of Pareto optimality would rule out any possibility of a transition to a market socialist economy. This explains my personal antipathy toward the concept, and my interest in poking intellectual holes in it. One of the less sensible manifestations of this interest was "A Simulation-Type Experiment on Pareto Optimality." It was the contention of this very short note-type manuscript that if one postulated a reasonable interpretation of the Pareto optimality conditions, one could show by numerical experimentation that violating these conditions had a random effect on the welfare of the entities: there was no consistent movement either up or down. Of course, practically any economist scanning this paper would consider it practically certain that one or both of two basic flaws were present: either the allegedly "reasonable" formulation of the Pareto optimality conditions was faulty, or the numerical simulation methodology was faulty. In retrospect, I would have to concur with this judgment. In any case, I can now appreciate the folly of trying to challenge Pareto optimality on the basis of numerical computations.

In my youthful exuberance (and also because at that point I had no "reputation" to lose), I submitted this half-baked specimen successively to three leading economics periodicals: the *American Economic Review*, the *Journal of Political Economy*, and *Econometrica*. The only one of the three to obtain a referee report on it was *Econometrica*. In February 1969, the paper was rejected. The amazingly polite referee report started out by saying "Unfortunately this is not an acceptable paper," made a few bemused comments about the methodology, and concluded with: "Having said this, he [the author] specifies various sets of parameter values for his model, under both all-firms-face-same-prices and all-firms-do-not conditions, which he then solves for cost figures. It turns out that changing prices leads to a change in costs which implies that we should ditch the notion of Pareto optimality." Enough said: the referee did not consider it necessary to elaborate *why* Pareto optimality should probably *not* be "ditched" on the basis of my flaky "Simulation-Type Experiment."

I had better luck with the other manuscript, "An Appraisal of Langian Socialism," which was a concise summary of the principal content of Chapters 6 through 10 of the "rough draft": "The Lange Economy Outlined," "The Pricing Issue," "The Investment Issue," "The Checking Problem," and "Modern Firm Theory and Langian Socialism." The initial submission of this lengthy manuscript was to the *Journal of Political Economy*, but that wasn't as hopelessly optimistic as it might seem. This was because shortly before my submission, the *JPE* had published a lengthy article by Abram Bergson entitled "Market Socialism Revisited" (October 1967). This article contained an analysis and evaluation of Oskar Lange's market socialist proposal: it was essentially an expansion and updating of Bergson's 1948 article "Socialist Economics" in the AEA's *A Survey of Contemporary Economics*. The appearance of this article at this time in a major economics forum proved, as nothing else could, that Langian market socialism was still of "current interest" to the economics profession, and hence was a legitimate topic for further contributions. If the *Journal of Political Economy* had accepted my "Appraisal" paper for publication, I could have gone to my dissertation committee with this irrefutable evidence that what I was saying about Langian market socialism was indeed competent and of interest to the profession. Unfortunately, that buoyant hope was quickly eliminated when in October 1968, I received a polite rejection from the *JPE*.

Rejection by the *Journal of Political Economy* of "An Appraisal of Langian Socialism" was not the end of the line for that particular "pp" (my abbreviation for "publication possibility"). I still had hopes that I might get it published in a reputable journal, and that would thereby end the foot-dragging by my dissertation committee. In actual fact, the paper was indeed eventually published—but far too late to assist me in my campaign to obtain the doctorate. Moreover, given the nationalistic prejudices among U.S. economists, not all of them would concede that the publication had been in a "reputable" journal. Be that as it may, of all the numerous articles on market socialism I published in subsequent years, only one was drawn entirely from dissertation material: "An Appraisal of Langian Socialism," published in the *Indian Economic Journal* (January-March 1973). By the time this was published in early 1973, it was far too late to have any effect on my quest for the Ph.D., which had been successfully concluded almost two years previously when Northwestern awarded my doctorate in August 1971. The publication of this particular article was one of the more curious episodes of my academic career.

Even after its rejection by the *JPE*, I had sufficient residual confidence in the project to undertake some revision during the spring of 1969, and more importantly, a neater typing job. In May of 1969, I sent it to the other side of the world: to the *Indian Economic Review*. In those early days, I was not as assiduous about record-keeping as I later became, and I have been unable to ascertain, specifically, why the *Indian Economic Review* was chosen for submission. I can only surmise that they had recently published one or more articles about Oskar Lange. Or perhaps because it was widely assumed that those Indian people were keen on socialism. Whatever the reason, the article was sent through the postal mail to India, and India, part of the "inscrutable East," took an inscrutably lengthy time to pass judgment on my submission. In the fall of 1972, more than three years following submission, a small airmail envelope from India showed up in my mailbox, and the message within informed me that, regrettably, they would not be able to publish "An Appraisal of Langian Socialism." So that was the end of that: this manuscript would join my pile of never-published manuscripts. No problem, because by that time I had my Ph.D. in hand from Northwestern University, and the paper's primary purpose was thereby moot.

Another year passed. Then, in the fall of 1973, another airmail letter arrived from India, this one from the *Indian Economic Journal* informing me that they were pleased to be publishing "An Appraisal of Langian Socialism." I never bothered trying to ascertain what had happened. My guess is that someone at the *Indian Economic Review* liked the piece, and even though it was rejected there, he sent it along to the *Indian Economic Journal*, where it encountered an editor who liked it. India is a great country, the *Indian Economic Journal* is a great economics journal, and I am proud to have been one of its contributors.

Since it had been mandated by my committee that my dissertation address the "bureaucratic" problems of Langian socialism, those problems contributing to the "administrative costs" of the system, I could not simply assert that virtually all of these problems would disappear if the market socialist system discarded the specifics of the Langian plan, and instead adhered to the principles of the pragmatic market socialist plan. In the original "Rough Draft," Chapter 11 was entitled "The Pragmatic Socialist Alternative": this brief chapter described the basic concept, provided a few provisional institutional details as well as a bit of theoretical formulation, and argued that this market socialist alternative would avoid the bureaucratic problems of Langian market socialism as they had been discussed in the previous chapters. The committee was quite definite that this chapter would have to go: this particular concept of market socialism was unknown, there was no literature on it, and therefore there was no place for it in my dissertation.

Oh well, one does what one has to do. Although there were others, the two most obvious bureaucratic problems with Langian socialism were: (1) the CPB (Central Planning Board) pricing system; (2) the "production rules" of the business enterprise: first, the quantity of production must be set so that the marginal cost of production equals the price of the commodity, and second, at that quantity of production, the factors of production (e.g., capital and labor) must be set to minimize the average cost of producing that quantity of production.

As for CPB pricing, I cannot help observing that "Central Planning Board" was a remarkably poor terminological choice by Lange in view of the fact that his system was explicitly intended to avoid the evils of central planning. Why not call it the Central Pricing Board? That would even use the same initials: CPB. In any case, the idea was that the business enterprises would not have independent authority to set the prices on the commodities they produced. Instead they would send inventory change reports to the CPB. If inventories throughout the industry were rising, the CPB would decrease the price of that commodity. If inventories throughout the industry were falling, the CPB would increase the price of that commodity. One of Lange's fiercest critics, Friedrich Hayek, pointed out that in the modern economy there are millions and millions of commodities, and there are myriad price changes on these myriad commodities every year. So, obviously, the CPB would have to be a giant bureaucracy, and even then it couldn't keep up with the necessary price changes. The proliferation of irrational disequilibrium prices would soon bring the economy grinding to a halt.

There were arguments that could be deployed against Hayek's apocalyptic scenario. For example, during World War II, the United States had set up the Office of Price Administration (OPA) to control inflationary pressures. Compared to the other expenses of World War II, those associated with the OPA were quite modest, and the OPA's activities certainly did not bring the U.S. economy grinding to a halt during World War II—even though these activities were basically intended to forestall prices from rising to their equilibrium levels. Of course, the simplest way of getting around the perceived problem was to allow the firms to keep control over the prices they set for their own products. Under ordinary conditions (i.e. in peacetime), inflationary pressures would not be excessive. But this was not something I could emphasize, because CPB pricing was an integral part of Lange's scheme, and my dissertation, by order of the committee, was restricted to Lange's scheme.

Lange's production rules were straight out of a microeconomics textbook. The biggest problem with them is that economic decision-making by firms as described in microeconomics textbooks, has very little in common with actual business decision-making in the real world. To start with, the typical business firm in the textbook produces a single commodity, whereas the real world economy is dominated by large corporations producing a wide range of products. In the textbook, the marginal cost of producing that one commodity is a straightforward concept, whereas in the real world of multi-product corporations, the costs of the various products are interconnected, so that the true marginal cost of any one product would be difficult to ascertain. In fact, real-world corporations are normally quite unconcerned with marginal costs, as their attention is instead focused on average costs. Furthermore, they are just as much concerned with marketing as they are with production: they spend as much time and effort on how best to sell their products as they do on how best to produce them. When one imagines how the typical contemporary corporation executive would react to being told that from now on, the objective is: "set *q* (quantity) so that MC (marginal cost) equals *p* (price) and minimize the AC (average cost) of producing that *q*," one can only envision bemusement and befuddlement. If such a rule were enforced too stringently, it seems likely that there could be a serious paralyzing effect on business, and consequently a seriously deleterious effect on overall economic performance.

But this was not how the "Langian production rules" were treated in the evaluation of Lange's market socialist plan undertaken by Abram Bergson and other critical commentators. As the rules themselves were based on the textbook view of the world, so also was their critique. Bergson first noted that there was no "observable success criterion" by which it could be conveniently ascertained by an outside observer whether or not the publicly-owned firm was adhering to the Langian production rules. To enforce the production rules, therefore, it would probably be necessary for the government to organize and deploy a massive "army of auditors." These auditors would need to examine operations within each and every one of the thousands of publicly-owned firms in order to guarantee that the rules were being obeyed.

Of course, it could be observed that in the contemporary capitalist economy, an "army of auditors" is already in existence: hundreds of thousands of CPAs busily checking that corporation executives are carrying out their responsibilities in a conscientious and legal manner. This presently existent "army" has been necessitated by the empirically irrefutable separation of ownership and control first described by Adolf A. Berle and Gardiner Means in their landmark *The Modern Corporation and Private Property* (1932). The modern accounting profession, numbering millions of accountants in the United States alone, is the natural consequence of the fact that progress in production technology has created large corporations, sometimes gigantic corporations, that dominate economic activity. These corporations are bureaucracies, and in that sense there has already occurred "bureaucratization of economic life"—like it or not. These corporations are absolutely essential to efficient production, but they do concentrate a great deal of authority in the hands of their high executives. Something needs to be done to ensure that these executives do not utilize this authority to unduly favor their own interests over those of other members of society. Thus one has applicable accounting rules enforced by an "army of auditors," and applicable legal rules enforced by an "army of law enforcement personnel." These "armies" are obviously necessary in today's economic real world, but is it sensible to have yet another army to enforce Lange's production rules?

In his 1948 essay "Socialist Economics," Abram Bergson suggested a possible solution to the problem. Instead of the production rules, the managers of the publicly-owned firms could simply be instructed to maximize profits. Profits are an externally visible success criterion that is already in use within the private ownership capitalist economy. It is used by the capital owners to assess the success of the corporation executives responsible for day-to-day management of the privately-owned corporations. In the same way, it could be used under socialism by the personnel of the public ownership agency to assess the success of the corporation executives responsible for day-to-day management of the publicly-owned corporations. A salient advantage of profit maximization, according to microeconomic theory textbooks, is that under perfect competition, the firm equates marginal cost to price in order to maximize profits, and in so doing satisfies the conditions for Pareto optimality. Thus profit maximization leads to Pareto optimality: there is no need for a marginal cost pricing rule if the firm is instructed to maximize profits, an observable success criterion. To reiterate, this is true *if* the firm is perfectly competitive.

Unfortunately, Bergson continues, a problem arises if perfect competition cannot be assumed. According to those same microeconomic theory textbooks, if the firm is imperfectly competitive (and observation of the real economic world suggests that imperfect competition is widely prevalent), the firm will not equate marginal cost to price, but rather will equate marginal cost to marginal revenue. In other words, the firm managers have an incentive to "cheat": they can earn higher profits by violating the marginal cost pricing condition for Pareto optimality. Thus, alas, if the economy is to enjoy the benefits of Pareto optimality, it will be necessary to send out that same "army of auditors" to make sure the firm managers of the imperfectly competitive firms (presumably the large majority of firms) are abiding by the marginal cost pricing principle. Thus this effort to make an end-run around the army of auditors problem will result in running up against that same army of auditors. Bureaucracy once again raises its ugly head.

One obvious solution to the perceived problem is simply to specify profit maximization as the success criterion of the publicly-owned firms and to abandon marginal cost pricing. This would mean abandoning the possibility of achieving Pareto optimality—but so what? After all, if it is true (as it probably is) that most real-world business enterprises in the existing capitalist economy are imperfectly competitive, then according to the accepted wisdom of economic theory textbooks, the existing capitalist economy is not Pareto optimal. Complaints about the performance of the real-world capitalist economy abound, but the various performance deficiencies alleged by critics are never, to my knowledge, attributed to failure to achieve Pareto optimality. Pareto optimality is one of those ideas of little interest to anyone other than specialists in theoretical welfare economics. And even they don't take it too seriously in a practical sense—as evidenced by the fact, among other things, that they were *not* electrified by Lange's argument that a market socialist economy could achieve Pareto optimality whereas the equivalent capitalist economy would not. Without pausing a single moment to think about it, they assumed immediately that the administrative ("bureaucratic") costs of enforcing the Langian production rules on imperfectly competitive firms would greatly exceed the benefits bestowed by Pareto optimality. So how great could these supposed benefits be?

Close to three years elapsed between my passing the oral prelim and being advanced to candidacy in November 1968, and being awarded the Ph.D. in August 1971. During that interval, the dissertation draft went through five iterations before being deemed acceptable by my committee. The original "Rough Draft of a Proposed Dissertation to be entitled Economic Efficiency and Langian Socialism" contained no mention of Lange's concern about "bureaucratization of economic life," but it dealt thoroughly with the pricing issue and the rule checking issue, as well as some others of lesser significance. Starting with the first iteration under the new title "The Administrative Costs of Langian Socialism," and continuing through the succeeding iterations, these issues were cast as "bureaucratic" issues. The new terminology did not make a lot of sense, in that the substance of these issues remained the same despite the difference in interpretation. But continually harping on "bureaucracy" in relation to Langian socialism was what my committee wanted, and I was in no position to oppose their preference.

In one sense, however, the requirement that bureaucracy be a major concern was useful in the sense that it helped me to fatten up the dissertation by adding many more citations to the reference list, thus responding to Karl de Schweinitz's concern that I incorporate more "relevant literature." As one might expect, there exists a substantial sociological literature on bureaucracy, and some of it contains preliminary efforts at quantitative approaches. Of the mathematical appendices I added, the longest was entitled "Size-Induced Inefficiency," wherein I essayed mathematical approaches to such hypotheses as Parkinson's Law (as the size of the organization increases, its administrative overhead grows more than proportionately to its productive base). Some fairly sophisticated-looking equations resulted, but quite likely they were fundamentally vacuous. During the spring of 1969, I developed two articles from this appendix: "Bureaucratic Inefficiency" and "Analytic Aspects of Size-Induced Inefficiency." I submitted these to journals such as *Administrative Science Quarterly*, without success. The basic problem, I suspect, was that the models were so abstract that there was no obvious way to test them empirically. Also, sociology journals are not so enamored of mathematics as economics journals.

During the period in which I was working on the dissertation, I cranked out almost a dozen papers, some of them related to the dissertation, most of them not. I kept hoping that if I could achieve just one or two publications, or even an accepted manuscript to be published later, this might instill more confidence in me among my committee members, and render them more amenable to approving my dissertation. Unfortunately for this hope, not a single one of the papers I wrote during the period of dissertation work was ever published. Eventually I got the hang of it and started publishing quite abundantly. But not until well after the dissertation was history. Since only publications can provide truly compelling evidence of professional competence, and since I was given my Ph.D. before I had scored one single page in print, I can only surmise that my committee gave me the benefit of the doubt: they approved my degree before I could provide any compelling evidence of professional competence. Possibly they were motivated to this tolerance by the increasingly evident fact that I was never going to give up: that I was going to keep pestering them forever—until they signed their names to the necessary documents. In fairness both to them and to myself, however, I believe I did provide them with enough solid evidence to support a "reasonable expectation" that someday I would mature into a good economist.

Those years of dissertation work were quite stressful. There were some grueling episodes during that period, during which my thesis committee was no doubt sorely tempted to terminate my degree candidacy. But progress continued steadily. At one of the meetings, there was a major breakthrough when it was decided that all the mathematical appendices should be deleted from the dissertation. Even I had to admit that they were not adding anything substantive, and while de Schweinitz found them wholly incomprehensible, both Fisher and Wright found them irritatingly dense. Although the latter two had the mathematical knowledge to do so if it had been absolutely necessary, they did not have either the time or the inclination to slog through the derivations to ascertain whether or not they were free from mathematical error. By jettisoning the mathematical appendices, Fisher and Wright were absolved of the tiresome responsibility to check my math, while it freed me from worries about making mathematical errors. It was a win-win decision. The only minor downside for me was that the dissertation would not provide an opportunity to hone my math skills.

With the math appendices gone, the page count was reduced below what I needed for a normally sized dissertation. I went searching for additional topics in the professional literature that might, with a certain amount of bending, pulling, and stretching, seem at least tangentially relevant to Oskar Lange's market socialist proposal. I was especially interested in topics outside the field of economics, because practically every topic in economics was being developed using mathematical modes of inquiry. I needed more material that could be adequately conveyed using "words only."

I did already have the "bureaucracy" literature, and although I could not avail myself of either my own or anyone else's efforts to explain the evils of bureaucracy using mathematics, there was still plenty of "words only" material on which to call. Professional sociologists are fully aware that the term "bureaucracy" is simply another word for "organization" and hence is inherently neutral. But to the great general public, the term is pejorative: it connotes the inevitable downside of organization that very often organizational requirements come into conflict with individual preferences. The term is thus handy as a smear.

Aside from the popular and professional literature on bureaucracy, I needed more grist for the mill. This was gathered from topics far and wide, often with rather tenuous links to the economic literature on Lange's market socialist plan. Some examples are as follows: (1) industrial organization literature on the relationship between firm size, market structure, and technological innovation; (2) public choice literature on the provision and administration of public goods; (3) literature on the comparative economic performance of nationalized industries such as (at that time) the British railway system; (4) results from theoretical welfare economics such as the Arrow Impossibility Theorem; (5) centralized pricing under Soviet central planning; (6) centralized pricing as handled by the U.S. Office of Price Administration during World War II; (7) Berle-Means literature on separation of ownership and control; (8) psychological literature on motivation and behavior; (9) law enforcement literature, especially as it pertains to the suppression of white-collar crime; (10) behavioral economics literature questioning the "rationality" assumption of human behavior; (11) auditing activity by the U.S. Internal Revenue Service; (12) antitrust law enforcement by the U.S. Department of Justice. Again and again, I argued that upon close consideration of the possible bearing of these various areas of study on Langian market socialism, they indicated that the "bureaucratic burdens" of Langian socialism would not be nearly as substantial as supposed by various critics of the proposed system.

I think it is safe to say that none of the three faculty members on my dissertation committee had ever previously devoted any serious consideration to Oskar Lange's market socialist proposal. They subscribed to the conventional consensus view among mainstream economists that Lange's proposal was "interesting in theory but unpromising in practice." One implication of this judgment was that given the degree of support for the capitalist status quo among all elements of society, it was absurd to believe that Lange's ideas could be made the basis for a serious political challenge to the capitalist status quo. Inasmuch as it is comforting to believe that there are good reasons for an apparently unchangeable status quo, the committee would have preferred that my delving into the bureaucracy issue would add additional weight and substance to the conventional consensus view. Even though I agreed basically that the Langian plan was "unpromising," I hated to see this opinion being extended to any and all alternative plans of market socialism, especially the pragmatic. Since I was forbidden from supporting—or even mentioning—pragmatic market socialism, I took out some of my frustration by suggesting at various points in my dissertation that "bureaucratic" complaints against Langian market socialism were being given far more credit than they deserved, and that alternative market socialist systems were feasible for which these complaints would be even less relevant.

In fact, in the "Summary and Conclusions" section of the final version of the dissertation, I expressed this viewpoint more or less openly. I doubt that any of my dissertation committee members ever read my dissertation closely enough to realize that in it (in the "Summary and Conclusions" section and at other locations), I was questioning the conventional consensus judgment on Langian market socialism. Even if they had noticed this, they probably would not have cared. After all, the readership of most Ph.D. dissertations, aside from their authors and their committee members, can usually be counted on the fingers of one hand. So whatever I had to say about Langian socialism would almost certainly have absolutely no bearing on its standing among mainstream economists.

From the beginning of my candidacy, I had been under a strict injunction to avoid any mention of "pragmatic market socialism," my own preferred alternative to "Langian market socialism." The initial "Rough Draft" had a chapter entitled "The Pragmatic Socialist Alternative" that I was instructed to delete. It is perhaps evidence that the committee did not pay too much attention to the final version of the dissertation that I "sneaked into it" a fair amount of discussion of what was effectively pragmatic market socialism. During my explorations in the literature, I had come across a perfectly reasonable pretext for doing this: pages 138-141 in Ludwig von Mises' book *Socialism: An Economic and Sociological Analysis* (revised edition, Yale University Press, 1951), wherein the author discusses and rejects the "proposal of some of the younger socialists" for an "artificial market." Mises did not reveal the identity of these "younger socialists" nor have I been able to ascertain it, which raises the possibility that the "artificial market" idea was part of an oral tradition that had never before made its way into print. Mises described the "artificial market" as follows:

> The advocates of the artificial market, however, are of the opinion that an artificial market can be created by instructing the controllers of the different industrial units to act as if they were entrepreneurs in a capitalistic state. They argue that even under capitalism the managers of the joint stock companies work not for themselves but for the companies, that is to say, the shareholders. Under socialism, therefore, it would be possible for them to act in exactly the same way as before, with the same circumspection and devotion to duty. The only difference would be that under socialism the product of the manager's labors would go to the community rather than to the shareholders. In such a way, in contrast to all socialists who have written on the subject hitherto, especially the Marxians, they think it would be possible to construct a decentralized rather than a centralized Socialism.

Clearly the "artificial market" concept is a reasonable approximation to pragmatic market socialism as I had always envisioned it. In fact, I even permitted myself a passing mention of the supposedly verboten term, when I wrote, on page 72 of the final version of my dissertation:

> Both Mises and Hayek, in their discussions of calculation under socialism, often consider the case of a market socialism in some respects more advanced than that of Lange himself. They are quite prepared to accept that the socialist authorities are attempting to implement a system that might be termed "pragmatic socialism." Such a system, in pricing, inter-firm competition, investment, etc., is supposed to operate exactly like capitalism, with the single exception that the property-return generated by the allocation process goes to the state rather than to individual capitalists. Firms are instructed to maximize profits and managers are evaluated in terms of their success in this regard. Firms have full control over their own prices. Finally, the socialist investment banks are instructed to maximize the return on loaned-out capital.

The only fudge in the foregoing quote is that as far as I know, Mises and Hayek did not "often" consider this case. It would have been more accurate to say that they "made mention" of it in a couple of locations. But I was using Mises' quote to establish that there *was* a "literature" on pragmatic market socialism. True, this particular literature consisted of a very few pages in some very obscure locations—but this was a quantum jump beyond no literature at all.

Ludwig von Mises was one of the best-known twentieth century critics of socialism. Whatever form of socialism you cared to mention, from Soviet socialism to liberal socialism to Langian socialism, he was against it, and he explicated the reasons for his distain at great length. Only a tiny fraction of his denunciation of socialism was directed at the artificial market (i.e. pragmatic market socialism), but this tiny fraction was of great interest to me personally, because I was not in fact advocating any form of socialism other than pragmatic market socialism. Much of my voluminous published work on market socialism is basically an attempt to refute the Mises argument against the artificial market. But many important components of the refutation were briefly introduced in a dissertation sub-section entitled "Weak Effort Incentives" running from page 92 through page 108: (1) the separation of ownership and control which suggests that the "real work" of capital management is performed mostly by corporation executives and not by stockholders or other capital ownership groups; (2) the backward-bending supply curve of capital management effort which suggests that very wealthy capitalists have little incentive to capital management effort because their capital property incomes are high even if they provide little or none of it; and (3) the possibility that under contemporary capitalism capital property return is basically an unearned Ricardian rent, because the function relating capital management effort to capital property return is of a "plateau" nature, according to which a very small input of capital management effort suffices to achieve very close to the asymptotic upper limit on capital property return.

My oral examination (otherwise known as the "oral defense" because it is envisioned as the meeting at which the candidate "defends" the completed dissertation against questions and objections from the dissertation committee members) was scheduled for 11 AM on Wednesday, June 30, 1971, in the economics department offices in Kresge Hall. It is ordinarily a formality, because if there had actually been any serious questions or objections regarding the dissertation, the candidate would not have gotten this far. But of course there had been nothing about my personal quest for the Ph.D. that had been in the slightest "ordinary," so I was hardly confident of the outcome. In fact, I was distinctly anxious.

The actual meeting was held in Colin Wright's office, because it was a bit larger and had a blackboard. I launched into an outline of my magnum opus. I got as far as Chapter II before Wright cut in. Apparently the few pages he had read had been the opening pages of Chapter II. Like de Schweinitz and Fisher, he thought I had been much too verbose. He suggested a reduction of the first five pages into five sentences that he found more satisfactory. All three of them went on record to the effect that "the meat of the matter" was being buried in a mass of irrelevant and dubious digressions. The thing that worried me, of course, was that when they got through stripping away all the irrelevant and dubious digressions, they would discover that "the meat of the matter" had been illusory and non-existent. Then it would be back to the drawing board.

Fortunately it did not go that far. There were no serious complaints about the "substantive content," such as it was. The comments were superficial and mainly had to do with material that should be deleted. I had no problem with the suggested deletions, because I realized that I had gotten rather too wordy. The previous January Professor de Schweinitz had said he wanted "more content," but I could see that I had overdone it. The final version of "The Administrative Costs of Langian Socialism" was 261 pages in length, down by 68 pages from the previous draft of 329 pages. I doubt very much that any of the three professors on my dissertation committee ever looked at the final version.

The final version of my dissertation was delivered to the Northwestern University Graduate School on Monday, August 9, 1971. Upon arriving at the Northwestern campus that day, my first stop was at the Department of Economics, where the expected envelope with the necessary signed documentation was waiting. Then onward to the Graduate Office. My offerings were taken by a kindly-looking, white-haired lady. She commented helpfully that my dissertation was a big one, and apparently nicely typed. I had everything, they checked my graduate card, and assured me that I was indeed finished.

And so there it was—the great day of liberation. After having served nearly four years in "Dissertation Purgatory," I imagine my sentiments were somewhat akin to those experienced by a prisoner being released from jail. Not after a lengthy sentence, to be sure—perhaps thirty days for disturbing the peace.

4

PUBLISH OR PERISH

As utilized in higher education, the phrase “publish or perish” is metaphorical rather than literal. Faculty members are not stood up against a wall and shot if they fail to publish. But the phrase does suggest, strongly and accurately, that if a faculty member at a college or university does *not* publish an adequate amount in the professional literature, the consequences will definitely be dire. Fortunately, the consequences will not be so dire as to be fatal—aside from a tiny minority who are so demoralized by their inability to publish an adequate amount in the professional literature to be awarded tenure, that they actually commit suicide. I am not personally aware of any such cases, but presumably they must have happened from time to time during the long history of higher education.

On the other hand, there has been at least one well-publicized case in the recent past of tenure denial leading to a homicidal outburst. On February 12, 2010, at a biology department meeting at the University of Alabama at Huntsville, assistant professor Amy Bishop pulled out a 9-millimeter handgun and shot six of her colleagues, three fatally, in retaliation for tenure denial the previous year (it is customary, in cases of tenure denial, to allow the faculty member one final “terminal year” in which to find another job). On September 24, 2012, two and a half years later, Bishop was sentenced to life in prison without the possibility of parole. If the death penalty had been applied, which was a definite possibility since Alabama happens to be one of the more liberal states of the United States in terms of dealing out capital punishment to murderers, this could have been cited as a case where failure to publish sufficiently led (indirectly) to the person perishing.

To a faculty member in higher education, failure to publish can be fatal to other desiderata aside from physical survival: to one’s self-esteem, to one’s hopes for tenure, to one’s prospects in the higher education system, to one’s prospects in the broad area of life-in-general. In my own case, failure to have published an adequate amount in the professional literature would have been fatal to my hope of making a significant number of people aware of my ambitious ideas for improving the future prospects of humanity. In other words, these hopes would have *perished* if I *did not publish*. In that sense, "publish or perish" was indeed apt. While physical survival was not at stake, nevertheless a great deal was.

To achieve a stable, reliable, long-term career at most American colleges and universities, a necessary but not sufficient condition is possession of a doctoral degree. But once the Ph.D. is in hand, there remains another obstacle to be surmounted: tenure. Requirements for tenure vary widely according to the prestige of the institution. At the highest end of the scale, at such elite universities as Harvard, Stanford, the University of Chicago, and the like, it is not simply a matter of publishing anything at all anywhere at all. Rather it is necessary: (1) to publish work in the leading journals in the field, (2) to publish a *substantial quantity* of work in the leading journals in the field, and (3) to publish a substantial quantity of work in the leading journals in the field that is *widely recognized as highly significant to the discipline*. Needless to say, this is not easy to accomplish. If you picked at random one Ph.D. from the current crop of new Ph.D.s produced at universities in the United States and throughout the world, the chances would be extremely small that that individual could measure up to such standards.

At the other end of the spectrum are low-prestige community colleges and four-year colleges where the principal criterion continues to be possession of a doctorate. According to the hoary humorism, these are places where "a Ph.D. and a smile" are sufficient to get one tenured. The latter 1960s and early 1970s witnessed a sea change in the academic job market. In most fields, supply (the number of new Ph.D.s) was catching up with and surpassing demand (the number of new job openings). From a sellers' market (favorable to new Ph.D.s), there was quite a rapid transition to a buyers' market (favorable to hiring institutions). Accordingly, standards for tenure were raised. Formerly it was the case at low-prestige community colleges that instructors were not expected to have doctorates, but now doctorates became necessary. At mid-level colleges and universities such as my own Western Illinois University, formerly a "Ph.D. and a smile" was sufficient for tenure, but now new hires were expected to show at least a modest amount of research productivity resulting in professional publications. The changing job market enabled institutions of higher education across the prestige board to raise the standards for tenure.

In order to understand the significance of tenure in the higher education system, it is also necessary to understand the higher education system itself. Many people are attracted to careers in higher education because of the benefits therein. Among these benefits are *not* particularly high rates of financial remuneration. In fact, salaries are quite modest by the standards of several other professions that require a significant amount of education. Even highly successful professors, some of them Nobel Prize-winners, earn salaries that would elicit only a contemptuous sneer from the typical mid-level corporation executive or money manager. The major benefits of an academic career are non-monetary. One of them is the long summer vacations: two months or even three months during the year during which the professor is entirely freed from the daily responsibility of meeting classes. Another advantage is that most of the people one encounters in a "typical day at the office" are students—healthy, attractive young people normally with positive, optimistic attitudes. Allied to this is the fact that these healthy, attractive young people are normally fairly deferential to their professors. Although good performance on exams and other assignments is the principal criterion of a student's success, it doesn't hurt to be on good personal terms with one's professors.

But above all these other benefits is that of *job security*. Of course, in order to attain this particular benefit, the professor must be tenured. And prior to being awarded tenure, the professor must endure several "probationary" academic years, usually six in number, though in some cases it is less, and in some cases more. In the case of six-year probationary periods, a decision on tenure award is made in the sixth year. If the decision is negative, the professor is usually entitled to one "terminal year" of employment in which to find another job. After that, the professor is dismissed. An adverse tenure decision is inevitably a gut-wrenching psychological setback, and quite often it spells the definitive end of the person's hopes for an academic career.

For higher education faculty, the joy upon being awarded tenure is comparable only to the joy of successfully completing a Ph.D. program. For most people in our society, having a "guaranteed job for life" is a hopeless dream. Most people are forever at risk from such factors as redundancy, bankruptcy, or unsympathetic bosses. There are far more safeguards against unfair dismissals than there were 50 or 100 years ago, but the safeguards are still not overly reliable. If one is "unfairly" dismissed, normally there is little one can do about it. Among the homeless alcoholics wandering around in the slums of every major city, at least a few are likely to be formerly highly paid and respected corporation executives. On the other hand, extremely few are formerly tenured professors. Indeed, the level of job security among tenured faculty in higher education is, for good reason, highly enviable to those in most other professions.

According to the official party line, the principal value to society of the institution of tenure is to protect faculty against unjustified dismissal for controversial viewpoints expressed in their published writings. To fire people for unconventional opinions would be an infringement upon their natural right as a citizen to free speech. To forestall such iniquitous inequities, the institution of tenure is necessary. I like the comment on this rationalization by Adam Winkler, a constitutional law professor at UCLA, in his blog commentary on the Amy Bishop case entitled "Crazy for Tenure":

> Tenure is usually said to be necessary for academic freedom. Scholars, the argument goes, can write about any topic without fear of reprisal from university officials. The truth is that only a handful of professors write in areas controversial enough to incite university interference. Most professors write about cold-button issues like animal behavior, string theory, theoretical mathematics, or medieval Spanish poetry. This is not the stuff of great controversy. Professors usually can't even persuade their own mothers to read their scholarship.

I agree with Prof. Winkler's view of the *actual* function of tenure:

> Tenure is most valued by professors as a form of compensation. Universities can pay a pittance because they throw in lifetime employment and the autonomy to write on whatever topic the professor wants. That immunity from the marketplace has tremendous value, especially for people whose interests aren't prized by consumers. Without tenure, the medieval Spanish poetry professor has nowhere else to go.

I might add to this, for example, that without tenure, specialists in (and enthusiasts for) market socialism (such as myself) have "nowhere else to go." Of course "nowhere else to go" is an exaggeration. Conceivably I might have followed a career as a corporation executive or a money manager. But that probably wouldn't have allowed sufficient time for research and writing on such topics as market socialism. And even if I had done the research and writing, there was still the issue of getting the material published. Publishers of professional writing are much reassured by an author's academic affiliation. If an author cannot list an academic affiliation, the material is unlikely to be seriously considered for publication.

Following the award of tenure, the pressure to get more publications is greatly reduced—but it never completely disappears. To begin with, few faculty members are comfortable with being regarded by their colleagues as "deadwood," which is assuredly what will happen if years, or even decades, drift by without further publishing. If one manages to get into this unenviable situation, one can protest all one wants that one's teaching responsibilities, or service responsibilities, or social responsibilities, or family responsibilities, or whatever other responsibilities might be available, leave no time for research and writing—but it will be to no avail. It will be widely assumed, whatever excuses might be offered, that the basic reason for lack of productivity is laziness and/or incompetence. But beyond the maintenance of status and self-respect, there are some other motivations to keep working at publishing, albeit they are of relatively minor importance.

Publications might be necessary for promotions and the attached salary increments, though the extremely limited opportunities for promotion make this a minor consideration for most faculty. Leaving aside the rank of instructor (used for non-tenure-track faculty), there are only three levels: assistant professor, associate professor, and full professor (or simply "professor"). New hires, whether with Ph.D. in hand or ABD, normally start as assistant professors. The starting salary, which varies widely over disciplines (to the great dismay of egalitarians within the profession), has a very strong influence on lifetime earnings. Normally promotion to associate professor goes hand in hand with award of tenure. After associate, there is only rank left: full professor. Even at the lesser institutions, promotion to full professor almost always requires some amount of post-tenure productivity—it is not simply a matter of years-in-rank. If one observes that a certain faculty member remains at the associate professor rank for many years, even for decades, this is virtually conclusive evidence of negligible or zero productivity. With acceptable productivity, the number of years between promotion to associate and promotion to full is roughly the same as between initial hiring and promotion to associate: approximately six years. In my own case, I was a little bit in advance of the average: I started at WIU in 1968, was promoted to associate professor in 1974, and then promoted to full professor in 1978. Age-wise, I was 25 when I started, 31 when promoted to associate, and 35 when promoted to full. Therefore I was at the highest rank, with no further opportunities for promotion, while I was still a good 30 years shy of what is usually considered retirement age. My experience in this regard is fairly typical. Relative to the long advancement ladder normally available in corporate enterprise, the advancement ladder in higher education is severely truncated.

At some times and places, "merit" might assume a role in the determination of salary increments—although simple seniority (years in service) is normally the principal determinant. The egalitarians in the profession tend to be strongly opposed to merit on grounds that it is unfair, inequitable, and strikes at the roots of faculty harmony and collegiality. The kernel of substance in this complaint is that in evaluating the respective worth of faculty research publications, inevitably a considerable degree of subjective judgment is involved. On the other hand, even the most adamant egalitarians have to agree that in some objective sense, the value of different contributions does vary. But they assert that the evaluation processes involved in merit determinations are usually highly unreliable.

If a particular faculty member is dissatisfied with the rate of increase of his/her salary, and believes that he/she is being unfairly and illegitimately underpaid, there is only one effective recourse: go out into the open market and endeavor to find another job. Many faculty members who do this (such as I did at certain points during my early career at Western Illinois University) are likely to find that outside one's immediate circle of friends and colleagues at one's present place of employment, it is a cold, dark world out there. The outside world does not know what a fine fellow you are, or how great is your future promise. It will not take seriously any allegations you may offer that you are an excellent teacher. Above-average student evaluations don't count: they can easily be "purchased" by awarding students excessively generous grades. Written testimonials from students are also of little value. Even if they are highly laudatory, this might just mean that you are personally likeable and do a good job of making your courses entertaining. But entertainment is not the same as education—in fact, the two are likely to be in opposition.

In actual fact, there is only one thing that will definitely impress those people in the cold, dark, outside world with the ability to offer you a faculty position at another institution of higher education. Publications. You can't acquire publications by being a nice person, by being helpful, cooperative, supportive, amusing, entertaining, and so on and so forth. For publications it is necessary to be both competent and industrious. Publications are an accurate, unbiased, objective indicator of competence and industriousness. But not just *any* publications. They should be in top-tier journals, or possibly—at a minimum—in second-tier journals. Third-tier or lower journals do not count for much—in fact, they may be worse than useless. Thus the publications that got you tenure in the first place are probably not going to get you job offers from other universities, especially if those other universities are ranked significantly higher than your current university.

Interest among tenured faculty in acquiring additional publications varies widely. A small minority are undeterred by the possibility of being deemed deadwood by their colleagues. They read their daily newspapers, meet their classes, go home early to their families, and undoubtedly lead full, rich lives outside of the workplace. At the other extreme are the small number of intense eager beavers who score three or four publications each and every year, many of them in the better journals, and occasionally include a book among the articles. They spend far more time in their campus offices than the norm, often show up early and leave late, and are frequently found in their offices even on weekends. Presumably their family lives cannot possibly be so full and rich, but they have the compensation of being regarded with high respect by their faculty colleagues. The majority of tenured faculty will be found somewhere in between these two extremes. At an intermediate-level university such as Western Illinois, the typical faculty member in this middle range will be content with a journal article every year or two, and might also have a book in the works, with an expected completion date normally some years off in the future.

Ever since an early stage in my own higher education career, I have maintained fairly complete records on my research and writing efforts and resulting publications. In the area of journal articles I have an Excel spreadsheet named articles.xlsx, which covers most of my projects from May 1967 through March 2015. (A small number of replies and comments are not included.) For almost every article project I ever undertook during that interval, I recorded the following information: a sequence number according to the date the original manuscript was completed; manuscript title; initials of any co-authors; number of alternative titles; number of revisions; number of submissions; number of rejections; indicator of publication (0 if unpublished, 1 if published); date of publication (if published); and the lag in months between the date the manuscript was finished and the date when it was published. In separate Word files I keep information on each article project: journals to which it was submitted, dates of submissions, dates of rejections, dates of revisions, and if published, name of publishing journal and date of publication.

According to the articles.xlsx spreadsheet, during that 49 year interval, I completed 155 article manuscripts, of which 92 were published—usually after several submissions and a substantial lag. In terms of summary statistics, there were 476 separate submissions, 386 rejections, and the average length in months between completing a manuscript and seeing it in print was 27.74 months. This latter is no doubt something of an underestimate, because many professional journals experience publication lags, and the date on the journal issue is often six months or more prior to the actual date of publication.

My overall success rate, the number of journal publications divided by number of projects (92 divided by 155), in percentage terms, was 59.35 percent. An alternative success rate, the number of journal publications divided by number of submissions (92 divided by 476), in percentage terms, is far less impressive: 19.33 percent. My average annual productivity rate (92 published articles divided by 49 years) was 1.877, a little less than two per year. I don't believe I'm being immodest when I say that that is not a bad rate, considering that it applied over such an extended period of time, and that my university was not known as a "research institution." On the other hand, I must be candid in admitting that none of my articles appeared in top-tier journals, and only a few appeared in second-tier journals.

I was a slow starter, in that out of my first 15 article projects, 13 were never published. Between May 1967 and March 1970, I cranked out the following 13 unpublished article manuscripts:

"A Note on Optimal Debt Management Policy" (May 1967): 1 rejection.
"A Simulation-Type Experiment on Pareto Optimality" (March 1968): 3 rejections.
"Pragmatic Socialism as a Form of Market Socialism" (Fall 1968): 1 rejection.
"Income Distribution, Progressive Taxation, and the Average Propensity to Consume" (Fall 1968, with Roger Leonhard): 5 rejections.
"An Alternative Test for the Liquidity Trap" (Fall 1968): 3 rejections.
"Analytic Aspects of Income Equality" (Fall 1968): 3 rejections.
"Some Considerations on the Welfare Economics of Income Equality" (Spring 1969): 1 rejection.
"Bureaucratic Inefficiency" (Spring 1969): 3 rejections.
"Analytic Aspects of Size-Induced Inefficiency" (Spring 1969): 3 rejections.
"Dynamic Stabilization with Tax Policy" (Spring 1969): 1 rejection.
"Managerial Emolument and the Separation of Ownership and Control" (Spring 1970): 2 rejections.
"A Very Long-Run Growth Model" (Spring 1970): 1 rejection.
"A Constructive Criticism of the Phillips Stabilization Method" (Spring 1970): 1 rejection.

What I don't know, and will never know, is whether or not there were actually some worthwhile ideas in that crop, and the reason none of them found their way into print was inadequate presentation. In those long-ago days, there was no such thing as computer word processing, computer-generated graphics, and computer-assisted mathematical expressions. My graphs were hand-drawn, and my typing was amateurish. The equations were particularly bad: any Greek letters or mathematical symbols had to be emplaced by hand. Aside from sub-standard presentation, I did not do a very good job of situating these contributions within the literature. The available reference tools were primitive: the *Journal of Economic Literature* of the American Economic Association, a print resource, had only just begun publishing. I'm not claiming that with better presentation, any of these titles would necessarily have been published—but at least there would have been a higher probability of publication for some of them.

There were two articles produced during that period of time that did escape the ignominy of non-publication:

"An Appraisal of Langian Socialism" (August 1968): 3 rejections, published in the *Indian Economic Journal*, September 1973.

"Mathematics Requirements and Major Enrollment in Departments of Economics: An Empirical Investigation" (March 1969, with Michael Pledge): 1 rejection, published in *Illinois School Research*, September 1972.

Both of these articles were published well after I had finished degree requirements for the Ph.D. at Northwestern and was no longer in the uncomfortable ABD status at WIU: the first, two years after, and the second, one year after. So neither of them was useful for the purpose they were originally intended. "An Appraisal of Langian Socialism" was the only published article I managed to extract from a dissertation draft, and the strange tale of its appearance in a journal published on the other side of the world from the United States was recounted above in the "Union Card" chapter.

It was during the 1970s that I finally—at long, long last—found the range for journal articles, and began publishing at a respectable rate. According to the articles.xlsx spreadsheet, there were 26 article projects for which the original manuscript was completed between 1971 and 1979, and of these, 20 were eventually published. Specifics are as follows:

"A Statistical Estimate of Optimum Population in the United States" (June 1971): 2 rejections, published in the *Nebraska Journal of Economics and Business*, Winter 1973.

"Investment Propensities under Capitalism and Market Socialism" (June 1971): 5 rejections, published in the *Revista Internazionale di Scienze Economiche e Commerziali*, October 1978.

"On the Potential Efficiency of Market Socialism" (January 1972): 1 rejection, published in *ACES Bulletin* (Association for Comparative Economic Studies), Summer 1976.

"Capital Management under Market Socialism" (June 1972): 5 rejections, published in the *Review of Social Economy*, October 1974.

"A Note on the Perverse Supply Curve of the Cooperative Firm" (December 1972): 1 rejection, unpublished.

"Economic Performance of Public and Private Enterprise: The Case of U.S. Electric Utilities" (August 1973): 2 rejections, published in the *Journal of Economics and Business*, Fall 1975.

"The Definition of Elasticity of Substitution" (November 1973): 4 rejections, unpublished.

"Langian Pricing and Inflation Control" (December 1973): 2 rejections, published in *Metroeconomica*, 1977.

"A Dynamic Optimization Model of the Soviet Enterprise" (February 1974): 0 rejections, published in *Economics of Planning*, 1973.

"The Generation Gap and Optimal Economic Growth" (March 1974): 5 rejections, published in *Socio-Economic Planning Sciences*, August 1976.

"A Numerical Search Technique for Optimal Capital Accumulation Programs" (May 1974): 1 rejection, published in *Socio-Economic Planning Sciences*, February 1975.

"A World Economic Equalization Program: Results of a Simulation" (August 1974): 1 rejection, published in the *Journal of Developing Areas*, January 1976.

"Pareto-Efficient Factor Reallocation: A Simulation Approach" (November 1974): 1 rejection, published in *Review of Business and Economic Research*, Fall 1975.

"Is the Death Penalty a Deterrent to Homicide? Some Time Series Evidence" (December 1974): 3 rejections, published in the *Journal of Behavioral Economics*, Summer 1976.

"A Survey of Market Socialist Forms" (February 1975): 0 rejections, published in *Annals of Public and Cooperative Economy*, April-June 1975.

"Capitalist Institutional Evolution and Market Socialism" (August 1975): 2 rejections, unpublished.

"Decision-Making in State Controlled Firms: The Lessons from Market Socialist Theory" (February 1976): 1 rejection, unpublished.

"The Social Dividend under Market Socialism" (February 1976): 0 rejections, published in *Annals of Public and Cooperative Economy*, January-March 1977.

"A Practical Proposal toward World Union" (March 1976): 3 rejections, unpublished.

"An Empirical Evaluation of Diffusion Models: The Case of Automobile Ownership in the United States" (August 1976): 3 rejections, unpublished.

"An Old Controversy Renewed: Introduction to the *JBE* Capital Punishment Symposium" (September 1977): 0 rejections, published in the *Journal of Behavioral Economics*, Summer 1977.

"The Microeconomic Efficiency Argument for Market Socialism Revisited" (February 1978): 0 rejections, published in *Journal of*

Economic Issues, March 1979.

"Testing the Deterrent Effect of Capital Punishment: A Reduced Form Approach" (February 1978): 5 rejections, published in *Criminology*, February 1982.

"Student-Teacher Evaluations and Student Achievement: Evidence from a Project in Principles of Economics" (May 1978, with James F. Niss): 3 rejections, published in *Journal of Economics* (Missouri Valley Economic Association), 1979.

"Optimal Redistribution in the Interdependent Economy: A Simulation Study" (May 1978): 5 rejections, published in *Public Finance*, 1983.

"An Integration of the Accounting and Economic Approaches to Cost-Volume-Profit Analysis under Uncertainty" (July 1978, with Penelope J. Yunker): 5 rejections, published in *Journal of Business and Economics*, January 1982.

The optimum population research embodied in my first published article in the professional literature ("A Statistical Estimate of Optimum Population in the United States") was typical of a great deal of my subsequent research on a variety of issues. I have always been drawn to research topics that have a strong bearing on important real-world policy issues. What could and should be done about population is an example of such an issue. I tend also to want to tackle problems that are widely regarded as too complex and complicated to be susceptible to useful, productive analysis. In order to tackle problems that are evaded by most other economists, and to derive specific, meaningful results bearing on these problems, I very often have had to resort to innovative methodologies that had never before been brought to bear. Of course, this makes my work vulnerable to charges that it is unconventional, unorthodox, unprecedented, atypical, without proper foundation, and so on and so forth. Innovation, of course, is generally considered to be a good thing. However, according to the various referees who have been responsible for the numerous rejections of my article submissions over the years, I am very often *too* innovative. All I can say in my defense is that I have consistently employed methodologies that seem to work, that seem to get results. That my researches do in fact possess some redeeming strengths is indicated by the fact that despite the many rejections, I have after all amassed over the years a substantial body of published work.

The period of time during which I achieved my initial breakthrough on article publications through the publication of "A Statistical Estimate of Optimum Population in the United States," also saw two other significant developments in my professional career: I started work on a large book containing my ambitious ideas and proposals for making the world a better and safer place for the human race, and I took my first tentative steps into the job market with the objective of "moving on up" in the academic firmament. As it turned out, my first effort at a large book turned out to be no more than a learning exercise: it was never published (although parts of it were included in another book published several years later). With respect to my job search activities, they also were unproductive: I remained at Western Illinois University for my entire working career.

Throughout my three years as an ABD and afterwards, even though I had a heavy teaching load and was constantly involved in a range of outside activities, nevertheless I worked very hard at producing and placing articles in the professional literature. But throughout that time there was always at the back of my mind the need to start work, as soon as possible, on a book. Articles would be useful for securing my professorial position, but in order to reach beyond academia to the general public, I needed a book. And not just any book: it had to be a large book, a compelling book, a bestselling book. This book would convey an improved, purified distillation from my prior "New World" and "Plan Alpha" projects: divested of irrelevant side-issues and overblown rhetoric, instead focused on the essential issues, and conveyed in calm, collected, judicious prose. The mad enthusiasm of callow youth would be replaced by the prudent wisdom of seasoned maturity.

I started making preliminary organizational notes for a large book project during the summer of 1971, at about the same time I was putting the finishing touches on my doctoral dissertation. But I did not do any actual writing for it until a full year later. During the summer of 1972, Penny and I took the second of our numerous trips to Belgium to visit her family. Perhaps carried away by our status as "honored guests from America," I indulged in a bit of puffery to Penny's family about this amazing book that I was soon going to start writing. But when I mentioned that among other things, this book would outline a solution (pragmatic market socialism) to the ideological conflict that fueled the Cold War, the principal reaction seemed to be a sort of smirking skepticism. Although quite understandable, this rather irritated me, and I decided I should get started on the writing right away. Of course, summer vacations in locations far from home are not favorable to productivity, and so I only managed to scratch out a few handwritten pages. But it did break down the natural inertia that impedes the commencement of any large, intimidating project. As soon as we returned to Macomb for the 1972-73 academic year, I commenced a serious writing program, which was maintained throughout the year.

For quite a while I was uncertain what to title this magnum opus, this "big book" (abbreviated "BB" in my diary). My initial thought was *The End of the Nightmare*, a reference to ending the Cold War which threatened humanity with the nightmare of nuclear holocaust. But then I thought the implication of this title might be too restrictive. The vision was not confined to ending the Cold War: it went beyond that to a global economic development program, and even beyond that to the foundation of a federal world government. The working main title was changed to *Pragmatic Utopia*, with sub-title to be devised later. The combination of "pragmatic" with "utopia" I thought would be an attention-getter, since the two concepts are generally assumed to be fully contradictory to one another. But everyone to whom I mention this title, even to those most sympathetic (e.g., my spouse Penny), thought it was a terrible idea: it would get attention all right—but the wrong kind.

Eventually I had to agree. My thought had been that this book was *not* proposing a full-scale, literal utopia which would be the equivalent on the earthly plane to the mythical Garden of Eden. Rather it would be *as close as we could get* to such a condition, given the constraints under which we must necessarily operate, constraints such as limited natural resources, and the physical and psychological limitations of human nature. In economics, the idea of "constrained optimization" is fundamental, as for example in the case of the household that must maximize its utility subject to a budget constraint with a fixed amount of income. My idea was that with the implementation of such advances as pragmatic market socialism and federal world government, humanity would be in a position to achieve the maximum social welfare given the inevitable constraints. The situation would not and could not be literally ideal, but it would be the best attainable under the circumstances. But eventually I concluded that this interpretation of *Pragmatic Utopia* was far too subtle, far too nuanced. My wife—and numerous others—were quite right.

Finally, well into the writing of the BB, specifically in January, 1973, I finally settled permanently on a revised title: *The Grand Convergence: Economic and Political Aspects of Human Progress*. This title expresses the concept of three separate but mutually supportive convergences: ideological, economic, and political. Ideological convergence refers to the transition from democratic market capitalism in the non-communist world and oligarchic planned socialism in the communist world to democratic market socialism in both worlds—the economic component of which would be some form of pragmatic market socialism. Economic convergence refers to the transition from abject poverty in the Third World and great wealth in the First World to a high level of affluence in all parts of the world. Political convergence refers to the transition from the quasi-anarchic contemporary international system based on national sovereignty, to a federal world government capable of providing a strong political foundation for a higher level of security and prosperity throughout the world. There would be temporal interdependency between these three convergences: first, ideological convergence would end the Cold War and free up a large quantity of economic resources previously used for military production for reallocation to a global economic development program; second, this reallocation would enable economic convergence in terms of rising living standards throughout the world, but especially in the poorer nations; and third, as economic convergence continued, conditions would become more favorable for the establishment of a stable and benign federal world government.

Although there have been some modifications in this vision with the passage of time and changes in world circumstances, much of it remains just as pertinent to the world of today as it was to the world of the 1970s. Obviously, the biggest change by far in world conditions between now and then, was the collapse of the Soviet Union in the early 1990s, and the abandonment of Marxist ideology by its successors in the Commonwealth of Independent States, and by its satellite nations in Eastern Europe. The renunciation by all these countries of their former messianic aspirations toward the elimination of capitalism and its replacement by communism throughout the world, had a marvelously beneficial effect on international relations. Most historians consider it to have marked the definitive termination of the Cold War. With the two leading nuclear superpowers of the world, the United States and the Soviet Union, no longer at ideological loggerheads, the threat of nuclear holocaust receded to a level that most people consider insignificant.

It cannot be seriously argued that the prospects of humanity were not immensely improved by the end of the Cold War as it was known during the decades from the fifties through the eighties. On the other hand, humanity still confronts serious problems, uncertainties, and hazards. For example, despite the ending of the Cold War several decades ago, the United States and the Russian Federation still consider it necessary to maintain nuclear arsenals of such huge destructive potential that if they were ever unleashed, it would be catastrophic for global human civilization.

It is necessary to remember that the scourge of persistent competition among sovereign nations leading regularly to warfare was not introduced in 1917 when the Bolshevik revolution in Russia unleashed communist ideology into real-world international relations. Persistent warfare among nations long predated communism, and there is a possibility that it may well postdate it as well. Also, it should be kept in mind that communism has not yet entirely disappeared as a potentially troublesome force in international politics. Although much moderated from the hardline communism of Stalin and Mao, communism is still influential in some Asian nations, most notably in the People's Republic of China, as well as in Vietnam and North Korea. But even if these last vestiges of communism were to disappear forever, that would still leave the sovereign nation-state system. The combination of the sovereign nation-state system with nuclear arsenals could eventually be fatal to the interests of humanity.

Much of the vision that was elaborated in *The Grand Convergence: Economic and Political Aspects of Human Progress*, the unpublished manuscript I wrote during the 1972-73 academic year, is still quite relevant today. As a matter of fact, I recycled that same title in a book published by Palgrave Macmillan in 2010. *The Grand Convergence* was (is) a good title, and I'm pleased that I eventually had an opportunity to use it on a published book. In my personal record-keeping system, I apply the label "Grand Convergence I" to the unpublished manuscript of 1972-73, and "Grand Convergence II" to the published book of 2010. Whereas in Grand Convergence I, the tripartite convergence envisioned was ideological, economic, and political, in Grand Convergence II the ideological component was jettisoned as no longer relevant owing the historic transformations of the early 1990s. The two convergences elucidated in Grand Convergence II are economic and political.

During the winter and spring of 1973, the pages of Grand Convergence I piled up rapidly: initially handwritten (this was long before the advent of word processing), then typed. I began thinking about how to present the project to the publishers. It would have been nice to have had the entire thing completely finished and neatly typed before making my initial approach. But as the draft material accumulated, I realized that this was shaping up to be a very substantial tome indeed, probably in the vicinity of a thousand pages or more. Even if it had all been straight text, it would have been an intimidating typing job, but in addition to text I was anticipating incorporating numerous tables and figures. For a while I even thought about adding an analytical appendix filled with a large number of equations. But I soon abandoned the analytical appendix on grounds that even without it, the book was already becoming dangerously bulky.

As the spring of 1973 began transitioning into summer, I found that I was simply too impatient to wait until I had a polished final version before approaching the publishers. I was doing most of the typing myself, and in those days before word processing, tables were especially difficult to format properly using a typewriter. And the placement of figures within the text created still another set of problems. I came up with the idea of a "Grand Convergence Sampler." The Sampler would contain a generous selection of sections from the book, all neatly and uniformly typed, of about 250 pages in all. A limited number of figures would be included, but no tables. The Sampler plus the table of contents would provide a potential publisher with all the information necessary to make a decision.

Even before I made my first submission, I realized that publication of this relatively gargantuan tome was a long shot. To begin with, the text alone, without including any tables and only a few figures, came to 921 pages. Adding the numerous tables and figures would likely increase the page count by at least another 100 pages. On top of that, there was my lack of status: here I was an assistant professor of economics at a boondocks college no one had ever heard of, and my résumé listed exactly one publication—forthcoming at that. And on top of that, the book was presenting arguments for institutional reforms that almost everyone among the likely readership was totally against: market socialism, global economic equalization, world government. It wasn't that the publishers were interested in "suppressing" such heretical proposals. It was just that they could not imagine that an adequate market existed for such a book. Perhaps if *The Grand Convergence* had been written by a renowned "public intellectual" such as John Kenneth Galbraith, the outcome would have been different. But—no disrespect intended—John Kenneth Galbraith did not possess the requisite imagination.

Between the early summer and late fall of 1973, I submitted the Grand Convergence Sampler to no less than 26 publishers. Most of them were courteous enough to "regretfully" decline interest. To their credit, not one of them replied to my submission: "You must be joking!" A book submission requires, in addition to a prospectus and writing samples, a covering letter. My covering letter went through several iterations: a typical example was the one that went to Martin Kessler of Basic Books:

> Dear Mr. Kessler,
>
> I have forwarded to you under separate cover an outline and some excerpts from a book which I have recently completed, entitled The Grand Convergence: Economic and Political Aspects of Human Progress. I would be gratified if you would devote to this booklet your usual careful editorial consideration.
>
> The book itself, which is the result of several years of thought and study by a university teacher in economics, is intended to be a serious contribution to the literature on general world problems. It presents a series of guidelines for the amelioration of some of the more pressing

> of these problems. The guidelines are rather considerably more detailed and specific--while not (hopefully) sacrificing practicality--than is usual in related literature. The guidelines are illuminated and supported by a considerable amount of background material drawn mostly from the social sciences, in particular economics. Whether or not the reader is made sympathetic to the proposed guidelines, some of which would be admittedly rather controversial, I would hope that reading and contemplating the background material would in itself provide considerable enjoyable mental stimulation and informational value for the typical intelligent reader. While a small amount of the background material is slightly technical, the vast majority of the exposition can be easily followed by the general reader with some interest and previous reading experience in social scientific literature.
>
> The primary market for this book would obviously be much more limited than that for something like Son of Valley of the Dolls. But on the other hand I suspect that the evaluation of the sales potential should not be unduly pessimistic. First of all, the book should sell, at a minimum, at least as well as a purely technical book intended primarily for library sales plus purchase by a few specialists--and for essentially the same reasons. But there is in addition a potential general trade market that with effective exploitation could be quite appreciable. There are a lot of politically and socially concerned adults and students around who could be induced to purchase and read a book like this. The book is not so dry and technical that the overwhelming majority of these people would be discouraged. If even a small part of this group could be tapped, the book could do quite respectably. Also the nature of the book is such that there is always a slight possibility at least that it could really catch on, in which case the investment could justify itself many times over...

The Table of Contents for *The Grand Convergence* did not include page numbers, since the existing manuscript was not sufficiently finalized at that point for pagination. Instead there were page counts for each section. The organizational structure was that of 12 chapters over five parts. The number of text pages was 921, but obviously between the large number of tables and figures still to be added, the total page count, had the book been published, would probably have considerably exceeded 1,000.

By far the largest amount of material devoted to a single topic was that pertaining to socialism: 430 pages out of 921. More than 10 years earlier, as I was grappling with the "New World" concept as a freshman student at Fordham University, I perceived the ideological confrontation between East and West over the issue of socialism versus capitalism as the critical logjam holding up the river of progress. If humanity could get past this obstacle—break up the logjam—then marvelous advances would become possible. The most plausible and attractive answer to the problem was some variant of pragmatic market socialism, a system that would combine the public ownership principle from socialism with the free market principle from capitalism. In order to make this concept fully comprehensible to the reader, it was necessary to provide a substantial amount of background on such topics as the history of the socialist idea, Soviet socialism, public enterprise, and the socialist critique of capitalism. Much of the socialist critique had been rendered null and void by real-world developments: most importantly, the development of Keynesian anticyclical policy in the aftermath of the Great Depression of the 1930s almost certainly eliminated catastrophic business depressions of the sort that Karl Marx had predicted would precipitate the collapse of capitalism.

Nevertheless, there was one aspect of the socialist critique that remained as valid under contemporary capitalism as it ever had been: the extremely unequal distribution of unearned capital property income. But for this criticism to be taken seriously, it must be shown that a system of pragmatic market socialism would function at least as well, and possibly better than, the contemporary capitalist economic system. To answer this question in the affirmative, the pragmatic market socialist proposal was then elaborated and defended. Although in later work I amplified in much detail both the proposal itself and its defense, the basic elements of the argument are covered comprehensively in Chapters 7 and 8 of the 1973 manuscript. Some of this material was in fact taken directly from a manuscript entitled "Capital Management under Market Socialism" which I had completed in June 1972, and which was eventually published in the October 1974 issue of *Review of Social Economy*. I included the graphs from that article but omitted the mathematical expressions. It was technical material, but not advanced technical material, and this analysis was so critical that I deemed it worth the risk.

Aside from pragmatic market socialism, there was one other visionary proposal in the 1973 *Grand Convergence* manuscript that I consider as relevant and important today as it was back in 1973: federal world government. The exposition of the world government proposal was contained in the first section of the relatively brief final Chapter 12. Although in my subsequent writings, the case for world government came to the fore and was greatly amplified, the basic institutional elements of what I later designated the "Federal Union of Democratic Nations" were already present in the 1973 manuscript. The discussion of world government in that manuscript clearly manifested my clear awareness that even in the absence of ideological disagreements, global economic inequality constitutes a fundamental impediment to the foundation of a stable, effective, benign federal world government. This was true in 1973, and it is still true today. This is an unfortunate situation—but inevitable. It can only be dealt with by means of such institutional features as the retention by member nations of the rights of free exit and independent military power. This is what is meant by a "properly designed" federal world government. One of the most important reasons why there is no such thing in the contemporary world as a politically significant movement toward world government is that so many of the people who proclaim their firm adherence to the world government goal seem totally oblivious of the problem that extreme economic inequality among the nations poses to stable, effective, and benign world government.

As mentioned, my writing *The Grand Convergence* during the 1972-73 academic year was a "learning exercise," because the manuscript was never published. To call it a "learning exercise" implies that I did in fact learn some things that were helpful in getting later books published. Among these some of the most important were the following. First, do not go overboard with the use of tables and figures, and especially do not incorporate tables and figures (with attribution) from published sources. In later manuscripts I often included a substantial number of tables and figures, but they were all of my own devising, and related directly to important points in the text. Another lesson learned was the advisability of having a complete manuscript in hand before approaching the publishers—except, of course, for the index, because the final pagination has to be settled before the index can be added.

Also it is important to reduce or omit relatively extraneous topics. Here, of course, judgment is required. When one is arguing for reforms that have not yet appeared in the real world, such as pragmatic market socialism or federal world government, there is extremely little evidence—not to say none at all—that bears directly, exactly, totally, and precisely on the proposed reform. All the real-world evidence that can possibly be brought to bear is, as a lawyer would say, *circumstantial*. It is at best *probative*—not conclusive. None of the evidence that can possibly be adduced amounts to *proof*, in a literal sense, that these reforms would be beneficial. Nevertheless, evidence is evidence, even it is indirect and circumstantial, and setting the standards for relevance unrealistically high would mean that virtually nothing could be said about controversial issues.

That said, there are some topics whose bearing on the question of interest is so remote and tangential, that to include them is a waste of both the author's and the reader's time. An example of such a topic from the 1973 *Grand Convergence* manuscript is population. A considerable amount of attention was devoted to arguing that at the present juncture in the long-term history of humanity, further population growth is inadvisable from the standpoint of individual human wellbeing. That was true then, and it is still true today. But the fact remains that even if population continues growing at a brisk rate over the next 50 to 100 years (as it probably will), this will probably not seriously affect the feasibility and desirability of such reforms as pragmatic market socialism, a global economic equalization program, and federal world government. Sooner or later, some form of purposeful population control might well become necessary to preserve humanity from disaster. But this problem probably will not become critical for another three or four human generations.

My "New World" and "Plan Alpha" writings from the 1960s had insisted that all the reform concepts being put forward therein were tentative and provisional, and that what I was asking for was not necessarily that they be put into practice, but rather to propose that they were sufficiently plausible to be subjected to serious study by a large interdisciplinary research team. This approach was continued in the introductory pages of the 1973 *Grand Convergence* manuscript. But a permanent lesson learned from that project was that this was probably not a good idea. It made me, the author, seem too hesitant and uncertain. Of course I did not want to come across as a ranting zealot—it was vital that I be perceived by the typical reader as an informed, sensible, intelligent, judicious, and realistic person. But there is a happy medium between an excessively strident tone that will strike the reader as dogmatic, and an excessively tentative tone that will strike the reader as nerdy. During the latter months of 1973 during which one publisher after another was declining interest in my submission, I formed an irrevocable resolution that never again would I say anything about a foundation-funded interdisciplinary research organization.

Another resolution was that I would strike a more positive note in the opening paragraphs of whatever future book I would undertake. The first few paragraphs of the 1973 Grand Convergence I manuscript were excessively defensive in tone—veritably apologetic. I can only surmise that when I was writing those first few paragraphs, my mind was under the influence of the overwhelming amount of skepticism and borderline hostility I had elicited over the prior decade whenever I had made any effort whatsoever to impart to anyone at all my ideas about improving the world. Before I concluded that I lacked the personal charisma to get these ideas across in oral conversation, I had initiated innumerable debates with innumerable individuals. Very quickly, it seemed, they got to the point of disagreeing with virtually everything I said. So what I was trying to do, in the opening pages of Grand Convergence I, was to avoid getting immediately into a debate. What I wished to say was something like this: "I know you will have doubts about what I want to tell you. I have doubts myself. But let's try to look at this together, in a spirit of mutual endeavor." The intention was to cultivate curiosity and rapport with the reader, to avoid instant confrontation. But, alas, apparently I did not achieve this purpose.

There follows a few examples selected from the 26 rejection letters I received from various publishers during the latter part of 1973:

> From Virginia Hilu of Harper & Row (June 29, 1973): "Several of us in the trade department have carefully reviewed your manuscript THE GRAND CONVERGENCE: ECONOMIC AND POLITICAL ASPECTS OF HUMAN PROGRESS. It is obviously the result of much thought and effort, however, we do not feel that we can make an offer to publish. It is the kind of book that should best be considered by a university press and I suggest you approach the Princeton University Press, MIT, or Harvard."

> From Kimberly Wiar of the University of Chicago Press (November 28, 1973): "Thank you for sending your manuscript THE GRAND CONVERGENCE: ECONOMIC AND POLITICAL ASPECTS OF HUMAN PROGRESS, to the Press for consideration. We have now had the opportunity to peruse the work and to discuss it at an editorial meeting, and I regret to say that the consensus is that we ought not to pursue publication. Although your attempts to discuss 'general world problems' and to formulate a research proposal are certainly laudable, it seems to us that the work would be much more appropriate for the list of a commercial publisher."

> From Peter Robinson of Praeger Publishers (August 3, 1973): "Thank you for your submission of The Grand Convergence: Economic and Political Aspects of Human Progress. Unfortunately, after consultation with our editorial board as well as our production and marketing departments, the consensus is that the market for your book would be too narrow to justify our placing your book on our list. We wish you good fortune in placing your book with another publisher and thank you for thinking of Praeger."

> From Martin Kessler of Basic Books (October 23, 1973): "I must apologize for having held on to your manuscript, THE GRAND CONVERGENCE: ECONOMIC AND POLITICAL ASPECTS OF HUMAN PROGRESS, for such an unconscionably long time, but we have been exceptionally busy of late. Your manuscript was most seriously considered here, but while we found much in it to admire, and agree with the general thrust of your argument, we were forced to conclude that the message of the volume was not sufficiently novel to jus-

> tify substantial professional or trade sales, and not sufficiently systematic or geared to course requirements to make us very hopeful of substantial college adoptions."
>
> From Dennis O'Toole of Harcourt Brace Jovanovich Inc. (December 12, 1973): "Thank you very much for allowing us to consider THE GRAND CONVERGENCE: ECONOMIC AND POLITICAL ASPECTS OF HUMAN PROGRESS. We found your manuscript very interesting, but unfortunately it seems to fall into a field too highly specialized for a general publisher such as Harcourt. Perhaps it would be more logically placed with one of the university presses."

Even at the time, I found it somewhat amusing that the commercial presses were pointing me to the university presses while at the same time the university presses were pointing me to the commercial presses. In any case, the book acquisition editors seemed to be very similar to the journal editors in that most of the free advice they deigned to provide was basically useless. On the whole, the situation was highly demoralizing.

As anyone who has ever experienced rejection can attest (and most of us have experienced it at one time or another in our lives), the experience is psychologically painful. Consider a common example. Outside of traditional societies in which arranged marriages are common, and given the way the mating game normally proceeds in non-traditional societies, it is up to the male to initiate contact with prospective female mates. Consequently, most adult men have had the experience, at one time or another, of telephoning an attractive female prospect to ask for a date, and being told that she was extremely busy at present, and would probably remain so for the next several weeks or months. The feeling that the poor fellow gets in the pit of his stomach is basically the same as that which an author gets upon reading a rejection letter from a publisher. It carves off a little bit from one's self-respect, a small part from one's soul. One can take a positive view of it: after all, humility is a virtue, and nothing cultivates humility so much as rejection. But in the final analysis, that is small consolation for the pain.

As related above, my initial efforts at article publications were highly unsuccessful: out of my first 15 completed article manuscripts, only two eventually made it into print. I consoled myself with the thought that all these article projects focused on very minor topics in the larger scheme of things. But the ideas elaborated in the Grand Convergence I manuscript could hardly be considered minor topics in the larger scheme of things. In fact, they *were* the "larger scheme of things." True, the ideas were thoroughly original and innovative, and for that reason inevitably controversial. But I had elaborated and defended these ideas in great detail, using every bit of information I could possibly muster. I had given the project everything I had. Surely I had gotten the vision across. Surely even the most skeptical reader could not fail to comprehend and appreciate the vision. But as the rejection letters gradually arrived, one by one, throughout the later months of 1973, I began to absorb an awful reality: No, what I had done was *not* enough. *The Grand Convergence* was unpublishable. Despite its potentially world-historical message, it was never going to see the light of day in print. It was a failure.

A failure of this magnitude tends to induce an introspective frame of mind in an individual, an unusual degree of self-examination and self-assessment. The failure of Grand Convergence I to be published raised a veritably terrifying possibility. Perhaps these grand ideas I had developed for improving the prospects of humanity really were total nonsense—just as they were perceived to be by almost all of the dozens, if not hundreds, of people to whom they had been presented over the previous decade. Perhaps the problem was that I was simply too dense, too simpleminded, too obtuse to understand this.

Well, naturally this was something I could not accept. I couldn't possibly be *that* stupid or misguided. After all, I was Phi Beta Kappa, had graduated from Fordham magna cum laude, had an M.A. from the University of California at Berkeley, and a Ph.D. from Northwestern University. Nor was I ignorant: I had read widely in economics, history, political science. My intelligence may not be outstanding, but it is certainly above average. And my fund of relevant information is surely far greater than the norm. I had actually *studied* these proposals, thought about them deeply. They were solid proposals—of that I was confident. But why couldn't other people see this? As much as I would have preferred to do so, I could not, on the basis of objective evidence, attribute it to my greater intelligence. So what *was* it?

I came to the conclusion that it was *Vision*. In a basic physical sense, vision refers to the ability to see things with your eyes. But in the expanded sense, it refers to things you can see *in your mind*. I could see in my mind that such reforms as pragmatic market socialism and federal world government—provided they were properly designed—would be beneficial, that they could and would contribute favorably to the future prospects of global human civilization. Moreover, I had very strong, clear ideas about their proper design. Given proper design, these things were definitely practical, feasible, doable. My unusually generous endowment of *Vision* enabled me to see clearly what others could not see. That was the answer. It was a reassuring answer. The difficulty, of course, lay in sharing this particular vision with those of lesser visionary capabilities, since the proposals ran so contrary to certain deeply imbedded preconceptions in society against both socialism and world government. *I* could see and understand that these particular preconceptions were *mis*conceptions. But would I ever be able to get *other people* to see and understand this?

Was this Vision of mine a blessing or a curse? If it proved forever impossible to share the ideas stemming from it to any appreciable extent, if it meant that I faced a lifetime of being deemed at best a harmless crank and at worst a malign prophet, then most people would consider it a curse. On the other hand, maybe someday, one day, I would be able to lift the blinders from the eyes of my fellow human beings, and share my ideas with them. If that day ever came about, and the future prospects of humanity were thereby significantly improved, then my Vision would be perceived to have been a blessing.

I was (and am) extremely fortunate to be a citizen in good standing of the United States of America. Given the high regard among the United States population for rights of free speech, and our toleration and respect for new ideas, I had a far better opportunity to share my ideas than might otherwise have been the case. At other times and places in recent human history, submitting something like the 1973 *Grand Convergence* manuscript to publishing houses could have resulted in a midnight visit from the political police, and summary consignment to a concentration camp—or worse. Instead of that I got polite letters from publishing houses praising my effort but regretfully declining interest in publishing it.

Within the enlightened American milieu in which I have lived my life, not many people have perceived in me a malign and possibly dangerous prophet. The vast majority of those who have been exposed to my visionary thinking regard it as a praiseworthy endeavor, as something which speaks very well of my humanity and my good intentions. The snag is that it is all so totally unrealistic, so completely impractical, so uselessly idealistic. Being generally regarded as a harmless eccentric bothers me if I think about it, but I try not to think about it. Certainly it is far better than being burnt at the stake for heresy, or being shot at dawn for treason.

I came forward out of this setback with no appreciable damage to my underlying determination. In past history, many important figures encountered early setbacks, yet continued working at whatever grand design inspired them, and eventually succeeded in achieving their objective, to the greater benefit of humanity. So I would follow in their footsteps. I would not give up. I would continue trying. I would write more books, better books, publishable books—books that would effectively convey my vision of a better future for all of us. It was 1973, I was 30 years old, and I was just getting started!

5

The Vision in Print: Articles

Throughout my career the overriding objective has been a large, best-selling book laying out a grand-scale vision of global progress. Before the fall of communism in the Soviet Union and Eastern Europe during the early 1990s, the vision consisted of pragmatic market socialism in the West leading to ideological harmonization, ideological harmonization leading to disarmament and a global economic development program, a global economic development program leading to a stable, effective, and benign federal world government. The first step in the progression was to be pragmatic market socialism in the West. Following the fall of communism in the Soviet Union and Eastern Europe, the role of pragmatic market socialism as a first step was eliminated. The vision was then modified to include the simultaneous launch of a global economic development program and a federal world government. A simultaneous launch would be feasible if the envisioned federal world government were "properly designed," by that meaning that it would constitutionally incorporate, among other things, the reserved national rights of free withdrawal and independent military forces.

The original pre-fall vision was laid out, with minor adjustments, in *World Union on the Horizon: The Case for Supernational Federation* (University Press of America, 1993). The adjustments were required by the fact that publication of this book slightly post-dated the fall. The post-fall vision (entirely omitting pragmatic market socialism) was laid out first in *Political Globalization: A New Vision of Federal World Government* (University Press of America, 2007), and somewhat later in *The Grand Convergence: Economic and Political Aspects of Human Progress* (Palgrave Macmillan, 2010), the title of which was recycled from the unpublished manuscript of 1973. Unfortunately for my intentions, all three of these books were published and marketed as "scholarly contributions," and as such had a virtually imperceptible effect on both professional awareness and general public awareness. "Instant oblivion" is the term I invented to describe their fate.

All along, the articles on which I worked were intended as precursors to books. This could be said even of articles which had nothing to do with visionary ideas. For non-visionary articles, their purpose was to demonstrate to acquisition editors for book publishers that I was a sufficiently competent economist to be able to place articles in the professional literature—thus lending credibility to the hypothesis that I was also sufficiently competent to produce publishable books. With respect to articles on visionary topics, this basic purpose was supplemented by the further purpose of working out various details that might later be incorporated into books. I discovered by experience, however, that usually the articles got into such specialized and intricate detail that not much of them could be directly utilized in books, owing to space considerations alone, not to mention that the intended readership of the books was not confined to professional economists. Nevertheless, the fact that these articles were directly or closely related to visionary concepts made them exceptionally interesting to me. Unlike the non-visionary articles, these might actually make a significant, appreciable difference to the future prospects of global human civilization. On the other hand, each of these articles necessarily dealt with only one small component of the overall concept. But it was the overall concept that possessed the real power, not the individual components. According to the old saying: "The whole may be greater than the sum of the parts." Only a book, which would combine a number of diverse components, could hope to convey adequate appreciation of the overall vision.

By actual count, of the 155 manuscripts completed between 1967 and 2011, some 48 were on market socialism and closely related topics such as capital wealth distribution (of which 29 were published), and some 25 were on world government and closely related topics such as global economic development (of which 15 were published). In this chapter I will provide salient details on the more important of the article projects.

Pragmatic Market Socialism

Having been mentally and emotionally drained by the prolonged effort to finish my dissertation, I took an extended break from creative endeavors during the 1971-72 academic year: I accomplished very little beyond meeting my classes. However, there was one fairly significant exception to this general pattern of lassitude. I completed two manuscripts during that year that specified a formal model of capital management effort under capitalism versus under pragmatic market socialism. The first manuscript, entitled "On the Potential Efficiency of Market Socialism," was completed in January 1972, and eventually published in the *ACES Bulletin* (Association for Comparative Economic Studies) in Summer 1976, approximately four and a half years later. The second manuscript, entitled "Capital Management under Market Socialism," was completed in June 1972, and was eventually published in the *Review of Social Economy* in October 1974, a little over two and a half years later. In other words, the manuscript that was completed first was published almost two years *after* the publication of the manuscript that was completed second.

Of the two papers, the route of "Capital Management under Market Socialism" toward publication was more typical, and since this article was an important milestone in my professional career, being the very first time anything related in any way to my visionary ideas saw the light of day in print, I will provide here a capsule summary of its history. For each of my article projects (with a few minor exceptions), their history was recorded in a "Summary Record," first in handwriting, then typed into Word files. These files provided the raw material for the Excel spreadsheet articles.xlsx. The "Summary Record" for "Capital Management under Market Socialism" is as follows:

Capital Management under Market Socialism

Main period of work: Spring 1972.
Manuscript completed: June 1972.

Submitted to *Western Economic Journal*, June 1972.
Rejected September 1972.

Submitted to *Southern Economic Journal*, September 1972.
Rejected December 1972.

Revision work: December 1972 – January 1973.
Revision completed: January 1973.

Submitted to *Quarterly Journal of Economics*, January 1973.
Rejected March 22, 1973.

Sent copy to Abram Bergson for comments, March 1973.
Replied June 1973 with generalities.

Revision work: September 1973.
Revision completed: October 1973.

Submitted to *Kyklos*, October 1973.
Rejected November 1973.

Submitted to *Review of Social Economy*, December 1973.
March 1, 1974: Paper still in review process. OK if I submit it else-

where?
Submitted to *Journal of Economic Issues*, March 1, 1974.
Rejected by *JEI*, March 15, 1974.
May 9, 1974: *RSE* will publish it in October issue if I reduce it from 31 to 15 pages.
Revision/condensation submitted May 17, 1974.
Appeared in October 1974 issue.

For each of my article projects I retained a folder containing the various versions of the paper, and related correspondence. From the folder for "Capital Management under Market Socialism," the following are some highlights: The initial version was only 16 typed pages in length, but it contained two complicated-looking sections: one of them containing analysis of some algebraic examples for the manager utility function and the capital management effort production function (components of the model), and the other containing extensions into uncertainty analysis and dynamic analysis. Both of these sections were eliminated from the final published version. I gradually learned from experience not to add mathematics unless they are absolutely central to the analysis. Mathematics complicate matters for editors and referees, because they are usually far more difficult to fathom than straight prose. Moreover, many of the mathematical expressions in the first version were exceptionally messy-looking with numerous hand-drawn characters. In the pre-word processing era, emplacement of mathematical expressions in a manuscript using a typewriter was frustratingly difficult, and the result often quite amateurish-looking. When equation editors were added to word processing programs starting in the late 1980s, authors could emplace beautifully typeset equations and other mathematical expressions into their manuscripts. It was thus easier to produce manuscripts that appeared publishable.

The first rejection letter, dated September 25, 1972, from Alice Vandermeulen, editor of the *Western Economic Journal* (later *Economic Inquiry*), was as follows:

Dear Professor Yunker:

I am sorry to have to report that several referees have read your manuscript, and they all advise against acceptance. The consensus seems to be that the first and last parts don't hang together very well. The feeling is that you have "a microeconomic exercise involving maximization of managerial efforts under various degrees of response to pecuniary incentives and job insecurity, which can at best be taken as an extension of the Lange model, rather than a reinterpretation of the complete model. The beginning analogy of the administratively imposed rule for optimal production, involving a tradeoff between the

> cost of regulation and its benefits, seems poorly linked to the rest of the paper."
>
> Although you realize that editors are only brokers in expertise, my own hunch is that you should lock your dissertation in a drawer and write what seems to be the heart of whatever you think your contribution to be. Much of what you work out with calculus could be said with a mere citation to "capitalist" literature.
>
> Thank you for giving us the opportunity to see your paper.

Even for that more gracious era, this was an unusually cordial rejection letter. However, I could only smile ruefully at some of the misconceptions it conveyed. As often happens, the referees' potshots were well wide of the mark. In no way could pragmatic market socialism be deemed an "extension" of the Langian approach—it was fundamentally different. And although job insecurity was mentioned in the paper, it was not incorporated into the basic capital management effort model. Prompting Prof. Vandermeulen's comment about "locking my dissertation in a drawer" was the fact that I had listed "The Administrative Costs of Langian Socialism" among the references. She apparently thought that the article was based on my dissertation, and she surmised that it contained a lot of "filler material," as dissertations often do. As a matter of fact, however, none of the mathematical analysis in the article had appeared anywhere in any of the various versions of my dissertation. The math was all developed during the academic year after the Ph.D. had been completed.

The next rejection letter from Vincent Tarascio, editor of the *Southern Economic Journal*, dated December 13, 1972, was a far more typical example of the genre:

> I am sorry to report that our referee does not feel that your paper represents a substantial contribution to the literature, and he has recommended that it be rejected.

Whether any given piece of research, of whatever it might consist, represents a "substantial" contribution to the literature, is obviously a subjective judgment. Authors usually feel that their work represents a substantial contribution to the literature. Referees often disagree. If so inclined, authors can appeal to editors against referee judgments. Such appeals are almost never successful. Ordinarily editors have far more contributions than they can possibly publish, so they are usually quite content to receive from referees recommendations to reject.

The first revision eliminated the section on algebraic examples but retained the material on uncertainty analysis. By adding more background material to forestall any misapprehensions that pragmatic market socialism was an "extension" of Langian market socialism, the new version comprised 22 typed pages, up from 16. The next submission, to the *Quarterly Journal of Economics*, was definitely a long-shot submission. The *Quarterly Journal of Economics* is a top-tier journal edited at a top-tier university: Harvard University, no less. It was hardly a shock , therefore, when it was rejected.

At this point I decided to appeal for assistance to Abram Bergson, a Harvard professor, and at that time without a doubt the world's leading authority on market socialism generally and Langian market socialism in particular. Quite possibly he had been the referee on my submission to the *Quarterly Journal of Economics*. In response to my request for input, Professor Bergson replied as follows:

> Dear Professor Yunker:
>
> I am returning herewith your MS on "Capital Management under Market Socialism." The question on which you are focusing strikes me as an interesting one, but I wonder whether the essentials could not be brought out more clearly and more briefly than they are now, for the exposition somehow seems unduly involved. Please see also the comments which I have inserted on the margins of the MS.
>
> The foregoing are purely personal opinions and should not be construed as representing in any sense the opinions of the QJE. Actually I myself was not the QJE referee for your essay.

This was an encouraging response, in that in Prof. Bergson's opinion I was focusing on an "interesting" question, and the only advice was to try to convey the essentials "more clearly and more briefly." This advice pertained to presentation—not substance. Not least of the value of this letter from Prof. Bergson was that it enabled me to add the following acknowledgement note to subsequent versions of the paper:

> The author would like to thank Professors Abram Bergson and Karl de Schweinitz for helpful comments and suggestions on a prior draft.

Karl de Schweinitz had not provided any input on this particular manuscript, but he had had plenty to say on my prior work on market socialism. The next revision was expanded to 31 typed pages and featured distinctly improved typing. For example, in place of α and β, I substituted a and b, so that I would not have to hand-write the Greek letters. (Later on, it became a simple thing to use Greek letters, by changing the characters to the Symbol font.) There followed two more rejections before I struck pay dirt.

Finally, there came a letter from William Waters, editor of the *Review of Social Economy*, dated May 7, 1974, offering to publish my paper if I would cut it down from 31 to 15 typed pages. Under the circumstances, this was an offer I could not refuse. Of course it was difficult cutting so much out of my carefully considered and painstakingly crafted prose. But authors of contributions to the professional literature get used to this sort of thing: even though there are dozens if not hundreds of economics journals, there is always an incredible amount of competition for the available space. The irony is that often the same referee who demands that certain "important omitted considerations" be added to a revision, will at the same time demand that the allegedly overblown text be reduced in length. This creates a difficult tightrope for the author to negotiate. At least I was not asked to cut out all the math. This was the abstract I provided for the published version of the article:

> The common understanding of the "incentives problem" of market socialism is that if imperfectly competitive firms are given a profits incentive, they will have a motivation to violate the Langian efficiency rule MC = p, while if no profits incentive is established and only rules stated, there will be no observable success criterion for firm managers and they will be consequently uninspired in the performance of their duties. This issue is only relevant to the peculiarly Langian objective of establishing greater microeconomic efficiency in the socialist economy than in the capitalist. Another possibility is that of a socialist economy which would be equivalent to capitalism in Pareto efficiency terms--its potential advantage over capitalism would then be confined to greater equity in the distribution of property return. The "incentives issue" here is whether or not the capital stock will be managed with the same effectiveness under socialism as it is under capitalism, given that the socialist capital managers would not receive nearly as much of the total property return as do the capitalistic capital managers. This paper analyzes the problem with the aid of a mathematical model of the utility-maximizing capital manager. The Mises-Hayek allegation that a reduction in the retention coefficient will reduce capital management effort is specified formally, and the socialist reply to this allegation is discussed.

The 1976 *ACES Bulletin* article is more comprehensive than the 1974 *RSE* article, but the sections on capital management effort are very similar, based as they are on the same theoretical model. The notion that capital property income (the major components of which are dividends, interest, and capital gains) is unearned income dates far back, to the initiation of the socialist critique in the early nineteenth century. Karl Marx utilized the labor theory of value, which was cutting-edge economics in his time, to justify the view that capital property income is essentially unearned, in the same sense that David Ricardo argued that land rents ("Ricardian rents") are unearned.

Later on in the nineteenth century, possibly to some extent in response to Marx's complaints about capitalism, the marginal productivity theory of factor earnings was extended to capital: just as wages and salaries are a legitimate marginal product return to labor, so too dividends, interest, and capital gains are a legitimate marginal product return to capital. During the first half of the twentieth century, Oskar Lange, who holds undisputed claim to being the "father of market socialism," argued that while dividends, interest, and capital gains are indeed a legitimate marginal product return to *capital*, this does not justify the claim of capital property *owners* to these capital property income streams. These income streams (according to Lange) are quite clearly the result of the productivity of *inanimate capital itself*, and have nothing to do with any alleged effort on the part of animate capital property owners.

This situation might not be a problem if capital property ownership were relatively equally distributed over the population. But under contemporary capitalism, the distribution of capital property has become grossly unequal. Thus there is highly unequal distribution of apparently unearned capital property income streams. Clearly this is an injustice—*unless* it is somehow true that capital property income streams are earned, in some sense or other, by their receivers under capitalism. Lange proposed a market socialist blueprint according to which capital property income streams would be collected by a public agency and distributed among the general population as a social dividend. Otherwise the market socialist economy would operate almost exactly the same as the market capitalist economy that preceded it. As it happened, however, the specific blueprint for market socialism proposed by Oskar Lange is subject to certain deficiencies (e.g., lack of an observable success criterion for firm managers) that are rectified by the alternative blueprint for "pragmatic" (as opposed to "Langian") market socialism.

My intention in these papers was to tackle the question of whether or not capital property income is earned income within the context of the pragmatic market socialist blueprint—using formal economic theory. Over the many decades that capitalist apologetics has been deployed against the socialist threat, there have been two primary arguments offered to the effect that capital property income is earned income: that it is a return to capital management effort (the term most favored for this concept in capitalist apologetics is "entrepreneurship"), and that it is a return to the sacrifices of saving. There are a few other arguments, most notably that it is a return to "risk-taking." But when examined closely, as I did in "Risk-

Taking as a Justification for Property Income" (*Journal of Comparative Economics*, March 1988), it becomes apparent that the risk-taking argument is fundamentally a variant of the capital management effort or saving arguments.

Both the "Potential Efficiency" and the "Capital Management" articles explicated a formal model of capital management effort. To my knowledge, a *formal* approach to this question was unprecedented. No one prior to myself had proposed "capital management effort" (symbolized by *e* or *E*) as an economic variable to be examined. The significance of this innovation should not be underestimated. This is because within the discipline of economics, two things are required for any proposition to be taken seriously: (1) it must be shown to be a possibility by means of formal analysis of a reasonably specified mathematical model; (2) it must seem *intuitively plausible*. My own published work on market socialism has positively demonstrated, based on reasonably specified economic models, that a pragmatic market socialist economy *might* out-perform a technologically equivalent capitalist economy. Note the emphasis on the word "might." I never argued that a pragmatic market socialist economy *would definitely* out-perform a technologically equivalent capitalist economy. Nevertheless, many economists apparently have great difficulty in accepting even the "might" proposition, because it is so much in conflict with their strong intuitive preconceptions.

The model of capital management effort developed in the related papers "On the Potential Efficiency of Market Socialism" and "Capital Management under Market Socialism" was the starting point, the "kernel" if you will, for a substantially more elaborate model I developed in the mid-1980s and beyond: the *els* model. The abbreviation "*e-l-s*" stands for capital management effort *e*, ordinary labor *l*, and saving *s*. The earlier model might be designated simply the *e* model. Both the *e* model and the *els* model come to the same two conclusions: First, on the basis of analysis of these models, it is theoretically indeterminate whether capitalism or pragmatic market socialism would perform better. Second, there are some serious considerations, brought to light by these models, that suggest that pragmatic market socialism might indeed perform better than capitalism.

The capital management effort model starts with the assumption that the typical capital manager is like every other human participant in economic processes: he or she is a utility maximizer. The utility of the capital manager is a function of income and leisure. In a standard labor supply model, labor is the total amount of time available, less that devoted to leisure. Labor produces income as the product of time spent laboring, multiplied by the wage of labor. In the equivalent capital management effort supply model developed in the articles under consideration, we simplify by assuming that the person specializes in capital management effort and does not provide any labor. (In the more advanced *els* model developed in later research, this simplification was relaxed: a person may provide both capital management effort *and* labor.) For the capital manager, capital management effort produces capital property income through a standard production function displaying diminishing marginal productivity of capital management effort: the function is illustrated graphically as a concave increasing curve (upward-sloping and bowed over). The capital manager maximizes his or her utility subject to the constraint of this production function, just as an ordinary laborer would maximize his or her utility subject to the budget constraint that income is the product of wage of labor times amount of labor provided.

The pragmatic market socialist concept is that the economy would function exactly the same as the capitalist market economy with one key exception: private capital owners would be replaced by agents of a public ownership agency tentatively designated the Bureau of Public Ownership (BPO). This name is inspired by the real-world United States Bureau of Land Management, the federal government agency tasked with managing publicly-owned land "in the public interest." (This name, by the way, confronts head-on the "bureaucratic bugaboo" habitually unleashed against socialism by skeptics. The Bureau of Public Ownership would be comparable to the U.S. Internal Revenue Service—in other words, a "bureaucracy," but a bureaucracy very energetic, determined, and effective in carrying out its socially sanctioned mission.) The Bureau of Public Ownership would take over all ownership rights inherent in capital instruments such as stocks and bonds that are currently owned by private households. In essence, therefore, the capital management function in the economy would be shifted from private capital owners to the corps of BPO agents. Private appropriation of capital property return would be replaced by the social collection and disposition of this return.

What would be the effect of this change and this change alone? At the one extreme, there is the view that capitalists are pure rentiers, completely passive, that is to say in the traditional socialist rhetorical epithet, "parasites." If this were true, the BPO need only be a collection box for property return payments and still the goal of pragmatic market socialism—a level of economic performance no less efficient than that attained under capitalism—would be fully achieved. At the other extreme, there is the view of skeptics such as the Austrian economists Ludwig von Mises and Friedrich Hayek: namely that capitalists are quite active in overseeing the management of their capital property, and that this activity is motivated by the capital property return to be produced thereby. That is to say, effective control over the capital stock is supposedly in the hands of the capitalist owners and not the managerial executives, and the effort of this control group toward effective capital management is directly proportional to the return that can be expected to accrue to that effort. Thus if capitalists were replaced by BPO personnel, unless the BPO personnel were allowed to keep for themselves the entire capital return, the situation thus being equivalent to capitalism, they cannot be expected to put out the same effort in capital management as their capitalist predecessors. As a result, capital will be less effectively managed, capital property return will be lower, and economic efficiency will be correspondingly reduced.

The extreme view of *complete* passivity on the part of capitalists may not be completely accurate. In order to motivate the personnel in the BPO to perform effectively their economic role in the economy, the pragmatic market socialist blueprint specifies that they be allowed to retain personally some fraction of the property return that accrues to the agency. On the other hand, there would be little point in socialism if this proportion were very substantial, say higher than one tenth to one fifth of the total property return. The question is then: Assuming that capital managers under pragmatic socialism (the BPO personnel) only receive a fraction of the capital property return generated by business enterprises using the capital stock, is capital likely to be managed as effectively as under capitalism?

Using the mathematical methodology of comparative statics, the analysis demonstrates that the answer to this question is theoretically indeterminate: it could go either way. The actual outcome would depend on the numerical values of certain model parameters which economic science has as yet no means of measuring.

As a pro-socialist interested in advancing the case for pragmatic market socialism, of course, I did not want the reader of these articles to be left with the impression that nothing worthwhile remained to be said on the issue of whether capital property return is earned or unearned than that "economic science gives us no answer." While it is true that economic science cannot give us an iron-clad, yes-or-no answer, there are some important pieces of evidence, some of which can be backed up with formal theoretical analysis, that suggest that the answer to this question is most likely *no*, capital property income under contemporary capitalism is *not* earned. Specifically, that society can enjoy the same level of economic efficiency even though those entrusted with the capital management function (the BPO agents) would receive personally only a small fraction of the amount which is currently being appropriated by the capital owners under capitalism.

Some of this evidence, and the analysis based upon it, goes well beyond the exposition contained in the early articles "On the Potential Efficiency of Market Socialism" and "Capital Management under Market Socialism." Some of the points that were expanded and elaborated in later work were briefly mentioned in these early articles. An important example of such evidence is the separation of ownership and control, a topic of keen interest ever since the publication in 1932 of *The Modern Corporation and Private Property* by Adolf A. Berle and Gardiner C. Means. From the commonsense appearance of things, it is the corps of corporation executives who do the actual work of managing the capital stock owned by their respective corporations. But corporation executives are hired employees similar to assembly line workers—albeit paid a lot more. This obvious, factual separation of the management function from the ownership condition makes it difficult to believe that the various stockholders and bondholders, who are the formal owners of the corporations, are doing anything of any critical importance.

I well recall how my father, a corporation executive, used to scorn the stockholders—they have to be paid their due, he would say, but they do absolutely nothing meaningful to assist the corporation executives with their efforts to manage their corporations, to make them profitable. Later on, when his son started spouting socialistic sentiments, my father quickly backtracked, claiming that after all, the stockholders—or maybe their ancestors—were indeed very fine people who had made magnificent entrepreneurial contributions to the economic success of the nation, and therefore it was perfectly right and just that they be paid their due. I remember my cheeky younger sister Ruth once informing my Dad that one of the reasons she did not take a lot of his beliefs seriously was that he also believed—or said he did—in an afterlife. I would suggest that belief in the proposition that stockholders, as capital owners per se, make an important contribution to economic processes, is somewhat akin to belief in an afterlife. Of course, apologists for capitalism can argue that commonsense appearances to the contrary, stockholders do make a vital contribution to economic processes. But their arguments are reminiscent of arguments of religionists that the afterlife exists, arguments that seem to reduce to: "I do so much *want* this to be true, that it simply *must* be true!"

The implication of the separation of ownership and control, in terms of the capital management effort model, is that it supports the view that the capital management effort production function is sharply bent over: a very small input of capital management effort suffices to achieve near the maximum level of return, and further increases in capital management effort have an imperceptible increasing effect on return. I used the term "plateau production function" to describe this case, because a graphical depiction of rate of return as a function of capital management effort suggests the edge of a plateau. In this case, the utility-maximizing equilibrium position of the capital manager would show a very low level of capital management effort—nevertheless, the capital property return accruing to this very low level of effort would be close to the maximum possible return.

The separation of ownership and control also suggests that owing to the atomization and dispersion of ownership claims over individual corporations among a host of unrelated, disorganized owners, the level of accountability exercised by the capital owners over the corporation executives has been seriously attenuated. One evidence of this is the inflated salaries and benefits that the highest corporation executives award themselves. Of course, it is not difficult to find economists who will attest firmly that these inflated salaries and benefits accurately reflect the value of this type of labor to the larger society. After all, what other way to explain them? This viewpoint might bring to mind the favorite maxim of the goofy Dr. Pangloss in Voltaire's novel *Candide* (1759): "All is for the best in the best of all possible worlds!" Of course, to those who have not fully surrendered their common sense to capitalist apologetics, another plausible way to explain these inflated salaries and benefits is that they are quasi-rents accruing to the *effective* capital ownership rights (as opposed to *legal* capital ownership rights) exercised by high corporation executives.

Pragmatic market socialism would possess a degree of institutional flexibility in dealing with capital management authority that is not available under capitalism. One possibility, for example, would be to consolidate all property rights over a specific corporation into a single BPO agent. A disorganized mass of stockholders would be replaced by a single person, thus enabling a degree of cohesion in the exercise of authority not known under contemporary capitalism (except in the rare cases of solely-owned corporations). The implications of such a consolidation of capital management authority were carefully considered in such later contributions as "The Microeconomic Efficiency Argument for Socialism Revisited" (*Journal of Economic Issues*, March 1979) and "Agency Issues and Managerial Incentives: Contemporary Capitalism versus Market Socialism" (*Research in Political Economy*, 1994).

Other important issues were not mentioned at all in the two early articles, "On the Potential Efficiency of Market Socialism" and "Capital Management under Market Socialism," or hinted at only tangentially. For example, no attention was devoted to the question of how the social dividend would be distributed to the general population under pragmatic market socialism. The initial impression that one might naturally derive from the writings of Oskar Lange and other proponents of market socialism is that the social dividend should be divided equally among all households: every household would get the same amount. An alternative distribution principle is that social dividend be disbursed to households in proportion to their labor incomes (wages and salaries—or in the case of retired households, pension income). In other words, households with higher labor income would get more social dividend income. As one might expect if one thinks about it, these different principles of social dividend distribution could have an important effect on overall economic performance.

The original capital management effort model was a partial equilibrium model that examined only the individual household, not the larger economy. General equilibrium models, in contrast, encompass the entire economy, albeit usually with significant simplifications to make them amenable to meaningful analysis. My first venture into general equilibrium territory for purposes of studying the pragmatic market socialist option was a manuscript completed in December 1985 entitled "The Equity-Efficiency Tradeoff under Capitalism and Market Socialism." This manuscript attained an all-time record high number of rejections (9) before finally being published in the *Eastern Economic Journal* (January-March 1991). While the underlying model did not incorporate capital management effort provided by households, the research did incorporate a major innovation: empirical estimates of both the distribution of capital wealth and the distribution of labor income in the United States in 1963. A standard labor-supply model represented the households, and the overall model incorporated linear income taxation by the government, the so-called "negative income tax" function because if the household's market income is sufficiently low it would receive a subsidy (a "negative tax"). This function is a simplified representation of real-world tax and welfare systems.

Using a computer, solutions were obtained for each numerical specification of the tax rate utilized in the linear income tax function. Utility levels could thereupon be obtained for the households, and total social welfare (sum of household utilities) computed. The specific social welfare function utilized, defined as the sum of household utilities, is known as the Bentham social welfare function, after the renowned nineteenth century philosopher of utilitarianism, Jeremy Bentham (1748-1832). It was found that the relationship between the tax rate and Bentham social welfare is dome-shaped: social welfare rises up to a peak level with the tax rate, then declines. The tax rate at which social welfare is maximized is the optimal tax rate—in terms of the Bentham measure of social welfare.

The numerical results indicated that for each tax rate of the linear income tax function, both total income of the population and Bentham social welfare is higher under socialism than it is under capitalism. Meanwhile, economic inequality, as measured by the Gini coefficient of consumption, is lower under socialism than it is under capitalism, for each tax rate. It follows that at the optimal tax rate, total income is higher under socialism than under capitalism, inequality is lower under socialism than under capitalism, and social welfare is higher under socialism than under capitalism. The reason for this is that if capital property income, instead of going largely to a small proportion of the population (the empirical data indicated that under capitalism, 88.57 percent of capital property income is received by the wealthiest 10 percent of the population), is instead distributed as a social dividend supplement proportional to the household's labor income, this is an incentive to labor provision, and leads to more labor being provided by every decile of the population. This is turn leads to higher income and higher social welfare for every decile within the population—except for the highest (wealthiest) decile. The political implication of this result is that 90 percent of the United States population has a material interest in replacing the capitalist status quo with the pragmatic market socialist alternative.

It is not too surprising that this implication did not sit very well with some of the anonymous referees exposed to this paper during my prolonged search to find a publisher for it. Although the numerous negative referee reports I accumulated over the long period of time during which I was attempting to find a publisher for "The Equity-Efficiency Tradeoff under Capitalism and Market Socialism" were quite diverse, most of them reduced to variations on two basic themes: (1) the model was "oversimplified," and (2) the analysis ignored various "important considerations." And these two basic themes actually reduced to just one complaint: that the analysis ignored the two most important justifications for capital property income: that it was a legitimate return to capital management effort (e.g., entrepreneurship), and that it was a legitimate return to the sacrifices of saving.

My effort to rectify this shortcoming was the *els* model, which incorporated capital management effort e and saving s as primary factors of production provided by the private household, in addition to labor l. As one would expect, the *els* model is far more complicated than the model used in the "Equity-Efficiency Tradeoff" article. Among other things, this means that it must be studied exclusively using numerical solutions of numerical specifications of the model, and these numerical solutions must be obtained by iterative methods. From a practical standpoint, computer solutions are thus mandatory. But the qualitative results are comparable to those forthcoming from the "Equity-Efficiency Tradeoff" research—for what are arguably plausible numerical values of the model parameters. That is: For each tax rate of the linear income tax function, both total income of the population and Bentham social welfare is higher under socialism than it is under capitalism. Meanwhile, economic inequality, as measured by the Gini coefficient of consumption, is lower under socialism than it is under capitalism, for each tax rate. It follows that at the optimal tax rate, total income is higher under socialism than under capitalism, inequality is lower under socialism than under capitalism, and social welfare is higher under socialism than under capitalism.

My efforts to get this indication, and the *els* research on which it is based, into the professional literature, were long and involved, and will be discussed at various points in the following. The starting point was an unpublished manuscript entitled "A General Equilibrium Comparison of Capitalism and Pragmatic Market Socialism" completed in November 1987. Suffice it to say here that both the research and the indication are now available in the published literature—albeit in very obscure locations. But during the early 2000s I did come tantalizingly close to getting a major article on this subject into the illustrious *American Economic Review*. Had that effort been successful, the "pragmatic" approach to market socialism would likely today be far better known within the economics profession than it actually is. That harrowing episode (harrowing for me, that is) will be described in the section below entitled "Near Misses."

Many of my article projects initiated during the 1970s and 1980s were aimed at chipping away at various components of capitalist apologetics. To some extent, capitalist apologetics was (and still is) a muddled miasma of half-baked invidious comparisons of glorious capitalism with such "socialist" horrors as the gulag archipelago of Stalin-era USSR, or the dehumanizing cradle-to-grave welfare states of Scandinavia, or the hopelessly bungling inefficiency of public bureaucracies anywhere and everywhere. But within that miasma there exists a core of logically consistent and superficially plausible objections to socialism.

Most of these latter may be categorized as follows: First, there is the allegation that capital property income is earned income: a payment for capital management effort and/or a payment for the sacrifices of saving. Second, there is the allegation that when properly understood, the distribution of capital wealth is not excessively unequal. This is conveniently labeled the "people's capitalism" argument. Third, there are the "noneconomic" arguments in favor of capitalism, of which the most important is that capitalism is a bulwark of democracy. These arguments will be briefly evaluated in the later chapter on "Pragmatic Market Socialism." At this point, however, I will simply provide a chronological listing of my published articles, not previously mentioned in the current chapter, and not part of the *els* model research, that deal directly or indirectly with these various arguments (the article titles are usually sufficient to indicate which particular argument is addressed):

"Investment Propensities under Capitalism and Market Socialism," *Revista Internazionale di Scienze Economiche e Commerziali*, October 1978.

"The People's Capitalism Thesis: A Skeptical Evaluation," *ACES Bulletin* (Association for Comparative Economic Studies), Winter 1982.

"The Distribution of Lifetime Capital Property Income under Capitalism and Market Socialism," *ACES Bulletin* (Association for Comparative Economic Studies), Summer 1984.

"A Market Socialist Critique of Capitalism's Dynamic Performance," *Journal of Economic Issues*, March 1986.

"Would Democracy Survive under Market Socialism?" *Polity*, Summer 1986.

"On the Morality of Capitalism: In Light of the Market Socialist Alternative," *Forum for Social Economics*, Spring 1988.

"A New Perspective on Market Socialism," *Comparative Economic Studies*, Summer 1988,

"Some Empirical Evidence on the Social Welfare Maximization Hypothesis," *Public Finance*, 1989.

"Relatively Stable Lifetime Consumption as Evidence of Positive Time Preference," *Journal of Post-Keynesian Economics*, Spring 1992.

"Evaluating Changes in the Distribution of Capital Wealth," *Economic Inquiry*, October 1994.

"Capital Management under Profit-Oriented Market Socialism: An Explicit Function Approach," *Southern Economic Journal*, July 1996.

"The Adverse Economic Consequences of Extremely High Capital Wealth Inequality," *Journal of Post-Keynesian Economics*, Spring 1997.

"Inheritance and Chance as Determinants of Capital Wealth Inequality," *Journal of Post-Keynesian Economics*, Winter 1999.

"Growth Propensities under Capitalism and Profit-Oriented Market Socialism," *European Journal of Comparative Economics*, 2012.

Some of the above articles made no mention whatsoever of a possible market socialist alternative to contemporary capitalism, and even for those that did make explicit reference to market socialism, they dealt with only one aspect of the overall implications of this alternative. In essence they dealt with individual trees, not the forest as a whole. One of my objectives throughout the 70s and 80s was to place in the professional literature—preferably in a prestigious economics journal—a relatively comprehensive statement of the case to be made for pragmatic market socialism. This article would differentiate pragmatic market socialism from other variants of market socialism such as the Langian, would provide a fairly detailed description of the institutional blueprint, and would evaluate the various elements of capitalist apologetics in light of this blueprint. To accomplish this objective fully, obviously a book would be necessary. That book was in fact published in 1992 by Praeger: *Socialism Revised and Modernized: The Case for Pragmatic Market Socialism*. Prior to that book's publication, I wanted a published article that would essentially be an abridged version of the forthcoming book. Of course, getting an article such as that into a top-ranked journal, such as the *American Economic Review*, was virtually impossible. Quite aside from its ideologically unacceptable pro-socialist slant, it would be both too long and too subjective for a top-rated professional journal.

Nevertheless, hope springs eternal—even hopeless hope. In September 1985, I completed a large manuscript (117 double-spaced typed pages) entitled "The Case for Pragmatic Market Socialism" and sent it off for comment to 28 credentialed individuals, most of them economists. Considering the great length of the manuscript, I was perhaps lucky to have nine individuals respond with comments: Abram Bergson, Joseph Berliner, John Elliott, David Granick, Charles Lindblom, Jeffrey Miller, Warren Samuels, Howard Sherman, and Leland Stauber. The respondents were generally complimentary if not effusive, and mostly concurred on two salient points: (1) the paper expressed an innovative and interesting approach to the market socialism question, (2) the paper was far too lengthy and normative to be a serious candidate for publication, especially at the leading journals. The relatively small number of substantive suggestions concerned certain controversial areas that perhaps needed more consideration, but no one had any specific ideas about material that was superfluous, unnecessary, and a good candidate for excision. Prof. Bergson explicitly suggested that the manuscript as it existed was most sensibly considered as an outline sketch for a book, which is indeed what it was.

It required well over a year for all the comments to trickle in, but eventually, in the early spring of 1987, I was ready to try to bring the project to a conclusion. I sat down to a radical condensation of the paper, to a mere 50 double-spaced typed pages, and re-titled it "A New Perspective on

Market Socialism." I sent the result to Orley Ashenfelter, managing editor of the *American Economic Review*, along with a rather presumptuous covering letter. I figured that my chances with this paper at the *AER* were so vestigial in any case that I really did not have anything to lose.

Given the controversial nature and great length of "A New Perspective on Market Socialism," I have to admit it was given quite a fair shake at the *AER*. It was sent to no less than five referees, all of whom submitted comments. From one of the comments I derived a very important lesson for future reference. In the paper I had used the abbreviation "PMS" for "pragmatic market socialism." One of the anonymous referees, in a mocking mood, mentioned that "PMS" was also widely used for "pre-menstrual syndrome." The referee pointed out that just as PMS (pre-menstrual syndrome) allegedly severely degrades the condition of women suffering from it, so too PMS (pragmatic market socialism) applied to the United States economy would most likely have a similarly adverse effect. I would offer this word of free advice to anyone advocating any sort of specific social reform: Be very careful with your abbreviation. Certainly my own usage of that particular abbreviation was immediately terminated.

Although their specific remarks were quite varied, all five referees were agreed that "A New Perspective on Market Socialism" was not appropriate for publication in the *AER*. No matter, what could I have expected? When you add together the dominant consensus within the contemporary Western economics profession that socialism—*any* kind of socialism, market or otherwise—is highly unpromising, with the great length of the manuscript, and with the extremely high standards for publication in the prestigious *American Economic Review*, you realize that it would have been a veritable miracle if "A New Perspective on Market Socialism" had appeared in its pages.

Following this rejection, I concluded that it would not be worthwhile to submit the manuscript to any other first-tier journal, nor even to any second-tier journal. Only at a third-tier journal might referees be found who would not be so persnickety and where the paper might have a chance. So it went off to *Comparative Economic Studies*, formerly the *ACES Bulletin* (of the Association for Comparative Economic Studies), in which I had placed three earlier articles on market socialism. The single referee for *CES* had some suggestions for revision that actually caused a slight expansion of the paper to 55 double-spaced typed pages. The article, all 16,885 words of it, appeared in the Summer 1988 issue of *Comparative Economic Studies*. No disrespect intended to *Comparative Economic Studies*, but let's face it: its "impact factor" (assuming it could be measured) would have to be one thousandth or less than that of the *AER*.

Global Economic Development

According to diary entries made during the summer of 1974, it was an exceptionally hot and humid summer. Despite the torrid weather, on the whole I was in quite a positive, optimistic mood during that summer. In May of that year there had occurred a momentous breakthrough: "Capital Management under Market Socialism" had been accepted for publication in the *Review of Social Economy*, and was scheduled to appear in a fall issue. This would be the first time one of my writings on the visionary concept of pragmatic market socialism had gotten into print in a professional journal. I had plenty of follow-up projects on pragmatic market socialism on my to-do list, but the top priority, now that the ice had been broken on pragmatic market socialism, was to do something on a global economic development program. Pragmatic market socialism was the first stage of the grand design: once pragmatic market socialism had led to a reciprocal accommodation in the communist world on the issue of political democracy, the improvement in international relations would enable substantial disarmament, and a substantial proportion of the resources saved through reduced military spending could be reallocated to a global economic development program aimed at substantially reducing the level of global economic inequality.

A global economic development program on the monumental scale I envisioned would be completely unprecedented. Critics of foreign aid could be relied upon to ridicule the notion of a monumental global economic development program. They would say that not a shred, not a scintilla, not an iota of hard evidence existed that an unprecedentedly large-scale global economic development program would do any good. In a literal sense this was true—because a global economic development program on this scale had never been attempted. You cannot know for sure that a policy proposal would not be successful, if you have never implemented that policy proposal. Although even the most adamant skeptic of foreign aid would be hard put to deny this truism, the fact remains that the cost of "experimenting" with an unprecedentedly large-scale global economic development program would be unprecedentedly huge. Thus the more evidence that could be marshaled that such an experiment might be successful, the more incentive there would be to undertake it.

As might be expected, even as long ago as the early 1970s, economists had already done a substantial amount of statistical research on the effectiveness of real-world foreign aid. There was some evidence that it had a positive effect on the economic growth of certain recipient Third World nations, but the evidence was not very robust. And of course the research was on the existing, small-scale foreign aid programs. Economists tend to be a conservative group, and by and large they are averse to working on policy proposals that go far beyond anything presently existing in the real world. Therefore, if I wanted any worthwhile evidence on the kind of project I had in mind, I would have to produce it myself.

In the summer of 1974, I commenced work on a hypothetical global economic development effort far beyond anything ever before attempted in the real world. Those were the days of running Fortran programs on the campus mainframe computer using input entered on 80-column IBM punch cards. Luckily for me, the campus mainframe was located in Morgan Hall, which was immediately adjacent to Stipes Hall, in which I had my office. I recall one evening chatting with Norm Walzer in the mainframe's Morgan Hall service room. I was starting to get promising results as I fine-tuned my Fortran program. In an expansive mood, I said to Norm: "That is the fate of the world being printed out over there." Norm grunted noncommittally. Norm Walzer was perhaps the most capable economist with whom I became acquainted at Western Illinois University. He was a grant-generating phenomenon, and he founded the Illinois Institute of Rural Affairs (IIRA) as a permanent public service organization affiliated with Western Illinois University. Norm's statistical researches were very much on down-to-earth matters: e.g., what small Illinois towns were spending on police and fire protection. Accordingly, he was good-naturedly skeptical regarding my grandiose research projects.

After some unpromising experimentation with using optimal growth theory, I started over with a very straightforward, ad hoc model in which contributions by the rich nations into the transfer fund would be determined by their populations and per capita incomes, while payments from the transfer fund to the poor nations would also be determined by their populations and per capita incomes. Basically, the richer the nation is in terms of per capita income, and the larger it is in terms of population, the more it would pay into the transfer fund; while the poorer the nation is in terms of per capita income, and the larger it is in terms of population, the more it would receive from the transfer fund. The formula for determining a rich nation's contribution into the transfer fund was so structured that it could only come from monetary flows not needed to support consumption: in other words, from a part of what would have been otherwise allocated to investment in "generalized capital." Generalized capital is an economic concept I proposed to deal with the issue: in addition to ordinary physical capital (plant and equipment), it encompasses human capital (the value of education and training inputs into the labor force), and social overhead capital (the value of roads, bridges, schools, and so on). With this change in approach, the simulation results improved markedly: now the results for all the variables of the model became believable. Or at least they would be believable to most competent economists looking only at the methodology itself, without bringing in fixed preconceptions about the relative uselessness of foreign aid.

By the end of July, I had a manuscript entitled "A World Economic Equalization Program: Results of a Simulation." As I can see now with the benefit of 20-20 hindsight, using "World Economic Equalization Program" to designate the envisioned large-scale global economic development effort was most likely a mistake. It would have been better if from the beginning I had called it the "Global Marshall Plan," a term I did not invent, but which I adopted several years later. There were two basic problems with "World Economic Equalization Program." First, the abbreviation WEEP. This was not as bad as PMS for "pragmatic market socialism" (for reasons mentioned earlier), but it was bad enough. In my youthful naivety I imagined the acronym "WEEP" would elicit images of tears of joy for humanity's at long last freeing ourselves from the blight of excessive differences in average living standards among nations. But in due course, I realized that foreign aid skeptics could and would take the acronym in another sense altogether: the tears would be tears of frustration at the huge waste of resources entailed by such a program.

The second problem with "World Economic Equalization Program" was the word "equalization," which is too closely associated with "redistribution" through a tax and welfare system. Thus the term could too easily suggest a Global Welfare State through which the living standards in both the rich nations and the poor nations would be equalized at a very low level, a level much closer to the existing living standards in the poor nations than to those in the rich nations. Recognizing this problem, from the beginning I was at great pains to disassociate the WEEP from the notion of a Global Welfare State. From the outset I endeavored to establish that the intended "equalization" was at a higher level of living standards than anything currently prevailing, even in the richest nations. The actual concept was that living standards in both the rich nations and the poor nations would continue to rise, but that living standards in the rich nations would increase at a slightly lower rate in order that living standards in the poor nations could increase at a much higher rate. From the beginning I ruled out the possibility—as politically impossible within the rich nations—of equalization occurring at living standards somewhere between those in the rich nations and those in the poor nations. Later on I devised the term "Crude Redistribution" to describe this latter idea. The term "Common Progress" I invented at the same time to describe what was actually being proposed (*all* nations advancing economically)—the diametric opposite of "Crude Redistribution."

At the time, however, blissfully unaware of these issues with the "World Economic Equalization Program" (WEEP), in July 1974 I sent the manuscript off to the *Journal of Conflict Resolution*, on the premise that economic inequality was a source of potential conflict, and hence a journal interested in reducing the sources of potential conflict might be interested in a large-scale global economic development program aimed at substantially reducing global economic inequality. Of course, if I had taken a close look at the articles the *Journal of Conflict Resolution* was carrying, I might not have been so optimistic. The journal's principal focus was on theoretical abstractions as opposed to practical ideas toward the reduction of potential conflict. The rejection letter from the managing editor of the *JCR*, Marguerite Kramer, dated December 9, 1974, read:

> I have just received the second evaluation of your paper "A World Economic Equalization Program" and, on that basis, regret to tell you that we will not be able to publish it in the JCR. While one reviewer was more encouraging than the other, they both found several of the assumptions to be arbitrary and questionable.
>
> That just weakens the whole thrust of the paper as far as we are concerned. Perhaps the enclosed comments will be of some use to you. Your topic and conclusions are certainly challenging and merit further analysis. Let me encourage you to submit the ms. elsewhere.

A referee's report was included, and it did indeed include a substantial number of varied complaints about "arbitrary and questionable assumptions." While I had to admit that some of the assumptions were "questionable," I could not accept that they were "arbitrary." In order to tackle any serious economic issue in a systematic way, it is necessary to specify a model, and a model necessarily incorporates a variety of specifications ("assumptions"). The specifications of the WEEP model were in no way arbitrary: they were all required to shed some light on a serious global problem. For example, the referee heaped particular scorn on my application of the Cobb-Douglas production function to represent a reasonable approximation to production relations within the six groups of nations. ("Are data presented to justify the use of C-D functions? No. One is presented instead a 'take-it-or-leave-it' situation. I prefer to leave it.") But in actual fact, Cobb-Douglas production functions were widely utilized in economics (and still are) to represent production relations within specific nations—on no better grounds that it was (and is) conventional to do so. The referee complained about unsubstantiated assumptions, but nowhere provided sensible reasons why these unsubstantiated assumptions would produce misleading results.

Oh well, if I worried too much about such pesky, close-minded referees, I would soon come down with a nasty stomach ulcer. The *JCR* managing editor had encouraged me to submit the manuscript elsewhere, and I was certainly amenable to this suggestion. This time, however, I decided to take advantage of an "in" I had right there on the campus of Western Illinois University. I decided to test the old adage that it is not so much *what* you know, as *who* you know.

During my early years at WIU, I had developed a cordial relationship with Spencer Brown, editor of one of the small number of reputable professional journals edited and funded by our university, the *Journal of Developing Areas*. Spencer was something of a character, given to turtleneck sweaters, medallions, mordant humor, and well equipped with the somewhat callous attitude toward aspiring authors required for an editor's peace of mind. I contributed a few book reviews to the pages of the *JDA*, but by far my more important contribution was as a referee. Any submission that looked dubious to Spencer he forwarded to me, in hopes that I might provide a reasonably plausible justification for rejecting the paper. I was mostly able to oblige him, though once in a great while I would surprise Spencer by recommending acceptance without revision.

On December 13, 1974, I hand-delivered the WEEP manuscript to Spencer, advising him that its conclusions were highly controversial, and so perhaps could he send it to referees he knew to be unusually open-minded? In late March, 1975, Spencer Brown provisionally accepted the paper for publication in the *Journal of Developing Areas*, subject to revision, on the basis of no less than six referee reports. Certainly Spencer did not give me a "free pass" on publication. All the referees agreed that this was eye-opening research that deserved to be in print, but most of them had ideas about how it might be strengthened. Luckily for me, none of these ideas amounted to starting over from scratch, and I was also given the option of incorporating as much (or as little) of the referee input as I wished, without the need for resubmission. The revision was submitted in April 1975, and it was published in the January 1976 issue of the *JDA*.

Although this was a major milestone, I was not entirely happy with the research as it stood then. There were various things I could do—without going back to square one—to improve the work and make its conclusions more forceful. Also, the *Journal of Developing Areas* was somewhat peripheral and not especially appropriate. A much superior outlet for the research would have been *World Development*, a highly reputable monthly journal devoted largely to growth issues. Owing to the press of other work, it took me a full ten years between the publication of "A World Economic

Equalization Program: Results of a Simulation" in the *JDA*, and completion of an upgraded version of the research in a manuscript entitled "A World Economic Equalization Program: Refinements and Sensitivity Analysis." The latter was submitted to *World Development* on May 19, 1986. On February 10, 1988, somewhat over one and a half years later, I received the following from managing editor Deena R. Khatkhate:

> I am now in a position to inform you that your paper, "A World Economic Equalization Program: Refinements and Sensitivity Analysis," is accepted for publication in World Development. It deals with an important subject, in a manner which is considered to be unconventional. I am sorry that it has taken such a long time to convey this decision to you, but I would like you to know that the delay occurred in large part because the referees were overburdened with other professional commitments. We are unable to press them for an answer since they work without any remuneration.

No apologies necessary! Even if reaching a decision had taken quite a long while, I could not complain if the eventual decision was favorable. The "Refinements and Sensitivity Analysis" paper was one of the very few of my manuscripts that sailed through to publication without one single rejection. On top of that it was published in a highly reputable journal. There have been very few days during my long career during which I actually felt ecstatic—one of them was February 10, 1988.

Although the paper continued to use the original six groups of nations defined on per capita income, there were some important enhancements. The principal "refinement" referred to in the title was the addition of a basic "validity test." The model was numerically simulated over a period of time in the past (1963-1983) during which the actual values of the variables were known. This showed that without a WEEP in operation, the model produced results in terms of per capita income growth reasonably close to the actual observed results. The "sensitivity analysis" in the title referred to showing how the numerical results would be affected by changes in the numerical values of the various parameters. Some ten years before, for example, a referee for the *Journal of Conflict Resolution* had complained about my "unsubstantiated" application of the Cobb-Douglas (CD) production function to represent production relations within the six groups of nations. In the later version, I utilized the Constant Elasticity of Substitution (CES) production function. The CD function is a special case of the CES function in which the elasticity of substitution is one (1). I was able to show that variations in the elasticity of substitution had no significant effect on the basic results, thus responding to that earlier referee's complaint. Of course, even in its improved condition, the WEEP research still involved numerous assumptions that could be reflexively criticized on the basis that they were "arbitrary." This would not be, however, because the assumptions themselves were so unreasonable, but because the results forthcoming from the assumptions were so remarkably optimistic.

So what were these "remarkably optimistic" results? Reproduced here are images of the three plots contained in the published version of "A World Economic Equalization Program: Refinements and Sensitivity Analysis." All three plots were included as separate panels of the single figure in the article: "Figure 1: Baseline Simulation Results," appearing on page 928 of the August 1988 issue of *World Development*. The figure herein is renamed "Figure 5.1: WEEP Model Baseline Simulation Results."

Panel A shows results in terms of per capita consumption for the six groups of nations over 35 years into the future, under the assumption that no WEEP is in operation. (The initial year for the simulation was 1983, the last year for which World Bank data was available at the time of the research.) The richest groups 1 and 2 show continued growth from an initially high level, while at the other end of the spectrum the poorest groups 5 and 6 show very little progress. The per capita consumption gap between the richest and poorest nations steadily widens.

Next, Panel B plots results in terms of per capita consumption for the six groups of nations over 35 years into the future, under the assumption that a WEEP is in operation. With a WEEP in operation, the richer nations would pay a certain percentage of their national incomes into a transfer fund, while the poorer nations would draw from the transfer fund to augment their stocks of generalized capital. In this case we see a pattern of convergence for all six groups of nations. Groups 1 and 2 maintain their positions as the highest income groups, but all the other groups show dramatic growth acceleration, so that by the end of the 35-year planning period, differentials in per capita consumption among all six groups of nations would be a small fraction of what they were at the start of the planning period.

What is even more remarkable than the convergence itself, is that it is brought about without inflicting a significant growth penalty on the rich nations. Panel C shows a comparison of the richest group 1 and the poorest group 6 under a situation of no WEEP (solid lines) versus with WEEP (dashed lines). The graph illustrates the remarkable progress of the poorest group at the expense of a modest retardation in the growth of the richest group. In fact, the growth retardation in the richest group is so modest that it would probably be unnoticeable.

Figure 5.1: WEEP Model Baseline Simulation Results

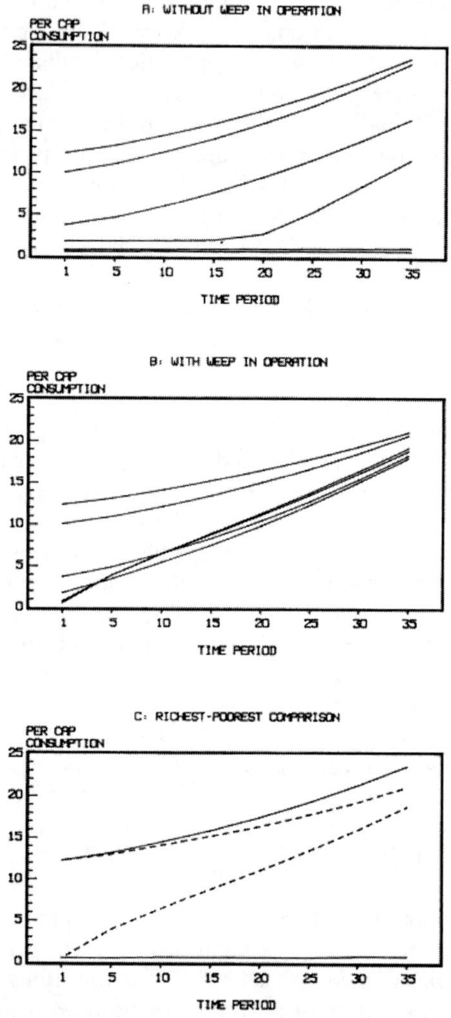

How could such a thing be possible? One does not have to be a professional economist to entertain suspicions that this result is simply too good to be true. The answer to the paradox lies in one of the oldest and most generally accepted assumptions of contemporary economic science: diminishing marginal productivity of a factor of production. In this case, the factor of production is generalized capital, comprising physical capital, human capital, and social overhead capital. Few economists would wish to suggest that the rich nations do not possess far larger stocks of generalized capital than the poor nations. According to the principle of diminishing marginal productivity, this means that if a given increment to generalized capital in a rich nation is instead transferred to and installed in a poor nation, the decrement in national output of the rich nation will be far less than the increment in national output of the poor nation. In and of itself, this conclusion is quite unremarkable. But when it is applied to what might be done to lessen the global economic inequality problem, the implications are in fact truly remarkable. They are indeed so remarkable that a great many of my fellow economists have great difficulty acknowledging even the *possibility* that they might be valid.

During the long interval between the time I submitted the "Refinements and Sensitivity Analysis" paper to *World Development* (May 1986) and its acceptance for publication there (February 1988), I presented it at the February 1987 meeting of the Missouri Valley Economic Association (MVEA) in Kansas City, Missouri. Presenting a paper at a conference is a way of getting an item on one's résumé that might never find a home with a print journal. Of course, once a print journal has published a paper, there is no longer much point in including it as a conference presentation, because it is well known that the standards for conference presentations are far lower than for journal publications. But in 1987 I had no way of knowing that this particular paper would be published in a journal in 1988.

The tight time constraints applied to paper presenters in conference sessions mean that an author has time only for a cursory description of the research. Then the discussants are called upon for comment. Professional economics being what it is, the comments are mostly potshots taken by people who don't have either the time or the inclination to study the work sufficiently to be able to provide useful constructive criticism. The session chairman assigned my WEEP paper to two discussants rather than the usual one. My diary entry for Saturday, February 27, 1987, describes the paper presentation as follows:

> The gap between my thinking and conventional thinking was once more brought home to me by the reaction of the discussants of my WEEP paper. According to the WEEP model simulations, a tremendous amount of equalization could take place in only 35 years, at the cost of only a modest rate of retardation in the growth rate of rich nation per capita consumption. At the same time, I show by sensitivity analysis that the result might collapse with different parameter values. Two discussants commented on the paper, as the session chairman had

> not done his job properly and assigned specific discussants to specific papers. Pat Gormely of Kansas State U. seemed to grasp the paper's methodology, was full of praise about the exposition and organization and my being candid about the possibility of failure—but he just couldn't shake the feeling that the baseline simulation was simply incredible, unbelievable, fantastic, inconceivable—in the literal sense of these terms. The other fellow, one Oleg Zinam of the U. of Cincinnati, was incensed by the whole thing. In the first place it used a mathematical model, and Zinam is one of these dinosaurs in the profession whose ignorance of math is matched only by his disdain for it. His contempt for my effort was not merely methodological but substantive as well. Everyone knows, according to Oleg, that the LDCs are culturally, socially and politically immured in poverty, that they are totally ungrateful for the foreign aid they do get, and if something like this were put into practice, most of the funds would end up in the Swiss bank accounts of the dictators and social elite of the LDCs. No mathematical model was capable of overturning this reality. That was that was that, as far as Oleg was concerned. He got quite agitated about it. Gormely was merely bemused and bewildered, Zinam was downright indignant at this presumptuous and misguided work of mine.

In fact, as Prof. Gormely acknowledged and Prof. Zinam ignored, I had indeed in the "Refinements and Sensitivity Analysis" paper explicitly acknowledged—and demonstrated—that the optimistic baseline simulation might be completely invalid. The key issue is the extent to which differences in per capita income between nations are a result of differences in stocks of generalized capital, as opposed to differences in total factor productivity. Of course, generalized capital stocks of nations are not currently measured. However, using data on per capita income and population, and an assumption regarding the initial capital-output ratio in the richest group of nations (actually in this data the richest "group" consisted of just one nation: the United States), one can estimate the stock of generalized capital in the United States, and by working backwards, the stocks of generalized capital in the other groups. This initial capital-output ratio specification (symbolized by k) can be considered a parameter of the model. Another important model parameter is the output elasticity of generalized capital (symbolized by α). In Table 4 ("Sensitivity Analysis") of "Refinements and Sensitivity Analysis," I showed numerically that if the k and α parameters take on sufficiently adverse values, the WEEP will be ineffective in equalizing per capita income among nations.

Another way of conceptualizing the key issue, which I developed in subsequent work, is in terms of the relative importance of generalized capital and total factor productivity in determining observed differences in national output among nations. Total factor productivity determines how much output a certain nation will obtain from its stocks of factors of production. Critics of foreign aid are asserting (although they are often not consciously aware that this is the nub of their argument) that the poor nations in actual fact have plenty of generalized capital—but owing to their lamentably dysfunctional political, social, and attitudinal characteristics, they make very poor use of these resources. In other words, they have low total factor productivity—not low generalized capital stocks. The alternative view is that total factor productivity is roughly the same in all nations, and the poor nations are poor because of their small stocks of generalized capital. If the latter view is true, then a WEEP would likely be very beneficial. If the former view is true, a WEEP would accomplish very little.

Which view is closer to the truth? There is little or no hard, scientifically reputable evidence bearing on the question. But to simply *assume*, as most economists have done and still do, that a World Economic Equalization Program would fail, is an obviously self-serving rationalization that is sadly unworthy of the higher qualities of human nature.

Subsequently, I continued researching the matter, and my efforts resulted in two additional journal articles, as well as two books: *Common Progress: The Case for a World Economic Equalization Program* (Praeger, 2000), and *Global Marshall Plan: Theory and Evidence* (Lexington, 2014). These books will be discussed in later chapters.

Federal World Government

The endpoint of the grand design, of course, was not pragmatic market socialism, nor was it a large-scale global economic development program. These were but steppingstones to the foundation of a stable and benign world government. Throughout the 1980s I worked intermittently on a large book manuscript with the working title *World Union on the Horizon*. Basically this book was intended to accomplish what I had failed to accomplish in the unpublished manuscript written during the 1972-73 academic year (Grand Convergence I, whose full title was *The Grand Convergence: Economic and Political Aspects of Human Progress*). *World Union on the Horizon* was to be a powerful statement of the overall vision, starting with pragmatic market socialism and ending with the Federal Union of Democratic Nations. But as the project neared completion in the latter 1980s, I gradually came to the realization that there was so much coverage of pragmatic market socialism in it and so little of world government that the working title did not make sense. So I changed the title to *Pragmatic Market Socialism: An Economic and Political Appraisal*.

Among the political aspects of pragmatic market socialism was that it might pave the way to a global economic development program and a federal world government. Unfortunately, by the time it was finally completed, the manuscript was far too bulky (1,338 pages) to be a viable candidate for publication.

When I eventually reconciled myself to this reality, I broke the *Pragmatic Market Socialism* manuscript into two parts. The material on pragmatic market socialism was condensed into a 337-page book entitled *Socialism Revised and Modernized: The Case for Pragmatic Market Socialism*, published by Praeger in 1992; and the material on world government was expanded into a 332-page book entitled *World Union on the Horizon: The Case for Supernational Federation*, published by University Press of America in 1993. So I did eventually get to utilize the "World Union on the Horizon" title that I had used throughout most of the 1980s to designate the large-scale book-in-progress. Good titles are difficult to devise—one does not want to waste them.

From the beginning way back in my Fordham years in the early 1960s, my ultimate objective had always been a large book, a powerful and persuasive book, a bestseller that would convey the grand design to a wide public—a public wide enough and influential enough that there would be a reasonable chance that the grand design could actually be realized in the real world. The decision on publication of this magnum opus would be in the hands of acquisition editors for the major publishing houses. How could I impress these people? Obviously I could not do it with my academic affiliation, which was modest at best. Thus I would have to do it by showing on my résumé a long list of published articles in reputable scholarly journals. The more closely related these articles were to my submitted book, the better my chances. Throughout the 1970s and into the 1980s, I was steadily accumulating published articles on pragmatic market socialism, along with many on other topics of a less controversial nature. I also had articles on the World Economic Equalization Program, albeit only two: one published in 1976 and the other in 1988. The one remaining gap pertained to world government.

Before publishing *World Union on the Horizon* in 1993, I had made two earlier efforts to publish a major article on the grand design, up to and including world government. The first project was never published, but the second did achieve publication, though not in the type of journal I would have preferred. My first published article on world government was "Practical Considerations in Designing a Supernational Federation," written in the summer of 1983 and published in *World Futures* in 1985. The "Practical Considerations" article was preceded by a paper entitled "A Practical

Proposal toward World Union," written in 1976 and never published.

The immediate impetus to the first project, "A Practical Proposal toward World Union," was the publication in the January 1976 issue of the *Journal of Developing Areas* of "A World Economic Equalization Program: Results of a Simulation." Now that I had some published work on both pragmatic market socialism and the global economic development program, it was time to take a crack at a major article outlining the entire plan, including world government. The resultant manuscript, completed in March 1976, ran to 68 double-spaced typed pages. I realized, of course, that the great length of the paper would be an impediment to publication, probably an insuperable impediment. But owing to the complexity of the subject matter and its inherently controversial nature, there wouldn't have been much point in trying to squeeze it all into a much shorter paper. At least if the ideas were presented within a reasonably comprehensive exposition, there was a chance they might be appreciated.

Nevertheless, it was hardly a surprise when the rejection letter from Nils Petter Gleditsch, dated May 11, 1975, started out by saying: "First, as you are no doubt aware, the article is much too long for the *Journal of Peace Research*." But lest I, the author, conclude that excessive length alone was the conclusive rationale for rejection, Nils Petter went on to propose a substantive deficiency in the paper:

> The originality of your paper lies primarily, it seems to me, in the concept of "market socialism," which I find highly interesting, although not totally convincing. Where your paper is deficient, in our view, is in the assumptions that (a) convergence has any chance at all of being accepted by the major powers, and (b) that convergence will necessarily lead to peace. The experience of China and the Soviet Union would seem to argue against it. In fact it can be argued that as nations (or systems) become more similar they compete for the same things to a larger extent and thus are more likely to be involved in conflict. I do not want to impose this alternative thesis, but this formulation at least points to a central research problem which is skipped in your paper.

What did Nils Petter Gleditsch mean by "the experience of China and the Soviet Union"? During the 1970s, the USSR and the PRC were growling at each other over their different interpretations of the proper course for the world Marxist movement, and there were those in the West who rather hoped that this growling would eventuate in them attacking each other with nuclear missiles and wiping each other out. More realistic observers thought this outcome unlikely, and of course it never happened. If there had occurred a nuclear holocaust during the 1970s, the principal antagonists would most likely have been the USA and the USSR, and a critical role in setting up the preconditions for the explosion would have been ideological disagreement over the relative merits of capitalism versus socialism. It is certainly possible that under some circumstances nations becoming "more alike" would make them more hostile toward one another in some respects, but this is not plausible as a general rule.

For example, when in the early 1990s, the Soviet Union abandoned Marxism, dissolved itself, and made haste to implement the capitalist economic system, the reduction in the ideological gap between Russia and the United States was regarded correctly as a major step in the right direction. There was no concern that Russia and the United States becoming "more alike" would make them deadlier enemies than they had been before. But what really irked me about Nils Petter's analysis was its wrong-headed interpretation of the thrust of my paper. Although I was well aware that it is almost invariably futile for authors to argue with editors, every so often I was unable to suppress the urge to respond. An excerpt from my May 18 letter to Prof. Gleditsch:

> The reason I bring this up is that to the extent that your letter commented on other aspects of my article besides its length, these comments do not amount to valid and substantive criticism of the article. Indeed, I can only surmise that the length of the paper must have discouraged a really careful and reflective reading of the manuscript.
>
> In the first place, while the term "convergence" is ubiquitous in both popular and scholarly commentary on the contemporary world predicament, my paper goes miles beyond the conventional banalities in specifying a precise and plausible scenario toward a World Union. At the risk of immodesty, I must insist that this is a really original and even unique piece of writing.
>
> I did not at any point say or imply that this convergence plan would <u>necessarily</u> (your word) lead to peace. My carefully explicated assertion in this paper is merely that it would <u>increase the probability</u> of a peaceful escape from the world crisis. Your speculation is noted that convergence might increase war-risk because as systems become more alike they might compete to a greater extent for the same things. Such a superficial—I might even say flippant—speculation as this (applied to the <u>current</u> international situation) betrays a very serious underestimate of the gravity and seriousness of the nuclear impasse. It is rather like a surgeon who, doubting his skill to remove a malignant cancer from a patient who will otherwise be doomed, attempts to rationalize that there is no need of an operation because the patient's body will of its own accord eliminate the cancer and form an immunity against further cancerous invasions, and the patient will thus be all the

> stronger and more healthy for not having had an operation.
>
> My paper is also deficient, according to the editorial staff, because it assumes that "convergence has any chance at all of being accepted by the major powers" (my emphasis). The judgment here of an a priori impossibility is clearly anti-scientific, as well as being shockingly negative as an expression of the attitude of people who are associated with a journal whose very name implies an optimistic, progressive, and innovative viewpoint on world problems.

Although I'm quite sure that Nils Petter Gleditsch was as well aware as I was of the usual sterility of argumentative exchanges between editors and authors, he was sufficiently irritated by my communication to reply to it. After first assuring me that I needn't be concerned about the possibility of offending him ("editors quickly develop a thick skin, even if they have not already acquired it as researchers"), he went on to say that they would happily reconsider a much shortened manuscript. But whatever the length of the manuscript, he doubted that it would be published, because the transformations it was proposing were simply far beyond the boundaries of conceivability. He did not say explicitly that it would be a mistake to try to make the world more homogeneous ideologically and economically because this would increase the risk of nuclear holocaust—but he did say that in order for my argument to possess any credibility, it would have to deal carefully and compellingly with the contrary view that increased homogeneity among the nations would increase tendencies toward hostility and warfare. But in my opinion (then and now), that would be like dealing carefully and compellingly with the proposition that aliens from outer space built the Egyptian pyramids. I doubted that anyone could do it—and I certainly knew I could not.

Next the paper went to *Alternatives: A Journal of World Policy*. The editor, Saul H. Mendlovitz, regretted that they were not able to publish it (for unspecified reasons), but wished me success in seeking publication elsewhere, and hoped that I would again consider *Alternatives* for future contributions. It sounded like a form letter, but possibly my paper had made a positive impression on Prof. Mendlovitz. This is because several years later when I requested from several well-known international relations authorities positive pre-publication comments on my forthcoming book *World Union on the Horizon*, he was one of those who responded affirmatively.

Next the paper went to *Co-Existence*, a journal edited in Glasgow, Scotland. Their rejection letter, dated October 14, 1980, once again cited excessive length as an insuperable obstacle to publication, but held out a small reed of hope: If I would submit a much shorter manuscript that focused solely the possibility that the establishment of pragmatic market socialism in the West might start construction of a viable bridge over the ideological chasm between the communist and noncommunist camps, they might have an interest in such a manuscript. It took me quite a while to respond to that friendly invitation, but eventually, in March 1982, I sent them a 37-page manuscript entitled "Ideological Harmonization as a Means of Promoting Authentic Detente: A False Hope?" In May 1982, they invited a revision, of which the only absolutely necessary feature would be shorter length. I sent them a 24-page condensation, which appeared in the October 1982 issue of *Co-Existence*.

The summer following the appearance of "Ideological Harmonization" in *Co-Existence*, I decided the time had come for another effort at a lengthy article that covered the entire vision—the "grand design"—from pragmatic market socialism, through global economic development, to federal world government. By this time I had far more in the way of published credentials than I had had back in 1974 when I wrote "A Practical Proposal toward World Union." The new manuscript, written during August 1983 and entitled "Practical Considerations in Designing a Supernational Federation," was 63 double-spaced typed pages in length, only marginally shorter than its predecessor, "A Practical Proposal toward World Union" (68 pages).

The "Practical Considerations" manuscript went off to *International Organization* on August 22, 1983. The submission elicited the following response from the editor, Peter Katzenstein, dated September 12:

> I have now had a chance to read your "Practical Considerations in Designing a Supernational Federation," which you sent me recently for possible publication in International Organization. I have also read through the various supporting materials that you included in the package.
>
> I fear that you have misunderstood the character of the journal. IO is not a policy-based journal, which would obviously be the correct forum for your paper; it is, rather, a journal of international political economy and international relations that concentrates on the advancement of our theoretical understandings of those two and related fields. I have therefore decided not to send your manuscript out to review by members of the Editorial Board--not, I hasten to add, because of any "inherent vice" (as the lawyers have it), but because it does not speak to the concerns of our constituency. Rather than waste a couple of months of your time for an answer that is inevitable, I would strongly recommend that you offer the piece to a policy-focused journal; for example, the Institute for the Study of World Order is just starting a new journal, World Policy, with a good deal of fanfare, and that would

> seem to me to be a much better "market" for this manuscript.
>
> While I'm sure that this will not be a welcome letter, I hope that you will understand that it is prompted by a wish not to waste your time. I do hope that, as your work brings you closer to IO's fields of interests, you will consider the journal as a forum for your future work.

I hate it—and you probably do too—when people tell you that you don't "understand" their argument, when the fact is that you understand it perfectly well—you just don't agree with it. Thus I was irritated by Prof. Katzenstein's speculation that I didn't "understand" that *International Organization* was closed to policy proposals. There was no reason why I should have reached that particular understanding. Nowhere in its "Instructions to Authors" did IO specify that it would not publish anything with a direct bearing on policy questions. And even if they had said that explicitly, what possible justification was there for it? Thus I was unable to quell the urge to respond, which I did as follows (September 16, 1983):

> Thank you for your letter of September 12, and particularly for the advice concerning World Policy. I have submitted "Practical Considerations in Designing a Supernational Federation" there. Perhaps I will have better luck than I did with International Organization. I'm not overly confident, however. The Institute for World Order also publishes Alternatives, an avowedly policy-oriented journal, which is nevertheless indistinguishable from all the other international relations journals such as International Organization.
>
> I must say that I find your editorial policy to be very questionable. It appears that when you looked at my paper, the initial question that entered your mind was not the appropriate question, namely: "Does this paper have potentially worthwhile ideas in it concerning the potential future course of international organization, ideas at least worthy of discussion and debate?" Rather the inappropriate question that seems to have dominated your thinking was: "Would publishing a piece of strongly stated and highly controversial policy prescription such as this besmirch the image this journal is attempting to project of impartial, scholarly, scientific objectivity?"
>
> Of course, all professional journals, in the field of international relations no less than in any other field, have a legitimate concern for maintaining professional respectability. But this concern should not be pushed to the extreme of erecting veritable barriers against policy-oriented work per se. Such barriers are particularly ill-advised in the area of international relations, in which the possibility of unimaginable catastrophe stares us directly in the face. Surely the need for genuinely innovative policy thinking is greater in international relations by far than it is in any other field. But the fearfulness of the present interna-

> tional situation seems to have shocked the international relations journals into a perverse state of timid conservatism bordering on mental paralysis, such that the vast majority of published articles have only the most tenuous and remote apparent bearing on the vital policy questions of the contemporary age. This timid conservatism operates as a potent deterrent to genuinely innovative thinking, and in fact, far from being neutral as regards policy, constitutes a very strong albeit implicit endorsement of the current policy status quo. This is terribly frustrating to a few individuals such as myself, who have been blessed (or perhaps cursed) with a certain amount of intuitive vision, and who can perceive clearly the potentially disastrous sub-optimality of the current policy status quo.

I rather expected a response from Prof. Katzenstein reiterating his negative views on my understanding, but I heard no more from him. Although I did not put much stock in his speculation that *World Policy* might be more receptive to the "Practical Considerations" manuscript, that was not a good reason *not* to submit it there. The rejection letter from the managing editor, Sherill Leonard, did allow that *World Policy* was certainly not closed to contributions on supernational federation, but she added that such work "would need to be well-grounded in the current political and economic debate in this country and abroad, and would need to take extraordinary care to appear politically relevant and feasible." The problem with this proviso is that there is extremely little treatment in the professional literature of the "current political and economic debate [on world government]," and the reason for this is the assumption by the vast majority of international relations specialists that no "politically relevant and feasible" case can possibly be made for any conceivable form of world government. At least this would explain why *World Policy* has never published anything on world government, either for or against.

With rejections from *International Organization* and *World Policy* in hard, I determined that the prospects of the "Practical Considerations" manuscript were not good with those kind of journals. After a suitable interval, on August 24, 1984, I sent the paper to *World Futures*—not the kind of international relations or international organization journal that I would have preferred—but obviously a journal with a focus on the future. A little more than a week later, the following communication arrived from associate editor John Harwood-Jones, located in Scarborough, Ontario, Canada:

> Your paper has just reached me. It definitely has a place in World Futures, and I do not think a condensation will be necessary.
>
> I have not had time to read it through, but it is important that I re-

ceive from you, as soon as possible, the enclosed copyright release form, signed by you. Such a form must accompany every submission to the printer, and the mail service between Canada and the United States, unfortunately, is quite slow.

I would appreciate it, therefore, if you would sign and return it to me as soon as possible. From what I have read, it will not require much copy editing, and I can get it off to the printer as soon as I hear from you. Because of its length it will have to go in Volume 21 3/4.

Thank you for your submission to World Futures.

I could hardly believe it! A little over one week from submission to acceptance?—unheard of! John Harwood-Jones, I think I love you!

As it happened, a very substantial interval elapsed between the paper's acceptance in August 1984 and its actual appearance in *World Futures*, Vol. 21(3/4), issued in December 1985. Not only was Mr. Harwood-Jones the accepting editor, he did a bit of copy-editing before sending the manuscript off to the printers in Hong Kong. He told me that the copy-editing was easy, but he recommended (for future reference) against so much hyphenation at the ends of lines because it might confuse the Chinese typesetters who might not be as comfortable with English as might be preferred. I responded apologetically that the superabundant hyphenation—and also my exceptionally narrow margins—were a consequence of my tactic of squeezing as many words as I possibly could on a page in order to reduce the page-count and hence reduce the likelihood of rejection based on excessive length. (This assumes that some editors might be fooled by such a tactic.)

Subsequently *World Futures* became a reliable outlet for my world government essays that were too speculative and/or normative for the mainstream international journals. In all I published four articles in *World Futures*, all of them quite lengthy by ordinary journal standards:

- "Practical Considerations in Designing a Supernational Federation" (1985, 60 pages, 24,164 words).
- "Federal World Government at the Dawn of the Third Millennium: Old Challenges and New Opportunities" (2000, 66 pages, 24,228 words).
- "Effective Global Governance without Effective Global Government: A Contemporary Myth" (2004, 31 pages, 16,065 words).
- "Recent Consideration of World Government in the IR Literature: A Critical Appraisal" (2011, 28 pages, 14,207 words).

The total word-count of these four articles is nearly 80,000, enough for a medium-length book. *World Futures* is a serious journal—not a "gee-whiz" techno-futurology publication—although frankly most of its contents are far more esoterically theoretical than my own relatively down-to-earth policy contributions. Although I would have preferred that they be published in mainstream international relations periodicals, I owe a considerable debt of gratitude to the editors at *World Futures* for their receptiveness to my offerings on world government. This receptiveness inculcated hope in me that my approach to the world government issue, despite so much expressed skepticism, was after all reasonably cogent and not entirely devoid of promise.

Near Misses

Although my primary personal "holy grail" throughout my adult life has been the publication of a bestselling nonfiction book that would attract a critical mass of attention to my innovative proposals toward the improvement of the global human condition (pragmatic market socialism, a Global Marshall Plan, and/or the Federal Union of Democratic Nations), there has always been a "secondary" holy grail in the form of publishing a major article on these proposals in a leading professional periodical. Only such a forum would be sufficiently prestigious to attract the attention of a significant number of influential people. Of course I was aware of the possibility that the attention thus attracted might be heavily skewed toward dismissive contempt, but at least there would be some possibility of a sympathetic reaction.

Of course no single published article, no matter how long and detailed, and no matter how high the status of the periodical in which it was published, would be capable of precipitating the attitudinal sea change among all strata of society to which I aspired. Such a seismic transition could only be brought about by a book—a bestselling nonfiction book that would spend weeks or months at the top of the charts. On various occasions I completed book-length manuscripts that I hoped might fill the bill. But I was fully aware of the fact that the judgment of an acquisitions editor for a prestigious publisher is not determined solely, or even principally, by the inherent quality of a submitted manuscript. It is also based on ad hominem considerations: to wit, what are the author's credentials? What are his/her educational attainments, employment history, previous publications? Perhaps most importantly: Does the author possess a "name"? In other words, among a random sample of potential readers of the book, how many would recognize the author's name? If the answer to this last question is "none" or "virtually none," then that would constitute quite a serious liability against the submitted manuscript.

Of course, considering the size and gravitas of the book manuscripts I was submitting as putative nonfiction bestsellers, my own credentials were decidedly modest. I had a Ph.D. from Northwestern University, but it would have been better if my Ph.D. had been awarded by Harvard University. I had professional employment as an economics professor at Western Illinois University, but it would have been better if the professional employment had been with Harvard University. I had a fairly lengthy list of article publications, and the list gradually lengthened as the years went by, but none of the articles had appeared in a first-tier journal, only a few had appeared in second-tier journals, and the large majority had appeared in third-tier or lower journals. Exactly how much of a liability this represented I did not know. How many acquisition editors at major publishers would be aware of the yawning prestige gap between, say, the *Journal of Political Economy* (definitely first-tier) and the *Review of Political Economy* (definitely third-tier)? It would seem safe to assume that few such editors would hold a Ph.D. in economics, and be likely to know the difference immediately. But if they investigated a bit, it might not take long for them to find out. Certainly it would have improved my chances of gaining the support of an acquisitions editor for a major publisher if I could boast at least a few publications in top-tier journals. Or even, perhaps, just one.

Alas, I never racked up even one single solitary publication in a top-tier journal. In fact, there were only two occasions in my life when I came within sight of my secondary holy grail of placing a major article in a top-tier journal. In 2003, I nearly placed an article entitled "A Comprehensive Incentives Analysis of the Potential Performance of Pragmatic Market Socialism" in the *American Economic Review*, the flagship publication of the American Economic Association. A few years later, in 2008, I nearly placed an article entitled "Beyond Global Governance: Prospects for Global Government" in *Foreign Affairs*, the flagship publication of the Council on Foreign Relations. Both the *American Economic Review* and *Foreign Affairs* are world-class periodicals, and arguably both of them are actually the single most influential journal, in their respective fields, in the entire world.

If these articles had been published, it might conceivably have made a perceptible difference to the course of history. At a minimum, it would have exposed thousands, perhaps millions, of people to ideas previously regarded by almost everyone as dangerously heretical. Perhaps many of these thousands, perhaps millions, of people would have fundamentally revised their view of the world—just as I had done back when I was a freshman student at Fordham University in the early 1960s.

Or—perhaps not. After all, during my career I became aware of a handful of articles in major periodicals that directly challenged conventional wisdom on highly controversial issues—and which had no more effect on the status quo than a flea in a hurricane. For example, the first article in a top-tier economics journal, with which I became acquainted at the time of its appearance, was "The Dynamic Inefficiency of Capitalism" by Kelvin Lancaster, in the Sept.-Oct. 1973 issue of the *Journal of Political Economy*. This article drew my immediate attention, because the title suggested a deficiency of capitalism which I had long believed might be correctable under pragmatic market socialism. Specifically, the concern of business executives under capitalism to maintain a satisfactory rate of return for the capitalist owners, could lead to a lower rate of capital accumulation than would occur under a market socialist system that would be primarily concerned with maximizing the welfare of the entire population, not that of a small minority of wealthy capital owners. This inspired certain institutional proposals within the overall pragmatic market socialist proposal, namely the National Investment Banking System (NIBS) and the National Entrepreneurial Investment Board (NEIB), that would be designed specifically to increase the rate of capital investment above that observed under capitalism.

Over the years I devoted a certain amount of effort to trying to develop a formal mathematical and statistical approach to this issue—although, I would have to concede, with indifferent success. Eventually I published three articles on the proposition that pragmatic market socialism might manifest stronger economic growth than capitalism owing to a higher rate of capital investment: "Investment Propensities under Capitalism and Market Socialism" (*Rivista Internazionale di Scienze Economiche e Commerziali*, 1978); "A Market Socialist Critique of Capitalism's Dynamic Performance" (*Journal of Economic Issues*, 1986); and "Growth Propensities under Capitalism and Profit-Oriented Market Socialism" (*European Journal of Comparative Economics*, 2012). All three of these journals are third-tier, and to my knowledge these articles have not inspired any further investigation into the matter. On the other hand, to say that it is not possible to back up this proposition compellingly at this time with theoretical and/or statistical evidence, does not negate the possibility that the proposition is basically correct and numerically significant.

Kelvin Lancaster's 1973 "Dynamic Inefficiency of Capitalism" article, by virtue of the fact that it was published in a top economic journal and embodied quite sophisticated mathematical analysis, did in fact inspire a modest theoretical literature. Although Lancaster's analysis is presumably technically correct (after all, it was published in the *Journal of Political Economy*), the analysis is cumbersome and unworldly. Nowhere in either the assumptions or the analysis is there anything comprehensible in terms of everyday casual empiricism and/or common sense. The upshot is that despite the description in the title of capitalism as "dynamically inefficient" in the title of a 1973 article published by the illustrious *Journal of Political Economy*, no serious questions about the legitimacy of capitalism have been raised on this point within the economics profession in the many years since its publication.

Later on, in 1992, there appeared in *Time Magazine* an article ("essay") that virtually electrified me when I first encountered it. This was "The Birth of the Global Nation," by Strobe Talbott, in the July 20, 1992, issue of *Time*, a piece which was seen and read by millions of *Time* readers. As of 1992, the only writing on world government that I had managed to get into print was "Practical Considerations in Designing a Supernational Federation" (*World Futures*, 1985). If I had to guess, I would say that my "Practical Considerations" essay was seen by perhaps fifty people, of whom only a small fraction would have undertaken to read it. I had completed the manuscript for the book *World Union on the Horizon: The Case for Supernational Federation* in May 1992, and I was in the process of trying to find a publisher for it when I spotted Strobe Talbott's "Birth of the Global Nation" in *Time*. Surely, I thought, this was an optimistic omen. Even though Mr. Talbott offered no meaningful discussion whatsoever on the institutional structure of a world government, nor on the pros and cons of such a government, the thrust of his brief two-page essay was that some form of world government was definitely in the offing—and that it will definitely be a good thing for everybody when it eventually comes about. I thought that surely such progressive sentiments, appearing as they did in a reputable mass-circulation newsmagazine, would augment the possibility that a major publisher would be interested in *World Union on the Horizon*. Unfortunately, that was not to be. Nor did Talbott's *Time* essay do the moribund world federalist movement any perceptible good. Mr. Talbott was given an award by the World Federalist Association, but the WFA continued its long-term decline.

As these examples demonstrate, none of the articles of which I am personally aware, that have appeared in top-tier periodicals and that have challenged conventional wisdom on highly controversial issues, have had any perceptible effect on the real-world status quo. Despite this evidence, I never wavered in my efforts to place articles on pragmatic market socialism, global economic development, and federal world government, in top-tier periodicals. After all, there is always a first time.

Comprehensive Incentives Analysis

I suppose I owe a debt of gratitude to Professor Peter Murrell, an economics professor at the University of Maryland. Not that I have ever received any direct support and encouragement from the fellow. He is definitely not a kindred spirit with a sympathetic interest in any of my visionary proposals for the improvement of global human civilization. I know for a fact that he thinks that pragmatic market socialism is a very unpromising idea, and although he never weighed in on the Global Marshall Plan or the Federal Union of Democratic Nations, I have little doubt that he would be equally skeptical of these ideas. In other words, he is a typical representative of the prevalent conventional wisdom against any and all ideas of this sort. Why, then, do I feel that I owe him a debt of gratitude? This is because he published in the professional literature some criticism of pragmatic market socialism, and this criticism was a catalyst to my developing a far more elaborate theoretical development of the concept than I might otherwise have done.

My work on pragmatic market socialism has tackled the question of whether or not capital property income is an economically and ethically legitimate earned return to capital management effort using three distinct, successively more comprehensive mathematical models. The central variable in all three models has been capital management effort e (or E), defined as all categories of human effort (corporate supervision, investment analysis, entrepreneurship, etc.) intended to increase the rate of return realized on financial or physical capital. The first model was a partial equilibrium model of utility maximization by the "representative" capital manager. This analysis constituted the substantive content of my first published article on pragmatic market socialism: "Capital Management under Market Socialism" (*Review of Social Economy*, 1974). The analysis was amplified in three additional locations in the published literature: "On the Potential Efficiency of Market Socialism" (*ACES Bulletin*, 1976); "A New Perspective on Market Socialism" (*Comparative Economic Studies*, 1988); and in the "Analytical Appendix" of *Socialism Revised and Modernized: The Case for Pragmatic Market Socialism* (Praeger, 1992).

The second model was a very small-scale general equilibrium model, involving only three primary factors of production: aggregate physical capital (K), aggregate labor (L), and aggregate capital management effort (E). The only location in the published literature in which this analysis appeared was in my article "Capital Management under Profit-Oriented Market Socialism: An Explicit Function Approach" (*Southern Economic Journal*, 1996). The *Southern Economic Journal* is widely acknowledged as a second-tier economics journal, and is thus the highest-status journal in which one of my market socialism articles ever appeared.

The third model was a medium-scale computable general equilibrium model that provided the technical basis for what was by a large margin the most comprehensive and sophisticated analysis of the potential performance of pragmatic market socialism I ever produced. There are three locations in the published literature in which this research is presented: (1) *Capitalism versus Pragmatic Market Socialism: A General Equilibrium Evaluation* (Kluwer, 1993); (2) Chapter 5 ("Application: An Evaluation of Capitalism versus Pragmatic Market Socialism") in *Capital Management Effort: Theory and Applications* (Ashgate, 2004); and (3) "A Comprehensive Incentives Analysis of the Potential Performance of Market Socialism" (*Review of Political Economy*, 2007). It would be difficult to say which of these three locations is the most obscure.

It is conceivable that neither the second model nor the third model would ever have been developed if it had not been for the catalytic effect of two articles by Peter Murrell published in the professional literature. The first of these was a comment on my 1979 article "The Microeconomic Efficiency Argument for Socialism Revisited" in the *Journal of Economic Issues*. Both Murrell's comment ("The Microeconomic Efficiency Argument for Socialism Re-Revisited") and my reply to it ("The Microeconomic Efficiency of Market Socialism: Reply") were published in the March 1981 issue of the *Journal of Economic Issues*. The second of Murrell's articles was "Incentives and Income under Market Socialism," published in the *Journal of Comparative Economics* in 1984. As a subscriber to the *JCE* at that time, I became aware of this second article as soon as it appeared, and immediately researched and wrote a reply to it, using the second of my three capital management effort models, entitled "Incentives and Income under Market Socialism: Another View." After considerable delay and an invited revision, the *JCE* eventually rejected my reply. But I was sufficiently confident of the substantive analytical content of the research that I doggedly pursued publication for many years, through several revisions, title changes, and rejections. Eventually, in 1996, some 12 years after the initial draft was written, the research was finally published in the *Southern Economic Journal* under the title "Capital Management under Pragmatic Market Socialism: An Explicit Function Analysis."

Of the six articles on market socialism that I published during the 1970s, the second most important, after "Capital Management under Market Socialism" (*Review of Social Economy*, 1974), was "The Microeconomic Efficiency Argument for Socialism Revisited" (*Journal of Economic Issues*, 1979). In common with all my early articles on market socialism, it went to great lengths to emphasize that the version of market socialism under consideration, pragmatic market socialism, was qualitatively distinct from the Langian market socialist plan proposed by Oskar Lange back in the 1930s. The principal implication of this difference was that the perceived shortcomings of Langian market socialism, such as the impracticality of marginal cost pricing, the lack of an observable success criterion for firm managers, and so on, could not sensibly be applied to pragmatic market socialism.

My 1979 *JEI* article argued that while the pragmatic market socialist economy could make no claim to being Pareto efficient, this was irrelevant—because the real-world capitalist economy was not Pareto efficient either. Aside from imperfect competition and external effects, there was an abundance of distortions created by the tax system and the business regulation system. Not that these "distortions" are necessarily dysfunctional. The tax system and business regulatory system are intended to address correctable problems. Their purpose is to "distort" a suboptimal condition into an improved condition—or at least a "less suboptimal" condition. Although the principal benefit of pragmatic market socialism would be a more equitable distribution of capital property income through the social dividend, a case could be made for supplementary benefits pertaining to economic efficiency. One of these was that the proposed institutional features of pragmatic market socialism would address the adverse effects of the separation of ownership and control on the effort incentives of the high corporation executives—these adverse effects reducing the overall efficiency of economic production.

Peter Murrell's comment took issue with my argument, on grounds that only Lange's microeconomic efficiency argument was deserving of respect. Any market socialist system that could not boast of achieving Pareto efficiency could not be taken seriously, and was therefore unworthy of consideration. In Murrell's case, this was a somewhat hypocritical position, since in various other contributions he maintained that in practice Langian market socialism would most likely be a disaster, notwithstanding its alleged Pareto efficiency. In other words, Murrell fully shared the prevalent mainstream judgment that for a variety of reasons, Langian market socialism was unpromising. His comment was therefore hardly a defense of Langian market socialism against the challenge of pragmatic market socialism. It was rather, in effect, an assault on any and all market socialist schemes.

The central thrust of Murrell's comment on my 1979 *JEI* article was that the fundamental, inherent, and uncorrectable flaw in pragmatic market socialism (as well as in Langian market socialism or any other form of market socialism) was that the diversion of capital property income received by capital property owners into social dividend income distributed to the general public would drive a wedge between the productivity of capital and the return paid to capital. The return paid to capital would be less than the productivity of capital, and the consequence of this distortion would be economic inefficiency. This argument relies on the blending together of capital with capital owner, thus endowing the capital owner with the productivity of capital. It ignores the physical and existential dichotomy between nonhuman capital and the human capital owner. It is oblivious to the self-evident distinction between nonhuman capital and human capital management effort—this distinction being at the heart not only of my own writing on market socialism, but (implicitly if not explicitly) that of all other proponents of the concept.

In May 1980, I received a communication from Warren Samuels, editor of the *Journal of Economic Issues*, informing me that they were planning to publish Professor Murrell's comment "The Microeconomic Efficiency Argument for Socialism Re-Revisited," and asking if I wanted to write a response. Of course I wanted to respond to this inane production of Professor Murrell! The editor enclosed along with Murrell's comment two referee reports on it that he had received. Both reports agreed that there were some serious flaws in Murrell's argument, but that the topic was interesting and worthy of further discussion, and that further discussion of it would be particularly valuable if I were given the opportunity to respond. I was especially delighted by the first of the two referee reports, a very brief report which in its entirety reads as follows:

> I have read the paper by Peter Murrell, "The Microeconomic Efficiency Argument for Socialism Re-Revisited." I don't remember the last time I read such a silly article. What is silly about it is the set of assumptions used, which are all totally unrealistic. If one accepted the assumptions, the argument is sort of amusing. Taken by itself, it is a totally useless argument in my opinion. On the other hand, if it were published with a good, lengthy reply by Yunker in the same issue, it would be fun, entertaining, educational and even useful for JEI readers. Otherwise, no.

What a joy it was for me to read that! At last, here was some tangible evidence that there were at least a few other people in the world who perceived the market socialist possibility in the same light I did!

Taking seriously this referee's suggestion that my reply should be "lengthy," my reply was 22 pages long (double-spaced typed). Professor Samuels, the *JEI* editor, said he enjoyed reading my reply, but it was too long: I would have to cut it down to 10 double-spaced typed pages. It was hardly a novelty to me to be required to trim my prose, so I did as Prof. Samuels directed. Some depth was lost, but 10 pages was sufficient to cover the nub of the matter, which was, essentially, this: Murrell claims capital = capital owner; I say capital ≠ capital owner. Or more precisely, Murrell says that the totality of the return to capital needs to be collected by the capital owner or capital will be inefficiently utilized in the productive process, while I say that the capital owner can be replaced by a capital manager (e.g., a BPO agent) who collects only a small percentage of the totality of the return to capital, and this will not result in the inefficient utilization of capital in the productive process. Murrell's comment, and my reply to it, appeared together in the March 1981 issue of the *JEI*.

This was not the end but rather the beginning of my debate with Peter Murrell on the matter. For many years I subscribed to the *Journal of Comparative Economics*, and in the fall of 1984 I encountered Peter Murrell's rejoinder to our previous exchange, in the form of a full-length article entitled "Incentives and Income under Market Socialism" (*JCE*, September 1984). As I read it, I recognized that it constituted a direct assault on the idea of market socialism in any form: Langian, pragmatic, or otherwise. The problem with any form of market socialism, in Murrell's view, was that it converted all or most of capital property return into a social dividend payment distributed among the general population, none of whom was involved in capital management. Thus capital would necessarily be applied in production in a less efficient manner, and overall economic performance would suffer accordingly. (No quantitative estimate was offered as to the extent of the alleged suffering.)

In contrast to his earlier "literary" (i.e. prose only) comment on my 1979 *Journal of Economic Issues* article, this time the argument was dressed up in mathematics. But the mathematics could not conceal the fact that it suffered from the same flaw as the "literary" argument: it assumed that the return to capital was the same thing as the return to capital management effort. This is a contestable assumption, to say the least. Basically Murrell's "Incentives and Income" article was a statement of the capital management argument against the potential efficiency of market socialism that I had addressed in my 1974 *RSE* article "Capital Management under Market Socialism."

Although I thought its conclusion was incorrect, the appearance of Murrell's article in a prestigious comparative systems journal energized me. At last here was a published statement of the capital management argument against market socialism—it provided a clear target against which I could respond. Within a few days after reading Murrell's article, I had developed a mathematical model of capital management effort that went well beyond my original partial equilibrium model, backed it up with a computer program capable of providing numerical solutions, and written a new paper entitled "Incentives and Income under Market Socialism: Another View."

I sent this paper off to the *Journal of Comparative Economics* in the optimistic belief that it would be a strong candidate for publication. But its chances of publication were not helped by the fact that the *JCE* editor submitted it to Peter Murrell for comment. Not surprisingly, Murrell's opinion was that my newest contribution failed to come to grips with the essence of his argument. The *JCE* editor said that an additional problem he had with my paper, in addition to Murrell's adverse opinion, was that it was much too long to constitute a comment on a published paper. I reworked the piece to present it as an original approach to the issue (which it was), rather than simply a response to Murrell, and re-titled it "The Optimal Distribution of Property Return under Market Socialism." However, this reincarnation of the research did not appeal to the *JCE* editor or referees, and the paper was rejected.

I did not give up on the project, although it required a very substantial length of time to be brought to published fruition. After a number of revisions, title changes, submissions, and rejections, the analysis was eventually published, many years later (1996), in the *Southern Economic Journal*: "Capital Management under Profit-Oriented Market Socialism: An Explicit Function Approach." Although I was happy to get this worthwhile piece of research into print, the fact was that I had long before concluded that its capital management effort model was indeed seriously deficient as a technical approach to the question of the potential performance of pragmatic market socialism. Perhaps it greatest single limitation was that—as had been the case with Murrell's 1984 "Incentives and Income" paper—it made no reference whatsoever to the empirical, real-world distributions of both capital wealth and labor income. These empirical, real-world distributions must certainly have a major impact on the relative performance question. It seemed commonsensical, therefore, that no model that excluded this vital factual data would likely be particularly informative on the question of interest.

By the fall of 1984 when I wrote my initial article challenging the argument advanced in Peter Murrell's "Incentives and Income under Market Socialism" in the *Journal of Comparative Economics*, I was becoming increasingly comfortable with the great technological innovation of the time: the microcomputer. Word processing was the single most important capability of the new technology, but a very close second was the marvelous increase in the convenience of computer programming. As anyone who has ever written programs for computers knows, a very onerous and time-consuming aspect of it is the debugging process. In the bad old days of submitting programs recorded on IBM cards to the mainframe computer located in the university computer center, even a relatively simple program might require several days to be fully debugged. With microcomputers, all that bother was a thing of the past. Instead of days to get a program debugged, it might take an hour or two.

Throughout my working career, one very important use of computer programs was to verify theoretical results obtained from mathematical manipulations. Very often the heart of the research is the derivation of optimization results, either for the maximization or minimization of some criterion variable, sometimes with constraints, sometimes without. If a great deal of calculus and algebra had been required to obtain a certain optimization result, my mathematical skills were not so reliable that I could absolutely trust the result without testing it numerically. Such testing was straightforward: write a program for the result, put in numbers, and by a simple application of sensitivity analysis, ascertain that the supposed optimum is indeed an optimum. Moreover, for those many models that are sufficiently complex to preclude explicit-function solutions, the model can be specified numerically and solutions obtained by iterative methods. Without computers, iterative methods would be impossibly time-consuming. Thus by the early 1980s, I was writing computer programs for the majority of my research projects. In addition to the greater efficiency in writing programs achieved through the use of microcomputers rather than mainframe computers, I was becoming more adept at devising models for the investigation of various economic questions. Some of these questions had nothing to do directly with the controversial issue of market socialism.

For example, one question of perennial interest is the proper degree of redistribution through the tax and welfare system. In the fall of 1985, I decided to have a go at this question using a small-scale general equilibrium model, and following almost a year of intermittent work on the project, I completed a manuscript entitled "Estimates of the Equity-Efficiency Tradeoff Using a Simple General Equilibrium Model." The model results included not merely the equity-efficiency tradeoff (the downward-sloping relationship between aggregate output and post-redistribution equality), but also the social welfare function (the dome-shaped relationship between the marginal tax rate and the social welfare measure). The paper suffered a total of four rejections before a revised version was at last accepted and published under the title "Some Empirical Evidence on the Social Welfare Maximization Hypothesis" (*Public Finance*, 1989).

According to my research records, my first submission of the "Equity-Efficiency Tradeoff" paper was in October 1986. In November 1986 I commenced work on a new project entitled "A General Equilibrium Comparison of Capitalism versus Pragmatic Market Socialism." During the several months during which I had been occupied with the first project, I had thought of it principally as a steppingstone to an economically sophisticated comparison of the potential performance of pragmatic market socialism relative to that of contemporary capitalism. In order to do this, I needed to expand the model I had utilized in "Equity-Efficiency Tradeoff" to include capital management effort (*e*), plus I needed nice, stable, plausible models for both the capitalist economy and the pragmatic market socialist analogue. I already had empirical estimates of the distribution of labor income, but in addition to that I needed empirical estimates of the distribution of capital wealth. It took a long time to work out the two model variants required: the capitalist variant was relatively simple, but the socialist analogue was far more complicated. Without a computer program with which to verify various mathematical results, it would have been veritably impossible to get anywhere. Both the capitalist and socialist variants were sufficiently complicated to preclude derivation of mathematically explicit model solutions. It was necessary to utilize numerical iteration to arrive at numerical model solutions. This methodology is only feasible using computer programs.

Basically a full year of intermittent work was involved before the completion of a manuscript entitled "A General Equilibrium Evaluation of Capitalism versus Pragmatic Market Socialism." Its first submission was to the *Journal of Political Economy* on November 6, 1987. Its first rejection came on January 14, 1988. The referee felt that the model was implausible, the results were implausible, and anyway the Austrian luminaries Ludwig von Mises and Friedrich Hayek had demonstrated conclusively decades previously that market socialism—*any* form of market socialism—would be economically catastrophic. Over the ensuing years, I would encounter various permutations and combinations of these basic sentiments, expressed by a variety of referees, sometimes very briefly, sometimes at considerable length. Did these various referees examine the research carefully and thoughtfully? Or did they skim through the paper looking for things they did not like, that struck them as vaguely dubious, and that would provide convenient pretexts for recommendations to reject? I suspected—and still do—the latter.

According to my records, in the 20 years between 1987 and 2007 I produced a grand total of seven different manuscripts presenting this research: (1) "A General Equilibrium Comparison of Capitalism versus Pragmatic Market Socialism" (November 1987); (2) "A General Equilibrium Evaluation of Capitalism versus Pragmatic Market Socialism" (January 1989); (3) "A General Equilibrium Evaluation of Capitalism versus Pragmatic Market Socialism" (second version, August 1993); (4) "Profit-Oriented Market Socialism: A General Equilibrium Analysis" (June 1994); (5) "An *els* Comparison of Capitalism versus Pragmatic Market Socialism" (June 2002); (6) "Pragmatic Market Socialism: A CGE Evaluation" (October 2002); (7) "A Comprehensive Incentives Analysis of the Potential Performance of Market Socialism" (January 2003). These seven manuscripts racked up numerous rejections before the last one was published in the *Review of Political Economy* (January 2007).

Although the basic model and the basic results were identical over all these manuscripts, there were some slight improvements in the theoretical model to eliminate some minor anomalies, the data was periodically updated to utilize data from more recent federal government data sources, the empirical basis was expanded from 10 deciles to 20 half-deciles, and there were some alterations in presentation intended to increase the probability of publication. Some of these alterations involved expansions, others condensations. As noted earlier, twice the results appeared in book publications prior to the 2007 *ROPE* article: the Kluwer book in 1993, and the Ashgate book in 2004.

If I am counting correctly, the various articles containing the research suffered a grand total of 18 rejections before the last version was accepted and published. To a professional academic anxious to see his/her research work in print, any rejection is demoralizing, but these particular rejections were especially painful for me, because the subject matter was so near and dear to my heart, and also because this was probably the most technically sophisticated research I would ever be able to produce on the potential performance of pragmatic market socialism. Because of these factors, I was determined to keep on trying.

One of the principal shortcomings of the research, as perceived by most of the referees, was that the *els* model was "unsophisticated" and lacked precedent in the literature. To counter this, I decided to write some articles that would utilize the capitalist variant of the *els* model, but would not mention that the model could be applied to evaluate pragmatic market socialism. Presumably this would enable the *els* model to be evaluated more objectively on its own technical merits. During the 1990s I produced four manuscripts of this sort: (1) "Evaluating Changes in the Distribution of Capital Wealth" (completed September 1992); (2) "An *els* Model of the Economy: With Applications to Optimal Taxation" (completed October 1995); (3) "Differential Taxation of Labor and Capital Income" (completed November 1995); and (4) "Application of the *els* Model: Optimal Tax Rate and Public Good Proportion" (completed December 1995). Although two of these papers eventually made it into print, on the whole the success of the gambit would have to be described as "indifferent." Between them, the four papers racked up an impressive number of rejections, and neither of the two that were published appeared in a top-tier journal: "Evaluating Changes in the Distribution of Capital Wealth" appeared in *Economic Inquiry* (October 1994), and "Application of the *els* Model: Optimal Tax Rate and Public Good Proportion" appeared in *Public Finance Review* (January 1999). These meager publications could hardly be used to substantiate the proposition that the *els* model had been "accepted" into mainstream economic theory.

In September 2002 I completed "Profit-Oriented Market Socialism: A CGE Evaluation." This was the immediate predecessor to "A Comprehensive Incentives Analysis of the Potential Performance of Market Socialism," the article that nearly made it into print in the pages of the esteemed *American Economic Review*. Although the essential substance of the research was the same as it had been in the first effort way back in 1987 with "A General Equilibrium Comparison of Capitalism versus Pragmatic Market Socialism," the 2002 "CGE Evaluation" paper was considerably improved relative to that first effort 15 years previously. Among other things, a number of technical anomalies had been ironed out, the data on distribution came from a recent edition of the Survey of Consumer Finances (a very authoritative U.S. federal government source), and I even went to the trouble of utilizing my word processing skills to format the paper exactly according to the style sheet utilized by the target journal, the *Review of Economic Studies*.

Toward the end of the fall semester of 2002, the *Review of Economic Studies* rejected "Profit-Oriented Market Socialism: A CGE Evaluation." Of course, predecessors of this paper had compiled a long list of rejections based on obtuse and/or hyper-critical referee reports. But without doubt the single referee report on "CGE Evaluation" earned the top award for brevity and stupidity. According to the referee's three-line report, this paper made no worthwhile contribution at all to the study of market socialism because it ignored the critical issue of incentives. This is like saying that the standard neoclassical theory of the household is without value because it ignores incentives, or that the standard neoclassical theory of the firm is without value because it ignores incentives. Such statements are never made, but if they were they would be immediately recognized as hopelessly obtuse. A very reasonable interpretation of household incentives is embodied in the motivation to maximize household utility subject to the budget constraint, and a very reasonable interpretation of firm incentives is embodied in the motivation to maximize profits subject to the production function. I'd seen that nonsense about "ignoring incentives" several times before, but this time it really got to me. I was furious.

At this point a digression may be in order to try to convey why I felt so aggrieved that this particular piece of research was having such an immensely difficult time getting into print in a good journal. It was not just that the model represented quite a respectable level of sophistication, and that the computer programming involved in the research was equally sophisticated. It was not just that market socialism was (and still is) a potentially important idea with a substantial professional literature—much of which I myself had contributed. It was also that the research was such a *fair and balanced* treatment of this extremely controversial idea.

This fairness and balance was clearly expressed at the outset, in the abstract that preceded the text:

> An evaluation is undertaken here of the economic performance of contemporary capitalism relative to that of a hypothetical market socialist alternative designated "profit-oriented market socialism." In most respects, profit-oriented market socialism would closely mimic the contemporary market capitalist economy. The major difference would be that the preponderance of profits and interest generated by the operations of publicly owned business enterprises would be distributed to the general public as a social dividend supplement proportional to household wage and salary income rather than in proportion to household financial assets. The basis of the comparison is a small-scale but comprehensive computable general equilibrium (CGE) model. This is termed the "*els* model" because it encompasses three primary factors of production: capital management effort e, labor l, and saving s. Numerical solutions of the model suggest that the critical issue is the numerical value of a model parameter (ν) representing the output elasticity of total capital management effort in the aggregate production function. If this parameter value is relatively low, then profit-oriented market socialism out-performs capitalism. If this parameter value is relatively high, then capitalism out-performs profit-oriented market socialism. The fundamental implication of the research is that the relative performance of a profit-oriented market socialist economy is an empirical question and not a theoretical question.

As is apparent, this was one of the manuscript versions of the research that used the more generic "profit-oriented market socialism" in place of "pragmatic market socialism." Accordingly, a "public ownership agency" (POA) replaced the "Bureau of Public Ownership" (BPO), and "POA agent" replaced "BPO agent." This terminological device was intended to conceal the fact that the author of the paper was none other than James A. Yunker, the inventor and chief promoter of pragmatic market socialism, a variety of profit-oriented market socialism. How successful this device was in concealing my authorship of the paper I do not know, but it would be obvious to any person reading it that its author must believe strongly in market socialism. No skeptic would undertake such enormous effort to "scientifically investigate" such an intensely controversial policy proposal. Nevertheless, here the author was—although obviously an advocate of market socialism—admitting frankly and unambiguously that this system might not work as well as capitalism.

There are two diagrams that neatly sum up the basic conclusions from the research. Variants of these diagrams appeared in every presentation of the research: the two published books and the one published article, and in all the several unpublished articles. Their appearance varied somewhat depending on the variables illustrated and the graphics software used to produce them. But their interpretation was always the same. The first of the two diagrams clearly illustrates the superiority of market socialism over capitalism indicated by the numerical solutions of the capitalist and socialist variants of the *els* model *under the benchmark set of parameter values*. The specific diagram used in the "CGE Evaluation" manuscript rejected by the *REStud* in 2002 is shown as Figure 5.2 below:

Figure 5.2: Nash Social Welfare Functions under Capitalism and Socialism

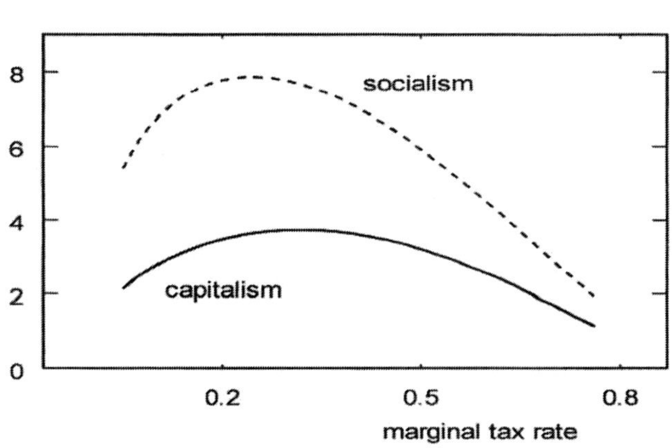

The dome-shaped curves show Nash social welfare (product of household utilities) as a function of the marginal tax rate of the income tax function. The higher the marginal tax rate, the greater the degree of redistribution. The peaks of the curves indicate the theoretically optimal level of

taxation and redistribution. If the rate of taxation/redistribution is pushed beyond that rate, social welfare declines. It is intuitively obvious that there is some optimal degree of redistribution. Computations using the *els* model enable a scientifically grounded estimate of that optimum. The solid curve shows results from the capitalist variant of the model; the dashed curve shows results from the market socialist variant of the model. As can be seen, for each value of the marginal tax rate, the socialist curve lies above the capitalist curve by a substantial margin. It is apparent, therefore, that *under the benchmark set of parameter values* used in the *els* model solutions, socialism out-performs capitalism.

But what about sets of parameter values other than the benchmark set? On the basis of a large amount of sensitivity analysis, it was ascertained that this result is highly robust against different numerical specifications of the parameters—with one key and critical exception. That exception is the elasticity of capital management effort in the aggregate production function, symbolized by the Greek letter ν (nu). The benchmark value of ν was set to 0.025. Given the nature of the aggregate production function, and empirical measures of the proportion of total national income in the United States represented by labor income (approximately 0.80), the theoretically permissible range of ν values is 0 to 0.20. Figure 5.3 following shows the Nash social welfare measure as a function of the numerical value of ν:

Figure 5.3: Nash Social Welfare as a Function of the Output Elasticity of Capital Management Effort (ν)

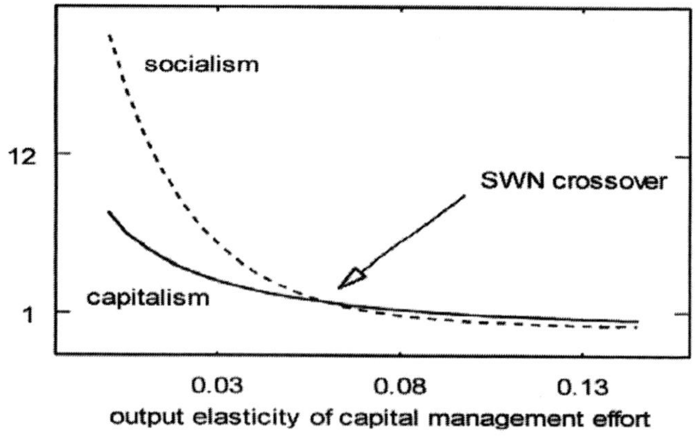

This diagram indicates that Nash social welfare under socialism is higher than that under capitalism for low values of ν, while it is lower under socialism than it is under capitalism for high values of ν. The "SWN crossover" point is the critical ν value that separates the two ranges. In the "CGE Evaluation" research, this value was computed to be 0.06031. Stated simply, if the actual value of ν is less than 0.06031, socialism works better than capitalism; if the actual value of ν is greater than 0.06031, capitalism works better than socialism. Clearly, it would be nice to have a solid, reliable estimate of the actual value of ν. But since there has never been any effort to measure real-world capital management effort, no such estimate exists.

Certainly the research results are consistent with common sense intuition. The value of ν indicates the extent to which capital property income may be legitimately interpreted as an earned return to capital management effort, as opposed to an unearned return generated by the marginal productivity of physical capital itself. The higher is ν, the more truth there is in the proposition that capital property return is an earned return to human effort; the lower is ν, the less truth there is in it. At the same time, it is intuitively plausible that to the extent that capital property income is in fact an earned return to capital management effort, then the market socialist economic system would tend to be inferior to capitalism. But to the extent that capital property income is not in fact an earned return to capital management effort, then the market socialist economic system would tend to be superior to capitalism.

Therefore, this research most certainly does not "prove" the proposition that market socialism would be better than capitalism. What it shows is the *possibility* that market socialism would be better than capitalism. But what it also shows is that this result depends on a parameter value that might not be an accurate representation of reality. There is really no need for a defender of the capitalistic status quo to attack the *els* model used in the research. He or she could simply say: "Well, it is obvious to any sensible person that capitalism is superior to market socialism. Thus it is obvious that to the extent that the *els* model is a reasonable approximation to reality, the real-world value of the ν parameter must clearly be in excess of 0.06031."

But no, that is not good enough for close-mindedly dedicated defenders of the capitalistic status quo, among whose ranks are the large majority of referees who have passed judgment on my various submissions to economics journals. To these people, any research at all which purports to demonstrate the possibility that market socialism might be superior to capitalism simply must be riddled with error. They might not know exactly where and what these errors are, but they are absolutely, religiously certain that they must be there.

But I was not ready to give up on this research. For my part, I was equally absolutely, religiously certain that this was good, solid research, and it deserved to be published in one of the better journals. Despite all the adversities, the plethora of rejections in the past, there simply *must* be a way to present this research that would make it publishable. After all, I had published a substantial number of articles on pragmatic market socialism in the past. That proved that there were at least a few referees out there who might appreciate this research, who could see its value, and who would recommend publication. To start with, a new title was in order. I replaced "Profit-Oriented Market Socialism: A CGE Evaluation" with "A Comprehensive Incentives Analysis of the Potential Performance of Market Socialism." There! With a title like that on the manuscript, let's see if any close-minded referee will even dare to dismiss the research as "failing to address incentives." In addition to the title change, I added some material here and there to demonstrate that the research most definitely and directly *does* address the incentives issue.

With these improvements augmenting its chances of publication, I decided I would take this most recent revision straight to the highest court in the land where economics is concerned. Shortly after New Year's Day, 2003, I submitted "A Comprehensive Incentives Analysis of the Potential Performance of Market Socialism" to the *American Economic Review*.

As we know, the lag between human insemination and human birth is nine months. That is approximately how long it took the *American Economic Review* to respond to this particular submission. In early September 2003, I received a postal communication from Timothy Besley, a professor at the London School of Economics and the *AER* co-editor who had been assigned my submission. All prior communications I had ever received from the *AER* had conveyed, regretfully or disdainfully as the case may have been, rejections of my submissions. But this one was different! I could hardly believe my eyes as I read Professor Besley's message to the effect that I was being invited to submit a revision of "A Comprehensive Incentives Analysis of the Potential Performance of Market Socialism." An invited revision! As I read through the two enclosed referee reports, my excited wonderment grew. The bottom-line evaluations of the two referees were as follows:

> From the perspective of one familiar with the historical debates and models, this paper is a breath of fresh air, and may serve as a benchmark for future empirical and theoretical research in this area. Despite the many equations and tables, this paper is a wonderful idea piece,

> and its conclusion regarding capital management effort is both plausible and well-founded. I understand that the *American Economic Review* does not normally publish papers of this sort, but I suspect that the paper will be valuable to a significant part of its readership, so I recommend publication.
>
> The paper is very carefully and clearly written for the most part, and readers will be able to follow the development of the argument, the specification of the model, and the derivation of the results without filling in lacunae or finding important issues unaddressed. The expositional level of the paper is very high compared to the norms for economic publications. In formal terms the argument is founded in an excellent understanding of static general equilibrium theory, and carried out with careful attention to detail and the accuracy of arguments. The author addresses the question of the adequacy of a static model to address this question with arguments that are plausible if not conclusive. Given the premise of the interest of the method and the argument, and the absence of any papers in the literature addressing these questions at this level of sophistication, it would not make sense to reject the paper because it fails to carry out its project using all the sophisticated tools of modern intertemporal economics.

The first report used the magic words "recommend publication," and while the second did not use those exact words, it came very close. Naturally both of the referees had some concerns, and offered suggestions in a spirit of constructive criticism. The co-editor, Timothy Besley, also had some concerns of his own, and he did not bother to provide any constructive criticism. Even so, the overall tenor of the communication was decidedly positive. If this had been almost any journal other than the exalted *American Economic Review*, I would have considered this article to be practically in the bag for publication purposes. But this being the *AER*, a favorable outcome was not nearly as probable. My attitude at the time was cautiously optimistic—with great emphasis on "cautiously."

With a certain understandable degree of fear and trembling, I commenced work on a revision. When the revision was submitted on September 27, 2003, via e-mail attachment, it was accompanied by a lengthy memo detailing my responses to the comments of the two referees and the co-editor. Although I was confident that the revision dealt effectively with all the specific concerns voiced by the referees and the co-editor, I recognized that there was still a serious problem with it—the problem of length. The original submission version was 46 pages long, containing 17,994 words. By the standards of most professional journals, this is an extraordinarily long manuscript. The revision was even worse: 61 pages long, containing 25,886 words. Therefore, it came as a disappointment but not as a surprise when on October 28, 2003, I received a brief e-mail from Timothy Besley informing me that the revision was far too long. I needed to cut it down to no more than 36 pages, including everything: abstract page, text, endnotes, tables, and diagrams. Drat! I dutifully carried out Besley's instructions, but it was like using a meat-ax. A truckload of valuable material had to be cut out. I coped as best I could by informing the reader at several locations that a longer manuscript containing the research (the 61-page first revision) was "available from the author upon request."

There followed three months during which I existed in a quasi-agony of suspense, before the ax descended. On January 26, 2004, I received a brief rejection letter from Timothy Besley, accompanied by an equally brief referee report. Damn! It was difficult to believe that this new referee report had come from one of the two original referees. During my long career in academia, I rarely protested negative editorial decisions and asked for reconsideration. But this was one of those rare occasions. After all, this was the *American Economic Review*. I doubted that I would ever get another opportunity even remotely comparable to this one. No sense in being shy when the stakes were so high.

Over the next several months, I conducted an increasingly edgy e-mail dialogue with Prof. Besley. It was fruitless. He steadfastly maintained the "party line" that the rejection had nothing whatever to do with the controversial subject matter of "Comprehensive Incentives Analysis"—that it was simply a matter that the paper did not rise to the high standards necessarily maintained by the *American Economic Review*. Of course, this position was flatly contradicted by the high opinion of the work expressed by the two original referees. My view was that the principal factor underlying Besley's attitude on the matter was apprehension that the publication of such a controversial paper in the *AER* would damage the high prestige of the journal. And as the person responsible for its acceptance, his own personal standing within the economics profession might suffer. But I also suspected that he would never admit this—even to himself.

My eventual sign-off to the dialogue was as friendly as I could force myself to make it. I thanked him for giving me several months of hope of scoring an *AER* publication on my favorite subject of market socialism, and assured him that I would follow his advice and pursue other publication possibilities. Shortly afterward, I submitted the manuscript to the *Journal of Political Economy* with the usual outcome. At that point I decided that the best possibility of getting this work into print in a professional journal in my lifetime was to submit it to the *Review of Political Economy*. Despite the similarity of names, there is an ocean of difference in the prestige levels of these two periodicals. Moreover, I had a friendly acquaintance with *ROPE*'s editor, Steven Pressman, who as editor of Ashgate's series "Alternative Voices in Contemporary Economics," had been responsible for the 2001 publication of my anthology *On the Political Economy of Market Socialism: Essays and Analyses*. Sure enough, "Comprehensive Incentives Analysis" was accepted (with revisions) and appeared in the January 2007 issue of the *Review of Political Economy*. Such a publication was slightly better than no publication at all. At least it got the research into print in a respectable—if not prestigious—journal.

Beyond Global Governance

With the collapse and dissolution of the Soviet Union in 1991, the potential importance of pragmatic market socialism as an ideological bridge between the communist East and the noncommunist West immediately went into steep decline. By the mid-1990s, it was becoming virtually certain that neither the ex-republics of the Soviet Union, nor the ex-components of the Soviet bloc in Eastern Europe, were going to return to the Marxist faith, to which they had once been so beholden. I was as conscious of this as anyone else who read the newspapers, and from a strictly logical point of view, I should have immediately abandoned any further work on pragmatic market socialism in order to devote myself one hundred percent to my other two visionary concepts: the World Economic Equalization Program (aka Global Marshall Plan), and the Federal Union of Democratic Nations. Nevertheless, I continued to devote an appreciable proportion of my time and resources to pursuing publication of work on market socialism. For example, my near-publication in the *American Economic Review* of "A Comprehensive Incentives Analysis of the Potential Performance of Market Socialism" occurred in 2003-2004, by which time it was obvious to all that Soviet-style socialism was as dead as the proverbial doornail, and gradually moldering away in its grave under a ten-ton slab of concrete.

So, one might ask, why did I continue working on market socialism? One answer is that I was propelled by the force of inertia—I had worked so long and hard on the subject that I just could not bring myself to abandon it entirely. Another factor is that I still had not published anything on market socialism in a top-tier economics journal—and unless and until that happened, the economics profession would remain virtually oblivious of a very plausible reform proposal which certainly deserves to be taken seriously.

Still, the fact is that while I did not entirely abandon market socialism, as the 1990s proceeded and we turned the corner into the third millennium, more and more of my time and effort was devoted to world economic development and federal world government. In terms of published contributions, however, the volume of my work in these latter two areas never came close to that on market socialism. One reason for this was that by the time my priorities changed, a great many of my best working years had already gone by. Another reason is that my professional training and background was in the field of economics, and federal world government is a subject regarded as falling within the purview of international relations, a sub-discipline of political science. There are substantive differences, not only in subject matter but also in methodology and terminology, between economics and political science. Thus I was at a great disadvantage, in trying to place my writings on world government in the more prestigious international relations journals, simply because I did not "speak the lingo," as it were. There was also the fact that just as most economists believed pragmatic market socialism was a very bad idea, so too most international relations specialists believed that federal world government was a very bad idea. In both areas, I was up against extremely formidable preconceptions.

In my writing on federal world government, I could not rely on results from a mathematical model, statistical data, computer simulations, and the like, to support my contention that a properly designed federal world government would likely be a benign and successful forward step in the political evolution of global human civilization. Thus I was deprived of any kind of scientifically grounded evidence on which to base my assertions. I was inevitably on much thinner ice in this area—and my publication record shows it. According to my records, from 1976 onward, I produced a total of 13 article manuscripts on world government, of which only seven appeared in journals, while six had to be retired unpublished. Of these latter six, however, I utilized three of them as chapters in the two anthology books containing my world government writings: *Rethinking World Government: A New Approach* (2005) and *Beyond Global Governance: Prospects for Global Government* (2014). So there were just three articles that were complete lost causes as far as seeing print was concerned.

My most intensive period of article writing on world government took place during the writing of *The Next Step: A New Vision of Federal World Government*. Following the disappointing outcome with *World Union on the Horizon: The Case for Supernational Federation* (1993), during the rest of the 1990s and into the 2000s, I worked intermittently on research and writing for *The Next Step*, finally completing a manuscript in May 2001. After much revision and condensation, the original 886-page *Next*

Step manuscript was eventually published in 2007 under the revised title *Political Globalization: A New Vision of Federal World Government* (404 pages).

Starting in the summer of 1999 and continuing through the summer of 2000, I wrote no less than eight new articles on world government topics. In chronological order by date of manuscript completion, they were: (1) "Federal World Government at the Dawn of the Third Millennium: Old Challenges and New Opportunities" (September 14, 1999); (2) "Putting the Cart before the Horse? The Relationship between General Disarmament and World Government" (December 5, 1999); (3) "Rethinking World Government: A New Approach" (December 10, 1999); (4) "Economic Inequality as an Impediment to World Government: Analysis and Proposals," (December 14, 1999); (5) "Voting Weights in a Potential Future World Government: Problems and Proposals" (December 17, 1999); (6) "World Government Revisited: A Post-Cold War Perspective" (December 26, 1999); (7) "Effective Global Governance without Effective Global Government: A Contemporary Myth" (May 30, 2000); (8) "Global Governance and Global Government: A Survey of International Relations Specialists" (August 10, 2000).

I had in mind that it would assist in finding a good publisher for *The Next Step* if I could list on my résumé a significant number of recent article publications on world government. It would assist even more if these articles were in good journals. I was not as well-informed on the relative status of relevant journals in this field as I was in my home field of economics, which covered my work on both pragmatic market socialism and global economic development. I had to use such casual evidence as I could muster on such things as the university location of the editorial office, and the affiliations of the authors. On this basis I concluded that the best academic journals in which to publish my world government articles would be *International Organization*, *World Politics*, *International Relations*, and *International Studies Quarterly*. Farther down the scale would be other international relations journals such as *Alternatives*, *Millennium*, and *Global Governance*. Then there was an entirely different category of periodical aimed at government officials and non-specialists in the general public with a special interest in the international situation: *Foreign Affairs*, *Orbis*, and *World Policy Journal*. The articles in these periodicals were less scholarly and more popular in orientation. Then there were "social science-oriented" journals such as *Journal of Peace Research*, *Journal of Conflict Resolution*, and *Conflict Management and Peace Science*. All of the above journals would be widely acknowledged as good, solid, reputable, mainstream journals.

Unfortunately, not one of the eight articles in the foregoing enumeration made it into the pages of any of the mentioned journals. At one time or another, all of these mentioned journals rejected one or more of my submissions. The only two journals which did publish some of those eight were *International Journal on World Peace* ("Rethinking World Government: A New Approach") and *World Futures* ("Federal World Government at the Dawn of the Third Millennium: Old Challenges and New Opportunities" and "Effective Global Governance without Effective Global Government: A Contemporary Myth"). I'm afraid that most knowledgeable people would put neither the *International Journal on World Peace* nor *World Futures* on a list of "good, solid, reputable, mainstream journals." I did not know for sure, but I strongly suspected that these would not be the kind of journal that would impress an acquisitions editor for a major publisher such as Oxford University Press or Norton. In any case, no major publisher was interested in *The Next Step*, and in order to get its much-condensed successor *Political Globalization* into print, I had to resort to the bottom of the barrel, University Press of America.

Unless I am miscounting from my records, the eight articles completed between the summer of 1999 and the summer of 2000 racked up a grand total of 33 rejections. Every one of these rejections was a blow to my pride and self-esteem. They elicited emotions of sadness and disappointment—but also indignation and anger. Aside from wounded pride, another reason for this reaction was my sincere belief that my contributions on world government were potentially very important to the future destiny of humanity. If a benign and effective world government could be established—assuming it was "properly designed" as I sincerely believed the Federal Union of Democratic Nations to be—this would significantly diminish the danger that at some point in the future the human prospect would be severely damaged, if not utterly destroyed, by a nuclear world war. Thus the potential benefit from world government was immeasurably greater than the most that could be expected of pragmatic market socialism or a Global Marshall Plan.

I have preserved in my files most of my correspondence with editors, including referee reports. It would be impractical to include here substantial quotation from these materials, but I will provide a single illustrative example to convey their flavor. This is taken from an anonymous referee report from *International Studies Quarterly* on "Putting the Cart before the Horse? The Relationship between General Disarmament and World Government":

> By trying to do too much, this paper does much too little. The author makes a convincing case that some earlier pieces calling for world

government called for world disarmament prior to the establishment of world government and that was one of the reasons for their lack of widespread support. In contrast to this, the author here argues for establishing world government prior to the elimination of arms. The author rightfully suggests that those earlier pieces came out of a particular systemic context and that that probably goes far in explaining their call for total disarmament.

But there are other reasons for opposing total disarmament, especially in a world of multiple nuclear powers. Those other reasons don't get adequately aired here. There are also many other reasons for opposing world government, including the proposals discussed here. And those don't get adequately discussed either. Even major critiques of world government written long ago, like that included in Raymond Aron's *Peace and War,* don't seem to merit mention...

In discussing earlier calls for world government, it's unclear why there isn't a discussion of Kant's *Perpetual Peace*, for surely that has gotten much more attention of late than Borgese or Isely. In a similar vein, the author's own proposal is for a Federal Union of Democratic Nations, but the author's notion of "democratic" is unspecified. Again, attention to Kant (or even those who build on Kant like Doyle or Russett) would have forced attention to this part of the author's own proposal.

The author discusses the fact that this piece should contribute to the evolving literature on global governance, yet there is nothing in this piece to indicate acquaintance with the most recent work on global governance (such as the book edited by Henson and Sinclair, or that by Prakash and Hart or that authored by Cable). More importantly, there is little indication of how this proposal meshes with the evolution of transnational social movements, NGOs, transnational advocacy networks, etc....

While we are told not to put disarmament first, we aren't told much about whether the European Union is a model to be emulated, whether there is much to be learned from functionalism or neo-functionalism, or whether there is an embedded theory here. While there is a passing reference to the Commission on Global Governance's report, there isn't any indication of why that Commission's view of a modified UN is not more acceptable than that of Clark and Sohn...

It's difficult to be supportive of the publication of this piece in its current form. It needs to be situated in a much broader, richer, and more recent literature and many of his assumptions need to be presented as problematics and thus arguments are to be made regarding them.

Upon reading referee reports such as this, I would experience a weary sense of futility. Does this individual not understand that a manuscript addressing all the multitude of "issues" and "problematics" relating to a potential world government would be impossibly lengthy? Not just too lengthy to be published as a journal article, but also quite possibly to be publishable as a book. In any case, I suspected that no matter how much *was* indeed addressed, a mindset such as this would not and could not be satisfied—there would always be more "concerns," most of them stemming from the unshakeable preconception that world government—*any* world government—must necessarily be a very bad idea.

In light of this never-ending barrage of criticism, you might well imagine my amazed excitement when on September 5, 2008, I received a letter from Catherine Harrington, a secretary at the Council on Foreign Relations, which contained the following riveting sentence: "If you would like to submit an essay to *Foreign Affairs* for consideration, please e-mail it to Senior Editor Daniel Kurtz-Phelan at dkurtz-phelan@cfr.org." Ms. Harrington's letter was a covering letter in a large box containing three copies each of my books *Political Globalization: A New Vision of Federal World Government* (2007), *Rethinking World Government: A New Approach* (2005) and *Common Progress: The Case for a World Economic Equalization Program* (2000). The covering letter explained that the CFR was retaining one set of this trio of books for office use, and the remaining sets were being returned to me. The sets were originally sent to all members of the editorial team at *Foreign Affairs* in September 2007, in support of a submission entitled "On the Practicality and Advisability of Federal World Government." That submission had been regretfully but expeditiously declined by Rosemary Hartman on the basis that a number of commissioned articles had arrived ahead of schedule and the journal was full into the foreseeable future. And now, a year later, here was *Foreign Affairs* actually *inviting* a submission!

There was absolutely no doubt about it: there was not a single periodical in the entire world, not excepting the top academic international relations journals, where one of my world government articles would be more widely exposed. The prospect was dizzying! Of course I immediately sent an e-mail to Daniel Kurtz-Phelan, attaching one of my available unpublished world government articles: "Beyond Global Governance: Prospects for Global Government." The substantive content of the "Beyond Global Governance" manuscript was virtually the same as that of "Practicality and Advisability" manuscript. They were even about the same length. In actual fact, "Beyond Global Governance" was my third submission to *Foreign Affairs*: in addition to "On the Practicality and Advisability of Federal World Government" in September 2007, I had sent them "World Government Revisited: a Post-Cold War Perspective" way back on December 27, 1999. The latter submission had been rejected on January 4, 2000—one week later. I must admit I have been impressed at how expeditiously *Foreign Affairs* shovels the blizzard of submissions they must receive back to their authors.

If *Foreign Affairs* actually published "Beyond Global Governance: Prospects for Global Government," it would be even a bigger deal—a *much* bigger deal—than if the *American Economic Review* had published "A Comprehensive Incentives Analysis of the Potential Performance of Market Socialism." Just a few years before, during the fall and winter of 2003-2004, the latter possibility had played havoc with my peace of mind. But if the virtually unimaginable had occurred and the *AER* had published "Comprehensive Incentives Analysis," the most likely result would have been my achievement of ephemeral notoriety as a latter-day exponent of market socialism. But just as Oskar Lange's 1930s advocacy of market socialism had no perceptible effect on the real world, that would almost certainly have been the outcome of my more recent advocacy of the idea. But the stakes were so much higher with the potential appearance of "Beyond Global Governance: Prospects for Global Government" in *Foreign Affairs*. Clearly, federal world government is potentially a far more important idea than pragmatic market socialism.

From my experience, *Foreign Affairs* deals with submissions far more expeditiously than does the *American Economic Review*. With the *AER*, I had been borne high on the wings of hope for exactly five months: from September 3, 2003, when I submitted the invited revision of "Comprehensive Incentives Analysis" to Timothy Besley, and February 3, 2004, when I received from him a rejection letter. With *Foreign Affairs*, the equivalent interval was somewhat under three months, from September 5, 2008, when I sent an invited submission to Daniel Kurtz-Phelan, and November 25, 2008, when my submission was rejected by Rosemary Hartman, a secretary at the CFR.

I rather suspected that Daniel Kurtz-Phelan was my sole supporter among the editorial staff of *Foreign Affairs*, but I was never so boldly undiplomatic as to inquire directly of him whether this was so. During the interval of hope and for a period of time afterwards, I conducted a friendly correspondence with Daniel Kurtz-Phelan. It was far warmer than my earlier e-mail correspondence with Timothy Besley. After all, Besley took full responsibility for rejecting "Comprehensive Incentives Analysis," whereas Kurtz-Phelan lobbied for "Beyond Global Governance." During my correspondence with the latter, I sent him a number of long-winded communications. His responses, while cordial, were invariably on the laconic side. One example of this was my "The Ax Falls" e-mail to Daniel on November 25, 2008:

> Upon returning home this evening, I found in my e-mail inbox a courteous note from Rosemary Hartman expressing regret that *Foreign Affairs* will not be able to utilize my paper. It seems that a number of commissioned articles have arrived ahead of schedule and there are other pressing issues arising from the results of the recently concluded U.S. presidential election. (Ms. Hartman's note was very similar to her earlier rejection note I received in September 2007, except that then the pressing issues arose from the ongoing U.S. presidential campaign.)
>
> Although a disappointment, at least this outcome was not an unexpected disappointment. Things like this have happened to me before. One time I had a major article on market socialism that made it to the invited revision stage at the *American Economic Review*, the world's foremost economic periodical. But in the end the sub-editor handling the paper decided that I had not responded adequately to referee comments. The paper was eventually published in the *Review of Political Economy*, an obscure periodical with negligible readership. Another time an editor at the U.S. branch of Oxford University Press nibbled half-heartedly for a while at my book *Rethinking World Government: A New Approach*, before thinking better of it. The book was eventually published by University Press of America, a third-tier publisher of highly specialized professional treatises. Predictably enough, the book disappeared instantly and without a trace following its publication by UPA. But the fact is that I can readily appreciate the attitude of the *AER* editor and the OUP editor—there is simply too huge a gap between the grandiose ideas espoused in my writing and my own rather humble professional credentials. I have a strong suspicion that if a paper such as "Beyond Global Governance" had been authored by, say, Colin Powell or Strobe Talbott, *Foreign Affairs* would be quite happy to publish it.
>
> I realized from the start that the prospects for publishing "Beyond Global Governance" in *Foreign Affairs* were quite dim, and following my custom in these situations, I have been consoling myself with such thoughts as "Be careful what you wish for—you might get it," and "There is much to be said for the quiet life." After all, it is clear that if my ideas on world government were to reach a larger public and attract significant interest, my personal life would change drastically—and not all for the better. While I would be able to bask in the approval and respect of some people, there would be many others who would loathe and despise me because my (in their opinion) thoroughly misguided proposals could be setting the stage for a horrific global tyranny under which the American people (among others) would be brutally

oppressed. I would be subjected to a barrage of criticism and vilification, and my actual physical safety might even be jeopardized. There would inevitably be a few who would think it would be a good thing if this incipient Antichrist (me) were put out of the way, and maybe one of them would take action. As a potential assassination target, I am about as "soft" as they get.

As for global human civilization, if my proposals for a Global Marshall Plan and a Federal Union of Democratic Nations continue to be unrecognized and ignored, this only means that the current unstable international regime will remain unstable, and there will be a higher probability of eventual disaster. But my wife and I are now in our sixties, and I often comment to her that "Most likely we will be safely in our graves long before things start really falling apart." So as far as me and my loved ones living peaceful, comfortable lives is concerned, the odds on that are no doubt higher if I remain just as unknown and anonymous as I am now.

Besides which, perhaps I *am* wrong about world government. I am not completely oblivious of the obvious implication of the fact that the overwhelming majority of humanity, from the political leadership and the intelligentsia on down, believes that any form of world government at all is both impractical and inadvisable at the present time, and will likely remain so into the foreseeable future. As I see it, there are two principal possibilities: either I am an unrecognized genius, or I am merely an unusually lucid crackpot. Of course I would prefer to believe the former, but I am sufficiently rational to recognize the distinct possibility that the latter is actually the case.

Although it ultimately turned out to be a rather painful false hope for me, I am nevertheless very appreciative of your good intentions, and very grateful for your efforts to bring my work to the attention of your fellow editors and the higher authorities (your "bosses") at the Council on Foreign Relations. And of course, if it ever comes about that the journal's inventory of worthy submissions is running a little low, feel free to call upon me to provide a few pages guaranteed to jolt your readers wide awake!

Daniel's reply to this was:

Sorry the news was not good. The best I can say is that the top editors (I'll refrain from using the sinister-sounding "bosses") gave your work a read and consideration. Best of luck placing the piece elsewhere, and happy holidays.

For obvious reasons, I was as reluctant to let this possibility go as I was reluctant to let go of the possibility that the *AER* would publish "Comprehensive Incentives Analysis." A few months after the above exchange, on April 13, 2009, I sent another lengthy appeal to Daniel Kurtz-Phelan under the subject "America's Public Relations." On April 16, Daniel replied with:

> Nice to hear from you. You make a decent case, but I'm sorry to say that it's extremely unlikely that something passed on once will get real consideration a second time. I'm happy to pass it up the chain, but I must say the odds are extremely long. On another note, I'm leaving *Foreign Affairs* shortly to join the Obama administration. I'll send out an email with new contact information soon, but at any rate, thanks for the opportunity to read your work.

I never heard anything more about the matter from anyone at the Council on Foreign Relations. That may have meant "No," or perhaps Daniel decided it would be a waste of time to "pass it up the chain." If so, I couldn't blame him. After all, it might not have been healthy for the Obama administration if it had become public knowledge that there was a "rabid one-worlder," Mr. Daniel Kurtz-Phelan, working in the U.S. State Department.

6

THE VISION IN PRINT: EARLY BOOKS

According to Wikipedia, "the Holy Grail is a vessel that constitutes an important motif in Arthurian literature. Different traditions describe it as a cup, dish, or stone with miraculous powers that provide happiness, eternal youth, or sustenance in infinite abundance. The term 'holy grail' is often used to denote an elusive object or goal that is sought for its great significance." This medieval legend marched on into the modern era, and variants of it are often featured in popular culture (e.g., *Indiana Jones and the Last Crusade*). No doubt many if not most of us have our own personal holy grails, varying in their nature but alike in being "an elusive object or goal that is sought for its great significance." In my own case, there has been throughout my adult life only one holy grail: a non-fiction bestseller containing a compellingly persuasive advocacy of one or more of my three visionary projects for a better world: pragmatic market socialism, a Global Marshall Plan, and the Federal Union of Democratic Nations.

It was a long, hard struggle, but eventually I did publish a number of books containing what I hoped would be "compellingly persuasive advocacies" of my visionary projects. The trouble was that none of them came within miles of being a bestseller. Between 1978 and 2018, I published a total of 15 books as follows (categorized by principal topic):

Pragmatic market socialism:

Socialism in the Free Market (268 pp., Nellen, 1978).
Socialism Revised and Modernized: The Case for Pragmatic Market Socialism (337 pp., Praeger, 1992).
Capitalism versus Pragmatic Market Socialism: A General Equilibrium Evaluation (152 pp., Kluwer, 1993).
Economic Justice: The Market Socialist Vision (391 pp., Rowman & Littlefield, 1997).
On the Political Economy of Market Socialism: Essays and Analyses (439 pp., Ashgate, 2001).

Capital Management Effort: Theory and Applications (271 pp., Ashgate, 2004).

Global Marshall Plan:

Common Progress: The Case for a World Economic Equalization Program (235 pp., Praeger, 2000).
Global Marshall Plan: Theory and Evidence (197 pp., Lexington, 2014).

Federal Union of Democratic Nations:

World Union on the Horizon: The Case for Supernational Federation (332 pp., University Press of America, 1993).
Rethinking World Government: A New Approach (279 pp., University Press of America, 2005).
Political Globalization: A New Vision of Federal World Government (404 pp., University Press of America, 2007).
The Grand Convergence: Economic and Political Aspects of Human Progress (246 pp., Palgrave Macmillan, 2010).
The Idea of World Government: From Ancient Times to the Twenty-First Century (128 pp., Routledge, 2011).
Beyond Global Governance: Prospects for Global Government (130 pp., University Press of America, 2014).
Evolutionary World Government: A Pragmatic Approach to Global Federation (347 pp., Hamilton, 2018).

The combined aggregate grand total for these 15 titles is a whopping 4,158 pages. Despite its volume, thus far this work has attracted no significant amount of attention. One image that continues to recur in my mind, concerning the publication of each and every one of these books, is that the effect of its publication has been equivalent to that of a single pebble tossed into the middle of the Atlantic Ocean. (Why the Atlantic Ocean? I don't really know. After all, the Pacific Ocean is even bigger.)

The phrase that I have used to describe the fate of every one of these 15 books is "instant oblivion." They sold a handful of copies, mostly to the largest university libraries, and elicited almost no reviews. I would estimate the total number of reviews to have been about a dozen, all in obscure professional journals. If I had to take a guess at the number of people in the world who have any acquaintance whatever with any of these books, it would probably be around 300, certainly not more than 500. In other words, I have never been able to reach a substantial audience.

Back in the 1960s and 70s during which I was first developing the ideas later put forward in these books, I would never have believed it possible that one could publish 15 books totaling 4,158 pages, and have the ideas within them remain almost totally unknown. What I did not realize, back then, was the sharp distinction, well known within the book publishing industry, between "trade titles" and "scholarly titles"—the latter otherwise known as "professional" or "specialized" titles. For the former, the publishers are aiming at a large market: 10,000 copies sold or more. For the latter, the publishers are aiming at a much smaller market. I cannot say exactly what the breakeven quantity sold is for these kind of books, but I would guess it would not be more than 500 copies. A "bestselling" scholarly book might sell as many as 2,000 to 2,500 copies. For a "trade title," on the other hand, 2,000 to 2,500 copies would be a resounding flop.

I suppose I should be grateful that there is a distinction in the book publishing industry between trade books and scholarly books. If the only kind of book that book publishers would consider publishing were trade books, the rather horrifying realization arises that I most likely would never have published even one single book. As things stand, numerous copies of my various books are out there, mostly far back in the stacks of the major university libraries, where they collect dust in lonely isolation. But at least they exist, and there is always the possibility that someday they will be "discovered," and consequently they might still have a beneficial effect on the future course of human history.

No doubt I should have been more aware of how high was the mountain I was trying to climb. After all, what makes a bestseller? First and foremost, bestsellers must be "good reads." What this normally means is a well-written, entertaining book that makes few demands on the reader's intellect or emotions. There should be little or nothing in conflict with the reader's current beliefs and preconceptions. As the reader reads, he or she should be continuously nodding and thinking: "Quite right! Yes, that is certainly true, I must fully agree with what the author is saying." Owing to the fact that my visionary ideas tend to go up against currently prevalent viewpoints, my books are not such that any contemporary reader, taken at random, who happens to encounter them will find them consistent with his/her current beliefs and preconceptions. Thus they are unlikely to be deemed "good reads."

Even at the outset, back in the 1960s and 70s, I thought I was reasonably well aware that what I was tackling would be very difficult to accomplish. As the years—and then decades—slowly passed, and as I continued to write and write and write—and eventually publish no less than 15 books adding up to no less than 4,158 pages, I gradually became more and more deeply aware of just *how difficult* was the task I had set myself. In fact, "difficult" is perhaps a somewhat inadequate term for what I had in mind.

Better, perhaps, would be "virtually impossible."

The trouble was (and remains) that my ideas for such things as pragmatic market socialism, a Global Marshall Plan, and the Federal Union of Democratic Nations, are so diametrically opposed to conventional judgments. It so happens that these conventional judgments are based on misunderstandings and misconceptions concerning the supposed evils of socialism, foreign aid, and world government. My specific proposals in these areas were formulated in full awareness of these supposed evils, and were explicitly designed to avoid them. In a word, the various well-known arguments against socialism, foreign aid, and world government, simply do not apply to pragmatic market socialism, the Global Marshall Plan, and the Federal Union of Democratic Nations. This is not to say that *no* sensible arguments can be made against these proposals—but it is to say that such arguments are quite weak when compared to the *imagined* strength of the well-known arguments.

From the original "New World" scheme of the early 1960s, pragmatic market socialism had been envisioned as the initial component of a grand design for improving the prospects of global human civilization. It required thirty years before I actually published a worthwhile book explaining and espousing pragmatic market socialism: *Socialism Revised and Modernized: The Case for Pragmatic Market Socialism*, published by Praeger in 1992. It so happened, however, that fourteen years prior to *Socialism Revised and Modernized*, the Nellen Publishing Company issued my first published book (1978) on pragmatic market socialism: *Socialism in the Free Market*. This book was derived entirely from material on pragmatic market socialism salvaged from the large unpublished manuscript written during the 1972-73 academic year: *The Grand Convergence: Economic and Political Aspects of Human Progress* (aka Grand Convergence I).

At the time, I had high hopes for *Socialism in the Free Market*. Unfortunately for those high hopes, the publisher Nellen turned out to be a shoestring operation conducted as a hobby by Eugene H. Nellen, whose day job was as a business professor at CCNY's Staten Island branch. Employees of the Nellen Publishing Company comprised exactly three people: Eugene H. Nellen, his wife Nancy, and one Robert A. Nicholas. Although I was promised the opportunity to inspect and correct the galley proofs, Mr. Nicholas never got around to sending them to me.

Thus when I finally received a copy of the completed book in October 1978, I was horrified. The book had been set in 8.5 Times New Roman type, a size normally utilized for footnotes. But the main problem was the incompetent copy editing and typesetting. The book was littered with typos, misspellings, and incorrect word usages. Some of the errors were veritable howlers. Over the next few days, with heavy heart I worked my way through the entire book. I tried hard to ignore editorial changes that I didn't like, but which could—using generous standards—be deemed correct. When completed, the list of errors with corrections ran to 32 single-spaced pages, documenting 544 errors over 240 pages of text. I sent the list to Eugene Nellen, with a covering letter threatening to disown the book entirely unless he had a corrected edition reprinted.

Reluctantly, Mr. Nellen acceded to my demand, and a corrected edition was eventually issued in December 1979. Unfortunately, it was almost as messy as the original edition. In those days, apparently, they did not have the electronic typesetting files that later became standard in the industry. Or if such files existed, they were not owned by the Nellen Publishing Company. Thus the corrections had been separately printed and pasted into position on the original printed galleys. Alas, the typeface of the corrections did not exactly match the original typeface: in fact, it was appreciably darker than the original, giving the effect of bolding. To a reader, the impression created by the sudden, inexplicable appearance of boldface in numerous locations, would have been analogous to the impression made by an orator who, for no discernible reason, suddenly starts shouting.

But long before the "corrected" edition was issued, I had effectively given up on *Socialism in the Free Market*. It was stillborn—a misfire. To begin with, even though it had been intended for a general reader, the text should have been backed up by a reasonable amount of documentation in the form of notes and references. I had plenty of documentation on hand, because by this time I had published several articles on market socialism in the professional literature. The main reason for dispensing with documentation was an effort to hold down the size of the manuscript. Next, there was the minuscule type size, which would not have been amiss in a telephone directory. Finally, even if the Nellen Publishing Company had had the resources to do a decent printing job, they would never have had the far larger resources necessary to support the book with a major promotional effort. I had hoped for a bestseller, but then as now, the editing and printing expenses of prospective bestsellers are minor relative to the marketing budget.

In fact, by late 1979 I had already been working for several months on a much larger book manuscript, intended to cover the entire vision from market socialism through to world government, under the working title *World Union on the Horizon*. According to the new plan, *Socialism in the Free Market*, at best, would have been a minor forerunner to this far weightier and more comprehensive contribution. The problem with corrections that did not match the original type was the final nail in the coffin of *Socialism in the Free Market*. There was no getting around the fact that the effort had been a complete failure, and in the future the less said about it, the better.

Following the *Socialism in the Free Market* debacle, my subsequent books, all 14 of them, were at least typographically respectable. Over the years, there were three "waves" of book publications. From the late 1970s and throughout most of the 1980s, I labored on a large manuscript, initially entitled *World Union on the Horizon*. The title was later changed to *Pragmatic Market Socialism: An Economic and Political Appraisal*, and the manuscript for it was completed in May 1988.

Although this manuscript proved too lengthy for publication, work on it provided the impetus to four books that were published from 1992 through 1997. These four books were the "first wave" of book publications, which will be described in the present chapter on "Early Books." Throughout much of the 1990s and into the 2000s, I labored on another large manuscript, initially entitled *The Next Step: A New Vision of Federal World Government*, and initially completed in May 2001. Later on the manuscript went through a number of title changes and alterations, before eventually being published in 2007, much condensed from the original draft, under the title *Political Globalization: A New Vision of Federal World Government*. The original *Next Step* manuscript was the impetus to a "second wave" of five books published between 2000 and 2007. A "third wave" consisted of another five books published between 2010 and 2018. The "second wave" and the "third wave" will be described in the following chapter on "Later Books."

The First Wave

During the fall semester of the 1978-79 academic year, I was on sabbatical. I had put in ten full academic years teaching at Western Illinois University, was competently performing my classroom duties, and had been continuously productive in research and writing for the last several years. According to the informal "once every seven years" principle, I was now fully qualified for a sabbatical.

The official stance of university administrators on sabbaticals is that they allow time for worthy, hard-working, hard-pressed faculty members to complete research projects which are then published to the benefit of humanity and the greater glory of the university. But there is nothing tangible backing up the official stance: professors are not subjected to financial or other penalties if they fail to publish research carried out during sabbaticals. In practice, sabbaticals normally amount to lengthy paid vacations, during which faculty refresh themselves with various forms of R & R, often involving travel. Still, in deference to the official stance, faculty are required to submit plans for research activity to be accomplished during their upcoming sabbaticals. It so happened that I had plenty of article projects available, some of which had already resulted in completed manuscripts, the topics of which could have been utilized for a research plan.

But I decided, perhaps a bit rashly, to be honest that my aspiration was toward something far more ambitious than just another article. In answer to the first query on the sabbatical application form ("Give a brief, layman's description of your proposed work"), I wrote:

> In today's world of nationalistic and ideological conflict, the concept of a world state is by turns invoked as the sole alternative to eventual nuclear disaster, and ridiculed and dismissed as a utopian illusion. For many years it has been my opinion that viable worldwide political unity in the relatively near future is far more practicable than most people believe. The two principal obstacles to international political unity at the moment are the ideological polarization between the Communist and non-Communist worlds, and the economic gap between the developed and underdeveloped worlds. I propose to show that opportunities exist, toward the elimination of both of these obstacles, which are inadequately understood at the present moment.
>
> The fundamental assumption is that a major worldwide disarmament agreement is possible literally at any moment, since the ideological conflict that motivates the arms race is the result of mental attitudes which are evolving in a hopeful direction. This refers to the "thaw" in international relations since the Stalin era, the "convergence" in the economic systems in East and West, and to the possibility of dramatic acceleration in this convergence if certain proposals which I make concerning the institutional realization of market socialism in the advanced capitalist nations are accepted. The release of economic resources from military expenditure would permit the expansion of capital aid gifts to less developed countries, resulting in the rapid acceleration of their development programs.

In response to following queries, I provided a thumbnail account of my efforts as far back as my 1960s essays, continuing through the large unpublished *Grand Convergence* manuscript from 1972-73, the incorporation of a substantial chunk of this manuscript into a book entitled *Socialism in the Free Market*, due to be published in 1978, and an existing 80-page article manuscript, completed in 1976, entitled "A Practical Proposal toward World Union" which had been submitted to the *Journal of Peace*

Research. On the whole, the five-page, single-spaced sabbatical application, submitted in October 1977, more or less bared my soul regarding my professional hopes and dreams. Looking back, I can see that that was a risky thing to have done. Or it might have been, had my claim on a sabbatical been weaker. Quite possibly, my five pages worth of soul-baring were never read by anyone. Quite possibly, the secretary in the provost's office who received the application took a quick look at the covering page, noted that I had been employed for ten years but had not yet received a sabbatical, and stamped it "Approved."

In actual fact, my fall 1978 sabbatical was probably more productive than is the norm for sabbaticals. I did what I had promised and got started on a large book manuscript that I hoped would realize my final objective (holy grail) of a non-fiction bestseller containing a compellingly persuasive exposition and advocacy of my grand design for human advance. My first attempt toward this objective had been the Grand Convergence I manuscript from the 1972-73 academic year. It had failed, but a substantial swatch of material from it had been used for *Socialism in the Free Market*, due to be released by the Nellen Publishing Company later that fall. Even before I became aware, later in the fall, of how badly Nellen had mangled *Socialism in the Free Market*, I was not very optimistic about the prospects of the book. Nellen was a very minor publisher, and moreover, *Socialism in the Free Market* contained far too much technical economics, and was far too narrowly focused on pragmatic market socialism. The really inspirational aspect of the grand design was the world government toward which it was ultimately directed. My intention in the fall of 1978 was to produce a large manuscript in which the case for world government would be developed in full and adequate detail—along with a plausible scenario, involving pragmatic market socialism, toward its foundation. The title of this book would be *World Union on the Horizon*.

As it happened, my achievement fell well short of what I had said in the sabbatical application: "I am confident that with one semester of uninterrupted effort, I could produce a complete or nearly complete book manuscript." I most definitely *did not* produce a "complete or nearly complete book manuscript." In fact, I barely broke ground for it. The sabbatical was in the fall of 1978, and it was only in 1985, seven years later, that I published in *World Futures* an article entitled "Practical Considerations in Designing a Supernational Federation" which was basically a somewhat condensed reworking of "A Practical Proposal toward World Union." As for a book, I eventually published *World Union on the Horizon: The Case for Supernational Federation* in 1993, some 16 years following the sabbatical. Moreover, the 1993 book was very much different from the book I was planning in the fall of 1978.

A completed manuscript for the book I planned in 1978 was finally finished and ready for submission to book publishers in June of 1988, almost ten years later. Ten years, of course, is a very long time for a book to be in development. The book took much longer to complete than I had anticipated, and it was also much longer than I had imagined it would be. The completed manuscript consisted of 1,338 double-spaced typed pages containing approximately 417,000 words. It was *not* entitled *World Union on the Horizon*; rather the title was *Pragmatic Market Socialism: An Economic and Political Appraisal*. Why the change?

Ironically enough, while my initial intention had been to de-emphasize pragmatic market socialism in favor of expanding the material on the world government proposal, when the time came, I found myself writing more and more and more about pragmatic market socialism. Possibly it was the fact that I am an economist, and had spent an enormous amount of time thinking about pragmatic market socialism. There was also the fact that the ideological impasse between communism and non-communism was the initial and main barrier to further progress. It was the logjam in the river of progress. If that logjam could be broken up, then the river could resume flowing freely. And pragmatic market socialism was the instrument with which I hoped to attack and break up the logjam. In any case, by 1986 I realized that if I was going to write as much on world government as I had already written on pragmatic market socialism, the result would be a massive, multi-volume tome that would almost certainly be unpublishable.

In its final form, *Pragmatic Market Socialism: An Economic and Political Appraisal* contained 12 chapters. Only Chapter 11 ("A Wider Perspective on the Issue") discussed the World Economic Equalization Program and the Federal Union of Democratic Nations. Chapter 11 contained approximately 38,000 words, whereas the great majority of the other approximately 379,000 words in the manuscript were focused almost exclusively on pragmatic market socialism. Given the disproportionate emphasis, using *World Union on the Horizon* as the title would have definitely been inappropriate.

Even though the final manuscript for *Pragmatic Market Socialism: An Economic and Political Appraisal* indeed constituted a very thick pile of paper, its size does not entirely explain why it required almost ten years to complete. The fact is that there was a lot going on that slowed me down and delayed completion of the book: a lot going on in both my personal life and my professional life, and also in the world at large. Probably the single most important reason for the long gestation period of *Pragmatic*

Market Socialism was the fact that I was constantly preoccupied with various article projects, many of which were directly related to the subject matter of the book. My master list of article projects shows some 43 new article manuscripts completed between 1978 and 1988, the interval during which I was working on the book: an average of almost four articles per year. The large volume of article work greatly constrained the amount of time I was able to devote to the book.

In addition, as the 1980s advanced, an extremely significant development was occurring in the wider world: specifically, the Soviets were talking more and more about fundamental economic and political reforms, reforms that could quite possibly guarantee world peace forevermore. From the point of view of humanity's basic survival probability, this was quite encouraging. On the downside for me personally, however, it suggested that perhaps the usefulness of pragmatic market socialism as a tool toward assuring world peace would soon be at an end. If the Soviets abandoned communism, such a transition would significantly reduce the impediments to world government. At the same time it would suggest that I had wasted a lot of time working on pragmatic market socialism. Well, perhaps the time had not been *entirely* wasted—after all, pragmatic socialism was a good idea strictly in its own right. But the work had not had the full value I had expected. Such ambivalent thoughts were running through my mind as I put the final touches on *Pragmatic Market Socialism: An Economic and Political Appraisal*.

Finally, the moment of truth approached. A plan of attack was formulated and put into action. Western Illinois University had two copy centers at the time, one in Sherman Hall for administrative use, and the other in Stipes Hall for academic use. At the cost of $107, I had 25 copies made by the Stipes Hall copy center of the proposal material: title page, table of contents, preface, and Chapter 1. I also made five copies of the full manuscript, all 1,338 pages of it, to send to any publishers who might be interested in the proposal material.

Although I never had any direct experience of an editorial office, it seems reasonable that quite often decisions on submitted manuscripts are based on the covering letter and the first few pages of proposal material. There follows, in order, the initial covering letter, the table of contents, and the first two paragraphs of Chapter 1:

> Dear Sirs/Madams:
>
> I am presently seeking a publisher for a recently completed book entitled <u>Pragmatic Market Socialism: An Economic and Political Appraisal</u>. This substantial volume, the culmination of a program of intensive thought and study commenced more than 25 years ago, will

perhaps ultimately be recognized as the single most significant contribution to the socialism-capitalism controversy made during the twentieth century.

You have every right to be skeptical of this statement--nevertheless I urge you to give this proposal your most serious attention. Enclosed herewith find the following: my professional resume, a detailed table of contents of Pragmatic Market Socialism, and a copy of Chapter 1.

As you can see from my resume, I have spent my entire working career as an academic economist at a regional university in the Midwest. My teaching responsibilities have mostly been in analytical economics courses. Since 1972, I have published nearly 50 articles in a wide variety of professional journals both in economics and other disciplines.

The proposals put forward in Pragmatic Market Socialism are extraordinarily bold and visionary. Despite this, they are sufficiently rational and coherent that I have been able to discuss them in numerous published articles in the professional literature. Appended to this letter is a list of those of my published articles which are directly relevant to the subject matter of Pragmatic Market Socialism. This lengthy list demonstrates that a great many qualified individuals have found this line of thought interesting and stimulating.

However, I have not yet achieved that critical mass of published writing necessary to project these ideas out of the realm of narrowly specialized discourse and into the wider arena of public discussion. My articles are widely scattered over a number of periodicals, and each one of them deals with a narrowly circumscribed topic--not with the concept as a whole.

One might envision the potential impact of a comprehensive development and examination of the entire concept within a single, large, handsomely printed volume. Pragmatic Market Socialism might attain the status of a seminal contribution--a classic--in which case sales of the book would remain strong for years and decades to come.

The entire manuscript is complete at this time, and I would be happy to send you a copy at your request. Thanking you in advance for your consideration of my proposal, I am,
Sincerely yours,

List of published articles directly relevant to Pragmatic Market Socialism: An Economic and Political Appraisal:

“Capital Management under Market Socialism,” Review of Social Economy 32(2): 196-210, October 1974.

“A Survey of Market Socialist Forms,” Annals of Public and Cooperative Economy 46(2): 131-162, April-June 1975.

"A World Economic Equalization Program: Results of a Simulation," Journal of Developing Areas 10(2): 159-179, January 1976.
"On the Potential Efficiency of Market Socialism," ACES Bulletin (Association for Comparative Economic Studies) 18(2): 25-52, Summer 1976.
"The Social Dividend under Market Socialism," Annals of Public and Cooperative Economy 48(1): 91-133, January-March 1977.
"Investment Propensities under Capitalism and Market Socialism," Rivista Internazionale di Scienze Economiche e Commerziali 25(10): 842-855, October 1978.
"The Microeconomic Efficiency Argument for Socialism Revisited," Journal of Economic Issues 13(1): 73-112, March 1979.
"The Microeconomic Efficiency of Market Socialism: Reply," Journal of Economic Issues 15(1): 220-227, March 1981.
"Ideological Harmonization as a Means of Promoting Authentic Detente: A False Hope?" Co-Existence 19(2): 158-176, October 1982.
"The People's Capitalism Thesis: A Skeptical Evaluation," ACES Bulletin (Association for Comparative Economic Studies) 24(4): 1-47, Winter 1982.
"The Distribution of Lifetime Capital Property Income under Capitalism and Market Socialism," ACES Bulletin (Association for Comparative Economic Studies) 26(2): 77-97, Summer-Fall 1984.
"Practical Considerations in Designing a Supernational Federation," World Futures 21(3/4): 159-218, 1985.
"A Market Socialist Critique of Capitalism's Dynamic Performance," Journal of Economic Issues 20(1): 63-86, March 1986.
"Would Democracy Survive under Market Socialism?" Polity 18(4): 678-695, Summer 1986.
"Risk-Taking as a Justification for Property Income," Journal of Comparative Economics 12(1): 74-88, March 1988.
"On the Morality of Capitalism: In Light of the Market Socialist Alternative," Forum for Social Economics 17(2): 23-39, Spring 1988.
"A New Perspective on Market Socialism," Comparative Economic Studies 30(2), 69-116, Summer 1988.
"A World Economic Equalization Program: Refinements and Sensitivity Analysis," World Development 16(8): 921-933, August 1988.
"Investment Analysis by the Individual Investor," Quarterly Review of Economics and Business, forthcoming. (With T. Krehbiel).

PRAGMATIC MARKET SOCIALISM: AN ECONOMIC AND POLITICAL APPRAISAL

Contents

Preface x

Part I: A Proposal for Pragmatic Market Socialism
Chapter 1: Introduction
A. An Overview of the Proposal 1
B. An Overview of the Study 29
Chapter 2: An Essay in Definition
A. Some Essential Terminology 100
B. Common Misconceptions of Socialism 119
C. The Essence of Socialism 141
Chapter 3: The Basic Proposals
A. Transition and Compensation 149
B. The Social Dividend 160
C. Exceptions to Socialism 168
D. The Bureau of Public Ownership 175
E. A Critique of Alternative Market Socialist Plans 188
F. The Protection of Democracy 204
G. Pragmatic Market Socialism and Contemporary Capitalism: Elements in Common 219
Chapter 4: Auxiliary Proposals
A. Introduction 257
B. Investment 261
C. Industrial Concentration 279
D. Taxation 292
E. Regulation 300
F. Inflation 314
G. Anticyclical Policy 329
H. Employment 337
I. Pensions 344
Chapter 5: The Benefits of Socialism
A. A Disclaimer of Utopianism 349
B. Equalized Distribution of Property Return 376
C. Higher Economic Efficiency 404
D. More Authentic Democracy 451

Part II: A Critique of Capitalist Apologetics
Chapter 6: An Overview of Capitalist Apologetics
A. Introduction 469
B. Characteristics of Capitalist Apologetics 481

C. Challenging Capitalist Apologetics 511
Chapter 7: Return to Capital Management
A. Introduction 520
B. The Capital Management Argument....................................... 528
C. Marxian Exploitation Theory... 540
D. Non-Marxist Theory of Unearned Property Return............... 552
E. Theoretical Formulation of the Capital Management Problem 569
F. The Separation of Ownership and Management 595
G. Institutional Investors and Capital Markets 613
H. Non-Capitalist Production in Non-Communist Nations 634
I. Non-Capitalist Production in Communist Nations.................. 656
Chapter 8: Return to Saving
A. Introduction 676
B. A Theoretical Formulation of the Saving Problem 705
C. The Potential Need for Government Intervention.................. 735
D. An Addendum: The "Return to Past Labor" Variant............. 747
Chapter 9: People's Capitalism
A. Introduction 753
B. The Distribution of Current Capital Wealth........................... 766
C. The Distribution of Lifetime Capital Wealth 795
D. Determinants of Capital Wealth Mobility 809
Chapter 10: Non-Economic Arguments for Capitalism
A. Capitalism as a Bulwark of Democracy 867
B. Capitalism and the Quality of Life... 910

Part III: Concluding Thoughts
Chapter 11: A Wider Perspective on the Issue
A. Introduction 956
B. Ideological Harmonization and Authentic Détente................ 968
C. A World Economic Equalization Program 1014
D. The Federal Union of Democratic Nations.......................... 1039
E. Conclusion 1073
Chapter 12: On the Question of Implementation
A. The Basis for Hope.. 1082
B. The Human Interest Society... 1088
C. The Role of Economists... 1099
D. Beyond Economics.. 1117
E. A Final Word 1122

Analytical Appendix
A. Marxian Exploitation Theory 1127
B. The Capital Management Problem 1131
C. The Saving Problem 1149

D. A World Economic Equalization Program 1165

Notes 1179
References 1273
Index 1312
About the Author 1338

Chapter 1: Introduction
A. An Overview of the Proposal

In this book I propose to re-examine the issue of socialism versus capitalism in light of the pragmatic market socialist alternative. The basic idea of pragmatic market socialism is neither original nor complex. But perhaps owing partially to its very simplicity, it has not yet been systematically developed, either by social scientists or ideologues. In the mountainous literature on socialism, whether it be professional or polemical in nature, references to the pragmatic market socialist concept are rare and usually tangential. It has been my primary aim, throughout my career as an academic economist, to rectify this situation. Starting with the publication of "Capital Management under Market Socialism" in the *Review of Social Economy* in 1974, I have produced a steady stream of articles on the various issues and questions raised by the pragmatic market socialist alternative. Although my personal judgment on the pragmatic market socialist alternative is certainly favorable, I have endeavored to avoid a dogmatic and excessively enthusiastic tone in my writing on the subject. My position is certainly not that any reasonable and objective judge must perceive the preferability of pragmatic market socialism over contemporary capitalism. Rather it is merely that the case to be made for pragmatic market socialism is sufficiently impressive to merit serious and deliberate consideration by all those with some genuine larger concern over the contemporary human condition and the future prospects confronting mankind.

The motivation behind pragmatic market socialism is as elementary as the concept itself. It is to preserve all that is healthy, positive and productive about the modern market capitalist economy, while purging it of the ethical perversity embodied in the extremely unequal distribution of unearned property return. By "property return" is meant various forms of non-labor income, principally dividends, interest and capital gains. In the modern market capitalist economy, labor income, principally wages and salaries, is quite unequally distributed—but inequality in labor income distribution is veritably dwarfed by inequality in property income distribution. An excessively large proportion of property return is received by extremely wealthy capitalists, many if not most of whom founded their capital fortunes on inheritances. The

> contemporary capitalist system makes possible the phenomenon of the inheriting playboy or playgirl—the individual who inherits great wealth and then proceeds to live a lifetime of ease and luxury, without ever making a positive social contribution in the form of work. It is difficult to refrain from applying the terrible epithet "parasite" to individuals in this category. While opinions differ as to the prevalence of the phenomenon under contemporary capitalism, it cannot reasonably be denied that the phenomenon exists under contemporary capitalism. And while the defenders of capitalism may argue that there is no serious harm in the phenomenon, they can hardly assert that the phenomenon possesses positive social value. Indeed, for the vast majority of us who *must* work in order to eat, it seems natural and legitimate to ask the question of whether a viable alternative might exist to a system which tolerates economic parasitism.

The first proposal mailing went out on June 14, 1988, and was sent to five publishers: Macmillan, St. Martin's, Allen and Unwin, Oxford UP, and Basil Blackwell. When none of the first five expressed interest, the second mailing went out on August 12, 1988, to Auburn House, Westview Press, Cambridge UP, Ballinger, M. E. Sharpe, Kluwer, MIT Press, Lexington, Norton, and Columbia UP. The second mailing was "enhanced" in two ways: (1) the covering letter was addressed to specific editors; (2) there was a slight change in the beginning and the end of the covering letter. As to editors' names, back in those long-ago days, one did not have the Internet as a source for a prodigious amount of specific information. I had purchased a print copy of *The Literary Marketplace*, only to find that it contained information only for those publishers who had responded to their questionnaire—and many if not most of them had not. I telephoned one publishing house to ask to whom specifically I should send my proposal. This inquiry apparently astonished whoever it was I was speaking to, but it eventually elicited the unhelpful information that it should be sent to the "editorial department."

By the time of the second mailing, I had concluded that submitting book proposals to the "editorial department" was probably not the optimal way to proceed. Thereafter, by any means necessary, I obtained the names of specific editors for each publishing house to whom the proposal was submitted. I also made some changes to the initial and concluding paragraphs of the covering letter. Finally, owing to the prodigious length of the manuscript, I also mentioned that I would be amenable to some degree of condensation should that be necessary.

Whether the offer to condense the manuscript did any good in terms of publication probability, I don't know. But even if it did have a positive effect, it was not strong enough to elicit a contract. Still, compared to the publication effort on *The Grand Convergence* some 15 years earlier, the publication effort on *Pragmatic Market Socialism* was considerably more professional and (so it seemed at the time) far more promising. This time the entire manuscript was complete at the time the proposal was submitted, even to the inclusion of a draft index. My professional credentials were much stronger, consisting as they did of approximately 50 journal articles, of which almost 20 were directly related to the subject matter of the book. Moreover, the submitted proposal material for *Pragmatic Market Socialism* was far less bulky and intimidating than the "Grand Convergence Sampler" had been.

However, the two books did have some very important characteristics in common: they contained highly controversial proposals for the improvement of the human condition, they were extremely long, and their author was totally unknown to the general public, and only marginally known within the economics profession. Perhaps if the book had been authored by the likes of John Kenneth Galbraith or Michael Harrington, it would have been published. I'll never know.

The third and final proposal mailing was sent out on March 19, 1990, to Rowman & Littlefield, Basil Blackwell, St. Martin's, Lynne Rienner, Basic Books, Greenwood Press, Routledge Chapman and Hall, Johns Hopkins UP, and M. E. Sharpe. The rejection letters from the publishers elicited by all three of these proposal mailings were almost invariably polite, often complimented the project, and usually offered best wishes for its publication elsewhere. Somewhat over half the letters mentioned the length of the manuscript as a major impediment to publication. The rejection letter from Spencer Carr of Westview Press, dated August 19, 1988, was typical of the genre:

> Thank you for your letter and proposal to publish your study of market socialism. I regret that we cannot express interest in the project. Partly it is that we cannot agree with you about the degree of interest in market socialism at this time. But primarily the economics of publishing is such that it is impossible for us to even consider publishing what would probably be an 800 page book on this topic. I know that you have put an enormous amount of work into this project, and I hope that you find a publisher, perhaps a university press, able to take a different view of it.

Of the 23 publishing houses to which the unsolicited proposal material was sent, only one requested to see the full manuscript. That request, dated May 7, 1990, came from Simon Winder, executive editor at St. Martin's Press. After almost two full years of having demoralizing rejection letters slowly drift in, one every month or so, my hopes were nearing rock bottom. Nevertheless, they were somewhat revived by this nibble from St. Martin's. My covering letter for the full manuscript was quite upbeat about the potential interest of the subject matter, plus I laid particular emphasis on my willingness to drastically condense the manuscript.

On June 13, Mr. Winder responded that while they found the topic to be quite interesting, and they appreciated the effort that had gone into the project, in the end they simply could not consider such a massive manuscript. In response to my offer to reduce the size, he said that such a drastic reduction would be necessary that it would have to be a very different book. He concluded by saying that should I ever produce a much smaller book on market socialism, St. Martin's would be happy to consider it.

In actual fact, the idea of breaking down the 1,338 pages of *Pragmatic Market Socialism: An Economic and Political Appraisal* into two or more much shorter books had been percolating in my mind ever since the first rejection letters on the early submissions started drifting in during the summer of 1988. One book would be devoted to pragmatic market socialism, and another to world government. But it wasn't until the summer of 1990, two years later, that I finally started work on this plan. There were the usual reasons for the delay: most importantly, continuing work on a sheaf of article projects. Finally, in the summer of 1990, galvanized by the short-lived hope aroused in May by St. Martin's request to see the entire manuscript of *Pragmatic Market Socialism*, I resolved that the time had come to move on—to start work on the successor volumes.

Socialism Revised and Modernized

The first successor volume was *Socialism Revised and Modernized: The Case for Pragmatic Market Socialism*. Work on this new manuscript proceeded from the late summer of 1990 to December of that year. I could have used material taken verbatim from the 1,338-page *Pragmatic Market Socialism* manuscript, but I decided to write the new manuscript from scratch. So much condensation would have been required that I thought it easier just to compose new prose. However, the concepts, proposals, and arguments were exactly the same as those in the large manuscript. I included in the new manuscript not only most of the "Analytical Appendix" (renamed "Analytical Models") from the big *Pragmatic Market Socialism* manuscript, but added to it a very substantial "Theoretical Appendix" consisting of an adaptation of a large, unpublished article manuscript for which I had been trying to find an outlet for years: "A General Equilibrium Evaluation of Capitalism versus Pragmatic Market Socialism." This article was based on the most theoretically sophisticated research I had ever done (and ever would do) on the question of the relative performance of pragmatic market socialism versus contemporary capitalism. Since I was having great difficulty finding a publisher for this article (among its other liabilities, as perceived by editors and referees, was its great length), maybe I could "slip it into print" as part of a book.

The completed manuscript came to a mere 493 double-spaced pages, a very big improvement over the 1,338 pages of *Pragmatic Market Socialism: An Economic and Political Appraisal.* Of course, I had not forgotten the interest in the large book displayed by Simon Winder of St. Martin's Press several months earlier. As I had promised, on January 4, 1991, I sent off the entire manuscript of the new and improved (i.e. shorter) treatment of pragmatic market socialism to Mr. Winder. Unfortunately, shorter length was not sufficient to change their minds. Mr. Winder's expression of regret was dated January 21, 1991:

> I have now had a chance to read your revised manuscript.
>
> I am afraid that we must continue to decline publication. Our problem is simply that we cannot see a large enough audience which we can reach. Your book would seem much more at home with a publisher such as Hill & Wang or Basic Books or Pantheon who have a reputation for producing large, thoughtful books in this field. We really just do not have that reputation ourselves and your book would be lost on our list.
>
> I am sorry we are unable to help and I am returning your ms under separate cover. Good luck with placing it elsewhere.

Rats! Oh well, it is not that I had had little previous experience with expressions of regret from potential publishers. After all, after continual battering, one's ego begins to form a certain amount of protective armor. Immediately I set to work, and on February 1, a proposal mailing was sent off to no less than nine potential publishers. To Westview Press belongs the distinction of being the first to reject this new offering. (The total number of rejections from the February 1 mailing was five—three publishers never responded.) Spencer Carr's unusually sympathetic rejection letter, dated February 7, reached me on February 11:

> Thank you for your letter and proposal to publish your manuscript on pragmatic market socialism. I have enjoyed reading through your admirably well prepared prospectus, and I am convinced that you have useful, even important, things to say.
>
> But I regret that, for some of the very reasons specified in your own evaluation of today's intellectual climate, I do not see sufficient market to make this project work in the context of a commercial press program. I think it would be difficult to gain the attention of the people

> who would most profit from reading this book.
>
> I suggest that you try university presses with congenial lists, and SUNY, Temple, and Rutgers come to mind first off. I wish you well placing this with one of these or some other appropriate publisher.

Oh no, I thought—here we go again: the usual apologetic sentiments, combined with the usual useless advice.

But then, around the middle of February, something unexpected happened. I had sent the proposal to Cynthia Harris, executive director of Greenwood Press, and Ms. Harris wrote back to say she had forwarded the proposal to one of their subsidiaries, Praeger Publishers, who might have an interest in it. A few days after I received this communication, a letter arrived from James R. Dunton, editor-in-chief at Praeger, asking me to send him the entire manuscript. Could this be it?! Could this—*finally*—be it?! Better not get too excited. After all, shortly before, Simon Winder of St. Martin's had looked at the entire manuscript, and had regretfully declined interest. That could well be the outcome this time around.

And then, on March 18, 1991, it happened! A letter arrived in the office mail from James R. Dunton. From much experience I had learned that rejection letters come in very thin envelopes—the typical rejection letter takes up only a small part of one sheet of letterhead. This envelope was different: it was much fatter, indicating that there was something more than one page inside. Taking it back to my office for privacy, I held it up to the light and peered at it. I could see a bit of print—something about a "royalty schedule." Wow! They definitely do *not* talk about royalty schedules in rejection letters! I ripped open the envelope and beheld the following glorious message:

> I have now had an opportunity to review your work, and it looks quite good. I have had a contract immediately drawn up, therefore, and enclose it herewith.
>
> Please review the agreement carefully, and should you have any questions, do not hesitate to call. Otherwise, merely sign on page four, where indicated, and return the document directly to me for countersigning. You will then receive a copy of the fully-signed agreement, and our joint endeavor will have begun.

At that time, both my wife Penny and I had window offices on the fourth floor of Stipes Hall. As she was chairman of the accountancy department, Penny's office was much bigger than mine and had a lot more window frontage. Our respective offices were on opposite sides of the building, less than a minute's walk apart. Thus whenever anything interesting happened to one of us, he or she would immediately head over to the other's office to share the news. When I handed Mr. Dunton's letter to Penny, her eyes opened wide and she got all red in the face. Some men are blessed with steadfastly supportive wives—I have been one of them.

Both Penny and I recognized this development as a very big step in the right direction—but there were a few things about it that kept our joy from being completely unrestrained. For one thing, I had had the experience, back in 1978, of getting a book published (*Socialism in the Free Market* by the Nellen Publishing Co.) that was so miserably produced that I normally did not even include it on my professional résumé. But my biggest single immediate concern was Clause 21, typewritten at the end of the printed contract, specifying that the author must provide "camera-ready copy" for the entire book. In later years I became more than familiar with camera-ready copy (CRC)—in fact, I have provided CRC for most of my published books. But at the time the concept was new to me, and I was shocked and horrified. Praeger was a reputable publisher, and I knew for a fact that most of their books were beautifully typeset. But I also knew that not all of them were.

In fact, there were two books in particular that Praeger had published that had been authored by people I knew well: my wife, and my father. In 1982 Praeger had published Penny's dissertation: *Transfer Pricing and Performance Evaluation in Multinational Corporations: A Survey Study*, and in 1983 they had published my father's post-retirement contribution to business how-to literature: *Integrating Acquisitions: Making Corporate Marriages Work*. What worried me was that neither Penny's book nor my Dad's book had been professionally typeset. They were in the "Praeger Special Studies" category, for which the authors provided typed pages. Any experienced reader will instantly recognize the difference between typed pages and typeset pages, and the former suffers badly from the comparison. A typed book is something less than a "real" book.

My immediate thought was, I am faced with a serious quandary here: either I give them typed output, in which case the book is doomed from the outset, or I give them typeset output obtained—at enormous expense—from a professional typesetting firm. Because of this and other concerns, I did not immediately sign and return the contract enclosed with Mr. Dunton's letter. Instead, on March 19, 1991, the day after receiving the contract offer, I wrote him a lengthy letter, the opening paragraph of which was as follows:

> Thank you very much for your letter of March 13, 1991, and for the enclosed contract concerning Socialism Revised and Modernized: The Case for Pragmatic Market Socialism. Naturally I am very anxious to sign a contract and get on with it. Before doing so, however, I would

> very much like to clarify a few points. Although I don't want to seem like a difficult author, the fact is that for me, this book is the work of a lifetime. As I approach that great watershed of 50 years of age, it has become fully apparent that pragmatic market socialism is the only important economic idea that I will ever have. Therefore this book is the only chance I will ever have to make a significant impression on economics in particular and on social science generally. It is especially important that the printed book reflect the effort which I the author have put into it, and that it represent something of my aspirations with regard to the various concepts and proposals with which it deals.

I can envision only too clearly how James R. Dunton's eyes must have rolled around in their sockets at this impertinent missive. Talk about an uppity author! Looking back at it, I must offer my sincere gratitude to Mr. Dunton for not immediately canceling the contract offer.

Following the initial paragraph, I went into great detail about my concerns, and offered much specific advice on how they should regard this book, and how they should produce and market it. First and foremost, they should recognize that *Socialism Revised and Modernized* is far more than the usual scholarly treatise—it might well become a trade bestseller, such as *The Affluent Society* by John Kenneth Galbraith or *The Other America* by Michael Harrington. But in order to realize its full potential, I wrote, it must be a substantial volume—not significantly condensed from the present manuscript. Also it should be popularly priced: something in the $30 to $40 range, rather than the $60 to $100 range applied to many academic books. Last but not least, it must be *typeset*. With respect to typesetting, I had had no prior experience with desktop publishing (DTP), and I doubted my ability to master this technology sufficiently in the available time to produce acceptable output. And so on and so forth.

I'm fairly sure that James R. Dunton did not read this entire letter, and it is probably a good thing that he did not. A few days after sending it off, I received a telephone call from him (in my diary, I commented that it was rather like getting "a telephone call from God"), in which he claimed he hardly knew where to begin to respond to my *very* long letter—perhaps it would save time if I just asked him a few questions orally, to which he would respond, likewise orally. The telephone call lasted about ten minutes, and while I wouldn't go so far as to say that Mr. Dunton "read me the riot act," he was quite firm and decisive. In my diary, I paraphrased his overall tone as being somewhat along the following lines: "Listen up, you insignificant pipsqueak of a no-account author. You are a complete twerp if you don't realize how lucky you are to get this opportunity. Take it or leave it—and if you leave it, we won't lose any sleep over it." So that was that. Of course, I had had far too many rejection letters in the past on my various book submissions to leave it—I took their offer. Following that telephone call, I decided that it would be in my best interest to be a "good little boy" as a Praeger author: ready, willing, and eager to please, whatever their desires might be. I did my best to adhere to this principle over the following year, although I'm sure the people at Praeger who became familiar with me did not consider me an especially docile and compliant author.

To his credit, James R. Dunton's tone was not peremptorily dictatorial throughout our telephone conversation. On the critical issue of typesetting, for example, he assured me that desktop publishing had come a long way in the last few years, and they were finding that nearly all of their authors were providing CRC that was indistinguishable from professional typesetting. He was confident that I would have no problem with this aspect of the process. Possibly I might have to hire a specialist, but it was more likely that I could handle the chore myself. He added that an advantage for the author was the ability to have complete control over the appearance of the printed output. And within a short period of time, I ascertained for myself that Mr. Dunton was indeed quite correct on this critical matter.

My first thought was Raylene Prentice, of WIU's Center for Business and Economic Research, an operation directed by Dick Hattwick, an economics department colleague. Mrs. Prentice was responsible for typesetting the *Journal of Behavioral Economics*, which at that time was being published by Western Illinois University. Neither the content nor the typesetting of the *JBE* could be considered first-rate, but the latter seemed basically adequate. Mrs. Prentice typeset a few pages from my book, including some fairly complicated mathematical material, as an example of what she could accomplish. Her samples were fairly impressive, but she would be working off regular hours as an independent: thus her doing the entire book would involve quite a hefty expense.

I asked her what she was using, and she told me the software was Ventura Publisher from Xerox, and the hardware was a Hewlett-Packard LaserJet III. It so happened that a LaserJet III could be purchased for about $1,400, and Ventura Publisher for about $600. So for an outlay of around $2,000, I would have everything I needed to do the job myself. Penny agreed that it would be a worthwhile investment in the future, and so I went ahead with the purchases. The DOS-based Ventura Publisher desktop publishing program had quite an abbreviated commercial lifespan. The first version was released in 1986, and within about ten years it was pretty much obsolete, its capabilities having mostly been incorporated into various Windows-based word processors that were easier to use. But at the time, unexpectedly confronted as I was by the need to provide camera-ready copy for *Socialism Revised and Modernized*, it was a godsend.

On the downside, Ventura Publisher was not notable for ease-of-use, and it required several weeks of hard work as I climbed painfully up its steep learning curve. One of Ventura's selling points was that it could import files from several major word processing programs, and any editing changes in Ventura could then be written back into the original word processing files. The problem was that *Socialism Revised and Modernized* had been written using ChiWriter—which was not a "major" word processing program. So this particular "selling point" was not relevant to my case. ChiWriter could export ASCII files that could be imported as straight text by Ventura Publisher, but any editing changes in the Ventura files could not be written back into ChiWriter files. Another downside was that mathematical expressions had to be written into Ventura files using a rather complicated text editing system that frequently involved a great deal of trial-and-error to get the expressions exactly right.

As one might expect, getting material from ChiWriter into Ventura Publisher was a laborious chore. Nevertheless, I used this procedure not only for *Socialism Revised and Modernized: The Case for Pragmatic Market Socialism*, published by Praeger in 1992, but also for *Capitalism versus Pragmatic Market Socialism: A General Equilibrium Evaluation*, published by Kluwer Academic Publishers in 1993, and for *World Union on the Horizon: The Case for Supernational Federation*, published by University Press of America, also in 1993. In fact, within a couple of months of commencing my desktop publishing activity, I was envisioning eventually applying the methodology to two large future projects. One would be a typeset rendition of the "big book" (*Pragmatic Market Socialism: An Economic and Political Appraisal*), and the other would be a compendium of my published articles on market socialism to be entitled *On the Political Economy of Market Socialism: Essays and Analyses*. I never got around to the first of these, but I did accomplish the second, which was published by Ashgate in 2001. However, *Essays and Analyses* was not done using Ventura Publisher—by that time I was using Microsoft Word for Windows, whose typesetting capabilities were on a par with those of Ventura, while being much easier to use.

In my March 19 letter to James R. Dunton, I had raised three specific issues relevant to my perception of *Socialism Revised and Modernized* as a potential trade bestseller: size (it had to be a substantial tome), price (it should be low), and typesetting (I preferred that they take care of that). In the subsequent telephone consultation on March 21, Mr. Dunton laid out the "facts of life" re publishing my book, such as they were and would remain. First and foremost, I should get it through my head once and for all that my book could never be a trade bestseller. There was no such thing as a mass market for it: it was a scholarly contribution pure and simple, with a very limited market among libraries and a handful of specialists. He envisioned a first printing of 1,000 copies, and he doubted very much that the first printing would sell out. (As far as I know, he was right about that. I only received one royalty statement from Praeger: as of June 1993, it had sold 309 copies.) On the typesetting matter, I was told that that had to be done by me, it could not and would not be done by them. On the price matter, I was told that pricing was a matter for the publisher to decide, and any input from the author was unlikely to be helpful.

With respect to length, the submitted manuscript was 493 typed pages long, while the contract specified that the final version was to be no more than 500 typed pages in length. One might have thought, therefore, that there would be no problem about length. But there was. The specification in the contract was for 500 *double-spaced* pages, and this created a problem, since a fair amount of material in the original submitted manuscript had been single-spaced: quotes, notes, and references. All this single-spaced material would now have to be double-spaced. The upshot was that to accommodate the iron-clad "double-spacing throughout" commandment, a substantial amount of material had to be jettisoned. The main thing to go was the Theoretical Appendix ("A General Equilibrium Evaluation of Capitalism versus Pragmatic Market Socialism"), but that wasn't enough. In addition, the scholarly apparatus (notes and references) had to be pruned considerably. In typeset form, the final published version of *Socialism Revised and Modernized* was 337 pages long; if all the deleted material had been retained, it probably would have been closer to 375 pages. One takes what one can get.

By the middle of April 1991, copies of the signed and countersigned contract were in both my files and Praeger's files. The physical book itself became available in April 1992, approximately one year later. My relations with the various people at Praeger who became involved with my book during that year, starting with James R. Dunton, editor-in-chief, and going all the way down to Beth Wilson, the copy editor assigned to my manuscript, remained basically civil, but they were hardly warm and cuddly. Apparently it hurt their feelings that I was not particularly happy about my book being treated as a scholarly treatise of interest mainly to library acquisitions personnel. They found it difficult to understand how I could possibly envision my book in any other way. Their point of view on the issue was nicely summarized in the following ex cathedra pronouncement in James R. Dunton's letter to me dated February 26, 1992:

> Thank you for your letter of February 17. I am a bit concerned that you remain so troubled by our approach to your book. I took great pains to explain to you how we viewed this book and how it would be handled before I agreed to publish it. We discussed this at some length over the telephone on at least two occasions prior to the publishing contract being signed. And the approach we have subsequently taken is precisely that described at the outset.
>
> As indicated in my letter of February 11 and in earlier conversations, we consider your work to be a fine addition to the scholarly literature, and we are proud to be publishing it. We do not, however, consider it to be a trade book -- not in terms of commerciality of topic, style of writing, or name recognition of the author -- not by any criteria. This distinction is at the heart of the publishing decision. The list price of $45.95 for this book, therefore, has been set based upon (1) a recognition of the type of book it is, and (2) the economic realities of publishing such scholarly works.
>
> As to the matter of price elasticity which you raise once again, we have found there to be very little in this sort of publishing. And we do have some experience in the matter. (Please be assured that if the simple price elasticities you describe were at work in scholarly publishing, we and our competitors would be taking advantage of them. To the contrary: the prices for our scholarly books fall squarely in the middle range when compared to those of our competitors.)
>
> To conclude then, our pricing of and approach to your book is appropriate, indeed typical for the sort of scholarly work that it truly is. Such an approach does not mean that we deem your book or any other of our scholarly works to have "poor sales prospects." Rather, it means that we have a realistic and objective view of the market for the books we publish. And that view is based upon long experience.
>
> Perhaps understandably, authors sometimes lack the degree of realism and objectivity which their publishers must maintain. In those instances, publisher and author must simply agree to disagree and, hopefully, focus upon more productive matters. Given that this issue has been so thoroughly explicated both prior to and since you made the decision to place your book with Praeger, I would hope we could now move on. Yours is a good book, and there is much yet to do.

Well, of course I couldn't be too upset about this pronouncement. After all, Mr. Dunton had allowed that *Socialism Revised and Modernized* was a "good book" and they were "proud to be publishing it." By this time I had already submitted camera-ready copy for the entire book, and having done it myself I was quite satisfied with it, and unless there was some kind of weird accident at the printing factory, I could not possibly suffer a repetition of the horror of finding out (as I had with *Socialism in the Free*

Market back in 1978) that the publisher had mangled my book almost beyond recognition. *Socialism Revised and Modernized* would be a respectable book that I could put on my résumé without apology. And there were plenty of books left in me. This book was a good start, and hopefully my future books would do better. Maybe one of them would be the holy grail: a non-fiction bestseller.

There was nothing I could do about the price, and in fact it was later raised to $55 from the $45.95 mentioned in Dunton's February 26 letter (he explained that production costs had run higher than expected, and their pricing formula was partially cost-plus). And there was nothing I could do about their attitude toward my book. Its "marketing" consisted mainly of including a short description of it on various distributed lists. For example, on page 54 of the Greenwood Publishing Group's Spring 1992 catalogue for "Social and Behavioral Sciences," it was described as follows:

> This timely volume advocates pragmatic market socialism and offers a penetrating critique of the entire range of capitalist apologetics. As Yunker envisions it, market socialism would virtually duplicate the everyday economic functions of market capitalist economies, such as the United States', but with public ownership of large, established corporations, profits being distributed among the entire labor force. Pragmatic market socialism would be a means of enhancing economic justice and fairness without sacrificing the efficiency advantages of free enterprise and the market economy.

This mini-blurb was on a page describing their *four* new books on "Economic Theory." On each page of this 84-page catalogue, there were between three and four new book descriptions. If we take 3.5 as the average number of new book descriptions per page, that implies there were 294 new book listings in that one catalogue. Since this was just the Spring 1992 catalogue, that implies that Greenwood Publishing Group was pumping out approximately 600 new books per year. It is little wonder, therefore, that my book was "lost in the crowd."

Never having experienced it myself, I sometimes wonder what happens when a literary agent or acquisitions editor in New York City stumbles on a manuscript that he or she believes has been written by "the next Ernest Hemingway" or maybe "the next Alvin Toffler." If a few influential book reviewers can be got on board, then presumably the author is summoned to the headquarters of McGraw-Hill or Knopf or Norton or whatever other lucky big-time publisher is involved, and some sort of publicity blitz is planned: a nation-wide book-signing tour, appearances on TV talk shows, the formation of a fan club. Of course there was none of that for *Socialism Revised and Modernized*, and presumably none of that either for any of the other books churned out by Greenwood in 1992.

Since I had not provided any monetary subsidy toward the publishing costs of *Socialism Revised and Modernized*, I did not have too much difficulty persuading my wife Penny, the accountant and chief financial officer of our household, to let me invest some of our own money on a self-financed marketing effort. Praeger had no objection to letting me spend my own money on marketing projects, though of course they needed to approve whatever copy I intended to use. Copy approval was no problem, and they authorized me to proceed with their blessing. From the spring of 1992 through early 1993, I spent a little over $5,000 financing such gambits as: (1) in May 1992, a "personalized" bulk mailing of a four-page book description to 560 members of the Association for Comparative Economic Studies; (2) in September 1992, a bulk mailing of a tri-fold leaflet on the book to 5,000 randomly selected members of the American Economic Association; (3) a half-page advertisement in the September 1992 issue the *American Economic Review*; (4) a half-page advertisement in the December issue of the *Journal of Economic Literature*; (5) a full-page advertisement in the program of the 1992 annual meeting of the Allied Social Sciences Association (ASSA); (6) a full-page advertisement in the January 1993 issue of *Dissent*; (7) approximately 20 copies of the book for complimentary distribution to selected individuals. Among those receiving complimentary copies were the six economists who had provided pre-publication comments, seven economists who were authors of economic systems textbooks, plus Jeffrey Sachs of Harvard University who was providing economic wisdom to the ex-Soviet Union, Lawrence Klein of the University of Pennsylvania who was providing economic wisdom to the People's Republic of China, and the Honorable Vladimir P. Lukin, Russian ambassador to the United States.

Socialism Revised and Modernized was basically an espousal of a socialist economy. Although it was a specific socialist economy miles apart from most people's conception of a "socialist economy," I realized that since the large majority of the population of the Western world feared, hated, and despised anything remotely resembling socialism in the pure, public ownership sense, it was going to be very difficult to persuade people to read the book. It would be of great assistance toward this end if I could get one or more reputable authorities to provide a reasonable facsimile of an endorsement of sorts.

As soon as I had the signed Praeger contract in hand, I went ahead with my optimistic plan of getting a notable authority to provide a supportive foreword. Abram Bergson of Harvard University was the foremost living authority in the United States on market socialism, and in the past he had provided comments on two of my market socialism articles. So he was the first person I approached (via postal mail). Bergson begged off on the basis that he had recently undergone eye surgery and was unable to read very much. The next person I approached was Lester Thurow of the Massachusetts Institute of Technology, a well-known and much-published critic of the socioeconomic status quo, author of *Generating Inequality* (Basic Books, 1975). I'm not sure that *Generating Inequality* was a bestseller in the general sense, but it was certainly a bestseller within the category of books that criticized the socioeconomic status quo. To my knowledge, Lester Thurow had never explicitly recommended any form of public ownership socialism, but pragmatic market socialism was surely consistent with many of the objectives he proclaimed. Alas, Lester Thurow was far too busy to consider providing a foreword for my book. With two declines in hand, I decided to abandon the quest for a foreword. The basic problem, I suspected, was that anyone sufficiently well-known to provide a useful foreword would almost certainly be reluctant to risk his treasured reputation by endorsing a socialist proposal being put forward by a virtually unknown economist.

I thought, however, that I might have better luck with pre-publication comments—and indeed I did. Of the eight economists from whom I requested pre-publication comments, six of them were kind enough to provide them. Pre-publication comments are much easier than forewords—they do not require so much writing, and they are considerably less forceful as endorsements. These are the six pre-pub comments I obtained for *Socialism Revised and Modernized*:

> Abram Bergson, Harvard University: A welcome addition to comparative systems literature. The detailed and comprehensive blueprint for market socialism is distinctly novel and illuminating.
>
> Howard Sherman, University of California-Riverside: This book swims with success against the current; it describes and defends, with a rigorous yet readable argument, a model of socialism that revives the socialist vision in a very concrete and attractive manner.
>
> John Burkett, University of Rhode Island: In *Socialism Revised and Modernized*, Professor Yunker presents a comprehensive and serious case for a type of market socialism that differs from capitalism primarily in providing a more egalitarian distribution of income. The system proposed in this book differs radically from traditional Soviet-type central planning and is immune to many criticisms of the latter. The book deserves the attention of all those concerned with economic systems and income distribution.

Joseph Berliner, Brandeis University: The dramatic abandonment of Soviet-style central economic planning has cleared the way for serious discussion of democratic and efficient forms of socialism. Professor Yunker presents a sophisticated challenge to the economic and ethical legitimacy of capitalism and offers a novel and interesting alternative in his proposal for "pragmatic market socialism."

Louis Putterman, Brown University: Could a market system really function with public control of investment, and with no private return to savings? James Yunker makes an interesting case that it could. For those who have wondered about the moral parity of capital incomes with labor earnings but assumed private profit to be necessary to the economic mechanism, Yunker provides stimulating food for thought.

Jan Tinbergen, Erasmus University: Although the laissez-faire system seems to have shown its superiority to Soviet-style centrally planned socialism, it is a misunderstanding that all types of socialism have been shown to be inferior. An optimal social order should combine incentives toward efficiency with a minimum of inequality. Yunker's creative proposal for pragmatic market socialism is presented with caution. He shows the possibility of a socialist system that would be superior to the contemporary capitalist mixed system. Studies of this type are what we need. Yunker's book deserves many readers.

As is apparent, these comments could all be described as guardedly positive concerning the proposed pragmatic market socialist economy. If I had to summarize their tone, it would be something like: "This is an interesting policy proposal which is worthy of thought and study. Conceivably—just conceivably—it might work as the author imagines it would." Hardly an enthusiastic endorsement, but under the circumstances, I was happy to get what I did.

Not all my efforts to publicize *Socialism Revised and Modernized* were fruitful. I wrote to the president of the Association for Comparative Economic Systems requesting that at the next ASSA meeting there be a session, possibly a panel discussion, on pragmatic market socialism. There was no response to that suggestion. On January 21, 1992, about three months prior to the book's issuance, I submitted no less than three new, especially written manuscripts that, had they been accepted, would have spread awareness of pragmatic market socialism. To *Challenge* went "Last Call for Socialism"; to *Dissent* went "Pragmatic Market Socialism and the Purposes of Socialism"; and to *Annals of Public and Cooperative Economy* went "Pragmatic Market Socialism: An Introduction." None of these articles was published. My submission tactic may have backfired. I wanted to impress on the editors that pragmatic market socialism was a serious idea, and to that end I included with the submission such items as my professional résumé, the advertising material carrying all six pre-publication comments, and even the galley proofs for the book itself. I suspect that the reaction of the editors to all this was: "This pragmatic market socialist concept seems already to have gotten a lot of print exposure. So we don't need to provide this author with even more free advertising for his book."

Whatever the big-time publishers do to try to make one of their promising projects into a national bestseller, or perhaps a worldwide bestseller, was not done by Praeger for *Socialism Revised and Modernized*. Of course, Praeger did not do that for any of their books, so I could not hold that against them. Leaving aside the possibility of a veritable miracle, I could not expect that my book would be reviewed in the *New York Times Book Review* or the *London Times Literary Supplement*. The best I could possibly hope for would be a review in the *Journal of Economic Literature* (*JEL*), a publication of the American Economic Association, which is about as authoritative among economists as is the Bible among born-again Christians. Unfortunately, no *JEL* review of it was ever published. It did get a short annotated listing in the "New Books" section, which amounted basically to a cut-down version of the book's table of contents. The listing did include the information that there was both a "Subject Index" and a "Name Index." That was good, because with *JEL* listings, a notation of "No Index" is code for "This is not a professionally reputable book, and should be avoided by any professional who values his/her time."

Reaction to the publication of *Socialism Revised and Modernized* was so limited that perhaps "reaction" is too strong a term. Perhaps "ripple" would be more accurate. The book garnered a handful of listings and reviews in various obscure locations. As far as I know, there were only three full-scale reviews: in *Comparative Economic Studies* (Spring 1993), in the *Review of Social Economy* (Summer 1993), and in the *Journal of Economic Issues* (September 1993). Perhaps the fact that I had previously published articles in all three of these journals made them more receptive to reviewing the book. Most of the listings and reviews were basically noncommittal descriptions, and at most echoed the cautious evaluations contained in the pre-publication comments. But there were some misinterpretations, usually based on the social democratic precept that public ownership of capital does *not* define "true socialism." But there was at least one openly skeptical reaction. A brief, three-paragraph review by William Thomas, in a Foreign Policy Research Institute publication, was concluded as follows:

> Despite claims to the contrary, Yunker's arguments are colored by a raw faith in interventionism. (Not least is his belief that some legisla-

> ture will write a nationalization law that fits his design precisely.) And of course his sweeping measures would, if enacted, have disastrous economic effects. Still, it is noteworthy that Yunker's work makes strikingly modest claims when laid beside the historical promises of socialism. This strengthen his proposal, but it also exposes the decline of the socialist project.

As I read this, I could not help thinking about the psychological phenomenon of "projection": attributing one's own shortcomings to others. "Raw faith" indeed! Any reasonable person who reads *Socialism Revised and Modernized* carefully will have to concede that I never express "raw faith" in anything, including pragmatic market socialism as a reform of the existing capitalistic status quo. All I claim is that the system is sufficiently promising to merit a provisional real-world experiment with it, with the intention of returning to the capitalistic status quo should its performance prove disappointing. Obviously, Mr. William Thomas would be adamantly opposed to such an experiment, because, as he says: "And *of course* [Yunker's] sweeping measures would, if enacted, have *disastrous economic effects*" (italics added). "Of course"?! "Disastrous economic effects"?! One would have to search long and hard for a better expression of "raw faith" in the virtues of the capitalistic status quo.

Over the many years since the publication of *Socialism Revised and Modernized*, I have had a few (very few) communications from people who find the concept of pragmatic market socialism somewhat intriguing, to the point that they felt impelled to initiate a dialogue with the author. Usually the dialogues were about problems they personally perceived in the proposal, with which I had not, in their opinion, dealt convincingly. Almost always I responded equably to these inquiries, and continued the dialogue for as long as the other party remained interested in it. I could do this only because the number of such inquiries was vestigial—perhaps two or three per decade. But I have never, ever, received what I would consider a "fantasy fan letter" along these lines: "I think pragmatic market socialism would be an enormous step forward! Is there anything at all that I personally can do—anything at all—to help you make this possibility a reality?"

World Union on the Horizon

The main reason why the failure of *Socialism Revised and Modernized* to make a noticeable impression did not have an especially demoralizing effect on me was that even before the book appeared in April of 1992, I had already "moved on," as the expression has it. Immediately after submitting draft camera-ready copy to Praeger in December 1991 for *Socialism Revised and Modernized*: *The Case for Pragmatic Market Socialism*, I commenced work on a new book: *World Union on the Horizon: The Case for Supernational Federation*. The substantive content was drawn largely from Chapter 11 ("A Wider Perspective on the Issue") in the large unpublished manuscript from 1988: *Pragmatic Market Socialism: An Economic and Political Appraisal*. Chapter 11 provided the kernel, but a good deal of work was involved in expanding this kernel into a substantial book. The original manuscript was written using ChiWriter, but already I was anticipating typesetting the material (should it become necessary) using Ventura Publisher, with which I had become fairly adept. For the main title, "World Union on the Horizon," I used the original title of the "Pragmatic Market Socialism" manuscript, before the title was changed to better reflect the main body of content. I had high hopes that *World Union on the Horizon* would be far more attractive to publishers than *Socialism Revised and Modernized* had proved to be. As much as I was reluctant to admit it, the disintegration of the Soviet Union did seem to have put the final nail into socialism's coffin. This historic development lent considerable support to the hoary conservative dogma that "socialism can't work—it never has and it never will." To my mind, this was a ridiculously simplistic viewpoint—not to mention incorrect—but it seemed to be firmly held by a very large number of people.

World government, on the other hand, was an entirely different matter. Unlike "socialism," it had never "collapsed" as it had in the Soviet Union—because it had never been tried. The end of the Cold War, as welcome as it was, reduced the short-term threat of nuclear war, but it did not end it. The superpowers did not divest themselves of nuclear weapons; rather they maintained an adequate sufficiency of them to devastate the planet—should it become necessary to use them. Nuclear war remained a deadly threat to the future prospects of humanity. But a properly designed federal world government, such as the Federal Union of Democratic Nations, could significantly reduce this threat without running the risk of degenerating into global tyranny. My new book, *World Union on the Horizon*, would explain all this, possibly in a manner so vivid and compelling that it would rise to the top of the non-fiction bestseller lists.

The degree of faith I had in this new project was such that I definitely wanted to keep it out of the hands of Praeger Publishing. I did not want Praeger to "bury" it as a scholarly treatise, such as they had done with *Socialism Revised and Modernized*, when it was in fact an appeal to the entire world population of intellectually upscale non-fiction readers with an interest in the future of the human race. This potential market was so vast that if even a small part of it could be tapped, this could make *World Union on the Horizon* a runaway bestseller. But this could only happen if it was considered a "trade title" by its publisher, and Praeger had decided irrevocably that it did not wish to compete in the trade market. The problem was that in the contract I had signed with Praeger, one of the clauses stipulated that the author must first submit his/her "next substantial work" to Praeger. Only if Praeger declined to publish it, could it then be submitted to other publishers. If I abided by that contract provision, and Praeger elected to publish *World Union on the Horizon*, then it would be a dead duck from the start, just as *Socialism Revised and Modernized* had been.

To make absolutely sure this would not happen, my "next substantial work"—which I *did* submit to Praeger, as per the contract—was a slightly cut-down version of *Pragmatic Market Socialism: An Economic and Political Appraisal*. I deleted the third part ("Concluding Thoughts"), and deleted everything occurring elsewhere in the manuscript that made reference to that third part. The notes and references sections were also trimmed of anything having to do with the third part. The page-count on the resulting manuscript still ran to over 1,100 pages—relative to the 1,338 pages in the original *Pragmatic Market Socialism* manuscript. Although a significant reduction from the original version, it was still sufficiently lengthy that I was pretty confident that Praeger would not be interested. I printed out the whole thing, boxed it up, and sent it off to James R. Dunton.

My plan succeeded. In early May 1992, Mr. Dunton declined interest, saying, "Concerning your next work, PRAGMATIC MARKET SOCIALISM, I am afraid that at 1,100 manuscript pages it is far too long to be seriously considered for commercial publication." I believe that was the only time in my entire life that I received a rejection letter that I actually *wanted* to receive! The 1,100-page version of *Pragmatic Market Socialism* was never submitted anywhere else. Aside from the fact that it was almost certainly unpublishable, I had bigger fish to fry—hopefully *World Union on the Horizon* would succeed where *Socialism Revised and Modernized* had failed.

The manuscript for *World Union on the Horizon: The Case for Supernational Federation* was completed in early May 1992, and the first proposal mailing was sent out on May 22, 1992, to five big-time publishers: St. Martin's Press, Basic Books, Oxford University Press, W. W. Norton, and Alfred A. Knopf. At the time I was quite optimistic. In some respects, this new submission was better than anything I had ever submitted in the past. The proposal material for *World Union* was probably the most effective I had ever put together. The one-page cover letter was very direct and to-the-point. The cone-bound proposal booklet contained three parts: (1) contents, preface, and Chapter 1 in typeset form (using Ventura Publisher output—to demonstrate that I could provide CRC if necessary); (2) contents, preface, and Chapter 1 in typed form (using Chiwriter output—to demonstrate that I could provide the double-spaced output preferred by copy editors); and (3) author's résumé. From the paginated tables of contents, a potential publisher could ascertain that this was a relatively short book, well under 400 pages both typed and typeset. Specifically, the typeset version, minus the index, was 323 pages long and contained about 115,000 words. This was well within the comfort zone of most publishers. The preface contained a brief history of my thought and work on supernational federation over the preceding 30 years (perhaps a "human interest" story), and Chapter 1 provided an informal overview in Section A, and a detailed outline and synopsis in Section B (quite an efficient way, I thought, to introduce the book to a busy reader). Moreover, the subject matter was somewhat less objectionable than that of my recent submissions on pragmatic market socialism: pragmatic market socialism would pose a direct threat to the financial interests of wealthy capitalists, while supernational federation did not (and does not) adversely affect any specific, identifiable "group of losers."

Although still not very high, my professional status was higher than it had ever been in the past. I was a professor of economics (albeit at a lesser, regional institution) with a lengthy list of article publications and a substantial recent book: *Socialism Revised and Modernized*. Among my published writing was a considerable amount bearing directly on the submitted book, including, most importantly, "Practical Considerations in Designing a Supernational Federation" (*World Futures*, 1985). Last but not least, there was the excitement being generated by the reformist transitions in the communist world, especially in the ex-Soviet Union. There were brighter rays of hope now shining down from the heavens than at any time since the end of World War II. Perhaps *World Union on the Horizon* would be perceived as appropriate to the moment—as seeking to exploit the new opportunities for humanity that had lately opened up.

It did not require too much time for my hope-bubble to be punctured. The proposal material was sent out on May 22, 1992, and the first rejection letter, dated May 27, from Herbert J. Addison, vice president and executive editor in the New York office of Oxford University Press, was as follows:

> Thank you for your letter of May 22 and the proposal for your book "World Union on the Horizon: The Case for Supernational Federation."

> We spoke with our advisor in economics about the proposal. While we both agree that this would be a useful volume for its intended audience, we are pessimistic about finding a large enough audience to make publication at this time feasible.
>
> Other editors may disagree with our assessment, and I hope that you will submit this material to another publisher.
>
> We wish you every success in finding a suitable publisher for this project, and we thank you for giving Oxford the opportunity to consider your proposal.

Although rejection letters do not get much more pleasant than this, into my deep disappointment was mixed a certain amount of irritation. Why did they need to consult with their "economics advisor"?—the subject matter of this book had far more to do with international relations than economics. In any case, I had my suspicions that they had not bothered to consult with anyone, economist or otherwise. They did not have time enough for that. My proposal was sent to them late in the afternoon of May 22. The United States Postal Service is far more efficient than many people realize, but even so, the proposal could not have arrived in the Oxford offices before May 25. Since their response was dated May 27, that would hardly allow time for a skim reading of Chapter 1 (20,262 words), let alone a leisurely and reflective perusal of it. And while we are on the subject, why do publishers feel the need to insert the phrase "at this time" into their rejection letters? Is the author supposed to infer that if he had submitted his book a few months earlier, or perhaps a few months later, they would have been happy to add it to their lists?

Oh well, try not to be so bitter about it. After all—trying to be realistic for just a moment—what should I have expected? After all, imagine if *I* were an assistant acquisitions editor at a major publishing house, and that *I* were suddenly confronted with a proposal for a book advocating world government from an absolute unknown with marginal credentials. What would *I* have done? Even if the book had been authored by Henry Kissinger, I probably wouldn't have given it any consideration. After all, Kissinger was getting on in years, and was probably on the verge of senility—only thus could he have produced such a crackpot exercise in utopian fantasizing. It might have been worth my job to have passed the proposal up the editorial chain of command, thus wasting the valuable time of the higher-ups. Of course, I as the *author*, knew that this particular book was *not* a crackpot exercise in utopian fantasizing. But if I had been an assistant acquisitions editor for a major publishing house, who had probably devoted less than five minute's thought to world government over his/her entire lifespan, how could I have known that? So the question arose in my mind: Was there *anything* I could do to improve the odds?

Perhaps I could persuade some authoritative individual to take an interest in *World Union on the Horizon*, and intercede on its behalf with a major publishing house. During the summer of 1992 I sent off letters of appeal, enclosing the *World Union* proposal material, to three individuals whom I thought might possibly be willing and able to help: Amitai Etzioni, Gabriel Kolko, and Strobe Talbott. Amitai Etzioni and Gabriel Kolko had published important books back in the 1960s which had had a transformative effect on my worldview: respectively *The Hard Way to Peace*, and *Wealth and Power in America*. I never heard from Etzioni, but Kolko wrote to say that, regrettably, his publisher (Pantheon) was no longer doing "serious" books.

At the time, Strobe Talbott seemed like an even better bet: in its issue of July 20, 1992, *Time* magazine had published his two-page op-ed piece entitled "The Birth of the Global Nation." The gist of the piece was that if humanity is to survive, we had better establish an authoritative world state—sometime within the next 100 years or so. But he had no specific suggestions on how this marvel could or would be accomplished. Even though the end of the Cold War was the obvious immediate impetus to his *Time* essay, Talbott had no practical ideas whatever as to how such a thing as world government could be achieved within the foreseeable future. And I suppose he could not imagine that an unknown professor of economics at Western Illinois University could offer any useful insights on the matter. However, he was sufficiently considerate to write me the following note, dated August 6, 1992:

> I just received your letter and manuscript and hasten to reply. I'm leaving in the morning for a three-week trip, including to Asia, so I won't get a chance to look at your work until early September, I'm sure I'll find it enlightening, since I can tell from your gracious letter that we're very much on the same wavelength. However, I should also tell you, I'm afraid, that I won't be able to help you place it with a publisher. That's a major undertaking for even the best of books (I should say: for <u>especially</u> the best of books), and it's simply not in line with my own activities as a journalist. So while I will, when I get a chance, look at your manuscript, I would strongly urge you to look elsewhere for help in finding a publisher.

September came and went without my hearing anything further from Strobe Talbott. Perhaps he never "had a chance" to look at the proposal material for *World Union on the Horizon*, or perhaps he assumed that there would be no point in doing so. As for his endorsement of world government in the 1992 *Time* essay, many years later Talbott published a book entitled *The Great Experiment: The Story of Ancient Empires, Modern States, and the Quest for a Global Nation* (2008), in which the essay was mentioned but not elaborated on. *The Great Experiment* is something of a political history of state entities, with virtually nothing on specific ideas for institutional structures beyond the United Nations. It contains numerous references to "global governance" as it is currently understood—as having nothing to do with world government. Apparently the "global nation" has no need of a "global government." Concerning his 1992 "global nation" op-ed piece in *Time*, Talbott says simply (page 126): "The piece made me briefly popular with foreign policy liberals, and not so briefly, a target of brickbats from the right."

By the middle of July 1992, all five presses approached in the original proposal mailing of May 22 had responded that while my project looked worthy enough, it was "not quite right for us at this time" (or words to that effect). It was time to prepare another mailing. My plan was to try my luck again with some top-tier publishers, but I did not know the names of appropriate acquisitions editors (recall: this was pre-Internet). For want of a better idea, I telephoned the head offices of three different major publishing houses. At one of them, I got a name, but at the other two, haughty-sounding voices at the other end of the line informed me that they never consider submissions by authors: in order to be considered, a proposal must be submitted through a literary agency. I was advised that contact information for any number of literary agencies was available in *Literary Market Place*, a print publication available "in every library." I hustled over to the WIU library, and sure enough, there it was. It did indeed contain listings for a multitude of literary agencies, the majority of them located in the Big Apple. The proposal mailing of July 27 went to five literary agencies that, according to *Literary Market Place*, had an interest in serious non-fiction.

Within a month of that mailing, all five had responded—negatively. On the whole, the responses were even more cursory than those from the publishers. Mostly they did not bother to compliment the work. Also, in contrast to the publishers who often returned the proposal material at their own expense, the literary agencies informed me that if I wanted to get my proposal material back, I should send them an SASE (self-addressed stamped envelope). Heck, the reason I hadn't bothered enclosing an SASE with the original mailing was that SASE's were beneath my dignity: I was not some starving scribbler in an attic garret who could not afford to make as many copies of the proposal material as I might possibly need.

I concluded from this experience that it wasn't just the publishers who were mostly interested in sure-fire books by well-known authors, and who were strongly inclined to give short shrift to anything that did not fit into that category. The literary agencies seemed even less open to new work by unknowns than the publishers. This suggested a sort of Catch-22 situation in which the unknown author is trapped like a fly in a spider's web. You can't become a well-known author unless you publish a book with a major publishing house—but you can't publish a book with a major publishing house unless you are a well-known author. Well, of course, it couldn't be as bad as all that: otherwise no new author could ever get his/her work on the bestseller lists. And new authors were getting their work on the bestseller lists all the time. All it would take, presumably, is one perceptive acquisitions editor at a major publishing house. But would my work ever come across the desk of such a person? Apparently such individuals were not overly abundant.

The next two mailings I sent out (on August 12 and September 8) did not include any literary agencies. They went to a grand total of 12 different presses, ranging from such top-tier publishers as Viking Penguin and Harvard University Press, down to lesser operations such as Greenwood and Lexington. As the rejection letters continued drifting in from these mailings, my hope of getting *World Union* undertaken by a publisher with sufficient clout to make it a viable contender for the bestseller lists gradually faded away. By the time I finally got a nibble, I was well into a "first-come-first-served" frame of mind—any publisher at all was starting to look very good.

Curiously enough, just as had been the case with *Socialism Revised and Modernized*, I did not submit the book to the press that finally published it. I had submitted *Socialism Revised* to Cynthia Harris of Greenwood Press, and she passed it along to James R. Dunton of Praeger. Similarly, I submitted *World Union on the Horizon* to Jonathan Sisk of Rowman & Littlefield, and he passed it along to Julie Burnham of University Press of America (UPA). On October 15, 1992, I received a telephone call from Ms. Burnham saying that they had issued a contract on my book, and it was on its way through the postal mail. This development was a huge relief, but not a cause for unrestrained rejoicing. Although the name "University Press of America" sounded rather impressive, I had never heard of it. Obviously it was not in the same league as Harvard University Press or Oxford University Press. When Ms. Burnham told me over the telephone that they planned to use my own typeset material as CRC, that confirmed my suspicion that *World Union* would be handled by UPA the same way Praeger had handled *Socialism Revised*. Out the window went any hope that *World Union* might become a non-fiction bestseller.

That was not good—but it got worse. When the contract arrived, I was horrified to see that it contained the following provision: "23. The Author agrees to arrange for a bookstore(s) or organization(s) to guarantee purchase of 100 copies, including postage and shipping charges, of the Work." Oh drat!—having to provide camera-ready copy was bad enough, but having to guarantee the purchase of 100 copies made it far worse. In all likelihood, this meant that the author himself would have to buy 100 copies of the book. This was far too close for comfort to vanity press territory. Immediately I sent off a letter to Julie Burnham complaining that surely because of the broad appeal of *World Union on the Horizon*, it need not be subjected to the 100-copy rule. But even before Ms. Burnham had a chance to reply, I changed my mind, and sent her a signed copy of the contract. With a heavy heart, I bowed to reality. Up to that point, I had received more than a dozen rejections, and I decided to heed the ancient wisdom expressed in the old proverb: "A bird in the hand is worth two in the bush."

Fortunately for Penny's and my finances, UPA issued the book in both cloth (hardback) and paperback editions, and they were gracious enough to allow me to purchase 75 copies at the lower price for the paperback version (suggested retail price $27.50), and only 25 copies at the higher price for the cloth version (suggested retail price $56.50). As per the contract specification, the order was placed through a bookstore (the WIU University Bookstore), and when the 75 copies of the paperback edition and 25 copies of the cloth edition arrived at the bookstore the following summer, I wrote out a check for $2,739.59 and handed it over to the bookstore manager. If the full retail price had been charged, the amount would have been $3,475 (plus shipping), but instead the lower wholesale price UPA charged to the bookstore was applied to the transaction. Still, $2,739.59 made a noticeable dent in our finances. But it wasn't so much the money itself—it was the humiliation of having to subsidize my own book. I had to wonder nervously just how widespread was awareness of this particular business practice of University Press of America. To many if not most people, such awareness would convey the aroma of a vanity press—not a pleasant aroma.

On the other hand, I have to concede that UPA did an excellent job, using the CRC I provided them, of printing and binding, and the final product was just as respectable as Praeger's job on *Socialism Revised and Modernized*. They also took care of the technicalities (ISBN number, Library of Congress Cataloguing-in-Publication data, etc.), and included my book in their various catalogues. Sales of the book were not noticeably lower than sales of my other books for which I did not provide subsidies.

Alas, sales of all my books have been meager, whether or not I put up anything toward the costs of production. Also, I suppose it was a bit of a consolation having so many copies of the book in my personal possession, for use as complimentary presentations to friends, relatives, and influential people. To begin with, I needed to send inscribed copies to the four authorities who had been kind enough to provide the following pre-publication comments:

> Dietrich Fischer, Pace University: So long as much of humanity lives in misery, there can be no islands of peace and prosperity in our interdependent world. James A. Yunker's *World Union on the Horizon* addresses this central problem and proposes innovative solutions that need to be widely discussed.
>
> Jan Tinbergen, Erasmus University: Professor Yunker advances various original ideas toward implementing the urgently need worldwide cooperation. These ideas constitute an appropriate challenge to conventional attitudes and will help to start a fresh new debate.
>
> Walter Isard, Cornell University: We are by necessity moving toward a global system. Whether agreeing or not, the reader can gain valuable insights from Yunker's analysis of world union.
>
> Saul Mendlovitz, Rutgers University: This book performs a valuable service in providing an explicit constitution for a supernational federation sensitive to ideological differences, economic disparities, and the vexing problem of resurgent nationalism. A thoughtful and provocative work.

I had originally requested pre-publication comments from twelve individuals, and therefore my success rate was 33 and 1/3 percent. This was far inferior to my 75 percent success rate for *Socialism Revised and Modernized* (eight requests, six comments provided). Possibly this was because I was an economist asking other economists for a comment on the socialism book, whereas I had no professional credentials at all in political science or international relations. Or perhaps, contrary to my assumption, "world government" was an even more frightening concept than "socialism." After all, there has been a certain amount of real-world experience with systems describing themselves as "socialist," and although there were plenty of obvious liabilities with these systems, they were at least survivable. World government, on the other hand, was a completely unknown quantity—and it was (is) widely believed that any attempt to establish one in the real world would quite likely unleash a nuclear world war. But anyway, perhaps the relative paucity of pre-pub comments on *World Union* was not a serious liability. After all, Gabriel Kolko had responded to my request with the following: "I have an inflexible rule never to give pre-publication comments, write reviews for authors, etc. Apart from taking time, it really does nothing to sell or advance a book. Readers pay no attention to such things, and review editors ignore them."

During the publication process for *Socialism Revised and Modernized*, I had engaged in a protracted, somewhat acrimonious, and ultimately futile struggle to persuade the Praeger personnel to set a relatively low price on the book, in hopes of tapping a large trade market. After that experience, I simply did not have the heart to try the same thing with the UPA personnel. From the beginning, I resigned myself to letting them do what they thought best with respect to pricing and marketing *World Union on the Horizon*. As had been the case with the Praeger people, the UPA people had no problem with letting me do some promotional work on my own time and at my own expense. So I repeated the effort I had made with *Socialism Revised*: I solicited some pre-publication comments, and I undertook a bulk mailing of an advertising sheet on the book to potential customers. As indicated, the pre-pub appeal netted four somewhat vague but cautiously positive comments.

The advertising sheet was another of my Ventura Publisher projects. The front page was mostly devoted to a blurb-type appraisal of the book's potential significance. The addressees consisted of subscribers to two major international relations journals *(International Organization* and *World Policy Journal*), and of members of the World Federalist Association (WFA). No doubt there were a few duplications. The development director of the WFA, Mrs. Olga B. ("Bobby") Gechas, was somewhat concerned that selling their membership list might endanger the Association's non-profit status. But upon appeal to higher authorities, a compromise was worked out: they did not "sell" me the list, but gave it to me at cost of production, with the additional consideration of a voluntary donation. My total expenditure for the WFA membership mailing labels came to $610.

Taking into account all expenditures for mailing labels, costs of printing the various components of the mailing, and postage, the total investment came to approximately $4,700, of which the largest single item was $2,900 for 10,000 29-cent first-class postage stamps. Penny and I spent many hours in the basement of our home preparing the mailing, which despite our best efforts had a somewhat amateurish appearance—when compared to the typical slick commercial mass mailing items that clutter up peoples' mailboxes. The mailing went out in early October 1993: 4,500 pieces to subscribers to important international relations journals, and 5,500 pieces to WFA members. I had more ideas for additional promotional mailings, but my spouse Penny, always the voice of moderation in these matters, persuaded me that I should wait a few months to see whether this first mailing had reaped any noticeable benefits in terms of sales. First reports of sales were disappointing, and thus all further mailing ideas were scrapped.

It did not assist prospects for sales to libraries that the January 1994 issue of *Choice* (the acquisition librarian's "Bible") carried a listing which complained that *World Union on the Horizon* did not present a "convincing plan for achieving this goal [world federation]." The implication was that *World Union* was just another useless repetition of the same argument that had been continuously put forward by world federalists ever since the end of World War II (the "one world or none" argument)—an argument that had been steadfastly rejected ever since that time by the overwhelming majority of the population. I don't know whether the provider of that item, one A. J. Ward of the College of William and Mary, actually read my book, but I have my doubts. Surely if Mr. Ward had actually read the book, he would have noticed that it was proposing a specific type of world government not part of the traditional world federalist mindset.

Additional First Wave Books

The principal components of my "first wave" of book publications were *Socialism Revised and Modernized: The Case for Pragmatic Market Socialism* (Praeger, 1992) and *World Union on the Horizon: The Case for Supernational Federation* (University Press of America, 1993). There were two additional books completed around the same time that were in the nature of postscripts to these first two books: *Capitalism versus Pragmatic Market Socialism: A General Equilibrium Evaluation*, published by Kluwer Academic Publishers in 1993, and *Economic Justice: The Market Socialist Vision*, published by Rowman & Littlefield in 1997. All four of these titles were in a sense the progeny of the large project on which I had labored throughout much of the 1980s: the large, unpublished *Pragmatic Market Socialism: An Economic and Political Appraisal.*

Capitalism versus Pragmatic Market Socialism: A General Equilibrium Evaluation was an expansion to short-book length of an article manuscript that I had been unsuccessfully trying to publish in an important economics journal for a number of years. Along the way there had been some title changes, but the version I attempted to "slip into" *Socialism Revised and Modernized* as a "Theoretical Appendix" went by the title "A General Equilibrium Evaluation of Capitalism versus Pragmatic Market Socialism." That section of the manuscript had to be deleted to meet Praeger's length constraints. This particular research was obviously a technical contribution of interest mainly to economic theoreticians. Since there was certainly no question of this becoming the non-fiction bestseller of my dreams, my attitude toward it was relatively relaxed. The book manuscript was written using ChiWriter and then converted into typeset format using Ventura Publisher. At a mere 146 pages in length (minus the index), the typeset version was short enough that I could submit the entire book with the initial proposal.

The project was completed in December 1992 (several months prior to the April 1993 release of *World Union on the Horizon*), and there were two proposal mailings: on December 22, 1992; and on March 3, 1993. A total of ten submissions were made, mainly to top-tier university presses (Harvard, MIT, University of Chicago), but with a few directed to academically oriented commercial presses. Predictably enough, I had better success with the latter. I received a total of three publication offers, but I signed with the first press that showed an interest. In a letter received on March 8, 1993, Zachery Rolnik, economics editor at Kluwer Academic Publishers, asked me to suggest some referees for my book. I did so, apparently the referees were satisfied, and a contract was issued on June 24, 1993. They utilized my CRC, so the book was issued in September 1993. A lag of only three months between contract and book is an amazingly brief interval. As the book was basically a technical addendum to *Socialism Revised and Modernized*, I never expected much from it. This expectation was not reversed by the book's subsequent history. As of a royalty report issued in December 1996, it had sold 256 copies.

My aspirations were higher with *Economic Justice: The Market Socialist Vision*. Whereas *Capitalism versus Pragmatic Market Socialism* had been a short technical sequel to *Socialism Revised and Modernized*, *Economic Justice* was intended to be a full-length popular sequel. I stripped out of *Socialism Revised* all the technical content (tables, figures, equations), and rewrote it from scratch in a more informal, chattier style. By this time, I had finally moved on from Ventura Publisher. I used a Windows-based word processor called AmiPro, whose typesetting capabilities were on a par with those of the DOS-based Ventura Publisher. By this time also, it was quite clear that Eastern Europe and the various components of the ex-Soviet Union were never going to return to communistic planned socialism. Thus all mentions of pragmatic market socialism as a possible ideological bridge were eliminated. The new effort also included far more anecdotal material (e.g., regarding Oskar Lange's personal history) that might make it more attractive as a "good read" to my intended reader: an intellectually upscale college graduate with a serious interest in socioeconomic policy. Presumably there were enough of these people out there in the world that *Economic Justice* might just possibly, just conceivably, become a non-fiction bestseller. Accordingly, the publication effort was much longer than it had been with *Capitalism versus Pragmatic Market Socialism*. Similarly, the writing process was relatively protracted. Work on the manuscript was started in the fall of 1993 and continued through December 1994. With the book complete at 393 typeset pages (155,691 words), the first submission was sent to Simon Winder of St. Martin's Press on January 4, 1995.

With *Economic Justice*, I was in no particular hurry, and so I did not at first engage in multiple proposal mailings. It wasn't until October of 1995 that I finally gave up on the one-at-a-time approach. This was after both St. Martin's Press and The Free Press had taken months to issue a cursory rejection of my submission. Between the mailings of October 1995 and February 1996, I submitted proposals to a total of 14 presses across the spectrum from major trade publishers to minor commercial presses specializing in scholarly works. Predictably enough, it was one of the latter that eventually published the book.

On March 4, 1996, I was invited by Jonathan Sisk of Rowman & Littlefield to send the full manuscript for review, and a contract was issued on August 22, 1996. Although at that time Rowman & Littlefield was under the same corporate roof as University Press of America, it did not require authors to guarantee the purchase of a minimum number of copies. That was a blessing. It wasn't so much the money per se, as it was the ignominy of having to pay money to get my work into print. The book itself, using my CRC, was released in April 1997. The release included a hardbound version priced at $69.50, and a paperbound edition priced at $26.95. These were hardly "popular" prices, but Rowman & Littlefield had no aspirations toward the trade market. By this time I was reconciled to this reality, and so I merely shrugged my shoulders that the high price would automatically deter the huge majority of potential readers. As of 2015, *Economic Justice* had sold 440 copies, 196 of the hardcover edition and 244 of the softcover edition.

Unlike the first two books in the "first wave" of my book publications, I did not consider doing any promotional projects on behalf of the second two. Apart from the fact that my dear spouse Penelope was getting fed up with my throwing our money down the rathole, I was beginning to resign myself to the unlikelihood of ever achieving a non-fiction bestseller unless I could produce a manuscript very much different from anything I had done before. First and foremost, every manuscript I had produced up to this point was tainted by pragmatic market socialism. *I* knew that pragmatic market socialism was a very promising, very attractive proposal for the reform and improvement of the existing capitalistic status quo—but it was beginning to seem that there was absolutely no way, given my finite personal capabilities as a writer and polemicist, that I could ever break through the thick crust of anti-socialist preconception among all strata of society from highest to lowest. Of the four books in my first wave, three of them focused entirely on pragmatic market socialism: *Socialism Revised and Modernized*, *Capitalism versus Pragmatic Market Socialism*, and *Economic Justice*. And while the fourth one, *World Union on the Horizon*, was ostensibly focused on world government, nevertheless it devoted quite a lot of attention to the possibility that there might be some backsliding in the reforming ex-communist countries—and thus pragmatic market socialism might still have a role to play as a bridge over the ideological gap.

Economic Justice said nothing about a possible ideological bridge, but it was a full-scale, unapologetic advocacy of pragmatic market socialism as an "internal reform" of the existing socioeconomic system. Its message was apparently not being eagerly awaited by the populace. It did receive the expected listings in *Choice* and the *Journal of Economic Literature*, both of which were bare descriptions that could have been written based simply on the book's table of contents. To my knowledge, the book attracted a grand total of two full-scale reviews, both in relatively obscure journals: the *Journal of Economic Issues*, and the *Review of Social Economy*. They both complimented me for providing a relatively lucid, balanced, sensible, and readable market socialist proposal. But they also expressed great doubt that the proposal could ever gain traction with a significant number of people.

I was rather irritated by what I considered the somewhat flippantly dismissive tone of the *JEI* review, authored by Doug Brown of the economics department at Northern Arizona University—so much so that I sat down and wrote a six-page, single-spaced letter to Professor Brown protesting that some of his comments were both inaccurate and misleading. For example, he complained that nothing was said in *Economic Justice* on the critical issue of transition: how could the overwhelming prejudice against socialism ever be overcome? My letter pointed out that an entire 17-page section in the book ("Prospects in the Capitalist Heartland") explicitly addressed that very issue. Brown's review complained also that the benefits of pragmatic market socialism were so modestly presented that they could never inspire a significant political movement: in order to be effective, the appeal for pragmatic market socialism would have to be connected to such larger issues as environmental preservation. I pointed out that *Economic Justice* had argued at length that one of the major reasons why there were such deep-seated suspicions against socialism was that many advocates of socialism in the past had promised unrealistic benefits that were both unconnected to socialism and unlikely to be appealing to a wide range of people. Thus I purposely avoided claiming that pragmatic market socialism would, for example, automatically lead to better environmental policies. Doug Brown replied briefly to my letter, saying that he looked forward to having a fruitful dialogue with me in the future—but at the present moment he was too busy to engage in one. I never heard from him again.

Some years later, while checking the Web for information on my various books, I happened to come across an online "customer review" of *Economic Justice* on Amazon's U.K. site. The four-paragraph post was unconditionally complimentary as to the book's content and direction, but it concluded with the following doleful assessment:

> It is unfortunate that Yunker's thoroughly sensible, responsible advocacy for market socialism has been largely ignored for 20+ years, but no surprise: from what I gather reading this book, he simply has too much faith in the intelligence of his readers. Normally one would admire someone for this, and I certainly do, but the fact is that as long as people are more easily moved by poorly thought-out rhetoric, superficially impressive arguments, and all the rest of it—as long as these things are predominant, a book like Yunker's just won't convince the masses. A shame.

When I saw this, I had to ruefully concede its perceptiveness. My only qualification was that I would not attribute to deficient "intelligence" the imperviousness of the "masses" to the market socialist alternative. Most people are quite intelligent, in many cases more intelligent than me. The problem is a combination of limited information with misinformation. This combination results in defective judgment. Most people have never given any serious thought to socialism, because they assume there would be no point in doing so. The faith of the average person in the street today in the economic and ethical legitimacy of capitalism might be compared to the faith of the average European peasant in the fields, back in medieval times, in the absolute truth of the Roman Catholic religion, including heaven and hell, angels and devils, and an omnipotent Supreme Being with a close personal interest in every last human being, living or dead. Will this ever change? Who knows?

In any case, by the latter 1990s the evidence was becoming overwhelming that my personal crusade against capitalism, based on the pragmatic market socialist alternative, was a lost cause. I was like Don Quixote in Miguel de Cervantes' classic of Spanish literature: foolishly tilting—albeit with the most commendable of intentions—at windmills. It was time to change direction.

7

THE VISION IN PRINT: LATER BOOKS

Although pragmatic market socialism would have been—and still could be—a worthwhile reform of the contemporary socioeconomic system, my principal motivation for developing the concept was the possibility that it could form an ideological meeting point somewhere between communistic planned socialism and democratic market capitalism, taking what was good from both sides and discarding the rest. Public ownership socialism would be taken from the communist side, and the economic market and political democracy from the noncommunist side. Ideological harmonization was not the final objective, but rather only a steppingstone to the ultimate objective: a global economic development effort and the formation of a federal world government. Subtracting pragmatic market socialism from the overall plan left global economic development and federal world government.

The entire plan, including pragmatic market socialism, had been laid out in *World Union on the Horizon: The Case for Supernational Federation*, published in 1993. When *World Union on the Horizon* sank like a stone into the deep blue sea of unnoticed books, this combined with other evidences of pragmatic market socialism's lack of appeal, persuaded me to drop any mention whatsoever of pragmatic market socialism in any further writing I would be doing on global economic development and federal world government. While I did in fact publish some additional writing on pragmatic market socialism (there were still a few things left to be said on the subject), none of this writing made mention of global economic development and/or federal world government.

I have always been an industrious writer, and hardly has one book manuscript been completed when I am busily planning successor book manuscripts. By the mid-1990s, therefore, planning was well advanced for my next "big book": my next attempt at the holy grail of a large, influential, non-fiction bestseller. The substantive content of the next book would be virtually identical to that of *World Union on the Horizon* with respect to global economic development and federal world government—the major difference would be that there would be no mention whatsoever of pragmatic market socialism. But the new book would be different in some other respects as well, and hopefully these differences would further increase the probability that it would be successful.

On what did I base my hopes that the new book would not meet with the same fate of "instant oblivion" that met *World Union on the Horizon*? First and foremost, as a result of its background, *World Union* devoted quite a lot of attention to pragmatic market socialism as a potential bridge over the ideological gap between East and West. By the time was the book was finally published in 1993, the Cold War was widely assumed to be definitively concluded, and there was obviously no further need for an ideological bridge (even assuming one had been feasible). So the book seemed dated and out of touch with current events. The new book, in contrast, would focus exclusively on the economic and nationalistic impediments to world government—on the presumption that the ideological impediment was now virtually extinct.

In addition to its misplaced emphasis, the earlier book devoted almost no attention to comparing and contrasting the Federal Union of Democratic Nations proposal to other world government proposals, thus possibly generating the misapprehension that the Federal Union proposal was not fundamentally innovative. The new book would go into considerable detail on the historical background of the world government concept, and also on the "conventional" world government proposal of the post-World War II era, which envisioned (and still does) a militarily dominant world government operating among totally disarmed member nations. I have always fully agreed with the consensus among world government skeptics that such a plan, if implemented, would likely be a one-way ticket to global tyranny.

But if the evaluation of world government is in terms of a *limited* world government as opposed to an *omnipotent* world government, then the danger of global tyranny would be reduced to an acceptable level—a level well below the danger of eventual nuclear holocaust brought on by the sovereign nation-state system. While the short-term nuclear war-risk was greatly ameliorated by the decline of the Cold War, there were (and still are) large stockpiles of operational nuclear weapons constantly at the ready, and our long-term prospects—in light of the repeated lessons of history—are not so optimistic.

Moreover, my earlier exposition of the case for world government in *World Union on the Horizon* was mostly rather abstract and lacking in empirical content—perhaps the unconscious result of my own educational background and teaching experience in economic theory. The new book would endeavor to flesh out the abstract arguments with a considerable amount of historical and political detail. Many topical discussions in the planned book would be fully independent of other topical discussions. So it would not be necessary to read the entire book in order to attain a good grasp of its nature and contents.

Another plus was that in the new book I would be able to mention, at some appropriate point, a quasi-endorsement of the Federal Union of Democratic Nations proposal from a reasonably authoritative source. Although *World Union on the Horizon* had attracted practically no notice whatever at the time of its publication, I was later gratified that the British political historian Derek Heater, in his historical survey of world government thinking entitled *World Citizenship and Government: Cosmopolitan Ideas in the History of Western Political Thought* (St. Martin's Press, 1996), devoted a few pages to *World Union*, and characterized its world government proposal as "meaty and original." Although there were a few minor misrepresentations in Heater's treatment, it was generally accurate and quite favorable.

Finally, the material in the new book on the World Economic Equalization Program (WEEP) would be much improved over the analogous material in *World Union*. The *World Union* material had been based directly on my 1988 article in *World Development*: "A World Economic Equalization Program: Refinements and Sensitivity Analysis." Although *World Development* is a highly reputable economic journal, one of the potential shortcomings of the research as reported in that article was its very high level of aggregation: all the world's nations were allocated to one of only six categories defined on per capita income. A skeptic could, and probably would, speculate that the optimistic results of the baseline simulations probably would not hold up if there were not so much aggregation. Even before I started working on the manuscript for the new book, I decided it was time to confront this skeptical speculation head-on.

For many years, the World Bank had been providing a voluminous global economic database called "World Development Indicators." Nowadays this database is available for free download, but during the 1990s, it was offered for sale on a CD-ROM—at what most people would consider a reasonable price. Using data from this CD-ROM, I expanded the empirical data used by the WEEP model to 140 nations: all nations that had populations of one million or more as of 1970. The same optimistic baseline results using the 140-nation dataset were obtained, that had been obtained earlier with the six-category dataset. These optimistic results, therefore, could not be sensibly dismissed on the basis of the speculation that they were unreliable artifacts resulting from excessive aggregation.

Although the same economic model continued to be utilized in the larger research, a considerable amount of Visual Basic programming was required to process the much larger dataset and apply it in the WEEP model simulations. In all, from the initial data collection to completion of the final book manuscript, the project required a full year, from January 1998 through January 1999. Relative to my earlier books, the publication process was mercifully brief and untroubled. After a mere two rejections, a contract was issued on May 17, 1999, by Greenwood Publishing Group, on behalf of Praeger Publishers, for *Common Progress: The Case for a World Economic Equalization Program*. Once again I provided camera-ready copy (this time using Microsoft Word), and the book was issued in February 2000.

The Second Wave

The publication of *Common Progress: The Case for a World Economic Equalization Program* in 2000 marked the start of the "second wave" of my book publishing career. This second wave was concluded in 2007 with the publication of *Political Globalization: A New Vision of Federal World Government*. The latter book remains the largest of all my books on world government, and at the time it was published I thought to myself: "As far as a written espousal of federal world government is concerned, I will never be able to do any better than this book."

Even before *Common Progress* was issued, work was well advanced on another "big book" in the tradition of the unpublished manuscripts for *The Grand Convergence: Economic and Political Aspects of Human Progress* (1973), and *Pragmatic Market Socialism: An Economic and Political Appraisal* (1988). After considerable deliberation, I settled on the working title: *The Next Step: A New Vision of Federal World Government*. The writing of *The Next Step* required exactly 19 months: from October 15, 1999, through May 15, 2001. This was the first time that I made liberal use of the Internet to fill in factual data for a manuscript on which I was working. Instead of trekking to the library and rummaging through dusty tomes to locate various required facts and figures, I could effortlessly retrieve many if not most of them while seated comfortably at my own computer monitor located on my own desk within my own private office. It was marvelous. By this time also, I was utilizing Microsoft Word exclusively even for the initial drafting, using typeset format, the idea being that book publishers would be impressed by this evidence that the author was capable, if required, of providing acceptable camera-ready copy. And if the publisher later wanted a double-spaced manuscript for purposes of copy-editing, the files could easily be converted to that format.

During the early stages of writing *The Next Step*, I undertook a forced-pace flurry of article writing on world government, with two purposes in mind. One purpose was to "warm up" for the book project by getting my thoughts on world government clarified, crystallized, organized, and into prose. The other was the possibility of being able to list several recent articles on world government when I approached the book publishers. Between September 1999 and August 2000, I finished no fewer than eight new article manuscripts on world government topics, as follows:

1. "Federal World Government at the Dawn of the Third Millennium: Old Challenges and New Opportunities." Published in *World Futures* (2000). Later included in a collection of my articles on world government published in 2005: *Rethinking World Government: A New Approach*.
2. "Putting the Cart before the Horse? The Relationship between General Disarmament and World Government." Unpublished.
3. "Rethinking World Government: A New Approach." Published in the *International Journal on World Peace* (March 2000). Later included in the above-mentioned collection of articles on world government (2005), which utilized this article's title for the book title.
4. "Economic Inequality as an Impediment to World Government: Analysis and Proposals." Unpublished.
5. "Voting Weights in a Potential Future World Government: Problems and Proposals." Unpublished. But an expanded version entitled "Representation and Voting in a Potential Future World Government: Problems and Proposals" was later included in *Rethinking World Government: A New Approach* (2005).
6. "World Government Revisited: A Post-Cold War Perspective." Unpublished.
7. "Effective Global Governance without Effective Global Government: A Contemporary Myth." Published in *World Futures*, 2004. Later included in *Rethinking World Government: A New Approach* (2005).
8. "Global Governance and Global Government: A Survey of International Relations Specialists" (with Vincent Auger). Unpublished. But was later included in *Rethinking World Government: A New Approach* (2005).

In view of the lengthy lags in professional journal publishing, it would have been unrealistic to expect to get all eight of these articles into print prior to submitting the book, which was done in late May 2001. But I did reasonably well, in that two of the eight were in print by 2001, in time for listing on the résumé included with the initial submission. Of the six that were unpublished as of 2001, one was published in 2004, and two more were included in the book entitled *World Government Revisited: A New Approach* (2005). So only three never saw print at all.

Of all my book projects that eventually yielded printed output, the interval between starting the writing and seeing the final product released was the longest for *The Next Step: A New Vision of Federal World Government*. As mentioned, the writing commenced in May 1999. Following three title changes and two condensations of the original manuscript, the final outcome was *Political Globalization: A New Vision of Federal World Government*, released in August 2007: eight years and three months later. Both the writing and the search for a publisher were longer than with any of my other books. Throughout the period, I had a feeling that "this was it" and "it was now or never." In both the writing and the search, I gave it everything I had. Indeed, although I did publish several books on world government following the 2007 publication of *Political Globalization*, I still regard that book as the best work on the subject I ever accomplished. Later contributions were simply cut-down repetitions of the arguments put forward in *Political Globalization*. And *Political Globalization* was itself a much cut-down version of *The Next Step*. The original *Next Step* manuscript was 886 pages long in draft typeset format and contained 419,182 words. The published book *Political Globalization* was 404 pages long in typeset format and contained 192,570 words.

My experience with publishers has been that they tend to be obsessed with length. Specifically, they almost always want my manuscripts to be shortened. No matter how much I shorten them, they almost always want them shortened even more. No doubt there have been a few super-successful authors in our time for whom the publishers are willing to set aside all considerations relating to length. For example, Stephen King. When a new Stephen King manuscript arrived in a publisher's office, no doubt they sent it off to the printer without reading it or even counting the pages. Any book with the name "Stephen King" on it was guaranteed to be a bestseller. Unfortunately for me, my writing has never been in the same category as that of Stephen King.

During the writing of *The Next Step*, I tried to be as relaxed and unhurried as I could possibly bring myself to be. I made time for a number of article projects, and even for a substantial book project: *On the Political Economy of Market Socialism: Essays and Analyses*. This was something I had had in mind for quite a while. Over the years I had accumulated a substantial number of article publications related either directly to market socialism, or to closely related topics. Possibly I could interest a publisher in a compendium of these articles. The project seemed more promising than it would have been otherwise, because by this time I was fairly adept at using Microsoft Word to produce camera-ready copy even of quite complicated material involving tables, figures, and mathematics. For mathematics, I used an add-in to Word called MathType. Constructing mathematical expressions with MathType was much easier than with any equation editor I had ever used in the past.

During the spring of 2000, one of my larger projects was preparation of CRC for a compilation of 24 articles, of 692 typeset pages in length. This was obviously not a candidate for bestseller status, but it would be a means of consolidating my extensive work on market socialism—plus it would look good on my résumé. Without too much trouble, I found an academically oriented publisher to undertake it: Ashgate Publishing Ltd, a British firm headquartered in Aldershot, England. It was included in a series they were doing called "Alternative Voices in Contemporary Economics." Of course my work on market socialism was definitely not "mainstream," so I was quite fortunate that they were publishing "non-mainstream" books. They did have qualms about the prodigious length, and insisted that I cut it down significantly. The final published version contained 14 articles, and came in at 439 typeset pages. As Ashgate concentrated on highly specialized scholarly books for which there was no question of a wider market, they did not pay any royalties at all: rather the author received 20 copies of his/her book. I'm sure most Ashgate authors were like me in being quite content with this arrangement. *On the Political Economy of Market Socialism* was released in June 2001.

Not long afterwards, I had a second book published by Ashgate: *Capital Management Effort: Theory and Applications*. This book was both written and published *after* the search for a *Next Step* publisher had commenced. The writing was done during the spring and summer of 2002, with the manuscript finalized in August. Actually very little original writing was involved, as it was mostly a matter of copying and pasting from no fewer than eight articles I had completed from the late 1980s through the mid-1990s that utilized the *els* model (e = capital management effort, l = labor, s = saving). The project was extremely heavy in the use of MathType to produce the multitude of mathematical expressions required. The *els* model had been originally developed for the purpose of enabling a technical evaluation, using as much as possible from mainstream economic theory, of the potential performance of a pragmatic market socialist economy relative to that of the contemporary capitalist economy. Of the articles that utilized the *els* model, four related to this original purpose, while the other four made no mention of market socialism. While I had not yet found journal outlets for any of the four in the former category, I had found publishers for two out of the four in the latter category: "Evaluating Changes in the Distribution of Capital Wealth" had been published in *Economic Inquiry* in 1994, and "Application of the *els* Model: Optimal Tax Rate and Public Good Proportion" had been published in *Public Finance Review* in 1999.

A major motivation for this project was to provide a home for an article entitled "A General Equilibrium Evaluation of Capitalism versus Pragmatic Market Socialism," an adaptation of which was included as Chapter 5 in *Capital Management Effort*. Although I had hoped to interest a major university press in this book (from its title, an editor for such a press would not have guessed that it had anything to do with the controversial subject of market socialism), in the end it found a home with Ashgate, much farther down the prestige ladder from a "major university press." A publishing contract was completed in July 2003, and the book appeared in July 2004. Work on it had helped to make time pass faster as I tried to find a publisher for the all-important *The Next Step*—plus it was another nice item for my résumé. At this stage in my career (I was nearing retirement), a good-looking résumé with lots of publications was no longer potentially useful for getting a job at a better university, or even for retaining my employment at Western Illinois University. But it was potentially useful for finding publishers for my book projects, such as (at that moment) *The Next Step*.

The Next Step/Political Globalization

According to my spreadsheet books.xlsx, the lag between completion of the manuscript for *The Next Step: A New Vision of Federal World Government*, and publication of the book *Political Globalization: A New Vision of Federal World Government*, was 90 months (seven and a half years). As mentioned, this was by far the longest lag in my entire experience. During that 90-month interval, the book was submitted to 73 book publishers and 10 literary agencies: it was rejected by 72 book publishers and 10 literary agencies.

There were some publishers who received more than one submission. Between its New York office and its HQ office in Oxford, U.K., there were a total of 8 separate submissions to Oxford University Press (under various titles and to various editors), and if I am counting correctly from my records, there were a total of 11 different Oxford UP editors who passed on my offering. By and large, they complimented the project as "interesting" and/or "impressive," but regrettably it did not quite fit in with their current publishing direction at that time (or some such thing). None of those 11 OUP editors ever complained, "Hey, didn't you submit this same book to us before?" Actually, acquisition editors receive so many book proposals, and issue so many rejections after cursory consideration, that even if the book had gone to the same editor at some point in the past, he or she might well have totally forgotten about it.

As one might reasonably infer from the above information, Oxford University Press has always been my idea of a "dream publisher": historic, distinguished, and with sufficient clout in the trade market to launch nonfiction bestsellers whenever they find promising material. If I could only publish a book with OUP, my quest for the holy grail might finally be successful. So, with this thought in mind, my first submission of *The Next Step* went to Nancy Toff, Senior Editor for Reference and General Interest in the New York office of Oxford University Press. It is a measure of my optimism that I sent Ms. Toff not the usual thin book proposal (by this time, these were often sent by e-mail), but rather the full manuscript through the postal mail. I wanted them to get a feel for the full magnitude of this book, and seeing the full manuscript, and holding it in their hands, might assist toward this end. The following is the lengthy covering letter to Ms. Toff (dated May 17, 2001), and after that the book's table of contents:

> As mentioned in the Preface, the intellectual odyssey that culminated in the book presented here was sparked by a reading of *The Power Elite* by C. Wright Mills, published by Oxford University Press in 1956. That, together with the fact that you are often comfortable with larger books (as evidenced, for example, by the histories of Norman Davies), would make Oxford an especially appropriate publisher for this project.
>
> The book in question is entitled *The Next Step: A New Vision of Federal World Government*. In the hope that OUP will be interested I am enclosing a photocopy of the entire manuscript, which is complete in draft camera-ready form except for the Index. I am sending you the book itself, rather than a prospectus with a sample chapter, because of the very unusual nature of this book. There is no need to return the photocopy if you are not interested. I am also enclosing in support of this submission a list of directly relevant previous publications and my professional resume.
>
> *The Next Step* sets forth two interrelated proposals: (1) for the establishment of a limited world government tentatively designated the Federal Union of Democratic Nations; (2) for the initiation of a very

large-scale, world-wide economic development effort (a "global Marshall Plan") tentatively designated the World Economic Equalization Program. The proposed world government is limited in three critical respects: (1) in contrast to the conventional world government proposal, each member nation would retain the right to withdraw from the federation at its own unilateral discretion; (2) in contrast to the conventional world government proposal, each member nation would retain the right to maintain military forces under its direct control, armed with whatever armaments are deemed necessary, including nuclear weapons; (3) in contrast to the conventional world government proposal, the federation legislature would utilize a dual voting mechanism under which both the more populous poor nations and the less populous rich nations would have to achieve consensus on proposed legislation before it could be passed (the conventional world government proposal incorporates a voting mechanism in the legislature that would place dominant power in the hands of the more populous poor nations). But at the same time, the Federal Union of Democratic Nations would be a legitimate, full-fledged state entity qualitatively beyond the United Nations of today. It would have a permanent organizational structure, a capital city, a flag, and the highest officials of all three branches of government, legislative, executive and judicial, would be directly elected by the populations of the member nations. It would be authorized to levy taxes and to maintain permanent military forces under its direct control—albeit there would be certain limitations placed on these authorizations.

The current rejection of the world government possibility by the vast majority of the world's population, including the intelligentsia, the political leadership and the general public in all nations, is owing to the fact that the term "world government" is almost universally understood in terms of the conventional world government proposal, according to which the world government would necessarily be both militarily dominant and under the full democratic control of the entire world population, the large majority of which is quite poor by the standards of the most advanced nations. Thus world government is perceived as posing a dire threat of either totalitarian repression or devastating civil war. The limited world government described in *The Next Step*, on the other hand, clearly would not be subject to these hazards. Its principal liability, obviously, is that it would not instantly abrogate the threat of nuclear holocaust. But there are no feasible means by which such an abrogation could be accomplished. The Federal Union of Democratic Nations is not viewed as the "end of history," but rather as an organic part of history. That is to say, it would establish a much firmer and more reliable basis for evolutionary progress toward an international situation in which the threat of nuclear holocaust would indeed be vestigial. This is a genuinely innovative world government proposal, potentially of immense importance to the future of human civilization. If humanity ever becomes sufficiently aware and fully appreciative of this alternative approach to world government, quite likely there would exist a significant probability that such a government would in fact be established.

I have published several books recently with minor, academically oriented publishing houses. These presses envision a very small number of sales, mostly to the largest academic libraries. Their books lack dust jackets, are priced exorbitantly, and receive no marketing beyond being listed in a catalogue and sent to a small number of professional periodicals. As far as I am concerned, there would be no point whatever in having *The Next Step* published in this manner. If this were to happen, the book would meet with what can only be described as "instant oblivion," and would have no more effect on the world than a pebble tossed into the middle of the Atlantic Ocean. My objective, therefore, is to enlist a major publisher on this project, a publisher with the resources to produce this book handsomely and market it intensively, and also with sufficient confidence in the potential market for the book to price it popularly. Although the book is aimed primarily at international relations specialists and policy makers, it would also be of interest to a substantial percentage of the general non-fiction reading public. Although the book is quite long and a complete reading would involve a substantial time investment, the fact is that a very good idea of the book's contents can be obtained from the first chapter alone. The book also contains a multitude of highly readable "mini-essays" on a variety of topics, ranging from the real-world history of empires to the intellectual history of the utopian concept, so that the casual reader could "dip into it" at almost any page and find interesting, relatively self-contained material.

The publishing house that undertakes this title could be making a major contribution to intellectual history, and possibly to real-world history as well. The project could also be quite profitable. There are no guarantees of any of this, of course, but as you well know very few book publishing projects are assured of success. This book, clearly, has something new and different to say on an extremely important subject. Whatever the fate of this particular book in a commercial sense, you would have the satisfaction of knowing that in publishing it you are fulfilling the highest social responsibility of your industry.

The Next Step: A New Vision of Federal World Government

Contents

Preface ix

Part I: A New Approach to World Government
1. Federal World Government: Introduction and Overview 3
  A Miscalculated Risk 6
  The Vision Outlined 11
  A Scientific Approach 19
  The Chicken or the Egg? 27
  Pros and Cons Outlined 32
  Synopsis of the Argument 52
2. The Proposed Federal Union of Democratic Nations 87
  Federal Union Fundamentals 90
  The Three Branches of Government 99
  Critical Limitations and Authorizations 123
  Toward Genuine Global Governance 158
3. Some Historical Background on World Government 177
  Empires in History 181
  Contract-Based Universal Government 195
  From the Hague to Hiroshima 204
  The Postwar World Government Boom 216
  The Soviet Design for a World State 232
  Postwar Western Designs for a World State 268
  World Federalism Today 268
  The Global Governance Myth 278

Part II: Overcoming the Economic Impediment
4. World Economic Inequality 299
  The Global Economic Gap 307
  The Impracticality of Crude Redistribution 321
  Self-Sustained Growth: An Illusory Panacea 330
  Poverty as a Threat to Harmony 344
5. Foreign Development Assistance 367
  Foreign Aid: Basic Facts and Controversies 370
  From the Marshall Plan to the Nineties 381
  Assessing the Effectiveness of Foreign Aid 393
  A Global Marshall Plan? 417
6. A World Economic Equalization Program 431
  The WEEP Model 437
  WEEP Model Policy Simulations 448
  Evaluation of the Evidence 467
  Functioning of a Real-World WEEP 476

It Is Worth Trying 503

Part III: Overcoming the Political Impediment
7. The Issue of Nationalism 513
Nature and History of Nationalism 518
Personal Freedom and National Sovereignty 529
The Correlates of Nationalism 542
Why Federations Fail 560
8. The Progress of Internationalism 571
Treaties and Alliances 574
The League of Nations 586
The United Nations 595
The European Union 637
9. Taking the Next Step 651
The Utopian Smear 658
Risks of Action versus Risks of Inaction 689
Delusions of Impotence 721
Campaign of Enlightenment 733
A Summing Up 756

Notes 763
References 841
Index 887

It would have been interesting (though most likely demoralizing) to have been a "fly on the wall" capable of witnessing the reaction of the Oxford UP editorial staff when this bulky and highly self-important submission showed up in their offices. While it is possible that they merely chortled with glee, if I had to guess, I think it was more likely along the lines of weary resignation at yet another submission that they obviously could not publish, yet which was sufficiently ambitious and had been presented with sufficient panache that they did not want to offend the author with a curt dismissal. After all, just conceivably this was a book with a future—even though that future was not with Oxford UP.

The proposal was bounced around in their offices for a while—and finally bounced out. Nancy Toff sent me an e-mail saying that it wasn't quite right for her area, but she had forwarded the manuscript to Caspar Grunewald of Trade Reference. The Toff e-mail was soon followed by one from Mr. Grunewald who said it wasn't quite right for his area, but he had forwarded the manuscript to Dedi Feldman of Trade Academic. It was Ms. Feldman who had the gumption to put my submission out of its misery: she wrote that, regrettably, *The Next Step* does not "fit in with Oxford's current publishing direction."

Shortly after this dispiriting message appeared in my e-mail inbox, a large box arrived in the postal mail containing the manuscript itself—despite my telling them in the covering letter that they need not return it. The manuscript was in an apparently virginal condition—as if the large loose-leaf binder containing it had never been opened. Actually it *had* to have been opened, because the covering letter and some other supporting material had been inside the front cover of the loose-leaf binder—and it was missing. Somebody in the office (most likely a lowly assistant editor or secretary of some sort) probably skimmed the covering letter and contents page, but I wouldn't be surprised if no one at Oxford UP, including Nancy Toff, Caspar Grunewald, and Dedi Feldman, ever read even one paragraph from the body of the book. It was a big disappointment, of course, but hardly a stunning surprise. I'd been there many times before.

So I did not waste time making my next move. I made five copies of the contents, preface, and Chapter 1, and inserted them, along with my résumé, into thin loose-leaf binders. For my next round of submissions, I went the recommended sample chapter route rather than unloading the entire book on a potential publisher. The latter tactic had not done any good with Oxford UP. I made a few adjustments to the covering letter, such as dropping the complaint about the high-price-low-sales approach of my recent publishers. On June 5, I submitted the proposal to five presses: Harvard University Press, Columbia University Press, Oxford University Press (U.K. office), Princeton University Press, and W. W. Norton. For personalization purposes, the first paragraph in the covering letter for each of these presses was slightly different, complimenting them on being a "leading publisher in the area of international relations," and supporting this statement with an appended list of books cited in *The Next Step* that had been published by each publisher. I was able to get actual editors' names for three of the five presses, but the letters to Harvard UP and Norton were just to the "Editorial Staff." In any case, I wasn't sure that putting somebody's name on a cold submission did any good. I suspected that in most cases, the editor whose name was on the covering letter never saw the submission—rather it was handled by an assistant or a secretary.

Between June of 2001 and August of 2002, I submitted the proposal material for *The Next Step* to 26 publishers and 4 literary agents without getting the merest whisper of a nibble. On the basis of this disconcerting evidence, I decided that perhaps it was time to try something different. There were three obvious factors working against publication of this book: (1) it advocated world government, which was assumed to be a very bad idea by the overwhelming majority of people; (2) it was authored by a person totally unknown to the general public and possessed of rather modest professional credentials in the field of economics; and (3) it was very long. There was nothing I could do about (1) and (2), but (3) was another story—I could shorten the book. Of course it was no fun slicing out large quantities of prose over which I had labored long and diligently, plus the strength of the argument was unavoidably being weakened. The more I cut out, the more critics could complain that I was "ignoring important matters." But even worse than complaining critics would be no critics at all, which would certainly be the case if the book were never published. So in the fall of 2002, I bit the metaphorical bullet and took the metaphorical meat-ax to *The Next Step*. I cut out a total of 216,661 words, bringing the word-count down from 419,182 to 202,520. The single largest cut was in the scholarly apparatus. The original manuscript had separate sections for notes and references, totaling 55,441 words. The condensed manuscript dispensed with a separate section for references, and included the references within the notes, for a total of 16,206 words. The saving on scholarly apparatus was thus 39,345 words. In terms of pages, the total manuscript page-count was reduced from 886 to 472.

I decided also to change the title to *World Government Revisited: A Post-Cold War Evaluation*. Partially this was to enable submission to some of the same presses that had rejected *The Next Step*: hopefully they would not recognize this submission as simply a shortened version of something they had already rejected. (Once again, my initial submission of the revised and condensed manuscript went to an editor at Oxford University Press.) But also there was an element of "change for the sake of change." My state of mind was somewhat comparable to that of a manager of a baseball team suffering a prolonged losing streak. The manager does not know exactly why his team is losing, but there are several possibilities. So he makes several changes, not knowing whether any one of them will make a difference. Thus it was with me: possibly a shorter manuscript would help, and possibly a new title would help. Or possibly not.

On the basis of 20 fruitless submissions between November 2002 and August 2003, apparently neither the shorter manuscript nor the changed title had helped: nary a nibble. So by the summer of 2003, it was becoming quite apparent that the shorter *World Government Revisited* was no more attractive to publishers than the full-length *The Next Step*. At this point, I put a moratorium in effect on the publisher search in order to try a new gambit. In August 2003, draft CRC was completed for a compilation of six articles (three of them published at that time) entitled *Rethinking World Government: A New Approach*. If a major publisher could be persuaded to publish the compilation and it sold fairly well, then that major publisher might also be persuaded to publish *World Government Revisited*.

This gambit was thwarted because no "major publisher" could be induced to take an interest in *Rethinking World Government.* Quite aside from any other negative aspects pertaining to author and subject matter, I was informed by several publishers (including Oxford UP) that they tend to avoid publishing books containing material previously published in journals, because (so they said) libraries are averse to spending their limited acquisition funds on books containing material already available in their journals collection. Finally, after 15 fruitless submissions between September 2003 and June 2004, in order to avoid having the effort go completely to waste, I submitted it to University Press of America. UPA is not so fussy, because their "business model" of having the author pre-purchase 100 copies of his/her book as a condition for publication, reduces their financial risk. Back in 1993, UPA had done a competent job of printing and binding *World Union on the Horizon*, using the CRC I had provided, and in 2005, they did an equally competent job on *Rethinking World Government: A New Approach*. Once again, I had another item that "looked good on my résumé," plus 100 copies of the book to distribute at will to friends, relatives, and influential people.

With the compilation gambit failed, by the fall of 2005 it was time to resume the publisher search. Once again I tried a title change: *Toward a Better World: A New Vision of Federal World Government.* I stayed with *Better World* for a total of only six fruitless submissions, before in January 2006 making yet another title change: to *Political Globalization: A New Vision of Federal World Government. Political Globalization* was the "survivor title": it was the title used for the final version, published in 2007. Between January and December of 2006, there were a total of 21 submissions of the *Political Globalization* proposal material to publishers and 5 submissions to literary agencies. During that time there were two nibbles from publishers, but in both cases, after looking at the full manuscript, they declined interest. There was also one actual contract offer, but after consulting the Web, I concluded that the reputation of this particular publisher was a little too dicey, so I declined.

Of course I was aware of the fact that the reputation of University Press of America was also somewhat dicey, but apparently, judging from Web blogs, not quite as dicey as that of the just-mentioned press (which shall remain nameless). But as the months passed—and then the years passed—I had been thinking more and more about UPA. True, I had always regarded it as a last resort, but the situation was becoming desperate. Did I want this book in print, or not? UPA had done a good job of printing and binding with my two prior world government books: *World Union on the Horizon* (1993) and *Rethinking World Government* (2005), and from occasional searches in online library catalogues, I knew that these UPA books were held by a significant number of university libraries. Surely if it were widely assumed that UPA was a mere vanity press, these books would not be so widely held. On the other hand, I had no illusions that UPA could make a non-fiction bestseller out of anything at all, let alone a controversial polemic by an unknown such as myself. But I was at the end of my tether. Various tidbits of folk wisdom were running through my mind: "Half a loaf is better than none." "A drowning man will clutch at any straw." Etcetera.

And so, on January 2, 2007, I sent the proposal material to Joseph C. Parry, acquisitions editor for Lexington Books. Lexington Books was under the Rowman & Littlefield corporate umbrella—as was University Press of America. In my covering letter, I asked Mr. Parry to forward the proposal to UPA if he could not issue a Lexington contract for the book. I explained that although I wasn't entirely comfortable with UPA's requirement that the author place a pre-publication order for 100 copies of the book, I was sufficiently determined that this book be in print that I was prepared to invest as much money in it as was necessary. This assertion did the trick. Mr. Parry passed the proposal on to UPA, and on February 8, 2007, Patti Belcher, UPA's chief acquisitions editor, expressed an interest. Within the month, an initial contract was issued.

There followed a rather protracted interval of somewhat complicated negotiations prior to the completion of a final contract. While I was willing to invest quite a substantial sum of money in this book, I was determined that UPA charge a lower price for it than they otherwise would have. Personally, I have never had the opportunity to find out exactly what measures the major publishers take to try to achieve bestseller status for books they regard as promising. But one thing was obvious: among various other things, they would definitely set a relatively low price. There was (and still is) an ironclad principle operative in the book publishing industry: trade titles carry low prices; scholarly titles carry high prices.

A somewhat simplified and streamlined version of the negotiations is roughly as follows: Early on in the process, I was informed by Ms. Belcher that according to their standard pricing model, the retail price for a hardcover copy of *Political Globalization* would be $84. To enable a lower price, I would have to either purchase more than 100 copies, provide a "subvention," or a combination of the two. I would have preferred something like $29.95, but that would have involved much too high an outlay from the Yunker family financial resources. Ultimately I was able to get their retail price down to $50 by pre-ordering 300 copies of the book (rather than the usual 100) at the "would have been" retail price of $84, plus paying a subvention of $20,000 to cover their lost revenues from the lower actual price relative to the "would have been" price. Precisely what these "lost revenues" would be would depend on actual sales which could not be known in advance. So the $20,000 was just a rough estimate. In the final analysis, my total investment, counting the pre-publication order plus the subvention, was $45,200 (not counting shipping and handling expense for the 300 copies). Thus I am reasonably confident that University Press of America did not suffer a loss on its publication of *Political Globalization: A New Vision of Federal World Government.*

To say that my spouse Penelope was opposed to this outlay would be a ludicrous understatement. She regarded it as a complete waste of money: $50 was hardly a bargain price in the eyes of most book-buyers, and *Political Globalization* would never in a million years get any reviews in influential media, and thus sell any significant number of copies. Clearly it was doomed from the start, no matter how much money we put into it. I knew she was almost certainly correct, but sometimes sheer determination ("A man's gotta do what a man's gotta do") outweighs rational self-interest. There were two compensating considerations that averted an outright revolt within our normally happy household. First, upon my recent retirement (in 2005), I had collected a sort of bonus (unused sick days and so on) that amounted to approximately $55,000. Although we mostly followed the communal principle in our household finances, I argued that this was a special case: that $55,000 was "my" unexpected windfall, and therefore it was acceptable that I should use it for my own selfish purposes. Secondly, the entire payment to UPA was put on our VISA credit card, which resulted in a prodigious number of points. But for those two factors, blood might have been shed (metaphorically, of course).

In an effort to keep our subsidy from being even larger, I reduced the manuscript page-count by a modest amount (472 pages to 404 pages) by means of shrinking the manuscript word-count from 223,275 to 192,497 (a saving of 30,778 words), and reducing the main type size from 11-point to 10-point. Along with other cuts, the scholarly apparatus was reduced: the notes section containing references (16,206 words) was jettisoned in favor of a references section alone (6,285 words). In the original *Next Step* manuscript, the combined total of the separate notes section and references section had been 55,551 words. Plenty of additional scope now for complaints that I hadn't done adequate homework in writing the book. As for the smaller type size, I recall distinctly my elderly father's comment when I handed him a copy of the finished product: "I can't read this—the print is too small!" Oh well, one does what one can. Actually, that reaction from my father did not bother me all that much, because I was quite sure that he would not have read it even if the print had been super-sized. People do not like to read books with which they do not agree.

Although the odds were overwhelming that Penny's assessment that *Political Globalization* was "doomed from the start" was fully on-target, I did everything within the bounds of sanity to avert this virtual inevitability. During the spring of 2007, I solicited pre-publication comments from a number of reputable mainstream authorities for use in advertising. Of the ten individuals contacted, four were kind enough to provide the following comments:

> James N. Rosenau, George Washington University: What Yunker has to say on the question of world government, although highly controversial, is nevertheless genuinely innovative, interesting, and worthy of thought.
>
> Andrew Strauss, Widener University School of Law: This book makes a serious and original contribution to world federalist literature. Whether they agree with him or not, both the lay and the professional reader will find Yunker's style highly engaging and his argument challenging.
>
> Joseph E. Schwartzberg, University of Minnesota: Yunker's work is characterized by remarkable originality, theoretical rigor, and sophistication. Unlike many advocates of democratic federal world government, Yunker has a keen grasp of the problems created by the yawning economic inequalities within the contemporary global system, and of the need to reconcile fairly the fundamental interests of rich and poor nations.
>
> Scott Hoffman, Director, World Federalist Institute: James Yunker's *Political Globalization* fills a long-empty gap in world federalist writing: it sets forth in considerable detail a novel, plausible plan for moving beyond the anarchic global political structure that leads inevitably to war, terrorism, and environmental destruction. In the tradition of Grenville Clark and Louis Sohn's 1958 classic *World Peace through World Law*, Yunker argues that limited federal world government is both necessary and do-able. However, Yunker's treatment of the issue acknowledges the major political, economic and social changes in the world since Clark and Sohn. Addressing a new generation living in a new century, he makes a powerful new case for achieving genuine global governance through global federation.

These comments were utilized in a tri-fold advertising leaflet that on September 28, 2007, was bulk mailed to 2,320 U.S.-resident members of the International Studies Association, publisher of *International Studies*

Quarterly, *International Studies Review*, and *International Studies Perspectives*. Not counting the labor input of myself and my wife, the direct cost of this mailing was $1,361.50, including $425 for the ISA membership list, $350 for a USPS bulk mailing permit, and $586.50 for postage. To this should be added approximately $600 in indirect printing costs. The ISA provided an Excel spreadsheet file with the membership information, and this was used to print the addresses directly on the tri-fold leaflet. The leaflet used a color image of the cover of the book, and I decided to utilize my own Lexmark C510 laser printer, which had both color capability and duplex (two-sided) printing capability, to produce all 2,320 copies needed. Not only did this operation entirely exhaust all four toner cartridges, but it damaged the photo-developer cartridge which had to be replaced.

Just how many additional sales were elicited by this mailing I have no way of knowing, but judging from the aggregate sales figures it cannot have been many. As of a royalty report dated 12/2015, it had sold 439 copies, 139 over my pre-publication order of 300 copies. On the other hand, I do know precisely the outcome of another marketing gambit I undertook around this same time. I decided to take a shot at placing a 1,600-word op-ed piece entitled "Questioning Conventional Wisdom on World Government" in the *New York Times*. According to the *New York Times* Website, approximately 1,200 unsolicited op-ed contributions were arriving every week, so it was hardly surprising that mine did not make the cut. Whenever I think about it, I am filled with a mixture of amusement and irritation that there are so many "America First" mentalities out there among the citizenry who are convinced (or say they are) that the *New York Times* is part of the "liberal power structure" bent on subjecting the United States to a diabolical New World Order through which a diabolical omnipotent world state would gleefully oppress the people of the United States. I don't know whether there exists a "liberal power structure" in the United States, but even if so, it apparently has no interest whatsoever in boosting any sort of world government.

I had one last promotional effort to undertake before closing the book on *Political Globalization*. As soon as the book was issued in August 2007, a significant number of my 300 pre-ordered copies were distributed to various people. Inscribed copies went to a few relatives, as well as to the individuals who had provided pre-publication comments. A number of others had gone to book review editors of various influential periodicals, and to influential people whom I thought might be inspired to write a book review. But it had always been part of my promotional plan to wait for several months following publication, in order not to interfere with the immediate post-publication sales flurry, and then distribute the remainder to a selected sample of people who might have an interest in it.

On March 28, 2008, I completed a mailing of 223 parcels, each containing a covering letter and a complimentary copy of *Political Globalization: A New Vision of Federal World Government*. The addressees included 168 academics teaching international relations at major universities, 8 high officials in the United States Department of State (including Secretary of State Condoleeza Rice), 6 officials of the Council on Foreign Relations, 21 U.S. Senators (members of the Committee on Foreign Relations, among whom were Barack Obama and Joseph Biden—soon to become President and Vice-President of the United States), and 20 ambassadors to the United States from various nations. A few parcels were returned as non-deliverable, but most got through.

The feedback from this mailing was—not to put too fine a point on it—pathetic. There were approximately a dozen acknowledgements with thanks, two of which came from the offices of Barack Obama and Joseph Biden. As high-ranking Democrats and serious contenders in the impending presidential campaign of 2008, the public relations departments for both men were apparently in high gear. From Obama's office came an e-mail, but Biden's office responded through the postal mail, on letterhead, with a genuine facsimile of Senator Biden's signature. Senator Obama thanked me for my interest and thoughtfulness, and wished me success in my endeavors. Although Senator Biden's letter alleged that *Political Globalization* was "a welcome addition to my library, and it is with eagerness and anticipation that I look forward to reading it," I would be willing to bet $1,000 that neither he nor Obama ever saw the book, and $10,000 that neither senator had time to read even one page. I expect that people at that high a level of influence must receive hundreds of books and articles every year, whose authors believe their writings contain innovative and important information, insights, and recommendations. Perhaps a few of them actually do—but which ones?

My wife Penny was absolutely correct that "never in a million years" would *Political Globalization* be reviewed in any influential media. As far as I know, there were only three references to it in print media. The January-February 2008 issue of *The Futurist* contained a brief notice on it, among numerous other "new and noteworthy books." In Volume XIV:1 (2008), the *Journal of World-Systems Research* ran a short review by Linda Jasper of Indiana University Southeast. Among several other shortcomings, Ms. Jasper noted "Several claims are made that are not substantiated" and "There is a distinct lack of scholarship in *Political Globalization*." Perhaps this reviewer would have been happier with the much longer original version of the book (886 pages versus 404)—perhaps not. After all, I have always conceded that one cannot "prove" that a properly designed federal world government would be beneficial, as if this proposition were a mathematical theorem.

In its December 2009 issue, *Millennium: Journal of International Studies*, edited at the London School of Economics, ran a review article authored by one of LSE's post-graduate students at the time, Jerome E. Roos: "Integration and Transition." In addition to my *Political Globalization*, the review covered two other recent books: *Globalization/Anti-Globalization: Beyond the Great Divide* by David Held and Anthony McGrew, and *Globalization and Contestation* by Ronaldo Munck. The principal commonality among the three books was that their titles contained the word "globalization." As for my effort, Mr. Roos provided a very brief, one-paragraph description of some of the key features of the Federal Union proposal that was basically accurate, but then complained that the book had a tendency "to get bogged down in irrelevant details," and failed to come to grips with the "key challenges of the 21st century," such as "climate change, resource scarcity, rapid population growth, and extreme poverty." Of course, it was not the purpose of *Political Globalization* to propose foolproof schemes for overcoming all the world's problems such as climate change, etc. At this point there are no foolproof schemes in existence for overcoming these problems. Rather the purpose of *Political Globalization* was to argue that a limited federal world government would *increase the probability* that humanity will cope successfully with these problems in our future development. Apparently this purpose was too subtle for Mr. Roos to appreciate. His treatment of *Political Globalization* was concluded with:

> Although we may be nowhere near a situation where the governments of the world would be willing to cede a significant share of their national sovereignty in favor of a world government, the ideal of a united humanity is a dream worth pursuing, and global federalism an alternative worth exploring.

In other words, while we might pursue the dream, it remains a dream impossible to achieve within the foreseeable future owing to the impermeable roadblock of national sovereignty. But then—why bother pursuing it?

By the fall of 2008, it was becoming obvious even to an eternal optimist such as myself that *Political Globalization*, despite the fact that it was likely the best writing I ever had done and ever would do on the subject of world government, and despite my personal promotional efforts, had been a flop. So the question arose: What to do now? One option was to retire well and truly. Although I had been officially retired since the summer of 2005, I didn't *feel* retired, and I wasn't acting the way retired people are expected to act. I was teaching courses in an adjunct capacity, I kept my campus office, and I was working on various article projects—just as I had been doing for the last several decades. I could drop all that, acquire fishing equipment, subscribe to a daily newspaper, and join the little posse of retired WIU professors who met every morning at McDonald's, rain or shine, to grumble and commiserate about this and that.

No, I was not ready for that—perhaps I never would be. *Political Globalization* had been a flop, but that did not necessarily mean that another book, a different book, with the same message but a different presentation, could not be successful. Already, even before the dust had settled over the grave of *Political Globalization*, I was in the early planning stages for my next "big book," my next effort to attain my personal holy grail, a non-fiction bestseller that would make my personal vision of federal world government the whole world's vision.

At that point, my plans for my next "big book" were still quite vague. But there were a few points about which I was certain. First, although the next big book would be *big*, it would not be *as big* as my prior effort. No more approaching the publishers and literary agencies with the 886 pages of the initial *Next Step* manuscript of May 2001. Second, in an effort to impress upon the reader the urgency and relevance of the message, there would be more material "torn from today's headlines": that is to say, more reference to current events and less to historical events. Third, this time around I would avoid using the bugaboo term "world government" in the book's title. In fact, I already had the perfect title in mind: *The Grand Convergence: Economic and Political Aspects of Human Progress*. This would recycle the title I had used for the unpublished manuscript I had labored on so many years earlier, during the 1972-73 academic year. It had been a good title then, and it was still a good title now.

At the age of 65, I was obviously no longer a callow youth. But according to the newer standards of longevity, I was merely in "early old age," Thus the odds were favorable that I had a number of years left in which to pursue my objectives. As the baseball great Yogi Berra so memorably put it: "It ain't over 'til it's over!"

The Third Wave

As mentioned earlier, the 14 books that I published in the 26 years between 1992 and 2018 may be subdivided into three "waves." The first wave, from 1992 to 1997, consisted of the following four books: (1) *Socialism Revised and Modernized: The Case for Pragmatic Market Socialism* (Praeger, 1992); (2) *World Union on the Horizon: The Case for Su-*

pernational Federation (University Press of America, 1993); (3) *Capitalism versus Pragmatic Market Socialism: A General Equilibrium Evaluation* (Kluwer, 1993); and (4) *Economic Justice: The Market Socialist Vision* (Rowman & Littlefield, 1997). Not counting *Toward Genuine Global Governance: Critical Reactions to "Our Global Neighborhood"* (Praeger, 1999) because it was a co-editorship and not a sole-authorship, the second wave, from 2000 to 2007, consisted of a further five books as follows: (5) *Common Progress: The Case for a World Economic Equalization Program* (Praeger, 2000); (6) *On the Political Economy of Market Socialism: Essays and Analyses* (Ashgate, 2001); (7) *Capital Management Effort: Theory and Applications* (Ashgate, 2004); (8) *Rethinking World Government: A New Approach* (University Press of America, 2005); and (9) *Political Globalization: A New Vision of Federal World Government* (University Press of America, 2007).

As its title indicates, the present section will cover the third wave, from 2010 to 2018, consisting of a further five books as follows: (10) *The Grand Convergence: Economic and Political Aspects of Human Progress* (Palgrave Macmillan, 2010); (11) *The Idea of World Government: From Ancient Times to the Twenty-First Century* (Routledge, 2011); (12) *Beyond Global Governance: Prospects for Global Government* (University Press of America, 2014); (13) *Global Marshall Plan: Theory and Evidence* (Lexington, 2014); and (14) *Evolutionary World Government: A Pragmatic Approach to Global Federation* (Hamilton, 2018).

Chronologically, the first wave was completed entirely during the latter part of my working career. My working career commenced in the fall of 1968, but it wasn't until 1992, some 24 years later, that I published my first meaningful book. (The "misfire" of *Socialism in the Free Market*, published by Nellen in 1978, did not count as a meaningful book.) My full-time working career at Western Illinois University extended over 37 years, from the 1968-1969 academic year to the 2004-2005 academic year. Thus my first meaningful book publication occurred well into the second half of that 37 years.

The second wave encompassed the year of official retirement: 2005. *Common Progress*, *On the Political Economy of Market Socialism*, and *Capital Management Effort* appeared before 2005; *Rethinking World Government* appeared in 2005; and *Political Globalization* two years later, in 2007. I signed the "Irrevocable Election to Retire" document in September of 2003, which committed me to retire officially on June 30, 2005. Western Illinois University stopped paying me regular salary on that date (although they continued paying a much smaller adjunct salary for several years afterwards), and on July 1, 2005, SURS (State Universities Retirement System of Illinois) commenced paying me pension income. The publication of *Political Globalization* in 2007 was the culmination of a long slog toward getting this magnum opus into print, a long slog that had extended over more than six years from the date of completion of the initial manuscript in May 2001.

The five books in the third wave were all written and published following my official retirement in 2005. By the summer of 2008, one year after *Political Globalization* had been released to an uncaring world, I was ready to accept the hard fact that the book had been a flop. It had been installed on the dusty back shelves of a handful of libraries, where it was likely to remain undisturbed for all time. It had, alas, met with "instant oblivion." By 2008 I had been officially retired for three years, and the thought occurred to me, as it had many times before, that perhaps the time had come to admit defeat, to give up, to throw in the towel,. Perhaps it was time to embrace retirement as it was understood by most retired people. Perhaps I should abandon the cause, take a deep breath, and devote my life to various superficial distractions designed to keep ennui at bay for whatever limited amount of time remained. *No way!* The thought had barely formed itself in my mind before it was summarily dismissed.

The Grand Convergence

Even before the corpse of *Political Globalization* had gone completely cold, my thoughts were busy with a successor volume. I already had the perfect title: *The Grand Convergence: Economic and Political Aspects of Human Progress*. This utilized the same title I had used long before for the large manuscript on which I had labored diligently during the 1972-1973 academic year. At that time the grand design was still in a somewhat inchoate form, with the consequence that the manuscript was discursive, diffuse, unfocused—and very, very long. It turned out to be unpublishable. Although the manuscript had been unpublishable, the title was still as good now as it had been then. It had an imposing tone and an optimistic ring. Importantly, it omitted the bugaboo term "world government."

In addition to omitting "world government" from the title, the new book would have one additional compelling advantage over *Political Globalization*: it would be much, much shorter. I was hoping to keep the number of pages, in draft typeset form at 11-point Times New Roman, to about 200. During the fall of 2008, after I had definitely decided to write *Grand Convergence*, I had two other sources of hope that the book might be deemed a possible trade bestseller by a major publisher. First, at the invitation of Daniel Kurtz-Phelan, a senior editor at *Foreign Affairs*, I had submitted an article there advocating world government. Daniel's invitation implied that he personally felt that my world government thinking was worthy of exposure in what was certainly the most influential foreign relations journal in the United States, and possibly in the world. All he had to do was drum up sufficient support among the other editors, and this would be a dream-come-true of the highest order. Certainly acquisition editors for the prestige presses would be highly impressed by the fact that my ideas on world government had been given the imprimatur of publication in *Foreign Affairs*.

The second source of hope at that time was the fact that Barack Obama was a candidate for the presidency of the United States, and the polls indicated that he had a very excellent chance of being elected. John McCain was the fully respectable candidate put up by the Republican party in 2008, but it seemed logical to me that any Democratic candidate at all, let alone Barack Obama, would take a more progressive and forward-looking approach to foreign relations. He seemed to be the type of individual who would not necessarily sneer at a carefully crafted and cogently argued proposal for a limited federal world government—especially if that proposal had appeared in the pages of the highly reputable *Foreign Affairs*.

In early November 2008, Barack Obama won the presidential election by what was almost a "landslide" margin. That was a tick in the plus column of my hopes, but later in the month I had to put a tick in the minus column: despite Daniel Kurtz-Phelan's support, *Foreign Affairs* rejected my world government article. Oh well, by this time momentum had been established: there was no doubt that my next book was going to be *The Grand Convergence*, and it was not going to take very long to complete. I had written the first few pages in October 2008, and the entire manuscript was completed in April 2009. At 266 pages (not counting an index to be added later), it came out a little longer than I had wanted. Even so, this would be the shortest "big book" I had ever submitted to the publishers. (It was "big" in terms of substantive content, even if not in terms of number of pages and word-count.)

The fact that it required only about six months to complete was owing partially to its relatively diminutive size, and partially to the fact that it was simply a much condensed version of *Political Globalization*. In other words, the substantive content was virtually identical to that of *Political Globalization*: it was just that the content had been greatly boiled down, and packaged somewhat differently. The leitmotif of *Political Globalization* had been that economic and cultural globalization were proceeding at a rapid pace, and it was time that these facets of globalization be supplemented and supported by political globalization. Political globalization in the form of the Federal Union of Democratic Nations would be supplemented and supported in the economic realm by a Global Marshall Plan. The leitmotif of *Grand Convergence*, on the other hand, was that technological advances in transportation and communications were binding the world more tightly together than ever before in terms of economic and cultural interaction. But there were still huge disparities between nations in terms of economic living standards, and the force of nationalism still tended to set nations at odds with one another. The combination of economic disparities and nationalistic divisiveness was creating conditions conducive to a nuclear world war utilizing weaponry that was ready and waiting. The collapse of Soviet communism was welcome evidence of continuing ideological convergence on a global scale. But the time was ripe now for further consolidation of the human prospect by means of economic convergence via a Global Marshall Plan, and political convergence via the Federal Union of Democratic Nations. The combination of economic convergence with political convergence could be described as the "grand" convergence.

The table of contents for the new manuscript was as follows:

The Grand Convergence

Economic and Political Aspects of Human Progress

1	Looking Ahead: The Long View	
	Triumph or Tragedy	1
	A Long-Run Trend	6
	Nuclear and Other Nightmares	11
	What Should Be Done?	19
2	Political Convergence: Supernational Federation	
	A Pragmatic Blueprint	31
	Key Limitations and Authorizations	41
	Purposes and Policies	56
3	Economic Convergence: Global Marshall Plan	
	Economic Realities: Good and Bad	71
	Foreign Development Assistance	84
	World Economic Equalization Program	93
	Evaluation of the Program	107
4	On the Practicality of Federal World Government	
	Antecedents of World Federalism	115
	Twentieth Century Proposals	127
	The Heterogeneity Bugaboo	140
	The Issue of Nationalism	149
5	On the Advisability of Federal World Government	
	The Global Governance Myth	155

	The New World Order	166
	What Is the "Utopian Delusion"?	177
	Drift versus Direction	188
6	The Next Step: Summary and Conclusion	
	Outline of the Argument	199
	How Is It Possible?	213
	A Final Word	225
	Notes	229
	Index (to be added)	267

Eight years before, in May 2001, I had completed a relatively mammoth manuscript (886 pages; 419,182 words) entitled *The Next Step: A New Vision of Federal World Government*, later reduced to 404 pages (192,570 words) and published by University Press of America in August 2007 under the title *Political Globalization: A New Vision of Federal World Government*. During the more than six years between the completion of *The Next Step* and the publication of *Political Globalization*, I had expended a very large amount of physical, intellectual, and emotional energy on the quest for a publisher. And then after I had finally found a publisher, I laid out a noticeable sum of money approaching $50,000 in a futile effort to avoid having the book suffer the ignominious fate of "instant oblivion." The return on this substantial monetary investment had been disappointing to say the least, and I was determined that nothing like this was going to happen with *The Grand Convergence*. Just as I had put a relatively modest amount of effort into writing it, I was also going to put a relatively modest amount of effort into finding a publisher for it. And if in the end I had to resort to University Press of America—so be it. But of course I harbored the usual hope that this would not be necessary, and that *The Grand Convergence* would be published by an important press and become the non-fiction bestseller of my dreams.

My hope for this glorious outcome suffered a setback before I even started the search for a publisher. Most non-fiction bestsellers are published by a handful of large, highly prestigious, well-established publishing houses: Simon & Shuster, Random House, Alfred Knopf, Norton, Harper, and so on. When I commenced accessing the "Information for Authors" pages on the websites of these publishers, I made an unsettling discovery. Aspiring authors were instructed *not* to submit their work directly; no unsolicited manuscripts under any circumstances would be considered for publication; all submissions must come through authorized literary agencies. In retrospect, I suppose this was the inevitable consequence of microcomputer word processing: this technological advance had enabled hordes of aspiring authors to produce respectable-looking manuscripts, and the major publishers were being inundated with a tidal wave of submissions. In a fully understandable defensive measure, they had commenced using literary agencies to screen the huge mass of submissions. In the past, I had made numerous book submissions directly to the major publishers; apparently this was no longer an option.

There were still a few major publishers, most of them university presses, that were willing to consider unsolicited manuscripts. Among these was Oxford University Press (OUP), which had always been my most-favored potential publisher. OUP had sufficient resources and clout to shoot for bestseller status if they thought they had a promising candidate. Therefore, on May 11, 2009, I addressed an e-mail query to David McBride, Editor, Politics/Current Events (Trade), Oxford University Press USA. My experience has been that e-mail submissions are normally rejected much more quickly than postal submissions. Thus I was somewhat surprised that I did not soon hear back from Mr. McBride. The lack of response became so prolonged that on July 28, 2009, I sent printed submission materials through the postal mail. This finally produced the familiar—through hardly desirable—reply, dated September 22, 2009:

> Dear Professor Yunker:
>
> Thank you for sending me your proposal for *The Grand Convergence.* After reviewing the material carefully, I have unfortunately concluded that it doesn't fit with the current direction of my list.
>
> Please be assured that this decision in no way reflects on the potential quality of the work, but rather has to do with the consideration of my publishing program as a whole. My publishing commitments are extensive, and I unfortunately must limit the number of projects I take on. It is never an easy decision to forego what looks to be promising work, but I must concentrate on those topics and projects that I think Oxford can publish most effectively.
>
> Thank you for giving Oxford the opportunity to review your work. I wish you all the best in finding a suitable publisher.

This is standard rejection boilerplate in the publishing industry, designed to minimize hard feelings on the part of the author—who might just conceivably, by some quasi-miraculous quirk of fate, have submitted a worthwhile book, and one which, by some even more miraculous quirk of fate, might eventually be widely recognized as such.

I was determined that no matter what, I was not going to go through with *The Grand Convergence* what I had gone through with *Political Globalization*. Thankfully, my (metaphorical) prayers were answered. In fact, it was only the second submission, a postal mail submission on May 22, 2009, that eventually resulted in a publication contract. That submission went to Airié Stuart, Trade Editor for Current Affairs and Business at Palgrave Macmillan. But the contract was not issued for quite some time afterwards. There was an "expression of interest" on August 31, but it wasn't until October 13 that Palgrave Macmillan finally came through with a contract offer. Not willing to wait around twiddling my thumbs while Palgrave Macmillan took its own sweet time making up its mind—considering that the most likely outcome anyway would be a rejection—I went ahead and "submitted elsewhere," as the phrase goes. Between August 10 and September 3, I submitted a total of 16 times: 13 to literary agencies, and 3 to major university presses. I racked up 12 rejections from the literary agencies (one of them never responded) and 3 from the major university presses.

As I had feared, the literary agencies were ostentatiously uninterested. Oh well, I couldn't object too vehemently to the situation, since I myself was contributing to the overwhelming deluge of submissions. It would simply require too much time for the literary agency people to go searching through the mountains of submissions in search of the few worthwhile ones. Presumably the vast majority of books selected by the agencies for submission to the publishers are the work of established authors with a track record of success. A small minority of submissions from unknown authors are taken on by the agencies through a process of random selection akin to that utilized by state lotteries. The odds of an unknown author being taken on by a literary agency, I would imagine, are roughly comparable to the odds of winning a very large prize in a state lottery.

As far as I knew in the fall of 2009, as I anxiously awaited a verdict from Palgrave Macmillan, this was a long-established and highly reputable publisher. The original Macmillan Publishing Company had been founded way back in 1843, and ever since then it had been publishing work by world-renowned writers such as Matthew Arnold, Thomas Hardy, Rudyard Kipling, and many, many others. The famous economist John Maynard Keynes had been published by Macmillan. At one time or another, numerous other well-known presses came under the Macmillan aegis: St. Martin's, Henry Holt, Metropolitan, Farrar Strauss and Giroux, and so on. Palgrave Macmillan was one of several offshoots from the original Macmillan. As such, it was certainly a descendent from a long-established and highly reputable publishing company.

What I did *not* know then was that the major part of Palgrave Macmillan's current publishing operations are in the "scholarly" end of the business, far removed from the "trade" end. Unlike trade books, scholarly books are slated from the outset for high prices and low sales. No doubt there are some subsidiaries within the Macmillan family that are geared toward competing in the trade marketplace, and that have the resources and attitudes necessary to achieving non-fiction bestseller status for some of their titles. Alas, Palgrave Macmillan is not one of those. During the publication process for *The Grand Convergence*, my relationship with Palgrave Macmillan was basically the same as it had been with Praeger during the publication process for *Socialism Revised and Modernized* back in 1992. They refused to consider my earnest argument that with my book, they had a potential trade bestseller on their hands.

I'll have to admit that the editors at Palgrave Macmillan were honest about their perception of *The Grand Convergence* from the very outset. The first "nibble" I had from Palgrave Macmillan was in the form of the following e-mail, dated August 31, 2009, from Laurie Harting, executive editor for business and economics:

> My name is Laurie Harting and I am the economics editor at Palgrave Macmillan. The project that you sent in at the end of the summer has made its way to my desk and I wanted to follow up with you. I am interested in the project, but I do not see this book as having a trade (i.e. general readership) audience, rather the specialized audience of academics and researchers.
>
> I would be interested in sending this book out for review—if you are interested in looking at this project as a more scholarly, targeted work, please send me the proposal electronically and I will secure a reviewer.

Of course I was pleased and relieved to receive this communication, not least because it came from a publisher who would not—unlike University Press of America—be asking me to purchase copies of my own book as a pre-condition for publishing it. On the other hand, it was not comforting that Laurie Harting was in the economics and business area rather than the politics and international relations area, because the economic content of *The Grand Convergence* was definitely subsidiary to the political content. Moreover, Ms. Harting was immediately throwing cold water on the idea that this could be a trade book. Nevertheless, I was not in a position to pass up an opportunity such as this. Within an hour of receiving this e-mail, I responded enthusiastically in the affirmative.

Throughout September and into October, I fretted about whether the external reviewer would approve the submission. In trying to publish articles in professional journals, my hopes had frequently been shot down by a single hypercritical referee. It somewhat disturbed me that the reviewer would not get the entire book itself, but rather the proposal material only, which contained only one chapter out of six, plus supplementary materials including my own rosy assessment of the quality and marketability of *The*

Grand Convergence. Apart from the question of whether or not the reviewer would find these rosy claims believable, they were risky in another way. By using the fact that I had published earlier work on the same issues as evidence that there was a receptive readership out there, I was leaving myself open to the objection that I had already published a considerable amount of similar material, and thus there might not be sufficient originality in *The Grand Convergence*. Plus the fact that these prior publications were obviously unknown to the wider world argued against my hypothesis that there were a great many readers out there thirsting for a book of this sort.

But these were subtle questions pertaining to marketability. What *The Grand Convergence* did definitely have going for it, was that it was much, much shorter than *Political Globalization*. This may have been the decisive factor, because on October 12, 2009, Laurie Harting ended the painful suspense by sending me a "Good News" e-mail announcing that Palgrave Macmillan was prepared to issue a publication contract on the book. This was a great relief—but my joy was not completely unrestrained because Laurie's e-mail reiterated her earlier position that this was going to be a specialized, scholarly contribution. Still, a bird in the hand is worth two (or more) in the bush, and so I immediately accepted the offer with expressions of great and humble gratitude. I figured that later on, after the project was well into the editorial pipeline, I could make one last attempt to persuade them that they had a potential bestseller on their hands.

Following this exchange with Laurie Harting, things moved along expeditiously. As the end of October approached, I decided the time had come to make my pitch regarding their marketing strategy. On October 24, I sent an e-mail to Airié Stuart and Laurie Harting urging them to reconsider the matter and recognize *The Grand Convergence* as a potential trade bestseller. Airié Stuart left it to Laurie Harting to respond to this nuisance communication. I'll have to hand it to both these editors. No doubt they were sorely tempted to put this uppity author into his proper place with some harsh language. But they opted instead for what they no doubt deemed the gentle, sympathetic, caring approach. On October 27, the very next day, I received the following e-mail from Ms. Harting:

> Dear Jim,
>
> I appreciate your plea for rethinking our publishing strategy. I went through the manuscript last night and I honestly think the standing strategy is the right way to go. When we look at what works for the general market there are 3 common factors:
>
> 1. the message of the content and the intended audience (the broader the audience the less expensive the book—the more special-

ized the more expensive);

2. the content and style of writing—again the more basic and general, the cheaper;

3. the author's platform—meaning the author's ability to be in front of audiences that are the target audience for the book.

Jim—your book is well written with a message that I believe should be out there for an audience, but I do not think it is a broad market—it is a very specific market of those interested in reading about political economy. It is also written at a much higher level (i.e.: more complicated and with the understanding that the reader has a deep knowledge of political and economic issues and challenges)—the book is also very long (longer than I would like and should probably be cut anyway!)

Palgrave is experienced at being able to market to both the scholarly and academic audiences as well as the readers for this type of book—and Amazon is the great equalizer for readers who are seeking a specialized topic. I would suggest that if we do well in the hardcover—we would absolutely look to do a paperback 18-24 months after hardcover release.

Regards,
Laurie

There were any number of points in Laurie's communication that I might have challenged and disputed. But what was the use? Confrontations between unknown authors such as myself and editors at established publishing houses are basically analogous to confrontations between five-year-old children and robust adults. In such confrontations, might makes right, and neither the five-year-old child nor the unknown author have might on their side. I decided I had better drop the subject and allow matters to proceed as Palgrave Macmillan wished them to proceed.

Besides which, Laurie's aside that the "book should be cut anyway" worried me. Although they were definitely prepared to publish *The Grand Convergence*, the contract stated clearly that the work was to be "approximately" 100,000 words in length. As my proposal materials had clearly stated, the draft typeset manuscript contained a little under 125,000 words. In an October 25 e-mail to Laurie Harting, I noted the discrepancy, and said "I'm hoping that 125,000 words will fall within the 'approximately 100,000' stipulation." Laurie never said explicitly that the 100,000-word stipulation was non-negotiable and that 125,000 was not sufficiently close to it, but within a few days she sent some helpful suggestions about where best to make the necessary cuts. I took the hint. There was only one of Laurie's suggestions with which I could agree: it had to do with the endnotes. She said that would be a good place to wield the pruning shears vigorously, and I could not but agree. After all, how many book readers consult the notes? The condensed version of the book that I sent in through the postal mail in early December 2009 contained 100,086 words, a reduction of 24,601 words from the original total of 124,687. Of the reduction, 16,588 words came out of the endnotes.

Although I was by that time fairly skilled at providing camera-ready copy of neatly typeset material, they wanted to do the typesetting themselves, a preference that I was not so presumptuous as to question. The final printed product weighed in at 246 pages, relative to the 266 pages in the original version using my own typesetting. Thus cutting 24,601 words, or almost 20 percent of the total, resulted in a saving of 20 pages. Of course, to be fair, if I had included an index in the original submitted version, it probably would have been longer by another 8 to 10 pages.

I found it rather irritating that they were so obsessed about length, to the apparent exclusion of any considerations whatsoever involving aesthetics, balance, flow, rhythm, consistency, etc. They seemed to operate under the assumption that any book may be cut down to whatever size is convenient, without this having any perceptible effect on quality and/or marketability. Could this actually be true? They are apparently capable of making money from publishing books. Perhaps their attitude does make sense from a financial standpoint. Authors, on the other hand, are more concerned with publishing good books, as opposed to profitable books.

It required several months before the production process (which included copy-editing) was completed and the book was made available for sale in September 2010. In the interval I mounted a hunting expedition for pre-publication comments from reputable authorities. In this effort I batted .500 (not bad if I had been a baseball player): I sent out six requests for pre-publication comments, and got three. They were as follows, along with their attributions as they appeared on the back cover:

> "James Yunker offers in this work a provocative and nuanced argument for limited world government. His account is particularly notable for the sustained attention it gives to tyranny concerns, and for its accessible application of economic principles to issues related to global poverty and economic inequality. The book should be of interest to students of global governance and international relations more generally, but also those concerned with some possible means of addressing sustainable and globally comprehensive economic development."
> —Luis Cabrera
> University of Birmingham

> "At its core *The Grand Convergence* is a clarion call to take seriously the question of how the global system can be structured to overcome

the primary problems faced by humankind. This book makes a serious and original contribution to the literature on global governance. Whether they agree with him or not, both the lay and the professional reader will find Yunker's style highly engaging and his argument challenging."
—Andrew Strauss
Widener University School of Law

"Conventional wisdom argues that any sort of a global authority is unimaginable. James Yunker challenges this view by providing an innovative plan for a limited federal world government that goes beyond the United Nations, but not so far as to threaten legitimate national interests. This book constitutes a welcome antidote to prevalent complacency and wishful thinking about effective global governance in the absence of effective global government."
—Thomas G. Weiss, Presidential Professor of Political Science
The Graduate Center, The City University of New York

As related below, the third of these comments, from Thomas G. Weiss, eventually led indirectly to another book on world government published the very next year: *The Idea of World Government: From Ancient Times to the Twenty-First Century* (Routledge, 2011). But these comments were not sufficient to rescue the book from its fore-ordained fate. I suppose publication of *The Grand Convergence* might have earned Palgrave Macmillan a modest profit (they priced it at a stratospheric $120), but from my own viewpoint, the book was a flop—just another case of "instant oblivion." To my knowledge, not a single external review of *The Grand Convergence* has ever appeared anywhere, let alone in an influential periodical. Also to my knowledge the number of copies sold was a mere 230.

The Grand Convergence had in common with its predecessor, *Political Globalization*, that it was treated by its publisher as a scholarly contribution. The prices of scholarly contributions are deliberately set very much higher than the typical prices charged for trade titles, with the inevitable result (according to the economic principle of the downward-sloping demand curve) that their quantities sold are very low. No doubt there is a legion of frustrated authors, such as myself, who aim their work at a general audience—but who are then instructed by condescending editors that their work is actually suited only to a handful of libraries and specialists, and therefore it must be sold at a very high price, else the revenue from the small number of sales will not cover the cost of production. Thereupon the publishers set these high prices, and lo and behold, sales are minimal. This has all the earmarks of a self-fulfilling prophecy. Sales are not *inevitably* low—sales are low *because* the price is high. The axiomatic assumption of editors in the scholarly book component of the publishing industry is that the demand for the books they publish is highly inelastic: reducing the price per copy will not increase the quantity of sales to any appreciable extent, thus reducing the price will reduce sales revenue. But it stands to reason that in at least a few cases, this axiomatic assumption is wrong. Unfortunately, I was never able to convince an acquisitions editor that my books were indeed among those "few cases," that they would indeed make promising trade titles. Thus: instant oblivion.

The Idea of World Government

In early April 2009, as I was putting the finishing touches on *The Grand Convergence* prior to commencing the search for a publisher, I happened to become aware, through Web browsing, of Alexander Wendt's 2003 article in the *European Journal of International Relations*: "Why a World State Is Inevitable." I was delighted and excited—not because I thought that a convincing a priori case could be made that the establishment of world government was indeed predestined, but because here was a reputable international relations journal that was willing to publish an essay clearly in favor of world government.

One of the most impressive features of Wendt's inevitability article was the large amount of comment it had attracted in the international relations literature. Among the numerous commentators was Thomas G. Weiss, whose paper "What Happened to the Idea of World Government" had appeared in the June 2009 issue of *International Studies Quarterly*. This was no ordinary article: it was actually a presidential address that Professor Weiss had delivered to the 50th Annual Convention of the International Studies Association. He was decidedly unhappy with the fact that serious consideration of world government had been virtually banished from the international relations literature. He argued that the profession should follow the example of authorities such as Alexander Wendt in reviving discussion of the issue. On top of that, I was veritably astounded to see that my own work on world government was cited by Professor Weiss. The only thing that kept my ecstasy from being complete was that the brief mention of my work was seriously off-target. Despite this slip, here was a reputable authority who apparently shared wholeheartedly my own sympathetic interest in world government. Obviously it was necessary to contact this individual posthaste. On January 30, 2010, I sent him the following e-mail:

Dear Professor Weiss:

I recently encountered your Presidential Address to the 50th Convention of the International Studies Association ("What Happened to the Idea of World Government"), later published in *International Studies Quarterly* (2009). I very much agree that the disinterested and dismissive attitude toward the world government possibility within the contemporary international relations discipline is a shameful dereliction to duty that could conceivably, if we are very unlucky, have fatal consequences for the future prospects of the human race. The IR profession should be seriously examining the various ideas and proposals that continue to be advanced by world federalists such as myself, even though the "world government boom" of the immediate post-World War II period is long gone.

Your article (p. 259) cites my two recent books on world government: *Rethinking World Government: A New Approach* (University Press of America, 2005) and *Political Globalization: A New Vision of Federal World Government* (University Press of America, 2007). The reference occurs in the context of following paragraph:

> "Unlike earlier generations of international organization scholars, however, the goal of contemporary proponents of global governance is *no longer* the creation of world government (see Latham 1999; Yunker 2005, 2007). This is a dramatic change from the past when such thinking was not beyond the pale and actually not even far from the mainstream."

Although I appreciate the mention, I'm a little concerned that readers encountering this reference, and finding nothing else about my work in your article, might assume that I am content with the global governance concept, and am not to be found among the advocates of an actual, functioning world government. But the fact is that I personally am definitely *not* content with the global governance concept, as is strongly emphasized in one of the chapters of *Rethinking World Government* entitled "Effective Global Governance without Effective Global Government: A Contemporary Myth."

I rather wish that at some point in your article, you had mentioned that certain world federalist scholars (specifically myself), working outside the IR discipline, were doing serious, lucid, professionally reputable work in support of the feasibility and desirability of a properly designed federal world government. By "properly designed" I mean a supernational federation somewhere between the ineffectual United Nations of today, and the traditional world federalist ideal of the "omnipotent world state." In my opinion (and in the opinion of 99 percent of the contemporary human population), the omnipotent world state is definitely infeasible at this point in human history, because of the significant danger that it would quickly degenerate into totalitarian tyranny.

Consulting my records, I see that on July 28, 2005, you were among several well-known IR authorities to whom I sent complimentary copies of *Rethinking World Government* (which had just been published) with the request that I be given assistance with placing the larger book then in progress, *Toward a Better World: A New Vision of Federal World Government* (later published as *Political Globalization: A New Vision of Federal World Government*), with a reputable mainstream publisher that would treat it as a trade title. The assistance could be in the form of personally introducing the project to an acquisitions editor, or providing a favorable pre-publication comment or foreword. Alas, no assistance was proffered by you or anyone else, and in the end the larger book was published as a scholarly title (exorbitant price, minimal marketing) by University Press of America, and suffered the predictable fate of "instant oblivion."

Since your article "What Happened to the Idea of World Government" manifests definite sympathy toward world federalism, I will again request a degree of assistance, which will perhaps be more successful than the one I made back in 2005. I am attaching the file practic1.pdf which contains my article "On the Practicality and Advisability of Federal World Government." I realize that this is an "opinion piece" and as such is not suitable for publication in most mainstream IR journals. My impression is that *International Studies Quarterly* is somewhat less stuffy and pretentious than some other major IR journals such as *International Organization* and *World Politics*. Possibly if the "Practicality and Advisability" article was submitted to *ISQ* with your personal endorsement, it might be seriously considered by the editors there. After all, while it may be an opinion piece, it is a *scholarly* opinion piece!

My second request has to do with my latest book on world government, *The Grand Convergence: Economic and Political Aspects of Human Progress*. This has been approved for publication by Palgrave Macmillan and should appear sometime late in 2010. Palgrave Macmillan is the most prestigious press ever to have undertaken a book of mine, and I am very pleased about that. On the other hand, they are insisting on regarding it as a scholarly treatise. The anticipated very high price will deter reviews and limit sales, so that even though Palgrave Macmillan is much more prestigious than such as University Press of America, *The Grand Convergence* will most likely encounter the same ignominious "instant oblivion" fate as my prior books on world government.

I would be delighted to send you, at your request, a pdf file of *The Grand Convergence*, in draft typeset form. Alternatively, I could send you a printout through the postal mail. If upon examining it, you are willing to endorse it, a reasonably enthusiastic pre-publication comment would certainly help the book, and might possibly even get the editorial powers that be at Palgrave Macmillan to change their minds and publish this book as a trade title.

Thomas G. Weiss was perhaps the quickest draw I ever encountered in the context of e-mail correspondence. His reply to the above e-mail arrived on the same day I sent it:

Dear Jim Yunker,

Thanks for your thoughtful email. Sorry about the reference that seems to imply that you're happy with the existent system, I really just wanted to cite the two of you as exceptions. I should have made that clearer.

Do send along copies of the books so that I can place them in our library. As you clearly see, prices are important and the librarian would not purchase them. But it would be great if my students could consult them. So thanks in advance. In exchange, I will send along a copy of the final volume of the UN Intellectual History Project.

All ISA journals are refereed. ISQ is the oldest and stuffiest and toughest to be published in, which is why I wanted my piece to appear there. I can't pressure the editors to take pieces, you will certainly understand that. I would think that International Studies Perspectives would be more appropriate for your piece, or perhaps if it is shortened as a "global insight" (i.e., 3000 words in a kind of op-ed) in Global Governance.

If you send me a hard copy of your manuscript, I can consider doing a short blurb for the book, but you will understand that I need to examine the actual argument before so doing.

Even books on the UN do not have big markets and get very little play, so you can appreciate (even if you do not like) publishers' unwillingness to consider world government—alas, the problem to which my article refers.

Kind regards, Tom Weiss

It seemed a little strange that Professor Weiss's mention of myself and Robert Latham in the "What Happened" piece was allegedly intended as a reference to individuals who were dissatisfied with global governance and wanted actual global government. (I was familiar with the Latham article which was essentially just a complaint to the effect that the effectiveness of global governance was being overrated, but contained nothing to suggest that the author was favorable to any kind of global government.) I had to wonder whether Weiss had actually examined my two cited books, but just assumed what was in them. Or maybe it was a matter simply of careless scholarship. No matter, he seemed a kindred spirit with respect to world government, and I sensed that I could have a fruitful exchange of views with him. As a matter of fact, it soon went well beyond an exchange of views. There was a bit of back-and-forth, and then, on February 4, 2010, Professor Weiss sent me the following bombshell:

> Dear Jim Yunker,
>
> Thanks for your various packages. The librarian is pleased to have the additions of your books for our collection—which, as you mention, is difficult these days for even less expensive volumes than yours. They are now on my reading pile.
>
> I went back, however, and reread good parts of your volume on "Rethinking World Government." Let me say that it is always fun to be challenged. At the same time, there are some serious problems with this book. It has the problems of a set of essays (lots of repetition). On a substantive level, for instance, there are problems of interpretation: I think that "global governance" is both larger and weaker than your characterization (p. 201). On a data level, for instance, I would be hard pressed to find statistics to verify that the 20th century "witnessed an unusual amount of ideological and military conflict" or that "humanity is learning from its mistakes" (p. 75).
>
> But my real problem resides in the fact that your own prescriptive preference is so dominant—it does not merely come obliquely at the outset and the conclusion, but virtually every page reflects a passionate drumbeat—captured by the use of "my mission" and "my belief" (p. 5)—in favor of your Federal Union of Democratic Nations. A more distant and objective analytical perspective would marshal evidence to lead the reader to say, "Gosh, world government is not as zany a proposition as I thought." If I had been a referee, I would have said as much. This is not to say that a press should not have a book on world government, but an academic journal or an academic press should have a more dispassionate examination in which the information and argument presented makes the case, not the assertions of the author.
>
> In fact, in my Routledge "global institutions and issues series," I would entertain a proposal on "World Government Revisited, Problems and Prospects." It would have, I think, something like the following: Chapter 1. Early predecessors (Grotius, Kant, Tsar Alexander, League of Nations, etc.). Chapter 2. Post-World War II proposals (you have very short versions of this elsewhere). Chapter 3. Nature of contemporary problems and solutions (WMDs, climate change, terrorism, you name it) and how current IGOs try to address but can't. Chapter 4. Global Governance and other systems explained and other contemporary efforts and their shortcomings. Chapter 5. Moving ahead.

These books are short (50,000 words) and cheap ($20) and readable. In the above suggested outline, however, the first four chapters would contain at least 90% of the book. The concluding chapter could be future oriented and prescriptive, but not the rest.

Chew on this. Kind regards, tgw

"Chew on this" I certainly would—with delight! Here I was with the *Grand Convergence* book forthcoming in 2010 with the highly reputable Palgrave Macmillan, and now a possibility had emerged of another book with the equally reputable Routledge! At last I was getting my world government ideas published by well-known presses many rungs higher on the prestige ladder than University Press of America. From Professor Weiss's proposition, however, the Routledge book, if it happened, would be far less than I would have hoped for. Not only was it to be unusually short, but I would be allowed only very brief coverage of my own ideas. Still, this was a very exciting prospect. Without hesitation, on February 5, I fired back the following to Professor Weiss:

Dear Prof. Weiss:

Thank you for your recent e-mail suggesting the possibility that I contribute a volume to the Routledge Global Institutions series. I would indeed be honored to contribute to this ambitious and distinguished series. Without a doubt I can temper my natural enthusiasm for world government sufficiently to produce a mostly descriptive narrative account, of modest length (50,000 words or about 125 pages in 12-point typeset), of the history of world federalism from the earliest beginnings to the present day, a book that might be used as a supplement for courses in contemporary international relations. It would mostly cover the same ground as is covered in Chapter 3 of *Political Globalization* ("Some Historical Background on World Government"). The published version of Chapter 3 runs to 43,000 words over 88 pages (in 11-point typeset), but the initial version of that chapter, prior to condensation, ran to 60,000 words over 120 pages.

The title you suggest (*World Government Revisited: Problems and Prospects*) certainly resonates with me. In fact, an earlier version of a recently published article was titled "World Government Revisited: A Post-Cold War Perspective." Afterwards I changed the title to "Beyond Global Governance: Prospects for Global Government," and the paper was eventually published in the *International Journal on World Peace* (June 2009). I'm sorry to say that this journal is definitely not a reputable, mainstream IR journal. But getting back to the title, your suggestion seems to indicate a focus on the current debate (Wendt, etc.), but then your suggested coverage seems to indicate more of an overall intellectual history of world government, working up to the current debate. If the volume follows the latter approach, then I would suggest the following as a title, to which I have appended a tentative list of chapters:

The Idea of World Government:

From Ancient Times to the Twenty-First Century

1. Introduction and Overview (basic concepts, problems, prospects)

2. Historical Antecedents (Aristotle and Alexander, empires, Emeric Cruce)

3. From the Enlightenment to Hiroshima. (Kant, Hague peace conferences, League of Nations)

4. The Postwar World Government Boom (United Nations, Reves, Hutchins, Clark and Sohn)

5. The End of the Cold War (global governance: strengths and weaknesses)

6. The Current Debate (renewed interest, Wendt's inevitability thesis, etc.)

7. Problems and Prospects (current state of the world, overall evaluation of world government)

It is quite true that all four of my books on world government (counting the forthcoming *Grand Convergence*) have been unabashed advocacies. They are far more prescriptive than descriptive, and as such go against the grain of contemporary social science. No doubt this has been partially responsible for the fact that none of them have been published by a reputable university press. There were, of course, at least two other important operative factors: (1) the very strong contemporary consensus that the idea of world government is totally impractical and potentially very dangerous, (2) the modest institutional affiliation and professional credentials of the author.

You are certainly correct that I am passionate about world government. There are two innovations in particular that I am trying to bring into both the popular and the professional perception of world government: (1) a carefully crafted institutional proposal for a limited world government tentatively designated the Federal Union of Democratic Nations, (2) a carefully crafted proposal for a Global Marshal Plan to address the world poverty problem, tentatively designated the World Economic Equalization Program. In my sincere opinion, these two innovations, if fully understood and absorbed, greatly strengthen the case that can be made for world government. It pains me that so few people are willing to devote the small amount of time it would take to fully understand and absorb these innovations.

No doubt it would be more professionally reputable if I just "stated the facts and let the reader draw his/her own conclusions." But the innovations referred to above are not "facts" but are rather better described as "ideas" or "proposals." When Galileo attempted to show that the Earth revolves around the Sun, rather than the other way around, he had factual astronomical observations to adduce (these facts were ignored by his opponents). When Darwin attempted to show that species evolve over geological time, he had factual fossil evidence to adduce, among other things (again, the facts were ignored by his critics). Both Galileo and Darwin could write books filled mostly with factual evidence. They could spend more time stating the facts and less time arguing the point. But I don't have similar factual evidence to cite. Without my two non-factual original contributions (the Federal Union and Global Marshall Plan proposals), the case for world government is almost as weak today as it ever was.

Be that as it may, I am confident that I can write a short book on the intellectual history of the world government concept, of the sort that would be appropriate for the Routledge Global Institutions series. The book would devote only 3-4 pages to the original contributions mentioned above, and, unlike my previous books on world government, it would not be evidently and obviously tendentious, polemical, prescriptive, and argumentative. It could be read without undue discomfort even by people who subscribe to the current conventional wisdom regarding world government. Only a small proportion of the included material would raise substantive doubts concerning the standard justifications for disregarding the world government possibility.

Not counting the forthcoming title with Palgrave Macmillan, I have published a total of 10 books since 1992. In every single case, I wrote the book first ("on spec") and only when the manuscript was complete did I submit proposal material to potential publishers. I'm not sure I want to go this route yet again. Even for me, a 50,000 word manuscript is a bit of an undertaking. I'm not as young as I used to be. May I ask just how much in the way of proposal material would I have to submit in order for an acquisitions editor at Routledge to make the decision to issue a contract? The less, the better. My principal project at the moment is an article on Alexander Wendt's "inevitability" proposition. But unless something really big and unexpected were to come up, I'm pretty sure I could complete a manuscript, for the project described above, by late summer or early fall of this year.
Best wishes, Jim Yunker

I well realized that there was a certain amount of risk in sending the above e-mail to Thomas Weiss. Here I was proposing significant modifications of his initial thoughts concerning the title, organization, and content of the book I might be contributing to the Routledge Global Institutions series. From my past experience with editors, I had the feeling that they very much preferred communications from authors whose thrust might be summarized as: "Yes, boss! Sure, boss! Anything you say, boss!" But obviously Professor Weiss was a very busy man, and I sensed that his actual interest in, knowledge about, and enthusiasm for world federalism was rather less than he would have people believe. Thus I suspected that I actually had a clearer idea of what he had vaguely in mind than he did. I was relieved that he took my input in the constructive spirit it was intended, and readily acceded to my suggestions. Things moved forward rapidly. The book had not yet been written, so the first step was the preparation of a proposal. Professor Weiss provided me with the standard format for such proposals pertaining to the Global Institutions series, to which I adhered assiduously in writing it up.

Although Thomas Weiss, along with his colleague Rorden Wilkinson of the University of Manchester in the U.K., were co-editors of the Routledge Global Institutions series, they did not have independent authority to accept books for publication in the series. They could propose books to higher authority, and presumably higher authority would normally approve them—but not necessarily. In this case, the higher authority was Craig Fowlie, Publisher, Politics & International Studies, Taylor & Francis. Before going to Mr. Fowlie, Thomas Weiss needed to get his co-editor, Rorden Wilkinson, on board. Thomas sent Rorden the draft proposal, and the latter responded with a few comments that were passed along to me in an e-mail dated February 15, 2010:

> Dear Jim Yunker,
>
> We are going to proceed and submit this to the editors at Routledge who will be in touch, probably within a few weeks.
>
> It does not make sense to ask you to tweak the proposal further, but Rorden nonetheless wanted me to pass along his reactions because we both have to sign off on the book before it goes into production. So here are his quick thoughts for your perusal. We shall be back in touch.
>
> [From Rorden]
>
> I agree I think we'll have a book and quickly. I have a few reservations but I don't think he can reconcile them and it'll be an interesting and provocative book anyway (so we should go ahead).
>
> A few things that I think need mentioning:
>
> 1. There is a lot of late 19th century and early 20th century intellectualism around the idea of a world state that he not only doesn't mention, I'm not sure he's aware of – Leonard Woolf is the obvious one, but Keynes (economic consequences of peace), the Fabians and others also ought to be mentioned (which would rebalance the book away from an assumption that it was only one side of the Atlantic that was doing thinking about this – he's read your piece on this so I don't know how he's managing to make this mistake).

> 2. I get very upset by phrases like "communist menace". What he means is a Soviet threat to US interests. Communism per se had very little to do with what the Soviets were doing; and it really isn't helpful to be so unanalytical. He also gets the date of the Bolshevik revolution wrong.
>
> 3. He needs to read Mazower's *No Enchanted Palace* because despite saying he's going to be critical, he isn't! The idea of world government was used and disseminated for some very instrumental reasons, none of which he alludes to and which Mazower deals with (albeit not quite exhaustively).
>
> 4. Statements like English has by accident become a common global language are naive at the very least. He is obviously unaware that imperialism (both British and American) have had a good deal to do with this. He is also forgetting that Chinese isn't going away in a hurry.

As I read over Rorden Wilkinson's "input," I experienced a definite flutter of apprehension. These were just the sort of casual, off-the-cuff potshots by anonymous referees that had been responsible for innumerable rejections of my writings in the past. Often such comments made little or no sense—but they didn't have to. If an editor wants something to substantiate his natural impulse to reject, this sort of thing does well enough.

But then I took a deep breath, and reflected that this situation was very different from the usual situation with an unsolicited manuscript submitted cold to a journal editor or book publisher. First and foremost, I had Thomas Weiss on my side, and apparently Rorden Wilkinson did not wish to make a stink on the matter—he had said, after all, "we'll have a book" and "we should go ahead." All I had to do was to stay calm, avoid getting huffy or sassy, and reply to Rorden's potshots in a civil, professional, and timely manner. On the same day I received his e-mail, I replied to Professor Weiss as follows:

> Dear Prof. Weiss:
>
> Thank you for your recent e-mail. I'm pleased that you think the revised version of the proposal is adequate for submission to Routledge. It's not perfect of course (nothing ever is), but I think that further tweaking would get us well into the range of diminishing returns. The present version should be sufficient for the Routledge commissioning editor and editorial board to make an informed decision. Hopefully it will be favorable.
>
> With reference to Prof. Wilkinson's comments, I want to emphasize at the outset that I welcome any and all input, and will happily incorporate as much of it as I can. If you want I will send you drafts of chapters as I complete them (assuming Routledge decides to publish

the book). And if there are any specific wordings, phraseology, or statements that either you or Prof. Wilkinson feel absolutely must be changed as a condition for publication, I will certainly make those changes (although possibly not happily).

That said, let me try to respond to the four comments you passed along from Prof. Wilkinson.

1. I am certainly fully aware that the idea of world government did not originate in the United States. You may recall the first sentence from the brief description of Chapter 1: "The chapter will commence with a list of well-known historical figures who have allegedly advocated world government: Dante Alighieri, Desiderius Erasmus, Pope Leo X, Hugo Grotius, William Penn, Simon Bolivar, Jeremy Bentham, and many others." The only one on this list, from what later became the United States, is William Penn. In my 2007 book *Political Globalization*, I devoted four pages (pp. 345-348) to the world government thinking of the noted British author H. G. Wells. I will most certainly mention and hopefully discuss Wells. I appreciate the information that Leonard Woolf and the Fabians were also world government supporters, something of which I was not previously sufficiently aware. While it is a nice principle to give credit where credit is due, a rather restrictive constraint on this particular book is the approximately 50,000 word limit. That pretty much precludes the possibility of doing justice to more than a handful of the numerous individuals who have been important in developing the world government idea.

2. I appreciate the correction on the date of the Bolshevik revolution. It was indeed 1917 and not 1918. But I think the term "communist menace" is defensible, at least relative to "Soviet menace." What really worried the capitalist United States, as well as all the capitalist Western European nations, as well as numerous other capitalist nations around the world, about the USSR was not the elimination of tsarist autocracy, nor even its departure from the alliance fighting the Central Powers. It was rather its deep and sincere dedication to the goal of worldwide socialist revolution. It wasn't so much Russia itself that the West feared, it was the militant ideology of Russia. And I don't believe that Marxist ideology was just a cynical mask concealing aspirations toward imperialistic expansionism. Without the hard-line Marxist orientation of the Soviet government throughout most of the twentieth century, it seems obvious that twentieth century history would have been much different. Perhaps Soviet policies, both internal and external, were in some way a perversion of ideal communism. Be that as it may, the Bolsheviks proudly proclaimed themselves the "Communist Party of the USSR." In light of this, I think the term "communist menace" is sufficiently justified. Especially since in a book of 50,000 words covering the entire intellectual history of world

government, plus contemporary developments in the discussion of world government, one cannot afford to get too nuanced. (Still, I'll try to come up with something other than "communist menace." Perhaps "Marxist menace"? That has the advantage of being alliterative.)

3. Thanks for making me aware of Mark Mazower's new book *No Enchanted Palace: The End of Empire and the Ideological Origins of the United Nations* (Princeton University Press, 2009). It was only published in September of last year, so perhaps I can be forgiven for not yet being familiar with it. Since it is currently available from Barnes & Noble for a mere $20, I shall hasten to place an order for it. Your comment seems to suggest that proponents of world government (some of them at least) harbored somewhat nefarious motivations. Could it be that following the demise of colonialism, world government was perceived, at least by some, as a means of re-establishing colonial-style control over the Third World? No doubt many Third World citizens see it in just that way. The point is definitely worth discussion. I thought I recognized the name "Mazower." Turns out that not long ago I read his book *The Dark Continent: Europe's Twentieth Century* (Knopf Doubleday, 1999). Very readable, and very depressing.

4. In saying that English is approaching the status of a global language "by historical accident," I was only trying to convey that this status is not the result of any inherent superiority of the language itself. I think I know as much about the history of British and American imperialism as any other economist, and more than most. (In college I took an undergraduate minor in modern history, and I have been a "history buff" ever since. I find history fascinating—the only trouble is that there is so much of it!) Certainly this history explains the prevalence of English throughout the world, I'm not saying it doesn't. What is "accidental" is that the British and American empire-builders spoke English and not some other language. I suppose it would be politically correct to mention that while English is spoken widely throughout the world, this is largely owing to despicable behavior on the part of the British and American empire-builders of the past. But I'd rather not draw attention to this unfortunate history. Too much concentration on the various misdeeds of past generations is an impediment to the present generation moving forward. As for the Chinese language, I wish only the best for both the Mandarin and Cantonese variants of it. I doubt if it will ever seriously challenge English, as it is too complicated and lacks a simple alphabet. But if it does, good for it. What is important is that within a couple of hundred years, most of the world's population will be familiar with a single language, whatever that language might be. Finally, as for my being naive, as a proponent of world federalism I am accustomed to this particular accusation. Obvi-

ously I reject it.
Best wishes, Jim Yunker

It transpired that Rorden Wilkinson was similar to his series co-editor from across the Atlantic, Thomas G. Weiss, in being very much on-the-ball with response to e-mail communication. On the very next day, February 16, I was relieved to get the following friendly response from him:

> Dear Jim (if I may),
> Thanks for getting back to us. This looks like a good book. We're fussy editors (which we hope is why the series is a success and runs like clockwork) so forgive attention to detail.
> Look forward to having you on board.
> Best wishes, Rorden

So, apparently, I now had Rorden Wilkinson on my side as well as Thomas Weiss. (Both Professors Weiss and Wilkinson later provided supportive pre-publication comments for my additional books.) Things were definitely looking quite promising for *The Idea of World Government.* As I hoped they would, matters proceeded expeditiously thereafter. Craig Fowlie had no problems with the project, and a contract was duly issued and ratified by mid-April. Astonishingly enough, the contract even called for an advance of $1,000: $500 to be paid upon the author's signing the contract, and the remaining $500 to be paid upon delivery to and acceptance by the publisher of the completed manuscript. At last I was a member in good standing of the tribe of paid writers—just like Stephen King! (Though I suppose his advances had numerous additional zeroes in them.) The contract specified that delivery was to be on or before September 1, 2010.

Following contract formalities, I set to work on the book itself. Relative to my previous book projects, 50,000 words was a mere bagatelle. There was a wealth of relevant substantive material readily to hand. For example, the initial draft of *The Next Step*, completed back in May 2001, had a chapter entitled "Some Historical Background on World Government" that contained almost 60,000 words. The problem was to cut the available material down into something that would fit into the specified length. It wasn't easy. The actual writing commenced in early July and was completed by mid-August. Well before the September 1 deadline, on August 17, 2010, I transmitted the completed draft of *The Idea of World Government* to Thomas Weiss, Rorden Wilkinson, and others involved in the project, headed by a table of contents that listed the word-count for each chapter:

The Idea of World Government
From Ancient Times to the Twenty-First Century

	Chapter Title and Component Sections	Words
1	Introduction and Overview	3,884
	Government and World Government	
	Summary Outline	
2	Historical Antecedents	5,951
	Empires in History	
	The Decline of Empires	
	World Government as Empire	
	Contract-Based Universal Government	
3	From Perpetual Peace to the Great War	6,493
	The French Wars	
	The Concert of Europe	
	The Hague Peace Conferences	
	World War I	
4	From the Treaty of Versailles to the Nuclear Age	6,909
	The League of Nations	
	The Uneasy Truce	
	World War II	
5	The Ephemeral Postwar World Government Boom	8,162
	The United Nations	
	Heyday of World Federalism	
	The Omnipotent World State	
	The Cold War versus World Government	
6	The Post-Cold War Era	7,912
	The Soviet Collapse	
	Global Governance	
	The European Union	
	Resurgent Interest in World Government	
7	Is There a Future for World Government?	6,549
	The New World Order	
	Proper Design: The Key Question	
	The Federal Union of Democratic Nations	
	The Case for Evolutionary Progress	
	Notes	2,806
	Select Bibliography	827
	Total Words:	49,493

I had brought the project in at 49,493 words, some 507 words below the 50,000 stipulation! (This did not include the index, but Thomas Weiss had told me they didn't count index words.) I had the same proud feeling that I imagine a Hollywood producer feels at bringing in a movie under budget. On August 17, I also submitted the completed "Marketing Questionnaire for Authors and Editors." At this point the ball was now firmly in their court; *The Idea of World Government* had thus been "put to bed" at my end even before Palgrave Macmillan had issued *The Grand Convergence*. As the summer of 2010 gradually transitioned into the fall of 2010, during which time I received my author's copies of *The Grand Convergence*, I was feeling a blissful sense of peace and accomplishment. It required several months for copy-editing and production to be completed on *Idea*. I did not offer to provide camera-ready copy, since I was sure they would decline the offer. *The Idea of World Government* was issued in both hardcover and paperback editions in early February 2011.

My hopes had not been high that this book would be noticed, so I was not surprised that it wasn't. For one thing, *The Idea of World Government* was basically buried in a long series of books intended to describe (when taken all together, "describe" in excruciating detail) the international relations situation as it currently exists. My book was number 52 in the series. Given an average length of 125 pages, that implied 6,500 pages in the series so far. No sane human being would consider reading 6,500 pages on anything, let alone on international relations. No doubt once in a while an author of one of the Global Institutions books might venture a hint of an idea about how existent reality might be changed for the better. But certainly there was nothing in how the books were produced and marketed to suggest that they were designed to be a fount of innovative thinking. What made my book atypical, if not unique in the series, is that it was concerned with something not currently in existence in the world: a world government. What the book dealt with was a hypothetical concept not yet implemented—and moreover, assuming that the almost universal judgment on it was correct, it never *would* be implemented.

The vast majority of material in *Idea* was merely descriptive information on the intellectual history of world government, information that had little or no bearing on the question of whether or not a properly designed federal world government would be feasible and desirable in today's world. I suppose it might be taken as evidence in favor of world government that the basic notion of a universal state has been around for a long time. But even if so, this is exceedingly feeble evidence. For example, the idea has also been around for a long time that there exists an afterlife in which good, law-abiding, god-fearing folk will, following their deaths, go on happily conversing with one another and enjoying all kinds of pleasant entertainments and diversions for all eternity—and never ever, in all that inconceivably immense span of time, succumbing even once to feelings of boredom.

Simply as a history of world government thinking, *The Idea of World Government* was far inferior to Derek Heater's *World Citizenship and Government: Cosmopolitan Ideas in the History of Western Political Thought* (1996). As might be expected, very little of what historical personages had to say about world government applies to the contemporary world, for the simple reason that they all lived long before the contemporary world came into being. Any reader desirous of a focused analysis of the pros and cons of world government in the contemporary world would have been highly disappointed with *The Idea of World Government*. Such a reader would most likely have fallen sound asleep while plowing through an inchoate mass of irrelevant historical information. In the seventh and final chapter, I was permitted a section on "The Federal Union of Democratic Nations," a section that contained approximately 2,300 words. This section actually *was* a focused analysis of the pros and cons of world government in the contemporary world. But owing to its brevity, the analysis was necessarily so perfunctory and superficial as hardly to have much effect on a mind that was likely already heavily skeptical.

During my original correspondence with Thomas Weiss about the project, he mentioned that the typical Global Institutions book was intended to be published, in a relatively cheap paperback edition, for a price of $20. But by the time my book was issued in early 2011, that goal was slipping badly. In February 2011, I checked the Routledge website to discover that a paperback copy of *Idea* would set a buyer back $31.95. To add to the futility, the page-count was listed as "12." I immediately wrote an e-mail to Nicola Parkin, the assistant editor handling the project, alerting her to the situation. She responded quickly that "12" was simply a typo: it should have been "128." A correction was soon made on the website.

Since 2011 there has occurred a certain amount of inflation. As of 2019, a paperback copy of *The Idea of World Government* is available from Amazon for $42.52. Alternatively, it is available in hardcover for $126.60 (that might be attractive for a few very well-endowed libraries), and also in a Kindle e-book for $37.64 (for the budget-minded reader). These are typical of the prices set for scholarly books, which is why scholarly books register such pitiful sales relative to trade books. According to the most recent royalty statement I had from Routledge (12/2016), total sales of *Idea* as of then had been 464 copies, of which 86 were of the hardcover edition, 373 were of the paperback edition, and 5 were of the electronic Kindle edition. Such clairvoyance on the part of the editorial staff at Routledge: they assumed the book would sell only a handful of copies—and they were right! Does it ever occur to them that perhaps a few of the scholarly books they publish might sell a reasonable number of copies if they would set a reasonable price?

Oh well, not to grumble. Even though sales of *The Idea of Global Government* have not yet topped 500 copies, and probably never will, it was the bestselling book of all the books I've published. And after all, there is a certain amount of consolation in knowing that, at least in absolute numbers, there has been a reasonable amount of dissemination of my world government books. True, most of them are gathering dust way back in the stacks of the largest university libraries. But they exist, they are there, they are physical objects occupying a specific position in space and time. Someday they might be "discovered."

After completing the manuscript for *The Idea of World Government* in August 2010 and forwarding it Routledge for publication, I finally had time to resume work on additional world government articles. Both *The Grand Convergence* and *The Idea of World Government* were in the bag as far as publication was concerned. This was definitely a good thing, but the downside was that both books were being published as scholarly contributions. As such, the probability was vanishingly small that somehow or other, via some quasi-miraculous chain of events, against all odds, sales of one or both of them would explode, and I would finally achieve the non-fiction bestseller of my dreams. Still, I wasn't quite ready to give up just yet. Perhaps I had one more world government book in me, and perhaps that one book would finally hit the bulls-eye. I had no firm idea yet of what that book would consist, but perhaps a promising approach would crystallize as I developed new article projects. Within a few months, I had cranked out no less than four new articles on the subject: "Evolutionary World Government" (November 2010); "Inevitability versus Desirability: Recent Discussion of World Government in the IR Literature" (March 2011); "New Thinking on an Old Dream: Federal World Government" (April 2011); and "Should the United States Champion World Government?" (September 2011).

As it turned out, it was the first of these four articles, "Evolutionary World Government," that provided the seed from which a book with the same title developed: *Evolutionary World Government: A Pragmatic Approach to Global Federation*, published by Hamilton in 2018. Along the way, two other books were spun off from the same overall effort: *Beyond Global Governance: Prospects for Global Government* (University Press of America, 2014), and *Global Marshall Plan: Theory and Evidence* (Lexington, 2014). These three books, along with *The Grand Convergence* (Palgrave Macmillan, 2010) and *The Idea of World Government* (Routledge, 2011), fill out the "third wave" of my book publications.

The inspiration for the "evolutionary world government" project reached back to my earlier research and writing on socialism. One day (I don't remember exactly when) it came to me that a possible parallel existed between revisionist socialism and limited federal world government. Both were developments from what had been an impractical project for social advance, and represented efforts to make an impractical idea, through specific modifications, into a practical idea. The abstract of the initial draft of "Evolutionary World Government," submitted to *Millennium* on November 11, 2010, was as follows:

> Development of the concept of "evolutionary socialism" around the turn of the twentieth century had a major impact on political and socioeconomic trends throughout the century. Revisionist thinkers such as Eduard Bernstein abandoned the orthodox Marxist position that socialism must necessarily involve social ownership of the nonhuman factors of production, and that socialism in this pure sense could only be achieved through violent revolution. In so doing, they laid the basis for the later success of social democracy in Western Europe and throughout the world. This paper argues that an analogous concept, "evolutionary world government," might lay the basis for a successful world federalist movement during the twenty-first century. By abandoning the current world federalist ideal of the omnipotent world state, and envisioning as the immediate objective a limited rather than an unlimited world government, a solid foundation might be laid for gradual, evolutionary progress toward the long-run goal of an authoritative and effective, yet democratic and benign, federal world government.

This paper eventually found a home with *Peace Research: The Canadian Journal of Peace and Conflict Studies*. In the two years between the initial submission to *Millennium* and the submission to *Peace Research*, the paper racked up a total of four rejections: from *Millennium*, *International Studies Perspectives*, *International Journal on World Peace*, and *Global Change, Peace and Security*. Such a prolonged search for a publisher was not unusual, but what was unusual about this particular article was that it made it to invited revision stage at not just one but two reputable, mainstream international relations journals. These were the first two on the above list: *Millennium* and *International Studies Perspectives*. In both cases, I was initially quite encouraged by the fact that the editor's letter requesting a revision seemed fairly positive, and also many of the enclosed referee comments were of a basically positive nature. True, the referees all had numerous qualms and reservations, but over my career I had compiled a very good record on invited submissions: somewhere between 80 and 90 percent of them had eventually been published.

With the "Evolutionary World Government" article, both my invited revisions were substantial and were accompanied by detailed responses to referee comments. Thus it was more than normally painful that on second thought, both these journals decided against publishing. It was also more than normally painful that in both cases, the editors apparently tended toward the view that, in the final analysis, the case for world government cannot be proven beyond a reasonable doubt, as if it were a mathematical theorem—and thus they should not be publishing anything at all on the subject. One of the reasons this irritated me is the old truism that "you can never prove a negative." Thus while it is impossible to prove that world government would be desirable, it is equally impossible to prove it would not be desirable.

Had either *Millennium* or *International Studies Perspectives* accepted and published "Evolutionary World Government," it would have been the most prestigious journal ever to have published one of my world government papers. Even though the paper had a tough time getting into print, the fact that it had "nearly" been published in two highly reputable international relations journals provided much food for optimistic speculation. Possibly this paper could and should provide the initial seed for a substantial book. One positive consideration was that while the title did indeed use the scary term "world government," that term was preceded by "evolutionary." "Evolutionary" is a non-scary word: practically all sensible people are in favor of "evolutionary" change, especially when contrasted with "revolutionary" change. So as I continued trying to find a publisher for the article, I continued mulling over the possibility of expanding the project into a book.

Sometime toward the end of 2012, I had a new inspiration for another book, this one having the salient advantage that it would require a bare minimum of time and effort to produce. It would be a collection of five of my world government articles, plus one additional article on a potential global economic development effort: "Swords into Plowshares: Financing a World Economic Equalization Program."

The "Swords" paper had been researched and written in the autumn of 2002, and after three rejections had eventually been accepted and published in a 2006 issue of *Journal of Policy Modeling*. This paper was an offshoot from my World Economic Equalization Program (WEEP) research, but it was significantly different from my previous three articles and one book on the subject. All of my previous contributions on the subject had assumed that none of the WEEP financing would come from a drawdown of military spending by the rich donor nations. In this latest contribution, the WEEP would be *entirely* financed by resources redirected from military uses. The research was done several years after the demise of the Cold War had resulted in significant declines in military spending by many nations. The premise of the article was that this decline would continue, and the resources thus diverted, instead of being reallocated to consumption and internal investment, would be reallocated to a World Economic Equalization Program. The benchmark simulation showed results consistent with the earlier research: a dramatic amount of economic convergence among the rich and poor nations of the world, at the cost of a very minor reduction in the growth rates of per capita income among the rich nations.

This optimistic finding was tempered by another finding similar to that of the earlier research: that if certain critical model parameters took on sufficiently adverse numerical values, the simulation results showed little or no advantage from the WEEP. Thus the research certainly did not "assume" that a WEEP would be successful. If any "assumptions" were being made, they were being made by foreign aid skeptics who would summarily dismiss the WEEP research without knowing the first thing about it. The "Swords into Plowshares" paper said nothing about the world government possibility, but as always, any indications that significant global economic equalization was feasible, indirectly supported the feasibility of world government.

The other five papers in the collection, tentatively titled *Beyond Global Governance: Essays on Global Government*, all of which focused specifically on world government, were as follows:

"Beyond Global Governance: Prospects for Global Government." Following three rejections, this had been published in the June 2009 issue of the *International Journal on World Peace*.

"Recent Consideration of World Government in the IR Literature: A Critical Appraisal." Following three rejections, this had been published in the August 2011 issue of *World Futures*.

"Evolutionary World Government." This had suffered four rejections, but two of them had been after invited revisions from two reputable international relations journals, and was currently under consideration at *Peace Research: The Canadian Journal of Peace and Conflict Studies*, where it was eventually published in 2013.

"From National Sovereignty to Global Government: Is There a Plausible Transition Path?" This was a contribution to the 2007 "First Virtual Congress (online) on World Citizenship and Democratic Global Governance." It was not an especially promising candidate for publication in a print journal, but here was an opportunity to get this worthwhile effort published as a book chapter.

"Should the United States Champion World Government?" This paper had been written in September 2011 with *Foreign Affairs* in mind. It was a speculative extrapolation from the historical fact that two United States presidents had been instrumental in establishing the two twentieth century international organizations that might someday be regarded as precursors of a full-scale world government. Woodrow Wilson had been instrumental to the foundation of the League of Nations in 1919, and Franklin D. Roosevelt had been instrumental to the foundation of the United Nations in 1945. When the paper was written in 2011, Barack Obama was still in his first term as the President of the United States, and it did not seem impossible that such an intelligent and progressive individual—should he become sufficiently aware of the Federal Union of Democratic Nations proposal—might perceive that by taking the lead in the foundation of such a dramatic step forward in international organization, he might assure himself of favorable treatment in the history books of the future. Unfortunately, *Foreign Affairs* followed their standard operating procedure of rejecting anything having to do with world government.

It required only about a day to put the six articles into a consistent draft typeset format as the six chapters of *Beyond Global Governance: Essays on Global Government*. This was done in January 2013, along with preparation of proposal material. At that time, it could be said that three of the six articles in the collection had already been published in print media, one would be appearing in print in the near future, one had been included in an online conference, and only one remained unpublished in either print or electronic form. The fact that most of this material had appeared in reputable outlets I hoped would support my contention that it contained a far more plausible appeal for world government than could be found in the naive idealism of traditional world federalists. But there was a downside to admitting that most of it had appeared previously in print: according to six out of the seven rejection letters received prior to getting a contract on the book in November 2013, the principal alleged reason they were not interested is that the sales prospects were poor for collections of previously published material. When I finally did get a contract on *Beyond Global Governance*, it was from my old friend, University Press of America.

Although I would have preferred that *Beyond Global Governance* had been published by a better publisher, by the fall of 2013 I had pretty much despaired of this preference, and was happy enough just to get the book into print. In any case, assisted by the competent camera-ready copy I provided, UPA produced a handsome little hardcover volume of 130 pages, counting index and "About the Author." They set the price at $60, but my pre-purchase requirement was for only 50 copies, as opposed to the usual 100 copies. Thus it required a mere $3,000 from me to get the book into print, which, relative to some previous outlays, was a definite bargain.

Even before I finalized the submission material on *Beyond Global Governance*, I had decided that I would definitely expand the "Evolutionary World Government" article into a book with the same title. My initial title for this book was *Evolutionary World Government: The Impossible Dream Made Possible*. More than two years elapsed between the initial decision, in January 2013, to expand the article into a book, and the commencement of the actual writing, in March 2015. By the time I started writing the book, I had had second thoughts about the sub-title (too enthusiastic), and had adopted the more sedate "A Pragmatic Approach to Global Federation." This also had the advantage of utilizing one of my favorite words: "pragmatic." As to the seemingly excessive amount of time between deciding to write the book and actually starting to do so, it can be attributed to the usual quota of distractions. As usual, for example, I was trying to publish various articles, some of them having nothing to do with world government or any other visionary notion.

In addition to various articles, there were two book projects that had to be wrapped up before commencing *Evolutionary World Government: A Pragmatic Approach to Global Federation*. One was to find a publisher for *Beyond Global Governance*. As already mentioned, this was not as easy as I had hoped because the book was a collection of articles, the majority of which were already in print in journals. But during the course of my efforts to find a publisher for *Beyond Global Governance*, another major book possibility suddenly emerged, seemingly out of thin air. The emergence of this possibility is a good example of the sometimes rather convoluted paths taken by authors in their quest for publishers.

On September 16, 2013, I sent an e-mail proposal to Susan McEachern, Vice President and Editorial Director in International Studies, Geography, History, and Area Studies for Rowman & Littlefield. On October 2, Ms. McEachern replied with her regrets: "It has become so difficult to sell collections of previously published essays." By this time I had heard this refrain so often that I was on the verge of despairing of having the book published by anyone but University Press of America. I knew that UPA and Rowman & Littlefield were somehow related under the same corporate umbrella, so I e-mailed Ms. McEachern back with a request that she do me a favor by forwarding the proposal materials to UPA. Quite unexpectedly, Ms. McEachern replied that I should instead submit the proposal to Lexington Books, because it does not require a "buyback" from the author. Lexington Books was already on my list of potential publishers, so it certainly wouldn't hurt to try. On October 4, I submitted an e-mail proposal to Justin Race, Associate Acquisitions Editor for Political

Science and International Relations at Lexington Books. I never did hear from Justin Race. Instead, on October 23, 2013, I received the following e-mail from Joseph Parry, Acquisitions Editor for Economics at Lexington:

> Dear Dr. Yunker,
>
> My name is Joseph Parry, and I am the Acquisitions Editor for Economics at Lexington Books, and your proposal for Beyond Global Governance was forwarded to my attention. Thank you for sending us your proposal for consideration for publication, and for your patience while the work was under review. We regret that we have decided the project would not be right for Lexington Books.
>
> Our decision is not a judgment of the scholarly merit of the book, but rather of its market potential and fit with the needs of Lexington's current publishing program.
>
> The amount of previously published material is a major concern, and the only aspect of your proposed manuscript that I am interested in pursuing is your chapter on a global Marshall Plan (World Economic Equalization Program) as material outside of that chapter is more aligned with International Relations than Economics. If you are interested in speaking with me about possibly revising your proposal so that it's on the World Economic Equalization Program, I would be very open to that.
>
> If you are not interested in expanding the material covered in chapter 3 into a standalone volume, then I would then take the liberty of passing your materials to our sister company, the University Press of America. UPA's publishing arrangement enables them to publish scholarship that makes a significant contribution but that may have a small market. UPA requires authors to secure a pre-publication order of books. A UPA editor will contact you if they decide to pursue publication of your book.
>
> Please let me know if you are interested in revising the proposal so that it's just on the World Economic Equalization Program, or if I can pass your material onto UPA.
>
> Sincerely, Joseph C. Parry

I thought I recognized the name "Joseph C. Parry." Sure enough, a search of my records turned up the fact that several years before (in February 2007), as the acquisitions editor for Lexington Books, Joseph C. Parry had rejected *Political Globalization*, and without even asking me, he had forwarded the proposal to University Press of America. I was quite familiar with UPA and would much rather have had *Political Globalization* published by some other press. But after six years of fruitless effort, I was at the end of my rope. And so when later in February of 2007, I received an expression of interest from Patti Belcher of University Press of

America, I decided the time had come to resign myself to this book's fate.

So now, in 2013, much the same was happening: Mr. Parry was rejecting *Beyond Global Governance*, but was proposing University Press of America as an alternative outlet. As had been the case back in 2007, by this time my hopes on *Beyond Global Governance* had pretty much evaporated anyway, so I was content just to get it into print. But what was different this time was Mr. Parry's expression of interest in taking one of the chapters from *Beyond Global Governance*, and expanding it into a book. I hadn't planned on doing any more WEEP research/writing, but obviously it would be foolish to pass up such a golden opportunity. I quickly responded to Joseph Parry as follows:

> Dear Mr. Parry--
>
> I'm sorry to learn that *Beyond Global Governance: Essays on Global Government* is not right for Lexington Books, owing largely to its incorporation of mostly previously published material. I guess you did not buy my argument about the convenience to a reader interested in world government of the collection into a single location of several articles originally published in a variety of obscure professional periodicals. I also suppose that there are very few readers out there interested in world government anyway.
>
> Still, I would very much like to get this book into print, even if I have to invest a significant amount of my own money in the project. May I ask you to please forward the attached proposal to the appropriate editor at University Press of America. This proposal is slightly different from the one I submitted to Lexington earlier. I have decided to remove Chapter 3 entitled "Swords into Plowshares: Financing a World Economic Equalization Program," since it is so much different from the other five chapters. In its current five-chapter version, the length of the book would be about 145 pages including front matter and back matter. Maybe UPA would be interested in publishing it in a paperbound edition only.
>
> Your suggestion about a book-length expansion of the material in "Swords into Plowshares" interests me very much. I am attaching two more files for your consideration: marshall.pdf contains the typeset version of "Could a Global Marshall Plan Be Successful? Evidence from the WEEP Simulation Model," published in *World Development* in 2004, and bgg-swords.pdf contains the draft typeset version of "Swords into Plowshares: Financing a World Economic Equalization Program," published in the *Journal of Policy Modeling* in 2006, and intended to be Chapter 3 in the earlier version of *Beyond Global Governance*. These two articles would be the starting point for a book-length expansion tentatively entitled *The Global Marshall Plan: Theory and Application*.

Although the substantive content of the proposed book would overlap with the substantive content of these two articles, writing the book would require a significant time investment, in the order of four to six months. To begin with I would have to update the validation data. There will probably have to be some alterations in both the theoretical model (to incorporate recent related literature) and the computer programming. There would also be a significant time investment in providing camera-ready copy of material involving equations, tables and graphs. I wouldn't mind doing this work at all, if there were a sufficiently high probability of a book publication.

I should tell you, however, that back in 2000, Praeger published my book *Common Progress: The Case for a World Economic Equalization Program*. That book did not arouse any noticeable interest within the economics profession, and the proposed book *The Global Marshall Plan* could reasonably be characterized as a "mere updating" of *Common Progress*. The use of the term "Global Marshall Plan," in place of "World Economic Equalization Program," may—or may not—perk up interest and improve sales.

Please look over the attachments marshall.pdf and bgg-swords.pdf, and in light of the above information estimate what the publication probability with Lexington Books of *The Global Marshall Plan* might be. Should the estimated publication probability of this book be high enough, I will definitely embark on the project.

Best wishes, Jim Yunker

From this e-mail there eventuated two book publications in 2014: *Global Marshall Plan: Theory and Evidence* (Lexington Books) and *Beyond Global Governance: Prospects for Global Government* (University Press of America). In both cases there were slight variations in the published titles from the original titles. "The" was removed from "Global Marshall Plan," and the sub-title was changed from "Theory and Application" to "Theory and Evidence." The sub-title "Essays on Global Government" was changed to "Prospects for Global Government." This latter change utilized for the book title the same title utilized for the first included article.

Matters proceeded quite smoothly for *Beyond Global Governance*, likely because by this time I was an "old hand" as far as publishing with University Press of America was concerned. I was slightly irritated, however, when they told me the draft manuscript had to be "externally reviewed" prior to their issuing a formal contract. This was a novelty. Were they kidding? Or was this just an empty formality: a feeble attempt to avert suspicion that UPA was a mere academic vanity press? Too late for that, I thought to myself: the suspicion that they were a mere academic vanity press was already thoroughly established in the blogosphere. The only question was how far outside the blogosphere this suspicion had spread. In any case, I was not overly concerned about the matter, and was not at all surprised that my manuscript passed "external review" with flying colors.

Global Marshall Plan

Lexington Books does not require a "buyback" from their authors, and is consequentially a more reputable publisher. Having *Global Marshall Plan* published by Lexington would be considerably more impressive than having it published by University Press of America. Therefore, I was not surprised that they also required external review prior to publishing a manuscript. They were willing to issue a contract to publish, which in my case was done in November 2017, but a contract stipulation was that the finished manuscript would need to be approved by external review before it was actually published. So the author would have to go to the trouble of writing a full manuscript prior to receiving a definite decision to publish. On the whole, this arrangement was not all that much different from writing a manuscript "on spec," as I had done for all but one of my prior published books.

Still, outside of the fact that this would postpone my getting started on *Evolutionary World Government*, there was no good reason for declining the opportunity. Mr. Parry seemed committed to the project, even though I told him that there would be a "great deal" of overlap between this new book and *Common Progress* (Praeger, 2000). Actually I had to do quite a bit of work on *Global Marshall Plan*, even though the basic simulation model was the same one I had used for the 2000 book. The data had to be updated, the simulations re-run with the new data, and I utilized new and more sophisticated methods of measuring economic results than in the earlier research. On the whole, despite their similarities, I thought *Global Marshall Plan* was a substantive and significant improvement over *Common Progress*. The bottom-line results remained the same: rapid economic convergence with a WEEP in operation; virtually no economic convergence without a WEEP in operation. The principal caveat was also the same: If certain model parameters took on sufficiently adverse values, the simulations showed little or no progress toward global economic convergence.

There was one rather fundamental discontinuity between the "Swords into Plowshares" article that had initially been included in the *Beyond Global Governance* compendium, and the research reported in the book

Global Marshall Plan. The WEEP model in "Swords into Plowshares" had been based on the assumption that all funding of the development effort would come from reduced military spending by the rich donor nations. This approach was *not* utilized in the book: the book reverted to the original assumption, utilized in all my other prior published research, that the funds for the economic development effort would *not* come from reduced military spending, they would instead come from what would have been domestic investment in generalized capital. When first starting work (in December 2013) on a new computer program for the book, I included computation subroutines for both approaches: (1) drawdown of military expenditures, (2) no drawdown of military expenditures. But as the project developed, I soon realized that it would complicate the exposition unduly to discuss results from both approaches. On top of that, the numerical results from the two approaches were not all that different. Finally, a drawdown of military expenditure, as the sole means of financing a Global Marshall Plan, seemed politically unlikely. Therefore, I soon discontinued running simulations using the drawdown approach, and the book never discussed that alternative approach.

What was a more serious concern to me than this technical issue, was Lexington's need for an external review of the completed draft manuscript. There was (and remains to this day) an extremely strong prejudice, among both the general public and the economics profession, that any real-world Global Marshall Plan would necessarily and inevitably be nothing more than an extremely wasteful fiasco. This prejudice is almost as entrenched, in its way, as is the prejudice against public ownership socialism, in any way, shape, or form, and also against federal world government, in any way, shape, or form. Quite likely 75 out of any 100 randomly selected economists, would state firmly, without even looking at the manuscript, that any research at all that suggested that a Global Marshall Plan would be anything more than a disaster, must certainly be in dire error. And most of them would render such a verdict with a great deal of smug self-satisfaction. Obviously, this outcome was something I very much desired to avoid. Another thing I wanted to avoid was having the Lexington production department do the typesetting on this complicated and demanding manuscript. I was fairly sure that on the basis of my extensive prior experience with providing CRC for highly technical books, I could do the job more competently than their own production department.

The upshot from rather lengthy negotiations with Joseph Parry was they did get their external reviews—but they were provided by economists whom I had previously provided with information about the project, and from whom I had received basically positive feedback. On the matter of

CRC, in the end I was allowed to provide it, but only after submitting a large amount of sample work to their production editor.

The final product, issued in August 2014, contained 197 pages, 16 tables, 10 figures, and 40 numbered equations. For once, word-count was not a problem: the total word-count, including notes and index, came to 71,528. The chapter table of contents was as follows:

Global Marshall Plan:
Theory and Evidence

1. Global Economic Inequality	1
Is It a Problem?	5
Outline of the Study	20
2. Foreign Aid: History and Evaluation	35
Six Decades of Foreign Aid	39
Research on Foreign Aid	52
Viewpoints on Foreign Aid	60
GMP Aspirations	67
3. A Global Marshall Plan Model	79
Theoretical Specification	82
Numerical Implementation	89
Validation of the Model	99
Appendix: World Bank Dataset	107
4. Application of the GMP Model	113
Benchmark Policy Simulation	116
Burden of the GMP	128
Sensitivity Analysis	133
5. Summary and Conclusion	143
Evaluating the Research	148
The Implementation Issue	163
Why a GMP?	166
Notes	175
Index	191

The back-cover copy included the following two pre-pub comments, respectively by F. J. Rademacher and Rorden Wilkinson:

> James A. Yunker's *Global Marshall Plan: Theory and Evidence* is an important book because the world urgently needs new ideas. The original Marshall Plan worked wonders in Europe after World War II. Although the global situation is different in many respects from the situation back then, a Global Marshall Plan is perhaps our best option for coping with global economic inequality, a problem which the world community has thus far failed to address effectively. Based on a rigor-

ous theoretical and empirical analysis, Yunker makes a convincing case for trying out that option.
—F. J. Radermacher, University of Ulm, Germany

The scale of world inequality—within, across, and between nations, genders, and other social groups—is staggering. Unchecked, its onward march harbors the kind of social and political instability few have yet to comprehend. Yet, in much the same way we have done when it comes to tackling the other great ills of our time—war, environmental catastrophe, human insecurity, health pandemics, among others—we have eschewed serious, imaginative, and innovative thinking about how to improve, in more than a marginal way, the lived experiences of much of the world's population. That we can no longer sit on our hands while Rome proverbially burns has been made clear by many. James A. Yunker is one of the very few brave enough to take world changing ideas seriously, explore their potential, examine their application, and show their capacity to make a dramatic difference to the world in which we live. Brave, passionate, compelling, Yunker's *Global Marshall Plan* is essential reading for all.
—Rorden Wilkinson, University of Manchester

I very much appreciated Rorden Wilkinson's assertion that this book was "brave, passionate, compelling," and "essential reading for all." Perhaps if this evaluation had appeared in the Sunday *New York Times* book review section, it might have done some good. I had no real hope for that, since all Lexington's books are deemed contributions to the scholarly literature and marketed as such—if you can call a short listing in a large catalogue of recent publications "marketing." The book elicited one review that I know about: by Franz Josef Radermacher in the *European Journal of Development Research* (Volume 18(1): 2006). According to a royalty statement I received in December 2015, as of then it had sold a grand total of 127 copies, 114 hardback, and 13 electronic. I recall my Dad's favorite remark about small sums of money received unexpectedly: "Better than a kick in the head." Getting my book *Global Marshall Plan: Theory and Evidence* published was definitely "better than a kick in the head." But there was no getting around the fact that it was just another case of instant oblivion.

Evolutionary World Government

This brings us to the fifth and final book in the "third wave" of my book publishing history: *Evolutionary World Government: A Pragmatic Approach to Global Federation*. Even though I had definitely decided to write this book by January 2013, it wasn't until March 2015, owing to the various distractions described above, that I actually commenced serious work on the writing. The writing went quickly. This was because most of the substantive material was simply a rehashing of the arguments on world government presented previously in *Political Globalization: A New Vision of Federal World Government* (2007) and *The Grand Convergence: Economic and Political Aspects of Human Progress* (2010). The main innovation was the analogy between the "evolutionary socialism" concept developed by Eduard Bernstein and other revisionist socialists at the turn of the twentieth century, and the "evolutionary world government" concept implied by my proposal for a limited federal world government tentatively designated the Federal Union of Democratic Nations. To show clearly the analogy I needed to provide brief reviews of both the history of socialism and the history of world federalism. There was a goodly amount of the former in my earlier writings on socialism, and a goodly amount of the latter in my more recent writings on world government.

By October of 2015, I had a manuscript ready for submission. In draft typeset format, it contained 448 pages and 195,734 words. This was rather longer than I had wanted, and on the basis of a great deal of prior history, I was far less than enthusiastically optimistic that this book would at last become the non-fiction bestseller of my dreams. Nevertheless, having poured a considerable amount of time and effort into it, I had to try.

I decided this time to forego submission to literary agencies on grounds that the prospects through that channel were indeed dismal. Perhaps the odds would be somewhat better with the handful of major university presses that occasionally ventured successfully into the trade market. At the top of the list of presses in this category was—of course—Oxford University Press. My first dip of the toe into the soul-freezing waters of trying to get a book published was a diffident e-mail to Anne Dellinger (Associate Editor, Academic and Trade for International Politics, Oxford University Press USA), on October 20, 2015, inquiring if perhaps they would take a look at my book entitled *Evolutionary World Government: A Pragmatic Approach to Global Federation*. Ms. Dellinger responded politely to the effect: "Sure, why not?" So I immediately forwarded the proposal material.

As per usual, my hopes with Oxford University Press were highly ephemeral. Ms. Dellinger soon decided that although the "book idea was certainly interesting" and it was clear that I had "put a lot of work into it," unfortunately the project would not fit in well with the rest of her list, which was focused more on comparative politics. Although she had to pass on it, she did take the trouble to forward my materials to David

McBride, Editor for Politics/Current Events (Trade). He too considered them, but he too felt that this project wasn't quite right for his list. Within one week, the OUP possibility was dead and buried. A real shame, because both Anne Dellinger and David McBride had job titles involving the magic word "Trade."

Over the following several months, I presented *Evolutionary World Government* to several more major university presses: Harvard UP, Princeton UP, Yale UP, Cambridge UP, Cornell UP. Finally I decided to try my luck with Routledge, the press that back in 2011 had published *The Idea of World Government* in their Global Institutions series. Of course this time I was going to them with a much larger book, and without the support of Thomas Weiss. Still, I knew people there: in particular I knew Nicola Parkin, the assistant editor who had overall charge of my contribution to the Global Institutions series. Ms. Parkin was delighted to hear from me and promised they would give serious consideration to *Evolutionary World Government*. But she did want to know more about exactly why I thought this book might possess trade potential. There was an obvious whiff of skepticism in such a request. But in my response of June 6, 2016, I did my best to overcome Ms. Parkin's natural skepticism.

I then settled back to await a response. I waited and waited. Days went by, weeks went by, months went by. Had Nicola Parkin, a U.K. citizen, perhaps been run over by one of those big, red, double-decker busses that are so ubiquitous over there? I thought about making inquiries, but I didn't want to seem too impatient, too pushy. Finally, just following New Year's Day, 2017, I succumbed to imperious necessity and sent an inquiry. This time I got a quick response:

> Dear Jim,
>
> Many thanks for your email and happy new year. I am really very sorry that you didn't hear back from me sooner, I was under the impression that I had written to you a few months after we spoke last year, but I can find no trace of that email now I am searching for it and you clearly did not receive anything, so I can only assume something went astray at this end, my deepest apologies for this.
>
> After spending some time reading the material you sent over and considering in particular your aspirations for the trade market for the book, my feeling is that we are not the right publisher for you and my suggestion would be to approach a smaller independent (or perhaps university) press who have a firmer footing in the general readership market to ensure that this book makes the impact you are aiming for. I am sorry to be the bearer of bad news and wish you every success with the book.
>
> I hope to have the opportunity to work with you again.

Very best wishes, Nicola

Apparently my proposal had "slipped through the cracks" at Routledge, as the phrase goes, the operative meaning of which is that they simply forgot about it amid more pressing matters. As for Nicola's contention that Routledge does not have access to the trade marketplace, I found that hard to swallow. But I suppose it was more polite for her to say that than to say: "We simply do not think your book would appeal to a sufficient number of readers to make it a profitable undertaking." As for Nicola's suggestion that I should submit to university or "independent" presses, that had the usual zero value of advice provided by editors. I had already tried a number of university presses, and I had no idea what she meant by "independent" presses. "Independent" of what—the need to make money?

Nicola Parkin's sobering e-mail did compel me into some deep thinking, during those icy-cold days of January 2017 regarding the prospects for *Evolutionary World Government*. I soon came around to two critical decisions related to trying to find a publisher for the book: (1) eliminate all or most mention in covering e-mails, proposal documents, and the like, of my vision that this book might be a trade bestseller—in other words, resign myself to the overwhelming likelihood that if the book were published at all, it would be as a scholarly contribution; and (2) cut the book down in size from its current 448 pages to approximately 300 pages—since condensation will almost surely be a condition of publication. I set to work cutting the manuscript down to size, but I couldn't bring myself to cut 448 pages down to my initial thought of 300 pages. Instead I got it down to 386 pages. In terms of word-count, this represented a saving of 28,973: from 195,734 to 166,761.

My plan was for the first submission of the slimmed-down *Evolutionary World Government* manuscript to go to Palgrave Macmillan, the company that had published *The Grand Convergence* back in 2010. But upon investigation I found that Airié Stuart, the senior editor who had supervised the publication of *The Grand Convergence*, was no longer at the same desk at Palgrave Macmillan. In fact, she wasn't at any desk at Palgrave Macmillan. She had founded her own literary agency, the Stuart Agency, and I suspected that she would need more promising projects than *Evolutionary World Government* to pique her interest. Her successor at Palgrave Macmillan, as the editor most likely to take an interest in my offering, was Dr. Anca Pusca, about whom their website provided the following information:

> Anca Pusca is Editor of the International Relations and Security Studies list. She holds a Ph.D. from American University in International Relations, and was previously a Senior Lecturer at Goldsmiths, Uni-

> versity of London, and visiting professor at the CUNY Graduate Center and Columbia University. Anca welcomes cutting edge authored monographs, edited volumes, Handbooks and Palgrave Pivots on critical IR and Security Studies, as well as theoretical and case-study based work on Diplomacy, Human Rights, and Peace and Conflict Resolution.

I was especially grateful to have this information because I hadn't been sure whether "Anca" was a male or female name. I debated whether or not to reveal to Ms. Pusca Palgrave Macmillan's 2010 publication of *The Grand Convergence*. I doubted very much that that book had sold well enough for them to have a welcoming attitude toward further book submissions from me. On the other hand, almost certainly Ms. Pusca would check me out and thus become aware of *The Grand Convergence*. Thus, no sense in trying to hide anything. By this time Palgrave Macmillan had posted on their website a "proposal submission form" enumerating the questions that the author's book proposal should address. I revised my proposal material to what I hoped would be a reasonable approximation to what they had in mind, and on January 14, 2007, sent the following e-mail to Dr. Pusca:

> Back in 2010, Palgrave Macmillan published my book *The Grand Convergence: Economic and Political Aspects of Human Progress*. In view of this and much other evidence of Palgrave Macmillan's commitment to progressive publishing in the area of international relations, I am hoping you might be interested in a manuscript I have recently completed, entitled *Evolutionary World Government: A Pragmatic Approach to Global Federation*.
>
> Attached herewith is the proposal document, which contains Book Description (3 pages), Book Prospects (2 pages), Manuscript Status and Statistical Summary (1 page), Contents (2 pages), two sample sections (20 pages), and Author's Résumé (7 pages). The entire book, except for an Index to be added later, is complete at this time in draft-typeset format. Aside from four black-and-white figures depicting time plots, it is all straight text. With your permission I will send you the entire manuscript in a pdf file.
>
> The prevailing contemporary conception of world government, among both advocates and skeptics, is the "omnipotent world state," a conception that was totally impractical throughout the Cold War, and which remains so today. However, there exist more promising conceptions of a world government whose power and authority would lie somewhere between that of the omnipotent world state, and that of today's United Nations. To be politically feasible, a federal world government would have to be relatively weak at first. But the establish-

ment of a legitimate state entity at the world level would provide firmer institutional support for developing processes of global governance. The hope is that eventually, via a gradual evolutionary process, humanity's prospects would become more assured through the assistance of a highly authoritative—yet democratic and benign—world government.

In the past, I have published some books and articles in the professional literature that deal with the subject matter of this book. In fact, I recently used the title "Evolutionary World Government" for an article published in *Peace Research: The Canadian Journal of Peace and Conflict Studies* (2013). The book *Evolutionary World Government* represents a comprehensive, full-scale expansion of the ideas sketched out in the article.

I would very much appreciate your consideration of this book.
Sincerely yours, James A. Yunker

After the better part of a year and a half of fruitless questing after a publisher for this book, I was very much encouraged by the response:

Dear James (if I may),

Good to see this new proposal from you, and I'd be happy to consider it for my list. Since the full manuscript is available, would you be happy to share that with me at this stage? We find the more draft chapters available, the more useful the peer-review process is. I also wanted to check with you whether this has been submitted anywhere else, as we usually ask for exclusivity during the review process, as we at that stage are already committing ourselves to the project financially.

I'll look forward to reading the full manuscript and hopefully working with you on this new project.
Best, Anca

At last! An editor willing to consider putting my book on her list! Oh, to be on an editor's list—a consummation devoutly to be wished! Certainly this was very encouraging. On the other hand, there was that dread "external review" matter popping up again, like the hooded head of a deadly cobra. There was obviously going to be same threat that had existed earlier with *Global Marshall Plan*: the project might be cancelled owing to one or more negative external reviews. I thought about suggesting as external reviewers people who were aware of and basically sympathetic toward my work—people such as Luis Cabrera, Alexander Wendt, Thomas Weiss, and so on. In other words, I might try to guide them toward individuals likely to provide favorable reviews, as I had done earlier with *Global Marshall Plan*. But I quickly dropped the idea. Perhaps it was because I thought it would entail excessive delay if I had tried to vet external reviewers for *Evolutionary World Government* the same way I had for *Global Marshall Plan*. I was in more of a hurry with this book than I had been with previous books. I was getting older; time was running out. And so I sent Ms. Pusca a pdf file of the entire book and told her I would be anxiously awaiting the verdict of the external reviewers.

Although the verdict eventually handed down was favorable, a disconcerting amount of time elapsed before that happened. In an interim report Ms. Pusca sent me in March, she admitted that she was encountering a bit of difficulty in recruiting qualified people to do a review. Apparently a lot of international relations authorities have more important things to do with their time than review books about world government. But at last, on April 26, 2017, I received an e-mail from Anne Schult, Anca Pusca's editorial assistant for international relations and security studies, saying that they had in hand two external reviews sufficiently positive to enable them to move forward. The reviews were attached, and I read them with mixed feelings.

One of them was exactly the sort of review that we authors always desire but rarely get. The gist of it was: "Yes, this is good stuff. You have my blessing to publish it as is." The other referee, alas, was more "conscientious." He (or she) presented a lengthy list of recommendations in the spirit of "constructive criticism." Most of it had to do with matters of emphasis: some topics had been discussed in excessive detail, whereas others had been discussed in insufficient detail. According to the reviewer, I should cut out a lot of existing material, and at the same time add some new material. The quantity of the former was larger than the quantity of the latter. In other words, the book should be shorter—considerably shorter, substantially shorter. From my experience, this sort of recommendation is music to the ears of the typical editor. In general, editors are drawn strongly to the view that whatever the length of the book produced by the author, it would be a better book if it were a shorter book. I suspect that they do not need to read a book, or think about it, in order to arrive at this opinion. Maybe this comes from the fact that the nature of their work requires them to do a lot of reading. They get fed up with these long-winded authors who could and should get to the point much more quickly. If the authors would only do that, it would make their jobs a lot easier.

Of course, it wouldn't do to express such sentiments to editors. In my reply to Anca Pusca and Anne Schult, I expressed deepest gratitude for the extremely helpful reviewer suggestions, and assured them that I would immediately start on a revision/condensation that could not help but greatly improve the book. The previous January, I had already done some chopping: I had excised some 28,973 words from *Evolutionary World*

Government. It now seemed that that earlier effort was not going to be sufficient. Once again, during early May 2007, I hacked away at the manuscript. Once again, it was a tiresome chore, an unnecessary chore, and quite possibly a counterproductive chore. I hadn't put that material in the book just to increase the word-count, as if I were a penny-a-word writer of nineteenth century pulp fiction. Every word, every sentence, every paragraph, was in there for a purpose. It added to the argument, strengthened it, enhanced it. By the same token, taking it out reduced the argument, weakened it, un-enhanced it. But for the sake of getting the book published, this had to be done. At the cost of considerable mental anguish, this time my chopping resulted in a saving of 46 in terms of page-count (down from 386 to 340), and 21,678 in terms of word-count (down from 166,761 to 145,083).

Even before I had completed and submitted the revision/condensation, Anca Pusca came through with a contract offer. Apparently she had sufficient overall confidence in the project by now not to need to get any further external reviewer input. On May 17, 2017, I received a lengthy e-mail from her containing the terms of the contract. An actual contract document was not attached, but all the important features of the proposed contract were covered. My blood ran cold as I perused the second item of the contract offer, pertaining to "Word length and illustrations," as follows:

> The extent of the work will be approximately but not exceeding **90,000** words (including endnotes and bibliography) and no fewer than **65,000** words.

Oh, for Pete's sake! 90,000 words! After two major word-cutting surgeries, I had gotten *Evolutionary World Government* down to 145,083 words. And now they apparently were going to require another 55,000-word reduction?! What the hell did they want: a little paperback pamphlet that would tip the scales at one ounce, for which they would charge $85, $95, $105—who knows how much?! Rebellion stirred within my breast. After all, you can push a writer just so far. When you push him past his limit, he might turn on you like a snarling dog.

Plus, at that time I had an attractive alternative possibility in mind. It so happened that several months prior to this, shortly after I had submitted the *Evolutionary World Government* manuscript to Anca Pusca for external review and was anxiously awaiting the outcome of that, I had received, out of the clear blue sky, on January 30, 2017, the following cheery e-mail from one Holly Buchanan, previously unknown to me:

> Dear Dr. Yunker,
>
> Good morning! I hope this email finds you well. I acquire for

Hamilton Books, an imprint of Rowman & Littlefield. As part of a company-wide initiative to streamline our imprints, we have combined the University Press of America and Hamilton Books publishing programs under the name Hamilton Books. You previously published your book *Beyond Global Governance: Prospects for Global Government* with us, and I was wondering if you are working on any new projects.

Hamilton Books publishes a wide variety of high-quality nonfiction titles for scholarly and general interest audiences using an innovative model that combines the best features of self-publishing (quick decision making, a higher level of author control over the content, swift publication process) with the benefit of publishing with an established publishing house that will typeset, print, and market your book. We offer authors an expedited decision-making process, a rapid production process, high-quality books with full-color covers, worldwide distribution, thorough marketing to the appropriate audiences. All our titles are also released as e-books in addition to print copies.

Scholars at all phases of their career, from junior faculty to established and emeritus professors, benefit from publishing with Hamilton Books. We publish custom textbooks for use in your classes (and for use by other scholars) as well as research-based monographs and professional titles in fields throughout the humanities and social sciences.

I would love to hear about your current research and any book projects you are working on. I look forward to hearing from you.
All the Best, Holly
Holly Buchanan, Assistant Acquisitions Editor
Hamilton Books, An imprint of Rowman & Littlefield

So, I thought to myself, Rowman & Littlefield was dropping the UPA imprint, and applying the UPA model to "Hamilton Books." I had little doubt that this maneuver was principally motivated by an effort to escape the bad rap UPA had gotten in the blogosphere for being an academic vanity press. How successful this maneuver would be toward its intended purpose was anybody's guess. Still, this was good news to me, because I had always known that *Evolutionary World Government* might well end up with University Press of America. That it might end up with UPA under a different name was a bit better, because presumably it would take the bloggers a little while at least to realize that Hamilton Books was just University Press of America under a different name. I immediately wrote a friendly reply to Holly Buchanan, saying that I did in fact have a new manuscript under consideration at Palgrave Macmillan, but that if it was unsuccessful there, I would seriously consider submitting it to her. I mentioned also that I indeed felt a great deal of gratitude toward University

Press of America, because they had previously published no less than three of my world government books that numerous other publishers had disdained—and had done a very good job of printing and binding them.

While Hamilton Books might be an attractive alternative to Palgrave Macmillan, I was certainly not ready yet to burn my bridges with the latter—after all, a definite contract offer (a "bird in the hand") cannot be lightly dismissed. So over the next two days, I wrote two e-mails, one to Anca Pusca (May 18), and one to Holly Buchanan (May 19). To Ms. Pusca I said I was delighted with the contract offer, but I just had one small qualm pertaining to the proposed word-count. The manuscript, after its most recent condensation, now stood at about 145,000 words. I was afraid that cutting it down to 90,000 words would seriously compromise its effect. What about something a little higher, say 125,000 words? To Ms. Buchanan I wrote that I had received a contract offer from Palgrave Macmillan but they wanted me to cut the book down from 145,000 words to 90,000 words. That was something I was very reluctant to do, so I asked if Hamilton Books would be likely to undertake publication of a book of 145,000 words in length. I realized that I would have to agree to a pre-purchase order, but I was willing to put up a reasonable amount of my own money to have this book published at what I considered an appropriate length.

For a few days afterward, I pursued negotiations with both Anca Pusca of Palgrave Macmillan, and Holly Buchanan of Hamilton. In addition to the length issue, I needed to know what price they had in mind for this book. After a considerable amount of back-and-forth between myself and Anca Pusca, their final bargaining position came down to this: the absolute maximum word-count they could approve would be 120,000, and according to their standard pricing methodology, for a book of this length they would charge $129 for a hardbound copy. Things were less complicated with Holly Buchanan. They had no problem with a book of 145,000 words. If I would agree to a pre-purchase order of 70 copies, they would charge $90 for a hardbound copy: my investment would thus be $6,300. So it came down to this choice:

(A) Publish with Palgrave Macmillan: 120,000 words (need for condensation); $129 price; 6 author's copies at no charge; no subsidy publishing taint.

(B) Publish with Hamilton: 145,000 words (no need for condensation); $90 price; 70 author's copies at a cost of $6,300; subsidy publishing taint.

I decided to go with (B), and on May 24, I sent the following e-mail to Anca Pusca:

Hello Anca --

I've been doing some deep soul-searching over the past couple of days, and it is with my sincerest apologies for all your time I have wasted, plus that of other members of the Palgrave team, that I am withdrawing my submission of *Evolutionary World Government*. Before I started my effort to find a publisher for this book, I made up a list of presses I thought might be interested in it, some of whom have published one or more of my previous books. There are still a few presses on that list to whom I have not yet submitted. Perhaps one of them will be interested in publishing the book at its current length, and perhaps even with a possible trade market in mind, so that they might gamble on a somewhat lower price. I know this goes against my guiding principle that "a bird in the hand is worth two in the bush," and I have great misgivings that by burning my bridges at Palgrave, this book will never see the light of day in print. But my decision is final.

I think I mentioned in an earlier e-mail that since 1992 I have published a total of thirteen sole-authorship books under a total of eight different imprints. Of the thirteen, no less than six were focused primarily on world government. Every single one of those thirteen books, including the six on world government, was published as a professional treatise, and every one of them suffered a fate for which I have coined the term "instant oblivion." Very few of them got any reviews at all, and the few reviews they did get were all in obscure specialist journals. Whether they got reviews or not, none of them made any noticeable impression on the world—at least that I am aware of. I don't know whether *Evolutionary World Government* will be published or not, but I am quite certain that if it is published by Palgrave Macmillan—cut down even more and carrying a price that will deter all but a handful of potential readers—it will follow my previous six books on world government into instant oblivion. As far as I am concerned, at this advanced stage in my life (I am 73 years old), the difference between six unknown books about world government, and seven unknown books about world government, is immaterial.

But once again, let me offer my heartfelt apologies for wasting so much of your time and effort. Although *Evolutionary World Government* will not be appearing on your list, I am sure it is nevertheless a very impressive list. My best wishes for your continued success in the publishing industry.

Very sincerely, Jim Yunker

Anca's response to this was calm and philosophical, which is to her credit because I am quite sure she is rarely subjected to rejections from authors—as an editor, she is accustomed to dealing them out, not to receiving them. She said she was sorry I wouldn't be publishing with them, but she respected my choice. I responded with "Thank you for your understanding attitude." My May 24 e-mail to her had been a little less than completely forthright, because it suggested that I would restarting the publisher search from scratch, and that I still entertained the hope that I might find a publisher willing to treat the book as a trade title. But in fact, just before sending the above e-mail to Anca, I had received an e-mail from Holly with the above-described offer from Hamilton. So I would not be going into the cold outer world again with this book; instead I would be going into the warm, welcoming arms of Hamilton Books. There was no hope there of trade publication—but so be it. I had had enough with this particular book.

A salient advantage of going with Hamilton is that it relieved me of the onerous necessity of chopping yet more of my hard-wrought prose out of *Evolutionary World Government.* Against that advantage was the salient disadvantage that after all is said and done, Hamilton Books is a subsidy publisher, whereas Palgrave Macmillan is not. How many potential book purchasers would be aware of this fact and would take it into consideration in deciding whether or not to acquire the book? How many would be influenced by the lower price that Hamilton would be charging, relative to that of Palgrave Macmillan? To what extent would the asset of Hamilton's lower price compensate for the liability of Hamilton being a subsidy publisher? I did not know the answers to these questions then, I do not know them now, nor will I ever know them in the future. Like so many important decisions in life, this decision was made, necessarily, on the basis of incomplete information.

Hamilton Books, as the successor to University Press of America, did a very competent job of printing and binding. With the assistance of my own competent camera-ready copy (CRC), and with its colorful hardcover binding featuring an outline map of the world, it is a handsome exemplar of the printer's craft. I was not disappointed. The book was issued by Hamilton in January 2018, with the following contents page:

Evolutionary World Government
A Pragmatic Approach to Global Federation

Contents

1 Salvation or Damnation?
- Neither Utopia nor Dystopia 1
- Outline of the Essay 10

2 A Pragmatic Blueprint
- Need for Specificity 29
- Federal Union Fundamentals 33

	Major Issues	
	Representation and Voting	36
	National Right of Secession	40
	National Right of Armament	47
	Supernational Armament Authority	54
	Religion and Language	59
	Trade and Migration	61
	A Complementary Proposal	
	The Economic Problem	63
	A Global Marshall Plan	71
3	Brief History of World Federalism	
	Origins and Development	81
	The League of Nations	91
	The United Nations	97
	The Postwar World Government Boom	106
	The Cold War and Beyond	117
	Postwar Blueprints	120
	Since the Soviet Collapse	127
4	Brief History of Socialism	
	Early Development	135
	Karl Marx's Codification	138
	The Great Schism	142
	The Soviet Era	147
	Stalin's Dictatorship	150
	Western Attitudes	153
	The Post-Soviet Era	155
+	Socialism in China	161
5	Learning from the Past	
	Evolution – Not Revolution	167
	Origins of Evolutionary Socialism	180
	Bernstein's Contribution	187
	World War I and After	195
	Application to World Government	199
6	Could It Be Done?	
	The Chicken or the Egg?	207
	The Nationalism Issue	217
	Sovereignty and Freedom	220
	Internationalist Tendencies	223
	The Heterogeneity Bugaboo	230
	Religion	233
7	Should It Be Done?	
	A Scientific Approach	241
	Global Governance	250
	A New World Order?	255

The Boat Metaphor 268
8 Prospects
Summary of the Argument 281
Weighing the Risks 292
No Plausible Scenario? 299
Notes 317
Index 341

This was my sixth published book on world government, and almost certainly it will be my last on the subject. Back at Fordham University in the early 1960s, I concluded that the first step toward getting my innovative ideas on the subject the attention they deserved, was to get the ideas into print. It required several decades, but that first step was eventually taken.

8

PRAGMATIC MARKET SOCIALISM

In December 1991, the Russian people, for the second time in the twentieth century, abolished the existing politico-economic regime before achieving anything close to a consensus on what should replace it. The first time they did this was in November 1917, when the Bolshevik party, under the leadership of Vladimir Lenin, overthrew the Provisional Government that a few months earlier had overthrown and abolished the czarist regime that had ruled Russia for centuries. The consequences of the November 1917 Bolshevik Revolution included several years of bloody civil war, which following as it did more than three years of Russia's disastrous involvement in World War I, left the nation, now calling itself the Union of Soviet Socialist Republics (USSR) a virtually prostrated, depopulated, smoking ruin. On the basis of Russia's 1917 revolution, and many similar disturbances in modern history, historians have concluded that politico-economic transformations of the magnitude of those in 1991 in the USSR are frequently accompanied by civil war. Thus the world viewed nervously the prospect of a nuclear superpower in the throes of civil war. Luckily for the world, the Russian people, and the people in the various non-Russian SSRs, were sensible enough not to allow matters to degenerate into civil war. Apparently they realized that civil war—in the nuclear age—would have been an unaffordable luxury.

What had brought about this amazing transformation, which only a few years before would have seemed virtually inconceivable? Of course there was no shortage in the West of smug conservatives who maintained that the Soviet collapse was the inevitable outcome of the contradictions of socialism, of the fact that socialism—any kind of socialism—was a perverse, unworkable system destined to destroy any nation sufficiently foolish to experiment with it. But this particular simplistic viewpoint dated back to shortly after the Bolshevik takeover of the Russian empire in 1917. But why *now* the collapse—after 70 years of apparently rock-solid communist rule of the Soviet empire? Quite possibly the single most important catalyst was a crisis of confidence among the top communist party officials of the USSR.

And quite possibly the single most important factor underlying this crisis of confidence was the inability of the Soviet Union, after years and decades of trying, to achieve a level of efficiency and prosperity sufficient to enable its rank-and-file citizens to enjoy a standard of living equivalent to—let alone superior to—the living standards of the rank-and-file citizens of the leading capitalist nations. In an absolute sense, the Soviet population as of the 1980s was not enduring especially impoverished conditions. The living standards of the Soviet people were far above the subsistence levels prevalent within most Third World countries, such as India, that continued to abide by the private ownership principle of capitalism. As of the 1980s, Soviet living standards were comparable to those in such capitalist nations as Turkey and Argentina—but Turkey and Argentina were not subject to a withering barrage of scorn and ridicule because of the paltry living standards of their people. What made the Soviet Union the target of so much abuse from the West was that over several decades it had been stridently denouncing the Western capitalist nations as cesspools of poverty, economic exploitation, and social decay that should and would eventually crumble and collapse. Following the introduction of nuclear weapons into international relations after World War II, this confrontational attitude fueled a Cold War impasse that threatened to unleash nuclear holocaust. Had such a holocaust actually occurred, the Soviet people would have suffered as much as anyone else—and probably more than most. And this existential threat to all mankind was the direct consequence of Soviet adherence to hardline Marxism. Meanwhile, hardline Marxism in the Soviet Union was failing to produce living standards among the Soviet people even roughly comparable to those in the West. It speaks well of such high-level communist leaders as Mikhail Gorbachev and Boris Yeltsin that eventually their intelligence, and their consciences, induced them to recognize and acknowledge the error of Soviet policy—and to change it.

Although there was deep and abiding support for comprehensive economic and political transformation among all levels of the Russian population, as often happens with major changes, the "transition costs" turned out to be much larger than anyone had anticipated. During the late 1980s and early 1990s, the Russian economy slipped into a devastating depression fully equivalent to the Great Depression that had prostrated the capitalist world back in the 1930s. The resulting popular discontent culminated in the constitutional crisis of September-October 1993, during which the festering conflict between Russian president Yeltsin and the Russian parliament boiled over into street fighting and armed intervention by the Russian army. Yeltsin emerged victorious from the crisis, but this traumatic episode clearly demonstrated that the final form of the Russian political and economic system was not yet fully settled. Nevertheless, by the mid-1990s it was almost completely certain that the authority of the Communist Party of the USSR was gone—probably forever, and also that Soviet centrally planned socialism in the pure public ownership sense was also gone—also probably forever.

Since the 1960s days of the New World and Plan Alpha, pragmatic market socialism had been the linchpin of my own "grand plan" for improving the future prospects of global human civilization. I saw pragmatic market socialism as the critical first step of a comprehensive scenario leading ultimately to a stable and benign federal world government. Pragmatic market socialism would be the first step toward comprehensive ideological harmonization among the communist and non-communist blocs of nations. The second step would be the abandonment of central planning and the one-party state by the communist nations. In other words, both East and West would converge on democratic market socialism: the West from the starting point of democratic market capitalism, and the East from the starting point of oligarchic planned socialism. Once this ideological impasse had been surmounted, it would be time for the simultaneous initiation of a World Economic Equalization Program (aka Global Marshall Plan) and a Federal Union of Democratic Nations.

But if the communist East in the early 1990s was now abandoning public ownership socialism, central planning, and the one-party state—or at least the republics of the ex-USSR and the Eastern European satellite states were doing so—then the role of pragmatic market socialism as part of an ideological bridge between East and West was no longer relevant. The ex-USSR and the Eastern European nations were now coming over to democratic market capitalism of their own accord. Pragmatic market socialism was no longer needed for purposes of worldwide ideological harmonization.

After working intently for approximately 30 years on the development of a plausible pragmatic market socialist alternative to contemporary capitalism, it would be an understatement to say that I had mixed feelings about this. I would have preferred that the ex-USSR and the Eastern European nations adopt democratic market socialism rather than democratic market capitalism. In my view, they were throwing the baby out with the bathwater—the dirty bathwater being central planning and the one-party state, and the baby being public ownership socialism. I recall that in one of my letters to James R. Dunton, editor-in-chief of Praeger Publishers which in the spring of 1992 was preparing to publish my book *Socialism Revised and Modernized: The Case for Pragmatic Market Socialism*, I said that the pragmatic market socialist system was actually perfectly suited to current Russian conditions—but unfortunately, "it will be difficult to get their [the Russians'] attention." Alas, that book, and the ideas within it, did not get the Russians' attention, any more than it got the attention of any significant number of people in the West.

Although I had mixed emotions about the transformations in progress in the communist East, my predominant emotion by far was happiness that these changes were going to deal the Cold War a terrific blow from which it would hopefully never recover. Nevertheless, my relief at the imminent end of the Cold War was not as complete and unalloyed as that of most other people. This was because I was far more aware than most other people of two remaining obstacles to a benign future for humanity. Now that the first obstacle—ideological conflict—was finally in abeyance, that left two other obstacles fully intact: global economic inequality, and the sovereign nation-state system. Ideological conflict had become a major factor in international relations with the successful consolidation of the Bolshevik revolution in the early 1920s. But prior to the early 1920s, humanity had been inflicting continuous warfare on itself since the beginning of history. The rise of the nation-state in the modern era, accompanied as it was by impressive technological progress in weaponry, had made warfare even more devastating than it had ever been in the past. The modern era also witnessed rapid economic progress in a relatively small subset of nations, while economic progress in the other nations was much slower. Thus a widening gap was emerging between living standards in the First World nations, and those in the rest of the world. The traditional non-economic causes of hostility and conflict were now being further aggravated by resentments based on economic inequality. The rise of the theory of "economic imperialism" (the rich countries are rich *because* the poor countries are poor) was an outward symptom of this underlying reality.

It soon became apparent that although the decline in tensions with the effective end of the Cold War would bring about a substantial amount of disarmament, it would not bring about full disarmament. The same attitudes of mutual suspicion and mistrust that had animated nations against each other before the rise of ideology continued onward after the decline of ideology, and made impossible a level of mutual trust sufficient to enable large-scale disarmament. Thus in our time—fully decades after the end of the Cold War—the superpowers continue to maintain nuclear arsenals capable of crippling global human civilization, should their use ever become necessary.

Once it became clear, at the latest by the mid-1990s, that the fall of communism in the Soviet Union and Eastern Europe was permanent and irrevocable, my "grand design" was thereupon appropriately revised. No longer was pragmatic market socialism to be the first step on the road to a global economic development program and a supernational federation. My writings on the latter two visionary topics no longer made reference to market socialism in any form, pragmatic or otherwise. Henceforward, the case for pragmatic market socialism was entirely separate and independent from the cases to be made for a Global Marshall Plan and the Federal Union of Democratic Nations.

In the larger scheme of things, the Global Marshall Plan and the Federal Union of Democratic Nations are far more important than pragmatic market socialism. The Global Marshall Plan and the Federal Union of Democratic Nations might save global human civilization from a disaster of biblical proportions, from a disaster that might kill billions of people, reduce living standards of the survivors to bare subsistence, and possibly start the human species sliding down a slippery slope toward physical extinction. The benefits from pragmatic market socialism would be far more modest: greater economic equality and equity, possibly some increase in efficiency and average living standards, possibly a somewhat purer form of political democracy. While modest in comparison with avoiding a catastrophe of biblical proportions, the benefits from pragmatic market socialism, considered in and of themselves, would be quite impressive, and would dwarf the benefits from most of those proposed incrementalist reforms of the present day that are generally deemed reasonable, plausible, and politically possible.

From the mid-1990s onward, my research and writing efforts became focused mainly on world economic development and world government. But I did not entirely abandon work on pragmatic market socialism. There were still some aspects of the subject that I wanted to add to the published literature. And in the final analysis, quite aside from the possible international ramifications of a transition to pragmatic market socialism, the transition in and of itself, viewed entirely from the internal perspective of the citizens of those nations undertaking the change, would be significantly beneficial.

In the present chapter, therefore, I intend to provide a relatively brief, but reasonably comprehensive, statement of the case to be made for pragmatic market socialism. First, the proposal will be situated within the general history of socialism, with special attention to the more recent development of the market socialist concept by Oskar Lange and others, including myself. This will be followed by a relatively detailed blueprint of how pragmatic market socialism might work in practice. Concluding the chapter will be an evaluative section on the inherent weaknesses of conventional capitalist apologetics when confronted by the pragmatic market socialist alternative.

It is perhaps worthwhile to emphasize at the outset that the case for pragmatic market socialism to be made in this chapter, cannot be proven "beyond a reasonable doubt" as that phrase is understood in jurisprudence. Far less can it be proven according to the strict and absolute standard of "proof" as understood in mathematics and science. However, what I believe *can* be said "beyond a reasonable doubt"—assuming reasonable minds—is that there is nothing in the body of accepted theoretical and empirical evidence within the discipline of economics that constitutes compelling evidence that pragmatic socialism would *not* work as intended and desired, and that it would *not* achieve a higher level of social welfare than an equivalent capitalist economy. Of course, I will have to concede that there are any number of economists who would disagree with this proposition. To my mind, this shows that these economists do *not* possess "reasonable minds" when it comes to the potential performance of a socialist economy. They have been so influenced by capitalist apologetics that they are simply incapable of objective thought on the matter.

But I am sufficiently modest to admit the possibility that I myself may be wrong. This is why I am at pains to emphasize that pragmatic market socialism is put forward as a *provisional and experimental* step in the development of economic institutions. It is provisional and experimental because it is explicitly acknowledged that the existing evidence does not establish beyond reasonable doubt that pragmatic market socialism would be superior to contemporary capitalism. What the evidence suggests, rather, is that there is a *sufficiently high probability* that pragmatic market socialism would be preferable to justify an *experimental* implementation of the system. If the actual performance of the system were disappointing, then it would be abolished and capitalism restored. A trial period of approximately ten to fifteen years should be adequate to settle the question. Indeed, any social scientist with an adequate appreciation of the role of experimentation in scientific inquiry will probably recognize that the only truly reliable and compelling way to judge the performance of pragmatic market socialism would be by means of a trial implementation.

Of course, the experimental method is far more readily adaptable to scientific inquiry than it is to social policy. But one important reason for undertaking this particular experiment is that pragmatic market socialism would be so similar to contemporary capitalism that it is rightly regarded as a very minor and marginal evolution beyond the existing economic system. For the overwhelming majority of people, there would be no significant difference in their daily lives between pragmatic market socialism and contemporary capitalism. What this means is that should the new economic arrangements prove to be unsatisfactory on the whole, it would be a relatively easy matter to reestablish the previous economic arrangements. As I view the question, the only people who have sound, sensible, logical reasons for being against this experiment are wealthy capitalists apprehensive of what the experiment might show.

Background

The word "socialism" established itself in common usage in the 1830s. Officially adopted by a few of the various European reformist groups of the time, it gradually became applied to a variety of such groups. In the pre-Marxian era, the general tenor of socialist writing was relatively gentle. It was Karl Marx who insisted on a bitter class struggle with its inevitable climax in violent revolution. The earlier socialists were generally optimistic that the quality of their schemes for social improvement would be apparent even to the financially privileged. It was indeed often hoped that the owners through voluntary action would bring into being the needed reforms. There need be no compulsion involved. The ameliorative action, for example, as in Robert Owen's thinking, might consist of industrialists voluntarily lowering hours of work, raising pay, providing education, parks and recreational facilities, and decent housing for the urban proletariat. This would result in a happier, more cooperative working force whose productivity would greatly exceed what it had been before the enlightenment. The improvement of the lot of the poor, therefore, need not impinge on the welfare of the rich—it might even foster it. Karl Marx dismissed the main body of his predecessors, such as Robert Owen, as "utopian socialists": as unrealistic and impractical dreamers.

Karl Marx provided the most influential single statement in the history of socialist thought. The volume and intellectual power of Marx's work far over-shadows that of any other socialist. In a sense, Marx *founded* modern socialism, since many of his predecessors did not in fact emphasize the abrogation of the private property right with respect to the nonhuman factors of production. Marx not only insisted on this, he expected the abrogation to be attended by violent social upheaval. Obviously there was to be no financial compensation, no coddling of the former capitalists. In Marx's work, then, the idea of socialization became closely associated with that of violent revolution. An extreme viewpoint thus became the most important viewpoint within the socialist ranks. The basic ideas in Marx's system were first given expression in the *Communist Manifesto* of 1848. They were elaborated and detailed in the three hefty volumes of *Das*

Kapital (1867, 1885, 1894). Throughout this period, Marx was active politically as well as intellectually. He was an important figure in the socialist parties of the day. It seems fairly obvious that he rather hoped that the proletarian revolution would occur during his own lifetime.

Socialist parties following hardline Marxism did not gain power in any country until the Russian revolution of 1917. During the latter nineteenth and early twentieth century, a good deal of the revolutionary basis was being eroded because of a gradual, long-term improvement in the condition of the working class. The agitations of the socialist revolutionaries may well have been a fundamental cause of this—along with, of course, the great advances in productive technology that continued throughout this period. Technological progress enabled capitalism to improve the lot of its rank and file workers, and quite possibly the socialist threat induced it to avail itself of the opportunity. The improvement manifested itself both in growing real income and in growing security. Not only did wages and salaries increase, but there were steps in the direction of compulsory unemployment, sickness, and old age insurance. The working class unions played a foremost role in this easing of the material condition of the proletariat. Relations between the socialists and the unionists were uneasy. Many socialists frowned upon what they considered to be modest concessions by the capitalists, for fear that these vestigial improvements would divert workers from their resentments and thereby postpone the revolution. Other socialists were more willing to compromise.

A fundamental rift in the socialist ranks occurred when the "revisionists," under the leadership of figures such as Eduard Bernstein, renounced the traditional Marxist doctrine of the necessity of violent revolution. According to Bernstein and like-minded socialists, the improvement in working class conditions and the power of the capitalist state made such a revolution practically impossible. It was preferable to work politically within the framework of democratic capitalism to attain socialism peaceably and legally. The expropriation of the owners would then have the sanction of the voting public, not that of an unruly mob. Once the decision had been made to attempt to gain power through normal democratic channels, the temptation was established to water down the program in order to gain electoral support. It is a tedious business being a politician if one never sees the inside of an elected office. Thus expropriation tended to be replaced by nationalization with compensation, then economy-wide nationalization by nationalization of "key" industries, and finally nationalization was often abandoned altogether and replaced by emphasis on such things as progressive income taxation and expanded welfare programs. All the while, the parties and individuals involved never relinquished the "socialism" label. The word was simply too sacrosanct ever to be explicitly abandoned. The revisionist movement led by Eduard Bernstein and others lay the foundations for a number of "social democratic" parties throughout Western Europe and elsewhere in the world. Some of these parties, such as the German Social Democratic Party and the British Labor Party, have been quite successful at various times and places throughout the twentieth century and beyond.

During the early twentieth century, the influence of public ownership socialism might have faded out of modern history altogether if it had not been for the Russian revolution. This revolution gave the harsh early-Marxist version of socialism something which it had never enjoyed before—the support of an important nation-state. The Bolshevik triumph in Russia was something of an historical accident. If either the Bolsheviks or their opponents had behaved somewhat differently—the variations seemingly well within the range of possibility—the outcome might have been very different. For example, the late Romanov tsars might have been less rigid, and more willing to allow evolution toward a constitutional monarchy. Again, the revolutionary activity which had been so intense in Russia in the late nineteenth and early twentieth century would have been much less so had it not been supported by the nascent industrial capitalist class which was hoping to emulate the accomplishments of the French Revolution. They failed to notice that the revolutionaries they were helping financially and otherwise, were as much or more under the influence of Karl Marx as under that of the eighteenth century Enlightenment figures. Even all this might have failed to come to a head if Russia had been spared her disastrous participation in World War I. By 1917, the antiwar feeling in the rank and file of the army and society generally was the most potent single factor in Russian politics.

It was used by the Provisional Government to sweep the tsar from power. Once free of the incompetent tsarist yoke, so the Provisional Government reasoned, the people would be inspired to prosecute the war more vigorously than before, and this time successfully. They were wrong. The damage had already been done, and a political change at the top could not overnight make Russia into an efficient fighting machine. Most of the people—or at least a very large minority of them—wanted peace whatever the cost in national pride. The Bolsheviks promised peace. The other aspects of the Bolshevik program were much less relevant to the fact that they managed to engineer themselves into power. Once in power, they hung on tenaciously in spite of great social turbulence. They kept their promise and got out of the war. The territorial cost was immense, but most of it was recovered once Germany had been defeated by the remaining

Allied powers. The support of the peasantry was gained by expropriating and redistributing the land of the aristocracy. They also gained the support of the urban proletariat by expropriating the industrialists. By doing all this, however, they acquired a great number of mortal enemies. This was demonstrated by several years of desperate civil war following the Bolshevik coup in Petrograd.

By the early 1920s, however, the civil war had petered out and the Bolsheviks remained firmly in control of Russia. A new variable had entered the world power equation. There now existed a non-negligible national power that espoused undiluted Marxist ideology. Socialism, whatever its merits or lack thereof, could no longer be shrugged off contemptuously by unbelievers or blithely twisted into nearly unrecognizable mutations by wishy-washy "revisionists." Marxist "speculation" had suddenly become a reality. There had been a revolution, the property-owning classes had been unceremoniously dispossessed, and now a great nation was about to move off into uncharted socialist territory. The rest of the world looked on with curiosity, apprehension, and for some, a degree of hope.

Much of the Bolshevik leadership at the beginning was hopeful that their example would inspire their fellows in the more radical wings of the Western European socialist parties, and the Russian revolution would after all provide the first sparks that would ignite a world-wide revolutionary conflagration. Such hopes were soon disappointed. By the time the civil war in Russia had ended, World War I was finished and the golden opportunity for revolutionary activity had passed. Apparently the initial sparks in Russia would have to smolder for an indefinite period of time before they would ignite the greater socialist revolution.

That left the question of what socialism should properly mean in a country in which the industrial structure was still at quite an early stage of development. For several years after the civil war, while the overriding objective was recovery from the ravages of protracted warfare, the New Economic Policy (NEP) remained in effect. This scheme left the economy in a remarkably free and unsupervised state, and more closely resembled market socialism than any of the succeeding economic arrangements in the USSR. The peasants were freed from the mandatory deliveries of the civil war period, and the industrial managers were permitted to engage in commercial production with a minimum of direction by the nominal owner, the state. Economic recovery took place on schedule, and the right wing of the communist party saw in this general pattern of economic permissiveness the best plan for the indefinite future.

The middle wing of the party, which gradually became dominant under the leadership of Joseph Stalin, did not want to resign itself to long years of gradual economic development. First and foremost, there was too great an external danger. At any time the capitalist industrial powers of Western Europe and America might decide to eliminate the Soviet state. An adequate deterrent against this possibility could only be provided by the rapid development of a formidable internal industrial establishment capable of giving a powerful account of itself in modern war.

And thus in the latter twenties and early thirties, the great Russian economic development effort, inspired and directed by the Communist Party, was launched. The collectivization and industrialization effort of this period placed a huge strain on the Soviet people. To begin with, a large proportion of the peasantry was opposed to collectivization. Most of them preferred to work independently their own holdings which had been allotted them in the early days of the revolution, and to sell the produce for what they could obtain on the free market. Now all this was changed. Large numbers of individual holdings were melded into collectives with centralized administrations. Output was collected and sold commonly, and the proceeds more or less evenly distributed among the collective's membership. The more successful among the peasantry before collectivization resented being lumped together with their less prosperous neighbors. As a result of all this, the living standards of the rural population were reduced to a subsistence level. Resistance in some areas went as far as armed conflict, and the Soviet state met its severest test since the civil war.

The communist party planners were thoroughly determined, however. Collectivization was essential, they believed, to raise output in the agricultural sector, and this was the basic prerequisite for smooth development of the industrial sector. Once the initial opposition was crushed and the collectivized agricultural sector began functioning normally, output did rise, but not sufficiently to justify the optimistic projections of the planners. This agricultural deficiency was at the heart of the unexpectedly large economic sacrifices the Soviet people were forced to make during the thirties and thereafter. Although the Soviet Union was in fact succeeding in adding to its industrial capacity at a rate unprecedented in history, the cost was extremely high. As more and more and more of national output was directed into plan achievement in heavy industry and social infrastructure, the consumer goods sector shrank to a bare minimum. The working population was exhorted vigorously to maintain a supreme productive effort and not to resent the temporary scarcity in consumer goods. Such appeals can never be entirely successful, and the social strain caused by forced-pace industrialization was enormous.

Whether or not it was more the general social malaise or Stalin's paranoid personality that was to blame, there occurred in the late thirties an event that dimmed appreciably whatever glory had been achieved in the economic realm. This was an intemperate purge of the Communist Party of the USSR carried out at the instigation of the man who had come to dominate it, Joseph Stalin. The purge underscored the monolithic and anti-democratic dominance of the Communist Party in Soviet society. This is the other great and overriding characteristic of the Soviet experience. The first is rapid economic growth under socialism; the second is the undemocratic, elitist philosophy adopted by the communist leadership.

The development task in Russia was interrupted and disrupted by the climactic struggle of World War II. The Soviet government attempted to evade embroilment (most dramatically via the Nazi-Soviet Pact of August 1939), in hopes that the capitalist powers would exhaust themselves in internecine conflict. But Hitler's intention had all along been eastward expansion, and when he had to his own satisfaction succeeded in neutralizing his enemies in the West, he turned without hesitation on Russia. The invasion commenced on June 22, 1941. The ensuing struggle demonstrated the military power of the Soviet state, but the cost was staggering.

Taking advantage of postwar chaos, Soviet Russia set up satellite socialist states in the overrun Eastern European countries, and supported the Chinese Communist Party in its successful effort to gain power in China. As World War I had facilitated the establishment of the first socialist state, World War II facilitated a vast territorial and population expansion of the socialist empire. The sudden enlargement of the socialist sector on the world map thoroughly alarmed the remainder of the capitalist world. But by now any military intervention to eliminate the socialist threat had become a costly and problematic proposition. The emphasis would now have to be on the containment of further Communist expansion. Thus the commencement of the tense and bitter Cold War.

The term "market socialism" is of relatively recent origin, dating from the seminal work of the mainstream economist Oskar Lange (1904-1965) in the 1930s. Prior to Lange, it was generally assumed, both by pro-socialists and anti-socialists, that socialism and the market were contradictory, incompatible, and fully antithetical. Marx's famous phrase "anarchy of the market" epitomized the extremely negative attitude toward the free market which had been customary among traditional socialists. To Marx, private ownership of capital, the economic marketplace, and exploitation, were three inseparable and codependent facets of the capitalist socioeconomic system. Thus getting rid of one of them meant getting rid of all three. For their part, orthodox mainstream economists tended to glorify the market as the operative mechanism of the famous "invisible hand," a powerful metaphor advanced in Adam Smith's *Wealth of Nations*.

The consensus mainstream attitude today toward the economic market is that it is indeed, just as Adam Smith argued, a powerful engine toward economic efficiency and social welfare—but also that this is an engine that requires a substantial amount of social intervention and control in order to achieve optimal performance. This general consensus was well established by the second half of the nineteenth century. Ever since then, the precise nature and degree of social intervention and control which is most desirable has remained a subject of perpetual, intensive debate between conservatives (favoring less intervention and control) and liberals (favoring more).

The continuum of social intervention and control is in fact a smooth and infinitely differentiated continuum, so that it is a matter of purely arbitrary semantics at which point social intervention and control becomes so comprehensive and extensive that the economy is no longer properly describable as a "market economy" but rather as a "regulated economy," "coordinated economy," "planned economy," or some such term. The overall continuum of social intervention and control is in fact composed of a number of important subsidiary continuums, of which some of the more important are as follows: (1) the proportion of the total stock of capital and natural resources (i.e. nonhuman factors of production) which is publicly rather than privately owned; (2) the proportion of aggregate income which is taxed away and devoted to provision of public goods (police and fire protection, roads, national defense, etc.); (3) the proportion of aggregate income which is taxed away and devoted to transfer payments (agricultural subsidies, social security, welfare benefits, etc.); (4) the degree of progressivity of the tax and welfare system; (5) the degree of legal regulation of private behavior; (6) the degree of legal regulation of business activity.

According to the strict public ownership interpretation of socialism, only the first of these continuums would be the operative criterion for characterizing an economy as either "capitalist" or "socialist." For example, in the United States today, depending on how the "capital stock" is defined (using this term in the general sense as a proxy for the entire range of nonhuman factors of production), somewhere between 15 and 25 percent of this stock is publicly owned, and the U.S. economy is clearly a capitalist economy. Under a system of democratic market socialism, since most large, established business enterprises would be publicly owned—which implies that somewhere between 70 and 80 percent of capital stock would be publicly owned—the U.S. economy would clearly be a socialist economy. But if there were an approximately equal mix of public and private enterprise, say 40 to 60 percent of the capital stock publicly owned, then it might not be so obvious whether the U.S. economy should be characterized as "capitalist" or "socialist."

According to the social democratic interpretation, "socialism" is defined in terms of general social intervention and control, not in terms of the level of public ownership of capital. The level of public ownership of capital might be fairly low (the 15 to 25 percent currently prevalent in the United States), and yet an economy might be appropriately characterized as socialist if the position attained on the other continuums were sufficiently high (i.e. if a sufficient proportion of aggregate income were taxed away and devoted to public goods or transfer payments, if there were a sufficient degree of progressivity in the public revenue and expenditure system, if there were a sufficient degree of regulation of business activity, etc.). If we were to use this interpretation of socialism, it would make the determination of whether a nation were capitalist or socialist quite an arbitrary and subjective matter.

The United States, for example, is characterized by a substantial proportion of aggregate income taxed away and devoted to public goods and transfer payments, by a substantial degree of progressivity in the public revenue and expenditure system, by a substantial degree of regulation of business activity. Is the United States therefore "capitalist" or "socialist"? Far right-wing conservatives are fond of affirming (with horror) that the United States is indeed "socialist"; while far left-wing liberals are adamant that the United States has a long way to go before it could be considered remotely socialist. Neither side has any meaningful, quantitative grounds for these statements. The social democratic interpretation of socialism, involving as it does some unspecified weighted average of positions on a variety of continuums of social intervention and control, is inherently vague and obscure.

The question of whether the United States has a market economy or a nonmarket economy is in principle just as obscure and muddled as whether the United States economy is capitalist or socialist in the social democratic sense. But the general consensus is that the United States clearly has a market capitalist economy—the economy is capitalist rather than socialist, and is also market-oriented rather than nonmarket-oriented. Social intervention and control of the United States economy may be quite substantial, but it has not become so absolutely dominant that the market basis of economic activity has been suppressed and obliterated. At least this would be the judgment of all those other than those same far right-wing conservatives who would also assert that the United States is a "socialist" nation.

The reason for this situation, no doubt, is that it would be completely impossible to suppress and obliterate the market basis of economic activity, particularly where large-scale human societies are concerned. Any serious effort to do so, even if made by a powerful totalitarian state, would cause an immense amount of confusion, dislocation, and inefficiency, and would almost certainly be doomed to ultimate failure. The market is an essential integrative and coordinative instrument for the economic processes of production and distribution within any large and populous polity.

The typical understanding of "pure planning" among economists is an economic system which would have no money and no pricing of commodities, and in which all decisions on physical production, distribution, and consumption would be made within a single, hierarchically organized government agency. Nothing remotely approaching such a system has ever been witnessed throughout the entire course of human history. The most dramatic effort in modern history at centralization of economic authority and central planning of the economy was made in the Soviet Union during the Stalinist period. Soviet-style central planning involved a very significant degree of social intervention and control beyond what has been standard in the United States and the nations of Western Europe—but it still stopped well short of "pure planning." Under the Soviet system, money existed and was used, commodities were valued and exchanged according to monetary prices, households had considerable autonomy in deciding on where to work and how to spend their incomes, and managers of business firms had appreciable consultative input into production and distribution decisions. The operative meaning of "centrally planned socialism," as opposed to "pure planning," was set by the planned economic system established in the USSR in the late 1920s and early 1930s under the direction of the dictator Joseph Stalin, and which persisted, essentially unchanged, until the dissolution of the Soviet Union in the early 1990s.

The premise on which the market socialist idea is based is that there is a relatively high degree of independence between the various types of social intervention and control: that society possesses the option of setting itself at a relatively high level along one of the continuums mentioned above, while at the same time setting itself at a relatively low level along others. More specifically, that society possesses the option of setting itself at a relatively high level on the public ownership of capital continuum (a level as high as that witnessed in the Soviet Union throughout most of its history), and at the same time at relatively low levels on the other continuums (levels as low as those witnessed in the United States at the present time).

The concept of market socialism is still fairly unfamiliar both to traditional pro-socialists, and to traditional anti-socialists. It represents a fundamentally new, fundamentally revised concept of socialism—even though it is a fully sensible concept of socialism and is indeed fully consistent with the primary definition of socialism to be found in most dictionaries. At the beginning of the twentieth century, the term "market socialism" was unknown; but by the middle of the twentieth century the term was well established in mainstream thinking on economic systems. What caused this important development in the intellectual history of socialism? By far the single most important factor was an individual by the name of Oskar Lange.

Oskar Lange was a young man in his early 30s when he published a lengthy essay titled "On the Economic Theory of Socialism" in two installments in the *Review of Economic Studies* (October 1936 and February 1937). This essay was the principal component of a book of the same name, published by the University of Minnesota Press in 1938, which also contained essays by Benjamin Lippincott (the volume editor) and Fred M. Taylor. Taylor's short essay ("The Guidance of Production in a Socialist State") had been his presidential address to the American Economic Association in 1928, and had appeared in the *American Economic Review* in March 1929. The Taylor essay speculated that efficient production might conceivably be possible under social ownership of capital, but the speculation was rather vague, and the principal role of Taylor's essay in the book version of "On the Economic Theory of Socialism" was simply to legitimize Lange's contribution, which went into the problem of efficient production under socialism in far greater detail. The impact of Lange's essay on the economics profession was greatly augmented by Abram Bergson's article on "Socialist Economics," included in the American Economic Association's *A Survey of Contemporary Economics*, edited by Howard Ellis and published in 1948.

Two key factors contributed to the very substantial impact of Lange's seminal work on market socialism within the economics profession: (1) the difficult situation confronting Western capitalism during the 1930s; (2) Lange's personal prestige as a brilliant mathematical economist. With respect to the first factor, it must be recalled that the 1930s witnessed the worst economic catastrophe ever to afflict modern capitalism: the Great Depression. Between the stock market crash of October 1929 and the trough of the early 1930s, such a precipitous and calamitous economic decline had never been experienced before, and it has never been experienced since. As if the economic disaster were not enough in itself, during the early 1930s a painful contrast emerged between the capitalist world prostrated by the Great Depression, and the growing, vibrant socialist economy of the Soviet Union, then embarked on the first of its extraordinarily ambitious Five Year Plans. A mental projection of the existing trends in the early 1930s over an extended period would clearly suggest that socialism would eventually surpass capitalism. Both in the real world and in the intellectual world, capitalism went on the defensive.

The "window of opportunity" created by the Great Depression for re-invigorating the socialist critique of capitalism did not remain open for very long. In the United States, the Depression bottomed out just as the voters elected the vigorous, confident Franklin D. Roosevelt to the presidency. The actual fiscal input into the economy involved in the multitude of Roosevelt's New Deal programs was actually fairly limited, and the rate of economic recovery was only minimally above what would have transpired had the laissez faire-oriented Herbert Hoover remained in office. But the impression of an activist, caring national government reassured the citizens, and enabled them to better withstand the privation and uncertainties of widespread unemployment. As for the booming Soviet Union, the Moscow purge trials of the late 1930s severely discredited the economic achievements of the regime, giving credence to the arguments of conservatives that Soviet economic progress was being built on the blood and bones of a suffering population. As the 1930s drew to a close, concerns about a looming world war overrode social criticism. In any case, the last vestiges of the Great Depression were routed by the worldwide arms buildup inspired by the saber-rattling fascist powers of Germany, Italy, and Japan. When World War II finally descended upon hapless humanity, the various struggles for national survival eliminated any possibility for further development of the socialist critique of capitalism.

But by that time, Lange's contribution had had sufficient impact not to be entirely forgotten. The substantial impact of Lange depended not only on the disarray and ferment caused by the Great Depression, but also on Lange's considerable personal prestige as an economist. A native of Poland, Lange emigrated to England in the 1920s, and later went on to the United States. At that time, mathematical modes of inquiry were not as dominant in economics as they later became, but they were beginning to gain firm footholds throughout the discipline. Lange's education had included exposure to considerable higher mathematics, and he was well equipped to employ mathematical methods. Prior to writing "On the Economic Theory of Socialism," he had in fact published a substantial amount of "orthodox" research in economic theory and econometrics, and he was generally regarded as "one of our leading young economists."

Prior to Lange, there had been little in the way of meaningful communication and/or intellectual cross-fertilization between orthodox Western economists and proponents of socialism. Generally speaking, the economists and the socialists stood on opposite sides of the fence, hurling accusations and imprecations across at each other. Oskar Lange came as a veritable revelation to both sides. Here was an individual who was manifestly neither stupid nor ignorant of economic theory, yet who strongly and clearly advocated socialism in the strict public ownership sense. Lange's work demonstrated tangibly that orthodox economic theory is not necessarily sympathetic to capitalism and hostile to socialism.

In the "neoclassical" theory of production and distribution, capital receives equal billing with labor as a source of value, and the determination of factor prices according to their "marginal productivity" adds an extra dimension of analytical complexity not known in classical economics. But the basic neoclassical principle that "capital earns its return through its marginal product contribution to output" only necessarily constitutes a defense of the basic capitalist principle of direct appropriation by private households of capital property return, if one simply ignores the clear and manifest distinction between capital itself (i.e. the inanimate instruments of production), and those human individuals designated as "capital owners" under capitalistic definitions of ownership. In a direct physical sense, it is the inanimate capital itself which contributes to production, and whose marginal product is recognized in the form of capital property return. Under modern industrial capitalism, the human capital owners are *not* clearly and directly involved in the production process. As the inanimate machines whose productivity provides property income to wealthy capitalists roar upon the factory floor, those human capital owners are likely to be a thousand miles away—playing croquet upon the lawns of their estates.

While contemporary capitalist apologetics prefers to simply ignore the distinction between inanimate capital itself and human capital owners, to blend these two separate categories together into one seamless intellectual construct—if pressed, it is certainly capable of producing reasons why the wealthy capitalists playing croquet upon their lawns do in fact, appearances to the contrary, make a worthy contribution to production, and are therefore economically and ethically entitled to the capital property income they receive. The human capital owners are alleged to provide "capital management effort" in various forms—that form which is especially favored in capitalist apologetics being the noble activity of entrepreneurship. Besides that, the human capital owners provide the saving—allegedly at great personal cost to themselves—which is used to build the factories and machines which contribute directly to production. Finally, on top of it all, the capital owners are "risk-takers"—by investing their wealth instead of hoarding cash under their pillows, they are exposing themselves to dire risk of financial loss. For all of these reasons (and quite possibly many others—given sufficient time to fabricate them), the capitalist owner is held by capitalist apologetics to be fully worthy of his/her capital property income. The fact that intimate knowledge of neoclassical economic theory is *not* necessarily an obstacle to perceiving the invalidity of these justifications for capitalism was clearly demonstrated by Oskar Lange.

Lange's essay "On the Economic Theory of Socialism" provided a detailed market socialist alternative to the only form of socialism then known to be operative in the real world: Soviet-style central planning. Instead of the detailed instructions given to enterprise managers by the central planning authorities, Lange proposed that the managers of publicly-owned firms be given two simple rules: (1) produce as much of each output commodity as is necessary to bring its marginal cost of production into equality with its price; (2) produce output commodities in such a way as to minimize the average cost of production. The first rule determines the quantity to be produced of each output commodity; while the second determines the quantities of input commodities (factors of production such as various types of capital and labor) to be purchased by the firm and applied to the production of each output commodity. Although supplemented by additional proposals, the "production rules" constitute the heart of the Langian approach to market socialism.

Lange asserted that on the basis of both economic theory and apparent institutional realities, this proposed system of market socialism would work not merely as well as, but actually better than, market capitalism. According to Lange's argument, the imperfectly competitive nature of most of the contemporary capitalist economy means that this economy is inefficient by Pareto standards. There is no escape from this outcome under capitalism because the private ownership of firms guarantees that their guiding motivation will be toward the maximization of profit. In contrast, a market socialist economy could instruct firm managers not to maximize profits, but rather to follow the production rules (set marginal cost equal to price, and minimize average cost). Following these rules would indeed generate a situation that would satisfy the Pareto optimality conditions.

Obviously, Lange's work did not inspire a mass conversion of orthodox economists to socialism. While it was recognized that in principle socialism might possibly perform more effectively than had previously been assumed, most economists took refuge in the belief that an optimally performing market capitalist economy would outperform an optimally performing market socialist economy. Lange himself gave skeptics a powerful phrase to use against his proposal when he expressed concerns about the possible "bureaucratization of economic life" under Langian market socialism. He went on to say that owing to the development of mass production by mega-corporations, economic life had already been significantly "bureaucratized," and that publicly controlled bureaucracies were superior to privately controlled bureaucracies. This amendment of the "bureaucratization" qualm was largely ignored by later critics of Lange's proposal. It could well be that Langian market socialism would be taken more seriously today if Lange had further developed the plan and responded to the points raised by several critics such as Friedrich Hayek, Abram Bergson, and others.

As it was, however, Lange never added anything to the market socialist proposal set forth in "On the Economic Theory of Socialism." After writing his famous essay, Lange occupied himself for several years with "orthodox" research, mostly in the area of econometrics. The Russian-supported communist takeover of Poland in the aftermath of World War II presented Lange with a difficult personal decision. The establishment of communism in Poland had turned his homeland into a full-fledged socialist state in the public ownership sense. As a proponent of socialism, Lange was happy about that. Unfortunately, the socialist system enforced upon Poland by the Red Army followed the Soviet central planning model. Lange elected to return to his homeland. His status as a leading economist in the West assured him a high position in the Polish economic planning bureaucracy. No doubt he was hopeful that he might be able to influence the Polish socialist system toward greater market orientation. Unfortunately, it did not work out that way. Lange's personal prestige and influence was not so great as to enable any significant deviation from the central planning orthodoxy imposed by the Russians. Instead, Lange himself became deeply enmeshed in the practical problems of central planning.

While the specific proposal for market socialism developed by Oskar Lange is too much influenced by economic theory to be taken very seriously as a practical alternative to capitalism, Lange's work was in fact extremely influential in a larger sense: once and for all, it opened the minds of economists to the *possibility* of market socialism. Once this possibility had been recognized, the way was open to the development of other market socialist proposals of greater practicality. Such practical proposals for market socialism, in turn, have the potentiality of resurrecting the fundamental socialist critique of capitalism—of seriously challenging the capitalist status quo which today seems so unassailably rock-solid.

Blueprint

Transition and Compensation. Pragmatic market socialism envisions a society purged of the phenomenon of extremely large personal capital fortunes based primarily on inheritance and chance. At the same time this society would incorporate a market economy whose day-to-day functioning would virtually duplicate that of the present capitalist economy. The intention may be described as a nearly exact "socialist analogue" to contemporary market capitalism. The essential elements of such an analogue will be described here. As we know from the history of the Russian revolution of 1917, socialization without compensation is a blatant invitation to devastating civil war. Thus, we need first to consider issues of transition and compensation.

The implementation of pragmatic market socialism would require the transfer of those legal rights to capital property income which are currently owned by private households under capitalism, to a national government public ownership agency, tentatively designated the Bureau of Public Ownership (BPO). Unaffected would be capital ownership rights held by corporations and other organizations. Also, private ownership of small business firms and entrepreneurial business firms would be retained. "Socialization," in the sense implied by the pragmatic market socialist proposal, may be defined as the termination of the present distribution of privately-owned property rights to future property return flows reflecting the productivity of the nonhuman factors of production (capital and natural resources) utilized in large-scale, established productive activity. Such a termination is justified on the basis that the present distribution of such rights is extremely unequal, and does not accurately reflect the respective contributions to economic production that are being made by the various members of society.

It is important to recognize that the transitions described do not amount to a proscription on privately-owned "wealth" in general, but merely to a proscription on privately-owned *capital* wealth. Thus under pragmatic market socialism, a wealthy individual could own mansions and estates, yachts and private jets, Rolls Royce automobiles and Rembrandt paintings, and maintain savings accounts in the tens of millions of dollars. But such an individual could not receive property income in the form of dividends and capital gains on corporate securities, real interest on savings accounts, etc. In other words, pragmatic market socialism does not imply the termination of luxurious lifestyles—it merely implies the termination of the financing of luxurious lifestyles on the basis of unearned capital property income.

It would not be regarded as morally obligatory to compensate fully that value of investment assets representing appreciation since initial acquisition out of labor income, or representing initial plus appreciated value of inheritances. As larger capital wealthholdings almost invariably involve some combination of inheritance and appreciation, the percentage of capital wealth compensated would decline with the wealth level. However, the compensation schedule would be sufficiently liberal to avoid imposing undue material hardship on individuals previously mostly dependent on property income. The objective of avoiding any expropriation of labor income accumulations would be facilitated by a provision for full compensation of all small to medium size capital asset accumulations. Beyond a certain specified amount, a declining fraction of capital wealth would be compensated, with the proviso that full compensation would be paid for all capital wealth derived directly from the owner's personal labor income.

All compensation for surrendered investment assets would be paid using cash especially created for the purpose by the central banking system. At first glance, this suggests the possibility of rampant inflation. But in actual fact, any inflationary propensity would be minor. Small to medium size capital wealth accumulations mostly represent stores of value, so that their conversion to cash should not augment the propensity to immediate consumption. Large capital wealth accumulations, on the other hand, represent sources of significant property income to their owners. Although under socialism financial asset accumulations would no longer be sources of property income for their owners, the conversion of compensation cash into immediate consumption would be greatly constrained by a significant wealth effect. As only a part of large capital wealth accumulations would be compensated, the value of cash compensation would be considerably less than the prior value of the surrendered assets. Moreover, compensation cash would not yield a future property return. Wealthy capitalists accustomed to spending large amounts on consumption in the expectation of large future flows of property income may well be obliged to reduce their current consumption, lest spending out of compensation cash rapidly deplete it and leave their owners in serious financial straits. In sum, while it is clear that large-scale cash creation by the national government in the absence of the envisioned capital wealth transfer would be highly inflationary, this should not be allowed to create a false expectation of serious inflation resulting from the potential transition under consideration here.

Two types of business enterprise would definitely remain in private ownership under pragmatic market socialism: small business and entrepreneurial business. The exception to social ownership with respect to small business is mainly motivated by the heavy administrative burden that would be imposed on the Bureau of Public Ownership if it were responsible for evaluating the profit performance of the managers of the hundreds of thousands of small business enterprises in a large, modern economy. The exception with respect to entrepreneurial business is motivated by the possibility that private entrepreneurial endeavor might play a significant positive role in the dynamic performance of the economy.

While it is evident that the great majority of product and process innovations are undertaken by established firms in the modern economy, there have been many instances in the history of modern capitalism of an apparently beneficial catalytic impact of private entrepreneurial activity. For example, Bill Gates, the founder of Microsoft, comes readily to mind. It is intended that entrepreneurial activity be encouraged under pragmatic market socialism via the National Investment Banking System (NIBS) and the National Entrepreneurial Investment Board (NEIB). But some people might be skeptical of such "institutionalized" entrepreneurial activity. While it is quite possible that the significance of private entrepreneurial activity is exaggerated to the point of mythology in capitalist apologetics, there is sufficient plausibility that this activity is indeed important to merit an exception to the general principle of social ownership of business enterprise.

Therefore, publicly-owned financial intermediaries would not merely be allowed but would be actively encouraged to lend financial capital to entrepreneurial business enterprises founded by private individuals. So long as the founder-owner remains personally active as the chief executive of an entrepreneurial firm, it would remain privately-owned no matter how large and successful it becomes. The transition to public ownership would normally occur when the founder-owner volitionally departs from the management of the firm following upon its sale to an established publicly-owned firm. This is already the typical pattern under capitalism: a founder-owner builds up an entrepreneurial enterprise, and then realizes its capitalized value as personal gain by selling it to an established firm. As this standard pattern of private entrepreneurship would be duplicated under pragmatic market socialism, there is no reason for expecting pragmatic market socialism to be significantly less favored by private entrepreneurship than is the contemporary capitalist economy.

The Social Dividend. Under pragmatic market socialism, the Bureau of Public Ownership would receive property income on those investment assets currently owned by private households under capitalism. Such investment assets include primarily stocks and bonds issued by business enterprises, and bonds and notes issued by government agencies. Contractual arrangements for interest income and repayment of principal would be enforced by the BPO through the same legal channels currently utilized under capitalism. As for the profits of publicly-owned business enterprises, the division of these between dividends paid to the BPO (and other outside owners such as financial intermediaries), and retained earnings, would remain at the discretion of the executives of each corporation. The BPO would take over the formal legal powers vested in stock instruments, but in contrast to the situation under capitalism in which the board of directors of each corporation may in principle issue detailed instructions to the executives regarding production, pricing, disposition of after-tax profits, and so on, the BPO's powers would be legally confined to supervision of top executive remuneration, and evaluation of top executives in terms of summary measures of corporate performance. Thus the amount of property return it receives in each period would not be directly controllable by the BPO. The statutory articles under which it would be established would require the BPO to disburse the large majority of the property return it receives to the general public as social dividend income. A reasonable benchmark figure would be a minimum of 95 percent social dividend distribution, implying a maximum 5 percent retention percentage by the BPO.

It is essential that the net property return, after deducting BPO expenses, not be "plowed into" general public expenditures, and the benefit of public ownership of capital be realized in the form of lower taxes. For pragmatic market socialism to be politically feasible, it must be possible for each citizen to compare a direct and tangible social dividend income supplement to whatever direct and tangible capital property income supplement has been lost through the abolition of capitalism.

Current labor income (wages and salaries) would be the dominant basis for distribution of the social dividend fund. That is, employed individuals would receive social dividend income in proportion to their earned labor income. Retirees would receive social dividend in proportion to pensions and other contractual retirement benefits. Whereas under capitalism, property return is distributed to individuals in proportion to their personally owned accumulations of financial assets, under pragmatic market socialism, this return would be distributed to individuals in proportion to their personally earned labor incomes.

Admirers of capitalism continually dwell on the point that under socialism, deserving people would no longer receive interest income and other forms of property income. In arguing the case for pragmatic market socialism, therefore, it is vitally important to place heavy emphasis on the fact that under this particular socialist proposal, the loss to the private household of capital property income would be directly counter-balanced by the gain of social dividend income. At the present time, people tend to regard it as a serious liability of socialism that it would deprive them of property income—without ever considering the fact that the present-day capitalist system (relative to the pragmatic market socialist alternative) is depriving them of social dividend income. It is virtually certain that for the overwhelming majority of the United States population, the amount of social dividend income which capitalism is presently denying them is greater than the amount of capital property income which pragmatic market socialism would deny them. If ever the practical implications of this reality are finally recognized by the general public, the continuation of the present capitalistic status quo may be called into serious question.

There are two crucial numerical questions with respect to the social dividend under pragmatic market socialism: (1) What percentage of his or her labor income would the individual citizen receive in the form of social dividend income? (2) What part of the population would receive more social dividend income than they currently receive capital property income? The second question is addressed in the "Evaluation" discussion below. The first question is briefly considered in the following:

An extravagant upper estimate of the social dividend percentage would be national income less wage and salary income, as a percentage of wage and salary income. This would give a figure of upwards of 20 percent. Of course, such a figure would be a gross overestimate. To cite simply one consideration out of several, only about 25 percent of the corporate profits figure in national income accounting is actually distributed as dividends: the rest goes to taxes and retained earnings. A relatively conservative estimate made by the author of the amount of property return that would have been available in 1972 in the United States for social dividend distribution ("The Social Dividend under Market Socialism," *Annals of Public and Cooperative Economy*, 1977), represented 6.75 percent of the "compensation of employees" figure in the national income accounts. Taking practically every reasonable deduction into account, the social dividend percentage would almost certainly be a minimum of 5 percent, and it may well be substantially higher than this.

An important allegation of capitalist apologetics is that capital property income, in whatever amounts received by private individuals, reflects the personal contributions to society of the recipients. But the dominant role of inheritance and random variation under contemporary capitalism in generating the present highly unequal distribution of the stock of capital wealth (and consequently of the flow of capital property income) makes a mockery of this allegation. However, it has become ingrained in the public mind that an important positive function of property income is to reward the social contributions of individuals. An effort might be made under pragmatic market socialism to inject a measure of reality into this perception by means of earmarking a very small percentage of the social dividend fund, probably not to exceed 10 percent, for merit awards. Such merit awards would be bestowed on individuals who have made, in the judgment of disinterested committees, outstanding contributions in science, culture, and other areas of human endeavor.

Another allegation of capitalist apologetics cites what might be termed the "inspirational" role of property return. The existence of property return, so it could be argued, enables every person in society to dream about the possibility of someday being liberated from the onerous necessity to perform daily labor by means of accumulating a sufficient amount of capital wealth to live on the property income produced by the accumulation. It may or may not be admitted that without benefit of inheritances and/or extraordinary good luck, such dreams are very rarely fulfilled. But even if this is admitted, it may nevertheless be maintained that even that tiny and vestigial hope of "living off the interest" which capitalism extends to the non-inheritor is a very fine and worthwhile thing which would necessarily be abrogated by socialism.

The current popularity in the United States of state lotteries featuring substantial lifetime income awards suggests a solution to the problem (presuming it is a problem). The solution would be a BPO lottery featuring substantial lifetime income awards, in which chances would be purchased by means of individuals voluntarily authorizing the withholding of whatever proportion they wish of the social dividend payment to which they are entitled on the basis of their labor income. In contrast to state lotteries, the BPO lottery would not be considered a revenue source: the only deduction from the prize fund represented by duly authorized withheld social dividend would be for the administrative costs of the lottery. Thus, if it should by any chance be true that a considerable number of people derive significant comfort from the thought that extraordinary good luck might someday liberate them forever from the need to work for a living, such people could be as happy under market socialism as they are presently under capitalism.

Bureau of Public Ownership. According to basic economic theory, the critical consequence of private ownership of business enterprise is that these business enterprises are guided by a profit-maximization incentive. This incentive in turn conduces to a high level of efficiency in the operations through which business enterprises transform productive factors such as labor, machinery, and raw materials into finished goods and services. In the case of business enterprises which are financial intermediaries (banks, savings institutions, insurance companies, pension funds, etc.), the profit maximization incentive guarantees the efficient allocation of financial capital as between private households borrowing for consumption purposes, business firms borrowing for capital investment purposes, and government agencies borrowing to create social infrastructure and to cover other public expenditures. Private ownership of business enterprise is thus primarily defensible on grounds that the profit incentive thus imposed on business enterprises promotes economic efficiency. From an economic point of view, therefore, the principal positive function of the class of private capital owners is to enforce a strong profit maximization incentive among the corps of corporation executives responsible for the day-to-day management of the large corporate enterprises which dominate contemporary economic life. The mission of the Bureau of Public Ownership (BPO) would be to duplicate this positive role: to enforce upon the corporation executives who manage the publicly-owned business corporations a strong profit motivation.

The Bureau of Public Ownership would establish performance criteria according to which each corporation president would be evaluated for purposes of remuneration and retention. This applies alike to industrial corporations, mercantile corporations, transportation corporations, financial intermediary corporations, etc. These performance criteria would be strongly dependent upon the current property return produced by the corporation, including profits and interest payments, but some weight might also be attached to indicators of long-term profit potential such as sales growth, innovations, and cost reductions. Principles of remuneration for top corporation executives would be proposed by the corporation executives themselves, subject to approval by the BPO. Remuneration would be strongly dependent on profitability, but so also—possibly even more significantly from the point of view of the effort incentives of the top executives—would be job retention. Presidents of corporations exhibiting sufficiently deficient performance would be subject to dismissal. As dismissal of a corporation president would be a drastic action, the conditions under which this event would occur would be carefully prescribed, along lines indicated in the following.

It is envisioned that the Bureau of Public Ownership would be a two-tiered agency. The first tier would be a central office located in the national capital. One responsibility of the central office would be to collect property return from the publicly-owned business corporations and disburse social dividend payments to the working population. Another responsibility would be to collect an array of statistical information from the corporations from which corporate performance functions could be estimated. From such performance functions the expected performance of any given corporation could be estimated, along with a confidence interval around that performance level. A numerical rule would then be specified according to which: (1) if a given corporation's actual performance, relative to its expected performance, is above a certain critical upper level, then the corporation president must not be dismissed; while (2) if a given corporation's relative performance is below a critical lower level, then the corporation president must be dismissed. Between the upper and lower critical levels of relative performance, retention or dismissal would be principally at the discretion of that corporation's "BPO agent."

The second tier of the BPO would consist of a corps of BPO agents. Unlike the first tier central office, the second tier would be physically decentralized into perhaps 200-300 local offices, each office comprising a group of 10-15 agents. Also unlike the employees of the first tier central office, BPO agents would not be permanent employees of the agency. Rather BPO agents would be selected at random from a roster of qualified personnel ("qualified" in terms of considerable experience in business enterprise management) for a standard period of service of perhaps five to seven years. Only extraordinarily successful agents would be tapped for further service beyond the standard term. Each BPO agent would be assigned several corporations, and his or her remuneration would consist mostly of a small percentage of the property return generated by the corporations within his\her sphere of responsibility and paid over by these corporations to the BPO central office. To reduce propensities to concentrate solely on current property return, the BPO agent would continue to receive a diminishing percentage of these corporations' property return payments to the BPO for a period of several years after leaving the position. The responsibilities and retention percentages of BPO agents would be calibrated to make these positions highly remunerative.

While the BPO agent would be strictly prohibited from issuing any specific operating instructions or advice to the corporations within his/her sphere of responsibility, his/her assignment would be to study carefully the performance of these corporations. To facilitate this assignment, the BPO agent would enjoy unrestricted access to the accounting records and other documentation of the corporation. When the performance of a given corporation falls within the discretionary range described above, it would be the corporation's BPO agent who would dominate the decision on whether the corporation president is to stay or go. It is envisioned that a decision to dismiss would be subject to review by the members of the local BPO office involved, and also by an appeals board in the central office. But a very large majority of these review boards would have to dissent from a dismissal decision in order for it to be revoked. Most probably the successor to a dismissed corporation president would be selected by a committee composed of executives of the corporation, and once installed, the successor would be guaranteed a tenure of perhaps two to three years in order to have a fair opportunity to affect the corporation's performance.

The objective of pragmatic market socialism would be to achieve at least as much competition in the business sector as currently exists under capitalism. There would a strict injunction against any efforts by BPO personnel to organize, foster, or encourage collusive behavior among competitive publicly-owned corporations. Such efforts would constitute violations of existing antitrust laws in the United States, and it is envisioned that these laws would be strictly enforced on the BPO, both in terms of its central office personnel and its agents. A reasonable amount of monitoring of the activity of individual agents would be undertaken to discourage any temptations regarding the encouragement of collusion.

Of course, a well-known proposition from capitalist apologetics denies the possibility of meaningful competition among business enterprises under socialism because all firms would fall under the same public ownership aegis. A related proposition is that business inefficiency would be necessarily subsidized under socialism because it would be politically impossible to allow inefficient firms to become bankrupt and cease operations. It must be conceded that such assertions could be based on numerous traditional advocacies of socialism, whose authors have decried the "anarchy of the market" under capitalism, and who have perceived in bankruptcies merely one more proof of "wasteful competition." However, clearly the pragmatic market socialist proposal is based upon a very different viewpoint regarding competition and bankruptcies. Competition is viewed as a positive force in the economy, and the possibility of bankruptcy is regarded as providing necessary discipline toward the end of efficiency.

The argument may no doubt be proposed that competition is "logically impossible" under any form of socialism (including pragmatic market socialism) owing to public ownership of all firms. But such an argument is based upon an invalid presumption of monolithic uniformity of purpose and complete centralization of authority (the so-called "military model") within the public ownership agency. The BPO described in the foregoing would almost certainly be consistent with a high level of business competition. Even now there are many illustrations from the real world of the possibility of substantial competition between individuals and organizations which are "united" under the same overall formal authority. One thinks of rivalry between different subsidiaries of a conglomerate corporation, of inter-service rivalry among various branches of the military, of competition among employees of the same corporation for promotions, of competition among sports teams which are all part of the same league, of competition among students who are all members of the same professor's class. The level of observed competition is not so much determined by the existence or non-existence of formal overall authorities, but by the incentive systems confronting the human individuals involved in the process. Under the BPO proposal as set forth, high executives of publicly-owned corporations would have just as much incentive to compete with one another as do the high executives of privately-owned corporations in the contemporary capitalist economy.

The BPO envisioned by pragmatic market socialism is clearly based on the conventional consensus in orthodox Western economics that, on the whole, profit maximization by business enterprises possesses highly desirable efficiency properties. It is certainly possible to dispute this consensus, and many socialist writers in the past have done so. But such disputes lead off into a foggy speculative realm which is merely shrugged off—not to say entirely scorned—by the great majority of contemporary mainstream economists. This is not a realm which will be entered here—because there is no need to enter it. Even the most conventionally-minded economists will concede that the pursuit of profits by business enterprises can have some adverse side-effects, and that it is legitimate for society to try to control some of these by means of business regulation. Thus in the United States, there are numerous regulatory agencies such as the Food and Drug Administration, the Federal Trade Commission, the Environmental Protection Agency, and so on and so forth. These agencies would continue to operate under pragmatic market socialism in the same way, and for the same purposes they have currently under market capitalism. The pragmatic market socialist proposal is entirely independent of and neutral toward questions regarding the appropriate extent of business regulation by the national government and other levels of government.

Business Capital Investment. Capitalist apologetics has traditionally expressed the gravest concerns regarding the potential fate of capital investment and economic growth under socialism. One of these concerns is that owing to the termination of interest and other property return payments on private household savings accumulations under socialism, the supply of saving will dry up and society will confront a stagnant and decaying capital stock. Another concern is that if "government bureaucrats" are involved in the investment process rather than "entrepreneurs," capital investment funds will be allocated among competing uses in such a politically biased and/or haphazard manner that the dynamic performance of the economy will plummet to abysmal depths. These concerns will be addressed below in the following "Evaluation" section. The verdict reached there on these concerns is that they do not constitute sufficient grounds for the rejection of the pragmatic market socialist alternative. The fact is that the pragmatic market socialist proposal is based on a profound awareness of the critical importance of capital investment in a modern industrial economy.

At this point, two specific manifestations of this awareness will be briefly described as auxiliary proposals to the core proposals for a Bureau of Public Ownership, and for social dividend distribution of capital property return. First, it is proposed that a new category of national government expenditure be created: that of business capital investment. The annual appropriation for this purpose would go through the usual budgetary process. Whether that appropriation would be large or small would depend primarily on two conditions: (1) the level of voluntary private household saving attained under pragmatic market socialism; (2) the democratically determined judgment of the citizen body as to how much business capital investment is appropriate.

Second, it is proposed that two new national government agencies be created—independent of the BPO—for the disposition of this budgetary appropriation into the business sector: (1) The National Investment Banking System (NIBS); and (2) the National Entrepreneurial Investment Board (NEIB). These two agencies would supplement and not replace the investment activity carried on by firms under BPO ownership. BPO-owned firms would include nonfinancial corporations which "lend" investment funds to themselves via retained earnings, and financial intermediary corporations such as banks, insurance companies, pension funds, and so on, which lend investment funds to, and purchase securities from, other business corporations. However, the NIBS and the NEIB would be somewhat different from standard financial intermediaries, and through this difference it is hoped that a somewhat higher long-term rate of capital accumulation and economic growth might be achieved under pragmatic market socialism than that currently prevailing under capitalism.

That which would distinguish the NIBS and the NEIB from the standard BPO-owned investment channels would be that while the performance evaluation of executives of firms in the standard channels would be implicitly oriented to the rate of property return produced on the entire accumulated stock of business capital, the performance evaluation of NIBS loan officers and NEIB agents would be explicitly oriented toward *recent* business capital investment. NIBS loan officers would be evaluated not on the basis of the success of all past loans they have made, but only on the basis of the success of their recent loans, say those made within the prior two or three years. The purpose of the NEIB is indicated by its name: to establish entrepreneurial firms. By its nature, an entrepreneurial firm has no interest in the rate of return achieved on the physical capital accumulations of existing firms. Therefore, evaluating the success of an agency in terms of the rate of property return produced by entrepreneurial firms automatically implies performance evaluation in terms of recent capital investment. In addition to direct funding from the national government budget, the NIBS and the NEIB would also re-channel all property return received on their loans and investments into business physical capital investment. The NIBS would operate exclusively on the supply side of capital investment, while the NEIB would operate on both demand and supply sides. In addition to its direct appropriations and retained earnings, the NEIB could solicit funding for entrepreneurial firms from ordinary financial intermediaries under BPO ownership. It is anticipated that the activities of both the NIBS and the NEIB would strengthen investment propensities within the economy and lead to a higher rate of economic growth.

Evaluation

The conservative response to the socialist challenge posed by Karl Marx and other nineteenth century dissidents has been the development of an elaborate body of thought that I refer to descriptively as "capitalist apologetics." Various components of this body of thought can be applied to pragmatic market socialism on the basis of the proposition that public-ownership socialism, in and of itself, necessarily and inevitably involves various dysfunctional conditions. Among these dysfunctional conditions are comprehensive central planning of the economy, the proliferation of intrusive social regulation of individual behavior and business enterprise, pervasive political intervention in the running of individual business enterprises, extreme social egalitarianism as implemented through highly progressive taxation and a massive welfare state, and the suppression of authentically democratic processes. In the final analysis, all these kinds of arguments—when applied to pragmatic market socialism—are based on the same dubious proposition: "There can be nothing new under the sun." That is to say, more precisely: "There can be no new forms of socialism under the sun." For example, the same deficiencies that applied to Soviet socialism during the heyday of centrally planned socialism under the megalomaniac dictator Joseph Stalin, must necessarily apply to any and all socialist systems.

But the entire history of human civilization demonstrates that there *can* be new social forms under the sun. Humanity has gradually proceeded from a condition of primitive barbarism, under which the invariable guiding principle was "might makes right," to a highly evolved civilization, governed to a substantial extent by the rule of law and upholding high standards of individual rights, worth, and dignity. For example, modern history has witnessed the dramatic rise to prominence of mass democracies: large and prosperous nation-states in which the highest political authorities are periodically held accountable to the general population in free and open elections. Three hundred years ago, during the heyday of absolute monarchy in Europe, conservatives would have dismissed the concept of mass democracy as totally preposterous. Such a polity, they would have argued, would inevitably degenerate into mediocrity and stagnation owing to the social leveling carried out by irresponsible demagogues elected by the rabble. Either that, or the polity would quickly become engulfed in a brutal civil war as the better classes fought to retain their advantages. The conservatives of three hundred years ago were eventually proved wrong by events. Events proved that it is possible to have a viable, functioning, genuinely democratic political system within a large and stratified nation without social leveling and without civil war.

Conservatives today who argue that any socialist polity would inevitably degenerate into mediocrity and stagnation—if not worse—are following in the footsteps of conservatives three hundred years ago who argued that a democratic polity would inevitably degenerate into mediocrity and stagnation. It would be rash to predict that today's conservatives will be proved wrong on the issue of socialism in the same way that yesterday's conservatives were proved wrong on the issue of democracy. But there is at least a reasonable possibility of this. Today's conservatives are failing to recognize the possibility of new forms of socialism, and they are also failing to appreciate the developing social realities that are making these new forms of socialism increasingly attractive. When yesterday's conservatives dismissed the possibility of democracy, they had in mind the ideal concept of democracy (epitomized by the New England town meeting) and failed to foresee the institutional forms of representative democracy, as practiced today, that are capable of translating the democratic principle into a practical political system. When today's conservatives dismiss the possibility of socialism, they have in mind the ideal concept of socialism (complete socioeconomic equality), and they fail to recognize the institutional forms of market socialism that are capable of translating the socialist principle into a practical economic system. Yesterday's conservatives failed to perceive how the development of a substantial middle class could make representative democracy more and more feasible and desirable. Similarly, today's conservatives fail to perceive how the developing realities of contemporary capitalism (extreme inequality of capital wealth ownership, separation of ownership and control, institutionalization of capital markets, and so on) are making market socialism more and more feasible and desirable.

Dogmatic assertions that pragmatic market socialism would be heir to all the same problems, real and imagined, ever associated with socialism—either as a real-world institution in the communist nations, or as a hypothetical proposal infused with utopian delusions—are merely an effort to beg the question, to shut down the ordinary processes of critical thinking, to terminate the debate through direct appeal to prejudice and preconception. The concept of market socialism in general, including all forms from Langian to pragmatic, is a dramatic new development in the intellectual history of socialism. It represents an informed, thoughtful, reflective effort to learn from the mistakes of communistic socialism, social democratic socialism, and utopian socialism, to find a genuinely new direction for socialism, to develop a practical and workable form of socialism to replace the misguided and half-baked proposals of the past. The concept of pragmatic market socialism goes a step further in this direction: it refines the general idea of market socialism introduced by Oskar Lange, and makes it far more precise, practical, and workable. The fact that some advocates of socialism in the past have been totally unrealistic dreamers and crackpots is not a legitimate argument against pragmatic market socialism—any more than it is a legitimate argument against representative democracy that some unrealistic advocates of democracy in the past seemed to have thought that it would be possible to govern a large, complex nation along the same lines as a New England town meeting.

While much of what currently passes for the "case against socialism" is irrelevant or virtually irrelevant when applied to pragmatic market socialism, there does in fact exist a logically sound and reasonably plausible case to be made against this proposed economic system. My purpose in this section is to enunciate and respond to that case. The following four sub-sections of this section will deal respectively with the capital management objection to socialism (that socialism would provide inadequate incentives to capital management effort—to the detriment of economic efficiency), the saving objection to socialism (that socialism would provide inadequate incentives to saving—to the detriment of economic growth), the "people's capitalism" objection to socialism (that the actual distributions of capital wealth and capital property income are not unduly unequal), and the political objection to socialism (that socialism would threaten freedom and democracy). These four objections will be examined in light of the pragmatic market socialist proposal.

Capital Management Effort. Probably the single most widely perceived basic economic problem with socialism is an alleged absence of adequate financial incentives to effort. People would find that there is no appreciable monetary return to working hard or to other economically beneficial behavior such as the founding of new firms (i.e. engaging in entrepreneurship). Therefore they would decline to engage in this beneficial behavior: they would fail to work hard, they would fail to found new firms, and so on. As a consequence, economic efficiency and productivity would decline. The economy would stagnate and decay. Quite possibly it would eventually collapse completely.

It so happens that this author agrees that the most serious potential problem of pragmatic market socialism is indeed the possibility that financial incentives to effort would be inadequate. However, the "effort" referred to here is of a very specific variety and certainly does not encompass the broad range of "economically beneficial behavior." The pragmatic market socialist proposal is designed explicitly to maintain exactly the same, or at least closely comparable, financial incentives to effort over each and every category of economically beneficial behavior—with one important exception. That one exception is what is termed herein "capital management effort." If incentive problems would be significant under pragmatic market socialism, they would be confined to this particular category. Thus it is quite important that it be understood what capital management effort is, and what it is not.

Capital management effort is defined here as any and all active effort aimed at achieving a high rate of return on financial capital. Capital management effort, as thus defined, falls into two major subcategories: (1) corporate supervision (as distinct from corporate management); and (2) investment analysis. This definition will be duly elaborated as we proceed, but it will be helpful to enumerate, at the outset, what capital management effort is *not*.

First and foremost, capital management effort is not labor as defined in standard economic analysis. In standard economic analysis, labor is any sort of activity by a person which is directly compensated (paid for) by a second party, whether that second party is another person, or an organization such as a business firm or a nonprofit agency. Labor income accounts for approximately 80 percent of total national income in advanced industrial nations such as the United States. The great majority of the adult, working-age population is dependent upon labor income in order to sustain life. The two exceptions consist of a small minority at the low end of the income spectrum who are physically or mentally incapable of work and who subsist on welfare doles, and a still smaller minority at the high end of the income spectrum who possess a sufficiently large amount of financial capital wealth that the income on this wealth provides at least a comfortable living—in other words, individuals who are, by proper definition, "capitalists."

A widespread misconception about socialism is that the concept itself demands a great deal of equality in the distribution of total disposable income among households—that is, of income after taxes and transfers. A major input into this misconception has been the traditional program of social democracy, which envisions a very high degree of progressivity in the taxation of *all* forms of income, labor income as well as property income, and which calls for extremely generous welfare benefits to be distributed to the less advantaged elements of society. However, social democracy has nothing to do with "socialism" as defined in terms of public ownership of the nonhuman factors of production: capital and land (natural resources). In fact, by the strict public ownership definition applied herein, social democratic "socialism" is not socialism at all. There is nothing in the pragmatic market socialist proposal, either explicit or implicit, that would entail greater progressivity in the taxation of labor income or more generous welfare benefits. There is no intention to subject even very high labor incomes, such as those earned by successful doctors, lawyers, corporation executives, and movie stars, to a higher rate of taxation.

In the contemporary corporate economy, it is apparent that a high level of performance among the top tier of corporation executives is vital to the success of the economy. This means that the marginal productivity of this type of labor is very high, and its remuneration should accordingly be quite generous. But whatever the amount paid for it, managerial effort provided by corporation executives is a form of labor and is not capital management effort as defined here. The capital management effort argument for capitalism would be far more persuasive than it actually is, if this were *not* the case. When we consider the totality of human effort which goes into trying to achieve a high rate of return on capital, common sense, together with a rudimentary understanding of the way the modern corporate economy works, suggests that most if not all of this effort is provided by corporation executives. Whatever might be thought of the current remuneration of corporation executives, most people recognize corporate management to be a technically demanding and psychologically stressful type of work. If the rhetoric, which is utilized in capitalist apologetics to assert that capital property income is an earned return to the capital management effort of the capital owners, could be legitimately applied to corporation executives, then this assertion would be far more believable. But it may *not* be so applied. The remuneration of corporation executives, whether it is applied in the form of salaries, bonuses, or benefits, is deemed labor income in both national income accounting and individual firm accounting. This remuneration rewards a form of labor (managerial labor), which means that the net income of the firm after managerial labor expenses have been met—that amount which is paid out in the form of dividends and interest—cannot be legitimately represented as a reward to managerial labor.

Without a doubt the most highly favored of all the buzzwords of capitalist apologetics is "entrepreneurship." This concept is cited more frequently than any other as a justification for the contemporary capitalistic status quo. The possibility of accumulating a vast capital fortune is (allegedly) an absolutely indispensable incentive to entrepreneurial endeavor. The benefits of entrepreneurship (allegedly) fully justify an extremely unequal distribution of financial capital wealth and thereby of capital property income. An important question is therefore: Is capital management effort to be identified with entrepreneurship? Such an identification is *not* warranted, since there is not a one-to-one correspondence between the two concepts. There is, however, some degree of overlap.

The two basic subcategories of capital management effort have been described as corporate supervision and investment analysis. The typical entrepreneur engages in both of these: he or she first engages in investment analysis in order to ascertain what type of new firm might be profitably established, and then, after the firm has been established, he or she, in the capacity of owner, engages in corporate supervision. But also essential to the overall concept of entrepreneurship is personal involvement in firm management (as opposed to firm supervision). Firm management means that one spends long working days at the office studying specific marketing and production problems and issues, and making tough decisions as between competing courses of action. Firm supervision, on the other hand, means occasional perusal of audited financial statements to determine how profitable one particular firm is in relation to the average among similar firms. With respect to any one firm, the time/energy requirements of firm management are much larger than the time/energy requirements of firm supervision. A true and genuine entrepreneur is not an outside investor, a silent partner, a rentier who merely puts up investment capital but remains otherwise uninvolved. In other words, he/she does not merely engage in firm supervision. Rather he or she actually and personally *manages* the new firm. This means that some part of the total remuneration of an entrepreneurial owner-manager is actually a return to managerial labor, rather than to entrepreneurship per se.

Unfortunately, there are no statistics available by which it can be precisely determined what percentage of the total flow of capital property income goes to individuals who have, at some point in their lives, personally established and managed an entrepreneurial business firm. In all likelihood, this percentage is quite low, perhaps in the order of 5 to 10 percent. This would mean that 90 to 95 percent of capital property income goes to individuals who established their entitlement to this income by means other than personal entrepreneurship—by such means as inheritance, financial speculation, or some combination of the two. The representation of capital property income, in capitalist apologetics, as an earned return to the noble enterprise of entrepreneurship, is no doubt the single most blatant and egregious departure from honesty in an area heavily burdened by such departures.

It should be well noted, in relation to entrepreneurship, that the pragmatic market socialist proposal put forward herein calls the bluff of those who assert that capital property income is primarily a return to personal entrepreneurship. Recall that a central feature of the proposal is for private ownership of entrepreneurial enterprises, so long as the founder-owner remains personally involved in the management of the firm. Upon voluntarily relinquishing management, the founder-owner would sell his/her ownership share for its full capitalized value to some other firm, most probably to a publicly-owned firm operating under the authority of the Bureau of Public Ownership. If there is any truth in the proposition that capital property income is mostly a return to personal entrepreneurship, then it would soon be found out under pragmatic market socialism that very little capital property return was being received by the Bureau of Public Ownership from the population of large, established, publicly-owned business firms. Rather capital property return would be going mostly to the founder-owners of privately-owned entrepreneurial enterprises. Of course, it would require an exceptionally naive defender of contemporary capitalism to seriously expect this situation to actually transpire under pragmatic market socialism.

Entrepreneurship is by far the primary variation to be found in capitalist apologetics on the capital management effort theme—but it is only one of several important variations. It is important to see these variations for what they are: as simply repetitions and rewordings of the same basic argument. But as far as the basic purpose of capitalist apologetics is concerned, there is really no need to keep cloning this basic argument, because the basic argument, stated simply and without rhetorical adornment or quasi-mystical embellishment, is indeed a plausible and serious argument against the workability of pragmatic market socialism. It applies both to the current (or "static") performance of the system, and to its long-term (or "dynamic") performance.

The capital management argument commences with the unarguable, a priori proposition that capital, being inanimate, non-sentient, and devoid of intelligence and volition, cannot through its own effort apply itself effectively in production—as a human worker would do simply by seeking out his/her highest-paid job. This proposition applies both to physical capital currently being used by firms in production, and to financial capital—funds which are to be allocated to physical capital investment in the future. This means that human beings must "manage" both physical and financial capital, much as a theatrical agent manages an actor or an actress. In order to motivate these managers to manage capital effectively, they must be paid the marginal productivity of their capital management effort.

Under capitalism, private individuals *own* their respective shares of the total capital stock. This ownership right entitles them to payments made for the use of capital by business firms. These individuals thus have a strong financial incentive to see to it that the capital earns a high rate of return—which will only be the case if the capital is effectively utilized (if it is physical capital) or effectively allocated (if it is financial capital). Thus the rational self-interest of the capital owners leads to the efficient use of capital in the economy.

Under socialism, the physical capital stock, as well as the capital investment fund, is legally owned by the general population, rather than by individual capital owners. Clearly, the general population has an interest in the effective use of its collectively owned capital. But equally as clearly, the general population cannot directly provide capital management effort to ensure the effective use of its capital. Instead, the general public must delegate its ownership authority to various individuals who are expected to provide the capital management effort which was previously provided by individual capital owners. Under the pragmatic market socialist proposal, for example, these individuals would be the personnel of the Bureau of Public Ownership (BPO), the National Investment Banking System (NIBS), and the National Entrepreneurial Investment Board (NEIB). These individuals would be allowed to retain as personal income only a very small percentage, in the realm of 1 or 2 percent, of the total amount of capital property return received by their respective public-ownership agencies from business firms (dividends on stock shares in the case of the BPO, and interest on bonds in the case of the NIBS and NEIB).

In other words, capital owners under capitalism who receive 100 percent of the return on their owned capital (less income taxes) would be replaced by public ownership personnel who would receive a mere 1 or 2 percent of the return on their capital responsibilities. The inference may be immediately drawn that since the financial incentive to capital management effort under socialism would be only a small fraction of what it is under capitalism, then the supply of capital management effort under socialism would be only a small fraction of what it is under capitalism, and hence the efficiency of capital utilization and overall economic performance under socialism would be only a small fraction of what they are under capitalism.

This chain of reasoning extends a very widely accepted concept in modern economics, that of the upward-sloping supply curve of labor, to capital management effort. According to the upward-sloping supply curve of labor, increases in wages and salaries increase labor quantity (or, possibly, labor intensity), while decreases in wages and salaries decrease labor quantity and/or intensity. Does it not follow, therefore, that the supply curve of capital management effort is also upward-sloping, so that the much lower payment for capital management effort to the non-owning capital managers under socialism would generate much less capital management effort than is provided by the capital owner-managers under capitalism?

This does *not* necessarily follow. To begin with, there are fundamental, qualitative differences between the labor income earned by individuals and the capital property income received by individuals. Labor income results from the multiplication of a fixed wage or salary rate by the amount of time worked. There is thus a proportional relationship between labor income and time worked: a graph of labor income against time worked would show a straight line. Capital property income, on the other hand, results from the multiplication of a variable rate of return on capital against the amount of capital owned by the capital owner. The capital management effort provided by the capital owner affects only the rate of return on capital; it does not affect the amount of capital on which that rate of return is received.

The relationship between capital management effort and rate of return on capital is a form of production function: the input of capital management effort generates the output of rate of return on capital. Now it is a universally accepted proposition of contemporary economics that production functions are characterized by diminishing returns to a factor of production: equal increments in the factor of production will generate steadily decreasing increments in the output. This means that the relationship between capital management effort and the rate of return on capital (and, by extension, the amount of capital property income received) is not a straight line as it is in the case of the relationship between labor time and labor income. Rather it is "bowed over": more precisely, it is concave upward-sloping, it increases at a decreasing rate.

Let us consider the relationship between capital management effort and the amount of capital property income received by the capital owner under capitalism. The question may be asked: How much of that capital property income is a marginal productivity return to the capital management effort of the capital owner, and how much of it is a marginal productivity return to the capital itself? The socialist position is that all or most of this capital property income is a return to capital itself, and that little or none of it is a return to capital management effort.

For well over 150 years, neoclassical economics has been hammering away at the proposition that capital contributes *independently* to production. To some unknown extent, this emphasis was a reaction to the Marxian critique of capitalism, based on the classical labor theory of value, which asserted that capital derives its value entirely from labor, and that capital value represents only "embodied labor value." It would be unprofitable to become entangled in a philosophical disputation regarding the "ultimate" source of value. Labor is in fact a viable candidate for this honor, based on the simple truism that even a gigantic stock of state-of-the-art capital would be completely unproductive if there were no human labor there to operate it. But as a matter of fact, I have no problem whatever with the neoclassical proposition that capital contributes independently to production. This proposition simply implies that capital should be a priced commodity—that business firms (as well as government agencies and nonprofit organizations) should have to pay for its use. It does not necessarily imply that what is paid by business firms and other organizations for the use of capital should be distributed to private capital owners on the basis of their personally owned financial assets.

Capital property return paid out by organizations which use capital ought, on the basis of both economic and ethical principles, to be paid, in the form of capital property income (dividends, interest, etc.), to private capital owners *only to the extent* that it is a marginal product return to the capital management effort of the owners, and not a marginal product return to the capital itself. In light of more than a century of strong, not to say strident, emphasis in neoclassical economics on the independent productivity of capital, one might naturally surmise that what we have here, in capital property income, is a return to capital itself, and not a return to capital management effort. In fact, in the more than 150 years since neoclassical economics discovered the independent productivity of capital, there has never been a single mention made of the alleged capital management effort of the capital owner. As utilized in capitalist apologetics, the neoclassical proposition that capital possesses independent productivity translates directly into "the capitalist is worthy of his capital property income." Capitalist apologetics, in other words, simply ignores the distinction between capital itself and the capital owner. It blends the two together, endowing the human capital owner with the productivity, worth, and social value of nonhuman capital.

A strict application of the independent productivity of capital principle would leave no room whatever for capital management effort. In this view, there is no such relationship, of the sort described above, between capital management effort and the rate of return on capital. Rather the rate of return on capital would be a fixed amount set by the interaction of supply and demand in the market for capital, just as the wage on a certain type of labor is a fixed amount set by the interaction of supply and demand in the market for that type of labor. The capital management effort of the capital owner would be zero, and the amount of capital property income received would be the product of the market-determined rate of return on capital and the amount of financial capital held by the owner. If this were the case, there would be no need to provide financial incentives to the BPO agents and NIBS/NEIB investment officers under pragmatic market socialism in the form of personal retention of a proportion of the capital property return received by their agencies from their particular capital responsibilities. Rather these individuals could merely be salaried employees, and their jobs would essentially be no different from any other kind of salaried job.

As a matter of fact, it is fully possible that making all personnel of the public ownership agencies under market socialism, including agents of the BPO and investment officers of the NIBS and NEIB, simply salaried employees, would in fact work quite well in practice. As is the case with any other kind of salaried job, of course, BPO agents and NIBS/NEIB investment officers would have to be subject to at least some minimum threat of dismissal for incompetence or uncooperativeness. Even though it has not yet been meaningfully incorporated into economic theory, it is obvious that a critical incentive to effort in any kind of job is the possibility of being fired if the job is being performed too poorly. But given a reasonable probability of dismissal, it might well result in a satisfactory outcome if BPO agents and NIBS/NEIB investment officers were salaried employees.

On the basis of my own extended reflective study of pragmatic market socialism, however, I have concluded that it would be rash to completely discount the possibility of a positive relationship between capital management effort and the rate of return on capital, and to assume that the rate of return on capital is completely independent of any effort provided by the capital owner. There is certainly a possibility that capital management effort is indeed a significant factor in the economic equation, and we would not want to create a situation in which there would be no capital management effort at all provided under market socialism. Thus the pragmatic market socialist proposal does envision capital management effort being provided by BPO agents and NIBS/NEIB investment officers.

In my own theoretical work on pragmatic market socialism, I have argued that the abstract essence of the primary socialist rebuttal to be made to the capital management effort argument against market socialism, resides in a concept which I have labeled the "plateau production function." Simply stated, this is the proposition that a very small amount of capital management effort (as provided by capital owners under capitalism, or public-ownership personnel under pragmatic market socialism) suffices to achieve very close to the maximum rate of return on capital. That is, at very low levels of capital management effort, capital management effort has a very strong increasing effect on rate of return, but that strong effect soon dissipates, so that at higher levels of capital management effort, this effort has very little increasing effect on rate of return. A graph of rate of return against capital management effort shows a rapid rise toward an asymptotic upper limit. The appearance of this graph suggests one side of a plateau—thus the name.

There are three especially important implications of a plateau configuration in the production function relating capital management effort to the rate of return on capital. First, this function means that while capital management effort is important to the success of the economy, the economy does not need very much of it in order to be successful. Second, from the point of view of the individual capital owner under capitalism, it means that most of his/her capital property income is of a "producer's surplus" nature: that is, the utility value of this income far exceeds the disutility of the very small amount of capital management effort required to obtain it. Finally, it means that a pragmatic market socialist economy, which paid the capital managers of the BPO, NIBS, and NEIB only a very small fraction of the capital property return that was previously paid to private capital owners under capitalism, would nevertheless experience a level of capital management effort approximately equal to that experienced under capitalism, and hence a level of overall economic efficiency and productivity approximately equal to that of capitalism.

Among the two most important "coefficients" relevant to the potential performance of a pragmatic market socialist system, relative to that of the market capitalist economic system, are the "retention coefficient" and the "effectiveness coefficient." The "retention coefficient" refers to the proportion of capital property return which is retained as personal income by the capital managers. The "effectiveness coefficient" refers to a parameter which determines the economic productivity of any given level of capital management effort, whether that level be high or low. The value of the effectiveness coefficient is determined by other economic and institutional factors—apart from the retention coefficient—which would affect the overall performance of the economic system.

The retention coefficient under pragmatic market socialism would be dramatically smaller than it is under capitalism: the capital owners of capitalism retain 100 percent of capital property return (implying a retention coefficient of 1), while the public ownership personnel under pragmatic market socialism would retain only 1 to 2 percent of this return (implying a retention coefficient of .01 to .02). This reduction in the retention coefficient might well, at first glance, suggest a severe deficiency of capital management effort under market socialism. But in light of the possibility of a "plateau production function" relating capital management effort to rate of return on capital, the matter is perceived to be not so straightforward. The salient implication of the plateau production function is that already under capitalism, there is a very small amount of capital management effort provided by the capital owners, and thus even a very drastic reduction in the retention coefficient would not have a noticeable reducing effect on the total supply of capital management effort.

The "retention coefficient" would clearly be much smaller under market socialism than it is presently under capitalism. Whether this would or would not mean a much smaller supply of capital management effort depends largely on whether or not the plateau production function is a good approximation to the actual real-world function relating capital management effort to rate of return on capital. Now as to the "effectiveness coefficient," critics of socialism would allege that this too would be much smaller than it is under capitalism. In fact, not wanting to accept that the validity of capitalism might depend on such a mundane-seeming concept as "capital management effort," they are quite likely to assert that the "real problems of socialism" lie not so much in a low retention coefficient, as they do in a low effectiveness coefficient. When asked to justify this assertion, they will make reference to such factors as the following: the soft enterprise budget constraint under socialism; comprehensive central planning of the economy under socialism; the proliferation of intrusive social regulation of individual behavior and business enterprise under socialism; pervasive political intervention in the running of individual business enterprises under socialism; extreme social egalitarianism under socialism, as implemented through highly progressive taxation and a massive welfare state. All this, it is alleged, will make a terrible mess of the economy, so that it could be said that the "effectiveness coefficient" under market socialism would be a small fraction of what it is under market capitalism.

The basic problem with this assertion is that the factors just listed as determinants of socialist inefficiency are factors from which the pragmatic market socialist proposal has been explicitly disassociated. The pragmatic market socialist proposal does not call for central planning, it does not call for an expansion of business regulation, it does not call for a bigger welfare state—in fact, it calls for none of these things. To cite these kinds of things as reasons for a lower effectiveness coefficient under market socialism is to engage in the question-begging tactic of asserting that the real and perceived flaws of communistic socialism and social democratic socialism must inevitably apply to *any* socialist system—including the pragmatic market socialist system. This basic argument may be described as the "there can be nothing new under the sun" argument. It need not be belabored that this is an inherently feeble argument.

On the pro-socialist side of the ledger, meanwhile, there are indeed several sensible factors which suggest that the effectiveness coefficient would in fact be higher under pragmatic market socialism than it is currently under capitalism. This possibility supplements the possibility of a plateau production function in the relationship between capital management effort and rate of return on capital. There are at least four factors that could improve the economic effectiveness coefficient as a result of the implementation of pragmatic market socialism.

First, the translation of capital property income into social dividend income (distributed to households on the basis of household labor income) would increase the effective wage and salary payment to labor, and (presuming an upward-sloping supply curve of labor) lead to an increase in labor supply and consequently an increase in economic output. Second, the concentration of the outside ownership interest in a particular firm in the hands of a relatively small number of BPO agents would counteract the separation of ownership and control condition under contemporary capitalism, impose a higher degree of accountability on the top executives, and thus enhance their effort incentives. Third, the capital managers under pragmatic market socialism (selected as they would be from high-level business executives) are likely to be generally more capable than the capital owners under capitalism (who are often widows and inheriting children with no business experience). Fourth, the capital responsibility of the typical public ownership agency agent or investment officer could be set at a level to maximize his/her incentive to provide capital management effort—not so high that his/her income would be high even if rate of return were very low, and not so low that his/her income would be low even if rate of return were very high.

We may summarize by saying that there are two major conceptual rebuttals to the pro-capitalist proposition that inadequate capital management effort, owing to the low retention coefficient of the capital managers, would cripple the economic performance of pragmatic market socialism. First, there is the possibility that the production function relating capital management effort to rate of return on capital is of the plateau configuration, meaning that the input of a very small amount of capital management effort suffices to raise the rate of return to its asymptotic upper limit. The implication of this type of function is that the level of capital management effort is already very low under capitalism, so the fact that it would be equally low under socialism would be no problem. Second, there is the possibility that the effectiveness coefficient under pragmatic market socialism would be higher than it is under capitalism. A higher effectiveness coefficient would both increase the incentive to capital management effort of the capital managers and have beneficial effects on overall economic performance through other channels as well (e.g., by making high corporation executives more conscientious and assiduous in the performance of their duties).

Saving. Relative to the capital management effort defense of capitalism, the sacrifices of saving defense has one major advantage and one major disadvantage. The major advantage is that it makes intuitive sense to a broad range of the population, from super-wealthy capitalists down to lower-middle-class and working-class people of very modest means. Super-wealthy capitalists are to some extent better able than are ordinary people to appreciate the dubiousness of the capital management defense of capital property income, because they know from personal experience how minimal is the time and effort they devote to corporate supervision and/or investment analysis, in relation to the large amount of capital property income which they receive. But being human beings, they of course want to feel morally justified about this large amount of income. They are thus drawn naturally to the thought that by preserving their wealth, by *not* liquidating their financial assets and engaging in an orgy of consumption (buying a bigger mansion, a better yacht, more fur coats and diamond necklaces, spending even more time and money in Monte Carlo casinos, and so on and so forth), they are allowing the resources that would have gone into their own augmented personal consumption to instead be used more productively to build factories and schools, to finance research and development, and to assist generally in the economic development of civilization.

Of course, super-wealthy capitalists are likely to already be enjoying a lavish standard of life, and so the "sacrificial" aspect of saving, such as it is, is for them less intense. At the other end of the income scale, working-class or middle-class households of modest means might not be in a position to appreciate the dubiousness of capital management effort as a defense of capital property income, since they have such minimal experience with this type of income. On the other hand, because their standard of living is so modest, they are naturally extremely conscious of the "sacrifices of saving." There are any number of very desirable commodities, not necessarily in the "luxury" category, that might be purchased with their small hordes of savings, and thus it is a constant, severe temptation not to go ahead and liquidate these hordes in order to buy some of these commodities. In light of the constant effort required to fight off temptations to spend savings accumulations, the interest income on these accumulations seems to working-class and middle-class households certainly to be a fair and legitimate return—it makes the effort to preserve savings accumulations at least a little bit more palatable. And so, at both ends of the income spectrum, although for somewhat different reasons at each end, there is a good level of basic intuitive plausibility in the proposition that capital property income is an earned return to the sacrifices of saving.

The major disadvantage of the sacrifices of saving defense of capital property income, relative to the capital management effort defense, is that when one goes beyond superficial first impressions to a careful consideration of this defense, it becomes obvious that it possesses far less substantive content and apparent merit than does the capital management effort defense. Whereas capital management is an active behavior, saving is a passive behavior. This means that while capital management effort must be provided by individuals (e.g., BPO agents) and cannot be provided by "society as a whole," saving can indeed be provided by "society as a whole." More precisely, a part of national government tax revenues may be allocated to capital investment, thus accomplishing both saving itself, and transformation of the saving into investment, in one step. Therefore, if an adequate amount of saving is not being provided by private households under socialism, then—if society desires—additional saving can be provided socially out of tax revenue. The sacrifices of saving, such as they are, need not be assumed individually by private households; they may alternatively be assumed by all households acting in concert, that is to say, they may be assumed socially. Capital management effort is a better defense of capital property income than sacrifices of saving, because capital management effort clearly cannot be provided out of tax revenue.

The obvious and elementary possibility of social provision of saving for investment purposes is the primary flaw in using the sacrifices of saving as a justification for capital property income. A secondary but still very serious flaw is that it is by no means clear that private household saving would indeed be lower under market socialism. If private household saving were as high (or higher) under pragmatic market socialism as it is currently under capitalism, then there would be no need for further provision of saving resources out of tax revenue. Based on the evidence currently at hand, there is indeed a very substantial probability that this would in fact be the case.

In the skin-deep thinking about these matters which is typical under contemporary capitalism, there is a great deal of uncritical acceptance of the following closely related propositions: (1) interest (and other forms of property return) are a reward for saving; (2) a zero rate of interest under socialism (reflecting a zero rate of return on financial wealth in general under socialism) would reduce saving either to zero, or at least to a very low level. As to proposition (1), there are other rewards to saving aside from interest, so that the effect of the interest rate on saving may be very small, even negligible. As to proposition (2), even if it were accepted, for the sake of argument, that reducing the rate of interest to zero would tend to substantially reduce saving by private households, this does not necessarily imply that saving would in fact be less under socialism. There would be other changes associated with a transition to pragmatic market socialism, and these other changes might completely nullify the adverse effect on private household saving of eliminating capital property return on financial wealth. In any case, as already noted, a decline in private household saving does not necessarily imply a decline in aggregate saving: social saving out of tax revenue could be used to eliminate the shortfall caused by lower private household saving.

The idea that capital property income is a return to the sacrifices of saving dates back to the beginnings of capitalist apologetics in the early nineteenth century. During that time the English economist Nassau Senior (1790-1864) came up with the memorable term "abstinence" to refer to these sacrifices. This term was fiercely lambasted and ridiculed by Karl Marx, in one of the more colorful and effective passages in *Das Kapital* (Vol. I, Chap. XXIV, Section 3), on grounds that wealthy capitalists enjoying luxurious living standards cannot be sensibly represented as practicing "abstinence," since this term connotes excessively abstemious living standards. Later on in the nineteenth century, the Austrian economist Eugen von Böhm-Bawerk (1851-1914), probably the most important critic of Marxist economics of his era, came up with the notion of "time preference." Böhm-Bawerk's time preference argument is substantively the same as Senior's abstinence argument—it simply does not use the questionable term "abstinence." Senior had argued that saving is akin to abstinence, and therefore property return must be paid to individuals in order to induce them to undertake this highly unpleasant abstinence. Böhm-Bawerk argued that saving is saving, and does not imply, in the case of wealthy people, that they are experiencing abstemious living standards—but all the same, property return *must* be paid, even to wealthy people, in order to induce them to continue saving. The reason for this is given as "time preference": the alleged inherent preference in all human beings, at all times and in all places, for consumption now rather than consumption later. If there were not a return paid on savings accumulations, according to Böhm-Bawerk, then wealthy people would liquidate their capital assets and use the proceeds to buy even larger estates, still bigger yachts, and so on and so forth. In his famous dictum: The marginal productivity of physical capital explains why a rate of return *can* be paid to owners of financial capital; and time preference explains why it *must* be paid to these owners.

The proposition that consumption now is invariably preferred to consumption later is a naive—and invalid—extrapolation from the proposition that income *now* is invariably preferred to income later. The latter proposition is in fact almost certainly true, at least in a capitalist economy, because a certain amount of money received now can be—if the recipient does not wish to devote it currently to consumption—put into a financial instrument yielding a rate of interest. Thus the recipient will be able to consume the amount of money, plus accrued interest, later on. But it is a logical and empirical fallacy to conclude, from the invariable preference for income now over income later, that consumption now is invariably preferred over consumption later. Consumption is qualitatively different from income. Consumption always involves some sort of physical experience, and it is also inherently instantaneous.

That is to say, consumption cannot be saved in the same way that income is saved. If an individual were to receive his or her income in the form of one lump sum payment per year of, say, $50,000, there would be no problem. The payment could be deposited in a bank account and drawn upon throughout the course of the year. But if the person received, to cover his or her food needs for the year, a large pile of perishable foodstuffs, which would remain edible for only one or two days, this pile being equivalent to what he or she normally consumes in one year—then there certainly *would* be a problem. A person cannot eat enough food to last for a year in one or two days, and in the absence of replenishment of the pile, that person would soon starve to death. In the jargon of economics, this indicates a limited amount of "intertemporal substitutability" with respect to consumption. On the other hand, income enjoys the maximum degree of intertemporal substitutability: a dollar's worth of income can be spent today, tomorrow, a year from now, ten years from now—all with equal ease.

The idea of time preference has a great deal in common with the idea of risk-taking. Both ideas are superficially plausible defenses of capital property return which appeal to initial intuition, but which fail to hold up against a careful and critical examination. Neither idea emerged naturally from objective social scientific inquiry into the nature and functioning of society: rather both ideas were and remain transparent, ad hoc, ex post facto rationalizations for the receipt of capital property income by private individuals, ideas produced solely in response to the socialist challenge to the economic and ethical validity of capitalism. Both ideas are subject to the weakness that that which is proposed as the justification for capital property income is not a primary factor of production: risk-taking clearly does not contribute directly to production, and neither does saving. Only after saving has been converted into investment does it contribute to production. According to the proverb, "there is many a slip 'twixt the cup and the lip"—similarly there is many a slip between saving and investment, and only a part of ex ante (before the fact) saving becomes actual ex post (after the fact) investment.

As putative moral justifications for capital property income, both ideas suffer from the same fundamental flaw that there is an inverse relationship between the amount of capital property income received by the household, and that which is supposedly being compensated by capital property income. Wealthy capitalistic households receiving large amounts of capital property income are subject to *less* disutility from risk-taking owing to their greater ability to practice risk-spreading via portfolio diversification, and they also experience *less* disutility from saving (fending off time preference) because their current consumption standards are already so high. Finally, even if we were to grant that a certain measure of validity might attach to risk-taking and/or time preference, this would not necessarily justify the capitalistic mode of distributing capital property return produced by business enterprises to private households on the basis of household financial wealth. Just as the risk-taking of investment, such as it is, could be assumed socially, so too the sacrifices of saving, such as they are, could be borne by society as a whole.

Now it is factually true that under the pragmatic market socialist system, households would in general receive no property return on their financial assets. Such assets could be held only in the form of money (i.e. in cash and/or bank demand deposits). A certain household might be quite wealthy under this type of market socialism: for example, it might hold $10,000,000 in cash and bank demand deposits. The pragmatic plan envisions no restrictions being put on the amount of financial wealth which a given household may own. But it does envision the termination of property return payments on financial wealth. Under capitalism, on the other hand, a household owning $10,000,000 would invest it, and would receive during the course of the year, assuming a modest 5 percent rate of return, $500,000 in capital property income. Another household of more modest means, holding say $10,000 in financial assets, would receive, at the same rate of return, $500. Under pragmatic market socialism, neither household would receive any property return on its financial wealth, since this wealth could not be held in the form of "investments."

A household which started the year with $10,000,000 in cash and demand deposits would end the year with $10,000,000 (assuming no spending out of it), and a household which started the year with $10,000 would end it with $10,000. Capitalist apologetics asserts that capital property income is a very important reason for holding accumulations of financial wealth—in fact, it may very well be the *sole* significant reason (as in the dubious dictum: "people save in order to take advantage of the interest rate"). Therefore, capitalist apologetics would assert that under socialism, in which there would be no interest or other property return on investments available to private households, the hypothetical wealthy household with $10,000,000 would have no incentive to hold that $10,000,000, and the hypothetical modest household with $10,000 would have no incentive to hold that $10,000. Both households would go on a spending spree—the wealthy household might buy a new 250-foot ocean-going yacht, while the modest household might buy a little pre-owned motorboat.

Upon a little reflection, most readers will recognize the dubiousness of this prediction. Consider first the modest household. Upon a transition to socialism, small-scale holdings would be compensated 100 percent in cash. Thus if, for example, the household had been holding the $10,000 in certificates of deposit or an interest-bearing time deposit, this same amount would now be held in a simple demand deposit. Would the household, now deprived of $500 per year in interest income, rush out to spend the $10,000 which previously had produced that $500? Not necessarily. It could be that the $10,000 has been earmarked for retirement income purposes, or for providing a college education for the children, or for providing a bequest to the children, or just simply because the household feels more comfortable knowing that it has some "financial padding." Aside from the maintenance of existing savings accumulations, there is the question of further saving out of current income. This modest household will in all probability receive *more* current income under pragmatic market socialism than it had been receiving under capitalism. It will lose the $500 in capital property income which it had been receiving under capitalism, but it will gain some amount of social dividend income under market socialism. If it loses $500 in capital property income and gains $2,500 in social dividend income, it will have $2,000 more a year out of which to save. It may very well *increase* its level of saving.

Now consider the wealthy household, the one with $10,000,000 in financial assets under capitalism. The envisioned compensation plan would indeed be "fair and equitable"—but that does not imply full compensation of large-scale financial wealth based on a combination of inheritance and financial speculation. After socialization, this same household might be left with, say, $2,000,000 in demand deposits. Will the household rush out to spend the $2,000,000, since it will no longer bring in any capital property income? Not necessarily. Recall that under capitalism, the household had been accustomed to receiving $500,000 a year in capital property income on its $10,000,000 in investment assets. Most of that $500,000 a year was probably being spent on consumption—keeping up mortgage payments on the estate, paying the servants, etc. The household would have to confront the fact that it can no longer count on $500,000 a year in capital property income to sustain the style of life to which it was accustomed. In fact, if it went on spending $500,000 a year out of its current stock of $2,000,000 in financial assets, it could maintain this pattern for only four years. It need not be belabored that the household quite probably would *not* go on a spending spree. Quite probably it would instead start pondering ways to reduce expenses. In actual fact, the annual consumption spending of this wealthy household is likely to be considerably less after socialization than it was before.

These stories are intended to suggest that there is a lot more to saving than the interest rate. In the foregoing sub-section, I did not develop a formal economic theory of capital management effort, and so too in this sub-section I will not develop a formal economic theory of saving. (Interested readers may consult my contributions on these topics in the professional economics literature.) That would become far too technical. Some fairly general comments will have to suffice. It so happens that the existing economic theory of saving is not as comprehensive and well defined as one might expect of such an important economic category. In fact, the only model of saving which might be described as "standard textbook material" is a rather simplistic two-period model in which the household uses saving (or borrowing) as an instrument to allocate the total amount of income it receives over the two periods as between period-1 consumption and period-2 consumption. This model provides some insight into the effect of the interest rate and income (both in period 1 and period 2) on the level of saving. A basic result from this model is that the effect of the interest rate on saving is indeterminate. A rise (or fall) in the interest rate has competing substitution and income effects, and there is no a priori basis for presuming which effect will dominate. This indeterminacy exists even if time preference is incorporated into the model by specifying that period-1 consumption has a greater impact on intertemporal utility than period-2 consumption.

A fundamental postulate of the sacrifices of saving defense of capital property income is the "upward-sloping supply curve of saving as a function of the interest rate": the higher the interest rate, the higher the level of saving provided by private households. That this postulate is actually nothing more than a conjecture is demonstrated even by the rudimentary two-period model of saving discussed in practically every standard textbook of microeconomic theory. An upward-sloping supply curve of saving with respect to the interest rate would mean that the substitution effect of an interest rate change dominates the income effect. But there is nothing contrary to standard economic presumptions in the alternative conjecture that the substitution effect and income effect cancel each other out and the interest rate has *no* effect on saving, or in the alternative conjecture that the income effect dominates the substitution effect and the supply curve of saving is *downward-sloping* with respect to the interest rate.

Naturally the level of indeterminacy increases as we proceed to more complicated models. A more realistic model of household saving would cover an indefinite number of periods rather than just two periods. It would take into account the fact that households typically expect to retire at some point in the future, and so they must make provision for sustaining consumption during the retirement years. An increasingly popular assumption in more recent models of saving is that household utility depends not only on consumption of commodities, but also on the amount of financial assets owned: in other words, financial wealth is valued "for its own sake." There is also the complication of aggregation and general equilibrium: the relationship between the interest rate and aggregate saving, taking into account the production side of the economy, may be qualitatively different from the relationship between the interest rate and the saving of one particular household, abstracting from the production side of the economy. And then there is the dynamic element: the long-term relationship between interest rate and saving may be quite different from the short-run relationship between the two. As one might well imagine, it can all become very complicated. Be that as it may, the following informal comments are provided, in lieu of a formal analysis of the problem, to suggest that a substantial decline in the aggregate rate of saving of private households under pragmatic market socialism is not all that likely.

To begin with, there is the fact that the "upward-sloping supply curve of saving" (the so-called "classical" theory of saving) is purely speculative from a theoretical standpoint. But even if the supply curve of saving were upward-sloping, this would not necessarily entail a reduction in private household saving under pragmatic market socialism if one or both of the following is true: (1) the effect of the interest rate on private household saving, while positive, is numerically very weak; (2) the effect of the interest rate on private household saving would be swamped by other effects.

Most people do not consult data on interest rates when deciding on how much they will save. Saving is usually a long-term proposition, interest rates do not vary all that much over the long term, and what fluctuations in interest rates will occur in the future is unknown anyway. A much more important question for most people, in deciding on their saving, is: "How much can I *afford* to save?" The amount that they can afford to save is largely determined by their income level. It was on the basis of this simple observation that John Maynard Keynes, the initiator of contemporary macroeconomic theory, postulated that the influence of the interest rate on saving is numerically insignificant and is dwarfed by the influence of income on saving. It is therefore quite important to note that the vast majority of households under pragmatic market socialism will have incomes higher than those they have presently under capitalism. To begin with, the vast majority of them will receive more social dividend income than they currently receive capital property income. In addition, there is the possibility that owing to the fact that the social dividend distribution principle implies an increase in the effective wage or salary rate of every household, households will provide more labor, thus increasing aggregate output and total household income. Most households will have more income out of which to save.

Another important point is that the great majority of saving provided by working-class and middle-class households is in fact "life-cycle saving" earmarked for the provision of retirement income. Most households provide for their retirement either by participation in a government pension plan (such as Social Security in the United States), or by participation in a private pension plan, often partially underwritten by the employer. The pragmatic market socialist plan proposed here envisions no change in the terms and conditions of retirement planning. In particular, retirement plans would incorporate compound interest just as they do today under capitalism. One of the major exceptions to the principle that capital property income would not be available to private households would be the compound interest paid on retirement accumulations by financial intermediaries. Thus there is no reason to expect this very important component of private household saving to be affected by a transition to pragmatic market socialism.

One of the cruder themes in capitalist apologetics is that socialism would deprive people of the ability to provide for their retirement years by eliminating all private ownership of income-producing capital instruments such as stocks and bonds. The fact is that only a tiny proportion of the retired population receives substantial income from stocks, bonds, and the like. Most retired people live on pensions and annuities which terminate upon the death of the recipient and his/her spouse. For these people, retirement planning would be the same under market socialism as it is under capitalism. And the role of saving in this planning would be the same.

People's Capitalism. The term "people's capitalism" was invented in the 1950s by the U.S. Advertising Council as its contribution to the propaganda battle being waged by the capitalist nations against the worldwide communist menace. The thrust of people's capitalism is that the "rank and file" of society either have already become the owners of the capital means of production—or, alternatively, will soon become the owners of the capital means of production presuming present trends continue a while longer. In other words, the capitalist class is being absorbed into the general population; it no longer stands isolated as a small minority whose financial interests are substantially and permanently different from those of the large majority. Thus the fundamental basis for the socialist critique of capitalism is rapidly eroding also. Evidence for this historic transformation of capitalism was found by the Ad Council in the spread of common stock ownership among the population: as of the 1950s, a larger proportion of U.S. households owned common stock than had been the case in the 1940s and 1930s.

Of course, if one goes back to the late 1920s, when the American public succumbed to a veritable mania of stock market speculation, common stock ownership was comparable to what it was in the 1950s. Most of the 1920s small-scale investors in the stock market had their savings wiped out by the crash of 1929 and the subsequent prolonged depression of the 1930s. What happened on a grand scale in that era continues to transpire on a small scale to this day: as a rule, small-scale investors in the stock market lose money. In fact, it can probably be said that the stock market is and remains a highly effective institution for the continuous transfer of capital wealth from low- and medium-income non-capitalistic households to high-income capitalistic households. Small-scale investors do not have sufficient capital with which to adequately diversify their investment portfolios; also, they are far too conscious of the hard work which went into the slow and painful accumulation of their small hoard of savings. As a result, they are anxious and skittish investors. Time and time again, they panic, sell out, and take a loss. Meanwhile, the large-scale capitalistic investors, with widely diversified portfolios worth tens of millions of dollars, calmly wait out most temporary downturns in the values of specific assets, and normally refrain from selling assets unless and until they can make a good profit on the sale. This same pattern holds for the entire range of investment assets, although it is most pronounced in the case of common stock. Thus, owing to the workings of the stock market, the wealth of small-scale investors is diminished while that of large-scale investors is augmented. Far from being a harbinger of "people's capitalism" in any meaningful sense, increased participation by working-class and middle-class households in the stock market is probably a sign that the concentration of capital wealth in the hands of the super-wealthy capitalistic minority is on the increase.

For as long as we have had systematic statistical data on capital wealth ownership, the distribution of capital wealth has been fairly and accurately describable as "extremely unequal." Despite occasional upward swings in common stock ownership, such as the one which inspired the Ad Council to come up with the memorable term "people's capitalism," there is no verifiable long-term trend toward significant equalization of capital wealth. In fact, the more recent trend, over the last 50 years or so, has been a slow but steady further increase in capital wealth inequality. Furthermore, there is no verifiable long-term trend toward the reduction of capital property income as a proportion of national income. Thus, there is no basis for speculating that the problem of maldistribution of capital property income will eventually "cure itself" if we merely wait long enough.

The essence of people's capitalism, as a defensive tactic, is to obscure the hard and unpalatable fact of extreme inequality in capital property income distribution under contemporary capitalism. This is accomplished by various forms of misinterpretation and misrepresentation aimed at diminishing the awareness among the non-capitalist majority that they are not now, nor probably ever will be, members of the tiny capitalist minority. The illusion of relatively high equality in capital wealth is mainly achieved by blurring the distinction between capital wealth and noncapital wealth such as residential real estate and consumer durables. As a matter of fact, under contemporary capitalism many if not most forms of noncapital wealth are far more equally distributed than capital wealth forms. What this means is that the typical household will own an amount of noncapital wealth much closer to the average amount of noncapital wealth than is the case with respect to capital wealth. For example, if, hypothetically, the average amount of noncapital wealth over all households in the economy is $100,000 per household, and the average amount of capital wealth is also $100,000, a certain household which owns, say, $50,000 worth of noncapital wealth (50 percent of the average), is likely to own only $5,000 worth of capital wealth (5 percent of the average).

The distinction between capital wealth and noncapital wealth is very clear and important. Capital wealth consists of financial instruments such as stocks and bonds which yield tangible property income in terms of dividends and interest, and which are capable of yielding further capital gains income upon sale. Noncapital wealth consists of material goods such as homes and gardens, appliances and furnishings, books and pictures, clothes and jewelry, automobiles and other transportation equipment, stockpiles of food and medicine, and so forth. These are all valuable commodities which *may* be sold at a profit (yielding what the tax code deems a "capital gain"), but which definitely *do not* yield a tangible income flow of any kind. A person could own $10 million worth of noncapital wealth, but if that person chooses neither to work nor to sell any of the property, then that person would soon starve to death. On the other hand, a person who owns $10 million worth of capital wealth could choose not to work and also not to sell any of the property, and that person could nevertheless live quite comfortably on the property income (dividends, interest, etc.) generated by the capital wealth (stocks, bonds, etc.).

Thanks to the widespread success of that very basic form of people's capitalism misrepresentation which simply lumps together capital and noncapital wealth into one homogeneous mass of "property," there are uncountable millions of impoverished and semi-impoverished people in the capitalist nations, who own not one dollar worth of legitimate capital property, but who are nevertheless convinced that they themselves are "capitalists" whose personal property would be threatened by socialism.

A strong propensity to blend together capital wealth and noncapital wealth into "wealth" pure and simple is not confined to the hopelessly ignorant or naive. Educated economists, for example, like to talk about the "implicit income" of owners of residential property—if a house owner did not own the house, he or she would be forced to pay rent for a dwelling place, and this "what if" amount can be considered the owner's "implicit income." The obvious shortcoming of this bit of intellectual legerdemain is that a person could be receiving millions of dollars a month in implicit income, but if that person had no other source of income, that person would be starving. The idea simply does not square with a commonsense understanding of the term "income." For another example, the government statisticians responsible for reporting information on "wealth" concentrate almost entirely on "total wealth" or "aggregate wealth" rather than capital wealth. In other words, most of the information which they provide pertains to the sum of capital and noncapital wealth. Since noncapital wealth is much more equally distributed than is capital wealth, this approach diminishes the apparent degree of "wealth inequality" in society, and diverts attention from the extremely high level of inequality that exists with respect to capital wealth.

That the distribution of capital wealth is highly unequal has been "common knowledge" for a long time. For example, it was a basic presumption made by Karl Marx in his nineteenth-century critique of capitalism—and while Marx's many critics have discerned numerous errors and omissions in his work, by and large they have not challenged this particular presumption. Apparently the evidence from casual empiricism has been compelling: people living in lonely mansions on the hill tend to possess lots of stocks and bonds; people living in modest frame houses down in the town tend to possess very little of this sort of thing. But we are living today in an age of quantitative, numerical science, and if we are to contemplate something so seemingly drastic as a transition from capitalism to socialism, then we would want to have as precise an idea as possible of those conditions which determine the relative desirability of the transition. One of these conditions is the distribution of financial capital wealth under contemporary capitalism. Just exactly how unequal is it? And what are the implications of this inequality in terms of a potential transition to pragmatic market socialism?

Of all the advanced capitalist nations today, the amount of available information on the financial condition of the population is probably greatest for the United States. The following discussion pertains to the United States, but roughly the same situation holds for the other advanced capitalist nations: Canada, Australia, New Zealand, Japan, and the nations of Western Europe.

The most extensive and reliable information on the financial circumstances of U.S. households comes from tax returns. Since the imposition of individual income taxation by the federal government in 1916, a tremendous amount of information has flowed into Washington on income distribution. Owing to fairly stiff penalties for misreporting income, and to fairly active enforcement of the tax rules, this information is reasonably reliable. For several decades, the federal government has made a respectable effort to organize this information and make it available to the general public in the form of the annual series of Internal Revenue Service publications entitled *Statistics of Income: Individual Income Tax Returns*. From this source, for example, we may ascertain that at low- to medium-income levels, capital property income (primarily dividends, interest, and capital gains) is a very small component of total household income, while at very high income levels, capital property income becomes a very substantial component of total household income. From this information on the flow of capital property income, it is evident that ownership of the stock of financial capital is highly unequal.

If the federal government imposed taxes on household wealth, we would have far better information on wealth distribution than we do at present. There is no annual tax on household wealth comparable to the annual income tax, but taxation of wealth does occur at the time of the owner's death, in the form of estate taxes. This type of taxation is approximately as old as individual income taxation. Information on U.S. wealth distribution based on estate tax returns has not been provided to the public in as great a degree of detail, and for as long a period of time, as has been the case for U.S. income distribution based on income tax returns. But the Internal Revenue Service has since the 1960s been issuing an intermittent publication entitled *Supplemental Statistics of Income: Personal Wealth Estimated from Estate Tax Returns*. This publication verifies a high degree of inequality in the distribution of total wealth, including both capital forms and noncapital forms. The information is not as precise as would be desirable for present purposes, both because of the emphasis on total wealth rather than capital wealth, and because of the inadequate degree of detail provided concerning households in the highest wealth brackets. Information from estate tax returns has been used by economists such as Robert J. Lampman and James D. Smith to assess changes in U.S. wealth distribution over time. Through such contributions, it has been established beyond reasonable doubt that the distribution of total wealth (and by implication of capital wealth) has been highly unequal throughout the twentieth century.

Since the 1960s another very important source of information on U.S. income and wealth distribution has appeared: periodic surveys conducted by the Federal Reserve Board (FRB). The collection of financial information through surveys has certain strengths and weaknesses relative to its collection through tax returns. Since the information is not being provided for tax purposes, there is not an automatic incentive toward underreporting. Also, the survey questionnaires go into far more detail than do tax forms. On the other hand, since there is no incentive for responding to the surveys other than general public spiritedness, and since there is no legal penalty for providing incorrect information, either by accident or by intention, the surveys also have serious limitations as sources of financial information.

The first of the FRB's surveys was called the *Survey of Financial Characteristics of Consumers (SFCC)*; succeeding surveys have been called *Surveys of Consumer Finances (SCF)*. The *SFCC*, conducted in 1963, was quite unique in terms of the quantity of hard information made available to the public in accessible printed form. A 166-page statistical report carrying the title of the survey, authored by Dorothy S. Projector and Gertrude S. Weiss, was issued by the Board of Governors of the Federal Reserve Board in August 1966. Two years later, in November 1968, another 321-page statistical report, authored by Projector alone, was issued on the 1964 follow-up survey of respondents to the 1963 survey: *Survey of Changes in Family Finances*. The nearly 500 pages of tabular data issued on these two related surveys remains to this day the single most accessible and comprehensive source of information on U.S. wealth and income distribution.

Considerably less information has been provided on the more recent *Surveys of Consumer Finances*. A limited amount of very general information derived from these surveys has been published in the FRB's monthly, the *Federal Reserve Bulletin*. For example, the three articles in the *Federal Reserve Bulletin* pertaining to the 1983 *SCF* amounted to only 45 pages. The Federal Reserve Board offers raw data files of the information from its various surveys to researchers, but the demand for these files has always been somewhat limited. Only experienced programmers with access to advanced computer equipment have any hope of extracting understandable information from these files. And the incentive for doing so is not great in that the resulting information is not highly publishable—both because it is "uninteresting" (since it is already well known that capital wealth is very unequally distributed), and because it is "irrelevant" (since it is also well known that no viable cure exists for inequality in capital wealth ownership).

As to the speculation that the degree of inequality in U.S. capital wealth distribution is considerably lower in the latter 1990s than it was in the early 1960s, this speculation has been convincingly refuted by a small but significant amount of careful study utilizing the FRB's more recent data. For example, definitive research by Edward N. Wolff published in the *Review of Income and Wealth* indicates significantly *greater* capital wealth inequality as of the 1990s relative to the 1960s. This situation is not altogether unexpected, in view of the conservative counter-revolution against progressive taxation, public expenditure, and the welfare state.

The present author has utilized the printed data in the 1966 *Survey of Financial Characteristics of Consumers* in a considerable amount of published writing. The numbers derived from the 1966 *SFCC* report authored by Projector and Weiss are eye-opening to say the least. Here is one example. According to the report, the average amount of investment assets owned by all 57.9 million U.S. households in 1962 was $7,013. At the same time, the richest .1 million households (i.e. 100,000 households) owned an average amount of investment assets of $1,264,653. Thus the richest 100,000 households owned 180 times the average amount of investment assets in the economy. One implication of this is that the richest .17 percent of households (i.e. less than two-tenths of 1 percent) owned a full 31.14 percent of total investment assets owned by all U.S. households.

Figures such as these might be regarded by some people as excessively abstract, as devoid of any appreciable impact or immediacy, as irrelevant and meaningless. But it so happens that these particular figures do in fact possess tangible importance. What these figures mean is that the annual incomes of the large majority of United States citizens would in all probability be significantly higher under pragmatic market socialism than they are presently under capitalism. This is because the social dividend payment to the vast majority of citizens under pragmatic market socialism would be significantly higher than the amount they are currently receiving under capitalism in the form of capital property income.

Applying two different estimation methods to the data provided in the Federal Reserve Board's *Survey of Financial Characteristics of Consumers* to answer the question of what percentage of the population would be benefited by social dividend distribution of capital income, yielded 94.4 percent for the first method, and 94.2 percent for the second method. These estimates first appeared in "The People's Capitalism Thesis: A Skeptical Evaluation" (*ACES Bulletin*, Winter 1982), and later in Chapter 7 of *Socialism Revised and Modernized: The Case for Pragmatic Market Socialism* (Praeger, 1992). A conservative conclusion from these estimates is that assuming comparable economic efficiency as between market socialism and contemporary capitalism, over 90 percent of the U.S. population would receive more social dividend under market socialism than they currently receive capital property income under capitalism.

The essence of the people's capitalism defense of capitalism is to obscure and obfuscate this reality. This is mainly accomplished by means of the typical person's unawareness of such information as has been provided in the FRB's *Survey of Financial Characteristics of Consumers*. Even if the person is in fact dimly aware of this type of information, he or she is unlikely to understand and appreciate its practical significance in terms of the relative desirability of contemporary capitalism versus market socialism. This is owing basically to lack of awareness and understanding of the market socialist alternative.

Democracy. To this point we have been concerned with the economic objections to pragmatic market socialism. We have focused on the allegations that capital management effort would be inadequate under market socialism, and that saving would be inadequate under market socialism. We have also examined the "people's capitalism thesis" that the distribution of capital wealth is not unduly unequal. Backing up these economic objections is a very important political objection: that socialism of any kind, market or otherwise, is antithetical to freedom and democracy. In my writings on market socialism, I have sometimes employed the term "democratic market socialism" as a substitute for "market socialism" or "pragmatic market socialism." This alternative term implies the possibility of a market socialist system that would be politically democratic as well as economically efficient. But is this a legitimate presumption? Many people take the political objection to socialism very seriously—in some cases, even more seriously than the economic objections. Therefore it is vitally necessary to confront and respond to the political component of capitalist apologetics.

The political objection to socialism first gained significant credibility and widespread acceptance in the 1930s. At that time, capitalist apologetics was temporarily on the defensive owing to the painful contrast which had emerged between the Depression-prostrated capitalist nations and the booming Soviet Union, then in the early stages of its planned industrialization campaign. One argument of capitalist apologetics concerning the USSR of that period was that although Soviet citizens did not have to worry about involuntary unemployment, their living standards were still intolerably low by Western standards. Another argument was that the USSR was totally undemocratic, and as a matter of fact no population with democratic control over its government would have permitted its already low living standards to be further straitened by an industrialization campaign designed to benefit future generations. According to this latter argument, the industrialization campaign in fact clearly demonstrated just how undemocratic the Soviet Union really was. This argument received a tremendous boost owing to the purges of the latter 1930s. Large numbers of communist party officials, many of them having made important contributions to the Bolshevik victory during the revolutionary and civil war periods, were executed or banished to slave labor camps, often after having been forced to "confess" mythical treasonous activity during the course of humiliating show trials. Prior to the purges of the latter 1930s, it might have been possible to interpret internal dissension within the USSR primarily as a struggle between forward-looking progressives and backward-looking reactionaries. Such an interpretation became very difficult in light of the purges.

Stalinist tyranny in the Soviet Union did more to discredit the socialist alternative to capitalism than any other factor, either empirical or theoretical, throughout the entire history of socialism. To aggravate the harm, Stalinist tyranny was later on closely replicated in the People's Republic of China during the Mao era. Smaller-scale tyrannies have been prevalent throughout the communist world: in East Germany, North Korea, Vietnam, Cuba, and so on. The dismal political record compiled by communism throughout its history has quite possibly administered a fatal blow to the prospects of socialism, now and for all time. There is simply no way around the fact that the communist nations have, without exception, combined pure public ownership socialism with highly oligarchic and undemocratic political systems. The question is whether it will ever be possible for a sufficient number of people to understand that the empirical association of socialism with political oligarchy, as obvious and dramatic as it has been in the communist countries, does not indicate a causative relationship between the two.

To begin to see that socialism does not necessarily beget political oligarchy and tyranny, it is first helpful to recognize that capitalism does not necessarily beget political democracy. The most horrendous totalitarian regime of the twentieth century was established in Germany with the accession of Adolf Hitler to power in 1933. The Nazi regime in Germany persisted until its military defeat by the Allied powers in 1945. During that brief but terrible period, the crimes against humanity committed by Hitler's Nazi regime significantly exceeded those committed by Stalin's communist regime. The Soviet Union had a great burden on its historical conscience, but at least it was never guilty of anything so barbarically wanton as the murder of six million Jewish people simply on grounds of their religious affiliation.

Moreover, to its credit communism was imbued with a noble vision of social progress for all humanity. Nazism, on the other hand, aspired toward nothing more than a worldwide caste civilization in which the German people would be the highest caste—a base, selfish, and unworthy aspiration. Despite use of the term "socialism" in "National Socialism" (the official name of the Nazi political philosophy), capitalism remained unmolested in Nazi Germany. Wealthy capitalists had had a strong hand in bringing Hitler to power, because they perceived National Socialism to be preferable to various left-wing alternatives, including unalloyed communism. Once in power, Hitler repaid the favor by fully respecting private property in capital (except with respect to the minority of capitalists who happened to be Jewish). German business enterprise was subjected to close governmental regulation and direction during the Nazi era, but the personal wealth and luxurious living standards of non-Jewish German capitalists were not significantly infringed upon.

Although Hitler's Third Reich is by far the most dramatic example, there have been many other examples in modern history of nations which are capitalistic in their basic economic institutions, and at the same time are politically oligarchic and undemocratic—sometimes to the point where they are reasonably described as "totalitarian dictatorships." Owing to this situation, capitalist apologetics is not able to assert that capitalism is both necessary *and sufficient* for political democracy. However, because of the absence of any authentically democratic communist nations, capitalist apologetics can and does assert that capitalism is *necessary* to political democracy. In other words (according to this argument), the combination of economic and political power under socialism sets up conditions inimical to political democracy, and sooner or later political democracy is indeed strangled.

Although this proposition is in fact consistent with crude empiricism, as soon as one begins to study the history of communism in the modern world with a certain degree of attention, the dubiousness of the proposition becomes apparent. The fact is that the absence of democracy under communism is far more plausibly attributed to historical factors than it is to public ownership socialism in and of itself. None of the nations in which communism became established, from Russia in 1917 to Cuba in 1959, had had firmly established democratic traditions prior to their respective revolutions. Apart from the absence of democratic traditions, there was the suddenness and traumatic extremity of the communist social transformation. Under communist transitions, all privately owned capital wealth was immediately expropriated with no compensation whatsoever. And no consideration was ever given to the fact that some small-scale capital owners had personally accumulated their capital holdings out of legitimate labor income.

Unalloyed hard-core Marxism of the sort that inspired Lenin and his associates at the time of the Russian revolution, and which inspired the leaders of other communist revolutions, has always engendered a great deal of skepticism—not to mention fear and loathing—not only among the wealthy capitalistic elite, but also among a considerable proportion of middle-class and even working-class people. Therefore, only under the most extraordinary conditions has an internal communist revolution become possible. In the case of the Eastern European satellites of the Soviet Union, their "communist revolutions" were imposed by the invading Red Army, and were in fact very much against the popular will. In Russia,

China, and a handful of other cases, communist revolutions succeeded internally, but only amidst the extreme disruption and hardship engendered by warfare, and then only by the narrowest of margins. The extreme and uncompromising policy measures taken by the new communist governments (of which uncompensated expropriation of all capital wealth is only the most obvious example) instantly alienated large proportions of their respective populations. Communist revolutions have also aroused a great deal of anxious concern in the rest of the world. From the earliest days of the Bolshevik revolution in Russia, for example, there were urgent calls for massive armed intervention to crush out the menace of radical socialism before it had a chance to spread. These calls were not heeded at the time, but they instilled deep dread in the communist leaders of possible invasion by hostile capitalistic nations. The eventual invasion of the Soviet Union by Nazi Germany in 1941 lent additional weight to this dread. The fear of invasion was a constant factor throughout the histories of the communist nations.

One must also take into account the revolutionary and conspiratorial nature of the communist parties prior to their assumption of power. As hunted outlaws in their own land, they could not afford the luxuries of leisurely open debate and fully democratic decision-making in deciding upon party policies and activities. Rather the emphasis was on tight organization, strict discipline, and unquestioning obedience. Had these parties been otherwise, it is unlikely that they would have been successful in seizing and retaining power amidst chaotic revolutionary conditions. It is unrealistic and unfair to expect parties such as these, confronted with bitter hostility both within and without, to have established genuine political democracy in nations which had never had any appreciable historical experience with genuine political democracy.

An important milestone in the consolidation and formalization of the political argument against socialism was Friedrich Hayek's highly influential *The Road to Serfdom*, published in 1944. Much of the book's impact was due to its timing. In 1944, with World War II still raging, the democratic nations felt besieged by totalitarianism from both the right and the left. Hitler had just tried to conquer the world in the name of right-wing totalitarianism, and following the war, Stalin was likely to try to do the same in the name of left-wing totalitarianism. It was an emotionally intense period for all of humanity, and Hayek's *Road to Serfdom* addressed the primeval anxieties of many people. In the calmer retrospect afforded by close to a century of relative peace, Hayek's statement of the political case against socialism is more readily perceived as exaggerated and indiscriminate, especially when considered in the light of the market socialist possibility.

In *The Road to Serfdom*, Hayek uses the term "socialism" in a very broad sense to encompass any and all social infringements upon the laissez faire ideal, infringements such as public regulation of business, progressive taxation, and welfare programs. Hayek claimed that these infringements gradually weaken the independence, initiative, and self-reliance of the population. The population becomes passive and dependent, it becomes the human equivalent of a herd of cattle, it develops a "slave mentality." Once in such a psychologically debilitated state, the population becomes especially susceptible to the authoritative rhetoric of dictatorially inclined demagogues. It stands by quietly as these demagogues and their cronies destroy democracy and set up brutal totalitarian regimes. And by the time the population fully understands that the demagogue-turned-dictator does not have their best interests at heart, it is too late to resist. At the time he wrote *The Road to Serfdom*, Hayek was a political refugee from Nazism, and clearly the principal inspiration to the book was an emotional reaction against the horrifying Nazi social system in Germany and Austria. But the book was also fueled by Hayek's intense revulsion toward the communist tyranny in the Soviet Union. Along with many other social commentators, both at that time and since, Hayek placed great emphasis upon the remarkable similarities between Nazi totalitarianism and communist totalitarianism—even though the two systems ostensibly derived from opposite ends of the ideological spectrum.

Socialism in the strict public ownership sense obviously could not be blamed for the excesses of Nazi totalitarianism, since Nazi Germany, in contrast to the Soviet Union, had carefully preserved and protected its wealthy capitalist class. In actual fact, Hayek devoted very little attention in *The Road to Serfdom* to public ownership of business enterprise as a contributory factor to the slave mentality and political totalitarianism. On the other hand, he devoted a great deal of attention to the standard social democratic agenda of business regulation, welfare programs, and so on. The major weakness of Hayek's argument is the indiscriminate virulence of its denunciation of this agenda. Hayek clearly disapproved even of the watered-down social democracy of the Rooseveltian New Deal in the United States. He implied that the distance between Franklin D. Roosevelt and Adolf Hitler was not nearly as great as it might seem at first sight. To most people, this was going too far. *The Road to Serfdom*, when read carefully, is a book which appeals strongly only to the extreme libertarian fringe of the conservative movement.

In actual fact, a much more focused and effective statement of the political objection to public ownership socialism was provided by Milton

Friedman in *Capitalism and Freedom*, published in 1962. By 1962, the threat of totalitarianism appeared much diminished, and Friedman's book is not imbued with the same spirit of urgency and dread which permeated Hayek's *Road to Serfdom*. In actual fact, only a very small part of Friedman's book deals directly with the political objection to public-ownership socialism: the objection that public-ownership socialism combines political and economic power to the detriment of democracy. Most of *Capitalism and Freedom* consists of a conventional assault, based on standard laissez faire preconceptions, on various social interventions in the free market. Friedman expresses disapproval of such things as occupational licensure and minimum wages—although he does not follow Hayek's example in claiming that these kinds of things tend quickly to breed a slave mentality and thus create a strong predisposition toward totalitarian dictatorship of the Stalin or Hitler variety. In Friedman's view, things such as occupational licensure and minimum wages—while they do not generate an immediate threat of dictatorship—do indeed seriously curtail personal freedom, as well as significantly diminishing economic efficiency. As pragmatic market socialism is inherently neutral toward occupational licensure, minimum wages, and the like, the great majority of *Capitalism and Freedom* is completely irrelevant to it.

However, as mentioned, in one relatively brief section of the book, Friedman does provide a clear, focused, and intelligent statement of the charge that any sort of public ownership socialism—market or otherwise—would endanger democracy. Friedman's argument is simply a mirror image of the conventional argument against "bourgeois democracy" developed by communist ideologues during the Cold War propaganda struggle between the communist East and the noncommunist West. According to this traditional communist argument, the proudly-touted Western democracy is a sham and a delusion. Candidates for elective office are so similar as to be tweedledum and tweedledee. They all have exactly the same attitude on the one political issue with real substance: whether the economy should be capitalist or socialist. Specifically, they are all totally supportive of the capitalist status quo.

Anyone who might have a preference for socialism never has a chance in the political arena. Anyone daring to express pro-socialist views will be quickly dismissed from his or her employment on the instructions of the capitalists who own the firm. Thus reduced to poverty, the individual will be unable to engage in effective political activity. The media of communications are almost entirely privately-owned, profit-maximizing business enterprises. The capitalists who own these enterprises see to it that little or no sensible pro-socialist material is published or otherwise disseminated.

Finally, there is the direct control over the political process exercised by wealthy capitalists. Capital wealth provides some of these wealthy capitalists with both the leisure time and monetary resources necessary to run for and serve in elective government offices. A much larger number of wealthy capitalists do not become directly involved in the political process, but they use the tool of campaign contributions to ensure that only those candidates with what they consider "appropriate" (i.e. anti-socialist) attitudes have any reasonable chance of being elected to office.

One could take any typical expression of this argument penned by a communist ideologue from the Cold War era, replace the term "wealthy capitalists" everywhere it occurs with "high party officials," and one would have a reasonable facsimile of Friedman's political argument against socialism. According to Friedman, the party in power under socialism will use its economic authority to suppress opposition political parties and dissidents in general. It will utilize this authority with special energy and enthusiasm against political dissidents wanting the restoration of capitalism. Such individuals will be dismissed from their employment with publicly-owned corporations, and will thus become ineffectual owing to poverty. The publicly-owned media of communications will be required to prejudicially misrepresent the statements and viewpoints of political dissidents, and to uncover and expose their personal sins, faults, errors, and liabilities. As a result of all this, the incumbent political party will gain an insuperable advantage over the opposition. Elections might be held at the appointed times, but their outcomes will be predetermined by the dominant party. The political system will degenerate into a self-perpetuating oligarchy. Friedman is aware of the fact that this argument is simply an inversion of the traditional argument used by communist ideologues to assault Western democracy. But he claims that under capitalism, the capitalist class is not in fact sufficiently aware of its own self-interest, nor sufficiently well-organized, to have the kind of control over political processes alleged by the communist ideologues. On the other hand, says Friedman, under socialism the party in power actually *would* behave in exactly the manner envisioned of the capitalist class in the communist argument.

Although there has been a tendency among pro-socialists to dismiss this kind of argument out of hand, in actual fact it is sufficiently weighty to require serious consideration. Let us then examine the argument in the context of the pragmatic market socialist alternative. Let us assume that we are considering a market socialist system established in a nation with a strong and viable democratic tradition, such as the United States or the United Kingdom. Let us also assume that there is no change in the formal, established political institutions of society: e.g., the government would still be divided into legislative, executive, and judicial branches, there would still be regularly scheduled elections, and so on.

The danger to democracy perceived by Milton Friedman lies in national government control both of business enterprise in general, and of those specific business enterprises concerned with communications (newspapers, book and magazine publishers, radio and television stations and networks, and so on). Control of business enterprise in general would be used by the party in power to deny gainful employment to political opponents; and control of the media of communications would be used to destroy the reputations and credibility of these opponents. The mechanism for exercising this control would be the issuance of instructions to the relevant firm managers, these instructions backed up by the threat of dismissal for disobedience. One possible solution to both of these problems lies in cooperative market socialism. Under this form of market socialism, the national government would have no authority to hire and dismiss managers of corporations: rather these managers would be elected internally by the employees. This, of course, would immediately pull the plug on the scenario envisioned by Friedman. Another solution would be the regional ownership market socialist proposal of Leland Stauber. Under this form of market socialism, firm managers would be responsible to public ownership personnel appointed not by the national government, but by a host of local governments. It seems doubtful that a large number of more or less autonomous local governments could get sufficiently well organized to represent a serious threat to democracy through misuse of the public ownership authority.

Of course, the pragmatic market socialist proposal recommended in this book is something different from both cooperative market socialism and municipal ownership market socialism. It does indeed envision an important role for the national government in the exercise of the public ownership authority. However, certain modifications may be proposed in the basic design to mitigate any possible threat to democracy implicit in public ownership of most large-scale business corporations. The principal modification is to make all or most media corporations (newspapers, book and magazine publishers, radio and television stations and networks, and so on) into labor-managed, cooperative enterprises. This would eliminate any BPO control over their high-level managers: these managers would instead be elected by the employees in regularly scheduled, open elections. On the basis of presently available evidence, it seems to this author that a profit-maximization incentive enforced by an outside ownership authority will tend to result in a higher level of overall economic efficiency within the firm than will labor self-management. But owing to the critical importance of an independent media of communications in preserving political democracy, I think that in this case the economic efficiency consideration should give way to the political safety consideration. So from this point forward, the discussion will be based on the assumption that BPO agents would not be involved in the hiring and firing of media corporation executives. These particular executives would be responsible only to their employees.

The elimination of media corporations from the authority of the BPO would eliminate the possibility of direct instructions by incumbent national government officials to these corporations to prejudicially misrepresent the personalities, ideas, and policy proposals of opposition party members. Of course, indirect pressure might be brought via threats to withhold advertising by the regular publicly-owned business corporations. But this is a very indirect means of control, and it only applies to that part of the media dependent upon advertising revenues. In addition to guaranteeing objective reporting of opposition viewpoints, the independence of the media corporations will enhance the likelihood that efforts by the incumbent national government officials to economically harass opposition party members by denying them employment with publicly-owned corporations would be quickly and widely exposed.

It need hardly be emphasized that misuse of the public ownership authority by incumbent officials to gain political advantages would be a very serious criminal offense. It would be far worse than the taking of bribes, because it would directly threaten the integrity of the democratic process. Any government official found to have issued such illicit instructions to managers of publicly-owned corporations would be subject to immediate dismissal from office and lengthy imprisonment. It would be very dangerous for these officials to issue any such instructions. The chain of transmission would be quite long, and at every link there would be a strong possibility of whistle-blowing and exposure.

Let us imagine, for example, that a certain national government official, say the president of the United States, wants to see to it that a certain vociferous political opponent is dismissed from his/her employment with a publicly-owned corporation. Let us ignore, for purposes of simplicity, secretaries, aides, assistants, messengers, and so on. To begin with, the president has to give an instruction to the director of the national office of the BPO to effect the dismissal. The director of the national office has to transmit that instruction to the BPO agent within whose authority the corporation falls. The BPO agent then has to transmit the instruction to the chief executive officer of the corporation. The chief executive officer then executes the instruction by dismissing the political opponent.

None of the three intermediate people involved in carrying out this illicit order (the BPO national director, the BPO agent, and the corporate chief executive) has anything personal to gain from this dismissal. All of them have a certain amount of insulation against being illicitly dismissed themselves. For example, if the corporation involved happens to be quite profitable, by the rules its chief executive officer *cannot* be dismissed. If discovered to have participated in such a nefarious conspiracy, they would all be subject to severe penalties. And the likelihood of discovery would be substantial: at a bare minimum, the political opponent dismissed from his/her employment for no legitimate reason will raise a fuss. And even if one such conspiracy were indeed successfully carried out, how much would it help the president? The president of the United States, under any imaginable set of circumstances, will have tens of thousands of "vociferous opponents." It would be impossible to neutralize any appreciable fraction of them by such means as specified above. Any president who tried it would, with shocking rapidity, meet the same ignoble fate encountered by Richard M. Nixon in 1974. Nixon was forced to resign from the presidency in disgrace for misdeeds far less serious than trying to hamper opposition political parties through misuse of the public ownership authority.

Throughout the history of human civilization, democratic governance has been the exception rather than the rule. Even in the contemporary era, an era in which the idea of democracy has achieved almost universal acceptance and support among both the mass of society and the educated intelligentsia, the actual practice of democracy seems to be a frail reed, easily bent and easily broken. The terrible experience of twentieth century fascism is still fresh in our minds. Until very recently, all of the communist nations have been political oligarchies, and the progress currently being made toward the establishment of genuine democracy in the ex-Soviet Union and the Eastern European nations seems rather halting and uncertain. One-party states are commonplace throughout the Third World, even in nations which loudly proclaim democratic ideals. Under the circumstances, a high degree of concern, within those fortunate nations which are genuinely democratic at the present time, with the maintenance of conditions favorable to the preservation of democracy, is quite understandable. But at the same time, the preservation of democracy is not a serious argument against pragmatic market socialism. The establishment of this type of market socialist economy in a nation such as the U.S. or the U.K., nations which have enjoyed a long, strong democratic tradition, would not significantly increase the threat to democracy.

The scenario set forth by Milton Friedman, a scenario of gradual corruption of democratic processes through abuse of the public ownership authority, has nothing in common with the historical absence of genuine democracy within the communist nations. Stalin, for example, did not get at his political opponents by surreptitiously engineering their dismissals from the publicly-owned enterprises—rather he ordered them arrested by the secret police, and either executed or imprisoned in Siberian slave labor camps. Communist dictatorships, in common with all other dictatorships past and present, have been based on naked, brute force, and not on subtle, indirect subterfuges. Naked, brute force can always be utilized to destroy democracy, whether business enterprise is publicly-owned or privately-owned. It can be done whether economic living standards are high or low. At this very moment, there is nothing of any degree of tangibility preventing the armed forces of the United States from taking over the government. If those who control the instruments of force in our society ever become determined to do so, they could easily sweep aside the opposition and assume the reins of power—at least for a while.

Conservative economists such as Milton Friedman tend to have a rather unrealistic view of basic human nature. They tend to believe that people, always and everywhere, engage in a purely egotistical pursuit of their own short-run self-interest. But men and women are social creatures: a certain amount of altruistic concern for their fellow humans has been bred into them by natural selection, and reinforced by moral education both at home and in schools. If the me-first, numero-uno attitude which Friedman attributes to the leaders of the "party in power" under socialism, and which induces them to exploit the public ownership authority to preserve their personal hold on power, were indeed a realistic depiction of actual attitudes among humanity, then the U.S. military would long since have taken over the national government, as would have the military in every other nation in the world which is at present genuinely democratic.

Of course, any effort at the present time by high-ranking U.S. military officers to organize a conspiracy to overthrow the elected government and install a military dictator would quickly be exposed by other high-ranking military officers—or their subordinates—unwilling to participate in the conspiracy. The basic obstacle to such a conspiracy is the tremendous commitment among all segments of society, including the military, to the democratic principle of governance. Individuals proposing to contravene this principle for purposes of personal gain and/or power would be regarded with horror and contempt by the vast majority of the population. As a result, any high-ranking officer in the United States military who commenced discussions of a possible military coup with his colleagues would very quickly be arrested and hustled off to a psychiatric ward for observation. Even if some of these colleagues might be intrigued by the idea in an abstract sense, they would have to ask themselves how likely it is that moral qualms could be suppressed in every one of the thousands of military personnel who would have to be involved in the conspiracy in order for it to have any appreciable chance of success. Even one whistle-blower could terminate the conspiracy and create disastrous personal consequences for the conspirators. Under the circumstances, the safer course, for an officer asked to join a conspiracy, would be to blow the whistle and take the relatively modest rewards available to a "defender of democracy," than to risk everything for the remote possibility of being part of a ruling military oligarchy.

For the same reasons that it would be well-nigh impossible to organize a military conspiracy to take over the government of the United States at the present time, it would be well-nigh impossible for the party in power, under a potential system of pragmatic market socialism in the future, to eliminate the political opposition by means of misuse of the public ownership authority. There would be too much moral revulsion against such a thing among the entire population; too many individuals would have to participate; there would be too great a probability of exposure for it to be a serious temptation to the leaders of the party in power.

The notion that socialism and democracy are incompatible proceeds basically from the same fundamental misconception as does the notion that socialism and competition (among publicly-owned firms) are incompatible. This is the misconception that governments in general, and national governments in particular, are totally focused, monolithic, coordinated, and disciplined organizations which single-mindedly and obsessively pursue the personal self-interest of whatever human individual happens to occupy the pinnacle of the governmental power pyramid. In actual fact, governments are composed of many thousands of different persons, and each one of them has his/her individual interest and point of view. This conglomeration of diverse individuals cannot and does not behave like a column of army ants on the march. It is unduly pessimistic and cynical to imagine that there is a strong tendency in human society toward extremely totalitarian governments such as transpired during Hitler's rule in Germany and Stalin's rule in Russia. Actually, such horrific cases as these have been relatively rare exceptions to the rule throughout modern history. Normally, the degree of internal discipline and common purpose mustered by national governments has been relatively limited.

The two major contributors to the safety of democratic governance are absence of crisis and historical tradition. Crisis conditions, such as severe economic hardship in the aftermath of a lost war, tend to politically galvanize the population, to polarize it, to jeopardize democracy. Democracy flourishes best under conditions of peace, prosperity, and stability—conditions under which there are no major economic threats or military challenges immediately at hand, under which there is no urgent need to make important decisions which impact heavily on the private lives of citizens, under which most individuals are content to let things remain pretty much as they have been in the past. The pragmatic market socialist economy proposed in this book is a very cautious and limited step beyond the current market capitalist economy. Most people would experience a modest but appreciable financial gain, and the small minority of financial losers (the wealthy capitalists) would be paid a sufficient amount of compensation for surrendered capital property to keep them from becoming enraged political activists. There is simply no reason to expect such a system, peacefully implemented by strictly legal and democratic processes, to generate a sufficient amount of opposition to seriously endanger democratic institutions and processes.

The second major reason for optimism is that many of those nations for which the pragmatic market socialist proposal is especially well-suited are currently democratic nations with strong democratic traditions. In the United States, for example, the fervor of democratic convictions among the entire population, from the top of the socioeconomic spectrum to its bottom, is fully comparable to the fervor of religious convictions among the faithful. Almost every citizen is ready and willing to risk life, limb, and possessions in defense of democracy. Democracy is regarded as the political sine qua non of individual happiness and social welfare, as an indispensable ingredient of any higher form of human civilization. Owing to the strength of this conviction, any public official under market socialism who might endeavor to undermine democracy by misusing the public ownership authority for personal benefit would very quickly encounter a harsh fate.

To conclude this discussion of the political objection to market socialism, I will briefly mention the diametrically opposed proposition: that far from endangering democracy, pragmatic market socialism would in fact be quite likely to significantly improve the quality of democracy in contemporary society. Mention has been made in the foregoing of the traditional communist critique of "bourgeois democracy." According to this critique, the capitalist class exercises a veritable stranglehold over the political system and social decision-making—despite ostensibly free and open elections—owing to its control of the media of communications and its ability to deny employment to proponents of socialism. Except to the communist ideologues responsible for this critique, the proposition that the capitalist class "controls the government" and "rules society" is generally regarded as preposterously exaggerated. Nevertheless, upon sober reflection, most people will have to concede that there is at least some kernel of truth in the critique. It seems self-evident that wealthy capitalists have a disproportionate influence on political processes and social decision-making—although no consensus would probably be possible on precisely *how* disproportionate their influence is.

It need hardly be emphasized that wealthy capitalists are not typical citizens. Their great financial wealth makes them very different from the common run of middle-class and working-class citizens. There is not necessarily a perfect correlation between their interests and the interests of the general population. One would naturally expect wealthy capitalists to be unusually conservative, to be unusually skeptical of proposed changes in a status quo situation which they find very comfortable. On the other hand, this natural tendency toward conservatism might be mitigated, at least to some extent, by the greater personal security of wealthy people—they might feel less threatened by changes (of the right sort) than are individuals of more modest means. Whatever the differences may consist of, it seems inescapable that there would be differences in attitudes and preferences as between wealthy capitalists and the rest of the population. Owing to the disproportionate political influence of wealthy capitalists, actual social decision-making and public policies are likely to diverge somewhat from the optimum that would be settled on in the absence of this class. While it would be difficult to predict what policy changes might actually take place under pragmatic market socialism as a result of the elimination of the disproportionate political influence of wealthy capitalists, it seems likely that these changes would at least be in the right direction from the standpoint of the majority of the population. Quite likely there is thus a political gain to be had from pragmatic market socialism, as well as an economic gain.

9

FEDERAL WORLD GOVERNMENT

Aspirations among humanity toward federal world government became greatly intensified during the twentieth century. The devastating experiences of World War I (1914-1918) and World War II (1939-1945) brought into sharp focus two fundamental realities. First, jealously independent and self-righteously sovereign nation-states are strongly predisposed toward confrontation and warfare among one another. The great strength of this predisposition entails the limited effectiveness of diplomatic efforts intended to preserve peace and stability. Second, owing to dramatic progress in science and technology, in combination with the size and economic power of the largest nation-states, the sheer destructiveness of warfare has reached tremendous proportions, far beyond anything witnessed or even imagined throughout all prior human history. The devastation of two Japanese cities, Hiroshima and Nagasaki, by atomic bombs at the end of World War II, foretold of possible future wars of even greater destructiveness, of a level of destructiveness possibly so overwhelming as to set the human race sliding irrevocably downward toward physical extinction. Prior to World War I, it had been a fairly prevalent viewpoint in some quarters that warfare was "healthy" for human society, in the same way that dieting and exercise are healthy for human individuals. Following the experiences of 1914-1945, this viewpoint is now mostly confined to fools and psychotics.

In the years immediately following World War II, interest in world government reached a peak unprecedented in history. Just as the largest national governments had established peaceful and secure conditions over huge territories and vast populations, so too a world government might be able to do the same over the entire face of the planet. Such an outcome was especially urgent in view of the apparent capacity of nuclear weapons not merely to devastate human civilization, but to terminate it. But owing to the Cold War conflict which rapidly developed during the post-World War II years between the communist East and the non-communist West, interest in world government quickly evaporated. Amid post-war chaos, the communist ideological movement flourished. The Soviet Union exploited its military occupation of Eastern Europe to forcibly install communist governments in several countries: Poland, East Germany, Hungary, Czechoslovakia, and so on. At the same time, it provided military assistance to communist forces in China, enabling the establishment of the People's Republic of China in 1949. Inasmuch as the communist movement aspired toward the revolutionary overthrow of the capitalist socioeconomic system throughout the world, these developments aroused intense anxiety throughout the non-communist West. It was widely feared that a world government, if established, would quickly be subverted by the communists and turned into a tool of communist expansion. At the same time, the communists entertained an exactly analogous apprehension: that a world government would quickly be turned into a reactionary tool for the overthrow of communist regimes in Russia, China, and elsewhere. Given the anxieties of the time, it is not surprising that the world government movement quickly lost momentum. Within a very short period of time, pro-world government attitudes were confined to a tiny fraction of the population, a fraction regarded by the overwhelming majority as hopelessly misguided, naive, and utopian.

The communist ideological system, which is far from being extinct in the contemporary world despite the collapse and dissolution of the USSR in 1991, comprises several key elements that are highly repugnant to most non-communists: (1) the proposition that socialism (public ownership of capital property) is preferable to capitalism (private ownership of capital property); (2) the proposition that centralized coordination and control of the economic system is preferable to decentralized, free market allocation; (3) the fact that communist political systems are effectively undemocratic (despite protestations of communists to the contrary) owing to the refusal of the controlling communist parties to allow genuinely free speech or to authorize free competition for high-level elective positions; (4) official disapproval of religious belief and restriction of religious practices; (5) messianic aspirations of communist adherents toward the overthrow of capitalist societies throughout the world, with the aim of replacing them with socialist societies in the mode of the Soviet Union and the People's Republic of China. Since the dominant images in non-communist minds of the Soviet Union and the People's Republic of China were (and remain) based on such horrific episodes of unbridled totalitarianism as Stalin's Great Terror during the 1930s and Mao's Cultural Revolution during the 1960s, it is understandable that most non-communists were (and remain) quite willing to undertake an appreciable risk of premature death as a result of nuclear holocaust, than to permit themselves to be subjugated to such intolerable conditions.

As the Cold War progressed throughout the second half of the twentieth century, apprehensions among most people that a world state, if established, would become an instrument toward the imposition of communistic totalitarianism, were increasingly supplemented by a second apprehension of great consequence. This is the apprehension that were a world state to be established, it would become an instrument toward the imposition of a worldwide welfare state through which the populations of the rich nations would be impoverished. A world state, it is feared, would impose confiscatory taxation on the rich nations (the United States, the nations of Western Europe, and so on) for the purpose of providing generous welfare entitlements to the populations of the Third World nations of Asia, Africa, and Latin America. This could happen even if—or perhaps *especially* if—the world state was democratically organized, in view of the fact that the "teeming masses" of the Third World greatly outnumber the populations of the relatively small number of rich, non-communist nations of the First World.

This potential problem of world government came into much sharper focus as a result of the Cold War. According to the Marxist theory underpinning communist ideology, the coming socialist revolution will directly and dramatically benefit the impoverished proletariat. Since the impoverished proletariat is especially numerous in the nations of the Third World, the Second World nations (the Soviet Union, Red China, and their allies and satellites) looked to these nations for potential future support, providing military assistance and propagandistic encouragement to the communist movements within them. As a result, the First World nations became far more conscious of the economic gap than they had ever been in the past. Greater awareness of this gap contributed to increased apprehension that the principle of redistribution of income, widely accepted within nations (up to a limited point), might be extended to the international arena. Such an extension would be especially likely were all of humanity to be politically united within a single world government.

Thus, in the minds of the people of the First World nations, world government came to be perceived as a potential threat to their welfare even greater than the threat of unrestricted nuclear warfare. This latter threat was (and is), after all, not all that great (according to the predominant contemporary consensus). True, a full-scale nuclear war, if it were to take place, would be unimaginably horrible and destructive. But because of this there is an extremely small, almost microscopically small, probability that such a war will ever take place. Nuclear weapons are sufficiently abundant, and delivery systems are sufficiently reliable, that conditions of Mutual Assured Destruction (MAD) have been achieved. The costs of nuclear war would be so overwhelming to all nations involved, including those initiating the war, that no national leader will ever seriously contemplate launching such a war. Nuclear disaster would be so huge, so terrible, and so universal, that owing to the fundamental rationality of mankind, it will never occur. Of course, the possibility exists that this reasoning, as conventional and widespread as it may be, represents merely wishful thinking, and that when it is finally recognized as such (in the wake of nuclear disaster), it will be too late.

Humanity has not yet experienced a nuclear world war, but most of us believe that we have a fairly clear idea of what would be involved—and it would not be pleasant. Nevertheless, we believe that there are "fates worse than death," even worse than the especially horrible deaths that would be occasioned by nuclear world war. In the minds of most citizens of the United States, for example, to live under a communistic socioeconomic system would be worse than death. Equally so, it would be worse than death to live under the noxious burden of confiscatory taxation for purposes of funding a worldwide welfare state benefiting the poor countries. The option of helping to establish, and then participating in a world government, is rejected by the U.S. population on grounds that to do so would substantially increase the probability of being subjected to communism and/or confiscatory taxation at some point in the future.

Strictly speaking, it is not an either-or choice. Presumably at least a few people in the United States would opt for the communist socioeconomic system, and/or confiscatory taxation, if it were *an absolute certainty* that the only alternative to these was nuclear world war. But, of course, it is *not* an absolute certainty that nuclear world war will occur if the U.S. population declines to establish a communist socioeconomic system, and/or declines to support a worldwide welfare state funded by means of confiscatory taxation of the rich nations. Equally, it is *not* an absolute certainty that nuclear world war will occur if the U.S. population does not help to establish, and does not participate in a world government. What is involved, in rejection of the world government possibility, is a *calculated risk.* The people of the United States (along with most of the rest of the world population) have presumably carefully weighed up the relative costs and benefits of a world government, along with their respective probabilities, and have concluded that their future prospects are more favorable without a world government in existence than with one in existence.

As a freshman college student at Fordham University in the winter of 1961-1962, I developed an intuition that this particular calculated risk has been badly miscalculated. Within a very short period of time, the initial intuition solidified into a virtual certainly. As the years passed and I studied the various facets of the issue in greater and greater detail, nothing changed my mind. Throughout almost my entire adult life, up to and including the present time, I have believed firmly that the future prospects of humanity would be appreciably improved with a properly designed, functioning world government in place than without one. Furthermore, what is true of humanity as a whole is true of the human populations of each and every nation on the face of the planet. Federal world government should be the next step taken in the political evolution of human civilization. For the first time in history, we have the incentive and we have the means to establish a benign and effective world government. If we wait for "more propitious circumstances" to establish such a government, at best we will be significantly retarding human progress relative to what might be achieved, and at worst, we may inflict upon ourselves a disastrous future that will be even worse for being unnecessary.

This proposition relies only to a very minor extent on the traditional accusation among world federalists that humanity is seriously underestimating both the cost of nuclear world war and the probability that such a war will occur within the near future if we persist with the sovereign nation-state system of today. Although I personally happen to believe that both the costs and the probability of nuclear war are being somewhat underestimated (albeit I would leave out the "within the near future" part), the ineffectiveness of this argument has been convincingly demonstrated by history. Even at the height of the Cold War, when the nuclear threat was obviously far greater than it is at the present time, world federalists tried in vain in muster support for world government by brandishing the prospect of nuclear holocaust. In the judgment of the overwhelming majority of the population, in all walks of life and throughout the world, nuclear holocaust constituted an acceptable risk, as weighed against the greater risks inherent in world government. Following the collapse and dissolution of the USSR in 1991, the near-term threat of nuclear war has greatly receded, hence appeals for world government based on this threat will be even less effective than they were throughout the Cold War period.

The argument instead relies primarily on the proposition that humanity is seriously *over*estimating the risks that would be involved in world government. I hasten to add that this is true only of a *properly designed* world government. If one imagines a strongly authoritative and highly activist world government, a government which would interact with the governments of the component nation-states exactly as the federal government of the contemporary United States interacts today with the governments of the 50 component states, then there would indeed exist a very substantial probability of a disastrous outcome—at least as far as a large fraction of the world's population is concerned. If we imagine a world government possessed of a monopoly on nuclear weapons, it could, under extreme circumstances, threaten uncooperative nation-states with mass destruction should they persist in opposing the established policy of the world government. Even if nuclear weapons had been abolished, a world government possessed of a monopoly on "conventional" heavy weaponry would be in basically the same position as one possessed of a monopoly on nuclear weaponry. If we further imagine that the high officials of this world government have been democratically elected by the world population, most of whom are desperately poor by the standards of a handful of wealthy nations, it is not too difficult to perceive the possibility that the world government might decide that it would be beneficial to this impoverished majority to carry out very substantial income redistribution financed by heavy taxation imposed on the populations of the handful of wealthy nations.

Should this handful of wealthy nations refuse to pay the heavy tax assessments required by the redistribution program, the world government could threaten them with nuclear destruction. Or, presuming the world government refrains from anything so barbaric as threats of nuclear destruction, or is unable to make such threats because nuclear weapons have been abolished, it could threaten the wealthy nations with invasion by an army equipped with machine guns, tanks, and heavy artillery. If the only forces at the disposal of the wealthy nations consisted of police units equipped with small arms, these nations would be virtually helpless in the face of such a threat. No doubt pockets of armed resistance would remain in the wealthy nations, but these would be gradually whittled down by hordes of secret police and internal security forces unleashed by the world government. Dissidents of all kinds, whether engaged in armed resistance or mere verbal opposition, would be rounded up and shipped off to concentration camps for re-education—or elimination. The outcome would be a nightmarish period of terror and oppression comparable to that experienced by the Soviet people during the worst years of Stalinist tyranny.

Certain democratic nations, such as India, show a high level of political stability today despite the long-term persistence of a very high level of economic inequality. A fairly strong case might be made, therefore, that the "global welfare state" scenario would be extremely unlikely to materialize even if a potential future world government *did* possess a monopoly on both nuclear weapons and conventional heavy weapons, and even if the economic gap which exists today *were* to persist into the indefinite future. But the probability of such a scenario under those circumstances, while it might be small, would certainly not be negligible. Similar conflicts of interest might also develop on matters unrelated to economic living standards: on matters such as ideological, religious, or cultural differences.

As a result, it is absolutely necessary that any proposed world government, in order to be seriously contemplated by the human population, be subject to appropriate limitations and constraints designed to safeguard the vital interests of the various national populations, and to reduce the probability of a totalitarian outcome to an acceptably low level. The fundamental thesis which I have been advancing throughout my adult life is that, contrary to presently dominant opinion, a world government can and should be established—a world government that would represent an acceptable compromise between the competing objectives of protecting the essential short-term interests of the various national populations, and at the same time favoring the essential long-term interests of the entire human population.

The world government proposal which will be briefly outlined and evaluated in this chapter is for a world state somewhere between the United Nations of today, which is essentially little more than an assemblage of speechifying ambassadors, and the full-scale, highly authoritative, extremely centralized state entity (the "omnipotent world state") imagined by the typical world federalist from the latter 1940s through to the present time. The United Nations is certainly a step in the right direction, and its existence and operations have certainly yielded some benefits. But it was founded just as the Cold War between East and West was beginning, and the constraints on it that were necessitated by the realpolitik of that period effectively hobbled it as an instrument for peace in the contemporary world. At the same time, those world federalists who envision the instantaneous elimination of the threat of nuclear holocaust, as well as the threat of major wars fought with conventional weapons, through the foundation of a very strong, very dominant world government, are indeed hopelessly naive and unrealistic. Those world federalists may eventually be proved correct in their contention that what is actually naive and unrealistic is the conventional belief that the sovereign nation-state system of the contemporary world can be allowed to go on indefinitely into the remote future without the occurrence of disastrous wars. But if they are proved correct about this, it will be through the occurrence of those wars, and then, of course, it will be too late. Until those wars actually occur, it is most unlikely that the human race will recognize in them a threat equal to or greater than the threat of totalitarianism imposed by an omnipotent world state—unless it can be convincingly demonstrated that world government need not entail a serious threat of totalitarianism.

What the human race has not yet recognized is that a world state does not need to be "omnipotent" in order to make a worthwhile contribution to the future prospects of human civilization. The specific world government proposal which forms the basis for the general description and evaluation herein of the world government possibility, is designated the "Federal Union of Democratic Nations." This proposed name should *not* be taken to imply that membership would be restricted to nations that *presently* implement very high standards of democratic accountability, but merely that all member nations *intend* to implement these standards. The Federal Union would be a legitimate state entity: it would have a capital city and a permanent organization, its high officials would be directly elected by the citizens, it would possess the power to make binding laws and to levy mandatory taxes, it would raise and maintain military forces, and it would display the conventional emblems and trappings of state authority. On the other hand, it would be subject to several key restrictions that are certainly not typical of the nation-states of today. Two such restrictions are especially important. First, the member nation-states of the Federal Union of Democratic Nations would possess the permanent and inalienable right to peaceful and unopposed withdrawal from the Federal Union at their own unilateral discretion. Second, the member nation-states of the Federal Union of Democratic Nations would possess the permanent and inalienable right to maintain military forces of whatever strength and weaponry (including nuclear weaponry) are deemed necessary and appropriate by the governments of these nation-states. There are other characteristics of the proposed Federal Union of Democratic Nations that depart from the normal characteristics of present-day nation-states, and that would serve to weaken its authority and effectiveness relative to its component nation-states. But these two are definitely the most important.

Needless to say, it is not typical of either the formal or informal constitutions of existing nation-states to allow explicitly and unequivocally for the voluntary departure of component districts of the overall polity. In fact, extremely violent civil wars have been occasioned by separatist movements. One of the foremost historical examples of this was the Civil War in the United States from 1861 through 1865. Neither is it typical of formal or informal constitutions of existing nation-states to allow explicitly and unequivocally for the subsidiary governments of component districts to maintain whatever military forces they wish to maintain, armed with whatever weaponry they wish to provide these forces. On the other hand, quite often in the past the military forces of nations have been composed of units recruited largely from specific districts, and the governments of these districts have sometimes exercised effective de facto control over them. Indeed, one of the factors contributing to the length and severity of the U.S. Civil War of 1861-65 was the fact that the Southern states were able to take rapid control over elements of the United States Army located within their own borders and recruited mainly from their own citizens.

To the typical, conventional-minded world federalist of today, these two characteristics of the proposed world government—the right of member nation-states to withdraw at any time, and the right of member nation-states to maintain whatever military forces and weaponry they wish—would be deemed thoroughly unacceptable. In the minds of "traditional" world federalists, such characteristics would surely defeat the purpose of world government. Such a world government, to their way of thinking, would not represent a significant, meaningful, worthwhile advance beyond the United Nations of today, an institution which has proven, beyond a reasonable doubt, its incapacity to significantly reduce the danger of warfare. In their minds, in order to be truly effective in abolishing warfare, the world government would have to maintain a monopoly on heavy weaponry, and it would also have to be ready at all times to return errant nation-states forcibly to the fold.

Of course, from the outset I have always been emphatic that the Federal Union proposal is not addressed primarily to those who already believe in the cause of world government. At the present time, those individuals who advocate world government represent a tiny, veritably microscopic fraction of the total human population—a tiny fraction regarded by the majority as hopelessly ignorant or misguided, as simplistic enthusiasts pursuing impossible utopias. I would anticipate that most current proponents of world government will grasp the essential nature of the case for world government which I offer, and will recognize its validity, somewhat more readily and quickly than will the typical opponent of world government. But if the case can be grasped and appreciated *only* by those who already advocate world government, then nothing is accomplished. A tiny and impotent minority will remain a tiny and impotent minority. What I am trying to do is to reach beyond that tiny minority, out into the mainstream of human thinking, to reshape the consensus understanding of world government among all humanity. Therefore, it is not a major concern that most world federalists of the present day will not immediately recognize and appreciate the contribution to the future prospects of human civilization to be made by the proposed Federal Union of Democratic Nations.

Also from the outset, I have placed heavy emphasis on the proposition that the formation of a world government should be considered an *experi-*

mental venture. Although a strong case can be made that a properly designed world government would probably improve the future prospects of global human civilization, the case is not so compelling as to admit of no doubt whatsoever. It cannot be "proven," in either the legal sense or the scientific sense, that world government would be beneficial. If the early development of a real-world world government turned out to be unpromising, the experiment could and should be terminated, and the world government disbanded. That is why the principle of free voluntary withdrawal from the federation is so essential. With this principle in place, it would not require a unified decision on the part of the federation's member nations to terminate the federation. The termination could be smooth and gradual as more and more member nations opt to withdraw. If this were to happen, it would not be a healthy sign for the future of humanity. But in and of itself, the dissolution of the world government would not be a disaster. We would be back to where we are today—sadder but wiser, and otherwise none the worse for wear. Perhaps some practical lessons would be learned that will benefit humanity in our future development.

Background

In his book *World Citizenship and Government: Cosmopolitan Ideas in the History of Western Political Thought* (1996), Derek Heater traces the roots of the world government concept back to the ancient Greeks. But this refers to the *roots*. Professor Heater is quite clear that the contemporary concept of a world government did not begin to develop until the modern era, commencing approximately around 1500. Furthermore, seriously intensive development of the idea only commenced during the twentieth century.

An important document in the post-World War II world government boom was a 532-page compilation by Edith Wynner and Georgia Lloyd entitled *Searchlight on Peace Plans: Choose Your Road to World Government* (1944). Wynner and Lloyd undertook to enumerate and briefly describe a large proportion of existing theoretical plans for supranational political entities. Part II describes some 74 plans, from a 1306 proposal of Pierre Dubois to a 1905 proposal of Richard Bartholdt. If one reads through their list of brief descriptions, it becomes apparent that the earlier proposals, starting with that of Dubois, encompassed only the Christian nations of Western Europe, and were largely motivated by a warlike, crusading spirit: a tight political union of the Christian nations would enable a more effective military resistance to and subsequent conquest of the infidel territories, especially those of the Islamic Turks. However, a few of the plans provided considerable details on the mechanisms of political unification among the Western European nations, and these mechanisms, at least in principle, could be extended to encompass other regions of the world.

The first plan listed by Wynner and Lloyd that explicitly incorporates the entire world is attributed to the French monk Émeric Crucé, author of *The New Cyneas* (*Le Nouveau Cynée*), published in 1623. Although *The New Cyneas* is a remarkable work considering the date when it was published, it prefigures the modern notion of a world state chiefly in scope, rather than in institutional features. For example, as befits a work published during the rising age of absolute monarchy, it envisions that the subsidiary political units would all be hereditary monarchies of one sort or another. Also, the basic concept is really that of a universal mutual assistance alliance, later realized in the form of the League of Nations and the United Nations—neither of which were particularly successful in discouraging aggressive war, and neither of which constitutes a genuine world state in the modern sense.

In the approximately three centuries of modern Western European history between 1700 and the present time, there were two veritably catastrophic periods of warfare: the "French wars" between 1792 and 1815, and the "German wars" between 1914 and 1945. It would seem that proposals for supranational political organizations, up to and including literal world states, flourish most abundantly in periods beset by large-scale warfare. A numerical indication of this phenomenon is contained in the Wynner and Lloyd catalogue (Part II) of theoretical plans to unite nations from 1306 to 1905. Of the 74 plans from this 600-year interval enumerated in the catalogue, some 28 date from 1792 through 1821, a period of 30 years encompassing the French wars. Some notable historical figures are to be found among the proposers of the 74 plans put forward between 1306 and 1905: Dante Alighieri, Desiderius Erasmus, Pope Leo X, Hugo Grotius, William Penn, Jeremy Bentham, Johann Fichte, Immanuel Kant, Thomas Paine, Czar Alexander I, Count Henri de Saint-Simon, Napoleon Bonaparte, Simon Bolivar, Charles Sumner, Baroness Bertha von Suttner, William T. Stead. No implication is intended that these individuals advocated a world state as presently understood. For one thing, most of the plans conceived "political unification" in terms merely of a formally recognized super-alliance: for something along the lines of the League of Nations of the interwar years and the United Nations of the post-World War II years. Few if any plans extended qualitatively beyond the alliance concept to the state concept.

Coming forward to the "German wars" of the first half of the twentieth century, it was during the unprecedented, horrific carnage of World War I that an inspirational slogan emerged that this was going to be "the war to end wars." At the end of the war, a supranational political organization was established known as the League of Nations, whose purpose it was to make a reality of this slogan. The League of Nations was in fact a real-world implementation of the typical pre-1914 proposal for supranational political union: a super-alliance of such power and resources that no non-member nation would dare attack a member nation. For a variety of reasons, the League, obviously, was unsuccessful not only in preventing World War II, but also in either shortening the duration or moderating the ferocity of that conflict. In view of its inability to forestall World War II, it is easy to be contemptuous of the League of Nations. But contempt ought to be tempered with a certain amount of respect for this pioneering effort to establish an institutional underpinning for the principle of collective security and active cooperation among the nations.

Somewhere around the middle of the terrible World War II years between 1939 and 1945, as inconceivable economic resources were being devoted on both sides to destroying enemy property and lives, resulting in the maiming and killing of millions, but at a point where the Allied powers were starting, slowly and painfully, to get the upper hand over the Axis powers, an idea commenced to gain support: that of a new and greatly improved League of Nations to be known as the United Nations. The name "United Nations" is generally attributed to U.S. President Franklin D. Roosevelt, although as far back as 1918, one Theodore Harris had put forward a detailed blueprint for a world government to be known as the "United Nations of the World." The first official use of the term "United Nations" was in the Declaration of the United Nations of January 1, 1942, in which 26 nations pledged themselves to continue the war effort against the Axis powers until final victory was attained.

Although the United Nations did not prevent the post-World War II Cold War confrontation that threatened global human civilization with nuclear catastrophe for close to half a century, the United Nations embodied significant advances over the League of Nations. In addition to virtually universal membership (the United States and the Soviet Union were founding members), the United Nations, in contrast to the League of Nations, would make a far more systematic and determined attempt to eradicate the roots of warfare by fostering economic, political, and social progress throughout the world. In other words, the United Nations would undertake a "peace-building" mission as well as a "peacekeeping" mission. The theme of "a new beginning" was reinforced by abandoning the somewhat stodgy League of Nations headquarters in Geneva, and opening a shiny new glass-and-steel skyscraper on the East River in New York City, to serve as UN headquarters. Consisting as it does of large quantities of uplifting prose ("We the peoples of the United Nations, determined to save succeeding generations from the scourge of war, which twice in our lifetime has brought untold sorrow to mankind..."), the UN Charter is a far more elaborate document than was the old League Covenant. The Charter was soon supplemented by the Universal Declaration of Human Rights, adopted by the General Assembly on December 10, 1948. While this document has been described by many as a "pious wish list," it nevertheless clearly delineates the kind of human condition within world society to which any and all rational persons of good will aspire.

It would be possible go on at considerable length pondering the question of how much of a contribution, on the whole, the United Nations has made to preserving peace and fostering cooperation in the international sphere. At one extreme are those who assert that the UN has been a completely negligible factor in world politics, while at the other extreme are those who assert that it has made a major positive contribution. While questions about the practical effect of the United Nations on global realities might be debated endlessly without approaching any clear resolution, there is an important distinction to be drawn between the practical impact of the United Nations and the psychological impact, as well as between the short-term impact and the long-term impact. The fact that the UN's short-term practical impact has not been dramatic does not necessarily mean that it has not been effective in a psychological sense as a symbol of human unity, and that it will not ultimately prove to have been, in the long run, extremely important in a practical sense as well. Taking the League of Nations and the United Nations together, their history covers four fifths of the twentieth century. Throughout four fifths of the twentieth century, these organizations stood as clear indications of humanity's persistent desire for a benign global political unity that will effectively eliminate the human tragedy and material waste associated with warfare, and will raise human civilization to new heights.

The Postwar World Government Boom. Given the virtually immediate polarization of the world along ideological lines in the aftermath of the Second World War, the fundamental defects of the United Nations were obvious almost from the very beginning to both the "realist" majority and the "visionary" minority. The realist majority viewed the UN mainly as just another tool for the pursuance of national interests, but far less important as such than foreign ministries and war departments. The visionary minority—those people responsible for the ephemeral "world government boom" in the immediate aftermath of World War II—saw the UN as a hollow shadow of the federal world government that it ought to be. The realists envisioned the indefinite continuation of time-honored balance of power politics, UN or no UN. They also saw no reason why the advent of nuclear weapons should fundamentally alter this game. True, nuclear weapons were far more destructive than anything witnessed in the past—but in a way this was good because the threat of nuclear holocaust would reduce the incentives in nations toward provocative and belligerent behavior. So the increase in the destructiveness of weapons was counterbalanced by a decrease in the probability that they would be utilized. Since humanity was presumably no more threatened by warfare than it had been before the invention and dissemination of nuclear weapons, there was thus no compelling reason for a substantive departure from the familiar balance of power politics of the pre-nuclear age.

The visionaries were far less optimistic on this point. According to them, the development of nuclear weapons immeasurably increased the overall threat to human civilization embodied in warfare. While the prospect of nuclear destruction might somewhat reduce the propensity toward provocative and belligerent behavior among nations, it would by no means eliminate it, and sooner or later some nation would stray over the line separating peace from unimaginably devastating warfare. What was obviously needed, in the view of the visionaries, was a world government with direct control over a large and dominant military force, with the power of taxation, and guided by officials subject to direct democratic accountability to the people through free and open elections. For a brief period, this idea gained an appreciable amount of currency, and it was seriously entertained far more widely than had ever been the case in the past. But the post-World War II world government boom quickly fizzled, a victim of the intractable Cold War conflict among the communist and the non-communist blocs of nations. In very short order, the realist viewpoint was completely dominant that whatever might be the attractions of world government "in theory," it was completely infeasible "in practice," because of the yawning, unbridgeable, irreconcilable ideological gulf between communists and non-communists.

Public receptiveness toward the general concept of world government attained a sharply delineated pinnacle in the half-decade that separated the end of World War II in the summer of 1945 from the beginning of the Korean War in the summer of 1950. However, the sudden and dramatic ascent in public receptiveness toward world government was almost immediately followed by an equally sudden and dramatic descent. No doubt a decisive factor in the rapid deflation of world government hopes and aspirations was the confrontational attitude of the Soviet Union in the years following the close of the Second World War. But it is by no means certain that if the Soviet Union had been a capitalist nation—even a democratic capitalist nation—that a genuine world government would have been possible at that time. Quite possibly, the highly ephemeral post-World War II world government boom was largely a shock reaction to the first use of nuclear weapons in warfare—the atomic bombings of Hiroshima and Nagasaki in August 1945. But human beings are remarkably adaptive, mentally and emotionally as well as physically. Within a remarkably short space of time, most people had filed away the threat of dying in a worldwide nuclear holocaust in the same compartment as the threat of dying in an automobile accident. It was a regrettable but inevitable hazard of daily life—therefore there was nothing to be done about it.

During the short-lived post-WW II world government boom, while best-selling authors such as Emery Reves (*The Anatomy of Peace*) drummed up support for the general concept of world government, and academics such as Robert Hutchins and Giuseppe Borgese (members of the University of Chicago "Committee to Frame a World Constitution") worked busily on trying to develop a practical plan for world government, still others applied themselves to the practical organizational work of building mass support for world government. An organization labeling itself the World Movement for World Federal Government (WMWFG) held its first World Congress in Montreux, Switzerland, in 1947, and issued a Declaration describing in considerable detail what the delegates deemed the necessary characteristics of a world state:

1. Universal membership: The world federal government must be open to all peoples and nations.
2. Limitations of national sovereignty, and the transfer to the world federal government of such legislative, executive, and judicial powers as relate to world affairs.
3. Enforcement of world law directly on the individual whoever or wherever he may be, within the jurisdiction of the world federal government: guarantee of the rights of man and suppression of all attempts against the security of the federation.
4. Creation of supranational armed forces capable of guaranteeing the security of the world federal government and of its member states. Disarmament of member nations to the level of their internal policing requirements.
5. Ownership and control by the world federal government of atomic developments and of other scientific discoveries capable of mass destruction.

6. Power to raise adequate revenues directly and independently of state taxes.

Interestingly, it is not specified that the world government be subject to democratic control. It is specified, in point 1, that there be "universal membership" in the sense that membership would be "open" to all the nations of the world. Nothing is specified, however, with respect to nations that join the world federation and then decide at a later date to withdraw. However, a phrase included in point 3 ("suppression of all attempts against the security of the federation") may well be directed against such nations. This would be in line with the well-remembered fact (in 1947) that one of the first indications of the aggressive intentions of Nazi Germany and the other fascist nations was their withdrawal from the League of Nations in the 1930s. In any case, a "right of withdrawal" would be meaningless if nations had no armed forces with which to back up their decision to withdraw. And in points 4 and 5, it is clearly specified that the member nations of the world federation would be deprived of all heavy weaponry (i.e. weaponry beyond the requirements of "internal policing"), both nuclear and conventional.

It will never be known with certainty whether a genuine world government would have been founded in 1945 if it had not been for the ideological conflict between the Soviet Union and the Western capitalist nations. Aside from the ideological impediment, there was an economic impediment to world government, and that particular impediment was almost as important in 1945 as it is today. The economic impediment alone might well have precluded genuine world government in 1945, even if the Soviet Union had been a democratic capitalist nation similar to the United States, Britain, France, and others. And even aside from the economic impediment, there is the basic issue of nationalism which, according to some, would be virtually as important as it is now even if all the nations of the world were extremely homogeneous in terms of economics, politics, religion, culture, language, etc. Be that as it may, certainly the most dramatic and obvious impediment to genuine world government in the postwar years was the increasingly hostile confrontation between the Soviet Union and the Western democracies—the rapidly developing Cold War.

The tensions introduced into international relations by the strategic maneuverings of the two superpowers, the United States and the Soviet Union, each espousing diametrically opposed ideologies, were drastically exacerbated by the rapid escalation of the nuclear peril. The Soviet Union exploded its first atomic bomb in 1949, thus terminating the short-lived U.S. monopoly in nuclear weapons. Hardly had atomic bombs been perfected when they were superseded by hydrogen bombs of far greater destructive power. Both the United States and the Soviet Union soon accumulated thousands of nuclear devices. In the latter 1950s and early 1960s, the competition between the superpowers turned to so-called "delivery systems"—especially to the development of nuclear-tipped long-range missiles equipped with very accurate inertial guidance systems. Prior to the development of these missiles, nuclear weapons could have been delivered by conventional bombers of the type that had been used in World War II. World War II had clearly demonstrated that even with highly effective air defense, it was impossible to completely avert bombing attacks by a determined enemy. By the early 1950s, therefore, the possibility of mass destruction of the major cities of the world by airborne nuclear bombing was no longer a nightmare of the distant future—it was rather an existent reality. With the advent of ballistic missiles in the 1960s, the length of warning time prior to a nuclear holocaust was further shortened—from hours to minutes. People took a deep breath, reassured themselves with the thought that no one would be stupid enough to start a nuclear war, and carried on more or less as before. But the added psychic strain took its toll.

Among the casualties was any sort of rational thinking about world government. Fear and anxiety ruled out any degree of mental flexibility and imagination with respect to the concept. Both the opponents of world government (the vast majority) and the proponents of world government (the tiny minority) could imagine no world government other than an all-powerful state entity that would assume a complete and total monopoly over any and all nuclear weapons, as well as any and all "conventional" heavy weaponry. Opponents of world government were convinced that such an all all-powerful entity would very quickly produce a global totalitarian condition as bad as anything recently witnessed in the Nazi Germany of Adolf Hitler and the Soviet Union of Joseph Stalin. If the proponents of world government had any qualms on this score, they kept them to themselves. In their view, the basic survival of humanity took precedence over the possibility of tyranny. Not to mention the fact that as bad as global tyranny might be, the only thing worse would be the proliferation of local tyrannies over the entire face of the globe in the aftermath of a nuclear holocaust. No blueprint for a *limited* world government was ever considered, as the Cold War grew and matured, either by the opponents or the proponents of world government. The oppressive tensions of the period effectively shut down the reasoning and judgmental faculties of the human race—at least insofar as these faculties applied to international organization. Even highly sophisticated academic writers could not rise above either-or, black-or-white, night-versus-day thinking.

Since the Soviet Collapse. The beginning of the end for the Soviet Union is plausibly dated to the elevation of Mikhail Gorbachev, in March 1985, to the position of General Secretary of the Communist Party of the Soviet Union (CPSU). Gorbachev was a dedicated reformer determined to lift his country out of the economic stagnation and psychic ennui of the late-Soviet era. Throughout the Gorbachev period of perestroika (restructuring) and glasnost (openness), there were increasingly optimistic indications that both the Soviet people and their political leadership were seriously reconsidering their longstanding commitment to Marxist ideology. Apparently some critical mass of dissent from the traditional orthodoxy was eventually reached, the communist leadership suffered a crisis of conscience, a societal chain reaction ensued, and within an amazingly short period of time, the Communist Party had been ousted from the position of political leadership and social domination it had held since 1917. In December 1991, the Union of Soviet Socialist Republics transformed itself into the Commonwealth of Independent States (CIS), a loose confederation comparable, at most, to the British Commonwealth. The various component states of the ex-USSR, as well as the states of its Eastern European satellite fringe, began busily converting themselves into democratic capitalist nations in the image of the United States and the Western European nations. This astounding transition was all the more remarkable for being, on the whole, non-violent. The policy of containment, enunciated by U.S. President Harry Truman in 1947, had finally succeeded. The costs of a large and permanent military force, the continuing risks of the nuclear arms competition, the human and material losses imposed by the Korean war and the Vietnam war, among many other things, were finally justified.

Of course, the collapse and dissolution of the Soviet Union in 1991 did not totally and completely abrogate the problem of ideology in the modern world. The single most populous nation in the world, the People's Republic of China, containing over 20 percent of the world's population, continues to abide by socialist economic principles (albeit with considerable reliance on free market mechanisms) and oligarchic political institutions. Several other nations in the Far East, together with Cuba in the Western hemisphere, also maintain their allegiance to communist ideology. However, rhetoric in the remaining communist nations concerning the eventual collapse of capitalism and ascendancy of socialism has become very muted, and they have more or less completely forsworn providing covert military support for revolutionary movements within non-communist nations. The non-communist nations are fairly confident that it is merely a matter of time before the remaining communist nations follow the example set by the Soviet Union in 1991, and return to the democratic capitalistic world mainstream.

Throughout the Cold War, conventional wisdom had insisted that the ideological confrontation between the USA and the USSR, in and of itself, was sufficient to abrogate any possibility that there could be established a genuine world government with significant power and authority. It seemed plausible, therefore, that the end of the ideological confrontation would restore a certain measure of sympathetic interest in world federalism. In the early 1990s, there were indeed a few signs of this.

For example, in the July 20, 1992, issue of *Time* magazine, there appeared a two-page essay, basically an op-ed piece, entitled "The Birth of the Global Nation." The piece was written by Strobe Talbott, journalist and author of several books on nuclear disarmament negotiations, at that time an editor-at-large for *Time*, later Under-Secretary of State for the ex-USSR and Eastern Europe in the Clinton administration. Talbott briefly sketched the history of world government thinking and opined that world government would probably be a good thing, as evidenced by the following representative excerpt:

> The human drama, whether played out in history books or headlines, is often not just a confusing spectacle but a spectacle about confusion. The big question these days is, Which political forces will prevail, those stitching nations together or those tearing them apart? Here is one optimist's reason for believing unity will prevail over disunity, integration over disintegration. In fact, I'll bet that within the next hundred years (I'm giving the world time for setbacks and myself time to be out of the betting game, just in case I lose this one), nationhood as we know it will be obsolete; all states will recognize a single, global authority. A phrase briefly fashionable in the mid-20th century— "citizen of the world"— will have assumed real meaning by the end of the 21st century.

Talbott did not provide any systematic arguments to support the claim that world government would be beneficial. The author concedes he may be mistaken, and specifies a very long time frame ("next hundred years"), implying that the case for world government has no short-term relevance. The basic ideas expressed in Talbott's essay had been commonplace in world federalist writing ever since the bombings of Hiroshima and Nagasaki in 1945, and these ideas, per se, had not thus far noticeably budged the general consensus among humanity against a world state. Nor have they done so in the post-Cold War era. Still, the appearance in 1992 of pro-world federalist writing in a leading U.S. national news magazine was unprecedented, and quite likely it was made possible by the collapse of the Soviet Union the year before, and with it the apparent elimination of the ideological barrier to world government.

A handful of new books advocating world government appeared in the early 1990s, such as those by Ronald Glossop (*World Federation? A Critical Analysis of Federal World Government*, 1993), Errol Harris (*One World or None: A Prescription for Survival*, 1993), and myself (Yunker, *World Union on the Horizon: The Case for Supernational Federation*, 1993). But they were few in number, and none of them achieved widespread recognition even among academics and professionals, to say nothing of the general public. In the hundreds of articles and dozens of books published every year since the early 1990s on contemporary international relations and international organization, terms such as "world government," "global government," "world state," and the like, rarely appear, and when they do, more often than not it is in the course of a cursory dismissal. The following typical example is taken from *The New World Order* (2004) by Anne-Marie Slaughter:

> People and their governments around the world need global institutions to solve collective problems that can only be addressed on a global scale. They must be able to make and enforce global rules on a variety of subjects and through a variety of means... Yet world government is both infeasible and undesirable. The size and scope of such a government presents an unavoidable and dangerous threat to individual liberty. Further, the diversity of peoples to be governed makes it almost impossible to conceive of a global demos. No form of democracy within the current global repertoire seems capable of overcoming these obstacles.

Nevertheless, the historian Campbell Craig, in a 2008 article in *Ethics & International Affairs*, wrote of a recent "resurgence" of interest in world government. What evidence is there for this alleged resurgence? To begin with, during the mid-2000s, perhaps in response to the traumatic 9/11 event, there may have been a spike in the production of appeals for world government from world federalist enthusiasts whose strident "one world or none" message harked back to the 1945-50 world government boom. One example of this sort of thing was Errol E. Harris's 2005 book: *Earth Federation Now: Tomorrow Is Too Late*. Of course, if appeals of this nature went unheeded during the perilous decades of the Cold War, they were even less likely to be effective now that the Cold War was history and the threat of nuclear world war in the near future had greatly receded.

What may be more significant is that a trickle apparently began of more restrained and scholarly world government advocacies from authors with reputable academic credentials. The major emphasis in Craig's "resurgence" article was placed on a very unusual article by the eminent international relations authority Alexander Wendt, provocatively entitled "Why a World State Is Inevitable," published in the October 2003 issue of the *European Journal of International Relations*. Inasmuch as the question of inevitability is only sensibly considered with reference to existent reality, and as world government is not yet part of existent reality, Wendt's proposition is clearly not meant to be taken literally. As Wendt himself conceded, the allegedly inexorable natural trend of political amalgamation leading toward a world state, might be negated instantly by a nuclear world war or a large asteroid crashing into the Earth. Rather the proposition is deliberately provocative: intended merely to elicit additional serious thought about the world government possibility.

Wendt's inevitability essay has indeed been cited in a substantial number of subsequent professional contributions. But whether this attention will lead to a serious challenge to the existing strong consensus against world government remains to be seen. While most of these contributions seem at least somewhat sympathetic toward world government, none of them significantly amplifies or expands Wendt's argument. And if indeed the inevitability thesis is eventually recognized as a serious challenge to the mainstream consensus against world government, quite possibly the outcome will simply be a further refining of the conventional "case against world government."

In support of his argument that a world state is, as alleged in the title of his article, "inevitable," Alexander Wendt marshals an argument based on teleological reasoning. According to teleological reasoning, everything in the universe has a purpose toward which it inevitably tends. Just as human babies tend to fulfill their purpose by developing into human adults, so too global human civilization is tending toward its final purpose: a global state. The argument is clever and fleshed out impressively with concepts and factoids derived from a wide range of human knowledge. As a piece of erudite writing, Wendt's article is quite impressive. But it is more likely to be persuasive to a theoretical philosopher than to the typical international relations professional.

Be that as it may, Wendt offers skeptical readers of his inevitability essay two pieces of reasonably solid, practical evidence that a world state will eventually be established: (1) the very long-run historical trend toward greater and greater political consolidation that has brought humanity from the tens of thousands of small, autonomous tribal units of pre-history down to the 200-odd nation-states of today, several of which encompass populations in the tens and even hundreds of millions; (2) the fact that a world state would benefit both large nations (lower probability of debilitating wars with other large nations) and small nations (lower probability of being subjected to the oppressive hegemony of large nations). Both of these points are significant and worthy of consideration, but in and of themselves, they are far from conclusive.

With respect to the long-term trend toward ever greater political consolidation, the hard fact remains that almost all of this consolidation was brought about, in one way or another, by means of warfare. In the nuclear age, it seems unlikely that additional warfare offers a plausible avenue toward further political consolidation leading to a world state. One must also take note of the fact that there has been a considerable amount of political de-consolidation in the recent past, ranging from the dissolution of the great European colonial empires to the disintegration of the Soviet Union and Yugoslavia. It is sometimes suggested that perhaps the most plausible scenario toward the creation of a world government is a nuclear world war that would so devastate global human civilization as to finally impress upon humanity the need for a strong world government. However, what may be more likely in the aftermath of a nuclear world war, would be a long period of low-intensity warfare fuelled by persistent bitterness and hostility, among a host of small states presided over by what are today referred to as "local warlords."

With respect to the potential benefits of world government for both the large nations and the small nations, it must be acknowledged that these are definite potential benefits, and need to be taken into account in any sensible evaluation of the world government possibility. But potential benefits have to be weighed against potential costs. The contemporary consensus is that the potential costs of world government (totalitarian tyranny, bureaucratic suffocation, global civil war) far exceed the potential benefits. Simply enumerating benefits, while paying little or no attention to costs, is unlikely to be effective, given that the costs are so well known.

Although there are obvious difficulties with Professor Wendt's "inevitability of world government" article, the fact that the author is a recognized and respected international relations authority, and the fact that the article was published in a reputable, mainstream international relations periodical, may be quite significant. It is not too much to suggest that 50 years ago, with the Cold War still raging, no recognized and respected international relations authority would have dreamed of writing such an article, and no reputable, mainstream international relations periodical would have dreamed of publishing it. Therefore, the appearance of this article may be, in and of itself, an important indicator of increased receptivity toward the concept of world government, at least among academic professionals.

This is not to suggest, however, that "increased receptivity" is likely to extend to the "omnipotent world state" concept of traditional world federalist thinking. The case against the omnipotent world state is as strong today as it ever has been. But increased receptivity may enable more individuals to take seriously the possibility of a *limited* federal world government along the lines of the Federal Union of Democratic Nations.

Blueprint

In his 1975 article "A New Paradigm for International Legal Studies: Prospects and Proposals" in the *Yale Law Journal*, the eminent international relations authority Richard Falk advised against offering "blueprints for a future world order system" on the basis that such blueprints represent "the fallacy of premature specificity." A considerable period of time has elapsed between 1975 and today, and conditions are much different. Back in 1975, the Cold War was still raging, and most people in the West were fearful that if a world state existed, the USSR would attempt to take it over and utilize it as an instrument with which to impose communism on the entire world. For their part, communists in the USSR and elsewhere were fearful that a world state might be used to impose capitalism on the entire world. With the collapse of communism in the USSR in 1991, these particular fears have greatly subsided. What was premature in 1975 might not be premature now.

More importantly, Falk issued his "premature specificity" injunction in the context of a discussion of Grenville Clark and Louis Sohn's *World Peace through World Law* (3rd edition, 1966): a magisterial but ultimately ineffectual appeal for world government through the mechanism of a "strengthened United Nations." Clark and Sohn went through the existing United Nations charter, expanding it in great detail, and providing voluminous commentary on the expansions. Quite possibly the work of Clark and Sohn amounted to *excessive* specificity, but that is not the same thing as *premature* specificity. The fundamental problem that Falk had with the Clark-Sohn effort was that, despite its representation as a mere "strengthening" of the United Nations, it actually envisioned the transformation of the UN into a variety of "omnipotent world state." Clark and Sohn were insistent that the member nations must be completely disarmed, and that all heavy weaponry, especially nuclear weapons, must be concentrated under the sole control of the world government. Reasonably enough, Falk assumed that there was no possibility that the nations of the world would voluntarily disarm themselves in favor of an all-powerful world government, and he therefore dismissed the Clark-Sohn proposal as politically impossible.

This was the real problem Falk had with Clark and Sohn: it was not so much a case of their proposal being prematurely specific, as it was a case of their proposal being politically impossible. And it must be acknowledged that despite the ending of the Cold War as it existed in 1975, it is still the case today that the nations of the world will not turn over control of their weapons and armed forces to a world government. For world government to be politically feasible, it must not require this. What is needed now is a plan for world government—a blueprint, if you will—that is *not* tied to disarmament of the member nations. Such a blueprint is hardly premature at this point, rather it is vitally necessary if there is to be any significant advance within the foreseeable future beyond the dangerously unstable contemporary international status quo. While we do not want *excessive* specificity, we do need *appropriate* specificity.

Prior to the successes of the Wright brothers and others in the early years of the twentieth century, it was a fairly commonplace speculation that the problems of heavier-than-air flight were too great ever to be overcome by human ingenuity. No less a scientific authority than William Thomson Kelvin (1824-1907), better known as Lord Kelvin, is reputed to have proclaimed in 1895: "Heavier-than-air flying machines are impossible."

There are several problems involved in flight: lift, control, propulsion, power. Prior to the pioneers of the early twentieth century, several unsuccessful designs had been offered. A critical pre-condition for the successful solution of the overall problem was the development of small gasoline engines with a high ratio of power to weight. This solution to the power problem, in conjunction with solutions to the problems of lift, control, and propulsion (wings, ailerons, rudders, propellers), made flight as we know it today possible. Whether or not heavier-than-air flying machines were possible could not have been determined on the basis of speculations employing the general scientific principles of the early twentieth century. It required a workable design involving solutions to the various problems of lift, control, and propulsion, in combination with specific technological advances, to demonstrate conclusively that heavier-than-air flying machines were indeed possible.

Much the same is true with respect to world government. Whether or not a world government is possible and desirable cannot be determined on the basis of general principles from political and other social sciences. The fact that these principles suggest that *some* world government schemes are unworkable does not necessarily establish that *all* world government schemes are unworkable. As gasoline engines turned out to be the solution to the power problem of flight at the turn of the twentieth century, possibly the technological advances that have produced contemporary communications and transportation technology will turn out to be the solution to the analogous "power problem" of world government in the twenty-first century. Even the most convinced world government skeptics have to concede that modern communications and transportation have rendered null and void the coordination problems of large-scale political organizations in the distant past.

In current discussions of world government in the international relations literature, there is very little attention paid to specific institutional characteristics of world government. Perhaps this has something to do with the above-mentioned 1975 injunction against "premature specificity" of Richard Falk. Or perhaps it is because the editors and referees responsible for the professional literature have a low tolerance for institutional specifics pertaining to hypothetical world governments. If so, this is a dysfunctional attitude, in that specific design elements are indeed critical to a proper evaluation of whether world government should have a future in human history.

Past appeals for world government have sometimes been accompanied by specific institutional proposals, but more often have not. Some of the best-known, most elaborate and most adamant appeals for world government from the post-World War II period, such as *The Anatomy of Peace* (1945) by Emery Reves and *The Commonwealth of Man* (1952) by Frederick Schuman, are entirely devoid of any specific institutional proposals. These works lambaste in great detail and most unmercifully the notion that reliable international security may be achieved by any means short of world government—and yet they are completely silent on how that government ought to be organized.

In perusing the works of Emery Reves and Frederick Schuman, as well as others of a similar nature, one might well be reminded of Karl Marx's intemperate 19th century tirades against the capitalist economic system, tirades that were unaccompanied by any significant development of a specific socialist alternative. Marx disdained the task of "writing recipes for the social chefs of the future" on grounds that any socialist system was bound to be superior to the capitalist system, and furthermore, that the appropriate institutional structure of the socialist socioeconomic system would be transparently obvious to the architects of the revolution once the revolution had been successful. The subsequent history of socialism in the USSR under Stalin, and in China under Mao, clearly demonstrated that the socialist cure may well be worse than the capitalist disease. What the experiences of Stalin's Soviet Russia and Mao's Red China have demonstrated beyond reasonable doubt is that socialism, in and of itself and defined (according to most dictionary definitions) as public ownership of all or most capital property, is by no means *sufficient* to establish a social system preferable to the capitalist social system.

In the same way, world government is by no means sufficient to establish global conditions preferable to those currently prevailing under the sovereign nation-state system. Clearly, the world government cure *could* be worse than the international anarchy disease. It follows, therefore, that any appeal for world government that is not based on a specific blueprint for world government, is hardly likely to be persuasive. In order to avoid this problem, the present analysis is being based on a fairly detailed world government blueprint. Although appeals for world government unaccompanied by specific proposals outnumber appeals that are indeed accompanied by specific proposals, there has in fact been a sufficient number of the latter throughout the course of modern history as to constitute an important obstacle to focused consideration of world government.

In point of fact, world government proposals are not all created equal. Some proposals, if implemented, would almost certainly result in a higher probability of eventual global tyranny. When compared to the better-known proposals for world government enunciated since World War II, the proposal for a Federal Union of Democratic Nations conveyed herein, would, if implemented, result in a very low probability of eventual degeneration into global tyranny. The originality of this particular evaluation of world government is therefore rooted directly in the originality of the proposed blueprint for a Federal Union of Democratic Nations. Thus the need for a clear understanding of this particular blueprint.

Federal Union Fundamentals. The proposed name of the federation is the Federal Union of Democratic Nations (FUDN). The Federal Union of Democratic Nations would be a supernational government founded on the basis of a Federal Union Constitution. The name of the union implies that the member nations would all be democratic in nature. A fairly generous interpretation of the word "democratic" may be necessary, lest too many nations be denied membership on the basis that they are not sufficiently democratic. In a general sense, "democracy" implies that the government is responsive to the preferences of the people. But more specifically, it implies that high government officials are elected by the citizens in regular, open, contested elections, and that citizens enjoy strong and effective rights of free speech, free press, and free political organization. A substantial number of nations in the world today—even some that proclaim themselves to be "democratic"—do not exhibit all of these characteristics.

For example, the People's Republic of China is today regarded by many people as a political oligarchy under the effective control of a handful of high officials of the Communist Party of China. But it would be inadvisable to exclude a nation as large and important as China from the Federal Union on grounds that it is insufficiently democratic. If China were a member of the Federal Union of Democratic Nations, there would be stronger psychological pressure on the leadership to implement democratic reforms. The long-run objective would be to have every member nation maintaining very high domestic standards of democratic accountability of the government—but this long-run objective will be better served if considerable flexibility is practiced in the short run.

The proposed Federal Union would be a full-fledged, genuine, legitimate state entity with clearly defined geographical boundaries (assuming some non-member nations), a permanent and continuous governmental structure, the power to levy taxes and enact binding legislation, and the authority to maintain standing military forces under its direct command. As the name suggests, it would be a federal rather than a unitary form of government. This means that the member nations would maintain their separate identities, governments, and cultures, and would retain substantial independence, autonomy, and sovereignty in all matters that do not impinge significantly on the welfare of other member nations.

As a full-fledged state entity, the government of the Federal Union of Democratic Nations would incorporate the standard tripartite structure of legislative, executive, and judicial branches. It is suggested that world government elections be held on a quinquennial basis (every five years), and that the highest officials of all three branches of government be democratically elected directly by the citizens. Elections would either be "0 year elections" (2020, 2030, etc.) or "5 year elections" (2025, 2035, etc.). In "5 year elections," each of the Union Districts would elect its Union Representative to a 5-year term, and 5 seats on the 25-seat Union High Court would be up for election to 25-year terms. The "0 year elections" would be the same as the "5 year elections" except for the fact that in the former, the entire population of the Federal Union would also elect a single Union Chief Executive to head the executive branch for a 10-year term.

The legislature would be a unicameral body, designated the Union Chamber of Representatives, consisting of approximately 200 Union Representatives. The Union Chamber would have the power to make laws and issue policy directives within its area of authority, as well as the power to alter and amend the annual financial budget prepared by the executive branch. The Union Chief Executive would be responsible for preparing budgets, for enforcing laws and implementing policy directives approved by the Union Chamber of Representatives, and (through direction of the Union Security Force) for maintaining the internal peace and external security of the Union. The Union High Court would serve as a court of last appeal on those matters within its area of authority, including the constitutionality of legislation and policy directives approved by the Union Chamber of Representatives.

Although a unicameral legislature is envisioned for the supernational federation legislature, some of the virtues of bicameralism—without incurring its inherent unwieldiness and divisiveness—would be captured by the proposed "dual voting system." Whenever a vote is taken in the Union Chamber of Representatives, the measure being considered would have to be approved by a majority, possibly by more than a 51 percent majority, on two different bases: the population basis and the material basis. In the population vote, the weight given to the vote of each particular Union Representative would be proportional to the population of his/her Union district, relative to the total population of the Federal Union. In the material vote, the weight given to the vote of each particular Union Representative would be proportional to the financial revenues derived from his/her Union district, relative to the total financial revenues of the Federal Union. Union Representatives from the rich nations would be disproportionately represented in the material vote, while Union Representatives from populous poorer nations would be disproportionately represented in the population vote. Since measures would have to be approved on both the material basis and the population basis, only measures on which rich nations and poor nations could achieve a reasonable degree of consensus would have a chance of being approved by the Union Chamber of Representatives. This would protect the vital national interests of both the rich and the poor nations. Either category could in effect exercise a veto power.

The most obvious short-term motivation for the dual voting principle is to impede possible efforts by populous poorer nations to impose radical redistribution on the rich nations through a "global welfare state," and also to impede the rich nations from passing legislation that is unacceptable to the poor nations—for example, because it would recreate the exploitative conditions of the colonial era. But it is important to realize that if the per capita income among the various member nations of the Federal Union were relatively comparable, then the proportion of Union revenues raised in a given District would become proportional to the District's population, and no systematic differences would be observed between the population and the material votes. This is the long-run aspiration of the economic complement to the political Federal Union proposal: a Global Marshall Plan (to be described and evaluated later in this chapter). Until the economic equalization objective has been achieved through the operation of the Global Marshall Plan, the dual voting provision provides some of the benefits of bicameralism, in terms of ensuring adequate representation of different interests, without incurring the ponderous unwieldiness of bicameralism.

An obvious skeptical reaction to the dual voting proposal is that it would lead to legislative gridlock: the failure of the legislature to pass anything beyond the most trivial and unimportant legislation. Granting that this is a definite possibility, the question remains why this would be inferior to the present situation, in which any kind of global legislation at all is impossible because there is no such thing as a global legislature. If the rich nations and the poor nations would be unable to agree on anything even if they were united within a world government, it seems inescapable that they will also be unable to agree on anything if they are fully autonomous states under the sovereign nation-state system. At any rate, such extreme pessimism is clearly unwarranted. Even under the sovereign nation-state system of today, an appreciable amount of consensus has been achieved—on some issues—among the rich nations and the poor nations.

National Right of Withdrawal. One of the most fundamental objections to the proposal for a world federation under consideration herein is that any state entity that was not prepared to forcibly prevent the departure of its subsidiary units would lack what is perhaps the most basic and essential characteristic of a state. It is quintessential, in this view, of a state entity that it be completely determined to preserve its territorial integrity at all costs. However commonplace this viewpoint might be at the present time, it is not valid. A state, whether it be at the national or the supernational level, can be a legitimate, genuine, authentic, and effective political organization in the absence of any determination to utilize force to suppress independence movements in subsidiary regions.

Think, for example, of the nation of Canada. A very large and important province in Canada, the province of Quebec, has been toying seriously with the possibility of independence for several decades. The major basis for this separatist leaning is the fact that the predominant language among the population of Quebec is French, whereas the predominant language among the population of the rest of Canada is English. No knowledgeable person, either in Quebec, or in the rest of Canada, or in the rest of the world, expects that if Quebec does in fact ultimately declare its independence, the national government of Canada will employ its armed forces to keep Quebec within the Canadian federation. But the expectation that potential secession would not be opposed by military force does not mean that Canada is any less a nation. If Quebec leaves Canada, Canada would carry on as a nation with its 11 remaining provinces and territories, which together account for approximately 85 percent of the Canadian land area, and approximately 75 percent of the Canadian population. Although the loss of 15 percent of its land area and 25 percent of its population would not be a happy event for most English-speaking Canadians, one consolation might be that it would no longer be necessary for the nation to maintain two official languages.

What I would suggest is that if and when it is founded in the future, the Federal Union of Democratic Nations should regard possible secessions by individual nations much as the English-speaking population of Canada presently regards possible secession by the province of Quebec: as an unfortunate and undesirable eventuality that is certainly to be avoided if at all possible—but nevertheless as survivable and certainly not worth the costs that would be involved in its forcible prevention. There is actually no alternative to taking this attitude if the world government is to be established. If the Federal Union evolves as intended, within a relatively brief period there would be strong economic, social, political, and psychological links between the member nations and the supernational federation. Leaving the federation would by no means be costless to the nation, even though it would not have to fight for its independence.

Individual citizens, of course, do not have the right to declare themselves independent of the political authority of the locality in which they reside. When it comes, however, to large political entities declaring their independence from still larger political entities in which they had previously been incorporated, this is no trivial matter. Human history is filled with wars fought to gain or prevent independence. Contemporary viewpoints on specific wars of independence vary depending on both the individual and on the circumstances of the war. For example, most American citizens today regard the Revolutionary War of 1775 to 1783, which secured the independence of the thirteen original American colonies from Britain, to have been an unquestionably beneficial episode not merely for the United States but for world civilization as a whole. British citizens today, while not usually inclined to dispute the benefits, understandably tend to be less enthusiastic about them. Meanwhile, most American citizens today regard the U.S. Civil War of 1861 to 1865, which forcibly prevented the Southern states from leaving the Union, to also have been an unquestionably beneficial episode not merely for the United States as a whole, but for the Southern states as well. Citizens of the Southern states today, while not usually inclined to dispute the benefits, understandably tend to be less enthusiastic about them.

The United States Civil War of 1861-1865 was one of the bloodiest and most destructive wars of the 19th century. For skeptics of world government, the U.S. Civil War provides an instructive lesson on the probable fate of a future world government. Prospects for the success of the United States in 1788 (the year of the final ratification of the present U.S. Constitution) were highly auspicious. The thirteen original states of United States shared a common language, a common heritage, geographical contiguity, and had cooperated closely in waging the war for independence. And yet, despite all of these advantages, after only a little over seven decades of operation, the United States was engulfed in a bitter civil war brought about by the effort of the Southern states to establish their independence. How clear it is, therefore, say skeptics of world federation, that if such a federation were established, it would eventually dissolve and degenerate into bitter civil war.

There are two major flaws in the argument that a world government would necessarily follow the path followed by the United States into the Civil War of 1861-1865. First, the constitution of the world federation considered here (the Federal Union of Democratic Nations), in contrast to the United States Constitution, would explicitly allow member nations to declare their independence from the world federation at any time they desire. The U.S. Constitution was silent on the issue of whether member states would or would not be permitted to secede peacefully from the United States. Had the U.S. Constitution explicitly stated that any move by a state toward independence would be forcibly suppressed, it is quite possible that the Southern states, being fully aware of the fact that they would have to fight hard to achieve independence, would have been more susceptible to compromise. At the time the U.S. Constitution was formulated, however, there was a great deal of apprehension about the federal government being too strong, and therefore putting into the Constitution an explicit anti-secession provision might have eliminated any possibility of ratification.

On the other hand, had the U.S. Constitution explicitly stated that any move by a state toward independence would be unopposed by the federal government, it is quite possible that the Northern states, being fully aware of the fact that they would have no legal right to oppose secession, would have been more susceptible to compromise. Whether the U.S. Constitution had explicitly forbidden secession or explicitly condoned secession, quite probably the conflict between the Northern and Southern states would not have escalated to the point where secession actually occurred. It follows, therefore, that the provision in the Federal Union constitution explicitly allowing secession by member nations will, in all likelihood, prevent the escalation of conflicts to the point where actual secessions occur. And this provision, at the same time, makes it highly unlikely that in the unfortunate event that secessions *do* occur, they will be opposed with military force.

The second flaw in the argument that a potential world federation will follow the path the United States followed into civil war, is that it neglects the overriding role that the institution of slavery played in the degeneration of relations between the Northern and Southern states to the point of secession and civil war. What was not foreseen by the U.S. founding fathers was that the rise of cotton cultivation for export in the Southern states, during the early decades of the republic, would greatly enhance the profitability of slavery, thus giving that reprehensible institution a new lease on life. At the time the U.S. Constitution went into effect, it was widely assumed that the United States would fairly quickly follow the lead of the rest of the civilized world and abolish slavery. It was assumed that the abolition would be peaceful, because of the marginal profitability of slavery.

Unfortunately, the invention of the cotton gin by Eli Whitney greatly changed the business calculus of slavery. Soon, the manifest conflict between the political ideals of liberty and equality on which the nation was supposedly founded, and the economic self-interest of the Southern plantation owners, resulted in continuing acrimonious controversy which bedeviled the young republic. The slavery issue became a bitter moral issue, with each side accusing the other of base and unworthy motivations. When the Southern states eventually declared their independence, it was not because they were in immediate fear that slavery would be abolished by the new Republican presidential administration of Abraham Lincoln, but rather because they simply could not tolerate any more questioning and criticizing of slavery—and Lincoln's administration would certainly engage in a great deal of questioning and criticizing of slavery. And when the Northern states went to war to prevent Southern independence, it was not primarily to preserve the Union, as such, but rather to thwart the selfish determination of the Southern gentry to perpetuate the evil and demeaning institution of slavery. It was the incendiary issue of slavery which made the U.S. Civil War of 1861-1865 happen—not the innate unwillingness of state entities to permit subsidiary entities to establish their independence.

At the present moment in world history, there is no political issue on the horizon that will be as controversial and emotional, over the next several decades, as was the slavery issue in American politics in the decades leading up to the Civil War. There is no nation on the face of the globe, of course, in which slavery is legal. This is hardly to say that full racial equality has been achieved in every nation of the world. But the principle of full racial equality is accepted by almost all properly educated people, and gradual progress is being made in most nations toward the practical implementation of this principle. In addition, most of humanity seems to have made peace with itself on the matter of religion. None of the major organized religions in the world today has on its official agenda the suppression of all other religions throughout the world. Even in the handful of nations in which governance is dominated by clerics, there is no serious intention to export this system to other nations.

National Right of Armament. The standard view among world government traditionalists is that the establishment of the world state would be accompanied by the immediate and total disarmament of nations. Most weapons of mass destruction (such as nuclear weapons) would be dismantled and destroyed, but a small proportion would be taken over by the military arm of the world government. With the nations deprived of heavy armament, presumably the world government would not require a great deal of military power to maintain peace and order. No longer would human civilization lie in the shadow of nuclear holocaust. The problem perceived by the vast majority of the human population with this scenario, however, is that while human civilization would no longer lie in the shadow of nuclear holocaust, it *would* now lie in the shadow of global tyranny imposed by a totalitarian world government.

Therefore, it is an absolutely indispensable component of the present proposal for a Federal Union of Democratic Nations that the member nations possess a permanent and inalienable right to maintain whatever military forces and weapons—including nuclear weapons—that they feel it necessary to maintain, for as long as they feel it necessary. The hope is that slowly and gradually, nations will voluntarily disarm, until at some future point the armaments of nations will be reduced to a very low level which could legitimately be described as inconsequential. But the objective of major disarmament (as opposed to "complete" disarmament—which may forever be impossible) would be a very long-term goal of the Federal Union, to be pursued in a relaxed and unhurried manner.

The idea of reducing the threat of war through formal disarmament treaties among nations came into prominence in the latter part of the nineteenth century. The immediate impetus to this was the arms competition which developed among the major European powers in the wake of German unification at the time of the Franco-Prussian War of 1871. By 1900, all the major European powers, not just the superpowers, found it necessary to maintain large-scale military forces armed with increasingly sophisticated and destructive weaponry. To the more perceptive and prescient people of the period, the arms competition, in and of itself, was increasing the threat of war. And, of course, if war *did* occur among nations with such formidable military forces, the costs could be horrific.

Toward the end of the nineteenth century, therefore, appeals for international measures to slow or even halt the accumulation of military power were becoming increasingly common. In response, two Hague Disarmament Conferences were held, in 1899 and 1907. A planned third conference was cancelled, however, because the would-be conferees were busy fighting World War I (1914-1918). World War I did not terminate human civilization, as had been warned by some alarmists, but it certainly imposed a great deal of pain, suffering, death, and destruction upon human civilization. Although all of the major military powers had participated in the Hague Conferences of 1899 and 1907, little of substance had been accomplished. The Conferences not only did not forestall the advent of World War I, but they did not noticeably reduce the carnage of that conflict. No agreements had been reached limiting machine guns and other automatic weapons, artillery, bombs, airplanes, capital ships, or submarines. No agreements could have been reached regarding tanks, which were invented later on, during the course of the war. Despite an agreement not to use poison gas, poison gas was in fact utilized. Even if detailed provisions for the limitation of weapons had been agreed to at the Hague Conferences, it is doubtful that they would have had any effect. There was no provision for the enforcement of any of the agreements reached, and amid the increasing rancor and tension among the major European powers in the years just prior to 1914, the agreements would most likely have been ignored.

The futility of the Hague Conferences provides a lesson on the limited effectiveness of disarmament efforts—in and of themselves—in those situations where nothing is done (or can be done) to alleviate the root causes of hostility and conflict among nations. In medical terms, disarmament efforts are an effort to treat symptoms of the disease, as opposed to treating the disease itself. The disease in this case is the normal suspicion, distrust, hostility, and conflict that naturally emerges from a system of sovereign and independent nation-states, all of whom are keenly aware of their rightful and legitimate national interests, and all of whom are determined that deadly force can and will be utilized against any nation which presumes to challenge these interests. Arms races are a consequence of this bad attitude.

The post-World War I history of the twentieth century provides further evidence on the limited effectiveness of disarmament efforts in the absence of progress toward the amelioration of basic sources of conflict. The interwar period witnessed several multilateral disarmament conferences in the tradition of the Hague Conferences. The intention was to establish numerical limitations on all types of weapons: land, sea, and air. Any and all hopes along these lines quickly foundered on the determination of Germany, controlled from January 1933 onward by Adolf Hitler, to throw off the arms limitations imposed by the Treaty of Versailles following World War I. Hitler ordered the German delegation home from the Geneva disarmament conference, withdrew Germany from the League of Nations, and commenced a massive and comprehensive rearmament drive.

The aftermath of World War II was, in important respects, a carbon copy of the aftermath of World War I. Humanity was shocked and horrified by what it had just done to itself, and was determined to avoid future repetitions of catastrophic warfare. The advent of nuclear weapons intensified the sense of urgency. But just as hopes for major disarmament in the interwar period eventually foundered on German intransigence, hopes for major disarmament in the postwar period foundered on Russian intransigence. Germany had been forcibly disarmed after World War I, and more than a decade passed before it commenced the rearmament program which contributed to the onset of World War II. Russia, on the other hand, was a member of the victorious "Grand Alliance" of World War II. At the end of the war, it was armed to the teeth, and owing to the vituperative ideological conflict with the non-communist nations in which Russia was embroiled, it was highly disinclined to disarm. By 1950, Russia was a nuclear power, and by 1960 it was well advanced in missile technology. By the early 1960s, the basic groundwork had been laid for instantaneous nuclear Armageddon.

For more than 30 years, humanity lived in the shadow of nuclear destruction, of catastrophe far beyond anything experienced in the past, of an unimaginable setback so comprehensive and devastating as quite possibly to set humanity sliding irretrievably back toward barbarism or even physical extinction. As in previous times, disarmament negotiations were undertaken among the superpowers in an effort to reduce the risk. Some progress was made: for example, in the limited nuclear test ban treaty of 1963, the nuclear nonproliferation treaty of 1968, and the first Strategic Arms Limitation Treaty of 1972. Despite these hopeful signs, stockpiles of armaments, nuclear and conventional, remained huge. There can be little doubt that if these stockpiles had been utilized in an unrestricted world war, the damage to the human prospect would have been devastating, perhaps fatal.

The rapid decline of the Cold War in the aftermath of the collapse and disintegration of the Soviet Union in 1991 certainly improved the prospects for substantial arms reduction by the two nuclear superpowers, the United States and the Russian Federation, either with or without benefit of formal treaties. The various START treaties (Strategic Arms Reduction Treaty) of 1991, 1993, and 2010 ("New START"), between the same two nuclear superpowers as the SALT treaties, are quite ambitious, but have not yet been fully ratified and implemented. Even were the most optimistic objectives of these treaties to be realized, there would still be an adequate sufficiency of operational nuclear weapons available to inflict catastrophe on human civilization should they be utilized.

The same underlying rationale that justifies the United States and Russia maintaining large nuclear arsenals, despite the demise of the Cold War, would justify various other nations adopting the same rationale. Several nations have already taken the step. Hindu India and Muslim Pakistan have been at odds over Kashmir ever since independence and partition in 1947. Relations between India and China have also been fraught over the years. China, as the number two power in the communist camp, felt it needed nuclear weapons—for the same reason that Britain and France in the non-communist camp felt they needed them. Since China had nuclear weapons, India felt it needed them. Because India had nuclear weapons, Pakistan felt it needed them. Israel needs nuclear weapons to deter the surrounding Arab nations. Therefore, the surrounding Arab nations may need nuclear weapons lest Israel become expansionist-minded. Bosnia may need nuclear weapons to protect itself against Serbia, and vice versa. And so it goes. Most nations of the world have signed the Nuclear Nonproliferation Treaty of 1968. But that treaty is a slender reed on which to depend, because for a number of nations there are compelling reasons to acquire and maintain at least a minimum nuclear capability.

This is a difficult situation, and I am certainly not saying that the establishment of a world government along the lines of the Federal Union of Democratic Nations would quickly and radically improve the situation. The proposed Federal Union would allow its member nations to maintain whatever armaments they desire under their own direct control. It seems inevitable, therefore, that many militarily powerful nations—even if they join the Federal Union with a certain amount of commitment—will exercise their right to maintain substantial military forces. With little doubt, we can expect the nuclear powers to remain nuclear powers.

This is not a problem—in the sense that it is not an argument against world government. We are confronted with a choice between an armed world without a world government in operation, or an armed world with a world government in operation. The hope of every informed and reasonable person in the world today is that as international hostility and tension gradually fade, the level of armaments maintained by the nations will gradually decline. Both the threat of war and the potential destructiveness of war, it is hoped, will slowly subside. The argument put forward here is that an operational world government will increase the probability of this favorable outcome. The world state would facilitate the processes of communication and accommodation among nations that further the cause of benign global governance. At the same time, it would provide a potent symbol of the brotherhood of mankind and of the high aspirations of human civilization. With a functioning world government in operation, we would have a better chance of realizing our natural aspirations toward a world without war, and without the fear of war.

Religion and Language. The general rule in pursuing the long-term goal of ever-increasing peaceful cooperation and psychological solidarity among the citizens of the Federal Union of Democratic Nations is to maintain perpetual flexibility and toleration with respect to all matters in which diversity is either inevitable, or has no seriously adverse bearing on practical economic and political issues, but to work gradually toward uniformity in other matters.

An important example of the former is religion. Whether this is the result of divine purpose or human nature, humanity has developed a large number of diverse religious systems: Judaism, Christianity, Islam, Hinduism, Buddhism, and Taoism, to name only some of the more important. Within each of the major categories there are normally several subcategories. It is almost definitional that religious belief systems cannot be confirmed or contradicted by any conceivable appeal to either logical reasoning or empirical reality. Many if not most religious belief systems offer the believer some form of solace against the apparent personal extinction implied by the physical realities of death and decay: for example, that the spiritual soul's awareness, perception, and reasoning will continue onward into an afterlife following the death of the physical body. In view of the fact that personal survival may be at stake, religious beliefs are often accompanied by strong emotions and great determination to suppress opposed religious beliefs. No doubt it would be desirable, from a strictly rational point of view, that humanity organize a universal ecumenical council with the purpose of specifying the tenets of a single "true" religion acceptable to all people. The futility of such an undertaking will be obvious to most.

What this means is that if it is to survive and prosper, the Federal Union of Democratic Nations must exercise complete impartiality and neutrality with respect to religion, now and forever. It must practice an uncompromising separation of church and state. A strong basis for religious toleration has already been laid in the modern world. Centuries of history have taught humanity that religiously based conflicts are not only extremely costly, but also very unlikely to yield long-term advantages even to the winning side. Moreover, the contemporary individual is far more aware of the multiplicity of established, organized religions in the world than were individuals in past centuries. This in itself has weakened faith in the concept of a "single true religion," and has weakened the determination, even among sincere believers in a particular religious system, to convert others to that system. In the modern world, all the great religious systems have achieved a degree of accommodation with each other—none of them aspires to "world domination," as it were. None of them, therefore, are likely to perceive in a world state an instrument toward the universal imposition of a single religion.

While religion is an example of a matter in which diversity seems inevitable, but which need not have any adverse effect on the practical economic and political operations of the Union, language is an example of a matter in which considerable diversity exists at the present time, but this is a form of diversity which is neither inevitable nor neutral in its effects on economic and political operations. This is an area in which the Federal Union should indeed press forward—albeit at a gradual, unhurried pace—toward less diversity and more homogeneity. History has clearly demonstrated that a common language is a powerful force in support of both political unity and economic prosperity. It has equally clearly demonstrated that different languages are frequently a potent divisive force: more often than not, the curse of separatism (as in Canada's province of Quebec) is linguistically based. As a speaker of English, my own judgment on this matter is possibly biased. Nevertheless, it is plausibly arguable that in view of the present widespread dissemination of the English language throughout the world, there are compelling arguments of practicality and expedience in favor of the adoption of English as the official language of the Federal Union of Democratic Nations.

My own proposal is that not only should English be *an* official language of the Federal Union of Democratic Nations, it should be the *sole* official language of the Federal Union. There are several languages besides English that are widely spoken throughout the world, which would make it very difficult to specify the second official language. And once a second official language had been allowed, the arguments would be endless for a third, a fourth, and so on.

A possible compromise to facilitate the adoption of English as the sole official language of the Federal Union might be to require schoolchildren in English-speaking nations to study some other language to the same intensity that schoolchildren in other nations study English. According to the ancient proverb, "Misery loves company": thus the knowledge that schoolchildren in English-speaking nations were being subjected to the mental stress and strain of studying another language no less than their own children, might provide a sufficient amount of psychological solace to non-English speakers to induce them to accept English as the sole official language of the Federal Union of Democratic Nations. Even if this compromise were to be acceptable to most nations, it would probably require a period of many decades, if not several centuries, before the overwhelming majority of humanity becomes fluent in a single language. In this area as in others, patience must be the watchword.

Trade and Migration. It is a conventional policy of a modern nation-state to maintain a free trade area within its national boundaries. The close ties which this policy facilitates between all parts of the nation are not only economically beneficial, but they also augment psychological feelings of unity and shared purpose. Despite decades of multilateral conferences and bilateral negotiations, first under the GATT rubric (General Agreement on Tariffs and Trade) and now under the WTO rubric (World Trade Organization), the various legal and financial impediments erected by individual nations against international trade and investment remain a very significant drag on the development of the global economy. Therefore a primary task of the Federal Union during its early decades would be to oversee the full and comprehensive dismantling of various national impediments (tariffs, import quotas, and so on) to the free flow of physical commodities and financial capital between member nations.

This will not necessarily be an easy task, since in some cases tariff revenues constitute a significant source of national government revenue, while in other cases protection against foreign competition is very much in the financial interest of influential individuals and organizations. Owing to these factors, it may require a substantial period of time before the domestic free trade objective is achieved. However, progress in this area would probably be more rapid than has been the historical rate of progress under the sovereign nation-state system. The Federal Union might also participate in the processes of travel and trade by building and/or maintaining international highways and railroads, as well as airports and seaports.

It is also a conventional policy of a modern nation-state to maintain a high level of internal population mobility. This is also economically beneficial, both to individual citizens and to the nation as a whole, as well as augmenting psychological feelings of unity and shared purpose among the population. Unfortunately, this particular characteristic of the typical modern nation-state cannot be quickly and easily emulated by the Federal Union of Democratic Nations. The immigration barriers that have been established by the rich nations to restrain the flow of migrants from the poor nations must be kept in force until a higher level of economic homogeneity throughout the world has been achieved. The opinion is almost universal among professional economists, that the abolition of immigration restrictions, under the current condition of wide economic disparities between nations, would lead to a massive wave of migration from the poor nations to the rich nations, and that the probable result of such a massive wave would be a drastic reduction in the average living standards within the rich nations. In other words, it is believed that the effects of free migration would be basically equivalent to those of a global welfare state. The potential dangers from unrestricted immigration may be exaggerated but they certainly cannot be ignored. Therefore the elimination of barriers to human mobility within the Federal Union will have to await successful completion of the Global Marshall Plan to be discussed below. This will probably entail a period of at least several decades.

The Complementary Economic Proposal. Apart from the natural apprehensions induced by the daily possibility of instantaneous nuclear Armageddon, the decades of the Cold War instilled in humanity far greater consciousness than ever before of the global economic gap, of the tremendous gulf that separates the high average living standards in the minority of rich nations from the low average living standards in the majority of poor nations. This economic gap was a major factor in the geopolitical situation during the Cold War, as both the wealthier capitalist nations and the communist nations endeavored to win over the nonaligned Third World nations to their respective sides of the ideological struggle. In some Third World nations, such as Cuba and Vietnam, the appeal made by the international communist movement to the natural resentments among the poor against the rich, was obviously effective. On the other hand, most Third World nations avoided communist political takeovers. There is little doubt, however, that communist ideology was a divisive force within these nations, and also contributed to strained and distrustful relations between these nations and the wealthy First World nations.

Now that the ideological impediment to world government has declined to what many would consider a vestigial level, the relative importance of the economic impediment has become paramount. During the Cold War, the non-communist nations were leery of world government on grounds that it might be subverted by the communist nations and transformed into a tool of communist expansionism. At the same time, the communist nations were leery of world government on grounds that it might be subverted (from their point of view) and transformed into a tool of capitalistic reaction. Now that the Cold War has faded into insignificance, the rich nations are leery of world government on grounds that it might be controlled by the poor nations and transformed into a tool for the radical transfer of current income from the rich nations to the poor nations. At the same time, the poor nations are leery of world government on grounds that it might be controlled by the rich nations and transformed into a tool for the reestablishment of colonial-style economic exploitation of the poor nations. The principal obstacle to world government has in effect shifted from the East-West ideological conflict to the North-South economic gap.

Not that this situation is clearly recognized and openly acknowledged within either the rich nations or the poor nations. At the present time, discussion of the world government possibility among the intelligentsia, the political leadership, and the general public, is so limited as to be virtually nonexistent. People are so deeply convinced that world government is a utopian pipedream that they deem it unworthy of thought and discussion. Nevertheless, it remains the case that if world government is indeed a utopian pipedream, there should be plausible reasons why it would be undesirable. It contradicts the rationality of humanity to hold that world government is a utopian pipedream in the absence of plausible reasons why it would be undesirable. What, then, are these reasons? If required to respond to this question, the typical person would respond to the effect: "If there existed a world government to which my own nation was subordinate, foreign interests would impose oppressive conditions upon my nation and myself." But what, exactly, would these "oppressive conditions" entail? A citizen of a poor nation will tend to define oppressive conditions in terms of the reestablishment of colonial-style exploitation: the plundering of natural resources, the hindering of self-sufficiency and industrialization, and so on. Meanwhile, a citizen of a rich nation will tend to define oppressive conditions in terms of enforced redistribution of substantial amounts of goods and resources from the rich nations to the poor nations: an extravagant global welfare state. Oppression, for both, means primarily *economic* oppression.

According to World Bank statistical data, most of the Third World nations made respectable gains in per capita income during the latter part of the twentieth century and into the twenty-first, the principal exception being some nations in sub-Saharan Africa. On the other hand, economic growth has, on the whole, been stronger in the richest nations, with the consequence that the gap between the richest nations and the poorest nations has been getting wider.

Figure 9.1. Per Capita Income (PCY) Growth, 1980-2010, United States, Japan, China, India

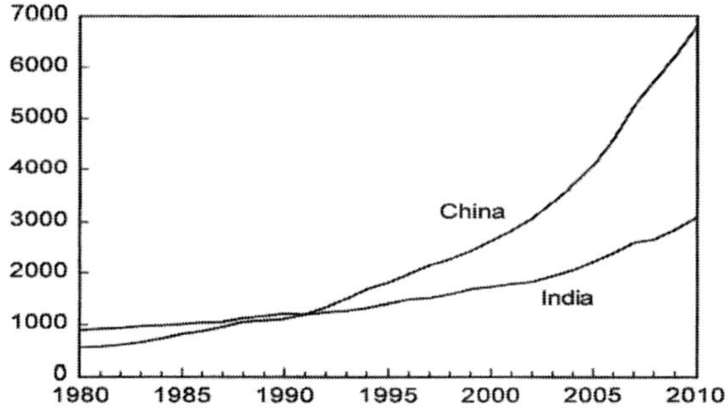

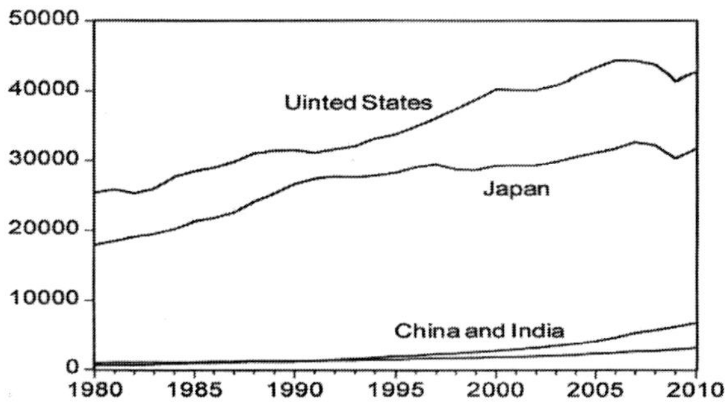

These points are illustrated by the upper and lower panels of Figure 9.1, based on data from the World Bank's *World Development Indicators* database. The upper panel shows economic growth in terms of per capita income (PCY) from 1980 to 2010 for China and India, where per capita income is defined as Gross National Income (GNI) per capita in constant 2005 U.S. $. Both the Chinese and the Indian plots show apparently healthy upward trends, albeit Chinese growth has obviously been considerably stronger over the latter part of the period. However, the lower panel shows economic growth in terms of per capita income from 1980 to 2010 for China, India, the United States, and Japan. Owing to the different units of measure on the vertical axis, the plots for China and India in the lower panel appear to be almost horizontal for much of the interval. This demonstrates that when the economic situation of low-income nations such as China and India is directly compared to the economic situation of high-income nations such as the United States and Japan, the magnitude of the problem becomes obvious. Not only is the existing economic gap very wide, but the gap is getting wider.

One might entertain reassuring thoughts about this situation. For example, the customary measures of national income and output exaggerate the economic gap because they take inadequate account of non-market production and consumption, and non-market production and consumption are relatively more important in the poorer nations. But such thoughts may well manifest little more than wishful thinking. While purchasing power parity (PPP) measures of per capita income show somewhat smaller differentials between the rich nations and the poor nations than the customary measures, the differentials are still extremely large.

Practical evidence of the extent and significance of the economic gap is found in the sad fact that the immigration services of the rich nations are perpetually engaged in a terrific struggle to curtail immigration from the poor nations. Few people doubt that if the restrictive immigration policies of the rich nations were relaxed, there would occur a tidal wave of immigration from the poor nations to the rich nations. Of course these policies, as necessary as they may be to preserving the prevailing living standards within the rich nations, are a perpetual thorn in the side of relations between poor nations and rich nations.

Granting that a great deal of economic inequality exists among the nations of the contemporary world, however, the question remains of just how serious a problem this is. Many historians and social analysts will argue that while existing world economic inequality is unfortunate and regrettable, it does not represent—in and of itself and in the larger scheme of things—a major hazard to the future prospects of human civilization. Various evidence might be cited in support of this proposition. To begin with, history provides an abundance of examples of warfare among peoples and nations that were quite homogeneous in terms of economic circumstances. For example, at the outbreak of World War I, living standards in the contesting nations of France and Germany were quite comparable. Indeed, the example of World War I, among others, suggests that geographical contiguity is a far more significant factor in the outbreak of warfare than economic inequality. Other factors that have apparently contributed to hostility and warfare in the past include racial differences, religious differences, ideological differences, and cultural differences. In light of all these other contributory factors, the role of economic inequality might have been relatively minor.

Clearly this argument possesses a degree of merit, to the extent that it makes us aware of the fact that economic inequality is only one of several contributory factors to international tension, hostility, conflict, and warfare. On the other hand, the fact that economic inequality is only one of several factors does not translate into the proposition that economic inequality is unimportant. History is full of plundering expeditions by poorer peoples desirous of appropriating the material possessions of richer peoples. One thinks of the barbarian invasions of the Roman empire, of the Viking depredations of the coastal areas of Britain and other European nations, of the Mongol invasions of China and Russia.

Nor is the economic incentive to aggressive warfare exclusively confined to the earlier periods of human history. The critical catalytic factor in the two world wars of the twentieth century was Germany's self-perception as a "have-not" nation. The critical factor in the buildup of tension that culminated in World War I was Germany's desire to possess an overseas colonial empire equivalent to that of Britain and France. The critical factor in the buildup of tension that culminated in World War II was Nazi Germany's desire to carve a huge land empire out of Eastern Europe and the Soviet Union, an empire which would have been equivalent to the overseas colonial empires of Britain and France. As a matter of fact, living standards in Germany just prior to both World War I and World War II, were equivalent to those in Britain and France, and they were certainly higher than those in Eastern Europe and the Soviet Union. This did not prevent Germany from considering itself a "have-not" nation in relation to such "have" nations as Britain and France. If nations that are deprived only in a psychological sense, as opposed to a legitimate material sense, can inculcate such emotions of (in their view) legitimate resentment, how much greater might this tendency be in nations which actually are seriously deprived in a legitimate material sense.

Historians and social analysts inclined to deprecate the role of economic inequality in generating international instability might acknowledge the significance in past history of plundering expeditions by poorer societies against richer societies, but they will argue that such expeditions are no longer feasible in the contemporary world owing to technological developments in weaponry. These developments have endowed the military forces of the rich nations with tremendous superiority over those of the poor nations. They might cite the Persian Gulf War of January-February 1991—in which the technically superior and better trained forces of the U.S.-led coalition slaughtered Iraqi forces with impunity—as an example of what would assuredly happen if a poor nation were ever imprudent enough to invade a rich nation.

Even assuming that this is true at the present time, and without commenting on the morality (or lack thereof) of this somewhat arrogant attitude, there are at least two important counterpoints to be made. First, this attitude neglects the continuing financial costs of supporting a military establishment sufficiently strong to deter aggression by poor nations for a prolonged period stretching into the indefinite future. Military expenditures by the rich nations have indeed declined significantly since the demise of the Cold War, but they have not declined as much as would have been possible in the absence of the large economic gap. If all or most nations had roughly equivalent per capita income, and thus the tendency toward economically inspired aggression were much lower, it might become possible for the rich nations to reduce military expenditure to only one or two percent of Gross National Product. The second point is that it is imprudent to assume that the military situation that holds today will persist indefinitely into the future. It is not impossible that a relatively poor nation will become a military superpower in the future.

Indeed, the People's Republic of China is an obvious candidate for this status. There are some interesting parallels between the PRC and Japan. When Japan joined the Axis in the 1930s and embarked upon its career of aggressive expansion that contributed to World War II, it was an "up and coming" nation that deemed itself, despite its ever-increasing material prosperity, a "have-not" nation. The fateful "Greater East-Asia Co-Prosperity Sphere" represented an effort by Japan to escape what it considered to be economic subservience to foreign interests. Should the PRC determine to pursue its economically defined national interests more aggressively in the future, history might repeat itself (albeit not in exactly the same way), with consequences that might be even worse.

A Global Marshall Plan. Possibly a major reason why so many people, not only among the general public but also among the intelligentsia and political leadership, have such a difficult time perceiving the true depth and significance of the world economic inequality situation, is that they are absolutely convinced that there is little or nothing that can be done about it. Resignation is a virtue, and psychologists agree that it is unhealthy to dwell upon serious problems that have no solution. Thus if the world economic inequality situation actually is impermeable, then it would be perfectly reasonable to ignore it or minimize it. On the other hand, if plausible means exist toward the amelioration or elimination of a serious problem, resignation is no longer a virtue but is rather a vice. Let us consider, therefore, whether any plausible means exist toward the amelioration or elimination of the world economic inequality problem.

From a purely technical standpoint, it would be possible to set up a global welfare state that would assure every living individual a substantial guaranteed minimum income, with the program financed from a progressive personal income tax. Clearly the costs of the program would fall mostly upon the populations of the rich nations, while the benefits would go mostly to the populations of the poor nations. In prior research, I examined the numerical implications of this policy, for which I coined the term "Crude Redistribution." Although the numerical implications of a global welfare state engaged in Crude Redistribution vary depending upon assumptions (e.g., concerning the disincentive effects of income taxation), even in the most optimistic scenarios, the tax rates necessary to finance such a program for any meaningful level of guaranteed minimum income, would be astronomical by current standards. Crude Redistribution is clearly politically impossible. Only if the rich nations were under military occupation following defeat by the poor nations, would they accede to such a program.

However, my purpose in demonstrating numerically the impracticality of Crude Redistribution was not to imply that the problem of world economic inequality has no solution. It was rather to compare and contrast, in a tangible way, the policy of "Crude Redistribution" with the policy of "Common Progress." Whereas Crude Redistribution envisions equalization of post-tax-and-benefit living standards across nations at a relatively low level somewhere between those of the rich nations and those of the poor nations (but closer to the latter), Common Progress envisions equalization of average national living standards at a high level even beyond those currently prevailing in the rich nations. The rationale for the term "Common Progress" is that economic progress is to be common to all nations, rich and poor alike. This concept could provide the basis for a politically feasible route toward equalization of average living standards across nations.

The concept could be implemented by means of an international foreign development assistance program on an unprecedentedly large scale. Basically the idea is simply that of a "Global Marshall Plan" (GMP), albeit on a far more ambitious scale both geographically and financially than the program that assisted the reconstruction of Western Europe following World War II. Another descriptive name for such a program is the "World Economic Equalization Program" (WEEP). Although WEEP and GMP are conceptually interchangeable, in my more recent writing I have gravitated toward the latter term. As an economist by profession, I have personally contributed a significant amount of preliminary research on the concept, comprising to this point two professional books and four professional journal articles.

The research involves computer simulation of a numerically implemented model of the global economy. These contributions demonstrate the distinct possibility that a sufficiently massive Global Marshall Plan might achieve a veritably dazzling level of success within a relatively brief period of historical time, on the order of 40 to 50 years. My most recent contribution on the subject is a book entitled *Global Marshall Plan: Theory and Evidence* (2014). The numerical results described in the following are derived from this latest iteration of the research.

Whether designated the World Economic Equalization Program (WEEP) or the Global Marshall Plan (GMP), the program must be based absolutely on the principle of Common Progress. Another key feature of the envisioned Global Marshall Plan is that it would be regarded from the outset as a *tentative and provisional* project, whose continuation beyond a trial period of perhaps 10 to 20 years would depend on dramatic material progress being observed in most participating nations. Of course, the conventional wisdom at the present time is that such a program would be doomed to abject failure: it would merely provide an opportunity for corrupt bureaucrats and dishonest businessmen to enrich themselves, and little or no improvement would occur in the living standards of the great mass of the population. Of course the possibility exists that this belief is merely a shallow rationalization for a policy of short-sighted selfishness, and as such is unworthy of the higher qualities within human nature. But if after a fair experiment, the pessimists are vindicated in their judgment of the uselessness of large-scale foreign aid, then the GMP would be quickly and permanently shut down, and the pessimists would then have ample opportunity to crow and gloat over their own wisdom and prescience.

The research reported in *Global Marshall Plan* utilizes conventional quantitative economic methodology. A production function is specified for each nation giving total output as a function of labor (proxied by population), generalized capital (which incorporates plant and machinery, social overhead capital, and education/training inputs into the labor force), and the total factor productivity coefficient. Output is then allocated to four uses: domestic consumption, domestic investment in generalized capital, military expenditure, and (in the case of the richer nations) a contribution into the "total transfer fund." The total transfer fund is then allocated over the poor recipient nations on the basis of poverty and population. For a given level of population, the lower the per capita income of the recipient nation the larger its share of the transfer fund; and for a given level of per capita income, the higher the population of the recipient nation the larger its share of the transfer fund. Transfer fund shares of the recipient nations are used to expand their generalized capital resources.

The dataset used for GMP model validation purposes was taken from the World Bank's *World Development Indicators* databank. This dataset consists of annual values from 1980 through 2010 (31 years inclusive) for total population *P* and for four comparable per capita income (PCY) measures for the 146 nations that were listed in the data source as having populations of one million or more in 1980. It was found from experiment that qualitatively the results from the simulations are virtually the same regardless of which particular World Bank measure of per capita income is utilized.

Once the mathematical structure of the model has been specified, a set of benchmark numerical parameter values are determined. These numerical values are set so as to achieve as close a fit as possible between the observed behavior of per capita income across nations over the "validation interval" extending from 1980 through 2010, and the computed behavior of per capita income from the GMP model simulation over the same interval. Although the GMP model does not track short-term fluctuations in national per capita income, for most nations it does a respectable job of estimating long-run trends between 1980 and 2010. With this validation of the model in hand, the research proceeds to the policy simulations: "what-if" experiments on the possible effects of a Global Marshall Plan.

The 1980-2010 validation simulation assumes that no GMP is in operation (none of the rich nations makes any contribution to the transfer fund). The policy simulations, on the other hand, assume that such contributions might be made, and covers the interval from 2010 through 2060. Therefore, the policy simulations estimate what might have happened had a Global Marshall Plan been commenced in 2010. The central implication from the research is that very rapid acceleration in the average living standards of the poor nations might be possible without excessive diminution of the rate of rise of average living standards in the rich nations.

The upper and lower panels of Figure 9.2 show projected per capita income growth in terms of Gross National Income per capita in constant 2005 U.S. dollars, over the policy interval from 2010 to 2060, for seven per capita income groups. The upper panel shows the situation without a GMP in operation; the lower panel shows the situation with a GMP in operation. Obviously the perfectly smooth curves shown in these graphs would not be observed over the coming decades. The GMP model does not incorporate the manifold sources of random variation in the real world. Nevertheless, the good fit between the GMP model results and the observed empirical results over the 1980-2010 validation interval gives us solid grounds for expecting that if random variation is suppressed, the real-world results might be well tracked by the model results. What the upper panel of Figure 9.2 suggests is that without a Global Marshall Plan in operation, we can expect continued widening of the economic gap between rich and poor nations. What the lower panel of Figure 9.2 suggests is that with a Global Marshall Plan in operation, there could be a remarkable narrowing of the economic gap within just a few decades. Furthermore, this narrowing would not be at the cost of a significant reduction in the rate of PCY growth in the rich nations.

Figure 9.2. Graphical Comparison: Weighted Mean PCY Growth for Seven Income Groups, Projected 2010-2060, with and without GMP

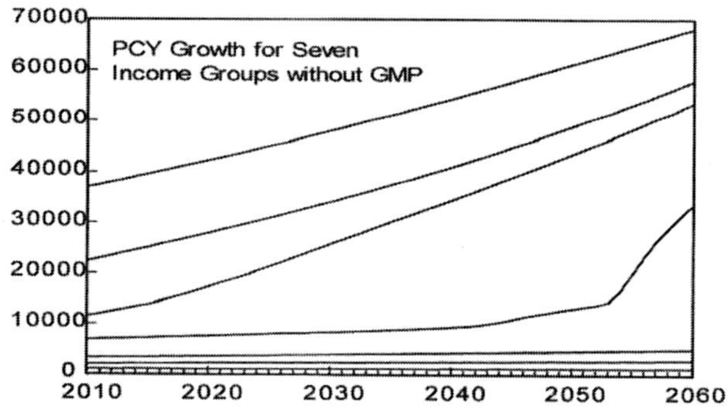

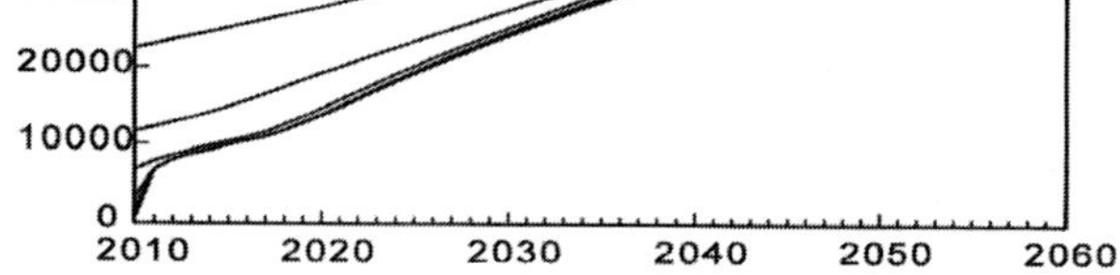

The conventional viewpoint in the world today, especially in the richer nations, is that a very large-scale economic development assistance program along the lines of the envisioned GMP would inevitably be a very expensive failure. Such a program would impact heavily on economic growth in the rich nations, reducing it very substantially. At the same time, improvement in the poor nations would be at best modest and at worst negligible. Therefore the natural reaction to the benchmark GMP model result described above stemming from this conventional viewpoint is that these results are simply too good to be true. Either the GMP model itself is in error (does not represent an adequate approximation to actual variables and relationships), or else the benchmark parameter values are in error (do not represent adequate approximations to actual numerical parameter values).

As for the model, it will have to suffice here to state that it is based on conventional and widely accepted economic principles (detailed technical arguments to this effect are provided in *Global Marshall Plan*, Chapter 3). The benchmark numerical values of the model's parameters are another story—it cannot be reasonably maintained that these values are "very conventional and widely accepted." The fact is that the theoretical content of contemporary economics is far more substantial than its empirical content. Whatever actual numbers are utilized for economic model parameters are normally subject to a considerable amount of uncertainty and error.

Therefore, in assessing the policy implications of any particular economic model, considerable weight is normally placed on sensitivity analysis: on the investigation of how changes in the parametric input into the model simulation affect the numerical output. The question addressed is: How robust are particular qualitative policy indications against changes in parameter values? Do these qualitative policy indications change dramatically if parameter values are changed slightly? If so, we deem the initial policy indications to be non-robust. On the other hand, do these qualitative policy indications remain basically intact despite substantial variation in the numerical values of the parameters? If so, we deem the initial policy indications to be robust. In the case of the present research, the initial policy indication is that a Global Marshall Plan would be highly beneficial. The sensitivity analysis utilized in this research explores in considerable detail the extent to which this indication is robust against parametric variation.

It is shown in Chapter 4 of *Global Marshall Plan* that for most of the 14 parameters of the GMP model, substantial variation in the numerical parameter value around the benchmark value does not materially affect the extremely favorable outcome. However, there are two principal exceptions to this rule, exceptions that were not unexpected. One of these relates to ξ, the parameter that determines the extent to which initial differentials in per capita income PCY are the result of differentials in total factor productivity A, as opposed to differentials in generalized capital stocks K. According to critics of foreign aid, a major reason for its ineffectiveness lies in the economically dysfunctional institutional and cultural characteristics of the recipient nations. This translates into the proposition that most of the observed differences in economic output among nations are not owing to differences in generalized capital resources, but are rather owing to differences in total factor productivity, itself a function of the institutional and cultural characteristics of the respective nations. Numerically this implies that the ξ parameter takes on a relatively high value. The other principal exception relates to χ, the parameter that determines how much of the recipient nation's share in the total transfer fund is effectively converted into generalized capital. The familiar proposition that foreign aid is mostly diverted by corrupt bureaucrats and dishonest businessmen into their own pockets and therefore generates very little benefit for the general population in the poor nations, translates into a relatively low value of the χ parameter.

The benchmark value of ξ is 0, indicating that *all* per capita income differentials are the consequence of K differentials rather than A differentials. This would be the most favorable case. As ξ increases toward 1, the model simulations demonstrate that the effectiveness of the GMP in reducing world inequality by raising output in the poor nations steadily diminishes. If $\xi = 1$, indicating that *all* per capita income differentials are the consequence of A differentials rather than K differentials (the least favorable case), then the GMP is in fact a complete failure: it has virtually no impact on world inequality. However, there are two important points revealed by the simulations with increasing ξ values. The first is that the ξ value has to become very large for the GMP to be completely ineffective. The second point is that the cost to the rich nations of the GMP program, in terms of reduced economic growth, is minimal whatever the value of ξ. In other words, the implication is that *if* the Global Marshall Plan is indeed a failure, this would be manifested in the poor nations failing to make significant economic progress, not in the rich nations experiencing a significantly lower rate of economic progress.

Results for the χ parameter are analogous to those just described for the ξ parameter. The simulations for χ variation show that χ has to take an extremely adverse value to render the GMP completely ineffective in raising output in the poor nations and decreasing world inequality; they also show that regardless of the χ value, the cost of a GMP to the rich nations, in terms of reduced growth, would be minimal. On the whole, therefore, it can be said that the qualitative conclusion that a Global Marshall Plan would be beneficial to humanity is quite robust against parametric variation of the GMP model.

No one is more aware of the limitations of economic models than economists themselves. In legal terms, any evidence forthcoming from either analytical or computational economic analysis must be considered "circumstantial." Nevertheless, results forthcoming from economic analyses are entitled to more weight than are the speculations, informed by prejudice and preconception, on which so much human decision-making is actually based. Critics of foreign aid regard it as a "proven fact" that foreign aid is ineffective. They point to the fact that billions of dollars of foreign aid have been disbursed over the last half-century—and the poor nations are still poor. This is analogous to saying that modern medicine is ineffective because people still inevitably die. The fact is that with the single major exception of sub-Saharan Africa, the Less Developed Countries (LDCs) have made considerable economic progress over the last half-century, and there is no compelling evidence that foreign aid was not a significant contributor to this progress. For example, several "Asian tiger" nations which registered truly dramatic progress, such as South Korea, were major recipients of foreign aid during their early growth.

For most LDCs, obviously, not as much economic progress has occurred as we would have preferred. Why is this? The suggestion which I offer is that the *amount* of effective foreign aid (netting out military aid and less beneficial aid forms such as food aid) has simply not been adequate to produce definitive success. Just as in nuclear physics a critical mass of uranium is required to commence a chain reaction, so too in development economics a critical mass of foreign aid is required to achieve a high degree of economic equalization across nations. In the past, the foreign aid effort of the rich nations fell far short of the necessary critical mass. "Billions and billions of dollars" of foreign aid is not necessarily so impressive when one reflects that there are billions and billions of poor people living in the contemporary world.

Among other things, the GMP model simulations compute for each contributor nation the percentages of GNP which the transfer fund contributions would represent. These percentages are much larger than what has been witnessed in the past, but they are by no means unmanageable. For example, according to the benchmark GMP model simulation, over the first 25 years of operation of the GMP, the United States would contribute approximately 3 percent of its GNP to the transfer fund. Between 2000 and 2010, United States defense outlays averaged slightly under 4 percent, well down from its Cold War high of 9.7 percent, set in 1968 at the height of the Vietnam War. Throughout the post-World War II era, the United States has devoted a substantial proportion of its national output to deadweight military purposes, and not merely has economic catastrophe been averted but the long-term economic growth of the nation has been quite strong. This is compelling evidence that the United States could devote a substantial proportion of its national output to foreign development assistance over the next few decades without incurring unacceptable economic costs. If the United States is capable of this, so too are the other wealthy nations.

The Global Marshall Plan and the Federal Union of Democratic Nations are complementary proposals. Of course, many of those with more conservative predispositions, even if they could be persuaded to seriously entertain the possibility of a Global Marshall Plan, would probably advise that the establishment of a world government be postponed until the success of the GMP had been demonstrated. That, in their view, would be the safer course. But as long as the world state under consideration incorporates the limitations previously discussed (the right of member nations to maintain military forces, and to secede at their own discretion, plus the dual voting system in the federation legislature), it would be sufficiently safe against the threat of Crude Redistribution. The existence of an operating Federal Union of Democratic Nations would contribute to a spirit of supernational patriotism throughout the world (if only weakly at first), and this spirit would enhance the likelihood that the Global Marshall Plan would be pursued long enough and vigorously enough to achieve final success.

Evaluation

For the most part, specialists in international organization do not consider that any form of world government will become feasible at any point within the foreseeable future, and therefore deem it unworthy of detailed consideration. Most discussions of world government in the professional and textbook literature are sketchy outlines of the progress of the concept in the history of ideas, to which is appended a cursory dismissal as far as the contemporary real world is concerned. The usual basis for the dismissal is the assertion that the contemporary human population is far too heterogeneous and diverse—economically, religiously, and ideologically—for peacefully attained universal political unity to be feasible. According to this conventional viewpoint, the only kind of state entity capable of encompassing and controlling such diversity would be a ruthlessly totalitarian regime determined to expunge and annihilate any and all vestiges of dissent.

In the well-known formulation of Kenneth Waltz, the degree of coercion necessary to hold a political system together is positively related to the heterogeneity of the population. The current world population is highly diverse—ergo, only a brutal totalitarian regime could hold its various components in check. In the following well-known passage from *Man, the State and War* (1959), Waltz applies the principle to suggest the imprudence of contemplating world government:

> Yet in the international as in the domestic sphere, if anarchy is the cause [of monstrous behavior], the obvious conclusion is that government is the cure… The problem, however, becomes a practical one. The amount of force needed to hold a society together varies with the heterogeneity of the elements composing it. World federalists write as though the only alternatives before us were unity or death. "World government is necessary and therefore possible," Robert Maynard Hutchins avers. But demonstrating the need for an institution does not bring it into existence. And were world government attempted, we might find ourselves dying in the attempt, or uniting and living a life worse than death.

Implicit in this passage, which is typical of the mainstream international relations literature, is an assumption that the essential *precondition* for successful world government is the attainment of a very high degree of socioeconomic homogeneity and psychological consensus among humanity. This assumption fails to recognize two critical aspects of the relationship between social uniformity and political unity: the *continuous nature* of the relationship, and the *interactive nature* of the relationship.

First, the relationship between social uniformity and political unity at any one point in time is a smooth and continuous relationship: the higher the degree of social uniformity achieved, the higher the level of political unity that may be established. To have a *very high* level of political unity in a world government—that is to say, an extremely strong, centralized, and authoritative world government (an omnipotent world state)—we would need a very high level of social uniformity. We are not here concerned with any such world government. If we are content with a *reasonable* level of political unity at the global level—that is to say, with a limited world government along the lines of the Federal Union of Democratic Nations—then we would *not* need a very high level of social uniformity.

Second, the relationship between social uniformity and political unity over a period of time is an interactive and mutually reinforcing relationship: the mere existence of political unity, albeit weak in the beginning, tends gradually to generate a higher level of social uniformity, and as social uniformity increases, it in turn permits a higher level of political unity. Thus the relationship over time between social uniformity and political unity is not static but dynamic: a mutually reinforcing, snowballing process is created that over time will tend toward a high (albeit far from "complete") level of both social uniformity and political unity.

Consider the traditional question: Which came first—the chicken or the egg? What makes the question absurd, and therefore humorous, is that *neither* the modern chicken nor the modern egg came first. The modern chicken-egg-chicken progression is the result of millions of years of slow, evolutionary development with roots in the primeval slime. Those who argue that it is necessary to have a high level of social uniformity prior to having an effective state are equivalent to those who would argue, in response to the chicken-egg question, that since chickens come out of eggs, then the egg came first. The problem with this argument, obviously, is that it is also true that eggs come out of chickens.

If we take social and attitudinal homogeneity to be the egg, and the effectiveness of state organization (i.e. political unity) to be the chicken, the relevance of the chicken-egg question becomes clear. A population which is politically united within the same state organization tends to become, over time, more socially and attitudinally homogeneous. Similarly, as a given population becomes more socially and attitudinally homogeneous, its state organization tends to become more effective—among other reasons, because it expends less resources on enforcing the majority will upon recalcitrant minorities. There is an ongoing, progressive, interactive, mutually reinforcing, snowballing process between the social and attitudinal homogeneity of a given population, and the effectiveness of the state organization within which it is politically united.

It is reasonably obvious, to all but the most enthusiastic proponents of world government, that the degree of homogeneity among nations today is insufficient to support a world state with an amount of practical and moral authority over the nations of the world analogous to that, for example, of the national government of the United States today over the 50 state governments. This means that an *extremely* powerful, effective, and authoritative world state is an impossibility at the present time. It does *not* mean that a *somewhat* powerful, effective, and authoritative world state is an impossibility at the present time. The constraints which are integral components of the proposed Federal Union of Democratic Nations would make this limited form of world government acceptable to many if not most nations of the world today—if and when they become aware of the possibility. If and when such a Union is established, it would then commence a long-term process of gradual evolution—just as did the United States—toward a higher level of homogeneity among its citizens, and a higher level of effectiveness in its operations.

In terms of the chicken-egg analogy, the "egg" which we have at the present time (the level of social homogeneity throughout the contemporary world), and the "chicken" which is capable of coming forth from this egg (the level of political unity which could be achieved by a world government established at the present point in history), are both fairly primitive versions of what we eventually hope to achieve. The ancient egg and the ancient chicken were virtually unrecognizable relative to their modern counterparts. But we should not (to utilize the well-known adage) allow the best to be the enemy of the good. It is certainly true that the world government that we could establish today would be far short of the ideal that might be imagined. Such a world government would not directly and immediately banish the threat of nuclear holocaust, would not directly and immediately banish such equally serious threats as genocidal outbreaks and accelerating environmental degradation. But these facts should not obscure the very high probability that a world government *would* establish a more secure institutional foundation for long-term efforts toward the reduction of such threats as nuclear holocaust, genocidal outbreaks, and accelerating environmental degradation.

The memorable "life worse than death" phrase from Kenneth Waltz dates from 1959, and the sentiment it expresses was echoed by any number of other authorities from the Cold War era. After the collapse of Soviet socialism and the dissolution of the USSR in 1991, however, world government skeptics could no longer rely on ideological conflict as a compelling argument against the feasibility of world government. Their dismissal of the concept had to be shifted to other "heterogeneities" aside from ideology. For example, in his one-page discussion of world government in his 1999 international relations college textbook, Mark Amstutz states:

> A stable world government needs a centralized governmental structure and widespread shared values and aspirations. A world federal regime will require the creation of both a central authority and strong social, economic, cultural, and political affinities. The dilemma of world government is this: the international system needs world government to reduce the threat of war, but the precondition for world government is world community, which can only be solidified through the political transformation of the anarchic world system.

Although the general thrust of the passage is obviously that world government is unlikely, the statement is not quite clear. What, precisely, is meant by "the political transformation of the anarchic world system"? If by this is meant "the establishment of a world government," then we would have a logical refutation of the possibility of world government along "Catch 22" lines: you can't have world government without world community, but you can't have world community without world government. This would constitute a sensible interpretation of the word "dilemma," but then the argument could be satirized as follows: "You can't have a chicken without an egg, and you can't have an egg without a chicken, therefore chickens and eggs are impossible."

On the other hand, if by the phrase "the political transformation of the anarchic world system," Professor Amstutz means "the achievement of a high degree of mutual toleration and cooperation among sovereign nations," this is not a "dilemma" but a "problem." More importantly, he offers no reason why the *present* level of mutual toleration and cooperation among sovereign nations is not sufficient to the establishment of a world government—*of a limited nature*. He cannot cite, as did the international relations authorities of the Cold War era, the ideological gap between the Soviet Union and the non-communist world.

He could cite, however, the issues dividing the First World and the Third World, i.e. the absence of "economic affinities" between the rich nations and the poor nations. As a matter of fact, although it was overshadowed during the Cold War era by ideological discord, the economic gap was always just as serious an impediment to world government as was the ideological gap. But even as the ideological gap need not necessarily have abrogated the possibility of world government during the Cold War period, so too the economic gap need not abrogate the possibility of world government during the post-Cold War period. What could have worked then, and what could work now, is a limited world government along the lines of the Federal Union of Democratic Nations. All that is needed to perceive this possibility is a certain amount of mental flexibility and vision.

Throughout most of the second half of the twentieth century, mankind lived in the shadow of nuclear catastrophe. There were massive arsenals of nuclear warheads and, particularly after the development of intercontinental ballistic missiles, extremely rapid and reliable means of delivery. If the decision had been made by top level officials that total war was necessary, then within a few hours, hundreds of millions would have been dead or dying, and much of human civilization would have lain in ruins. Proponents of world government, alarmed by this situation, urged the formation of a world state as a means of reducing this dire threat. But the decision had been taken, by the overwhelming majority in all walks of life within the Western non-communist nations, that the possibility of nuclear catastrophe constituted an acceptable risk in the interest of preserving the capitalistic way of life ("freedom") and preventing the imposition of communistic totalitarianism.

Proponents of world government were chided by mainstream authorities in the tradition of Kenneth Waltz, because they could provide "no plausible scenario" by which a benign world government could be established within an international community beset by intense ideological controversy. But the mainstream authorities themselves never troubled to provide "plausible scenarios" by which a world government in which the Western non-communist nations were founding members, could be subverted and turned into an instrument for the abolition of the capitalistic way of life and the imposition of communistic totalitarianism. Of course, the communist leaders were also concerned that a world government would be subverted (from their point of view) and made into an instrument for the abolition of the communist way of life. They also did not bother with constructing "plausible scenarios" by which this intolerable outcome would come to pass.

The Federal Union of Democratic Nations described herein could have provided, even at the height of the Cold War, a type of world government which might have been acceptable to both the communist and non-communist national leaders. Obviously, the founding constitution would have had to be neutral on the issue of capitalism versus socialism, just as most national constitutions throughout the world today are neutral on religion. It would have had to have been specified in the federation constitution that the Union "would make no law respecting the ownership of capital property." Thus the non-communist nations could have continued to uphold private ownership of capital, while the communist nations could have continued to specify public ownership of capital. This would not have prevented the communist nations from peacefully arguing the alleged virtues of socialism in an effort to persuade the populations of the non-communist nations; while at the same time the non-communist nations peacefully argued the alleged virtues of capitalism for an analogous purpose. This could have been done in much the same way that religious missionary efforts are conducted in the contemporary world.

The practicality of the proposed limited federal world government under consideration here is based upon one simple but profound insight: it is possible to create a meaningful and effective federal government without requiring its component political units to be militarily defenseless, and without forbidding them from detaching themselves from the union if that is their wish. Needless to emphasize, few national governments in the contemporary world would be comfortable about explicitly authorizing their subsidiary units (states, provinces, districts, and so on) to maintain whatever military forces they desire, and to declare their independence from the nation whenever they desire. Such liberties are commonly perceived as contradictory to the core principle of national sovereignty. The armed forces of subsidiary political units are typically regarded as potential threats to the authority of the national government. And history is littered with examples similar to the United States Civil War of 1861-1865, precipitated by unauthorized declarations of independence by the Southern states. These declarations were regarded as treasonous and were met with military force.

Nevertheless, we need not be imprisoned by the past. We need not be constricted within an intellectual straitjacket composed of traditional thinking about government and sovereignty. The fact is that the national governments of today are not at all comparable to a potential future world government. A potential future world government would be operating within a very different environment from that confronting the national governments of today. Therefore its institutional structure and operating procedures would, quite appropriately, be very much distinct from those of today's national governments. Human knowledge, understanding, and flexibility are advancing on many fronts. This is—or can be—as true in the area of political organization as it is in other areas. The world is changing, and we need evolving concepts of political organization to cope with the evolving world in which we live.

The proposal for a Federal Union of Democratic Nations is entirely and fundamentally innovative. Nowhere in the annals of world federalist thinking will be found a scheme of world government that allows the member nations to arm themselves as they please, and to withdraw from the federation whenever they please at their own unilateral discretion. The conventional world government scheme of today envisions what is descriptively termed the "omnipotent world state": member nations would be fully disarmed, and any move toward independence by a member nation would be instantly suppressed by armed force. Such a world state, it is true, would virtually eliminate the possibility of a sudden nuclear holocaust of the sort that has haunted the nightmares of humanity ever since the atomic bombings of Hiroshima and Nagasaki in 1945. Unfortunately, such a world state might also quickly degenerate into a totalitarian nightmare equivalent to what Hitler and Stalin inflicted on their respective nations during the worst years of the twentieth century.

In the years following the Second World War, world federalists put the case for an omnipotent world state before the court of global public opinion. The case was quickly and definitively rejected: fear of global tyranny trumped fear of nuclear holocaust. To this day, however, "traditional" world federalists continue to insist that the threat of nuclear holocaust is far more dangerous than the threat of global tyranny. Conceivably they are correct about this, but the only way they will be proved correct is if nuclear holocaust befalls the world. And then, of course, it will be too late. It has sometimes been suggested that only a nuclear holocaust will convince humanity of the necessity for an omnipotent world state. Rather more likely is that the embittered and impoverished survivors of a nuclear holocaust would be fragmented into a host of independent mini-states ruled by brutal warlords thirsting for revenge, who would thereafter make perpetual war upon one another with whatever weapons were available, as the human race slides inexorably toward a new dark age. Whatever the aftermath of nuclear holocaust might be, in the absence of nuclear holocaust, it is difficult to imagine how traditional world federalists will get the majority of humanity to change its mind on this issue and embrace the omnipotent world state—especially now that the ebbing of the Cold War has greatly diminished the immediate threat of nuclear holocaust.

Most traditional world federalists today would be inclined to dismiss such notions as the member nations of a world federation arming themselves as they please and leaving the federation whenever they please, as manifestly unworkable. They cannot imagine that such a world government would persist for any length of time and achieve anything worthwhile. They would predict that within a few years—a decade or two at the most—the federation would have splintered into its component nations, and humanity would be right back to where it is today, confronting the possibility of nuclear holocaust brought about by the inevitable suspicion and mutual hostility endemic to the sovereign nation-state system.

I would ask: *How can they be so sure?* How can they be so sure that a limited world government along the lines proposed would be so useless that it is not even worthy of experiment? The establishment of a such a world government would obviously be in the nature of an experiment. If the Federal Union of Democratic Nations soon flies apart from centrifugal forces, there would be no need for a central decision to dissolve it, since it would be effectively dissolved via the independent decisions of its component nations. If pessimistic skeptics are correct, and both the Federal Union (as well as its economic complement, the Global Marshall Plan) are failures, this would be a bad omen for the future of humanity on this planet. But from a realistic standpoint, we would be no worse off than we are today. We have little to lose and much to gain.

The Heterogeneity Bugaboo. During most of the second half of the twentieth century, human civilization teetered precariously over the abyss of nuclear Armageddon thanks to an ideologically fueled geopolitical confrontation between the communist and non-communist blocs of nations. Even during that perilous Cold War period, a limited world government along the lines of the proposed Federal Union of Democratic Nations would have been possible (above all, because member nations would have been able to retain their own independent armed forces), and had such a federation been formed, the better communication and closer cooperation it would have facilitated might well have hastened the end of the Cold

War and thereby reduced the terrible threat of instantaneous nuclear holocaust. But neither the intelligentsia nor the political leadership possessed sufficient vision to perceive the possibility. Instead, assuming that a world state must necessarily be omnipotent and claim a monopoly on large-scale armed force and weapons of mass destruction, the intelligentsia and the political leadership dismissed the possibility of world government on grounds that if the "other side" got control of such a government, they would immediately impose their odious economic and political system on "our side." This assessment was common to both sides: non-communist and communist. During the Cold War, therefore, the ideological gap was perceived as the primary impediment to world government.

Now that the ideological gap of the Cold War appears dead, and will hopefully never arise again from its grave to haunt humanity, the primary impediment to world government is the economic gap: the tremendous gulf that has opened up between economic living standards in the richest nations and those in the poorest nations. Not that this fact is explicitly recognized and openly acknowledged by either the general public or international relations experts. The latter speak of "heterogeneities" within the human population and the "lack of shared values," while the former are instinctively appalled by the notion that "foreigners" will gain any sort of meaningful control over their lives. Perhaps it is simply too crassly materialistic for the peoples of the rich nations to confess their fear of a global welfare state that will economically despoil them, and for the peoples of the poor nations to confess their fear that the re-imposition of colonial-style exploitation will economically despoil them. Both prefer to think that their apprehensions regarding world government are based on something higher than "mere economic self-interest."

Be that as it may, if we dig down past the various superficial rationalizations, it is fairly apparent that the North-South economic gap has now replaced the East-West ideological gap as the primary impediment to world government. Certain fundamental characteristics of the proposed Federal Union of Democratic Nations are designed to cope with the situation, most importantly, the dual voting system in the Union legislature, and the retained national rights to withdraw from the Union and to maintain independent military forces. These are short-term expedients, to enable the world government to be established and to commence functioning. In the long term, the only way to remove the economic gap as an impediment to successful world government, is to remove the economic gap itself—or at least drastically reduce it. This would be the goal of the proposed Global Marshall Plan (GMP) under the direction of a World Development Authority (WDA), an agency of the Federal Union. During its early decades, the top priority of the Federal Union should be pursuit of the global economic equalization effort to a satisfactory conclusion.

Although the existence of large economic differentials among the nations of the world is the primary impediment to successful world government at the present time, there are certain other impediments that need to be considered in assessing the practicality of world government. In a very general sense, any distinction at all within the human species can be perceived as an impediment to political unification. Among the most important of these distinctions are race, language, culture, and religion. Obviously, some of these impediments are more serious than others. But I would argue that even the most serious of them do not constitute a significant obstacle to federal world government, as long as the envisioned federal world government is properly limited.

The fact that race and language, in and of themselves, are not particularly serious obstacles to political unity, is clearly suggested by the several examples of successful nations that are quite diverse in terms of race and language. China and India are probably the most dramatic examples of very large nations within which there are numerous different languages and dialects spoken by substantial proportions of the populations. With respect to race, the United States "melting pot" is probably the single most important evidence that may be cited that considerable racial diversity is not necessarily an insuperable obstacle to political unity. The principal minorities in the U.S. are blacks, Asians, and Latinos. The presence of a substantial black racial minority in the United States today is the result of 400 years of slavery, an institution that represents the greatest historical stain by far upon the honor of the nation. It would be a gross misrepresentation of reality to claim that full racial equality of whites and blacks has been achieved in the contemporary United States. However, it would be equally blind to reality not to acknowledge the very considerable progress that has been made in this direction, as exemplified, for example, by the election to the U.S. Presidency of Barack Obama. The examples of China and India, among many others, show that linguistic diversity is not a serious obstacle to world government. The example of the United States, among many others, shows that racial diversity is also not a serious obstacle to world government.

Turning now to culture, we should recognize and acknowledge that most "cultural differences" are quite harmless. When we come to religion, however—often deemed to be an important component of culture—clearly the situation is not favorable. The horrific events of September 11, 2001, were instigated by Islamic extremists who were obviously motivated, to some extent, by religious enthusiasm. The 9/11 horror demonstrated that religiously aggravated hostility and conflict is hardly extinct in the modern world, despite the general advance of secularism. That event was a particularly dramatic example of a phenomenon that has often appeared elsewhere in the world. For example, India continues to be disturbed on a regular basis by Hindu-Muslim riots.

Against this background, it need hardly be emphasized that it is absolutely vital that religious freedom be recognized in the Union Constitution as a "fundamental human right," and that the Federal Union be constitutionally prohibited from passing laws or pursuing policies that favor any one religion over any other. It is not simply a matter of forbidding an established church; rather there must be erected a very high, very strong "wall of separation" between the state and any one religion or group of religions. In some ways this will be easier for the world government to accomplish than it has been for the national governments. This is because the amount of religious diversity over the entire world is much greater than the amount of religious diversity within any one nation. In many if not most nations, one religion has become dominant: for example, Christianity in the United States. But at the world level, there is no single religion that has achieved such dominance that the world government would be inclined toward favoring it.

The fundamental guarantee that the world government would not oppress any given nation in cultural and/or religious terms, whether that nation be primarily Christian, Islamic, or whatever, is the retained right of member nations to withdraw from the union at their unilateral discretion, along with the right to independent military forces. In the interest of the stability of the world federation, it would be advisable to maintain a high degree of flexibility on culturally oriented church-state issues within member nations. For example, if an Islamic nation wants to prescribe that only mullahs can hold political office in the national government, or to require that women keep their faces covered in public, then so be it. The Federal Union Constitution should specify clearly that the supernational government shall take no action against national customs, so long as these customs do not seriously infringe on basic human rights.

A Scientific Approach. Proponents of major social policy innovations in the past have tended to be extremely confident that the benefits of these innovations would far outweigh the costs. If they had any doubts on the matter, they kept these doubts to themselves. They argued the virtues of their proposals with an enthusiasm bordering on fanaticism, and dismissed critics and opponents as either mental incompetents or hypocrites in the pay of "vested interests." If they were heeded and their proposals implemented, then, quite often, various unanticipated and undesirable consequences would quickly surface, so that the net benefits of the transition would be less than expected, sometimes far less than expected.

In some cases, the proposed cure was indubitably far worse than the disease. One thinks immediately of Karl Marx, who proclaimed the socialist millennium with all the faith and zeal that one normally associates with religious fanatics. Within a few decades of Marx's death, what should have been the workers' paradise of the Soviet Union was transformed into a totalitarian nightmare presided over by Joseph Stalin. No doubt Stalin, who died comfortably enough of old age in 1953, after slaughtering millions of his own countrymen, never experienced any significant self-doubt. No doubt he convinced himself that his own personal survival and continued undisputed leadership of the Soviet Union was hastening the glorious socialist millennium promised by Karl Marx. From the ideas and idealism of Karl Marx to the concentration camps and firing squads of Joseph Stalin—such can be the disastrous outcome of sympathetic concern for all humanity and innovative social thinking.

Therefore, it needs to be reiterated once again, without qualification or equivocation, that no sensible person can be completely certain that the effect of a potential future Global Marshall Plan, or of a potential future Federal Union of Democratic Nations, would be favorable. It is extremely important that if either one or both of these initiatives is actually undertaken in the real world, it should be on a tentative, provisional, and experimental basis. It would be useless to deny that a non-negligible possibility exists that a Global Marshall Plan would be a complete failure, that there would be little acceleration in the growth rates of the poor nations and/or a serious decline in the economic status of the rich nations. If that happens (after a reasonable trial period), then the program should be cut back drastically or terminated altogether. It would be equally useless to deny that a non-negligible possibility exists that the Federal Union of Democratic Nations might be a complete failure, for a variety of reasons, including continued pursuit of a Global Marshall Plan which is clearly failing to achieve its mission. If that happens (again after a reasonable trial period), nations should withdraw from the Federal Union, until finally, having been reduced to an impotent rump state, the Federal Union voluntarily terminates its own existence. Such a dissolution would be sad and unfortunate, and an ill omen for the future of humanity. But peaceful dissolution would obviously be preferable to violent dissolution.

It is an absolutely central component of this proposal for a world government, therefore, that the world government practice an absolutely pure and unadulterated "open door" policy with respect to membership. The Federal Union must always remain ready to admit new nations to membership in the Union, and it must always remain equally ready to allow member nations to depart from the Union whenever they desire to do so. These principles must be clearly and unequivocally stated in the constitution which establishes the Union. The constitution must not only enshrine the permanent right of each member nation to withdraw from the Union at its own unilateral discretion, but it must also enshrine the permanent right of each member nation to maintain whatever military forces and armaments it desires, including nuclear. These military forces and weapons would provide a practical guarantee and a tangible safeguard for the constitutional right of free secession from the Union. These two interrelated reserved rights of the member nations are essential to the effective initiation of the Federal Union. Owing to these reserved rights, a large number of nations, including the larger and more powerful nations, will be willing to join the Union. Conceivably there could even be universal membership by all nations right from the start. Of course, the hope would be that the Federal Union would evolve smoothly and favorably, so that the member nations would become more confident and would gradually reduce the military forces under their direct control. The hope is also that the reserved right of secession would, in due course, become nothing more than an historical curiosity, since the benefits of maintaining membership in the Federal Union would be so clear and compelling that secession would become virtually unthinkable.

The formation of a world government along the lines of the proposed Federal Union of Democratic Nations should be looked upon as no more and no less than *a scientific experiment*. Such an experiment is the one and only way we have for achieving truly reliable, convincing, and compelling evidence on the potential performance of world government. Whether a world government would be a success or a failure simply cannot be determined, to any reasonably satisfactory level of certitude, by means of theoretical speculations and hypothetical musings based on the past history of human civilization. The current situation is simply too novel, too unprecedented, and too unparalleled for past history to provide more than circumstantial and inconclusive indications. The fact is that the only means by which we may ascertain whether a world state would make a positive contribution to the future development of human civilization is to set up a world state and then observe the outcome. What is needed is not more words but rather experimental *action*.

Whether progress has been achieved, in a fundamental social welfare sense, through the historical evolution of the institutions and operations of human civilization, might be debated by reasonable people. Most of us believe, for example, that the principle of representative democracy does in fact constitute a meaningful advance over the principle of absolute monarchy. But it cannot be proven, in a mathematically or logically rigorous sense, that thc average level of human happiness and self-realization is higher today under representative democracy, than it was in the past under absolute monarchy.

But where historical progress *has* been achieved, surely and incontestably, is in the area of science and technology. It cannot be reasonably disputed that a world in which automobiles and computers exist, is farther along than a world in which these things did not exist. Note that the argument is *not* that automobiles and computers necessarily increase human welfare in any meaningful way (though most of us believe they do). The argument is simply that automobiles and computers represent incontestable scientific and technical advance. And the point is simply that an essential component of scientific and technical advance has always been the experimental method. In the absence of experimentation, it is very doubtful that science and technology would ever have been capable of bringing forth such marvels as automobiles and computers.

What this means, in terms of world government, is that we will never be able to compellingly demonstrate either the desirability or the undesirability of federal world government without actually establishing a federal world government. This proposition may seem strange at first, because apparently neither the proponents nor the opponents of world government in the past have been sufficiently aware of it. Or if they were aware of it, they apparently feared that explicit recognition and discussion of this point would have weakened the case they were attempting to put forward, pro or con, on world government. But upon reflection, most people will hopefully recognize and acknowledge the high level of plausibility which characterizes the proposition. Of course, even if a person is prepared to assent to the proposition that only a real-world experiment with world government is likely to yield compelling evidence on the performance of world government, he or she might still regard such an experiment as far too risky to be undertaken. What I have attempted to do, in my work on world government, is to show that a real-world experiment with a *properly designed* world government would not in fact entail excessive risk, especially in view of the great benefits that might be garnered if the experiment is a success.

Needless to emphasize, in the past major social innovations have rarely if ever been proposed in experimental terms. Rarely have the proposers of such innovations offered arguments which could easily be satirized as equivalent to: "Try it—you *might* like it!" Neither have the opponents of these innovations considered it advisable to express their arguments in anything less than terms of complete certainty. However, to those in the middle ground, the perception may be that the proposed innovation may indeed be worthwhile as a means of establishing once and for all, by experimental means, whether or not the innovation is, on the whole, beneficial.

It may be found, after the innovation is adopted, that its overall effect is unfavorable. In that case, the innovation could and should be repealed, revoked, discontinued. An interesting case of this sort in United States history was the imposition of a national ban on the production, transportation, and sale of alcoholic beverages from 1920 through 1933. The ban was the outcome of long-term, organized efforts, dating back to the early nineteenth century, to limit the consumption of alcohol and thereby to curb the various social problems generated by drunkenness. A prohibition amendment to the U.S. Constitution was ratified by the requisite number of states by early 1919. The alcohol ban went into effect on January 29, 1920.

Within a short period of time, the costs of "legislating morality" became obvious. Millions of otherwise law-abiding citizens ignored the ban, resulting in a thriving illegal black market supplied by organized crime. Violence erupted in the streets as rival gangs fought to gain control over the illicit but lucrative trade. Corruption spread widely through the enforcement agencies as some of the abundant profits were diverted to bribes to gain the complicity of the police. The quality of illegal alcohol degenerated, leading to much death and disability among the consuming public. Anyone who wonders what the "war on alcohol" was like during the 1920s has only to look at the "war on drugs" being waged in more recent times.

After a decade of experience suggesting that in this case the cure was worse than the disease, the pendulum of public opinion swung against prohibition. The onslaught of the Great Depression in 1930 may have put the final nail in prohibition's coffin. To the other arguments against prohibition was now added the assertion that a legal liquor industry would add thousands of new, legal jobs paying taxable income. By the early 1930s, the repeal movement was in full swing. The Twenty-First Amendment to the U.S. Constitution, whose principal purpose was simply the repeal of the Eighteenth Amendment, was ratified before the end of 1933. And that marked the end of what Herbert Hoover, defeated in the election of November 1932 for U.S. President by Franklin D. Roosevelt, referred to as "the noble experiment."

Whether the episode had been noble or ignoble, Hoover's use of the term "experiment" is informative. Throughout the many decades prior to the 1920s during which the controversy had raged, advocates and opponents of prohibition had speculated endlessly about the probable effects of a national ban on alcoholic drink. Advocates forecast the moral regeneration of a nation no longer plagued by intoxication and alcoholism. Opponents forecast a narrow and joyless existence presided over by puritanical religious zealots. But no one *really* knew what would happen. When the pro-prohibition forces finally got the upper hand and pushed through the national ban, the anti-prohibition forces howled their lamentations. As it turned out, they should have shouted their hosannas. Within ten years, the compelling evidence provided by actual experience with prohibition swung the overwhelming weight of public opinion over to the anti-prohibition side of the controversy, and the national ban on alcoholic beverages was lifted. Ten years of actual experience with prohibition were worth more than ten decades of speculative controversy.

Opponents of world government today should keep this historical episode well in mind. Assuming they are correct, then very shortly after the the formation of a world government, its disadvantages and liabilities will begin to manifest themselves in a very clear and obvious manner. Perhaps, despite all the admonitions and warnings against attempting to make the world state into an instrument for the radical redistribution of current income, the high officials of the world state will set themselves resolutely toward this course of action. Against opposition to this policy, they will threaten to unleash the military and police forces of the world state. Clear evidence would then exist that the apprehensions and anticipations of world government skeptics were fully on-target. If this were to happen, then the world state would dissolve very quickly and very completely. Just as prohibition was abandoned as soon as its disadvantages could no longer be reasonably denied, so too the world state would be abandoned.

Of course, I myself do not believe that there is any significant possibility that were a world government to be established, its high leadership would be so foolish and misguided as to pursue policies which would inevitably be strongly opposed by substantial national populations. Into this category would certainly fall the policy of radical redistribution of current income. I have cited the example of prohibition of alcohol in the United States from 1920 through 1933 only to suggest that the formation of a world government need not be a final, definitive, irrevocable step. If a potential future world government were to be as unsuccessful in practice as was the policy of prohibition of alcohol in the United States during the 1920s, then that world government would quickly follow the same path into rapid oblivion as did that followed by prohibition.

But at the same time, most students of social policy recognize in the experience of prohibition in the United States during the 1920s an atypical case. The general rule is that innovative social policies—policies which are finally adopted after decades of vociferous controversy and bitter resistance—are successful rather than unsuccessful. The various vicissitudes and disasters confidently predicted by conservative opponents turn out to be groundless fantasies. Society carries on much as before, and after a while even most of the conservatives become fully reconciled to the changes, and recognize them to be beneficial not only to the larger society, but to themselves as well. Of all of the amendments to the United States Constitution, for example, only the Eighteenth was later repealed because its effects were obviously perverse. The Thirteenth Amendment, abolishing slavery, has not as yet had to be repealed. Nor has the Nineteenth, which granted the right to vote to women. If a world government is established in the real world, I am quite confident that it will soon be acknowledged as a positive development by all but a small handful of extremely inflexible mentalities. The key point is, however, that my own personal confidence on this score is *not* a vital component of the case to be made for world government. What *is* a vital component of this case is that it would neither be impossible, nor even especially difficult, to dissolve a world government which was not developing in a positive way.

A New World Order. Few people doubt that the world is currently a much safer place than it was fifty years ago. The abandonment of Marxist ideology by the components and satellites of the ex-Soviet Union has greatly eased tensions. Around the world, military spending and arms stockpiles have been reduced. The danger of instantaneous nuclear holocaust has been reduced to a level that many consider negligible and insignificant. The downside of these developments, as far as the future destiny of the human race is concerned, is the loss of a sense of urgency, the growth of complacency, and the dominance of a policy best described as "let's drift and see what happens." Not even the traumatic events of September 11, 2001, and those of its aftermath, have apparently dislodged humanity's strong consensus that the current international status quo situation is—if not the best of all imaginable worlds—at least the best of all possible worlds.

During the Cold War, it was routinely asserted that world government was no longer necessary to alleviate the threat of nuclear world war, because nuclear weapons had made such a war so immensely destructive that the rationality of mankind would forever preclude one from happening. Now that the Cold War is over, it might be asserted that world government is even more unnecessary because voluntary cooperation among the nations will accomplish anything worthwhile that a world government would have accomplished. In other words, informal "global governance" is just as efficacious as formal "global government."

Advocates of world government are typically dismissed as "utopian dreamers." But what may in fact be a "utopian dream" is that the development of cosmopolitan tolerance and mutual respect among sovereign and independent nations, subject to no higher political authority than themselves, will forever spare human civilization from a nuclear war for which the weapons are ready and waiting. Skeptics allege that humanity is not sufficiently rational to establish a world government. On what basis, however, do these skeptics also imply that humanity *is* sufficiently rational to forever avoid nuclear war under the sovereign nation-state system?

That the collapse and dissolution of the Soviet Union has generated a new world order is obvious. The salient question is whether this new world order will be stable and benign—or otherwise. There are warning signs, for those who have eyes to see them. In the United States, for example, unquestionably the greatest single military power in the world today, there are significant political forces in operation that are inclined to interpret the "new world order" as a giant conspiracy to enslave the United States. The recent election of the pseudo-populist, borderline xenophobic demagogue Donald Trump to the presidency of the United States has provided concerning evidence that these forces are indeed stronger than hitherto generally assumed. Certain extremists within these forces assert that it would be a sensible policy for the United States to "nuke" anyone or anything that represents a serious threat to U.S. national interests—and they see serious threats everywhere. Can these elements be kept under control forever? Would it be possible to keep them under control, for example, if an international terrorist organization manages to detonate a nuclear device in a major U.S. city?

That certain terrorist organizations would happily carry out such an action—were they in possession of a nuclear device—was incontrovertibly established by the horrific events of September 11, 2001. One is also reminded that the terrific cycle of violence during the twentieth century known as World Wars I and II, was precipitated by a single terrorist act: the assassination of Archduke Ferdinand and his wife in Sarajevo on June 28, 1914, by a teenage Serbian nationalist by the name of Gavrilo Prinzip, who died of tuberculosis in prison while World War I was still raging. Unfortunately, there are many people in the world today who share the reckless mindset of Gavrilo Prinzip. These people are ready and willing to light the fuse, and sooner or later they might be in a position to do so.

Meanwhile, there is unease in the rest of the world over what some perceive as unrestrained U.S. power. The "balance of power," on which all hopes for peace have hitherto depended in the modern era of national sovereignty—is now out of balance. Not everyone perceived in the 1991 Gulf War, for example, a heartening example of international solidarity against aggression by a nation under the control of a mini-Hitler. Some saw it as an ominous portent of global hegemony by the United States alone, or by an alliance among the small minority of wealthy nations. The 2003 invasion of Iraq by a "coalition" consisting almost entirely of the United States and Britain, generated a wave of protest not only in the Middle East but throughout the world. While few of the protesters would have denied that Saddam Hussein had degenerated into a vicious tyrant, they doubted that his regime presented such a clear and present danger to the security of the United States and its allies as to justify military invasion. The quick military victory of U.S. and U.K. forces in Iraq intensified apprehensions throughout the rest of the world that the United States, aided and abetted by a handful of its closest allies, was evolving into an international bully that would in future take upon itself the task of preemptively eliminating, via military action, all real and perceived threats to its national interests. No doubt those concerned that the United States might evolve into an international bully derived considerable comfort from the fact that postwar Iraq became a quagmire that swallowed up large quantities of U.S. human and material resources.

Many analysts view apprehensively the "undemocratic" Russian Federation, armed as it is with a vast nuclear arsenal, and heir to a long tradition of opposition to the foreign policies of the leading First World nations, especially the United States. One can only imagine, for example, what the consequences of 9/11 might have been if the USSR had not given up on communistic millennialism in 1991, and still had the same attitudes toward the West that it had had ten years previously. In 1914, Russia's opposition to what it regarded as intolerable Austrian impositions on Serbia to bring to justice the conspirators responsible for the assassination of the Austrian Archduke was instrumental in bringing on World War I. In 2001, the USSR's opposition to what it might have regarded as intolerable American impositions on Afghanistan to bring to justice the conspirators responsible for the 9/11 outrage might have brought on an even more terrible World War III. Fortunately for the world, the Russian Federation has been far less confrontational—for the most part—than its predecessor. Of course, Russia's reputation as a basically responsible, peaceful, law-abiding international citizen has recently been seriously damaged by its totally unreasonable and unprovoked military invasion of the Ukraine. This is exactly the sort of senseless "international incident" that has the capability of blossoming out into a nuclear holocaust.

Other analysts view the "rise of China" with misgivings (even though its current nuclear arsenal is only a fraction of Russia's), perhaps suspecting that China's evolution in the twenty-first century will parallel Japan's evolution into a violently destabilizing force during the first half of the twentieth century. For example, China's recent revival of its traditional (albeit thoroughly irrational) interest in absorbing Taiwan into the People's Republic is another unhealthy indication that these misgivings are not all that far-fetched. Were Red China to emulate Russia's invasion of Ukraine and attempt an amphibious invasion of Taiwan, this would be yet another senseless "international incident" capable of igniting world war.

This is not to forget the various rogue states plotting to enter the nuclear club. Such plotting may eventually have to be suppressed by direct military intervention. But not all the other nuclear powers may stand by quietly while the United States and its closest allies endeavor to curb nuclear proliferation throughout the world by military action. Last but not least, there is the fact that the ever-widening differentials in living standards between the rich and poor nations constitute an ever-hardening impediment to the kind of global action needed to avert the danger that overpopulation will degrade and eventually destroy the natural environment.

In Number 6 of *The Federalist Papers*, Alexander Hamilton, in response to the argument that there was no need for a closer political union among the thirteen original states because there was no foreseeable basis for future conflicts among them, wrote as follows:

> A man must be far gone in Utopian speculation who can seriously doubt that, if these states should either be wholly disunited, or only united in partial confederacies, the subdivisions into which they might be thrown would have frequent and violent contests with each other. To presume a want of motives for such contests as an argument against their existence, would be to forget that men are ambitious, vindictive, and rapacious. To look for a continuation of harmony between a number of independent, unconnected sovereignties in the same neighborhood, would be to disregard the uniform course of human events, and to set at defiance the accumulated experience of the ages.

Hamilton's 1787 argument concerning the original thirteen states is plausibly extrapolated to the 200 nations of the "global neighborhood" today.

Prospects. The case for world government is far stronger than is commonly recognized at the present time. Of course, this does understand a *limited* federal world government with, at a minimum, the following key attributes: (1) member nations would retain the right to maintain military forces, armed with both conventional and nuclear weapons, under their direct control; (2) member nations would retain the right to withdraw peacefully from the supernational federation at their unilateral discretion; (3) voting weight in the federation legislature would be determined in such a way that legislation must be acceptable both to the less populous rich nations and the more populous poor nations (the "dual voting" procedure).

Despite these limitations, the proposed Federal Union of Democratic Nations would possess the essential attributes and trappings of state authority: it would have separate, democratically elected branches for legislative, executive, and judicial functions, it would have a capital city and a permanent administrative apparatus, it would possess significant military forces under its direct control, it would have an appreciable power of direct taxation, it would have the essential symbols of political authority: a flag, anthem, and emblems. It would take an active role in global governance from the moment of its inception. Its early history would be devoted chiefly to the initiation, coordination, and successful prosecution of a very large-scale economic development assistance effort, termed the Global Marshall Plan (aka World Economic Equalization Program), designed to substantially narrow the economic gap between the rich and poor nations once and for all. A political agency of this significance would provide a powerful center around which to invigorate the positive impulses in humanity toward global community.

What is required might be described as a "campaign of enlightenment"—a campaign to make the majority of humanity aware of the fact that whatever may have been the case in the past, at the present time there is a reasonable preponderance of evidence in support of the desirability of world government as a means of strengthening the probability that human civilization will avoid disaster and continue its long-term advance. What are the odds that a sufficient amount of enlightenment can be achieved within the near future to make federal world government a practical possibility? Obviously, no one can provide a precise answer to this question. However, I would argue that the odds on this are much better than commonly believed at present.

The world government skeptic, of course, will proclaim the utter futility of speculating about either the overall strategy or the detailed tactics of a "campaign of enlightenment." Such a campaign, the skeptic will say, will never have a chance of developing into anything noticeable—and this not for just one reason but for two. First, there is the tremendous conservative bias at all levels of society everywhere in the world. Given the present climate of both intellectual and popular opinion, world government is simply too big and bold an idea even to be given consideration, let alone ever to be actually implemented. The second reason why a "campaign of enlightenment" is doomed from the outset, according to the skeptic, is the tremendous degree of apathy and disinterest among all segments of the population everywhere in the world. This is partly owing to the massive conservative bias against any hint of fundamental sociopolitical change—but it goes beyond that. People today are too busy with their personal careers, too preoccupied with their personal lives, and too overwhelmed by a tidal wave of information and entertainment emanating from the media, to have either the interest or the energy to undertake significant activity toward some higher goal or purpose.

In his time, Karl Marx railed against religion as the "opiate of the masses": as a deadening barrier against fundamental reform of the economic system. But nowadays, it can be argued, the "masses" are rendered inert not merely by religion, but also by popular culture, spectator sports, television and movies. Back in Marx's time, the leadership of the socialist movement did not come from the exploited "masses" but rather mostly from the middle and upper classes of society. Ironically, the leadership of the movement was not provided by those who stood to gain the most from a socialist transformation; it came rather from those with less to gain personally but better equipped with the knowledge and skills to effect social change. But today, the descendents of those socially responsible middle class and upper class people of the nineteenth century are far too concerned to protect their good names and reputations to even dream of becoming involved with anything so radical as a movement to establish world government.

What response may be made to these arguments? Although the alleged "conservative bias" and "apathy and disinterest" are closely interrelated in a practical sense, they are conceptually distinct and may be addressed separately. With respect to the degree of conservatism in the population, it can hardly be disputed that it has been appreciably higher during the second half of the twentieth century than it was during the second half of the nineteenth century. In fact, people living during the second half of the twentieth century (i.e. people alive today) tend to positively envy those people who lived during the second half of the nineteenth century. What a positive and optimistic time that must have been (or so we think)—when people had no hint of the twentieth century disasters to come: of the world wars, the totalitarian regimes in Germany, Russia, China and elsewhere, the threat of nuclear holocaust, and the danger of environmental collapse brought on by the population explosion.

But there may be a tendency here to exaggerate the impact of large social events upon the attitudes and emotions of individual human beings. Individual human beings are very adaptable, which means that they are not unduly upset by bad conditions nor unduly happy about good conditions. People today do not lie awake at night worrying about being killed in a nuclear holocaust, any more than they lie awake worrying about being killed in a car crash. By the same token, people in the nineteenth century did not happily congratulate themselves that they could not be killed in a nuclear holocaust—or in a car crash for that matter. Nor were people in the second half of the nineteenth century generally all that enthusiastic about the concept of social progress. No doubt some were enthusiastic, but certainly not all. There were plenty of political conservatives in those days, who were very conscious of such historical episodes as the Terror during the French Revolution, and who felt very much threatened by such things as the socialist movement codified by Karl Marx, and the general tendency toward extension of the voting franchise. Those conservatives could no doubt conjure up vivid images of civilization destroyed by the radical leveling policies of popularly elected demagogues. In retrospect, we look back to the latter half of the nineteenth century as an era of untroubled peace, plenty, security, and serenity. But it did not appear so to the people who were alive at that time.

In some ways, the people of today can look forward to the future with more confidence than could have the people of the nineteenth century. For one thing, the socialist menace is much reduced. Even though there are still a few important nations in the world that still subscribe to the communist form of socialism, none of the capitalist nations seems a likely candidate for any form of public ownership socialism, communistic or otherwise. In the view of the large majority of humanity, public ownership socialism has been thoroughly discredited both economically and politically—so much so that the people of the USSR, who vigorously championed the cause of socialism throughout most of the twentieth century, have themselves voluntarily renounced and repudiated it.

In the light of what we now know, the principle of political democracy also does not seem to be such a hazard as it was once regarded. The demagogues so much feared by nineteenth century conservatives have not come to power and thereupon destroyed civilization by means of their radical leveling policies. Even nations with a tremendous amount of poverty and economic inequality, such as India, are politically stable despite their democratic institutions. In the one case in the twentieth century where a demagogue came close to destroying civilization, leveling policies were not involved. In the case of the German Third Reich spawned by the demonic charisma of Adolf Hitler, the instrumentality through which German civilization was very nearly destroyed was involvement in international warfare—not implementation of excessively egalitarian domestic policies.

Therefore, while there may have been slightly more optimism and willingness to experiment in the latter part of the nineteenth century than in the latter part of the twentieth century, the actual difference might not be all that great. In any case, there is obviously a happy medium on the attitude spectrum between conservatism and progressivism. All but the most ideologically rigid conservative will admit that under certain conditions, certain changes become desirable; while at the same time, all but the most ideologically rigid progressive will admit that under certain conditions, certain changes would in fact be undesirable. According to the oscillatory theory of history, social attitudes toward change and progress swing like a pendulum between extreme conservatism and extreme progressivism. But a swinging pendulum tends over time toward a static, perpendicular position. It is not all that implausible that we humans are learning from our mistakes, that we are less subject either to extremes of conservatism or extremes of progressivism, and that the political pendulum is tending toward a static position over the happy medium.

The proposal for a limited world government in the form of the Federal Union of Democratic Nations quite likely does embody and manifest that happy medium. It is progressive in the sense that it would advance the level of international cooperation and coordination substantially beyond what has been achieved by the United Nations of today. At the same time, it is conservative because of the retained national rights to secession and independent military forces. These and other provisions of the plan would virtually eliminate the possibility that the world government would develop into a crushing global tyranny. The Federal Union would be a step forward, clearly, but not a radical step forward. Once they adequately understand this proposal, most people will hopefully perceive it to be the careful, cautious, evolutionary advance that it is in reality.

But what about the skeptic's allegation that the reigning apathy and disinterest among the human population stands as an impenetrable barrier against any significant part of the human population ever becoming aware of the inherent value and desirability of this form of limited federal world government? It cannot be denied that many people are very busy with their careers and their families, nor can it be denied that it is sometimes difficult to get the attention of very busy people. But it would be ridiculous to propose that people anywhere in the world—and particularly people in the wealthy, industrialized nations of the world—are so ground down and exhausted by work and family responsibilities that they are incapable of exerting themselves toward some great and noble purpose.

The skeptic points to the stultifying, deadening effect on human thinking and initiative of popular culture and spectator sports by conjuring up an image of inert couch potatoes gazing blankly at their television screens all evening. But the fact that this time is utilized for watching television rather than for sleeping demonstrates that most people possess untapped reserves of time and energy. Nor should the passive nature of some leisure time pursuits cause us to lose sight of the fact that other leisure time pursuits are quite active in nature. While some people spend a great deal of time watching spectator sports in stadiums and on television, many other people are out there participating in vigorous physical exercise. Many people also devote considerable amounts of leisure time to intellectual and cultural pursuits, as witnessed, for example, by the tremendous volume of book and magazine publishing. While it is true that people today experience a tremendous barrage of information from both print and electronic media, this does not necessarily mean that they have been battered by this barrage into a condition of indifferent passivity. They pick and choose from among this barrage what they will attend to. If something important happens, if some idea or movement comes along that is worthy of widespread attention and action, we have the communications media at our disposal to get the word out rapidly.

In short, I do not accept that apathy and indifference are the normal condition of humanity, nor do I accept that human beings are more prone to these attitudes in the contemporary age than they were in any prior age. In most ways, individual human beings today, as well as human society as a whole, are more flexible, fluid, and adaptable than at any time in the past. The human race as a whole is far better educated and informed than it has ever been in the past. We are far more aware of past history than we have ever been before. We recognize that humanity has made many mistakes in our past pursuit of progress—but we are also conscious of the fact that it is possible to learn from mistakes, that mistakes are necessary if any progress is to be made, and that the only truly final and fatal mistake would be to forsake progress for fear of making mistakes.

INDEX

ABD (All But Dissertation), 54-55
abstinence, 348
Addison, Herbert J., 211-212
Administrative Costs of Market Socialism, The, 65
Administrative Science Quarterly, 78
Advertising Council, 355
Affluent Society, The, 198
Afghanistan, 446
afterlife, 119, 273, 412
Agency Issues and Managerial Incentives, 120
agent (BPO), 328
Alighieri, Dante, 269, 386
Alpha Centauri star, 7
Alternative Voices in Contemporary Economics, 167
Alternatives, 141
American Economic Review, 126. 164-167
American Revolutionary War, 405
Amstutz, Mark, 431-432
anarchy of the market, 312
anarchy, 329
Anatomy of Peace, The, 390
Annals of Public and Cooperative Economy, 93, 206, 325
anti-charisma, 27
Antichrist. 175
anticyclical policy (Keynesian), 23, 29, 101
apathy and disinterest, 449
Appraisal of Langian Socialism, An, 71-73
Archduke Ferdinand, 445
Argentina, 302
armament, national right of, 408-412, 438
army of auditors, 75
Arrow Impossibility Theorem, 79
artificial market, 81-82
Ashenfelter, Orley, 126
Ashgate Publishing, 230
Asian tiger nations, 427
assumptions, 278
Atlantic Ocean, 178

balance of power, 445-446
bankruptcy, 329
Bartholdt, Richard, 385
BB (big book), 96
begging the question, 66, 334
Belcher, Patti, 240
Bentham, Jeremy, 121, 386
Bergson, Abram, 17, 56, 113, 316
Berle, Adolf A., 75, 119
Berlin, 9-10
Berliner, Joseph, 206
Bernstein, Eduard, 308
Berra, Yogi, 246
Besley, Timothy, 164-167
bestseller, characteristics, 179
Beyond Global Governance, 278-280
Biden, Joseph, 244
Birth of the Global Nation, The, 149, 394
Bishop, Amy, 84
blessing or curse, 107
blogosphere, 284, 295
Böhm-Bawerk, Eugen von, 348-349
Bolivar, Simon, 386

Borgese, Giuseppe, 171, 390
bourgeois democracy, 367, 374
bowed over, 340
Bowman, Charlie, 32-34
BPO agents, 328
Bronx (New York City), 1
Brown, Spencer, 131
Buchanan, Holly, 294-298
bulwark of democracy, 123
Bureau of Land Management, 23
Bureau of Public Ownership (BPO), 23, 117-118, 326-330
bureaucracy, 79
bureaucratization of economic life, 65-68
bureaucratic bugaboo, 117
Burkett, John, 205
Burnham, Julie, 215
business capital investment, 330-332
business depressions, 29, 101
business regulation, 330

Cabrera, Luis, 257, 292
calculated risk, 379
campaign of enlightenment, 448-452
Canada, 404-405
Candide (1959), 120
capital management effort, 116-118, 318, 334-346
capital management models, 150-151
Capital Management under Market Socialism, 110-114
Capital Management under Profit-Oriented Market Socialism, 155
Capitalism and Freedom, 367-368
Capitalism versus Pragmatic Market Socialism, 219-220
capitalist apologetics, 18, 24-25, 115, 123, 318, 332-334
Carr, Spencer, 193, 195
case against socialism, 334, 365
Case for Pragmatic Market Socialism, The, 125
Catch-22, 215, 431
Causes of World War III, The (1958), 14
Central Planning Board, 73-74
Checkpoint Charlie, 10
Chicago, University of, 390
chicken or the egg, 429-431
China, 28, 47, 98, 139, 204, 312, 363, 377, 393, 400, 402, 411, 417, 420, 437, 447
ChiWriter, 200
Choice, 219
Choose Your Road to World Government, 385
Christ, 27
circumstantial vs. probative, 102
Civil War (U.S.) 405-408
Clark, Grenville, 398-399
coercion, 428-429
Co-Existence, 141-142
Cold War, 4-5, 14-15, 45, 60, 97, 209, 225, 278, 291, 304, 367, 378-382, 391-392, 395, 415
collapse of Soviet Union, 4, 21, 97, 167, 250, 301, 377, 393
collectivization (Soviet), 311
Committee to Frame a World Constitution, 390
common language, 413
Common Progress, 227
Common Progress concept, 421
Commonwealth of Man, The, 400
Commonwealth of Independent States, 97
communism, early view of, 1-2
communist ideology, 377
Communist Manifesto, 307
communist menace, 6, 25, 269
Communist revolutions, 364-365
Comparative Economic Studies, 126, 207

competition, 329, 373
Complementary Economic Proposal, 415-420
computer programming, 156-157
computer simulation, 421-422
concave upward-sloping, 340
conservatism versus progressivism, 451
conservative bias, 449
conspiracy (Kennedy assassination), 36
Constitution (U.S.), 406-407
constrained optimization, 96
consumption, 349
containment, 5, 15, 312, 393
convergence, 96-97
cooperative market socialism, 24, 369
corporate supervision, 335
cotton gin, 407
Craig, Campbell, 395
Cranwell Prep, 1
critical mass, 427
Crucé, Émeric, 386
Crude Redistribution, 421
cure worse than the disease, 400, 439
curse of separatism, 413
Czar Alexander I, 386

Dante Alighieri, 386
Das Kapital, 307-308
deadwood, 87
defense outlays (U.S.), 427
delivery systems, 392
Dellinger, Anne, 288-289
democracy, 362-375
Dempsey, Jack, 51
de Scheinitz, Karl, 56, 61-62
diminishing returns, 340
disarmament, 171, 409-410
dissertation work, 57-83
Disssociative Identity Disorder (DID), 6
distortions, 152
diversification, 350
Doomsday prospect, 7-9
drawdown of military expenditure, 285
dual voting system, 403-404
Dubois, Pierre, 385
Dunton, James R., 196-199
Dynamic Inefficiency of Capitalism, The, 148-149

economic affinities, 432
Economic Efficiency and Langian Socialism, 63-64
economic gap (global), 378, 432
economic imperialism, 304
Economic Inquiry, 159
Economic Justice, 220-223
Economics: An Introductory Analysis, 16
effectiveness coefficient, 343-344
Einstein, Albert, 7
Eisenhower, Dwight D., 4, 10
Eisner, Robert, 56, 61
elasticity of capital management effort, 162-163
Ellis, Howard, 316
els model, 122-123, 158
employee control, 24
End of Empire, The, 270
End of the Nightmare, The, 96
English, 270, 413-414
entrepreneurial business, 322-323
entrepreneurship, 115, 318, 337-338
Environmental Protection Agency, 330
equality, 336
Erasmus, Desiderius, 386
Estimates of the Equity-Efficiency Tradeoff, 156-157
Evaluating Changes in the Distribution of Capital Wealth, 159

Evolutionary World Government, 287-300
existential threat, 25, 302
experiment with socialism, 32
experiment, 306, 384-385, 439-440
external review, 285

fairness and balance, 160
Falk, Richard, 398-399
fate worse than death, 379
father, disputes with, 29-30
Federal Reserve Board, 359-360
Federal Reserve Bulletin, 360
Federal Trade Commission, 330
Federal Union of Democratic Nations, 383-385, 401-408, 433-435
federal vs. unitary, 402
Federalist Papers, The, 447
Fichte, Johann, 386
Fischer, Dietrich, 217
Fisher, Walter D., 62
flight, 399
Food and Drug Administration, 330
Fordham University, 1, 54, 106, 138, 147, 300, 379
Foreign Affairs, 172-176
foreign aid, 427-428
Fortran, 128
Fowlie, Craig, 267
Franco-Prussian War, 408
French wars, 386
Friedman, Milton, 367-368
fruitcake, 57

Galbraith, John Kenneth, 99, 198
Gates, Bill, 323
General Agreement on Tariffs and Trade (GATT), 414
General Equilibrium Comparison of Capitalism and Pragmatic Marker Socialism, A, 123
general vs. partial equilibrium, 121
generalized capital, 128-129, 422
Genius at the Wheel, 50
German wars, 386
glasnost, 393
Gleditsch, Nils Petter, 139-141
global governance, 171
Global Institutions series, 273
Global Marshall Plan (GMP) concept, 420-428
Global Marshall Plan, 280-287
global welfare state, 129, 381, 402, 420-421
Glossop, Ronald, 395
Golden Rule Barber Shop, 49
good reads, 179
Gormely, Pat, 136
Grand Alliance, 410
Grand Convergence I vs. Grand Convergence II, 98
Grand Convergence, The, 96-106, 248-259
Grand Convergence Sampler, 99
Great Depression, 50, 101, 302, 316-317, 442
Great Experiment, The, 214
Greater East-Asia Co-Prosperity Sphere, 420
Greenwood Press, 196
gridlock, 404
Grotius, Hugo, 386
Guidance of Production in a Socialist State, The, 316
Gulf War, 419, 446

Hague Disarmament Conferences, 409
Hamilton Books, 295-296
Hamilton, Alexander, 337
Harrington, Catherine, 172
Harrington, Michael, 198
Harris, Cynthia, 196
Harris, Errol, 395

Harris, Theodore, 387
Harting, Laurie, 254-256
Hartman, Rosemary, 172
Harwood-Jones. John, 144-145
Hattwick, Dick, 199
have vs. have-not nations, 419
Hayek, Friedrich, 74, 365-366
Heater, Derek, 226, 385
heavier-than-air flight, 399
Heterogeneity Bugaboo, The, 435-438
heterogeneity versus homogeneity, 428-431
higher education system, 85-86
Hilu, Virginia, 104
Hiroshima, 4, 376, 394, 434
Hitler, Adolf, 11, 27,312, 363, 366, 373, 392, 410, 434, 446, 450
Hoffman, Scott, 242
holy grail, 146, 177
homogeneity versus heterogeneity, 428-431
Hoover, Herbert, 317, 442
Hungarian revolt (1956), 1-2
Hutchins, Robert, 390, 429

Idea of World Government, The, 259-275
ideological bridge, 167, 219-225, 303
ideological confrontation, 3
Ideological Harmonization as a Means of Promoting Authentic Detente, 142
impact factor, 126
implicit income, 357
Incentives and Income under Market Socialism, 151, 154
India, 72-73, 381, 411
industrialization (Soviet), 311
inevitability thesis, 396
inflation, 322
inheritance, 325
inspirational role, 326
instant oblivion, 108, 178, 225, 248, 251, 258, 261, 287, 297
institutional flexibility, 120
International Organization, 142-143
International Studies Quarterly, 170-171
Internet, 227
interpersonal comparisons of utility, 70
intertemporal substitutability, 349
Introduction to the New World, 21-22, 30-31
investment analysis, 335
invisible hand, 312
Iraq, 446
Isard, Walter, 217
Israel, 411

Japan, 420
Jasper, Linda, 244
job security, 86
Journal of Comparative Economics, 151, 154
Journal of Conflict Resolution, 130-131
Journal of Developing Areas, 131
Journal of Economic Issues, 153, 207
Journal of Economic Literature, 207
Journal of Peace Research, 139-141
Journal of Personal Progress, 20, 41
Journal of World Systems Research, 244
juvenilia, 2

Kahn, Herman, 7-8
Kant, Immanuel, 171, 386
Katzenstein, Peter, 142-143

Kelvin, William Thomson (Lord), 399
Kennedy, John F., 10, 35-37
Kessler, Martin, 99, 104
Keynes, John Maynard, 354
Khatkhate, Deena R., 132
Khrushchev, Nikita, 10
King, Stephen, 229, 271
Kissinger, Henry, 212
Klein, John J., 37-40
Kramer, Marguerite, 130
Kurtz-Phelan, Daniel, 172-176

labor theory of value, 341
labor, 335
Lampman, Robert J., 359
Lancaster, Kelvin, 148-149
Lange, Oskar, 16, 17, 22, 28, 41, 56, 61, 65-68, 71-75, 77-80, 115, 121, 152, 173, 220, 305, 312, 316-320, 334
language, 412-414
Last Call for Socialism, 206
League of Nations, 279, 386-388
learning exercise, 95, 102
legislating morality, 442
legislative gridlock, 404
length obsession, 257
Leonard, Sherill, 144
Level 7 (1959), 8-9
Lexington Books, 281
liberal power structure, 243
life worse than death, 429, 431
life-cycle saving, 354
limitations of economic models, 426-427
limited world government, 225
Lippincott, Benjamin, 316
literary agencies, 214-215, 253
living off the interest, 326
Lloyd, Georgia, 385
logjam, 100-101, 185
London School of Economics, 164, 245
lotteries, 326
Lukin, Vladimir P., 204

Man, the State and War, 428-429
managerial effort, 336-337
Mao, Tse-Tung, 363, 377, 400
marginal productivity theory, 115
marginal tax rate, 161-162
market socialism, 17-18, 312
Market Socialism Revisited, 71
marketing, 204, 218-219
Marx, Karl, 307-308, 400
material vote, 403
mathematical skills, 58
MathType, 230
Mazower, Mark, 270
McBride, David, 252, 289
McCain, John, 249
McEachern, Susan, 280
McEntire, Christian H., 49-51
Means, Gardiner, 75, 119
media corporations, 24, 369-370
Mendlovitz, Saul, 217
merit, 88-89
microcomputers, 155
Microeconomic Efficiency Argument for Socialism Revisited, The, 120
Microsoft Word, 200, 227
Microsoft Corporation, 323
migration (international), 414-415
military conspiracies, 372-373
military expenditures (U.S.), 427
military model, 329
military-industrial complex, 4
Milky Way galaxy, 7
Millennium, 245
Mills, C. Wright, 3, 12-14
miscalculated risk, 379-381
misery loves company, 414
Mises, Ludwig von, 80-82
Missouri Valley Economic Association, 135-136
Modern Corp, 119

Modern Corporation and Private Property, The (1932), 75, 119
Mohammed, 27
Montreux, Switzerland, 390
Mortensen, Dale, 56, 61, 62
multiple personality disorder, 6
municipal ownership market socialism, 369
Murrell, Peter, 150-151
Mutual Assured Destruction (MAD), 379

Nagasaki, 4, 376, 394, 434
Napoleon Bonaparte, 386
Nash social welfare, 161
National Entrepreneurial Investment Board (NEIB), 23, 148, 331-332
National Investment Banking System (NIBS), 23, 148, 33`-332
national right of armament, 408-412
National Socialism, 363
Nazi Germany, 363
necessary coercion, 428-429
negative income tax function, 121
Nellen, Eugene H., 180-181
neoclassical economic theory, 318, 341
New Cyneas, The, 386
New Economic Policy (NEP), 310
New England town meeting, 334
New Paradigm for International Legal Studies, A, 398
New Perspective on Market Socialism, A, 125-126
New World Oder, The, 395
New World Order, A, 444-447
New World Society, 26
New York City, 6,9, 203, 207, 232, 243, 287, 388
New York Times, 243
Next Step project, 227-246
Next Step, The, 168
Nicholas, Robert A., 180
no plausible scenario, 432-433
noble experiment, 442
noncapital wealth, 359
non-fiction bestseller, 177
Northwestern University, 42. 48, 54, 64, 83, 106, 147
nothing new under the sun, 332
nu (Greek letter □), 162-163
Nuclear Non-Proliferation Treaty, 411
nuclear war, 378-379, 391-392

Obama, Barack, 244, 249, 279
observable success criterion, 75
Office of Price Administration (OPA), 74
official language, 413
omnipotent world government (state), 225, 260, 382, 429, 434
On the Beach (1957), 8
On the Economic Theory of Socialism, 17, 316
one world or none, 219
One World or None: A Prescription for Survival, 395
one-party states, 371
op-ed piece, 243
open door policy, 439-440
opiate of the masses, 449
optimal marginal tax rate, 161-162
Optimal Tax Rate and Public Good Proportion, 159
optimum population, 94
oral defense, 82-83
Oswald, Lee Harvey, 36
Other America, The, 198
O'Toole, Dennis, 105
Our Time, 40-41
Owen, Robert, 307
Oxford UP, 211-212, 252, 288-289

Paine, Thomas, 386
Palgrave Macmillan, 253-254, 290-298
Pangloss, Dr., 120
parameter values (GMP model), 425-426
Pareto optimality (efficiency), 69-71, 152
Parkin, Nicola, 289-290
Parry, Joseph C., 281-283
partial vs. general equilibrium, 121
party line, 166
peace-building vs. peacekeeping, 387
Penn, William, 386
People's Capitalism Thesis, The, 361
people's capitalism, 123, 355-361
People's Republic of China, see China,
perestroika, 393
Persian Gulf War, 419, 446
Plan Alpha, 42-48
plateau production function, 119-120, 343
PMS abbreviation, 126
Political Globalization, 169, 239-246
political power distribution, 23
Pope Leo X, 386
population control, 46-48
population vote, 403
portfolio diversification, 350
postwar world government boom, 388-392
Power Elite, The (1956), 3, 12-14
pp (publication possibility), 72
Practical Proposal toward Supernational Federation, A, 139-146
Praeger Publishers, 196, 209-210, 227
Pragmatic Market Socialism and the Purposes of Socialism, 206
pragmatic market socialism, 22, 80-81
Pragmatic Market Socialism: An Economic and Political Appraisal, 138, 185-194, 210
Pragmatic Market Socialism: An Introduction, 206
Pragmatic Utopia, 96
premature specificity, 398-399
probative vs. circumstantial, 102
producer's surplus, 343
Prentice, Raylene, 199
pre-publication comments, 216-217, 242
Pressman, Steven, 166-167
Prinzip, Gavrilo, 445
probationary years, 86
producer's surplus, 343
production function, 340
production rules (Lange), 74-76
professional books, 179
professor ranks, 88
profit maximization, 330
Profit-Oriented Market Socialism: A CGE Evaluation, 159
progressivism versus conservatism, 451
progressivity, 336
Prohibition (of alcohol), 442-443
projected PCY growth, 423-426
projection, 208
Projector, Dorothy S., 360
proliferation (nuclear), 411
proper design/implementation, 2, 20, 45, 106-107
provisional, 439
Public Finance Review, 159
public ownership agency, 160
publications, 89-94
pure planning, 315
purges, 312-313, 362
Pusca, Anca, 290-298

Putterman, Louis, 206
Putting the Cart Before the Horse, 170-171

quasi-rents, 120
Quarterly Journal of Economics, 113
Quebec, 404-405
question-begging, 345
Questioning Conventional Wisdom on World Government, 243
quinquennial elections, 402

Rademacher, F. J., 286-287
radical redistribution, 443
random variation, 325
raw faith, 208
realist majority, 388-389
redistribution, 156
regional ownership market socialism, 369
rejection, 105
religion, 412-414, 437-438, 449
resurgent interest in world government, 395
retention coefficient, 343-344
Rethinking World Government, 238-239
retirement, 245, 248, 324, 351, 354
Reves, Emery, 390
Review of Economic Studies, 14, 159, 316
Review of Income and Wealth, 360
Review of Political Economy, 166-167
Review of Social Economy, 113-114, 207
revisionism, 308
Ricardian rent, 82, 115
Rice, Condoleeza, 244
rise of China, 447
risk-taking, 115-116, 318, 350
Road to Serfdom, The, 365-366
Robinson, Peter, 104
robust vs. non-robust policy implications, 425
Rock, Steve, 57
rogue states, 447
Roos, Jerome E., 245
Roosevelt, Franklin D., 279, 366, 387, 442
Rosenau, James N., 242
Roshwald, Mordecai, 8
Russian Federation, 446
Russian revolution, 309-310

sabbaticals, 182-183
sacrifices of saving, 353
Saint-Simon, Count Henri de, 386
Samuels, Warren, 153
Samuelson, Paul, 16
Sarajevo, 445
saving, 346-355
Schachter, Howard, 49
scholarly books, 179
Schuman, Frederick, 400
Schwartzberg, Joseph E., 242
science fiction, 6-7
Scientific Approach, A, 438-444
scientific progress, 441
Searchlight on Peace Plans, 385
secession (withdrawal), 404-408
self-fulfilling prophecy, 258-259
Senior, Nassau, 348
separation of ownership and control, 119-120, 152
separatism, 404, 413
Sherman, Howard, 205
Should the United States Champion World Government, 279
Shute, Nevil, 8
Simulation-Type Experiment on Pareto Optimality, A, 69-71
Sisk, Jonathan, 215
Slaughter, Anne-Marie, 395

slave mentality, 366
slavery, 407-408
small business, 322-323
Smith, Adam, 312
Smith, James D., 359
social democracy, 336
social democratic socialism, 314
Social Dividend under Market Socialism, The, 325
social dividend, 17, 122, 323-326, 361
social welfare maximization, 70
Socialism in the Free Market, 180-182
Socialism Revised and Modernized, 194-208
socialism, 313
socialism, meaning of, 2-3, 15, 28, 307
Socialism: An Economic and Sociological Analysis, 80-81
socialist analogue, 321
Socialist Economics, 17, 75-76, 316
Sohn, Louis, 398-399
Some Empirical Evidence on the Social Welfare Maximization Hypothesis, 156-157
Southern Economic Journal, 155
Soviet collapse, 301-303, 393-394, 445
Soviet Union, 362
specialized books, 179
specificity (appropriate versus excessive), 399
speed of light, 7
St. Martin's Press, 193-194, 195
Stalin, 9, 11, 31, 98, 123, 183, 310, 315, 332, 363, 367, 372, 377, 392, 400, 434, 439
Stauber, Leland, 369
Stead, William T., 386
stellar expansion policy, 45-46
Stephenson, Robert Lewis, 6
stock market speculation, 355-356
stockholders, 119
Strange Case of Dr. Jeckyl and Mr. Hyde, The (1886), 6
Strategic Arms Limitation Treaty (SALT), 410
Strategic Arms Reduction Treaty (START), 411
Strauss, Andrew, 242, 257-258
strengthened United Nations, 398
Strotz, Robert, 56, 61
sub-Saharan Africa, 427
subsidies, 216, 240-241
subvention, 240
Summary and Conclusions, 80-81
Summary Records, 110
Summer to Remember, A (1960), 11-12
Sumner, Charles, 386
supply curve of labor, 340
Survey of Consumer Finances, 360
Survey of Contemporary Economics, A, 56
Survey of Financial Characteristics of Consumers, 360
Swords into Plowshares, 277-278

Taiwan, 447
Talbott, Strobe, 149, 213, 394
Tarascio, Vincent, 112
Taylor, Fred M., 316
teleological reasoning, 396
tentative and provisional, 306, 422, 439
tenure, 85-86
terminal year, 86
terrorism, 445
Tervuren, Belgium, 1, 28
The Equity-Efficiency Tradeoff under Capitalism and Market Socialism, 121-122
Thomas, William, 207-208
Thurow, Lester, 205

Time Magazine, 149, 394
time preference, 348-349
Tinbergen, Jan, 206, 217
Toff, Nancy, 232
total factor productivity, 425-426
Toward a Better World, 239
trade (international), 414-415
trade books, 179
transfer fund contributions, 427-428
transfer fund, 128-129, 422
transition and compensation, 320-323
transition costs, 39, 302
Treadway, Peter T., 34
Treaty of Versailles, 410
tripartite government structure, 402
Truman, Harry, 5, 393
Trump, Donald, 445
Turkey, 302
Twentieth Century Council, 26, 48
two-tiered agency, 327-328

Ukraine, 446
Ulbricht, Walter, 10
unicameral legislature, 402-403
Union Chamber of Representatives, 402-403
Union Chief Executive, 402
Union Districts, 402
Union High Court, 402
unitary vs. federal, 402
United Nations, 49, 214, 233, 260, 265, 279, 382, 386-388, 398, 451
United Nations of the World, 387
Universal Declaration of Human Rights, 388
universal membership, 391
University of California at Berkeley, 42
University Press of America, 215-219, 239-241
Unsafe on Any Highway, 50
USSR, 123, 139, 269, 301, 303, 312, 315, 362, 377, 394, 398, 400, 431, 446, 450
utilitarianism, 121
utopian dreams, 445
utopian socialists, 307

validation test/simulation, 132, 423
Vambakos rooming house, 35
Vandermeulen, Alice, 111-112
vanity press, 216
Ventura Publisher, 199-200
Versailles, Treaty of, 410
Vietnam, 427
vision, 106-107
visionary minority, 388-389
Visual Basic, 227
Voltaire, 120
von Suttner, Baroness Bertha, 386

Waltz, Kenneth, 428-429, 431
Walzer, Norm, 128
war on alcohol, 442
war on drugs, 442
war to end wars, 387
Waters, William, 113-114
wealth effect, 322
wealth in general, 321
Wealth of Nations, 312
Weiss, Gertrude S., 360
Weiss, Thomas G., 258, 259-271
Wells, H. G., 269
Wendt, Alexander, 259, 396-398
Western Illinois University, 23, 57, 64, 85, 90, 128, 131, 147, 182, 186, 199, 213, 231, 247
Westview Press, 193, 195
What Happened to the Idea of World Government, 259
whistle-blowing, 370
Whitney, Eli, 407

Why a World State Is Inevitable, 259, 396-398
Wiar, Kimberly, 104
Wikipedia, 177
Wilkinson, Rorden, 267-271, 287
Wilson, Woodrow, 279
Winder, Simon, 193-194, 195
Winkler, Adam, 87
withdrawal (secession), 404-408, 438
Wolff, Edward N., 360
World Citizenship and Government, 226, 385
World Development, 132
World Development Authority, 436
World Development Indicators, 226, 422
World Economic Equalization Program (WEEP), 129-137, 421
World Federalist Association, 149
World Federation? A Critical Analysis, 395
World Futures, 144-146
world government, early view of, 2
World Movement for World Federal Government, 390
World Peace through World Law, 398-399
World Policy, 144
World Trade Center attack (9/11), 446
World Trade Organization (WTO), 414
World Union on the Horizon, 137, 168, 208-219, 224
World War I, 387, 408
World War II, 11, 312, 387, 410
World War III, 10, 446
worse than death, 379
Wright brothers, 399
Wright, Colin, 62
written prelim, 58-59
Wynner, Edith, 385

Zinam, Oleg, 136